Traynham

THE GREAT FRIENDSHIP

THE GREAT FRIENDSHIP

Soviet Historians on
the Non-Russian Nationalities

by LOWELL TILLETT

The University of North Carolina Press
Chapel Hill

To Anne

PREFACE

Writing on recent Soviet historiography involves inherent problems of organization and presentation. Since the historiographical upheaval which began in the 1930's, the Communist party's interference has been growing apace, but its directives are seldom specific and the dialogue between scholar and party theoretician is never candid. One can get only faint hints of the actual process by which the party demands are met. Thus the Western student of Soviet historiography is obliged to do a certain amount of speculation, and to involve himself in Soviet political developments in each period under consideration. It is not unusual to observe an interpretation changing under one's eyes, between the time research is done and the writing completed.

When a new interpretation is established and wins official favor, a number of related subjects come under scrutiny and must be reconciled with it. Ultimately the whole fabric of Soviet historical writing has been affected by the party's demands in a few areas. Because of the many facets of interpretation that are in a state of flux at a given time, it is almost impossible to describe the whole process. Perhaps this explains the unusual disjointedness of much that has been written in the West on the subject. Some of the works are collections of essays on a variety of subjects that are barely related (such as *Rewriting Russian History*, edited by C. E. Black, and *Contemporary History in the Soviet Mirror*, edited by John Keep). The one comprehensive work, Konstantin Shteppa's *Russian Historians and the Soviet State*, deals with such a bewildering assortment of subjects, authors, and views that the reader may frequently find himself at sea.

In this study I have adopted a novel organization which I hope will give as much coherence to the subject as the subject matter will permit. I have chosen one theme, which seems to me to be central in many of the historiographical controversies—the accommodation of historical interpretation to the exigencies of nationality policy—and have tried to describe the principal developments in the dialogue between party and scholar and the resulting changes.

Part One (the first twelve chapters) is a chronological account of
the background and development of the concept of the friendship
of Soviet peoples in history, restricted to the main issues and developments. In order to avoid cluttering this account with dozens
of side issues with which Soviet historians were concurrently involved, I have dealt with them separately in Part Two (Chapters
13-18) in a topical arrangement. This organization presents its
problems, but it seems to me that it is, to use the Soviet historians'
expression, the lesser evil. A secondary advantage of this organization is that the two parts of the work are almost independent
of each other; the reader who is primarily interested in the party's
role and the historian's response will find the account in Part One;
one who is interested in details of the reinterpretations in military,
cultural, and social history may be more interested in Part Two.

This study has certain limitations of scope which the reader
should be aware of at the beginning. In the first place, it is a
study of Soviet historiography and not of historical fact. I have
not attempted to determine the facts of Russian colonial history,
but have concentrated on two sharply contrasting Soviet versions
of that history, whose dividing line is about 1940. Since the earlier
version was revised under constant party supervision, the outlines of
the new history will show to what lengths the party has gone to
produce an interpretation that meets its ideological needs. A
balanced history of Russian colonialism, taking into account the
reactions of the non-Russian subjects, is perhaps unfeasible. The
written sources are largely unobtainable, and are in many exotic
languages.

This study is limited in other ways as well. I have tried to
treat several historiographical controversies in some detail, at
the expense of lengthy discussion of Marxian views of history, the
theory and practice of Soviet nationality policy, or broader problems of the Soviet historian. I have not given the tsarist historians'
versions of the questions at hand, although this would give the
book a third dimension, and allow the reader more comparisons.
But such a discussion would increase the book to unmanageable
length and would have only limited application to Soviet historiography. This study deals only with pre-revolutionary history,
since the changes of interpretation apply to the earlier period.
Another limitation of scope was imposed by necessity: undoubtedly
the works of non-Russian historians of the U.S.S.R., published in
their own languages, would reveal fine variations of interpreta-

tion and "bourgeois survivals." But this obviously cannot be attempted because of language barriers and the unavailability of materials.

There are two kinds of unusual sources used in this research which deserve some explanation—the pedestrian textbook, and Soviet studies that have been condemned and are not available in the West. Ordinarily one would not look for officially sanctioned interpretations in textbooks and survey histories, but the Soviet practice is unusual in this respect. Since the middle 1930's textbooks and survey histories have been prepared by whole brigades of historians, who have worked together to produce acceptable interpretations. Preliminary drafts have been widely read and criticized, sometimes by party officials themselves. These general works, therefore, can be said to be the historians' best estimate of the favored interpretation (except in some cases of defiance discussed below). There is another obvious advantage in seeking historiographical change in the textbooks: there are many editions that are only slightly changed by the scissors and paste method; one has only to read parallel passages to find the historians' response to party demands. As for the condemned books, the loss is not as great as it might seem. Hostile reviewers and critics in the U.S.S.R. have discussed them at length, quoting extensive passages from the most controversial sections of them. There are about a dozen books in this category that are of special interest to this study. I have mentioned in the notes that they were not available, and listed them in brackets in the bibliography.

Some of the party resolutions, book reviews, and articles have been translated in the *Current Digest of the Soviet Press* and in Marin Pundeff's *History in the U.S.S.R.: Selected Readings,* which was published after this research was completed. I have referred to these translations for reference purposes in the notes. They have been quoted directly only in those cases which are noted; elsewhere the translations are my own. Some of my research has previously been reported in three articles, on Shamil and Muridism (*American Slavic and East European Review*), on Russian colonialism (*Foreign Affairs*), and on Kazakh historical writing (*Problems of Communism*). Publication details are given in the bibliography at the end of this book.

A substantial part of this research was done under a fellowship from the Cooperative Program in the Humanities, operated jointly by Duke University and the University of North Carolina. Wake

Forest University and the Piedmont University Center gave financial support for the research and writing. Prof. Clifford Foust of the University of North Carolina has given me invaluable assistance by searching for Soviet materials and has read the manuscript and criticized it in detail. Prof. Thomas Mullen and my wife, Prof. Anne Tillett, have read portions of the manuscript and have made valuable suggestions. Prof. Richard Pipes persistently tracked down some monographs I was unable to find. I owe thanks to many libraries and librarians—especially to the Slavic Reading Room staff at the Library of Congress, to Mrs. Maria Lippert of the Institute for the Study of the U.S.S.R. in Munich, and to Mrs. Patty McIntyre, reference librarian at the University of North Carolina. Mrs. Emily Lincoln not only typed the manuscript but rendered valuable editorial assistance as well. Finally, I would like to acknowledge the last-minute assistance of two friends: Prof. David Hadley, who read the page proofs, and Hannelore McDowell, who drew the map.

CONTENTS

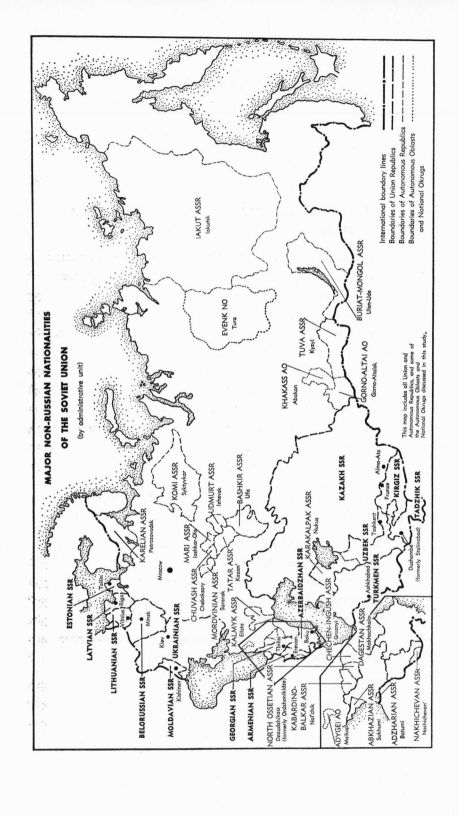

MAJOR NON-RUSSIAN NATIONALITIES
OF THE SOVIET UNION
(by administrative unit)

International boundary lines
Boundaries of Union Republics
Boundaries of Autonomous Republics
Boundaries of Autonomous Oblasts
and National Okrugs

This map includes all Union and
Autonomous Republics, and some of
the Autonomous Oblasts and
National Okrugs discussed in this study.

IAKUT ASSR
Iakutsk

EVENK NO
Tura

BURIAT-MONGOL ASSR
Ulan-Ude

TUVA ASSR
Kyzyl

KHAKASS AO
Abakan

GORNO-ALTAI AO
Gorno-Altaisk

KAZAKH SSR

Alma-Ata

KIRGIZ SSR
Frunze

UZBEK SSR
Tashkent

TADZHIK SSR
Dushambe
(formerly Stalinabad)

TURKMEN SSR
Ashkhabad

KARAKALPAK ASSR
Nukus

AZERBAIDZHAN SSR
Baku

CHECHEN-INGUSH ASSR
Groznyi

DAGESTAN ASSR
Makhachkala

NORTH OSSETIAN ASSR
Dzaudzhikau
(formerly Ordzhonikidze)

KABARDINO-
BALKAR ASSR
Nal'chik

GEORGIAN SSR
Tbilisi

ARMENIAN SSR
Erevan

ADYGEI AO
Maikop

ABKHAZIAN ASSR
Sukhumi

ADZHARIAN ASSR
Batumi

NAKHICHEVAN ASSR
Nakhichevan'

KALMYK ASSR
Elista

MORDVINIAN ASSR
Saransk

CHUVASH ASSR
Cheboksary

TATAR ASSR
Kazan'

MARI ASSR
Ioshkar-Ola

UDMURT ASSR
Izhevsk

BASHKIR ASSR
Ufa

KOMI ASSR
Syktyvkar

KARELIAN ASSR
Petrozavodsk

Moscow

ESTONIAN SSR
Tallin

LATVIAN SSR
Riga

LITHUANIAN SSR
Vilnius

BELORUSSIAN SSR
Minsk

UKRAINIAN SSR
Kiev

MOLDAVIAN SSR
Kishinev

PART ONE

The Making of an Historical Myth

CHAPTER **1.**

THE FRIENDSHIP OF
SOVIET PEOPLES: AN INTRODUCTION

"The friendship of the peoples of the Soviet Union with the Russian people has deep historic roots and a remarkable history." M. Mustafaev, in the journal Voprosy istorii, No. 9, 1951, p. 97.

Since the early 1930's Soviet historians have been painstakingly rewriting the history of their country under increasing supervision of the Communist party. Although the stated purpose of this undertaking has been the creation of a completely new "scientific" history, a "Marxist-Leninist" history, it has never been denied that the new interpretations are designed to support current political goals. The Soviet historian has been assigned a major role in the ideological struggle for the construction of a new Soviet society. He has enhanced the prestige and authority of the Bolshevik regime by producing party histories affirming the party's infallibility and the wisdom of its policies and actions from the beginning. He has helped to instill the new Soviet patriotism, which supposedly cuts across the lines of nationality to create a love of the multi-national state. He has tried to promote Leninist nationality policy, not only by touting the accomplishments of the Soviet period, but by rewriting the history of the Russian Empire in such a way as to reduce friction and violence among its peoples to a minimum, and to emphasize the positive results of Russian empire-building. It is this last task of the Soviet historian with which this study is concerned.

Anyone who has read one of the recent survey histories of the U.S.S.R., or of its constituent republics, is aware that the new

3

Soviet history has created a picture of the pre-revolutionary period almost as idyllic as that painted for the Soviet era. Under party prodding, the Soviet historian has made the alleged friendship of Soviet peoples retroactive to tsarist times, even to ancient and medieval times in some cases. This is not to say that the evils of tsarism are forgotten, but rather that the friendly relations of the peoples of the future Soviet family are emphasized. From the new point of view, tsarism is the challenge that evokes a heroic response from the multi-national masses of the Empire, culminating in the events of 1917. In the new history there is no mention of hostility among the peoples who now constitute the U.S.S.R. at any time in the past; there is instead an account of their continued mutual respect and helpfulness, and of a common struggle against enemies, both domestic and foreign. Furthermore, all peoples of the future Soviet state are said to have recognized the leadership ability of the Russian people, and to have benefited in many ways from their association with them. What emerges is a kind of historic common-wealth of peoples, fated by history to a common struggle which reached its victory in the October Revolution. This interpretation, in its broad dimensions and supporting arguments, which run counter to those of other historians (especially the first generation of Bolshevik historians), can only be described as an elaborate historical myth.

For all its dedication to science and technology, the first two-thirds of the twentieth century has been an unprecedented era for the creation of myths. And paradoxically, the most fervent myth-making has been done in the name of science; the author has been the totalitarian state, trying to justify its existence or verify the wisdom of its policies by the construction of historical myths. Suddenly we have witnessed the impact of a powerful and irrational new force in statecraft and politics—what Ernst Cassirer has called "the power of mythical thought."[1]

The new historical myths differ from the old ones both in kind and degree. Never before have the proponents of myths made such claims for the "scientific" bases of their theories. Mussolini's new Roman Empire, to be realized through the Fascist concept of man and the state; the Thousand Year Reich, based on concepts of race and geopolitics; the proletarian state and classless society, derived from the Marxist laws of historical development—all these

1. Ernst Cassirer, *The Myth of the State* (New Haven, Conn.: Yale University Press, 1946), p. 3.

grandiose plans have allegedly been grounded in fresh new scientific revelations.

Once a myth has been propounded in a closed society, it can be nurtured and developed through the almost unlimited controls at the disposal of the regime. The most eloquent spokesmen for the myth are published and rewarded; the critics are silenced. The constant re-examination and debunking of myths, so characteristic of the open society, is lacking, and consequently myths sometimes grow like wildfire, reaching absurd proportions. In such a climate, only the leader or the dominant party can check the myth's limits, and from the historical examples to date, they have done a poor job of it. In contemporary China, only Chairman Mao could convince his publicists that his works really do not hold the key to a better understanding of molecular structure, surgical techniques, oilfield operations, and the marketing of watermelons.

Bolshevik historical myths are especially elaborate, and have been affirmed with unprecedented argumentation. One reason is simple longevity: no other ideological dictatorship has been accorded a half century in which to fashion its version of history. More important, the Bolsheviks consider themselves the peculiar instrument of history. In their view, they are the carpenters who are following the blueprint drawn up by Marx and Engels, whose laws of historical development offer the key not only to a "scientific" interpretation of past developments, but a guide to current policies and future plans. While others, lacking the blueprint, flounder about, the Bolsheviks advance steadily and surely, confident that history itself is on their side.

Because of the Bolshevik identification with the historical process, history is both more political and more vital than in other societies. A "correct" understanding of history, in the party's view, can only strengthen its position and facilitate its future programs. No other regime has given so much attention to the writing of proper history textbooks. Beginning in 1934, the highest party spokesmen, Stalin, Zhdanov, and Kirov, began a series of commentaries on rejected manuscripts for history textbooks which set the guidelines for new ones. The textbooks produced under such guidance have gone through many editions, each adding refinements and bringing interpretations in line with current party thinking. Every new installment in the updating of history is considered to be more than merely a new interpretation: because history is "scientific," each new view is a discovery of a new truth, a victory for "Soviet historical science." The Bolshevik historian need not be defensive about holding interpretations designed to support the policies of the state, since historical truth and Bolshevik policy march together shoulder to shoulder. Indeed, the most favored Soviet historians are those who work actively to support state policies, and they are not modest in taking credit. As M. P. Kim, a leading historian, recently put it in a typical editorial, "It is the duty of Soviet historians to apply all their creative efforts and play a worthy role in the common pursuit of Communist construction."[2]

The proposition under discussion here is what the Soviets refer to generally as the friendship of peoples. The non-Soviet reader is likely to be acquainted with the term in its international application: the view that the popular masses of all countries, regardless of the regimes under which they live, are inherently friendly with each other because of their class interests, their common problems, and aspirations. In the Marxist view, quarrels and wars are made by the ruling classes, not by the masses. The term also has an important application to relations among the peoples of the Soviet Union. Since about 1930 Bolshevik propagandists have loudly asserted that Leninist nationality policy has created something entirely new in history—a multi-national society without national hatreds or hostilities. (It has belied its own argument by making frequent exhortations for Soviet citizens to further strengthen such friendship, a theme which continues to be widely publicized by the press a half century after the Revolution.) To the well-known propaganda technique of frequent and fervent repetition, the Bolshevik ideologists have added a historical dimension: they have more recently asserted that not only does no hostility *now* exist, but that it has *never* existed. This extension of the proposition into the pre-revolutionary past has been imposed in Soviet historiography only since World War II.

The obvious purpose of this new version of the history of the non-Russian peoples and their relations with Russians is to support Soviet efforts to solve lingering nationality problems. The complex of tensions generated in a multi-national state, consisting of dozens of peoples of different language, religion, and ethnic and historical background, was a major centrifugal force which threatened to

2. M. P. Kim, "O zadachakh izucheniia istoricheskogo opyta sotsialisticheskogo stroitel'stva v SSSR v svete reshenii XXII s"ezda KPSS," *Voprosy istorii*, No. 2, 1962, pp. 3-19 [hereafter cited as VI]. Quotation on p. 19.

pull the old Russian Empire apart. The Bolsheviks, who recognized the seriousness of the problem from the beginning, formulated a program that promised the non-Russian nationalities cultural autonomy and equality. But when the opportunity came, during the turmoil of the Revolution and Civil War, many of the non-Russian nationalities preferred complete independence to Bolshevik blandishments, and the fact that the Bolshevik leaders did not hesitate to put the pieces together again by force jeopardized the chances for the early success of the party's nationality program. Nationalism among the non-Russians has smouldered—and sometimes flamed up—ever since, as is indicated by the constant attention given to the question by the party's ideological authorities. Since World War II they have sent whole brigades of historians to attack the problem at its root: they want to change deep-set attitudes of the Soviet people, to create a citizenry that not only does not feel national hatreds but believes that they never existed in the Soviet family. This is a remarkable reversal of interpretation. Up to World War II, Soviet historians, like their party spokesmen, held that the Revolution was the great dividing line between darkness and light; before the Revolution, national hatreds were everywhere; after its success, the party's nationality policy created a friendship of peoples.

THE CLASS STRUGGLE AND THE FRIENDSHIP OF PEOPLES

Simple logic would seem to make friendship and warfare mutually exclusive. Since Russian colonial expansion was notorious for its brutality (especially as viewed by early Bolshevik historians), the task of reconciling the long-established interpretation with the party-imposed view of the great friendship was monumental, and almost every Soviet historian who wrote about the non-Russian nationalities was in serious error at one time or another as he groped for an acceptable interpretation. At one time in the early development of the myth, it appeared that the new Soviet history might go to the extreme of denying violence altogether. In the early 1950's large survey histories were written in which there were no direct references to tsarist conquests. The Russian advance was pictured as essentially defensive, undertaken to stave off imminent aggression from "foreign enemies," who threatened to conquer the non-Russian peoples. In many cases these peoples were said to have been annexed to Russia voluntarily, with no hint of violence. Resistance movements and revolts against the Russian masters were represented as efforts of feudal leaders to recover their old privileges, and were said to have had no mass support. In time Soviet historians worked out subtle arguments that enabled them to abandon such absurd positions (now attributed to the Stalin cult of personality), and to find a formula that would not only reconcile the irreconcilable, but would do so in the context of good Marxist concept and terminology. The answer was found in the re-examination of all these events as manifestations of the class struggle.

It should be noted at the outset that Soviet historians extol the friendship of *peoples,* not of governments or leaders. Herein lies the secret of the rationalization. The great utility of the term "the people" lies in its vagueness, its flexibility, and its favored place in the Marxist scheme of things. Just as the Western politician is confident that the people are on his side, and that his opponent is completely out of touch with them, so the Soviet spokesman can maneuver the term almost arbitrarily, attributing to the people that which is progressive and constructive. Furthermore, in the Marxist view, the people are the makers of history, the chosen instrument of the inexorable laws of historical development. Political decisions, no matter how arbitrary, are said to express their will; a "progressive" revolution, even when carried out by a small group of professional revolutionaries, is said to be their doing.

Soviet historical scientists, borrowing from the lexicon of the party propagandist, are notoriously vague in their references to the mass of humanity. Progressive historical acts are attributed to "the workers," "the peasants," "the masses." Reactionary deeds are laid to "the ruling circles," "feudal lords," "the imperialists," "the clergy." The size of each of these groups is so indefinite that the historian can, in many cases, almost constitute them arbitrarily. Each group can also be equipped with appropriate views on a given question. For the great sweep of history until very recent times, there are no census figures or public opinion polls to interfere with such exercises, and judging from Soviet writing on recent events (the Hungarian Revolution of 1956, for example), such empirical evidence would not stand in the way in any event. Thus the Soviet historian's attachment to the class character of historical events does not shackle him, as it might appear at first glance, but actually provides him great flexibility in the assignment of historical roles and the evaluation of events.

The new Soviet history of the non-Russian peoples of the U.S.S.R. abounds in vague references to these class groups. What does the Soviet historian mean when he writes about the acts of "the progressive people of Central Asia" early in the twentieth century? The terms are never defined, but the reader can soon learn from the context that the progressive people of that area at that time were those who were pro-Russian or revolutionary by a definition acceptable to the historian; they were not religious and did not belong to a nationalist group. Their progressiveness is unrelated to their numbers or their atypical place in society. Thus, when a Soviet historian states that "the progressive people of Central Asia and Russia undertook to unite the forces of their peoples in a common struggle against foreign aggressors and the power of their own tsar and khans," he makes a true statement if his definition of terms is accepted.[3] Likewise the much repeated assertion that "the best sons" of the Belorussian, Ukrainian, or Georgian peoples worked actively for union with the Russian state must be considered true, since by Soviet definition, anyone who opposed such a development would not be a best son.

In the Marxist view the class struggle has been a vital factor in the entire course of human history, except at its extreme chronological ends. One of the reasons for the apparently endless preoccupation with periodization is the assessment of the nature of the class struggle at a particular period, on which hangs the correct interpretation of many other events. Soviet historians have been obliged to find the class struggle even when it is not apparent and to base interpretations on its development. In the late 1940's, when the present interpretation was being formulated, one of the most common errors attributed to historians was their failure to see the class struggle in historical phenomena. This has led to the detection of class differences in unusual situations and forms. The Evenks of central Siberia have been divided into classes according to the number of reindeer herded by an individual, while Tatar historians, failing to find clear manifestations of the class struggle in one obscure medieval period, have declared that their ancestors were engaged in a class struggle in "passive form."[4]

3. G. Nepesov, "Vozniknovenie i razvitie turkmenskoi sovetskoi sotsialisticheskoi respubliki," *VI*, No. 2, 1950, pp. 3-24. Quotation on p. 4.
4. V. Uvachan, *Peoples of the Soviet North* (Moscow, 1960), p. 21; *Istoriia tatarskoi ASSR*, ed. N. I. Vorob'ev *et al.* (Kazan' 1955), I, 120. Another good example of an obscure class struggle is B. Rybakov's discussion of eleventh-century Kiev. Basing his views of a few phrases in the chronicles,

The dichotomy of Russian society is no Bolshevik invention. The concept of a dual Russia, in which the state and the populace opposed each other, was long held by both the *muzhik* and the intelligentsia. According to this view, the Russian state grew, not because of the will of the people or in their behalf, but in spite of the people and at their expense. The elements of "official Russia," the tsar, his court, and the bureaucracy, were so far removed from the daily life of the people that the state was considered to be an alien force in its own land. The two were considered not only to have entirely different ways of life, but separate cultures. In the view of the historian Kliuchevskii, this situation was only aggravated by Russian expansion, since it required more coercive measures and a greater sacrifice of the resources of the Russian people without giving them substantial material gains. The view that "the state swelled up; the people grew lean"[5] was advocated by both the Slavophiles and the Populists, and was easily adapted to the framework of Marxism by the Bolsheviks. Lenin himself penned the statement by which the old concept came to be linked with the new. Writing on the nationalities question in 1913, he held "official Russia" exclusively responsible for all hatred between peoples, and remarked that "there are two national cultures in every national culture. There is the Great Russian culture of the Purishkeviches, Guchkovs and Struves—but there is also the Great Russian culture typified in the names of Chernyshevskii and Plekhanov."[6]

Drawing on both the old concept of dual Russia and the Marxist class principle, Soviet historians have postulated a system of class alliances that is the shibboleth of the friendship of peoples idea. They maintain that in the course of Russian expansion among the non-Russian peoples, two alliances were struck, dictated by the class interests of the rulers and their subjects. At the upper level, the local leaders (kings, khans, or feudal lords), as well as the local

he rationalized: "The chroniclers, who observed life through the windows of a monastery cell or the prince's palace, did not like to record riots and uprisings: they understood their task to be only to write down accounts of battles and describe the bravery of warriors. Therefore very little is known of the class struggle in the period of early feudalism; not even an approximate picture can be gained from the episodic mention of separate events that is found in the chronicles" (B. Rybakov, *Early Centuries of Russian History* [Moscow, 1965], p. 92).

5. See Robert C. Tucker's essay, "The Image of Dual Russia," in C. E. Black (ed.), *The Transformation of Russian Society* (Cambridge, Mass.: Harvard University Press, 1960), pp. 587-605.

6. V. I. Lenin, *Polnoe sobranie sochinenii* (Moscow, 1958-65), XXIV, 129.

clergy and aristocracy, formed an alliance with the tsar's generals and officials. All of them were interested in exploiting the masses and extending their privileges. At the lower level, the non-Russian masses were hostile to the Russian ruling class, whom they regarded as a new class enemy, in addition to their indigenous rulers. But the remarkable thing about this interpretation is that the non-Russian populace did not resent the coming of the common Russian people, even when their arrival involved their dispossession from hereditary lands. Soviet historians contend that the masses, Russian and non-Russian, also struck an alliance in the colonies, instantly became friends, and strengthened their class struggle against their oppressors. Thus the friendship of peoples is dated from the moment of first acquaintance.

The alliance of the ruling classes has always been a thesis of the Soviet historian, and has undergone no substantial change in the historiographical revolution attending the promulgation of Soviet patriotism. But the alliance of the oppressed has come into view only recently. In the historical studies on the non-Russian peoples published in the 1930's, one can find a well-formulated version of the alliance of the exploiters, without a trace of an alliance of the exploited.[7] At that time Soviet historians agreed with their bourgeois counterparts that the non-Russian subjects of the tsar hated all Russians impartially. The lower alliance was accepted by Soviet historians only in the late 1940's, after much party prodding. Their acceptance of it was clearly an accommodation to the friendship myth.

The beauty of this interpretation is that it removes all hostility among the peoples of the Russian Empire from considerations of nationality, and puts it wholly into the category of the class struggle, in which hostility is considered to be honorable and constructive. The non-Russian subject did not fight with the Russian *per se;* he fought with his class enemy, who happened to be a Russian. National hatreds are thus all but eliminated, and subordinated to class hatreds. Stated succinctly, there was no hostility among the peoples of the future Soviet family. This view removes the necessity for eliminating wars and revolts from Russian colonial history. Such violence is laid to the class enemy,

7. E. Shteinberg, *Ocherki istorii Turkmenii* (Moscow-Leningrad, 1934), pp. 57-59; A. P. Okladnikov, *Ocherki iz istorii zapadnykh Buriat-Mongolov, XVII-XVIII v.* (Leningrad, 1937), pp. 18-19.

tsarist and local, and does not affect the cordial relations of the popular masses of all nationalities.

The Marxist view of the relationship of the popular masses to warfare was of fundamental importance to the working out of the friendship of peoples idea. Wars are also said to be a product of the class struggle, and they are just or unjust according to the role of the people. Although Marx and Engels established this thesis, it remained for Stalin to delineate the categories of warfare more precisely and to state the Bolshevik position on warfare. His view, which has not suffered in the recent reappraisals of his work, was stated in the *Short Course,* in which two kinds of wars are defined: "(a) *Just* wars, wars that are not wars of conquest but wars of liberation, waged to defend the people from foreign attack and from attempts to enslave them, or to liberate the people from capitalist slavery, or lastly, to liberate colonies and dependent countries from the yoke of imperialism; and (b) *Unjust* wars, wars of conquest, waged to conquer and enslave foreign countries and foreign nations."[8] It a letter to Maxim Gorky, Stalin made it clear that the Bolsheviks did not oppose all wars in principle: "We are not against *all* wars. We are *against* imperialist wars, as being counter-revolutionary wars. But we are *for* liberating, anti-imperialist, revolutionary wars. . . ."[9]

Thus the Soviet view of warfare transcends the traditional view of aggressive and defensive wars and puts them in the context of the class struggle. And although at the time Stalin expressed this view it probably would not have occurred to him that tsarist armies could wage liberating, anti-imperialist wars, this is precisely what later Soviet historical writers hold. The wars fought for the building of the Russian Empire are now viewed as largely defensive, their aim being to protect non-Russian neighbors from some external enemy or from their own internecine fighting. When wars waged by Russian leaders are acknowledged to be unjust (as in putting down peasant rebellions or "progressive" revolts of non-Russian peoples) they are attributed strictly to "tsarism," and the Russian people, even though they constituted the main striking force, are considered to be in no way responsible. The people initiate only just wars, such as national liberation movements or rebellions

8. *History of the Communist Party of the Soviet Union (Bolsheviks): Short Course* (New York: International Publishers, 1939), pp. 167-68.
9. I. V. Stalin, *Sochineniia* (Moscow, 1946–   ), XII, 176. Emphasis in the original in both quotations.

against exploitation. One of the thorniest questions Soviet historians have faced in recent years has been the re-examination of dozens of resistance movements and revolts of the non-Russian peoples, to determine whether they were of a progressive or reactionary character. The designation is based on the class nature of the leadership and its following, the causes and goals of the movement, and the involvement of foreign powers. The masses participate only in progressive revolts, the only exception being that they may be momentarily misled by cunning reactionary leaders.

Although it is axiomatic that the reactionary or progressive character of a particular movement is determined by the nature of the class struggle, the resulting interpretation is by no means inflexible. In practice the historian can work from either end of the proposition. In a number of cases to be discussed in this study Soviet historians have worked backwards: they have changed their views on the class struggle to fit a new interpretation of the nature of the event that was supposedly determined by it. Leaders who were formerly regarded as champions of the exploited have been moved over into the company of the class enemy when new considerations—frequently injected into historiography by current political policies—are emphasized. One of the best examples is the historic role of Shamil, the most famous of the resistance leaders, who directed a war against the Russians in the Caucasus for a quarter of a century beginning in 1834. Up to 1950 Soviet historians emphasized his popularity as leader of a movement for national liberation and independence, maintaining that his position was gained and held through democratic procedures. After 1950 Soviet historians, following directives issued by party spokesmen, emphasized that Shamil was the leader of Muridism, a fanatical Moslem sect, and of the feudal aristocracy of the mountain peoples. It was even asserted for a time that he did not have mass support, that his movement was of a feudal character. In the course of this discussion, the nature of the class struggle in the North Caucasus was itself changed, in the view of some Soviet historians. They maintained that the area was not in the early feudal stage, as previously held, but in the patriarchal-tribal stage, which is characterized by internecine fighting—thus reducing Shamil to the role of a tribal brigand.

THE ANATOMY OF THE MYTH

The friendship of peoples is currently set forth in all the Soviet histories of the U.S.S.R., in the histories of the Union Republics, Autonomous Republics, and local areas, as well as in numerous studies on the annexation of individual peoples, with a dull uniformity which has been reduced to formula. Indeed, one of the chief reasons for skepticism among outside scholars who are confronted with this idyllic piece of social history is the sheer quantity and variety of explanations and proofs the histories offer; they are like a row of heavy flying buttresses erected to support an extremely thin and fragile wall. The most important arguments in support of the view will be outlined here for two reasons: to show the sharp contrast with the view of the older Soviet historians, to be discussed in the following two chapters, and to make the subsequent discussion of the individual propositions meaningful in relation to the whole structure.

In the first place, the reader is impressed with the longevity and constancy of the friendship of the Russian and non-Russian peoples. Trading and cultural relations created such friendship in medieval times, and in a few cases even earlier. The new histories of the Caucasus area contain discussions of relations with the Eastern Slav neighbors to the north in the fourth and fifth centuries A.D. These beginnings are usually tenuous and unimportant, but even an expedition of a small company of traders or the visit of a Russian traveler is considered sufficient to "establish relations" between peoples, and the impression is sometimes given that intercourse was continuous after these first contacts.

The most important help the non-Russian peoples received was military aid against a variety of "foreign enemies." One gets the impression from the new histories that the Princes of Kiev and Moscow were always ready to ride off in any direction to rescue a weak neighbor from an aggressive foe. They rode to battle not for conquest, but in the cause of historic justice; indeed the "liberating and revolutionary traditions" of the Russian people won the lasting gratitude of their neighbors.[10] Even when the military aid resulted in the incorporation of the territory, it is not a question of ordinary conquest, since annexation is said to have been in complete accord with the wishes of the local people, who could see in this develop-

10. The expression is that of Anna Pankratova, one of the main architects of the myth, from her article "Velikii russkii narod i ego rol' v istorii," *Prepodavanie istorii v shkole*, No. 5, 1946, pp. 18-31.

ment an opportunity for a closer relationship with their protectors, the Russian people. One of the most far-fetched arguments in this connection is the assertion that the growth of the Russian centralized state was a solidly progressive phenomenon, of great significance to all Soviet peoples. The strengthening of the Muscovite state is given considerable space in the new survey histories of Moldavia, Estonia, and the Tatars; the battle of Kulikovo is a major event in the history of the Kazakhs. The impression is given that neighboring peoples saw the growing Russian state only as an ally and protector; there is no hint that they might have feared its military power or have been suspicious of its motives.

When it comes to the Russian acquisition of the largest empire in history, Soviet historians have introduced a number of explanations which soften the harshness of the earlier interpretation. They either deny a military confrontation between Russian and non-Russian peoples, or they introduce mitigating circumstances, such as the protection of the people against an enemy. A great majority of annexations of territory are now said to have been voluntary, in answer to the wishes not only of the local leaders, but of their people. In the case of the "three brotherly peoples"—Russians, Ukrainians, and Belorussians—the view is that a unified state was in development in the thirteenth century, when the invasion of the Tatars (a foreign enemy) disrupted it, and that all three peoples worked actively for the "reunion" achieved in the seventeenth century. Ivan IV's Kazan campaign of 1552, usually considered the first acquisition of a non-Russian people by the Muscovite state, is an example of the other type. In the new view (dating only from the early 1950's) the Russian army was sent to rescue the local populace from its natural enemy, the Golden Horde.[11] Evidence has been presented to show that the local people assisted the Russians who laid siege to their city. The expansion across Siberia is seen as a peaceful settlement of undeveloped lands by intrepid Russian pioneers, interrupted only by a few cases of military resistance by local tribal leaders, trying to preserve their privileges. The acquisition of the Caucasus and Central Asia is now regarded as a liberating effort to save these peoples from incorporation into an alien and oppressive state, by the Turks, Persians, and above all, by "British imperialism." The resistance to the Russian advance

11. For a discussion of the intricate problem of separating the Tatar people (friendly members of the future Soviet family) from the Golden Horde (the oppressive foreign enemy), see below, pp. 314-15; 341-42.

is characterized as reactionary feudal movements, aimed at maintaining the *status quo,* and impeding a progressive historical development. Only a few pitched battles of the old-fashioned sort
remain, principally in Central Asia. They are said to have been
fought against reactionary local leaders, who frequently had the
backing of the British. In any event, Russian acquisition of territory, regardless of the means, is considered a progressive historical
phenomenon. Soviet historical science has ruled out completely the
possibility that any of the non-Russian peoples might have been
able to maintain their independence and form a viable state of their
own. The only alternative was to be annexed to Russia or to fall
to some enemy.

Annexation to Russia is progressive for many reasons. The
local people gained political stability (tsarist oppression is acknowledged to have been better than feudal oppression or internecine
fighting). They enjoyed a higher standard of living, through
partial industrialization, improved agriculture, the building of railroads, and increased trade, which put them for the first time in the
world market. Expeditions of Russian scientists and engineers to
the colonies are no longer seen as acts typical of imperialism, but
as acts that were fully approved by the local population, and as
one more manifestation of the genius and helpfulness of the Russian
people. The non-Russian peoples made great gains through their
contacts with Russian culture, which is acknowledged to have
been superior to all the others, even the Georgian, Armenian,
Uzbek, and Tadzhik, which were at least a thousand years older.
The subject peoples went to school to the Russians at every level,
from the natives of Siberia, whose language was put into writing
for the first time by Russians, to the intellectuals of the more
advanced cultures, who sat at the feet of the great Russian "revolutionary democrats" of the nineteenth century. Finally, it is argued,
the ultimate benefit of annexation was that it put all these peoples
on the road to the Revolution, the socialist society, and eventual
communism. The arrival in the colonies of the Russian proletariat,
"the most advanced in the world," strengthened the class struggle
there, and quickened the arrival of the Revolution, which is now
viewed as a multi-national event. Of considerable importance is
the fact that annexation made possible the first contacts with
Bolshevik leaders, many of whom were exiled to these areas.

In all of this there is a strong resurgence of the doctrine of
Russian leadership, which in practice negates completely the

theoretical equality of peoples in the U.S.S.R. This is dramatized in the evolution of the term "elder brother" (*starshii brat*), referring to the seniority of the Russian people. The expression had its origin before the Revolution among the tsars' apologists, who tried to convince the colonial peoples of the Russian *mission civilisatrice*. It was scornfully rejected by early Bolshevik historians, who held it up as an example of hypocritical bourgeois rationalizing. But during World War II it began to reappear in editorials and speeches, and has become an honored term among non-Russian writers and speakers who ritualistically express their gratitude to the Russian people for help in the past and present.

Finally, the new history has taken the logical step of reducing historical friction among the non-Russian peoples themselves. The campaigns of medieval Georgian kings into Armenian lands, regarded as conquests before 1940, are now said to have been defensive efforts against the Turk, having the progressive effect of strengthening the medieval Georgian state. Moslem-Christian tensions and riots are played down, and are put in a class context when discussed at all. Historic alliances between various non-Russian peoples against their natural enemies are emphasized, and their cultural connections with non-Soviet peoples have been subordinated to ties with members of the present Soviet family. In the new view the non-Russian peoples were not only allied with the Russian people historically, but with each other.

With this sketch of the current interpretation in mind, let us look at what Bolshevik leaders and historians were saying on this subject during the first twenty years after the Revolution.

CHAPTER **2.**

EARLY SOVIET VIEWS
ON THE FRIENDSHIP OF PEOPLES

"Scratch some Communists and you will find a Great Russian chauvinist." Lenin to the Eighth Party Congress, 1919 (Polnoe sobranie sochinenii [*Moscow, 1958-65*], *XXXVIII, 183*).

"That was the time [before the Revolution] when Russia was cursed by all the peoples." Stalin to the Congress of the Peoples of Dagestan, 1920 (Sochineniia [*Moscow, 1946–], IV, 394*).

"In the past, we Russians—I am a Great Russian, as full blooded as one can be—in the past, we Russians were the biggest robbers that could be imagined." Pokrovskii's concluding remark to the First All-Union Conference of Marxist Historians, 1929 (Trudy pervoi vsesiouznoi konferentsii istorikov-marksistov [*Moscow, 1930], I, 494-95*).

During the early years of Soviet power, the question of the friendship of peoples was one of political rather than historiographical content. The writing of an acceptable Marxist-Leninist history of the Soviet peoples was an academic question for the future, but current relations between Russians and non-Russians were of critical importance, especially during the period of the Revolution, Civil War, and the formation of the U.S.S.R. The following examination of early Soviet views on this question will show the extent to which the Soviet historian has been obliged to reinterpret or "forget" the immediate Soviet past. If the evidence of the first decade of Soviet power were to be entered in court, it would destroy the myth: it would show that the friendship of Soviet peoples, which is supposed to have existed before the Revolution, did not in fact exist by 1930.

THE QUESTION OF GREAT RUSSIAN CHAUVINISM

One of the most persistent and urgent problems on the nationalities front after the Revolution was the question of Great Russian chauvinism, by which the Bolsheviks meant the tendency of Russians to take a superior or haughty attitude toward non-Russians, and to dominate them politically and economically. The party's continuing attention to this question for more than a decade after coming to power was an acknowledgment of a wide gap between theory and practice: the Revolution had not brought about a sharp reversal of attitudes between peoples of different nationality. In their urgent statements and resolutions on Great Russian chauvinism party leaders admitted that hatreds between Soviet peoples were in fact so strong as to endanger the entire revolutionary program.

The whole question of the party's struggle against Great Russian chauvinism, which so clearly refutes the more recent Soviet view that the friendship of peoples was already consolidated at that time, has understandably been overlooked in the new Soviet history, in which space is devoted instead to "the brotherly help of the Russian people" for the non-Russian nationalities, "the struggle of all Soviet peoples" for the establishment of Soviet power, and the "voluntary" formation of the U.S.S.R. When the theme is discussed, some of its essential features are skirted. The reader gets the impression that it was a minor problem when in reality it was of great importance, and that it was confined to a few leaders, mainly non-Bolshevik, when the truth is that it was largely a problem within the Bolshevik ranks and was very widespread, involving all levels of people.[1] Lenin made these points

1. The withering away of the issue is so complete that the younger Soviet students of history may well wonder what Great Russian chauvinism was. The standard college textbook on the history of the U.S.S.R., to take one example, makes two references of one sentence each to it (see *Istoriia SSSR, Epokha sotsializma: [1917-1957 gg], Uchebnoe posobie* [Moscow, 1957], pp. 258, 294). The party histories are almost equally brief, the question being referred to in a sentence or two in connection with the resolutions of the party congresses (see *Istoriia vsesoiuznoi kommunisticheskoi partii [Bol'shevikov], Kratkii kurs* [Moscow, 1938], pp. 246, 251; *Istoriia kommunisticheskoi partii sovetskogo soiuza* [Moscow, 1959], pp. 332-33, 356, 428). In none

quite clear in the same speech in which he modified Napoleon's
quip about scratching a Russian. He sharply criticized Bolsheviks
(calling Piatakov by name) for their superior attitudes towards
the other nationalities, adding that "the Bashkirs distrust the Great
Russians because the Great Russians are more cultured and have
employed their culture to rob the Bashkirs. That is why the term
Great Russian is synonymous with the terms 'oppressor' and 'rogue'
to the Bashkirs in those remote places. This must be taken into
account, it must be dealt with, but it will be a lengthy process."[2]

The universality of Great Russian chauvinism is indicated in the
wording of a resolution of the Twelfth Party Congress (1923),
which referred to its prevalence in the Ukraine, Belorussia, Azerbaidzhan, to Turkestan in general as well as specific references to
the Uzbeks and Kirgiz. The resolution specified that "relations
between the working class and the peasantry are hindered mainly
by remnants of Great Russian chauvinism found both in the party
and Soviet organs."[3]

The later cursory references to the question also give the impression that it was a result of the conditions of the New Economic
Policy, although it was a serious problem before the NEP was
introduced, and persisted long after it. A party spokesman complained in 1929 that "we find still among our officials a haughty and
contemptuous attitude towards the cultures of the more backward
peoples" and added, "It must be emphasized that certain sections
of the Russian working population are infected with Great Russian
chauvinism even today."[4] The last of three party congress resolu-

---

of the above references is any definition given, and by mentioning Great
Russian chauvinism in the context of the struggle with opposition groups the
impression is given that the party was not infected. The recent *Soviet Historical Encyclopedia* is slightly more helpful, but also misleading. In an
eleven-paragraph article on "Great Power Chauvinism," one paragraph is
devoted to the issue inside "the ranks of the CPSU" without giving details.
Most of the article is concerned with the phenomenon elsewhere—Napoleon's
empire, Austro-Hungary, and the contemporary U. S.—and the Russian
problem is distorted by an introductory sentence stating that "the Bolsheviks
unmasked the Great Russian chauvinism of tsarism, the landlords, the bourgeoisie, the petit-bourgeois parties, the bourgeois provisional government . . ."
(see *Sovetskaia istoricheskaia entsiklopediia* [Moscow, 1961–   ], III, 242-44).

2. V. I. Lenin, *Polnoe sobranie sochinenii* (Moscow, 1958-65), XXXVIII,
183.

3. *KPSS v rezoliutsiiakh i resheniiakh s"ezdov, konferentsii i plenumov Ts.
K.* (7th ed., Moscow, 1953), Part 1, p. 559.

4. G. Aleksandrov in *The Masked Class Enemy*, as quoted by Sergius
Yakobsen, "The Rise of Russian Nationalism," *Nationalism: a Report by a*

tions calling for the elimination of Great Russian chauvinism was passed at the Sixteenth Congress in June, 1930.[5]

The real status of the friendship of peoples in the pre-revolutionary period and the first decade of the Soviet regime (in contrast to the current view) can be sketched in the writings of two authoritative spokesmen: Stalin, who is doubly useful to our study as the chief theoretician and administrator in the nationalities area, and Mikhail N. Pokrovskii, the dominant Soviet historian of that period. Neither of these men devoted as much as a short article to the theme of the pre-revolutionary friendship of peoples, for the simple reason that the concept did not exist at the time. But in the context of their statements on the nationalities problem, in its political and historical aspects, their views emerge clearly, and are in complete agreement.

STALIN ON THE FRIENDSHIP OF PEOPLES

The Soviet myth on the friendship of peoples was formulated at a time when the words of the leader were not only desirable, but obligatory, in scholarly works. But the Stalin quotations on this theme, as mined by Soviet scholars, are of unusually low-grade ore: they are short, vague, and not to the point; or they come from the period after World War II. Anyone who analyzes Soviet literature on this subject will soon be aware that the Soviet scholars have missed their best opportunity—to prove the thesis with statements of Stalin as Peoples' Commissar for Nationalities. Their failure to do so is simply because Stalin did not hold the same views in the 1920's as those enunciated in the 1940's, and although his references to the subject are numerous, a fair quotation of them would destroy the myth.[6]

Stalin (as well as Lenin and other Bolshevik spokesmen on the question) believed that Great Russian chauvinism was a legacy of

---

Study Group of the Royal Institute of International Affairs (London, 1939), p. 74.

5. *Istoriia kommunisticheskoi partii sovetskogo soiuza* (1959), p. 428.

6. Statements of Lenin that are applicable to the friendship of peoples idea would seem to be even more uncommon. In 1954 N. Matiushkin, a popularizer of Soviet patriotism, published a pamphlet titled *V. I. Lenin on the Friendship of Peoples.* This forty-page work is a rather rare phenomenon: a Soviet work on Lenin with a scarcity of Lenin quotations. In the forty pages the author cites Lenin eleven times, in a majority of cases in one sentence or phrase. Not a single one of these quotations is directly on the subject. See N. Matiushkin, *V. I. Lenin o druzhbe narodov* (Moscow, 1954).

tsarism. He argued that capitalism, by its very nature, bred national hatred, and that communism, by contrast, offered the only possibility for friendly cooperation of peoples of different nationalities. The Revolution was therefore the great dividing line between darkness and light, and any thought of a pre-revolutionary friendship of peoples would have been unthinkable.

Stalin stated his view of the ties between capitalism and national hatred clearly in the theses on the national question for the Tenth Party Congress (1921): "If private property and capital inevitably disunite people, stir up national strife and intensify national oppression, then collective property and labor just as inevitably unite people, undermine national strife and abolish national oppression. The existence of capitalism without national oppression is just as unthinkable as the existence of socialism without the liberation of oppressed nations, without national freedom."[7]

A month after Stalin published this statement he restated his view to the Party Congress, tying the proposition to Russia and making it quite clear that an alliance of the working class of different nationalities would have been impossible under tsarism:

> Obviously, the only regime capable of solving the national question, i.e. a regime capable of *creating conditions for ensuring the peaceful coexistence and fraternal cooperation of different nations and races [natsii i plemen]*, is a regime of Soviet power, a regime of the dictatorship of the proletariat.
>
> It hardly needs proving that under the rule of capital, with private ownership of the means of production and the existence of classes, the equal rights of nations cannot be secured; as long as the power of capital exists, as long as the struggle for the possession of the means of production goes on, there can be no equal rights for nations, just as *there cannot be cooperation between the working masses of the nations.* History tells us that the only way to abolish national inequality, *the only way to establish a regime of fraternal cooperation between the working masses of oppressed and non-oppressed peoples,* is the liquidation of capitalism and the establishing of a Soviet structure.[8]

7. I. V. Stalin, *Sochineniia* (Moscow, 1946–), V, 19.
8. *Ibid.*, V, 38. Emphasis added. Another reference to this theme can be found in Stalin's speech to the Tenth Congress of Soviets in December, 1922 (*ibid.*, V, 145-55).

Not only did Stalin tie the friendship of peoples to a Soviet regime, he also drew his class lines in such slovenly fashion that the "Stalinist" line of 1920 would be clearly labeled "bourgeois nationalist" three decades later. He blamed national hatreds on tsarism and capitalism (one of the few propositions to survive without any revision), but in passing he specifically denied one of the premises of the later myth: that such national hatreds existed *only between classes*, as opposed to national groups of the same class. Stalin was of the opinion (like everybody else at the time) that the oppressed non-Russians hated all Russians impartially, without any particular regard to class. Thus, in an article of 1919, after listing the evils of tsarist nationality policy, he noted that such a program "aroused in the Eastern peoples a feeling of distrust and hatred of everything Russian."[9] The following year, in another article on the urgent nationalities problem, Stalin drew up a similar catalog of reactionary tsarist measures, concluding that "by all these means tsarism implanted among the local national masses the deepest kind of distrust, which sometimes passed over to hostility for everything Russian."[10] This quotation, which was cited by B. G. Gafurov in the 1949 edition of his *History of the Tadzhik People* (and was criticized by a reviewer, though without direct reference to its author, of course), was scissored out of a long passage which otherwise remained untouched in the 1952 edition.[11]

Lest there be any doubt that Stalin's references to the "hatred of everything Russian" are meant to express the hatred of one proletarian for another, one has only to search for more explicit statements. In the theses for the Tenth Party Congress, Stalin cited an important accomplishment of Soviet nationality policy. He said it had "changed completely the relations between the working masses of the different nationalities in Russia, struck at the root of the old national hatred, removed the grounds for national oppression, and won for the Russian workers the confidence of their brothers of other nationalities, not only in Russia, but also in Europe and Asia."[12] In the theses for the Twelfth Party Congress (1923), also written by Stalin, the complaint was made that the

9. *Ibid.,* IV, 237.
10. *Ibid.,* IV, 356.
11. B. G. Gafurov, *Istoriia tadzhikskogo naroda v kratkom izlozhenii* (Moscow, 1949), I, 417; *ibid.* (2nd ed., Moscow, 1952), pp. 396-97.
12. Stalin, *Sochineniia,* V, 20.

Russian Communists themselves were the worst offenders in re-
taining the old national hatreds, although more than four years had
passed since the Revolution.[13] Stalin also referred here to all kinds
of hatreds among the non-Russian peoples—"Georgian chauvinism
(in Georgia) directed against the Armenians, Ossetians, Adzharians
and Abkhazians; Azerbaidzhani chauvinism (in Azerbaidzhan)
directed against the Armenians; Uzbek chauvinism (in Bukhara
and Khorezm) directed against the Turkmenians and Kirgiz"—a
theme that would later be dropped in favor of the friendship myth.
Finally, he referred to the "distrust of the working masses" on the
international level when in 1921 he sponsored a new slogan on the
self-determination of peoples. The special merit of the slogan, he
stated, was that it "removes all grounds for suspicion that the
workers of one nation entertain predatory designs against the
workers of another nation, and therefore creates a basis for mutual
confidence and voluntary union."[14]

Most numerous among Stalin's statements negating the friendship myth are his many references, in passing, to the need for
creating friendly relations in the future and his acknowledgment
of very modest beginnings in the field. In 1919 he noted that the
peoples of the East "are beginning to regard Russia as the bulwark
and banner for the liberation from the chains of imperialism;"[15]
in 1920 he was talking about the "need to establish definite relations, definite ties between the center and the border regions . . .
to rally the border regions around the proletarian center . . . to put
an end to the estrangement and isolation of the border regions. . . ."[16]
In 1922 Stalin concluded his speech to the Tenth Congress of
Soviets by stating that "five years ago the Soviet power succeeded
in laying the foundation for the peaceful coexistence and fraternal cooperation of peoples,"[17] and in 1923, after recommending
"prolonged assistance" by the Russian proletariat for the non-
Russian peoples to the Twelfth Party Congress, he stated that
"otherwise there can be no grounds for expecting the establishment
of proper and lasting cooperation of peoples. . . ."[18]

Stalin's references to the question could be multiplied many
times over, but this would not change the essential and consistent

13. *Ibid.*, V, 189.
14. *Ibid.*, V, 52-59.
15. *Ibid.*, IV, 237.
16. *Ibid.*, IV, 351-63.
17. *Ibid.*, V, 155.
18. *Ibid.*, V, 188.

view that the Revolution had marked the beginning of friendship and that progress had been slow and laborious thereafter. Even in the middle thirties, Stalin would speak to the collective farmers of Central Asia about the "friendship between the peoples of the U.S.S.R.—a great and serious conquest [*zavoevanie*]" of the party, and refer to it not as an accomplishment, but as a task yet to be finished.[19]

A reading of Stalin's works from the October Revolution to the time of the formation of the U.S.S.R. will yield only one statement which might be construed as supporting evidence for the later line on the friendship of peoples. Speaking to a party meeting in Tbilisi in July, 1921, he tried to emphasize the seriousness of the current nationalities problem by remarking that the situation had been better in the past:

> I remember the years 1905-1917 when complete fraternal solidarity could be observed among the workers and laboring groups of the Transcaucasian nationalities in general; when fraternal ties bound the Armenian, Georgian, Azerbaidzhani and Russian workers into one socialist family. Now, on my arrival in Tbilisi, I was struck by the absence of the former solidarity between the workers of the Transcaucasus. Among the workers and peasants nationalism has developed, a feeling of distrust for their comrades of other nationalities has intensified: anti-Armenian, anti-Tatar, anti-Georgian, anti-Russian and every kind of nationalism is now widespread. The old ties of fraternal confidence are severed, or at least greatly weakened. Evidently the three years of the existence of nationalistic governments in Georgia (Mensheviks), in Azerbaidzhan (Mussavats), in Armenia (Dashnaks), have left their mark.[20]

How are we to reconcile these remarks with other statements of Stalin that are in such direct contradiction? Their exaggeration is obvious: during most of the period in question Stalin was not in the Caucasus to observe such "fraternal solidarity," and the accuracy of the term "one socialist family" would not be accepted at face value by today's most ardent supporters of the friendship myth. The most logical explanation seems to be that Stalin's reference to the "good old days" was a tactical move to put the blame for the current situation on his political enemies. He had come home to

19. Quoted in *Druzhba narodov RSFSR* (*Materialy v pomoshch' propagandistu i agitatoru*) (Leningrad, 1938), p. 3.
20. Stalin, *Sochineniia*, V, 95-96.

make a speech to his old comrades, and it may be that we see here an early glimmer of the nostalgia that was to become an ingredient of the Stalin cult of personality.

POKROVSKII'S VIEWS

Like Stalin, Pokrovskii was both a thinker and a doer. He not only established the first distinctively Bolshevik interpretation of Russian history, but he took the first steps in the direction of harnessing "historical science" to the party. The posthumous careers of these men also have interesting parallels: both men were made the object of a planned denunciation shortly after their deaths, and both were subsequently very painstakingly and selectively rehabilitated. The legacy of their ideas and techniques, as they have been carefully winnowed by their successors, persists in the Soviet Union today.

Pokrovskii did not write extensively about the relations of Russians and non-Russians, but his running commentary on tsarist colonialism, scattered through several of his works, makes his position clear. His observations—generously peppered with typical Pokrovskii sarcasm—constitute the harshest indictment of the Russian Empire that has ever been published. His views were essentially in agreement with the Bolshevik interpretation of his day (indeed, it was he more than anyone who established its fine points), but they did differ in degree. No other Bolshevik, whether for lack of erudition or eloquence, succeeded in damning the Russian Empire so effectively.

Russian colonialism was Pokrovskii's *bête noire*. He could think of no better historical example of the manifold evils of colonialism than the story of Russian expansion. Unlike Russian historians before and after him, he saw no mitigating circumstances or positive by-products of Russian colonialism. He did not fully accept the universal rationalization of later Soviet historians —that annexation to Russia had set the stage for non-Russians to share the benefits of the first successful proletarian revolution. Pokrovskii went no further than to acknowledge that the Revolution "could serve as some compensation for all the suffering" these people had endured.[21] He thought that Russian expansion was motivated by the most primitive greed for booty and land, and

21. M. N. Pokrovskii, *Russkaia istoriia s drevneishikh vremen* (Moscow, 1933), I, 250.

that the Russians had no cultural advantages to offer their new subjects—all the more reason why annexation to Russia was, for the non-Russians, an unmitigated tragedy, an "absolute evil."

In his view, the Russian Empire had been built exclusively on aggression. He did not detect a single case of "voluntary annexation" and sometimes rebuked his Bolshevik colleagues, even the non-Russians, for being too lenient on tsarism. At the First All-Union Conference of Marxist Historians, he declared that he was "somewhat shocked" by the "soft tones" of a report by the Georgian historian, F. Makharadze, on Georgia's annexation to Russia. Asserting that Georgia was for Russia merely a *"place-d'armes* against Turkey," he said it was "annexed by forceful measures without exception. To say that the Russians were defending Georgia, that they came to protect her, is as bare faced a lie and hypocrisy as to say that we were protecting Bulgaria."[22] He also rejected the view that Russian expansion into Mordvinian lands in the 1370's was without violence. The area "was surrendered to Russian colonists as booty and plunder. Great Russia was already formed. It was not a peaceful settlement of southern lands by 'cultured' Slavs. It was rape and oppression of a rather densely populated agricultural land."[23]

Pokrovskii believed that the beginnings of the Russian Empire were much earlier than the conquest of Kazan in 1552, the traditional date given by historians. In a well-known passage in his *Russian History from the Most Ancient Times* he stated that "the Russian Empire was called a 'prison of peoples.' We know now that this applies not only to the Romanov state, but also to its predecessor, the patrimony of the heirs of Kalita. Already the Grand Duchy of Moscow, and not only tsarist Moscow, was the 'prison of peoples.' Great Russia was built on the bones of 'aliens,' and it is no great consolation to the latter that eighty per cent of its blood flows in the Great Russians."[24]

He could not see the threat of other colonial powers as a

22. *Trudy pervoi vsesoiuznoi konferentsii istorikov-marksistov* (Moscow, 1930), I, 493-94; the same view is expressed in *Russkaia istoriia v samom szhatom ocherke* (Moscow, 1934), III, 223. Pokrovskii could not foresee that his successors would undermine his argument completely by arguing that the Russians were protecting Bulgaria by liberating her from the Turks.

23. 'Vozniknovenie moskovskogo gosudarstva i 'velikorusskaia narodnost,' " *Istorik-Marksist* [hereafter cited as *IM*], Nos. 18-19, 1930, pp. 14-28. Quotation is on pp. 23-24.

24. *Russkaia istoriia s drevneishikh vremen*, I, 249.

justification for Russian expansion. For him the British threat
was no greater for the peoples of the Caucasus and Central Asia
than the Russian threat. The free peoples of the Caucasus were
surrounded by a den of wolves—Russians, Persians, Turks, British,
and French—and he looked on them all with fine impartiality. Indeed, judging from his occasional statements comparing British rule
in India with Russian rule in her colonies, one might conclude that
he would have regarded British control of these areas as the lesser
of the evils. He thought that Russia's advance into the Caucasus
was strictly for strategic reasons, growing out of her rivalry with
Persia. He rejected the idea, later held by Soviet historians, that
the peoples living in the area preferred the Russians to other
conquerors. The defiance of the people, in fact, made the Russian
victory much more difficult than it would have been otherwise.
Russia won because of her favored geographical position and her
willingness to pay the military costs.[25]

One of the worst features of tsarist colonialism, in Pokrovskii's
view, was that it left the fate of the new subjects in the hands of
the conquering generals, who followed a consistent policy of cruelty
and sometimes looked upon the local people as cattle.[26] The
general appearance of Central Asian cities, years after the Russian
conquest, was that of an armed camp. By comparison British rule
in India seemed benign.[27] Pokrovskii had only contempt for the
Ermolovs and Kaufmanns, who would be regarded not unkindly
as governors by later Soviet historians.[28] For him, General Kaufmann was responsible for pillaging, burning, and murder in Central
Asia, the author of the notorious order of the day: "Shoot, shoot,
shoot!"[29] One of the main factors in prolonging the wars in the
Caucasus was "careerism" among the officers. After the close of the
Napoleonic wars, promotions came slowly for Russian officers, but
the mountain wars gave them the opportunity to rise more rapidly
through the ranks, and they were sorry to see the campaigns end.[30]
In Central Asia officers organized pointless campaigns against

25. *Diplomatiia i voiny tsarskoi Rossii v XIX stoletii* (Moscow, 1923),
pp. 179-81.
26. *Ibid.*, p. 205.
27. *Ibid.*, pp. 320-21.
28. *Ibid.*, pp. 184-95, 327-36; *Istoricheskaia nauka i bor'ba klassov* (Moscow, 1933), I, 227-30.
29. *Diplomatiia i voiny*, p. 331; *Istoricheskaia nauka*, p. 229.
30. *Diplomatiia i voiny*, pp. 205-6.

people who were giving no trouble because they knew they would receive great rewards, official and unofficial.[31]

What would be even more difficult to reconcile with the future friendship myth was Pokrovskii's low regard for the Russian common soldier, who in the new view is generally regarded as a mere instrument for carrying out reactionary tsarist colonial policy and is not in any way held responsible for its excesses. Pokrovskii's common soldier enjoyed "plain plunder" and killing. "The war with the mountain people," he said, "was actually a good opportunity for pillaging everything, especially by the Cossacks, and in doing so they pleased their officers."[32] Among Pokrovskii's many accounts of the soldiers' butchery, looting, destruction, and desecration of temples are three stories related by the painter Vereshchagin after his trip to Central Asia emphasizing Pokrovskii's view that the common soldier was, if anything, even more cruel than his officers. In one of them, Russian soldiers enter the house of an old woman, who greets them in a friendly way. They notice something moving behind the furniture and discover a sixteen year old boy. "We dragged him out, naturally, and killed him, along with the old woman." In another story two soldiers are arguing about which one will bayonet a four year old child, but when their officers pass by they are obliged to come to attention and the child crawls away to freedom. In the third story, some soldiers hear cries from a native house and fire several volleys through the walls, without bothering to look inside to see about the fate of the occupants.[33]

In contrast to his low opinion of the Russian conquerors, Pokrovskii had great respect for the leaders of resistance movements against the tsar's military forces. In view of his usual disregard for the role of individuals in history, his treatment of Shamil to the length of almost twenty pages in his *Diplomacy and War in Tsarist Russia in the Nineteenth Century* is indicative of his admiration for the mountain leader. He regarded Shamil as a hero and a capable leader in an unequal struggle. Shamil's movement was viewed as "democratic," although it was closely tied with a fanatical religious sect. Even Shamil's military dictatorship toward the end of his career was justified on the grounds of military necessity.[34]

Pokrovskii described the various means by which some non-

31. *Ibid.*, pp. 329-30.
32. *Ibid.*, p. 205.
33. *Ibid.*, p. 332.
34. *Ibid.*, pp. 211-29.

Russians, who were usually militarily defenseless, had escaped the
Russian conqueror. Such cases are especially inimical to the
friendship myth, and when retained by later Soviet historians, the
interpretation has usually been reversed. In some areas of Central Asia he noted that the inhabitants "voluntarily emigrated"
beyond the reach of the Russians, who tried to prevent them from
fleeing to Persia[35] (newer accounts have peoples fleeing from foreign enemies to the Russians, but never in the opposite direction).
He stated that some people on the Persian border who fell under
Russian control "could hardly wait until, finally, they were liberated
from Russian slavery by their free brothers"[36] and that the Azerbaidzhanis were temporarily "saved" from Russian annexation by
European pressures.[37] The new history has much to say about
liberating people and saving them from their enemies, but these
acts are performed exclusively by Russians.

When Pokrovskii referred to Russia's "civilizing mission" in
the Empire, his remarks were full of sarcasm. He put quotation
marks around such terms as "protectors" and "enlighteners" when
referring to the Russians.[38] The military governors, he wrote,
were careful to create a "sentimental legend" about the cultural
benefits received by the non-Russian subjects of Russian rule.[39]
Pokrovskii's main reason for denying the validity of the cultural
mission was that he considered Russian cultural attainments to be
of a very low order, inferior in most cases to those of the conquered peoples. He indicated that the Georgians gained nothing,
since their culture was unrelated to the Russian culture and was a
thousand years older.[40] He even held the extreme view that the
Tatar invaders of the thirteenth century were "a rather highly
organized, semi-settled people in a higher stage of material culture
than their Russian foes."[41] Whatever Pokrovskii's errors may have
been, none of his critics could ever accuse him of Great Russian
chauvinism.

When the "Pokrovskii school" was condemned by the party in
the late 1930's, his harsh views on tsarist colonialism were not
primarily at issue, since that interpretation persisted for some time.

35. *Ibid.*, p. 188.
36. *Ibid.*
37. *Ibid.*, p. 179.
38. *Ibid.*, p. 206; *Russkaia istoriia v samom szhatom ocherke*, III, 223.
39. *Diplomatiia i voiny*, p. 329.
40. *Russkaia istoriia v samom szhatom ocherke*, III, 222-23.
41. "Vozniknovenie moskovskogo gosudarstva . . .," p. 24.

But it is safe to say that if he had not fallen in the 1930's, he would surely have fallen in the 1940's, when the new views on Soviet patriotism, Great Russian leadership, and the friendship of peoples turned his interpretation inside out. Later on Soviet historians would find it convenient to make him the scapegoat for all the erroneous views of his day about the relations of Russians and non-Russians before the Revolution. His extremely harsh interpretation makes the contradictions between the first and second generation of Soviet historians all the more glaring.

TSARIST BRUTALITY IN THE EARLY SOVIET VIEW

Pokrovskii was by no means unusual among Soviet scholars in the severity of his judgment of tsarist conquests. Whereas tsarist expansion may have been characterized in some areas of Siberia as a comparatively peaceful settlement of Russian peasants in the vast stretches of plentiful land, it was best known to the world for its brutality. The tsars' conquering generals had made no secret of their calculated policy of terrorizing the population as a means of controlling it. Eyewitnesses, both Russian and foreign, were shocked by the extent of the cruelty, and their sensational accounts were soon well known.[42] Perhaps the best known statement on the matter is one which Curzon attributed to General Skobelev, one of the conquerors of Turkestan: "I hold it a principle that in Asia the duration of peace is in direct proportion to the slaughter you inflict upon the enemy. Strike hard, and keep on striking till resistance fails; then form ranks, cease slaughter and be kind and humane to the prostrate enemy."[43]

The early Soviet view was, if anything, even more extreme than those interpretations built on the eyewitness accounts. The Bolshevik hatred for the tsarist regime was not soon forgotten. In

42. The best known of the accounts of foreign observers in Central Asia were the American consul Eugene Schuyler's two volumes entitled *Turkistan: Notes of a Journey in Russian Turkistan, Khokand, Bukhara and Kuldja* (New York: Scribner, Armstrong, 1877); Lord George Curzon's *Russia in Central Asia in 1889; and the Anglo-Russian Question* (London: Longmans 1889); and the accounts of the Hungarian scholar Arminius Vambery, especially *Western Culture in Eastern Lands: a Comparison of the Methods Adopted by England and Russia in the Middle East* (London: John Murray, 1906). Among the tsar's subjects were the painter V. V. Vereshchagin, and Chokan Valikhanov, the Kazakh poet, who broke with the Russians in protest against such policies.

43. Quoted by Olaf Caroe, *Soviet Empire: The Turks of Central Asia and Stalinism* (London: The Macmillan Co., 1953), pp. 79-80.

drawing a contrast between tsarist and Soviet policies these writers
went out of their way to emphasize the ruthlessness of the tsarist
conquests. In one of the earliest accounts, Georgii Safarov, a
Bolshevik emissary to Turkestan, wrote in 1921 that the coming of
the Russians to Central Asia might be compared to the coming of
Tamerlane or Genghis Khan.[44] Museums and picture albums presented cartoons and paintings of Russian soldiers shooting natives,
of places of execution, and of natives displaying the heads of Russian soldiers.[45] The history journals, such as *Istorik-Marksist* (*The
Marxist Historian*) and *Bor'ba klassov* (*The Class Struggle*) presented articles on tsarist colonialism, although the topic was written
about less frequently than tsarist diplomacy and the working class
movement. Archival materials were occasionally published in
Krasnyi arkhiv (*The Red Archives*). The first edition of the *Great
Soviet Encyclopedia*, in its articles on the history of the non-Russian
peoples, preserved the prevailing view that tsarist expansion was
always achieved by violence, spoke of the policy of "impoverishment and extinction of the Kirgiz,"[46] and represented resistance
movements as progressive.

The early Soviet histories of the non-Russian areas also preserved this interpretation of tsarist colonialism and contained no
hint of a developing alliance between the working peoples of
different nationalities before the eve of the Revolution. One of
the most important of these is S. V. Bakhrushin's *Essays on the
History of the Colonization of Siberia in the Sixteenth and Seventeenth Centuries*, which, while free of the polemical language of
Pokrovskii, convincingly indicts tsarist colonialism from the more
solid ground of archival materials. Bakhrushin saw Russian expansion to the Pacific as typical colonial conquest, undertaken for
economic and military goals at great cost in the lives, property, and

44. G. Safarov, *Kolonial'naia revoliutsiia: opyt Turkestana* (Moscow, 1921),
p. 42.

45. K. Ramzin, *Revoliutsiia v Srednei Azii v obrazakh i kartinakh* (Moscow,
1928); see also the special issue of *Problems of the Peoples of the U.S.S.R.*
[hereafter cited as *POP*], No. 19 (Autumn, 1963), pp. 5-51. Vereshchagin did
a number of paintings and cartoons depicting the Russian conquest of Central
Asia, several of which are reproduced in these two works. In 1965 I searched
diligently through the dozens of pictures in the Vereshchagin room of the
Tretiakov Gallery in Moscow without finding any trace of violence between
Russians and Central Asians, although the violence of the Tatars was presented.

46. *Bol'shaia sovetskaia entsiklopediia* [hereafter cited as *BSE*], 1st. ed.,
XXXII, col. 377.

customs of the local people. He did not accept the validity of the civilizing mission and found little evidence of close cooperation between the Russian settlers and the native population. The eventual economic gains were described, but they were not presented as a historic justification for Russian colonization. The work was characterized by a detachment and objectivity that would not be possible in later Soviet works.[47]

Some of the early works on the history of Central Asia, undertaken by Marxist historians (Bakhrushin was not a Marxist in the 1920's), were more polemical in nature. The harshness of the tsarist conquest of Turkestan was emphasized by P. G. Galuzo in his *Turkestan as a Colony* (1929), which was also characterized by sympathy for all resistance movements, even when under religious leadership, and by flat statements about violence between the native population and ordinary Russian people.[48] E. Shteinberg, in his *Sketches on the History of Turkmenia* (1934), argued that tsarist colonialism was much more reactionary than other cases because Russia herself was "a barbaric, half Asiatic, feudal, gendarme" state, transmitting all her evils to her colonies, while the colonies of other nations, such as India under the British, were receiving advanced capitalist institutions.[49] S. D. Asfendiarov, whose *History of Kazakhstan* appeared in 1935, was perhaps the most outspoken of all. "Russian capitalism, like all the rest," he stated, "grew on the blood of millions of workers; its history 'was written in the chronicle of mankind with the flaming tongue of sword and fire.'" Bringing this oratorical indictment to earth with a charge of genocide, Asfendiarov said, "That dark period in the history of tsarist Russia was accompanied by the horrors of the extermination of whole peoples of Siberia (Ostiaks, Voguls and

47. S. V. Bakhrushin, *Ocherki po istorii kolonizatsii Sibiri v XVI i XVII vv.* (Moscow, 1927). An earlier survey history of Siberia is a straightforward account of conquest and exploitation. See V. I. Ogorodnikov, *Ocherk istorii Sibiri do nachala XIX stol.* (Irkutsk, 1920), Vol. I; *ibid.* (Vladivostok, 1924), Vol. II.

48. P. G. Galuzo, *Turkestan-koloniia* (*ocherk istorii Turkestana ot zavoevaniia russkimi do revoliutsii 1917 goda*) (Moscow, 1929), especially pp. 38-41. Galuzo had already published these views in a detailed study, "Pereselencheskaia politika tsarskogo pravitel'stva v srednei Azii," *Kommunisticheskaia mysl'*, No. 2, 1927, pp. 22-47; No. 3, 1927, pp. 9-78; No. 4, 1927, pp. 25-49.

49. E. Shteinberg, *Ocherki istorii Turkmenii* (Moscow-Leningrad, 1934), p. 51.

others), by the horrors of pillaging, killing and violence in relations
with Tatars, Bashkirs and other national groups."[50]

Asfendiarov's book constituted Volume I of a projected two-
volume history of Kazakhstan. He did not live to publish the second
volume. The victim of a crushing review in 1936, he soon disappeared during the purges. He was charged with "bourgeois
nationalism" for his failure to draw clear class lines and his idealization of counter-revolutionary Kazakh leaders and groups. It is
interesting that the author of the fatal review did not mention
Asfendiarov's interpretation of tsarist colonial policy: as of 1936
party ideologists and "bourgeois nationalists" were in complete
agreement on that subject.[51]

Thus it is apparent that up to the middle 1930's Marxist and
non-Marxist historians, whether within the U.S.S.R. or outside,
were in rare agreement in their view of the basic nature of Russian
colonialism. The main historians mentioned here—Bakhrushin, Galuzo, Shteinberg, and Asfendiarov—did have differences of opinion
about fine points of interpretation, some of which will be discussed
later in this study. With the exception of Bakhrushin, their works
were rendered obsolete by the drastic reinterpretations following
World War II. When the complete works of Bakhrushin were
published in the 1950's, his ideas on this subject were "corrected"
by the technique of the editorial footnote, by which the reader was
frequently advised that words mean the opposite of what they
seem to mean (see Chapter 15 below, pp. 348-50).

50. S. D. Asfendiarov, *Istoriia Kazakhstana* (*s drevneishikh vremen*),
(Alma-Ata, 1935), I, 110.
51. T. Ryskulov, "Protiv izvrashcheniia istorii kazakhskogo naroda i
kharaktera oktiabria v Kazakhstane," *Revoliutsiia i national'nosti,* No. 6, 1936,
pp. 62-67.

CHAPTER **3.**

THE BEGINNINGS
OF THE FRIENDSHIP MYTH

"They [the Ukrainians] did not know that a fate worse than that under the szlachta awaited them in the future at the hands of the Muscovite dvorianstvo and its autocrat—the 'white tsar.' " The consequences of the annexation of the Ukraine, from a 1928 textbook on Ukrainian history (M. Iavorskii, Istoriia Ukrainy v styslomu narysi [Kharkov, 1928], p. 58).

"The Ukraine's incorporation into the Russian state was for her a lesser evil than seizure by the Poland of the Pans or the Turkey of the Sultans." The 1940 view, from the Pankratova textbook (Istoriia SSSR, ed. A. M. Pankratova [1st ed. Moscow, 1940], I, 189).

"The Ukraine's incorporation into the Russian state signified a reunion of two great brotherly peoples which was to save the Ukraine from seizure by Poland and Turkey." The same passage, as rewritten for the 1947 and subsequent editions.

Although the concept of the friendship of Soviet peoples in pre-revolutionary times came into currency only during the World War II period, some of its elements can be traced back to the late 1920's. One can find already at that time a discussion of several of the premises of the future myth, as well as the appearance of the methods by which historical interpretation would be controlled by the exigencies of politics, in part by nationality policy. It would be a mistake, however, to look at the increasing party pressures on historians as another example of Soviet long-range planning

with consistent goals. On the contrary, the party's leadership in
this area has been haphazard in the extreme, depending on the
political situation at a given time. The most unsettling factor in
the Soviet historian's professional life has been his inability to
anticipate the political trends of the immediate future. Around
1930 Soviet historians were called on to combat Ukrainian nationalism. A decade later they were engaged in inculcating patriotism
through a respect for past leaders and military traditions, which
brought in its wake a resurgence of nationalism. Five years later
they were busily attacking "bourgeois nationalism" among the non-
Russian peoples, which involved condemning them for their respect for the distinctive features of their past and their military
leaders. Soviet historians seem to be engaged endlessly in tearing
down what they have just painstakingly constructed.

This uneven development, always tied to current policy, is
illustrated by the Soviet interpretation of some of the elements of
the future friendship myth as they existed in the 1930's when
Soviet historiography was beginning to eliminate individual interpretations in favor of a solid front.

THE PURGE OF THE UKRAINIAN HISTORIANS

The first extensive party attack on non-Russian historians
was the purge of the Ukrainian "nationalist" historians in the early
1930's. Although this ideological campaign did not directly involve
the friendship of peoples idea, it concerned some of its basic propositions, and one of its persistent problems, the eradication of
"bourgeois nationalism." This chapter in Soviet historiography has
been more fully described elsewhere[1] than the later ones, with
which this study is directly concerned, and discussion of it here
will be confined to an outline of issues and events, with some observations about their bearing on the future myth.

This first party battle with non-Russian historians is as instructive for what it neglected to consider as for what it held vital to a
Marxist interpretation. The party demanded at that time that historians give more attention to writing from a fiercely class position;

1. Olexander Ohlobyn, "Ukrainian Historiography, 1917-1956," *The Annals
of the Ukrainian Academy of Arts and Sciences in the United States*, V-VI
(1957), No. 4, 360-63; Hryhory Kostiuk, *Stalinist Rule in the Ukraine: A Study
of the Decade of Mass Terror* (1929-1939) (Munich, 1960), pp. 49-53;
Robert S. Sullivant, *Soviet Politics and the Ukraine, 1917-1957* (New York:
Columbia University Press, 1962), pp. 182-85, 197-98.

that they begin to emphasize what Ukrainian and Russian history had in common, rather than the Ukraine's separate existence; that they elaborate the Bolshevik role in the period of the Revolution. At the same time it largely ignored questions such as the progressiveness of annexation to Russia and Russian-Ukrainian cultural relations. Still other components of the future myth were discussed and an interpretation was arrived at which was diametrically opposed to the later view. What is now Great Russian leadership was still condemned at that time as Great Russian chauvinism. Tsarist policies in the Ukraine continued to be seen as an example of the evils of colonialism. The historic role of several Ukrainian figures began to be examined, but in many cases the assessment was in sharp contrast to that which would eventually be adopted.

Ukrainian intellectual life enjoyed a decade of comparative freedom during the brief life of the Ukrainian Republic and the New Economic Policy. In the general renaissance, one of the outstanding areas was the study of history, headed by the most distinguished of Ukrainian scholars, Mikhail S. Hrushevskii (Mykhailo S. Hrushevs'kyi), who, after heading the Central Rada briefly, went into exile in Vienna, then returned in 1924 to head the History Section of the Ukrainian Academy of Sciences. His monumental *History of Ukraine-Rus*, which was published in Kiev beginning in 1928, became the focal point of party criticism. The main objections were that the history emphasized the separate existence of the Ukrainians and Russians historically, and that it ignored class concepts.[2] For several years Hrushevskii's History Section existed independently of Marxist influences. In the late 1920's its membership did not include a single Marxist. The attempt to write a Marxist history of the Ukraine was undertaken in an entirely separate institution, the All-Union Association of Marxist-Leninist Institutes (*VUAMLIN*), headed by Matvei Iavorskii. By avoiding controversial issues, Hrushevskii managed to outlast Iavorskii, his principal critic, though not for long.

Iavorskii's main criticism of Hrushevskii, which was summed up in his report to the First Conference of Marxist Historians (1929), was that he had ignored the role of the class struggle in the processes of history, and that he had taken a nationalist viewpoint.[3] Iavorskii's own interpretation was laid down in a series of textbooks on

2. *Trudy pervoi vsesoiuznoi konferentsii istorikov-marksistov* (Moscow, 1930), pp. 426-35.
3. *Ibid.*

Ukrainian history which were widely used between 1922 and
1929.[4] Although he emphasized class in his approach to his subject,
Iavorskii did not meet party requirements as they were stated by
1930. He continued to present the history of the Ukraine apart from
Russian history, and in this view he received the public support
of Pokrovskii. In his final remarks to the Conference of Marxist
Historians, Pokrovskii derided the theory of "one and indivisible
Russia," agreeing with Iavorskii that it was a legacy of the historians of Imperial Russia.[5] After returning home from the conference, however, Iavorskii also came under attack for his nationalism. The sixth printing of his *Outline History of the Ukraine* was
halted, and although he continued to work for four more years, his
influence was finished. The party's differences with Iavorskii were
summed up in the *Great Soviet Encyclopedia*, which, in an article
published in 1931, labeled his interpretation as "nationalist-kula-
kist": "Its basic tenets were: (a) an attempt to interpret the whole
of Ukrainian history as a struggle of the people for a state of their
own; (b) the presentation of the Ukrainian bourgeoisie and the
kulaks as a revolutionary force . . . ; (c) the idealization of Ukrainian petty-bourgeois parties; (d) the rejection of the historical
preparation for the dictatorship of the proletariat and hence a
denial of such a proletarian revolution in Ukraine."[6]

Thus Iavorskii was placed in the same category as Hrushevskii.
Although he had written from a class viewpoint, he had not drawn
his lines sharply enough; in particular he had not written the kind
of simplified history in which the Bolsheviks and the masses stand
as a solid front against all "counter-revolutionaries." He had also
made the revolutionary movement too distinctively Ukrainian, and
Pokrovskii's support for his view that the Ukrainians had had a
history of their own had been of little help—indeed this criticism
of Pokrovskii's protégé was an early indication of the decline of the
latter's influence. Just before his death in 1932, Pokrovskii joined
those who were "unmasking" Iavorskii's "vulgarization of Marxism."

Although these issues were considered important in the early
1930's, other Iavorskii views, which today would be equally heretical, went unchallenged. In view of what has happened later, his

4. M. Iavorskii, *Narys istorii Ukrainy* (Kharkov, 1922); *Korotka istoriia
Ukrainy* (Kharkov, 1923), appearing in Russian translation as *Kratkaia istoriia
Ukrainy* (Kharkov, 1925); *Istoriia Ukrainy v styslomu narysi* (Kharkov,
1928).
5. Kostiuk, *Stalinist Rule*, p. 50.
6. *BSE*, 1st ed., LXV, col. 328; quoted in Kostiuk, *Stalinist Rule*, p. 50.

interpretation of certain events is instructive. The Treaty of Pereia-slav (now regarded as the central event in Ukrainian history, by which the peoples were forever united) is dismissed in a couple of sentences in his textbooks. In Iavorskii's interpretation Moscow promised "to assure Cossack autonomy forever" and to give the cities self-government.[7] His references to an independent Cossack state in later pages is an additional indication that he regarded the treaty as something much less than the instrument of the "reunion" of the two peoples, as the future Soviet interpretation would have it. The Ukrainian people were said to have approved the treaty, but under a misapprehension: "[Moscow's] system, though no better than that of the *szlachta,* was still not known to the Ukrain-ian working people, and therefore they leaned toward Moscow, because they knew that their faith was the same, and they would be rid of the *szlachta.*" But they were destined for a still worse fate under the *dvorianstvo* and the "white tsar."[8]

In his textbooks Iavorskii gave about equal space to Bogdan Khmel'nitskii (now the greatest statesman in Ukrainian history) and Ivan Mazepa (now the arch-traitor), treating them both as crafty representatives of their hated class.[9] In his de-emphasis on indi-viduals in history and his class outlook, he had considerably revised the view of Hrushevskii, who treated both men as substantial na-tional leaders, but as opportunists. Already in the 1920's, these two Ukrainian leaders had become the first of a large number of non-Russian leaders whose historic roles would shift because of the strict demands of Soviet historiography.

Early in 1931 Hrushevskii was attacked again, this time from the highest level in an article in a Ukrainian party journal. Among other things, he was accused of being hostile to Ukrainian-Russian friendship. This was apparently the first time that a major his-torian was condemned on such a charge. At that time, however, this was a minor theme, a vague suggestion of things to come. More important, as of 1931, were charges of bourgeois nationalist con-ceptions and ideological neutrality, which amounted to support of counter-revolutionary forces.[10] Hrushevskii was accused of belong-

7. *Kratkaia istoriia Ukrainy,* pp. 57-58; *Istoriia Ukrainy,* p. 58.
8. *Istoriia Ukrainy,* p. 58.
9. *Kratkaia istoriia Ukrainy,* pp. 54-57; 60-62. Mazepa's portrait, presented here, is probably one of the last published in the U.S.S.R.
10. Sullivant, *Soviet Politics,* p. 184, discussing an article by A. Khvylia, "Burzhuazno-nationalistychna trybuna" (*Bil'shovyk Ukrainy,* No. 6, 1931, pp. 46-58).

ing to a nebulous Ukrainian National Center and was deported to
the vicinity of Moscow, where he continued to work under surveil-
lance. At the time of his death in 1934 the Postyshev purge of
Ukrainian intellectuals had already closed most of the history
faculties. Although the party was urging the production of a
Bolshevik history of the Ukraine, nothing acceptable appeared
before the eve of World War II, and these textbooks were soon
made obsolete by the ideological changes of the war. The first
history of the Ukraine to last long enough to be used by one class
of students through its university career was published only in 1956.

THE SEARCH FOR A TEXTBOOK

The party's role in the interpretation of Ukrainian history
had been essentially negative. It had labeled certain ideas as
nationalistic, and in some cases had destroyed the historians who
held them. Beginning in the early 1930's there were indications that
the party would engage in the construction of a new history to
serve its own purposes: the appearance in 1931 of the new journal,
Bor'ba klassov, with its goal of "militant education of the masses";
Stalin's angry letter of the same year to the journal Proletarskaia
revoliutsiia, in which he protested the publication of an article
on party history and suggested his own version; the shakeup in the
branches of the Academy of Sciences in the non-Russian republics,
in which some history faculties were eliminated altogether; the end
of radical experimentation in curriculum and the return to the
obligatory use of textbooks.[11]

The resolution of the Central Committee and Sovnarkom "On
the Teaching of Civic History in the Schools of the U.S.S.R." of
May 16, 1934, marks a new intensification of the party's role in the
writing and teaching of history. Although its provisions were
of a very general nature, it is the key document in the Thermidorian
Reaction of the Bolshevik historiographical revolution as led by
Pokrovskii. It denounced the "abstract, schematic nature" of history
textbooks and teaching in recent years and called for new textbooks

11. Stalin's letter is in the Sochineniia (Moscow, 1946–), XIV, 84-102;
the decrees on curricula (1932) and textbooks (1933) are in Sbornik rukovodiashchikh materialov o shkole (Moscow, 1952), pp. 59-70. Excerpts from
the letter and decrees have been translated in an important new work on
Soviet historiography: Marin Pundeff (ed.), History in the U.S.S.R.: Selected
Readings (Stanford, Calif.: The Hoover Institution, 1967), pp. 91-97. See
also Anatole G. Mazour, Modern Russian Historiography (2nd ed., Princeton,
N. J.: D. Van Nostrand Co., 1958), pp. 194-95.

which would present important facts in chronological order. In order to train new cadres in historical science, the history faculties at the Universities of Moscow and Leningrad were to be restored that fall.[12] Though this decree did not specifically prescribe the content of the textbooks, it set the stage for a more active party role, and indicated the critical importance of historical writing as a support for the state.

Soviet historians did not have to wait long for more specific advice. It came in the form of observations on two rejected textbook manuscripts or *makety* (literally, dummies or mock-ups) signed by Stalin, Zhdanov, and Kirov, and dated August 14, 1934. Four of their comments relate to the future friendship myth and its supporting arguments, and give the most comprehensive view of the party position at that time. Heading the list of objections to one of the rejected manuscripts was the complaint that it was not really a history of the U.S.S.R. but was basically another history of Russia.[13] Thus the coordination of the histories of all Soviet peoples into a single synthesis was decreed from the highest authority. Henceforth the authors of survey textbooks on the history of the U.S.S.R. have faced the formidable task of coordinating the history of such diverse peoples as the Belorussians and the Iakuts, the Georgians and the Evenks. As the U.S.S.R. expanded in the World War II period the synthesis became still more complicated as Moldavia, the Baltic republics, and Tuva were added, with their historic ties to the Turks, Germans, and Chinese. Such histories of the U.S.S.R. attempt a synthesis of the history of all these peoples not from the time of their annexation to Russia or the Soviet Union, but from earliest times. The mere appearance of the history of all these peoples in ancient and medieval times in one book creates an impression that they had much more in common than

12. *Izvestiia*, May 16, 1934; translated in Mazour, *Modern Russian Historiography*, pp. 197-98.

13. *Pravda*, January 27, 1936. Publication was delayed for eighteen months. Shteppa believes that they were submitted to the Central Committee in March, 1934, and that the decision on the original decree on history was made as early as 1932. The phrase "history of the peoples of the U.S.S.R." had apparently first been employed at the Conference of Marxist Historians, when a section was organized under that heading. However, the papers read at the session indicate that the purpose was not to coordinate the histories but to give more emphasis to the histories of the non-Russian parts of the U.S.S.R. See Konstantin F. Shteppa, *Russian Historians and the Soviet State* (New Brunswick, N.J.: Rutgers University Press, 1962), pp. 50, 124-25. Excerpts from the Stalin-Zhdanov-Kirov observations have recently been translated in Pundeff, *History in the U.S.S.R.*, pp. 100-5.

was actually the case. Even if the Soviet historian had been given
no further instructions, he would have emphasized whatever meager
common points he could find in order to give his history some
semblance of coherence. However, the artificial synthesis that has
been achieved by the Soviet historian does not result from such
causes alone. In future years the party would instruct historians to
look for and emphasize the common links, and at the same time
to subordinate and eventually "forget" some facts that would stand
in the way of such an interpretation. The illusion is furthered by the
habitual anachronistic usage of the terms "Soviet," "Soviet Union,"
and "U.S.S.R."[14] References to "Soviet peoples," even in ancient
times, can be found in the new histories.

The new coordinated history textbooks also enjoyed a monopoly
in the elementary schools. The study of the history of the non-
Russian republics was subordinated to the history of the U.S.S.R.
From the time of the purge of the Ukrainian historians for nationalistic interpretations in the early 1930's up to 1960, there were
generally no independent courses and no textbooks on the history
of the non-Russian republics. The non-Russian pupil learned about
the history of his people only in the context of the courses on the
U.S.S.R.

This opinion of Stalin, Zhdanov, and Kirov on the need for
coordinating the history of Soviet peoples was the only one to
survive in the long run. The other three opinions relating to the
friendship of peoples were soon reversed, as the political winds
shifted. As evidence of the ephemeral nature of historical interpretations—even when given from the ideological source—these observations deserve to be quoted at length:

> [1] The summary does not emphasize the annexationist-
> colonizing role of Russian tsarism, together with the Russian
> bourgeoisie and landlords ("tsarism—prison of peoples").

> [2] The summary does not emphasize the counter-revolu-
> tionary role of Russian tsarism in foreign policy from the
> time of Catherine II to the 1850's and later ("tsarism, as
> the international gendarme"). . . .

> [3] The summary does not reflect the role and influence of
> Western European bourgeois-revolutionary and socialist

14. One notable example occurred in Molotov's speech of August 1, 1940,
explaining the incorporation of the Baltic Republics. Ninety per cent of
these people, he said, had previously lived in the U.S.S.R. (*Pravda,* August
2, 1940).

movement on the formation of the bourgeois-revolutionary movement and the proletarian-socialist movement in Russia. The authors of the summary evidently forgot that Russian revolutionaries considered themselves pupils and followers of well known leaders of bourgeois-revolutionary and Marxist thought in the West.

The inclusion of these complaints shows not only that the party leaders in 1934 had no intention of creating the myth of the 1950's but also that they were not even able to lay down an interpretation that would survive the normal life expectancy of a textbook. The first two propositions began to be revised almost immediately under the pressing need to create a Soviet patriotism with historic roots. The revision of the third proposition on the influence of Western Europe was even more ironic: one of its authors, Zhdanov, would turn it inside out, in a spasm of vituperation unequaled in a dialogue with scholars. Unfortunately, the "cosmopolitan" poets, composers, playwrights, and historians of the late 1940's were not allowed the luxury of reminding Zhdanov of his *dictum* of the previous decade.

Soon after these indications of the party's concern for the writing and teaching of history, several commissions were created to carry out reform at the regional level. The composition of these commissions—party ideologists and historians—was yet another indication of increasing party supervision. They were to examine textbooks, direct the writing of new ones, and revise curricula. The four commissions established for Central Asia engaged in sharp controversy. At a conference in Samarkand in 1936 party forces tried to direct Central Asian historians toward a new emphasis on the common elements in the history of the peoples of Central Asia. They met with sharp opposition, however, from local historians who questioned the interpretation. One of the leaders of the opposition was Asfendiarov, whose *History of Kazakhstan* had just been published. He and several other Central Asian historians who opposed the change were shortly condemned as bourgeois nationalists and disappeared in the Stalin purge of the late 1930's.[15]

On January 27, 1936, *Pravda* devoted a major part of its space to the question of improving instruction in history. It published six articles in all, including copies of the party resolutions and

15. G. A. von Stackelberg, "The Tashkent Conference on the History of the Peoples of Central Asia and Kazakhstan, 1954," *Bulletin of the Institute for the Study of the U.S.S.R.*, I (1954), No. 2, 8-13.

observations since 1934. In a front-page editorial, the party organ
made the clearest statement to date about the urgent political lessons to be learned from a proper study of history. The editorial
stated that "history is a powerful weapon in the struggle for socialism" and indicated that the main result of studying Marxist-Leninist
history would be a clear view of the class struggle: "The popular
masses of the U.S.S.R. must know the real history of mankind, the
history of the enslavement and liberation of the working masses;
they must know where we came from and where we are headed,
because this will multiply tenfold the conviction of workers and
collective farmers of the inevitable victory of socialism and will
give them a knowledge of the conditions of this victory."

The occasion for *Pravda's* presentation on history was its announcement that the Central Committee and Sovnarkom had
established still another commission of twelve, headed by Zhdanov,
for the purpose of examining history textbooks for universal adoption. The first task of the commission was to examine *makety* for
new textbooks on the history of the U.S.S.R. and recent general
history.[16] In March, 1936, another resolution set up a contest for
the best textbook on the history of the U.S.S.R. at an elementary
level, with a large prize (100,000 rubles) offered to the winning
collective. Those wishing to enter the competition had to be real
Stakhanovites: the deadline for entries was July 1.[17]

When the commission's decision was announced, on August 22,
1937, the winning textbook, *A Short History of the U.S.S.R.*, edited
by A. V. Shestakov,[18] had already been rushed to press for use all
over the Soviet Union in the third and fourth grades during the
new school year. The first printing, reportedly ten million copies,
must be something of a record in the history of publishing. In
announcing the decision the judges took occasion to mention twelve
"common errors" found in many of the forty-five unsuccessful textbook projects which had been presented in the contest. The errors
were discussed here for the obvious edification of historians who

16. Text of the resolution in *Bol'shevik*, No. 3, 1936, p. 62; as well as
Pravda, January 27, 1936.
17. Text in *Direktivy VKP (b) i postanovleniia sovetskogo pravitel'stva o
narodnom obrazovanii. Sbornik dokumentov za 1919-1947 gg.* (Moscow-
Leningrad, 1947), pp. 188-90. In view of the short time between publication
of the decree and the deadline, it seems likely that publication was delayed,
and contestants had gone to work earlier. In any event, the results were
not announced until August, 1937.
18. *Kratkii kurs istorii SSSR*, ed. A. V. Shestakov (Moscow, 1937).

would be writing about these subjects in the future. Several of these observations have a bearing on the budding friendship myth, and show the stage of the rationalization as of 1937.

Except for one objection to the organization of the histories (some authors had still failed to achieve a synthesis of the history of all the peoples of the U.S.S.R.), all the errors had involved subtle, but vital, points of interpretation. Historians were warned that the presentation of historical events in colors of pure black and white would no longer be acceptable. Many phenomena were comparatively progressive or reactionary in relation to their historical context. As an example, the Zhdanov commission noted that many historians had not recognized that the Orthodox church and the monasteries had played a progressive role in medieval Russia, particularly in bringing "written language and certain elements of higher Byzantine culture" to the Slavs. The historians were also criticized for not recognizing the positive role of Khmel'-nitskii in "his struggle against the occupation of the Ukraine by the Poland of the Pans and the Turkey of the Sultans" (the dominant theme of the future—the progressive essence of "reunion" with Russia—is nowhere referred to). The historians had also been confused in their interpretation of the countless rebellions and uprisings which run through Russian history and which were by no means all progressive. The report registered astonishment that some historians had even idealized the *strel'tsy* mutiny (*miatezh*) against Peter the Great, even though it was "aimed against the effort of Peter to civilize his contemporary Russia."

All these "corrections" would be echoed in later years when the concept of the friendship of peoples was being established in Soviet historiography. But the most far-reaching observation was one written by Stalin himself relating to another subtle point about the Russian acquisition of Georgia and the Ukraine:

> The passing of Georgia under the protectorate of Russia at the end of the eighteenth century, as also the Ukraine's transfer to Russian rule, is regarded by the authors as an absolute evil, without regard for the concrete historical circumstances of those times. The authors do not see that Georgia at that time had two alternatives—either to be swallowed up by the Shah of Persia and the Sultan of Turkey, or to come under a Russian protectorate, just as the Ukraine also had at that time the alternative—either to be absorbed by the Polish Pans and the Sultan of Turkey,

or to go under Russian control. They do not see, that the
second alternative was nevertheless the lesser evil.[19]

Thus the "lesser evil" formula was introduced into Soviet historiography. It was a formula which made it possible to look
upon the building of the Russian Empire as a comparatively progressive historical development, without at the same time changing
the interpretation of Russian colonialism as reactionary. It would
be used ritualistically by Soviet historians until 1951, when it would
be debated and discarded for a more positive interpretation.

It hardly needs noting that all these "errors" of the Soviet historians resulted from their adherence to interpretations that had
been accepted for almost two decades. The Church had been
regarded as reaction incarnate; Khmel'nitskii was still labeled, in
an article in the authoritative *Great Soviet Encyclopedia*, published
in 1935, as "a traitor and clear enemy" of the Ukrainian people;[20]
the rebellions were overwhelmingly interpreted as progressive mass
movements; the building of the Russian Empire was still "an
absolute evil." Here is a good example of the illusion of relative
motion which occurs when the party changes its mind. Others
move; the party stands steady as a rock.

How well did the Shestakov textbook measure up to the party's
expectations? The fact that it was awarded only a second prize
(75,000 rubles)—the first prize being vacated—indicates that there
was much room for improvement in the minds of the judges. The
authors had coordinated the histories of the major peoples of the
U.S.S.R. into a very compact volume (216 pages), and had cautiously rehabilitated Russian historical figures such as Ivan IV and
Peter the Great, but also had given considerable space to their
reactionary deeds, as well as the progressive ones, which left the

19. *Direktivy VKP (b)*, pp. 200-1. In view of future uses of this passage,
the careful wording should be noted. The term "progressive" is not yet
employed to describe the annexation of Georgia and the Ukraine. Note also
the bland terms for the annexation, "passing under the protectorate" and "to go
under Russian control"; the joyful escape from the "external aggressor" is
not mentioned until later.

Stalin's direct authorship of this formula was verified twenty-five years
later by the historian Nechkina, who stated that Stalin edited the entire report.
Nechkina also said that "the formula of the 'lesser evil' was personally
added by I. V. Stalin," which suggested that the original report had contained nothing on the subject. See M. V. Nechkina, "K itogram diskussii o
periodizatsii istorii sovetskoi istoricheskoi nauki," *Istoriia SSSR*, No. 2, 1962,
pp. 57-68. The quotation is from note 5, p. 74.

20. *BSE*, 1st ed., LIX, Cols. 816-18.

book's usefulness for promoting the new Soviet patriotism in some doubt. Some of the party's views, as stated in the observations on the twelve errors, were fulfilled so precisely as to suggest that the authors had seen the party's objections earlier and had made appropriate revisions. This was especially true in the book's interpretation of the role of the medieval Orthodox church and its interpretation of the *strel'tsy* rebellion.[21] The treatment of two other subjects—the role of Khmel'nitskii and the question of the annexation of the Ukraine and Georgia—was less satisfactory, and probably accounts for the book's failure to win first prize. Khmel'nitskii might be considered a positive figure if one read between the lines, but he was not specifically praised. He was presented as a feudal lord and opportunist who turned to Russia only after the Poles had beaten him at his own game of maneuvering for political power. The annexation of the Ukraine was presented as the substitution of one oppression for another.[22] The book presented a similar view of the annexation of Georgia. After an account of the devastation of Georgia at the hands of the Persians, it stated cryptically that "the king of Georgia appealed to Paul I for aid. To the capital of Georgia, Tbilisi, tsarist troops were sent; in 1801 Georgia finally was united with Russia. The devastating raids of the Persian shahs on Georgia ceased."[23] A passage describing Russia's oppression of the Georgians followed, presented in somewhat more detail than the passage on Persian rule. That Georgia had bettered herself, even by the modest requirements of the "lesser evil" formula, was not apparent.

The "lesser evil" formula made its debut at a particularly unfortunate time for Soviet historians, who had just redoubled their efforts to show the character of tsarist colonialism in darkest hues. The result was that the "lesser evil" was an even greater apparent contradiction than it might have been, and historians understandably represented annexation of non-Russian lands as only an ever so slightly "lesser evil," limiting themselves to the cases specified by the party directive.

The new condemnation of tsarist colonial policy had begun in 1935 with publication of archival materials relating to Kamchatka, Iakutia, and Azerbaidzhan.[24] In August, 1936, *Bor'ba klassov*

21. *Kratkii kurs*, ed. Shestakov, pp. 18, 61.
22. *Ibid.*, pp. 50-52.
23. *Ibid.*, p. 79.
24. *Kolonial'naia politika tsarizma na Kamchatke i Chukome v XVIII veke.*

devoted the major part of an issue to articles on tsarist colonialism. One article on the tsarist conquest of Turkmenia was illustrated with a cartoon showing General Skobelev with eight Turkmen heads bleeding on the tips of spears and a painting depicting the Russians storming the Central Asian stronghold, Geok-Tepe.[25] Another article described the cruelty of the Cossacks in the Caucasus, illustrated with a cartoon showing two native heads on a blood-stained document entitled "Report on Pacification."[26] A third article opened with the statement that "the history of the Buriat-Mongol people is full of horrible pages written in blood" (a quotation from a speech made in the Kremlin earlier in the year), and featured a cartoon called " 'Voluntary' Conversion of Aliens," showing a Russian soldier manhandling a Buriat, forcing him to bow before a priest.[27] Other articles in subsequent issues described the tsarist conquest of Kazakh lands and colonial policy in Armenia.[28] The most common theme in these articles was the reference to blood and agony. With the added impact of the illustrations, they blackened tsarist colonialism more effectively than even Pokrovskii had been able to do.[29]

An extension of the "lesser evil" formula would have been difficult to reconcile with this interpretation of tsarist horrors, and the historians made no attempts to speculate on its application beyond the Ukraine and Georgia. Even in the case of Siberia, which would be resolved later with comparative ease by accounts of

Sbornik arkhivnykh materialov (Leningrad, 1935); *Kolonial'naia politiki moskovskogo gosudarstva v Iakutii v XVII v. Sbornik dokumentov* (Leningrad, 1936); *Kolonial'naia politika rossiiskogo tsarizma v Azerbaidzhane v* 20-60 gg. XIX v. (Moscow, 1936).

25. I. Rabinovich, "Zavoevanie Turkmenii tsarskimi voiskami (1883-1885 gg.)," *Bor'ba klassov*, No. 8, 1936, pp. 1-11.

26. K. Sivkov, "Epizody iz istorii kolonial'nogo ogrableniia Kavkaza (XIX vek)," *ibid.*, pp. 24-35.

27. P. Perepechenova, "Kreshchenie Buriat," *ibid.*, pp. 110-14.

28. V. Lebedev, "Iz istorii zavoevaniia Kazakhstana tsarskoi Rossiei (1730-1732 goda)," *ibid.*, No. 10, 1936, pp. 60-65; S. Markosian, "Kolonial'naia politika tsarizma i Armiane v XVIII veke," *ibid.*, No. 11, 1936, pp. 92-98.

29. It was characteristic of the piecemeal revision that Pokrovskii's views on tsarist colonialism were not mentioned in the concerted attack on him, although one of his critics, A. L. Popov, found fault with his views on tsarist diplomacy. Pokrovskii's alleged error was to regard the tsar as a mere *gendarme*. Quoting Engels, Popov declared that Russian diplomacy "gained more than Russian armies in extending the boundaries," that "it made Russia great, powerful, and feared, and opened for her the road to world power." See A. L. Popov, "Vneshniaia politika samoderzhaviia v XIX veke v 'krivom zerkale' M. N. Pokrovskogo," in *Protiv antimarksistskoi kontseptsii M. N. Pokrovskogo. Sbornik statei* (Moscow, 1940), II, 210-390.

peaceful trade and settlement, no change was made in the older view. In several new historical works on Siberian peoples that appeared during these years, the old views of "aggression" and "conquest" prevailed.[30] They described prolonged resistance, and characterized native revolts as justifiable wars for freedom, even when their aim was to kill all the Russians in the area. There was no hint that annexation was preferable to continued tribal anarchy or raids from neighboring peoples. There were as yet no cultural advantages for the Siberian peoples through association with the Russian settlers; the Church continued to be an oppressor; the civilizing mission of the Russians was still regarded as a bourgeois concept.[31] A. P. Okladnikov repeated the charge that the "great power historians" had tried to create an apology for tsarism by writing about "the cultural mission of the colonizers and conquerors, the lofty government principles and acts of the Russian government, as, for example, bringing the blessings of civilization to the 'savages'."[32]

SOVIET VIEWS ON THE EVE OF WORLD WAR II

Konstantin Shteppa, who was teaching history in a Soviet university in the 1930's, later wrote that the appearance of party-sanctioned history textbooks at the university level in 1940 was "almost a godsend" for teachers who had been trying to deduce acceptable interpretations from recent party pronouncements. The handful of guiding interpretations had been vague and sometimes contradictory; their broader application was by no means clear. The new textbooks on the history of the U.S.S.R., written by whole "brigades" of scholars and subjected to intensive criticism before publication, "indicated the line and gave protection against mistakes and deviations."[33] However, as Shteppa went on to note,

30. P. T. Khaptaev, *Kratkii ocherk istorii buriat-mongol'skogo naroda* (Ulan-Ude, 1936), pp. 28-33; V. G. Kartsov, *Ocherk istorii narodov severo-zapadnoi Sibiri* (Moscow, 1937), pp. 33-38; A. P. Okladnikov, *Ocherki iz istorii zapadnykh Buriat-Mongolov (XVII-XVIII v.)* (Leningrad, 1937), pp. 385 ff.; S. A. Tokarev, *Ocherki istorii iakutskogo naroda* (Moscow, 1940), pp. 39-64; F. A. Kudriavtsev, *Istoriia buriat-mongol'skogo naroda* (Moscow-Leningrad, 1940), pp. 39-60.

31. Khaptaev, *Kratkii ocherk istorii buriat-mongol'skogo naroda*, pp. 33 ff.; Tokarev, *Ocherki istorii iakutskogo naroda*, p. 50; Kudriavtsev, *Istoriia buriat-mongol'skogo naroda*, chap. iii; *Kolonial'naia politiki moskovskogo gosudarstvo*, p. xxix.

32. Okladnikov, *Ocherki iz istorii zapadnykh Buriat-Mongolov*, p. 15.

33. Shteppa, *Russian Historians*, p. 135.

this was a false security, since textbooks proved to be extremely
unstable (one of them, the second volume of the *History of the
U.S.S.R.*, edited originally by Pankratova, went into its twentieth
edition twenty-one years after it appeared).

By the eve of the War the history of the U.S.S.R. was being
taught at three levels in Soviet schools, and textbooks had been
written for all of them. The Shestakov textbook was used in the
third and fourth grades; another series, under the general editorship of A. M. Pankratova, was used in the eighth, ninth and tenth
grades,[34] and the third series, written and edited by a whole galaxy
of Soviet historians, was published for use in the universities.[35]
The interpretations found in the original editions of these textbooks
were, in many cases, farther from the interpretations held today
than those of the most criticized "bourgeois falsifiers."

As far as the emerging concept of the friendship of Soviet
peoples is concerned, the new textbooks, like the local histories and
monographic studies of the period, are characterized not only by
interpretations which were soon considered erroneous, but also
by internal contradictions resulting from the piecemeal revision
of earlier views. Before surveying some of these interpretations,
it might be well to review the pertinent party guidelines of the
late 1930's, and to imagine some of the questions the historian must
have had about their implications.

It was obvious that the general direction of the party's campaign for the improvement of the teaching and study of history
was toward a new patriotism that would weld disparate Soviet
peoples together, as a support for a nationality policy which lagged
behind its goals. More urgently, it was to be a spiritual anchor for
the anticipated military conflict. This Soviet patriotism was of a
new variety: it was supposed to cut across the lines of nationality,
the traditional hallmark of patriotism, and create a love of country

34. *Istoriia SSSR*, ed. A. M. Pankratova (Moscow, 1940), Vol. I [to
1700]; *ibid.* (Moscow, 1940), Vol. II [1700-1900]; *ibid.* (Moscow, 1941),
Vol. III [1900 to present]. Although these volumes went through many printings with minor changes, there was no substantial revision of them until the
early 1950's. They are available in an English translation produced in the
Soviet Union: A. M. Pankratova (ed.), *A History of the U.S.S.R.* (Moscow,
1947-48), Parts 1-3.
35. *Istoriia SSSR*, ed. V. I. Lebedev, B. D. Grekov, and S. V. Bakhrushin
(Moscow, 1939), Vol. I; *ibid.*, ed. M. V. Nechkina (Moscow, 1940), Vol. II.
There is a slightly abridged translation of the first half of the second volume:
M. V. Nechkina (ed.), *Russia in the Nineteenth Century: Volume II of the
History of Russia* (Ann Arbor, Mich.: J. W. Edwards, 1953).

for a relatively new multi-national state. In many of its pronouncements on historical interpretation the party was calling for the new patriotism to be based on the historical heritage before the Revolution. This involved some kind of rehabilitation of the history of Old Russia, but the extent of the reinterpretation was by no means clear. The handful of specific interpretations which had been given provided no reliable guide for other cases, and led to painful reconsiderations of other questions, like a chain reaction out of control. To make his situation more complicated still, the historian had to be able to ground all his second thoughts in Marxism-Leninism.

The result of all these perplexities was that Soviet historians revised their views only on subjects about which they had specific instruction and retained older views elsewhere, leaving the contradictions for the future to resolve. The problem can be illustrated by the question of the rehabilitation of historical figures. A new view of Khmel'nitskii had been called for by the Zhdanov Commission, and elsewhere party spokesmen had mentioned Peter the Great, Aleksandr Nevskii, and Dmitrii Donskoi. It is no coincidence that all these figures were military men, whose rehabilitation was vital for instilling a new pride in the military heritage, an essential part of patriotism. Obviously the view of these men as members of the exploiting class was no longer a deterrent to their reputation. But how far should the rehabilitation of military leaders be extended? It was desirable to look with favor on those who had protected the *rodina* (motherland) against invaders, but what about equally famous generals whose reputations rested on the conquest of non-Russians who were now in the Soviet family? The historians were selective in their praise: the Kutuzovs and Nakhimovs were made heroes; the Ermolovs and Kaufmanns remained villains. The Russian common soldier was more completely rehabilitated, his cruelties against non-Russians being charged against "tsarism." In the campaign against Pokrovskii, which was going on at the time, A. L. Popov reflected the predominant view: "Pokrovskii forgot that often, on the field of battle, the ignorance and lack of talent of the tsarist generals were outweighed by the steadfastness and heroism of the Russian soldier."[36]

The rehabilitation of Khmel'nitskii must have puzzled historians. According to the Zhdanov Commission's remarks, the new view was adopted because Khmel'nitskii had saved the Ukraine from

36. Popov, "Vneshniaia politika," p. 322.

Poland and Turkey. Did this also mean that he was being re-habilitated as a national hero, a symbol for the Ukrainian people to rally around? If so, what should be done about other non-Russian national heroes? Here the party's guidance was not very instructive. Khmel'nitskii was an easy case: he had led the Ukraine to union with Russia, and his military deeds were aimed mostly against foreigners. But what about national heroes whose fame was made by resisting Russians, who had opposed annexation to Russia? The answer was not apparent.

In this connection the nature of the resistance movements came up. The party warned that rebellions had to be re-examined, but used as an example the *strel'tsy* rebellion which was a mutiny of the tsar's own soldiers. What interpretation should be given to rebellions of non-Russian peoples attempting to free themselves from the Russian Empire, whose lands now constituted the Soviet *rodina*? How should the historian view the revolt in Central Asia in 1916, a revolt against the constituted authority in time of a war for survival of the *rodina*? This problem was made more perplexing by the ambivalent attitude toward a strong centralized Russian state that attended the new patriotism. If the development of a strong Russia had been progressive historically, what was to happen to interpretations of the non-Russian resistance movements that were aimed at weakening it? The historians did not tackle this problem immediately. Beginning with Shestakov, they spe-cifically labeled the *strel'tsy* rebellion as reactionary, gave more space to the development of Muscovy, but at the same time main-tained that the other rebellions and resistance movements were progressive mass movements. In 1939, the popularity of the best known of the resistance leaders, Shamil of the Caucasus, was car-ried a step further in a book by S. K. Bushuev, *The Struggle of the Mountain Peoples for Independence under the Leadership of Shamil.*[37]

What were the larger implications of the party's modest state-ment about the Church as a civilizing force? It gave no hint of the larger rehabilitation of the Church that was to come in the war years. The historians did little more than comply with the letter of the statement. The Pankratova textbook, for example, acknowl-edged that the Church was a significant factor in the cultural life of Kiev Rus', and went a modest step further by stating that the

37. S. K. Bushuev, *Bor'ba gortsev za nezavisimost' pod rukovodstvom Shamilia* (Moscow, 1939).

Church was an important support for the Kiev princes. But as for later periods, the view persisted that the Church was the tsar's agent for Russification and was an enemy of all progressive ideas.[38]

The most complicated puzzle of all was the "lesser evil" formula, which raised more questions than it answered. In this instance too the party had chosen comparatively uncomplicated examples: Georgia and the Ukraine had been annexed by negotiation, with a minimum of violence. Should the formula apply also to non-Russian peoples who were involuntarily annexed after long colonial wars? And did the statement of the formula, taken together with the new respect for the military and the rehabilitation of leaders such as Peter the Great, portend a general revision of the nature of tsarist foreign policy? Here the guidelines were contradictory. As recently as 1936, Stalin, Zhdanov, and Kirov had objected to the failure of historians to see "the counter-revolutionary role of Russian tsarism in foreign policy." But this statement was also unclear, since the time limits mentioned ("from the time of Catherine II to the 1850's and later") might or might not exempt other periods. The complicating factor was that tsarist diplomacy and colonialism were inextricably tied together, and a complete revision of the latter, the most disreputable part of Russian history, was too breathtaking a change to be undertaken unless specifically demanded. Partial and selective revision was illogical, but it was the historians' own lesser evil.

The new textbooks on the history of the U.S.S.R. were extensively reviewed and discussed in 1940. They were generally well received—the exception being the first volume of the textbook at the university level, whose editors were at work almost immediately on a second edition. In the reviews and two conferences that were held on this book, many flaws were discussed and improvements suggested.[39] Several of these points were related to the treatment of the non-Russian peoples. In general the authors were commended for having attained a synthesis of the history of Soviet peoples, but their work was declared to be very uneven. A common error here was that the history of the non-Russian peoples during the period of the Russian Empire had been slighted (in the

38. *Istoriia SSSR*, ed. Pankratova (1940), I, 41.
39. Reviewed in *IM*, Nos. 4-5, 1940, pp. 100-7; *Istoricheskii zhurnal*, Nos. 4-5, 1940, pp. 132-40 [hereafter cited as *IZ*]; *Pravda*, February 12, 1940. Discussions reported in "Ob obsuzhdenii I toma uchebnika dlia vuzov po istorii SSSR," *IM*, Nos. 4-5, 1940, pp. 107-13; "Itogi obsuzhdeniia uchebnikov v institute istorii A N," *ibid.*, No. 9, 1940, pp. 144-48.

case of the Transcaucasus, twenty-eight pages on pre-Mongol times, three pages on the post-Mongol period). There was also a general lack of discussion of Russian influence and cultural relations. The role of the non-Russian masses in the tsarist period had not been fully developed. The critics were not pleased with the discussion of Ivan IV and Peter the Great. The most persistent complaint was that British colonial policy in the Near East had not been developed adequately. This point is of interest here because the "British threat" to Russian security would eventually be the main device by which Russian colonial and foreign policy would be recast in a largely defensive framework, with the non-Russian peoples looking to the Russian bear to help them in their fight with the British lion.

If these points are examined against the setting of growing patriotism and changing Soviet foreign policy, it will be seen that the criticism indicates not so much the "errors and shortcomings" of the book as the inevitable slippage on the transmission belt between the party engine and the scholarly machine. It is understandable that the authors, writing at a time when the whole range of views on Russian diplomacy, colonialism, and relations with the non-Russian peoples was undergoing a change, would be cautious in their discussion of them. It was impossible for them, writing in 1938, to gauge the extent of the rehabilitation of Ivan IV or Peter the Great in 1940.

The case of the Soviet interpretation of British policy illustrates most graphically the historian's dilemma when he must tailor his interpretations to fit current foreign policy. The fact is that the Soviet viewpoint on Britain in that period, regardless of the historical event in question, was heavily influenced if not determined altogether by a precise timetable of current happenings, the key dates being August 23, 1939, and June 22, 1941. Before the German-Soviet Pact, Britain was regarded as a potential ally against Hitler, and even though the U.S.S.R. had returned to a rather neutral position in the spring of 1939, the Soviet historian had no reason to damn Britain as a colonial power. After the pact, Britain again became an "imperialist" power and a major threat to the peace. All the other textbooks of this period appeared late enough to accommodate to this development, but the 1939 volume was beyond recall. After the German invasion, Britain became an ally again, and historians no longer found fault with British colonialism. The shoe was now on the other foot: the Nechkina and Pankratova textbooks of 1940 were "erroneous." The collective that was at work on a second edition of the unsatisfactory 1939 volume did not succeed in getting out a revision in the spring of 1941 (it appeared in 1947); otherwise they would have been in the same embarrassing position as before. Wartime conditions did not permit the periodic updating of interpretation of these textbooks to fit foreign policy developments. However, it is worth noting that the history of Kazakhstan, published in 1943, did not mention the British threat to Central Asia, although later histories concentrate on it as the major threat of a "foreign enemy" in the nineteenth century.

The growing Soviet patriotism is reflected in the history journals, particularly the *Istoricheskii zhurnal* (*Historical Journal*), whose articles were semi-popular in nature. During 1940 the journal published articles on great Russian heroes and battles, from Aleksandr Nevskii and the Battle of the Ice to the Civil War, whose Bolshevik heroes enjoyed new popularity. Several articles were obviously aimed at creating a new interest in the military history of the non-Russian peoples. One of these is remarkable, in view of future interpretations. It was "The History of the Peoples of Central Asia in the Course on the History of the U.S.S.R.," by K. Novonashennaia.[40] It was a guide for eighth-grade teachers, with suggestions for sources and points of emphasis. Though it did not refer to the Pankratova first volume specifically, it is clear that it was intended as a corrective for that account, which had been criticized in reviews. Novonashennaia devoted most of her article to the struggle of Central Asian peoples against "foreign enemies," Arabs and Tatars, without even mentioning resistance to Russians, which was the textbook's major emphasis. She thus accomplished an extremely rare achievement: an article on the history of non-Russian peoples, written in 1940, which could have been reprinted unchanged in 1950 or 1960. But her accomplishment was primarily one of omission—either by craft or luck. It is probable that she omitted discussion of resistance movements against the tsars because by 1940 she could see that the subject was controversial and potentially dangerous for Soviet patriotism. If other teachers were looking to *Istoricheskii zhurnal* for guidance on these lines, they would not have found it, since the journal also published three other articles in 1940 that presented the older view that the

40. K. Novonashennaia, "Istoriia narodov Srednei Azii v kurse istorii SSSR," *IZ*, No. 10, 1940, pp. 108-14.

resistance movements were of a national liberation character.[41]

The only non-Russian leader to be popularized before World War II was Khmel'nitskii, and this was done at the specific suggestion of the Zhdanov Commission. Compared to the hero worship of the *hetman* which would prevail after 1944, his rehabilitation at this point was quite modest. The following characterization, from Osipov's popular biography of 1939, shows that Khmel'nitskii's military role was considered progressive, but he had not lost the stigma of his class outlook: "Bogdan Khmel'nitskii was unquestionably the national hero of the Ukrainian people, his name being the military banner of that people at the time of the great struggle for overcoming the foreign yoke. However Khmel'nitskii in his domestic policy did not fulfill the hopes and wishes of the broad popular masses."[42]

The same cautious view was taken in a textbook on Ukrainian history, published on the eve of the war.[43] The annexation of the Ukraine was considered the lesser evil: the exact words of the Commission were used. There was no explanation why union with Russia was preferable to union with Poland or Turkey, and Russian oppression after annexation was not softened: "The tsarist government, in helping the Cossack *starshina* [the officer class] to exploit the national masses, at the same time thirsted to strengthen its rule in the Ukraine and to change it into a colony."[44] This was precisely what the Polish Pans had previously done. Khmel'nitskii was rehabilitated, but only in the circumscribed terms of the directive, and with a clear *caveat:*

> In evaluating the role and place of Bogdan Khmel'nitskii in the history of the Ukraine, it should not be forgotten that he was a member of the Cossack *starshina,* who saw as his first task, not the liberation of the Ukrainian peasant

41. The articles were on the Bashkir rebellion of the 1770's (*ibid.*, No. 11, 1940, pp. 77-88); The Chechen rebellion of 1877 (*ibid.*, No. 12, 1940, pp. 61-77) and Isatai Taimanov, 1836-38 in Kazakhstan. Isatai would continue to be considered the leader of a national liberation movement throughout the later reinterpretations. The interesting feature of this article is that the author, A. Iakunin, still held that the rebellion involved Russian troops, who put it down. The later interpretation would place Taimanov's revolt primarily against local feudal leaders (*ibid.*, No. 10, 1940, pp. 75-81).

42. K. Osipov, *Bogdan Khmel'nitskii* (Moscow, 1939), p. 6.

43. *Istoriia Ukrainy. Korotkyi kurs* (Kiev, 1940); also in Russian (1940) and Ukrainian of identical title published in Kiev in 1941. Page numbers in the following notes are from the 1941 Ukrainian edition, the only one available to me.

44. *Ibid.*, pp. 92-93.

from feudal exploitation, but on the contrary, he himself handed over properties to the *starshina*, to the Ukrainian *szlachta*, to the monasteries, and quelled peasant protests aimed against his social policy. But in essence this does not determine Khmel'nitskii's place in Ukrainian history. Before the Ukrainian people at that time was the question of life or death; either to free itself of the yoke of the Polish *szlachta* or die. The great merit of Khmel'nitskii for the Ukrainian people lies in the fact that he led the war of liberation against *szlachta* Poland and united the Ukraine to Russia.[45]

The instrument of that union, the Treaty of Pereiaslav, which would later be described at length as the most important event in Ukrainian history, was disposed of in a couple of sentences, in the manner of Iavorskii.[46]

The textbook also met minimum requirements on the role of the medieval Church, which it acknowledged as important in establishing the Slavic form of writing and the introduction of Byzantine culture. At the same time it noted the role of Christianity in the oppression of the people: "[Vladimir] understood that Christianity was an excellent support for establishing domination of the masses by the rising feudal class, because it taught the holiness of the ruler's might, and subjection to the yoke of their exploiters."[47]

On the question of the cooperation of the Russian and Ukrainian peoples, which would be of paramount importance in the future, this history contained very little. It mentioned cooperation of Ukrainian and Russian peasants in revolts, especially that of Stenka Razin. In the topic on annexation, its comment was brief and modest: "This unification had great meaning for the Ukrainian people. The common efforts of the Ukrainian and Russian peoples in the course of the past decades had thrown back the raids of Poland of the Pans and the Turkey of the Sultans. The economic and cultural ties of the Ukrainian and Russian peoples became stronger."[48]

What a small bud of the future flower!

45. *Ibid.*, p. 92.
46. *Ibid.*, p. 90.
47. *Ibid.*, p. 27.
48. *Ibid.*, p. 91.

CHAPTER **4.**

THE WAR YEARS

"*It must be noted, as a shortcoming in the work of the local publishing houses, that there is an almost complete lack of books on national heroes, on the participation and military cooperation of the various peoples of our country in popular, patriotic wars against foreign conquerors, on the love of the motherland and love of freedom of these peoples. Meanwhile there exists, among all the peoples of our motherland, a burning desire to know more about the heroism of their ancestors, about the participation of their sons in patriotic liberation wars.*" M. Morozov and V. Slutskaia, in Propagandist, *No. 17, 1942, p. 46.*

"*They [the authors of* History of the Kazakh S.S.R. (Alma-Ata, 1943)] *present the history of the Kazakh people exclusively as a process of forming military traditions in the struggle of the Kazakhs for their independence. All phenomena and events which are considered in the book are evaluated from this one-sided and therefore incorrect point of view.*" M. Morozov in Bol'shevik, *No. 6, 1945, p. 74.*

In the year and a half between the German invasion of June, 1941, and the Soviet victory at Stalingrad, the Bolshevik regime faced its most critical trial since the Civil War and its aftermath. The struggle for survival during World War II not only put the system to a crucial military and economic test; it also brought nationality problems to a critical stage. Around the western and southern rim of the Soviet Union, the government lost control of a number of the non-Russian populations—the Baltic peoples,

Belorussians, Ukrainians, Moldavians, and several small groups who inhabited the Caucasus. In other non-Russian areas, the hatreds created by the recent forced collectivization of agriculture and the Great Purge, as well as stubborn resistance to Russian domination and Bolshevism itself, made the reliability of these peoples doubtful. Facing up to the absolute necessity of maintaining a united front against the invader, and acting in the knowledge that some segments of the non-Russian population had greeted the Germans as liberators, Soviet authorities made concessions and compromises with doctrines no less sweeping than those of the New Economic Policy in the early 1920's.

Two new orientations in Soviet ideology during the War were of fundamental importance to the future development of the historiography of the non-Russian peoples. The relaxation of controls, brought about partly by an inability to maintain them, and partly as a concession to win the allegiance of the non-Russians, made it possible for historians to write more freely than they had since 1930. At the same time the party actively promoted Soviet solidarity by a variety of ideological appeals, even when they were in conflict with well-known Marxist-Leninist precepts. These included a new emphasis on patriotism and nationalism, a new respect for military traditions, and even an accommodation with the Orthodox church.

Much had been said about Soviet patriotism, but it existed largely in the party poster and the *Pravda* editorial. In their eagerness to secure the allegiance of non-Russian subjects, the ideological authorities tried to instill a new patriotism based on military tradition, with Russian military exploits as a leading element. But the scheme had a fatal flaw. Russian nationalism was not exportable to the non-Russian peoples. Nationalism in a multi-national state is a centrifugal, not a unifying, force. Although the emphasis was placed on military cooperation between Russians and non-Russians, and on Russian military aid for the other peoples of the future U.S.S.R., the result was that the non-Russian peoples turned their attention to their own military traditions and heroes, to struggles against the Russians, and not in alliance with them.

The *Zhdanovshchina* of the late 1940's liquidated the new ideological policy, as cleanly as the Soviet measures of the late 1920's liquidated the NEP. But there was an important difference: Soviet ideological authorities apparently liked certain themes which had been popularized during the war on the subject of Russian and non-Russian cooperation; they not only retained them, but imposed them in Soviet historiography without regard for the cost in credibility or scholarly labor. The war years are, therefore, the important growing years for the friendship of peoples myth.

PATRIOTISM BY FORCED FEEDING

Anyone who examines the Soviet press for a few months on either side of June 22, 1941, becomes aware of the urgency of the nationalities question as the Soviet Union went to war. The terminology of Soviet patriotism, which had been coming into currency for the last three or four years, seemed to explode, with the obvious political goal of binding Soviet peoples together for the conflict. From the beginning the press referred to the conflict as the "patriotic war."[1] References to the rodina, to "military traditions," to friendship and unity, seemed to increase tenfold. The term druzhba (friendship) now began to take an invariable adjective, nerushimyi (unbreakable or inviolable).

The sheer volume and repetition of the unity theme in Soviet pronouncements at this time suggests that all was not well. There was much boasting about the friendship of peoples and the accomplishments of Bolshevik nationality policy.[2] In Stalin's first public statement on the War, he spoke of Soviet solidarity at length, and called off a list of twelve Soviet peoples whom he said Hitler hoped to enslave.[3] Although the peoples included in Stalin's list seem to have been chosen at random, the Soviet press repeated it verbatim dozens of times in the following weeks, with exhortations on unity and friendship which were thinly disguised entreaties for Soviet peoples to forget their differences.[4] Only rarely did a

1. The term otechestvennaia voina (literally "fatherland war") has its own evolution. It had earlier been used to refer to the Russian war against Napoleon. This terminology was dropped by early Soviet historians, and as late as 1937 the Shestakov textbook referred to "the War of 1812" (Kratkii kurs istorii SSSR, ed. A. V. Shestakov [Moscow, 1937], p. 80). By the time the Nechkina text appeared in 1940, the older term was restored (Istoriia SSSR, ed. M. V. Nechkina [Moscow, 1940], II, 76 ff.).

2. The growth of nationalism during this period is discussed in the first part of Alexander Werth's Russia at War: 1941-1945 (London: Barrie and Rockliff, 1964).

3. Pravda, July 3, 1941.

4. For example, the next issue of Bol'shevik carried the list in an article, and two shorter lists containing the same peoples (Nos. 11-12, 1941, pp. 3, 10, 13, 19). The list was repeated in Shcherbakov's speech in January (ibid., No. 2, 1942, pp. 7-17).

The casual nature of the Stalin list of peoples is suggested by the fact

Soviet spokesman refer openly to the other side of the question, as did A. S. Shcherbakov, a Secretary of the Central Committee, in a speech of January 21, 1942, when he stated that "The German Fascists, at the beginning of their aggressive war against our country, counted on quarrels [*drachku*] between the peoples of the U.S.S.R. They hoped to divide peoples—Lithuanians against Belorussians, Ukrainians against Russians."[5]

Whatever the fine points of distinction may have been between the new Soviet patriotism and old Russian nationalism, they were soon lost sight of in the great emergency. The Soviet experience of a little over twenty years, containing many elements of bitterness, could hardly serve as a historical base for genuine love of country. Without much regard for what Marx or Lenin had said on the subject,[6] Soviet ideologists called for emphasis on prerevolutionary military greatness—which meant Russian greatness, almost to the exclusion of the other nationalities—with all the attendant evils of Russian nationalism, which could hardly serve the cause of Soviet unity. The theme of Russian leadership of the Soviet family emerged, modestly at first, and later with tremendous force. In the early days of the War, the Russians were regarded as *primus inter pares*, as stated in a much copied expression from a *Pravda* editorial entitled "The Great Friendship of the Peoples of the U.S.S.R.," referring to "the great Russian people, the first among the equal peoples of the U.S.S.R."[7] The dominant military role of the great Russians was soon being asserted and praised, notably in Shcherbakov's speech early in January, 1942: "The Russian people, the first among equals in the family of peoples of the U.S.S.R., bears the main burden of the struggle with the German invaders."[8] The term "elder brother," which had been rejected by the early Bolsheviks as an expression of the apologists for tsarism, now began to appear with increasing frequency in the Soviet press. Before the end of 1941 Emel'ian Iaroslavskii wrote an article in *Pravda* en-

that it included only one Central Asian people (Uzbek) and one A.S.S.R. (Tatar). The peoples on the list were neither the most vulnerable, nor could they be considered the most unreliable.

5. *Bol'shevik*, No. 2, 1942, p. 10.

6. As far as I can find, the first systematic attempt to give Leninist views on the new patriotism was expressed in an article in *Pravda*, February 1, 1942, by which time the basic lines were well established.

7. "Velikaia druzhba narodov SSSR," *Pravda*, July 29, 1941.

8. *Bol'shevik*, No. 2, 1941, p. 10. The "first among equals" phrase became a standard formula for a while. It occurred in *Pravda* editorials of December 29, 1941, and February 21, 1942.

titled "Bolsheviks, the Heirs of the Best Patriotic Traditions of
the Russian People," which was so blatant in its Russian nationalism that it might well have offended Soviet readers of non-Russian
origin.[9] In his argument that the best of the past was now represented by the Communist party, he did not acknowledge even a
small role for the non-Russian heritage, and seemed to ignore the
fact that some Bolsheviks might not be Russian. His points were
emphasized by topical headings in bold type:

> The Russian People: The Great Builder
> The Russian People: Versatile Artist
> The Russian People: Bold Reformer
> The Russian People: An Industrious People
> The Russian People: Bold Inventor, Persistent Researcher,
>   Fearless Pathfinder

This article anticipated Stalin's famous toast to the Russian people
of May, 1945, to the point of similar wording on Russian bravery,
inventiveness, and patience.

The leading vehicle for the infusion of patriotism in the early
days of the War was "the great military traditions of our ancestors."
Other trappings of patriotism—songs, poems, and landscapes—
would get their due, but with the Red Army in a fight for its life
and a civilian population caught in the clutches of war, the immediate demand was for a confidence in ultimate victory inspired
by accounts of heroes and their actions. Leading historians were
immediately called into service. Within days articles on heroes and
battles, written by Tarle, Bakhrushin, Pankratova, Derzhavin, Picheta, and others, began to appear, and within weeks pamphlets on
these subjects, written to the express needs of the time, rolled from
the presses.

The careful selection of battles and heroes in these early war
pieces illustrates the close connection between policy and historical
writing at a given moment; it also shows the growth of the friendship myth. Battles had to be chosen which would not offend allies
or neutrals. Examples of Russian victories against the Germans
were to the point, and two cases involving German invasions were

9. E. Iaroslavskii, "Bol'sheviki—prodolzhateli luchshikh patrioticheskikh
traditsii russkogo naroda," *Pravda*, December 27, 1941. Some people were
indeed offended by the nationalistic statements of the time. See Alexander
Werth's account of the reaction of the writer, Lidiia Seifullina, who declared
that she would henceforth call herself a Tatar after one of Stalin's speeches on
Russian greatness (*Russia at War*, p. 739).

chosen—the Battle of the Ice (1242) and the German occupation of the Ukraine in 1918. These, along with the "Patriotic War of 1812," were discussed almost exclusively in the early months of the war. The latter invasion, which contained many close parallels to the current one, possessed the obvious advantage of ending in a great Russian victory. Although its main Russian military figure, Kutuzov, was lackluster in comparison with other Russian heroes, he was quickly popularized.[10]

The heroes who were to be made the symbols of the new patriotism were carefully selected from a precise list given by Stalin. At the conclusion of his speech in Red Square on November 7, 1941, Stalin stated that "in this war you must draw inspiration from the brave example of our great ancestors [*predkov*]—Aleksandr Nevskii, Dmitrii Donskoi, Kuz'ma Minin, Dmitrii Pozharskii, Aleksandr Suvorov, and Mikhail Kutuzov."[11] The press evidently considered this list to be definitive, and devoted its efforts almost exclusively to these six heroes, mentioning them in the same order as Stalin did.[12] Such obvious Russian greats as the rehabilitated Ivan IV and Peter the Great were passed over for a time; the only heroes to receive recognition in addition to these six pre-revolutionary military leaders were those who had fallen in the current war and the Bolshevik leaders of the Civil War.[13]

10. The historian E. Tarle, who had just written an article on the Crimean War for *Bol'shevik* (No. 6, 1941), in which Britain was the villain, quickly added an article on the campaign of 1812 (*ibid.*, Nos. 11-12, 1942) and a pamphlet, *Mikhail Kutuzov.*

11. *Pravda,* November 8, 1941.

12. On November 10, *Pravda* ran an editorial on Stalin's speech repeating his list verbatim. It held rigidly to the list in later editorials on December 27 and February 11, 1942. Three weeks after the Stalin speech *Pravda* began a series of articles on the heroes: Minin and Pozharskii (Nov. 25), Nevskii (Dec. 24 and July 30, 1942), Kutuzov (July 31, 1942) and Suvorov (August 1, 1942). *Bol'shevik* called for patriotic pamphlets and books, but confined itself to Stalin's six heroes (P. Fateev, "Knigi dlia naroda," *Bol'shevik*, No. 6, 1942, pp. 59-64).

13. Aleksei Tolstoi had made brief reference to Ivan III and Ivan IV in his article "Rodina" (*Pravda*, November 7, 1941), and N. Neonidov mentioned bogatyrs, Decembrists, Peter the Great, Bagration, and Ermolov in his article "Patrioticheskaia ideia v istorii nashei rodiny" (*Bol'shevik*, No. 10, 1942, pp. 27-45). But these exceptions seem to prove the rule; the latter were barely mentioned in long lists of Russian notables.

The cult of Bolshevik military leadership received a tremendous boost at this time. See especially M. Leonov, "Boevye traditsii bol'shevizma vdokhnovliaiut krasnuiu armiiu v bor'be s vragom," *Bol'shevik*, No. 14, 1942, pp. 8-17, and Iaroslavskii in *Pravda*, December 27, 1941, cited above.

By early 1942 popular pamphlets on the six heroes had been
published in large editions.[14] The selection of these figures and
the omission of others is an important clue in the development of
the friendship myth. All those selected were Russian, and the
common factor was their role in defending Russian soil. The exclusion of Khmel'nitskii must have been puzzling, since he had
already been rehabilitated in the role of ally of Russia against
foreign aggressors. But from a propaganda point of view, his popularization at this point would have meant little, since much of the
Ukraine was already occupied and Ukrainian readers were out of
reach. Khmel'nitskii was to be held in reserve for the proper
moment and used as a symbol of Russian-Ukrainian unity as the
Germans were being routed from Ukrainian soil in the fall of 1943.[15]

The popularization of Russian heroes to inspire Soviet patriotism
raised a disturbing question. Were non-Russian heroes, who had
defended their homelands, also to be glorified? The answer was
not given in the discussion, except as it might have been deduced
from the silence of the press. This was a vital question, since one
of the thorniest problems of Soviet historians in the subsequent
months was their inability to discern the difference between a
popular hero and a reactionary class enemy. Historians might have
noted with profit a telling clue, also on the side of omission,
contained in the accounts of a number of meetings of representatives of the Soviet areas occupied by the Germans. These meetings,
which were held in various places (Saratov, Kazan, Moscow) beginning in November, 1941, were reported conspicuously and in a
set format in *Pravda*.[16] Each meeting featured short reports by
several prominent representatives of the people, a greeting to Stalin,
and a greeting to the people at home. References to friendship

14. Six of the early pamphlets were reviewed by S. Bushuev in "Muzhestvennye obrazy nashikh velikikh predkov," *Bol'shevik*, No. 8, 1942, pp.
57-64. The only author of note was Tarle, whose *Mikhail Kutuzov* had appeared late in 1941. In this early pamphlet campaign for the popularization
of heroes, there seems to be only one pamphlet of a sizeable printing on a
figure not on Stalin's list. This was S. Borisov's *Bagration*, and its largest
printing (15,000) was small by comparison to those of the others.

15. See below, pp. 75-76.

16. The first report was entitled "Meeting of Representatives of the
Ukrainian People," and was reported in *Pravda* on November 26, 1941; reports of others with similar titles were on Belorussia (*ibid.*, January 20,
1942); Latvia (*ibid.*, March 3, 1942); Estonia (*ibid.*, March 24, 1942);
Moldavia (*ibid.*, March 31, 1942); Lithuania (*ibid.*, April 29, 1942); North
Caucasus (*ibid.*, September 1, 1942); Transcaucasus (*ibid.*, September 6,
1942).

with the Russians (in the Soviet period) abound in these reports, as well as praise for their great historic figures and their recent military struggles. But specific mention of their national military heroes is conspicuously absent. The sole exception seems to be a passing reference to "the glorious Bogdan" by the Ukrainian writer Aleksandr Korneichuk.[17] The most conspicuous omission came when the speakers at the meeting of the peoples of the North Caucasus dwelt at some length on the fighting traditions of the region without mentioning Shamil, who was still the most prominent non-Russian hero in the 1940 textbooks.[18] This meeting was given the most prominent place by *Pravda* (an entire page plus an editorial), which even hinted at the Shamil movement without giving it a name: "The enemy does not know that the Caucasus was always a country of powerful and bold peoples, where in the struggle for independence the people produced fearless fighters." An editorial of the following day indirectly referred again to Shamil in its peroration, calling on the people to resist the advancing Germans: "The mountains of the North Caucasus are covered with great and heroic traditions. Courageous and fearless ancestors look now on their sons and grandsons."[19] But the hero of the Caucasus was never specifically mentioned. When it came to naming names, *Pravda* mentioned only Stalin, Kirov, and Ordzhonikidze.

With the benefit of hindsight, one might conclude that Soviet historians could have detected from these omissions that non-Russian military heroes were not to be rehabilitated, and could perhaps have deduced from the context the reason: any recollection of fighting against the Russians, rather than military cooperation with them, could only damage the concept of friendship. This was only one of the straws in the wind, however; there were other, more direct factors that seemed to support an opposite interpretation, as we shall see.

Before leaving the subject of omissions, it is worth noting some others which illustrate the uneven development of the friendship myth at this stage. When one looks back on the statements of the early war period, comparing the Soviet statement of the case for the friendship of peoples with that of the 1960's, it is apparent that some elements of the myth were well advanced, others were be-

17. *Ibid.*, November 26, 1941.
18. *Ibid.*, September 1, 1942.
19. *Ibid.*, September 2, 1942.

ginning to find expression, and still others were completely absent. The doctrine of Great Russian leadership was well developed, but was restricted largely to military leadership. Very little had yet been said about Russian cultural leadership of the non-Russian peoples, which is logical, considering the pressures of the times. The doctrine of Bolshevik leadership during the Revolution and Civil War was also growing rapidly, although it was also largely confined to military themes. Statements referring to Russian military aid to the non-Russian peoples (which is a step beyond Russian military leadership for its own sake) were either missing or very modest. When one reads the accounts of Aleksandr Nevskii that were popular at that time, with today's emphasis in mind, one is struck by the excellent opportunities that were passed up. The Novgorod prince does not go out to rescue the Baltic peoples, he goes to hold Russian lands which have been invaded.[20] By the middle of 1942, the newer note was being struck. The Germans, said a *Bol'shevik* account, thought victory would be easy. They did not take into account the Latvian people's "close military coopera- tion with other peoples and their great neighbor the Russian peo- ple, for the rebuff of the impudent German attackers. At the Battle of the Ice, in 1242, Aleksandr Nevskii dealt the Order a crushing blow, driving it out of Russian lands."[21] The popularization of close military cooperation between peoples seems to have developed first in connection with the Napoleonic campaign. The Shestakov textbook (1937) had discussed mass resistance by the Russian people, but said nothing about cooperation (pp. 80-81). The Nechkina textbook (1940) developed the idea of the "people's war," and described the fighting of Lithuanians and Belorussians, and later of Cossacks and others (pp. 84-86). But there is no emphasis on the fact that they fought in close contact with Rus- sians.[22] By late 1942 the concept of cooperation had developed further. In a review of one of the new works on the patriotic re- sistance to Napoleon, Bushuev noted that "all the people of Russia of that time rose against the attacker, remaining true to the cause. In the army led by the genius Kutuzov, Lithuanians, Belorussians,

20. A. Novikov, "Aleksandr Nevskii," *Pravda*, December 24, 1941; S. Bushuev, "Aleksandr Nevskii," *Propagandist*, No. 1, 1942, pp. 42-44.

21. Ia. Kalnberzin, "Latyshskii narod v bor'be s nemetskimi zakhvatchikami," *Bol'shevik*, No. 14, 1942, pp. 27-34.

22. In this account Nechkina does note in passing that Bashkirs, Kalmyks, Crimean Tatars, and other nationalities fought in the ranks of "the Russian Army."

Ukrainians, Bashkirs, Kalmyks, Georgians and others fought shoulder to shoulder with the Russians."[23]

The most conspicuous omission concerns the historical depth of the friendship of peoples. There were occasional references to military cooperation before the Revolution, but real friendship was still dated from the revolutionary period. This omission now appears glaring, in view of the presence of much of the argument and even the language of later times. A *Pravda* editorial on "The Great Strength of Leninist-Stalinist Friendship of Peoples," for example, remarked that "the great Russian people, elder brother and first among equals in the united Soviet family, gave enormous help to the other peoples. With that help the formerly exploited peoples achieved their liberation, their economic and cultural development." But the editorial confined itself to the period of the Revolution and just afterwards, citing Russian aid in the construction of *kolkhozy*—hardly the best example of solidarity with non-Russians.[24] The failure to note historic friendship is all the more conspicuous because most of the articles refer to military defense in the distant past. A *Bol'shevik* article, "The Peoples of the Caucasus will Never Be Slaves," discussed Armenian struggles against Genghis Khan, Tamerlane, and the Turks, but went on to remark that "in tsarist Russia also the gendarmes stirred up hatred by the butchery of Armenians." As for the "unbreakable military friendship of Soviet peoples," it was dated strictly from the period of the Revolution. Discussion of the "help of the brotherly Russian people" began with the examples of Stalin, Kirov, and Ordzhonikidze.[25] Some of the accounts were more precise in establishing dates for the friendship of peoples. M. Korneev's "Friendship of Peoples of the U.S.S.R.— the Guarantee of Our Victory," a pocket-sized pamphlet for agitators at the front, opened its discussion with Lenin's "Declaration of the Rights of the Toiling and Exploited People,"[26] and an article in the journal *Propagandist* in the middle of 1942, after dwelling on historical examples of separate military defense, de-

23. *Bol'shevik*, Nos. 16-17, 1942, p. 61.

24. V. Kruzhkov, "Velikaia sila leninsko-stalinskoi druzhby narodov," *Pravda*, February 21, 1942.

25. A. Azizian, "Narody Kavkaza nikogda ne budut rabami," *Bol'shevik*, No. 15, 1942, pp. 28-37.

26. M. Korneev, *Druzhba narodov SSSR—zalog nashei pobedy* (Kuibyshev, 1942), chap. i. The declaration was also considered the beginning point by A. Gorkin, in "Osnova prochnosti i istochniki sily sovetskogo stroia," *Bol'shevik*, No. 16, 1942, pp. 11-25.

clared that "for almost a quarter of a century the peoples of the
Soviet Union have lived a free life, in close union and unbreakable
friendship. The basis of this great friendship between the peoples
of our country was secured already during the days of October,
1917."[27]

In the middle of 1942 the propaganda emphasis on military
traditions reached a new intensity. Party spokesmen Iaroslavskii
and G. Aleksandrov wrote articles calling on historians to mobilize
the military greatness of the past and send it into battle.[28] *Pravda*
published two leading editorials on military traditions and their role
in Soviet patriotism. Military traditions were called "a rich arsenal,"
"the banner under which fighters go into battle," "the source of the
steadfastness and courage of our fighters."[29] At the end of July
the creation of the new Orders of Suvorov, Nevskii, and Kutuzov
was announced, to the accompaniment of new articles on these and
current Soviet heroes.[30] The curious thing about all this is that the
original Stalin list of six heroes was not significantly expanded.
The first of *Pravda's* editorials concluded with a restatement of
Stalin's six heroes; the second mentioned the battles of Poltava and
Sevastopol but supplied no new names.[31]

One exception to this cautious approach was an article on
popular military literature in *Propagandist*.[32] The authors, M.
Morozov and V. Slutskaia, found three shortcomings in the works
that had been produced to date. The first, which was quoted at the
head of this chapter, was that almost nothing had been written on

27. N. Anan'ev, "Velikaia sila nerushimoi druzhba narodov SSSR," *Propagandist*, 11-12, 1942, pp. 16-21.

28. E. Iaroslavskii, "O blizhaishikh zadachakh istoricheskoi nauki v SSSR," *IZ*, No. 6, 1942, pp. 17-24, and "Za boevuiu, dokhodchivuiu, pravdivuiu agitatsiiu," *Pravda*, July 10, 1942; G. Aleksandrov, "Otechestvennaia voina sovetskogo naroda i zadachi obshchestvennykh nauk," *Bol'shevik*, No. 9, 1942, pp. 35-47, and "O reshaiushikh usloviiakh pobedy nad vragom," *Pravda*, July 13, 1942.

29. G. Aleksandrov, "O reshaiushikh usloviiakh," and "Boevye traditsii sovetskikh voinov" [unsigned], *Pravda*, September 17, 1942.

30. See the series of articles in *Pravda*, July 30-August 1, 1942.

31. Neither the Northern War nor the Crimean War provided heroes suitable for all-out popularization. Pamphlets on Peter the Great appeared in small printings during the early years of the war and were not reprinted in large quantities until 1944 and 1945. There was also a limited popularization of Admiral Nakhimov.

32. M. Morozov and V. Slutskaia, "Broshiury mestnykh izdatel'stv o geroicheskom proshlom nashego naroda i o geroiakh velikoi otechestvennoi voiny," *Propagandist*, No. 17, 1942, pp. 46-48.

the non-Russian heroes[33] and the military cooperation of these peoples. Secondly, they complained that the publishing houses in the Union Republics and Autonomous Republics turned out "pale compilations" based on the production of the central publishing houses, and that "frequently the richest local archives and other materials are not used at all." Finally the authors supplied a list of "our military commanders [*polkovodtsi*] of the past." Pointing out that the publishers had so far produced works "only on the great ancestors," they called for popular pamphlets on "Bagration, Brusilov, Frunze, Chapaev, Shchors, Parkhomenko, Lazo, Kotovskii, Dundich and many other glorious commanders."

This list of heroes was conservative. Bagration was a colleague of Kutuzov, and Brusilov was the only successful Russian general of World War I without a reputation as a counter-revolutionary. Both had been the subject of pamphlets in modest printings. The others were Bolshevik leaders in the Civil War, whose place among heroes was well established. But this article, with its call for the non-Russian publishing houses to popularize heroes, was apparently interpreted by some historians to mean that all heroes were to be remembered. There were restrictive clauses, however: the authors called for works on heroes in the context of "patriotic wars against foreign conquerors" and of "the military cooperation of various peoples of our country." Some historians of the non-Russian peoples apparently failed to note that this would exclude national heroes who had fought against the Russians.

In response to the general call for popular works on military traditions, new works on Russian heroes began to appear. By the end of 1942, Tarle's short book on Nakhimov had appeared,[34] as well as pamphlets on Ivan the Great and Ivan IV. Vipper's biography of Ivan IV was republished at this time. The emphasis in the latter works was on the role of the Ivans in establishing a

33. The term *natsional'nyi geroi* is not completely clear in itself, but from the context it is clear that it refers to non-Russians. The authors complain that the *natsional'nyi geroi* have not been publicized, although they mention the books about the Russian heroes. Along with the emphasis on heroes, there is frequent mention of commanders. It is possible that the article was written in response to *Pravda's* leading editorial of December 1, 1942, "Komandir —organizator boevogo uspekha." Although No. 17 of *Propagandist* would normally be a September issue, it went to press on December 4. I am unable to find a similar appeal for the popularization of national heroes in other party publications.

34. E. V. Tarle, *Pavel Stepanovich Nakhimov* (Moscow, 1942).

strong central government, which could withstand all foreign predators—another growing theme.[35]

THE ILL-FATED *History of the Kazakh S.S.R.*

The publication of longer scholarly works was severely restricted by the War, but a few survey histories of the non-Russian peoples appeared. Their authors responded to the leading ideological theme, the emphasis on military traditions, and for this reason alone the books were short-lived. The most discussed of these works was the ambitious *History of the Kazakh S.S.R.*, which appeared in 1943.[36] It touched off a controversy about the history of non-Russian peoples which would continue for several years.

In at least one small way, the War brought favorable conditions for writing the history of the non-Russian peoples. Many of the historians of Moscow and Leningrad were evacuated to the non-Russian areas, and took a leading part in work there. Iaroslavskii noted in 1942 that this circumstance provided a good opportunity for large collectives of historians to utilize the archives of the Union Republics to produce survey histories from a Marxist-Leninist viewpoint. He coupled this observation with a statement on current needs: such works must engender Soviet patriotism and "strengthen the feeling of friendship among the peoples of the U.S.S.R.; they must serve, like all our science and literature, as a block against the smallest traces of racial hatred, against the smallest survivals of the reactionary past in the consciousness of the people."[37] It will be recalled that the article of Morozov and Slutskaia had also called for the use of local archives for the popularization of national heroes.

The writing of the *History of the Kazakh S.S.R.*, judging from the subsequent discussion, was a pilot project in the Soviet historiography of the non-Russian Republics. It was produced under the collective auspices of three institutes: the Institute of History of the Academy of Sciences of the U.S.S.R., the Kazakh branch of the Academy, and the Kazakh branch of the Institute of Marx, Engels, and Lenin. The large collective of Moscow, Leningrad,

35. The three works on the Ivans were reviewed collectively in *IZ*, Nos. 3-4, 1943, pp. 90-95. The reviewer, S. Pokrovskii, stressed their role in building a strong central government.
36. *Istoriia kazakhskoi SSR. S drevneishikh vremen do nashikh dnei*, ed. M. Abdykalykov and A. Pankratova (Alma-Ata, 1943).
37. Iaroslavskii, "O blizhaishikh zadachakh," p. 19.

and Kazakh historians who worked in Alma-Ata realized fully that they were seeking to establish interpretations that would serve as examples for the writing of the history of other Soviet republics, especially those of Central Asia. The party's role in the project was large; the Russian co-editor, the indefatigable Pankratova, acknowledged the help of the Central Committee of the Communist party of Kazakhstan, which had discussed every chapter of the book during a two-month period. The other co-editor, M. Abdykalykov, was one of the secretaries of the Kazakh party.

Soviet historical writing on Kazakhstan had been more extensive than that on the other Central Asia republics, but it had failed to meet party requirements. Two sizeable histories of the Kazakhs in the pre-revolutionary period had been attempted by Soviet historians. Asfendiarov's *History of Kazakhstan,* as has been noted, was quickly condemned in the middle 1930's. M. P. Viatkin's *Outlines of History of the Kazakh S.S.R.* was a victim of timing, among other things.[38] Written in 1940, during the period of growing patriotism, but before it had reached its wartime crescendo, Viatkin's history dealt generously with the Kazakhs' heroic past, devoting whole chapters to three of the revolts of the eighteenth and early nineteenth centuries. But it went to press less than a month before the German invasion, and met the unhappy fate of being condemned for a decade, and for diametrically opposite reasons. During the war years, Viatkin's views on patriotic themes and military traditions were not nearly ardent enough for party approval; in the post-war years the presence of Kazakh military traditions in the book made it a bourgeois nationalist work. The author eventually published a long letter of apology, acknowledging his "gross errors" in interpretation in this history, as well as many others in the course of the next decade, including his role as one of the authors of the 1943 history of Kazakhstan.[39]

The party's call for patriotism through emphasis on military traditions was answered in the new history of the Kazakhs. The whole middle of the book was devoted to a series of military movements that were characterized as "the struggle for independence and political unification." Their leaders, who had been consistently regarded as revolutionary and progressive leaders, in spite of their class origins as sultans and khans, were given new greatness.

38. M. Viatkin, *Ocherki po istorii kazakhskoi SSR* (Moscow, 1941), Vol. I.
39. M. P. Viatkin, "Pis'mo v redaktsiiu," *VI,* No. 2, 1952, pp. 157-59.

Numerous illustrations showed Kazakhs bearing arms against their traditional enemies—sometimes Russians.

The new history appeared in the summer of 1943, and was reviewed with complete favor in *Pravda* on July 10. The reviewer, A. V. Piaskovskii, a specialist on Central Asia, considered the book to be an important addition to the accomplishments of Marxist-Leninist scholarship. He referred briefly to the book's treatment of subjects which soon were to be condemned (feudal relations, periodization, the evaluation of revolts) without challenging a single one. Caught up in the spirit of the time, he spent a third of his review praising the authors' elaboration of the role of the Kazakhs in the current war.

We know a great deal more than usual about the preparation of this book and the controversies among its authors because of the report of a discussion of the newly published work held by the editors of *Istoricheskii zhurnal* on October 12, 1943.[40] The place of the meeting is not given, and neither is the reason for calling it. It seems likely, from the defensive tone of many of the speakers, that some party criticism had already been heard, and the historians, under conditions of comparative freedom, were explaining their positions and making a collective defense. The twenty-seven participants, from the collective of editors and authors and the Institute of History of the Academy of Sciences, constituted an assembly of notables in Soviet historical scholarship. There were no party representatives at the meeting, and editor Abdykalykov was never mentioned. The participants included the other editor, Pankratova, and Grekov, Bakhrushin, Bernshtam, Kudriavtsev, Viatkin, and Picheta. Their remarks, for the most part, supported well established interpretations, or those recently called for by party spokesmen. In many cases they admitted that they were sailing uncharted seas, and explained the careful reasoning upon which their interpretations were based. In view of what happened to these interpretations in a short time, the arguments of this little-known meeting take on great significance, both as a candid statement of a group of distinguished Soviet historians on several important questions, and as an indication of the historian's predicament in trying to anticipate the party line. It would be safe to say that never have so many Soviet historians pinned themselves to the wall so thoroughly in the course of six pages of print. In less than two years they would

40. "Obsuzhdenie v redaktsii 'Istoricheskogo zhurnal' knigi 'Istoriia Kazakhskoi SSR,' " *IZ*, Nos. 11-12, 1943, pp. 85-90.

all regret that the report was published, and the journal itself would be liquidated for its general laxness, of which this discussion was symptomatic.

The crucial question of the interpretation of the Kazakh resistance movements was discussed at the outset by Pankratova, who revealed that there had been a sharp difference of opinion among the authors on the question. Some had thought that all these movements were of a national liberation character, and therefore progressive. Others had argued that all of them were reactionary. This appears to be the first time that several Soviet historians seriously considered that the resistance movements might be reactionary—an indication of the impact of the recent interpretations concerning the importance of the centralized state and the rehabilitation of tsarist foreign policy. It is also worth noting that the historians at this point were still inclined to put all movements in the same category. No one had yet considered that a formula might be found by which they would be divided, good and bad. In the end the long established view prevailed. "We reasoned first of all," said Pankratova, "that the struggle of every people for its national independence is beyond question a progressive factor." This interpretation, of course, had the added advantage of promoting the current emphasis on patriotism.

This strong point of the book, noted by several speakers, carried with it a potentially dangerous implication, illustrated by the statement of Kudriavtsev, the editor of *Istoricheskii zhurnal:* "We can in all truth say that this book actually inculcates patriotism, the will to fight, faith in victory, inspired by feats in the name of the motherland [*rodina*]. Therefore it is difficult to overestimate the political significance of the book." But whose motherland? The motherland of the Kazakhs in the early nineteenth century was not the Soviet motherland of 1943. The "struggle for independence" of the Kazakhs could only be regarded from the viewpoint of Russian nationalism as an enemy action, aimed at weakening the now hallowed strong Russian government. There could be no gainsaying the hard fact that the modern military traditions of the Kazakhs, which the party apparently wanted to popularize, were formed in campaigns *against the Russians.* In making this interpretation the authors of the textbook could only resort to the view that these were actions against the reactionary autocracy and not against the Russian nation as a whole. "All the national liberation movements appeared to be progressive," Pankratova noted, "because

they were directed against tsarist power, against tsarist Russia."
The counterbalancing view that there was no ill feeling between
ordinary Russians and Kazakhs in the colonial period was not
stated (and was not held in the book), though Bakhrushin and
Grekov observed that the book might have gone further in developing the progressive influence of the Russians who settled in Kazakhstan. Pankratova observed that "the struggle of the Kazakh
people for their independence proceeded with the warm sympathy
and even the help of the leading representatives of the Russian
people"—but this statement apparently referred to Bolshevik leadership on the eve of the Revolution.

The speakers at this conference discussed resistance movements
but not their leaders. There was only one passing reference to the
most famous of the Kazakh heroes, Sultan Kenesary Kasymov, who
had been praised at great length in the book. Kenesary's leadership of an eleven-year movement (1836-47) was presented in the
book as an outstanding example of the fight for independence and
the formation of a strong Kazakh state—both progressive themes.
His invasion of Kirgiz lands late in his career had been excused as
a means of extending and strengthening the state. But such a
positive interpretation was accomplished at the expense of two
other factors, which had to be ignored: he had waged his struggle
against future Soviet peoples—the Kirgiz and, more important, the
Russians—and his movement was feudal and separatist in character.
The reluctance of the authors of the Kazakh history to discuss the
hero whom they had extolled a short time earlier is perhaps another
indication that these points were becoming more sensitive within
the party.

Another thorny problem was the manner of annexation. Was it
"voluntary" or by conquest? Pankratova indicated that there had
also been a controversy on this point, and that the established view
had been held: "The whole course of this annexation shows that
the annexation of Kazakhstan to tsarist Russia is a result of the
conquest of Kazakhstan by tsarist colonizers." In this connection the
authors had made their most venturesome leap, a clear departure
from an established party interpretation. They had explicitly rejected the "lesser evil" formula. The reasons were not clearly given
in the discussion, but the dilemma of the authors can easily be
imagined. How could they inspire patriotism and a will to fight in
the Kazakh people in the midst of a war for life or death while
at the same time holding that annexation to a foreign power, under

some circumstances, is the lesser evil in the long run? They adopted the view that the "lesser evil" formula had a limited application. Georgia and the Ukraine, to which it had been applied, were annexed to Russia by treaty when they were being threatened by a third power. Kazakhstan was annexed by conquest, and a different set of conditions existed. The authors tried to avoid linking the Russian conquest and the progressiveness of annexation, the result of which would have made aggression a progressive historical event. They were silent about characterizing the annexation as such, referring instead to the eventual consequences of the act. Kudriavtsev put it indirectly: "It is necessary to deny categorically the interpretation of the annexation of Kazakhstan as a reactionary phenomenon." The clearest statement was made by Pankratova, who remarked that "It is necessary to emphasize that the inclusion of Kazakhstan in the orbit of Russian influence, putting it on the path to capitalist development, had a progressive influence on the further development of Kazakhstan." Compared to what Soviet historians—including Pankratova herself—would write on this subject in the near future, this was mild indeed.

Although the overwhelming majority of the interpretations defended in this discussion would shortly be revised under party criticism, a few of the views survived. In addition to their discussion of the progressive role of Russians in Kazakhstan, the speakers referred to benefits derived from the development of capitalism and trade in Kazakhstan and the influence of Russian culture on the Kazakhs. These themes were minor ones, however, and compared to their later emphasis they can be considered embryonic at this point.

The discussion yielded no important opposition to the interpretations expressed in the history. In general the work was highly praised for its erudition and style. A few minor technical points were raised, and Pankratova promised to take them all into account in the preparation of a second edition. She indicated that the authors could now continue their planned work on an elementary textbook for Kazakh schools and survey histories of the other Union Republics. These tasks, however, would prove far more difficult than she knew at the time.

The participants in this discussion were undoubtedly interested in a related historical subject that had occupied most of the front page of *Pravda* on the previous day. With the announcement of the creation of the Order of Bogdan Khmel'nitskii, the party had called for the all-out popularization of its first non-Russian hero. This step was taken in celebration of the liberation of the Ukraine, and Khmel'nitskii was represented as a symbol of Russian-Ukrainian unity. The Army newspaper, *Red Star*, observed that "the life of Bogdan Khmel'nitskii is an example of the decisive struggle for the brotherly union of the Ukrainian people and its elder brother, the Russian people. Khmel'nitskii clearly realized that the free and prosperous development of the Ukraine was possible only in the closest union with Russia."[41]

The tone of the popularization of Bogdan stands in sharp contrast to the reticence of the participants at the conference on Kazakh history to discuss their hero, Kenesary, and points up the important criterion for the selection of heroes. Bogdan was being remembered as a symbol of unity; Kenesary could hardly be viewed except as a divisive force in the history of the U.S.S.R.

THE PARTY'S NEW EMPHASIS

It seems likely that when these events occurred late in 1943 the party was already concerned about the backlash of nationalism among the non-Russians, which was an inevitable result of its campaign for the popularization of military traditions. The quarrels within the Soviet family were kept quiet, however, and the first public indication of trouble came almost a year later with the first of the Central Committee resolutions on the weakness of ideological work in the Tatar Republic. One indication of party policy in this period is the pattern of publication of the pamphlets on military heroes. The official state bibliography not only supplies information about titles and time of publication, but also indicates which languages the pamphlets were translated into, and usually the numbers of each printing.[42]

The all-out popularization of heroes was restricted to seven

41. Werth, *Russia at War*, p. 744. Werth has noted that the Khmel'nitskii order was not widely awarded, and that some officers turned it down because of the hetman's anti-Semitism. N. Petrovskii quickly published a short book and two articles on the "reunion" theme: *Vossoedinenie ukrainskogo naroda v edinom ukrainskom sovetskom gosudarstve* (Moscow, 1944); an article of the same title in *Bol'shevik*, No. 2, 1944, pp. 42-45; and "Prisoedinenie Ukrainy k Rossii v 1654 godu," *IZ*, No. 1, 1944, pp. 47-54. On Khmel'nitskii's changing reputation, see also B. Krupnycky, "Bohdan Khmelnitsky and Soviet Historiography," *Ukrainian Review* (Munich), No. 1 (1955), pp. 65-75, and Clarence A. Manning, "The Soviets and Khmelnitsky," *Ukrainian Quarterly*, III (1946-47), 10-15.

42. This discussion is based on a survey of *Knizhnaia letopis'*, 1941-45.

figures—Stalin's six Russians and Khmel'nitskii, who did not figure in the running at all until late 1943. More than a million pamphlets appeared on each of these heroes, and in some cases a half dozen authors were in competition. The most popular series appears to have been the work of V. Danilevskii and S. Borodin.[43] One million copies of the latter's *Dmitrii Donskoi* were printed at one time in 1942, and there were many other Russian and non-Russian editions. In comparison with these seven, the also-rans made a poor showing. Two pamphlets on Peter the Great appeared in modest printings early in the War, and were not reprinted until 1944. Ivan IV received similar treatment. A very modest place (1,000 to 15,000 copies per printing) was claimed for Bagration, Nakhimov, and *Brusilov's Breakthrough,* which concerned the campaign more than its leader.

The pamphlet production reached its peak at the beginning of 1942, slumped during that year, and was reduced considerably in 1943. This cannot be explained solely on the basis of war conditions, since it was still possible to produce printings of a quarter of a million in a few cases. By late 1943, the only large printings were for Khmel'nitskii, a special case. The failure to sustain the campaign suggests that the authorities may have had second thoughts about the whole idea.

The pamphlets were published largely in the Russian language, and even in the case of the other languages, Russian heroes were overwhelmingly featured. Soviet authorities were thus exporting Russian nationalism for the purpose of creating Soviet patriotism: Kazakhs, Dagestanis, and Tatars were encouraged to read about Nevskii, Minin, and Pozharskii, but not about their own military heroes. The thoroughness of the popularization, even for the smaller peoples, is impressive. Iakuts, Komis, and Karakalpaks all received pamphlets on the Russian heroes, translated into their languages.

In this tremendous flood of pamphlets, the non-Russian heroes were represented by less than 5 per cent of the total numbers (excepting Khmel'nitskii). This was not for lack of effort on the part of the local writers, but because of the restraining hand of the authorities who controlled the printing presses. We can never

43. V. Danilevskii, *Dmitrii Donskoi* (Moscow, 1942), *Aleksandr Nevskii* (Moscow, 1942), and *Dmitrii Pozharskii* (Moscow, 1942); S. Borodin, *Dmitrii Donskoi* (Moscow, 1942) and *Mikhail Kutuzov* (Moscow, 1942). All of these were published in several printings and translations in 1943 and 1944. Except for the first two listed, which are in the Library of Congress, they were not available to me.

know how many manuscripts were stillborn at the publishing houses, but it is possible to deduce from the official bibliography that some non-Russian writers made an attempt to popularize their heroes. While the pamphlets on the Russians were being reprinted dozens of times in Russian and other languages, the works of the non-Russian writers about their heroes were turned out in small editions and not reprinted. The most conspicuous case concerns Shamil, the most popular of all the non-Russian heroes at that time. Among the earliest titles listed in the bibliography in 1941 are *Shamil, A Sketch from the History of the Struggle of the Peoples of the Caucasus for Independence* by one N. Kroviakov, and three pamphlets by R. M. Magomedov (a Dagestani historian who would figure prominently in the Shamil controversy which developed later), *Shamil, the Youth of Shamil,* and *Imam Shamil.* If, at the end of 1941, anyone had asked which hero, in the whole galaxy of Soviet heroes, was represented by the largest number of titles, the answer would have been Shamil. But the answer would have been misleading in the extreme, as the publishing record indicates. Four thousand copies of the Kroviakov pamphlet were published in Groznyi (in the North Caucasus) but the pamphlet was never reprinted. *The Youth of Shamil* and *Imam Shamil* were published in Makhachkala (Dagestan A.S.S.R.) in editions of ten-thousand copies each, and never reprinted. *Shamil* was published in Makhachkala in three languages of the Caucasus in editions of one to three thousand copies and was also not reprinted.[44]

The other hero pamphlets on non-Russian figures were nearly all from the Caucasus area. The Georgians led the field, producing pamphlets on three of their monarchs, who could be remembered for their importance in building a strong state and defending it against foreign incursions. The pamphlets were on David the Builder and Queen Tamara, medieval monarchs who defended Georgia against the Turks, and King George V, who drove the Tatars out of Georgia. These pamphlets had small printings in the Georgian language. There was a pamphlet on David Bek, the eighteenth-century Armenian who led a rebellion against the Per-

44. N. Kroviakov, *Shamil'. Ocherk iz istorii bor'by narodov kavkaza za nezavisimost'* (Groznyi, 1941); and R. Magomedov, *Shamil'* (Makhachkala, 1941), *Iunost' Shamil'* (Makhachkala, 1941), and *Imam Shamil'* (Makhachkala, 1941). None of these were available to me.

Magomedov's efforts to popularize Shamil were confirmed in 1950, when the Dagestan Party Secretary quoted a passage in which he had recounted his failure to get articles on the hero published. See Chapter 7 below, pp. 146-47.

sians, and Babek, a ninth-century Azerbaidzhani defender against the Arabs. A pamphlet on Daniel of Galicia (thirteenth century) appeared in Russian and Ukrainian late in the war when that area was being retaken by the Soviet armies. Apparently, not a single hero of Central Asia was celebrated in the pamphlets.

The party began to take a more direct hand in guiding the development of the interpretation of the history of the non-Russians in the Central Committee resolution of August 9, 1944, "On the Organization and Measures for the Improvement of Mass Political and Ideological Work in the Tatar Party Organization." The resolution called upon local party ideologists to remedy the "serious shortcomings and mistakes of a nationalist character in the elucidation of the history of Tatary (the embellishment of the Golden Horde, popularization of the feudal-khan epic about Idegei), which detract from the special influence of the study and elucidation of the history of the mutual struggle of the Russians, Tatars and other peoples of the U.S.S.R. against foreign invaders, against tsarism and the landlord-capitalist yoke, and even on the history of socialist transformation of Tatary in the period of Soviet power. . . ."[45] The "embellishment" of the Golden Horde was serious enough, as an abstract proposition, but with the attempt of the Tatars to make a hero of Idegei, who had besieged Moscow for several weeks in 1408, matters had come to serious straits. In addition to the Central Committee resolution, the ideological authorities decided to fight fire with fire. As an antidote they ordered ten-thousand copies of a pamphlet on one of the Russian heroes in the Tatar language. Their choice was a natural: Dmitrii Donskoi, who had defeated the Golden Horde in 1380.

Shortly thereafter the Central Committee gave a similar warning to the Bashkirs. In a general resolution on the improvement of their ideological work, the question of historical interpretation headed the list of grievances:

> In preparing for publication the *Outlines of the History of Bashkiria*, and in the literary work *Idukai and Muradym, an Epic on Bogatyrs*, no distinction has been made between the fundamental national liberation movements of the Bashkir people and the bandit-like raids of Bashkir feudal leaders on neighboring peoples; the subjugation of

45. "O sostoianii i merakh uluchsheniia massovo-politicheskoi i ideologicheskoi raboty v tatarskoi partinoi organizatsii," *Propagandist*, Nos. 15-16, 1944, pp. 19-22.

the Bashkir workers by the Tatar and Bashkir feudal leaders is presented in an unsatisfactory way, idealizing the
feudal past of the Bashkirs. In the drama *Kakhym-Turia*
the history of the participation of the Bashkirs in the Patriotic War of 1812 is distorted, the Russians and Bashkirs
being pitted against one another in the war.[46]

Like the resolution on the Tatars, this one noted the importance
of the mutual struggle of Russians and non-Russians, and it stated
even more explicitly that interpretations in which the non-Russians
were viewed as fighting against the Russian people would not be
tolerated. Here was the kernel of the Party-sponsored interpretation that would turn the Soviet history of tsarist colonialism inside
out. But it appeared inconspicuously in the middle of a lengthy
resolution, and many historians tried for a time to ignore it or get
around it.

These statements, which came more than a year after the publication of the *History of the Kazakh S.S.R.*, revealed how "erroneous" its interpretations were. Meanwhile there was an ominous
silence about that volume. After the early—and abortive—*Pravda*
review, the book was not reviewed again in a Russian publication,
unless one might call the hatchet work of *Bol'shevik* in March, 1945,
a review. The *coup de grâce* was dealt, ironically enough, by the
same M. Morozov who had made the clearest call for the popularization of national heroes. He objected to the authors' emphasis on
military traditions (which had been the most consistent theme
among party demands since 1941). Such a thesis, he observed,
was one-sided, because it ignored the basic determinant as set
down in Stalin's *Short Course*, namely the mode of production. The
basic error of the authors was their failure to elucidate sufficiently
the nature of productive forces at each stage of Kazakh history.
A second and no less serious error was their failure to apply the
principles of the class struggle to the internal aspects of the Kazakh
resistance movements. They had without discrimination pronounced
all movements progressive, as struggles for independence, regardless of their leadership or goals. Morozov specifically denied the
progressive nature of two movements (those of Karatai and Eset
Kotibarov) because of their attacks on Kazakh villages, and pointed
out that Sultan Kenesary Kasymov's attack on the Kirgiz in 1847
was "a feudal war," and not a defensive move for the strengthening

46. "O sostoianii i merakh uluchsheniia agitatsionno-propagandiskoi raboty
v bashkirskoi partiinoi organizatsii," *ibid.*, Nos. 3-4, 1945, pp. 16-18.

of the Kazakh government, as the book had stated. The whole Kenesary movement, which lasted from 1836 to 1847, was not evaluated (a source of much future uncertainty!). At the same time Morozov declared that some uprisings against the tsars were "objectively" progressive, for example the 1916 revolt in Central Asia. The Pankratova collective was also criticized for abandoning the "lesser evil" formula. They had gone back to the Pokrovskii heresy—the "absolute evil." Surely they must have realized that the Kazakhs were also rescued from a greater evil than Russian annexation: conquest by the Dzhungarians, the Chinese, or the Khans of Khiva. Finally, Morozov declared that the authors had underestimated the positive influences of the Russians on Kazakh history. He particularly objected to the view that the Kazakh nation had been formed under the Mongol occupation. This development had in fact come under Russian influence.[47]

Under the impact of this blow, the Central Committee of the Kazakh party passed a resolution condemning the book and setting up machinery for the writing of another history of the Kazakhs.[48] Needless to say, the resolution made no mention of the role of the Communist party of Kazakhstan in the creation of the history. In this connection the exclusion of the co-editor, M. Abdykalykov, from all the discussion of the book's failings, is instructive. Abdykalykov was the Secretary of the Central Committee of the Kazakh Party for Propaganda and Agitation. He was probably placed in the collective for two reasons: to add another Kazakh name to the few in the group, and to act as a kind of political commissar between scholars and party. It was, however, his co-editor, Pankratova, who took all the blame and made the apologies.[49]

47. M. Morozov, "Ob 'Istorii Kazakhskoi SSR,'" *Bol'shevik*, No. 6, 1945, pp. 74-80.
48. "O podgotovke 2-go izdaniia 'Istorii Kazakhskoi SSR," *Bol'shevik Kazakhstana*, No. 6, 1945, pp. 49-51.
49. How completely the party protected itself in this matter is illustrated by the difficulty of my search just to identify Abdykalykov. Having noted that he was the silent partner in all the discussions of the book, I searched all the reviews and references to the book but was unsuccessful in finding any mention of his name. The Soviet bibliographies revealed only the negative information that he had apparently never written as much as an article or book review. The Library of Congress staff, who tried manfully to identify the co-editor of the most celebrated history of Kazakhstan, could only produce a list of some twenty likely places where his name did not appear. As the mystery deepened, I made a point to browse through every book on Kazakhstan I happened to see in search of the missing editor. The search came to a successful end four years later when I discovered a quotation from a wartime

THE MYTH AT THE WAR'S END

The nucleus of the friendship myth as it existed in 1945 is to be found in the two Central Committee resolutions and the Morozov article. There were three main points: (1) resistance movements and revolts in non-Russian areas were to be interpreted from a class viewpoint, and not from a standpoint of nationality; (2) Soviet patriotism was not to be identified with non-Russian nationalism—there must be no "idealization of the feudal past"; (3) there must be an emphasis on the mutual struggle of Russians and non-Russians against "foreign enemies," to the exclusion of violence between these natural allies.

Nevertheless, these principles were only broadly stated, and sometimes only implied. Their application to specific historical events had to be made by historians by a haphazard procedure of trial and error. To make matters worse, the party position was itself changing rather rapidly. This can be detected in the opinions of Morozov, who presumably represented the party's position at the time of each writing. Not only did he call for works on national heroes and military traditions in 1942 and then blast the historians' efforts to fulfil his wishes a short time later, his criticism of the Kazakh history would be definitely naive, and even bourgeois nationalist from the party's position five years later. He defended the "lesser evil" formula, which would shortly be abandoned for a more positive view. He did not contest the authors' view that the Kazakhs were annexed by conquest, although such a view was loudly condemned a short time later in favor of volunteer annexation. Most important of all, he specifically restated the old view that only under Soviet power had a friendship of peoples been attained, failing to see any evidence of a pre-revolutionary friendship. But we should not expect Morozov, any more than Pankratova, to have the gift of prophecy.

This last point is the most important element still lacking in the myth in 1945. The concept of the natural alliance of peoples before the Revolution, although referred to rather vaguely in speeches and editorials during the War, would not be established as a historical view for some time. This was the capstone of the edifice,

news report, stating that the Party Secretary had made a speech at a war rally in Tashkent in December, 1942 (*Kazakhstan v period velikoi otechestvennoi voiny sovetskogo soiuza* [Alma-Ata, 1964], pp. 371-72). The absence of biographical information on Abdykalykov in standard Soviet reference works suggests that he was purged.

and without it, the historian could hardly view the finished structure.

A further clue to the real motives of the party, as opposed to the Marxist-Leninist jargon of the pronouncements, is furnished by the fate of the other survey histories published during the war years. The Kazakh history was the most ambitious and venturesome undertaking, but there were other publications that also answered the call to remember military traditions. The main ones were a Ukrainian history textbook published in Ufa,[50] a *History of the Armenian People*, published in Erevan in 1944,[51] and *The Tadzhik People in the Struggle for the Freedom and Independence of Their Motherland: Sketches from the History of the Tadzhiks and Tadzhikistan*, published the same year in Stalinabad.[52] These histories possessed the same failings as the Kazakh volume: All struggles for independence were considered progressive, and there was an abundance of military tradition. In this respect the Tadzhik history, chapter for chapter, has more emphasis on military tradition than the Kazakh history. All these volumes had as little to say about the mode of production as a force in history as did the Kazakh history. The Ukrainian history would eventually be criticized (in 1947) but on different grounds; the Armenian and Tadzhik histories were never subjected to widespread criticism. In this light Morozov's leading point about production is sheer obfuscation; the party had changed its mind about military tradition and a new emphasis had to be found. But why did the other volumes, with their share of military tradition, escape the party's wrath? The answer—obscure in 1945— is quite clear in the light of subsequent events. The Ukrainians, Armenians, and Tadzhiks had built their military traditions fighting against Poles, Turks, Persians, Arabs, and Mongols. The Kazakhs, in their modern history, at least, had specialized in fighting Russians.

50. *Istoriia Ukrainy*, ed. N. N. Petrovskii *et al.* (Ufa, 1943), Vol. I.
51. *Istoriia armianskogo naroda*, ed. K. G. Kafadarian and M. T. Nersisian (Erevan, 1944), Vol. I.
52. B. Gafurov and N. Prokhorov, *Tadzhikskii narod v bor'be za svobody i nezavisimost' svoei rodiny. Ocherki iz istorii Tadzhikov i Tadzhikistana* (Stalinabad, 1944).

CHAPTER **5.**

THE RECONSTRUCTION
OF SOVIET HISTORICAL SCIENCE

"In the Great Patriotic War the Soviet peoples demonstrated how the indestructible friendship of peoples of the Soviet Union had a great significance in winning the victory, sealed by blood in the friendship of brotherly peoples. Therefore, our scholars—historians, ethnographers, literary writers— must in their works promote the flowering of the friendship of peoples inhabiting the Soviet Union by truthfully reconstructing [pravdilo vossozdavat'] their history." From a speech by party spokesman G. Aleksandrov, August 1, 1945 (Bol'shevik, No. 14, 1945, p. 17).

The early post-war years were the most chaotic in the experience of Soviet historians, who were obliged to make sweeping revisions of views to keep abreast of ideological developments, all the while acknowledging as their own errors the views that had either been prescribed or tolerated by the party a short time earlier. The party's ideological reconstruction was no less prodigious than the rebuilding of devastated Soviet cities, and was far more complicated. Unlike the Soviet builder, the historian was called upon to tear down some parts of his earlier work while simultaneously rebuilding others. And he lacked a workable plan: the architect's blueprints were so sketchy that the carpenter had to improvise the details and was unable to imagine the shape of the finished structure. The party's new views were expressed in such piecemeal fashion, and with so many apparent contradictions, that even the most attentive and compliant historians could not make sense of them. Furthermore, there was the disturbing time factor. A scholarly work may require years to write, still longer to be published and reviewed. In the rapidly changing ideological climate of the late 1940's, it was virtually impossible for the historian to anticipate the "correct" interpretation of the near future.

The rewriting of Soviet history proceeded in the most unfavorable climate imaginable. The scholar, who had to contend with unprecedented party interference, was constantly involved with the growing cult of Stalin, which meant the absolute authority of the *Short Course*. The *Zhdanovshchina* brought back the atmosphere of the terror and forced acceptance of absurd positions on Russian leadership, the greatness of Russian culture, and the worthlessness of that of the West.

One of the urgent tasks the party set for historians was the production of histories of the non-Russian peoples from Marxist-Leninist positions. Not a single attempt to write such a history had had more than a fleeting success—largely because of the party's own rapidly changing demands. For an ideology that places a high priority on history as a political and educational tool, the situation was deplorable. The non-Russian peoples, who represent about half of all Soviet citizens and who were the most in need of such guidance, were without a history. The process was complicated by the legacy of the comparative freedom of the war years: historians refused to conform to new party views without reasoning, talking back, and offering logical proofs. There was also in this period an unusual amount of disagreement between the Russian center and the non-Russian periphery; at times the non-Russian historian received support from the local party and Academy of Sciences branch against the central organs in Moscow.

THE PARTY'S INSTRUCTIONS

Many of the party shifts directly affected the development of historical writing on the non-Russian peoples, but the exact meaning of their impact could not be immediately ascertained.[1]

1. No attempt is made here to discuss the issues of post-war Soviet historiography except those having a direct bearing on the history of the non-Russians. For general surveys, see Konstantin F. Shteppa, *Russian Historians and the Soviet State* (New Brunswick, N.J.: Rutgers University Press, 1962), chap. ix; P. K. Urban, *Smena tendentsii v sovetskoi istoriografii* (Munich, 1959), pp. 5-33; Sergius Yakobsen, "Postwar Historical Research in the Soviet Union," *Annals of the American Academy of Political and Social Science*, CCLXIII (1949), 123-33; Rudolf Schlesinger, "Recent Soviet Historiography," *Soviet Studies*, I (1950), No. 4, 293-312, and II (1951), No. 1, 3-21; Georg von Rauch, "Grundlinien der sowjetischen Geschichtsforschung im Zeichen des

The overriding factor was the continued campaign for Soviet patriotism, with all the drive of the war years, but with a new emphasis and set of goals. Soviet patriotism was still seen as a binding force, not against an actual military threat to the existence of the Soviet Union, but as an instrument of nationality policy, aimed at eradicating those elements of "bourgeois nationalism" that had emerged during the war, as a direct result of the party's emphasis on national pride and military traditions. The drive lost none of its militancy, but it was modified for the purposes of the Cold War. Scholars were regimented to fight an ideological war against potential foreign enemies, political and cultural. The dire threats which lay just beyond Soviet borders were constantly conjured up as a reason for binding Soviet peoples ever closer together in their mutual defense of the socialist motherland.

The doctrine of Great Russian leadership, which had been growing during the War, now knew no bounds. Stalin had inaugurated the unlimited celebration of Russian national greatness in his famous toast on May 24, 1945, in honor of Red Army commanders. He proposed a toast to the Russian people, not to the Soviet people in general, and stated his reasons: (1) "It is the leading nation of all the nations belonging to the Soviet Union"; (2) "it earned in this war general recognition as a guiding force of the Soviet Union"; and (3) "it has a clear mind, a firm character and patience."[2] There was no longer any question of "the first among equals" or of "mutual enrichment" of the peoples, but rather a view of the Russians as teachers, civilizers, cultural leaders, and protectors of the non-Russian nationalities.

One important part of the Great Russian leadership theme was the sweeping reinterpretation of Russia's past, which had been started cautiously a decade earlier. The view on Russia's relations with European culture that had been imposed in the late 1930's was completely reversed. At that time close ties of the Russians (and even non-Russians) with Europe were emphasized, as a way of proving that these were not backward peoples, but were assimilating the best the West had to offer. Now the Russians had gone far beyond that, and were asserting that Russian culture had been far superior to that of the West and had nothing to learn from it.

Stalinismus," *Europa Archiv*, V (1950), 3383-88, 3423-32, 3489-94; G. Stackelberg, "Otrazhenie politiki SSSR v smene sovetskikh istoricheskikh kontseptsii," *Vestnik instituta po izucheniiu istorii i kul'tury SSSR*, No. 2, 1952, pp. 34-53.
    2. *Pravda*, May 25, 1945.

The result for the history of the non-Russian peoples was that their old ties with Europe and Asia had to be uprooted, and new ones with the historically superior Russian culture had to be established. It became a serious offense to suggest that the Russians (or Slavs in general) were in any respect inferior to their neighbors. The Norman theory on the origins of the Russian state, which had been rejected during the War, was now eradicated. Questions of ethnogenesis and the origins of the Russian state became matters of national pride. V. V. Mavrodin dated the origins of the Slavs "from the beginning of the third millennium before our era," and Grekov reasoned that since ninth-century Kiev Rus' was as fully developed as the state of Charlemagne, its origins must be dated back to the sixth century in Volynia.[3] The upshot of this was a new emphasis on the common origins of the "three brotherly peoples" (Great Russians, Ukrainians, and Belorussians), who were no longer regarded as peoples with a separate origin and history, but as branches of the "Old Russian State." Thus the coordination of the history of the Soviet family was moved a step further; any discussion of the "single stream" concept, which accorded Ukrainians or other peoples an independent history, was condemned as a "bourgeois nationalist" survival of the "Hrushevskii school."

Tsarist foreign policy was reviewed and seen in a new light, and the horrors of tsarist colonialism began to be discussed only in muted tones. The momentum of the drive was such that one of the ordinarily infallible authorities of Marxism could be "corrected" in stride. Stalin was congratulated for "a remarkable example of a creative Marxist approach to the problems of historiography," demonstrated in his letter "On Engels' Article 'The Foreign Policy of Russian Tsarism.'" In this letter Stalin had bluntly stated that Engels was in error when he considered Russia as "the last bastion of European reaction" in the 1890's. According to the editors of the leading historical journal, Stalin "proved beyond doubt that during the period under discussion the role of reaction's last bastion in Europe had shifted more and more from Russia to the imperialist bourgeois states of Western Europe."[4] This new interpretation,

3. Shteppa, *Russian Historians*, p. 215; Alexander Vucinich, "The First Russian State," in C. E. Black (ed.), *Rewriting Russian History* (New York: Frederick A. Praeger, 1956), pp. 123-42.

4. "Zadachi sovetskikh istorikov v oblasti novoi i noveishei istorii," *VI*, No. 3, 1949, pp. 3-13. The letter had been written to the Central Committee

coupled with the growing emphases on the virtues of the strong
Russian state, the cultural and economic blessings accruing to non-
Russians after annexation, and the dangers of "foreign enemies"
just beyond the border, served to establish the view that annexation of territories to Russia, regardless of the circumstances, was to
be regarded as a historically progressive phenomenon. As for
tsarist colonialism, its taint was too strong to be removed quickly,
but eventually a formula would be found which would make that
unnecessary.

Historians received the party's views in a most haphazard fashion
during this period. The large "scholarly conference," which would
be so characteristic of the 1950's as a coordinating device, was not
yet extensively employed. Neither the Institute of History of the
Academy of Sciences, which was frequently under fire, nor the
history journals could be relied upon. *Istoricheskii zhurnal* had been
liquidated at the end of the War, and the editors of its successor,
Voprosy istorii (*Questions of History*), were not on firm ground.
Some of the best established historians—Mints, Pankratova, Rub-
inshtein, Bakhrushin, and others—were groping their way under
severe criticism. The limits of permissible interpretation were
ascertained from piecemeal statements in political speeches, in
the party press, in book reviews, and in the ideological resolutions of
the Central Committee. The main sources were high party officials,
like Zhdanov, and spokesmen for the Agitation and Propaganda
Section of the party (*Agitprop*)—G. Aleksandrov, M. Morozov,
and K. Litvin, none of whom were historians. Acting under the
political pressures of the moment, these men set the limits; it was
left up to historians, through the painful processes of trial and
error and self-criticism, to arrive at workable formulations. These
bits of party advice were like individual pieces of a jigsaw puzzle;
they offered no more than a hint of the finished picture. They
were also sometimes confusing and contradictory.[5]

One of the earliest and most detailed pronouncements of the

in 1934 and publicized at appropriate times, on the eve of World War II
(*Bol'shevik*, No. 9, 1941, pp. 1-5) and in the postwar period.

5. A conspicuous example is Khrushchev's apparently authoritative article
on the "Stalinist friendship of peoples," which appeared in *Bol'shevik* at the
end of 1949, by which time the view was well established that such friendship
preceded the Revolution, sometimes by centuries. But Khrushchev not only
never mentioned pre-revolutionary friendship, but twice referred to the
fact that the Revolution had "created" the friendship of peoples. See N.
Khrushchev, "Stalinskaia druzhba narodov—zalog nepobedimosti nashei
rodiny," *Bol'shevik*, No. 24, 1949, pp. 80-85.

post-war period for the writers of local history came in a speech of
Aleksandrov, delivered on August 1, 1945, and later published in
Bol'shevik.[6] On the subject of Great Russian leadership he observed that Soviet historians had not emphasized the influences of
Kiev Rus' on Western Europe; they had not showed how the Russians had saved Europe from the Tatar; they had not sufficiently
uprooted the harmful Norman theory. The history of the U.S.S.R.
must be presented as a "unitary organic process. The history of
the different peoples can be correctly worked out and made intelligible only in relation with the history of the other peoples, and above
all with the history of the Russian people." He criticized the de-
funct *Istoricheskii zhurnal* for having published articles that indis-
criminately characterized rebellions and resistance movements as
either progressive or reactionary. He indicated that the journal
had indulged two extremes of interpretation, and that both were
anti-Marxist. In the wartime spirit of patriotism, with its emphasis
on strong central government, some writers had idealized tsarism.
The journal had published an article that designated the revolts of
Bolotnikov, Razin, Pugachev, and even the Decembrists as reactionary, because they were trying to tear down the Russian
government, whereas Aleksander Nevskii, Dmitrii Donskoi, Ivan
IV, and Peter the Great were trying to strengthen it. Aleksandrov
considered this proposition absurd; it must be corrected by an
examination of the class nature of each revolt. At the same time
not all military actions of the non-Russians should be considered
progressive. Here he referred to the Tatar idealization of Idegei,
showing that by application of the class principle such an error
could have been avoided: Idegei was "one of the most powerful
feudal lords of the Golden Horde." Perhaps even more to the point
was his observation that Idigei "attacked Russian towns and villages
and took thousands of Russians into slavery."

The most important point Aleksandrov made about the new
history of the non-Russian peoples was that the friendship of
peoples concept must be incorporated into it. His appeal to Soviet
scholars (quoted at the head of this chapter) was a typical piece
of *Agitprop* reasoning, utterly pragmatic, and in total disregard of
those stubborn facts that might bother the historian. Stripped of
verbiage, Aleksandrov's proposition and conclusion can be stated
as follows: "The indestructible friendship of peoples of the Soviet

6. G. Aleksandrov, "O nekotorykh zadachakh obshchestvennykh nauk v
sovremennykh usloviiakh," *Bol'shevik*, No. 14, 1945, pp. 12-29.

Union had a great significance in winning the victory . . . [in World War II]. Therefore, our scholars . . . must in their works promote the flowering of the friendship of peoples . . . by truthfully reconstructing their history." There was no doubt in the party man's mind that a "truthful reconstruction" of history would verify the friendship of peoples, which was axiomatic. It remained only for the historian to find how to do the job. It would be no exaggeration to say that Aleksandrov's *non sequitur* is the central thesis of the new Soviet history of the non-Russian peoples.

The first efforts of Soviet scholars to take positions that would promote the new party goals were woefully inadequate. Beginning in October, 1946, a series of attacks on "bourgeois nationalism" began to appear in the press of the national republics with a regularity that indicated a concerted central plan.[7] The drive covered a great variety of subjects, including literature, linguistics, philosophy, the theater, and music. It was part of Zhdanov's campaign to eradicate all "fawning before the West" in Soviet cultural life and to deepen Soviet patriotism, but it had the equally important goal of eliminating the non-Russian nationalism that had been intensified by the militant patriotism of the war period. Removing such "idealization of the past" was essential for Soviet nationality policy, which had as its unstated goal the quieting of differences and further cooperation of nationalities.

The failures of historians to produce a "scientific, Marxist-Leninist" history of Soviet peoples was of great concern to the party's ideological leaders. It always ranked high among the "tasks of historical science." In November, 1946, *Kul'tura i zhizn'* (*Culture and Life*) made a broad attack on history textbooks, whose authors had been slow to adjust to the new views. They were said to be weak in pointing out the advantages for the non-Russian peoples of incorporation into the Russian state. The textbooks still emphasized the "colonial yoke," and failed to point up such progressive phenomena as "the development of capitalism, the breaking up of patriarchal power, the development of new economic ties." They neglected to note "the creation of a single economic structure in Russia," a progressive historical factor. Furthermore the textbook authors had failed to see the "mutual struggle" of the Russian and non-Russian workers against their common enemy, tsarism, and had overlooked the many cultural benefits

7. Frederick C. Barghoorn, "Stalinism and the Russian Cultural Heritage," *Review of Politics*, XIV (1952), No. 2, pp. 178-203.

which had come through association with the Russians. Historical writing on the non-Russian peoples was one of six main deficiencies in the current plan of the Institute of History.[8]

It seems probable that this article was intended primarily for the eyes of the editors and authors who were preparing revisions of the major textbook series. New editions of the first volume of the college-level textbook and of Pankratova's first two volumes appeared in the next few months. The deplorable situation of the textbooks was admitted by all. During the War they had not been revised, and the editors were slow to attempt to incorporate the new views after the War. The result was that for the most part the interpretations of 1939 were still taught in the classrooms in 1946. The college-level textbooks had never been revised, and although the first post-war editions of the Pankratova text were marked "fifth edition" for the first volume and "sixth edition" for the second, they had not been extensively rewritten. For the most part their contents were simply reprinted; the heroism of Kenesary Kasymov and Shamil was retained in the 1947 editions, as was the harshness of tsarist colonial policy. A few changes were made by deleting a sentence here or adding one there. For example, the Pankratova textbook buttressed its treatment of the Battle of the Ice (1242) by adding a single sentence to an extensive passage: "The Russian people saved the Lithuanians, Estonians, and Latvians from destruction by the Germans." The textbooks were not thoroughly revised until the early 1950's.[9]

Teaching was as unsatisfactory as writing. The Deputy Minister of Higher Education, V. Svetlov, wrote in *Pravda* early in 1947 that teaching lagged far behind theory in all the social sciences. When it came to the teaching of history, his first concern was for the interpretation of the history of the non-Russian nationalities:

> In the teaching of history also serious shortcomings have not yet been eliminated. Scholars and teachers do not always properly repudiate anti-Party, nationalistic theories, which distort the history of the peoples of the U.S.S.R., and ignore the fact that the class struggle has played a decisive role in the development of peoples. In a number

8. N. Iakovlev, "O shkol'nykh uchebnikakh po istorii," *Kul'tura i zhizn'*, November 30, 1946.

9. A few makeshift arrangements had been devised to try to keep history courses *au courant*. Several textbooks, of the "course of lectures" type, were published soon after the war. There were also a few textbooks on the history of the U.S.S.R. for pedagogical institutions.

of cases, history teachers in the U.S.S.R. are forgetting to draw the attention of their students to the fact that the Russian people have played the leading role in the development of the peoples of our country. . . .

Svetlov went on to deplore "the erroneous treatment of the tsarist government's policy on the non-Russian nationalities," although he did not say specifically what the correct interpretation might be, remarking only that it was important that the students be reminded that the workers of all nationalities had fought together against tsarist autocracy.[10]

About the same time the party's battle against Ukrainian historiography was renewed. K. Litvin, a veteran of *Agitprop* work and the Third Secretary of the Ukrainian Communist party at that time, attacked three histories of the Ukraine written in the early war years.[11] It was apparent from Litvin's article in *Bol'shevik* that after almost twenty years of attack, the party still feared the views of Hrushevskii, whose ideas were said to permeate Ukrainian historical writing. These ideas were by now even more dangerous than they were in the late 1920's: they stood poles apart from the party's views on Russian leadership, the common history of Soviet peoples, and the role of the class struggle, all of which had been intensified during the War. Litvin reeled off the familiar errors of Hrushevskii, which he detected in the pages of the wartime histories. Classes were weakly developed; the formation of the Old Russian State was not elaborated; the Norman theory had not been eliminated; the "traitor Mazepa" was not sufficiently condemned; the common history of the "three brotherly peoples" was missing. In his detailed criticism of Hrushevskii, covering more than a third of the article, Litvin revealed party sensitivity to all suggestion of separateness and animosity between the Ukrainian and Russian people. Hrushevskii had tried to identify Ukrainians more with Western Europeans than with Russians. He had attempted

> . . . to place the Ukrainian people in opposition to their blood brothers, the Russian people, to tear apart their friendship formed in the course of centuries, to make them fight among themselves and thus to prepare a way and means for pulling the Ukraine away from Soviet Russia. . . .
> The centuries-old friendship of the Ukrainian and Rus-

10. V. Svetlov, "O prepodavanii obshchestvennykh nauk v vysshei shkol," *Pravda*, March 10, 1947.

11. The books were *Istoriia Ukrainy. Korotkyi kurs* (Kiev, 1941), the *Narys istorii Ukrainy* (Ufa, 1942), and *Istoriia Ukrainy* (Ufa, 1943), Vol. I. The last two were not available to me. Criticism of the 1943 volume was surprising, since it was edited by N. N. Petrovskii, the highly favored popularizer of Khmel'nitskii.

sian peoples, based on their blood ties, their common historical fate, economic and political development, their many centuries' mutual struggle against common foreign and domestic enemies, Hrushevskii attempts to present as a forced relationship of the Ukrainian people to a "northern orientation." At the same time, the necessity for renewing a German orientation, in his opinion, is dictated not only by traditions but also by "the spiritual kinship between the Ukrainian people and the ethnic elements and life of Western Europe."[12]

Such preachments could not fail to emphasize the party's perennial fear of Ukrainian nationalism. The Ukrainian party's Central Committee passed eight resolutions on questions of bourgeois nationalism in this period, one of which (August 29, 1947) was entitled "Concerning Political Mistakes and Inadequate Work of the Historical Institute of the Academy of Sciences, Ukrainian S.S.R."[13] It repeated the Litvin criticisms of the survivals of the Hrushevskii school and called for Marxist works on Ukrainian history.

In the same week in which the Ukrainian Central Committee resolution on history was issued, the Central Committee in Moscow passed a general resolution on ideological shortcomings in Armenia (August 27, 1947). The Armenian Central Committee convened a plenary session to discuss the resolution, at which thirty-one speakers appeared. Bourgeois nationalist distortions in historical writing were prominently mentioned, the most important of which was "the idealization of the past," making the older (pre-Russian) period appear as "a golden age in the history of the Armenian people."[14]

The most detailed party opinion on historical interpretation in these matters was contained in N. Iakovlev's harsh critique of the new editions of textbooks that had appeared in 1947. In the course of his discussion of manifold errors, he devoted several pages to the

12. K. Litvin, "Ob istorii ukrainskogo naroda," *Bol'shevik*, No. 7, 1947, pp. 41-56. For a discussion of related aspects of this article, see Yaroslav Bilinsky, *The Second Soviet Republic: The Ukraine after World War II* (New Brunswick, N.J.: Rutgers University Press, 1964), p. 205.
Litvin's views on Hrushevskii were repeated late in 1948 by Pankratova. See A. M. Pankratova, "'Kratkii kurs istorii VKP(b)' i zadachi sovetskoi istoricheskoi nauki," *Vestnik Akademii Nauk SSSR*, No. 10, 1948, pp. 17-30 [hereafter cited as *VAN SSSR*].
13. The resolution was discussed in a long article in *Radians'ka Ukraina*, October 3, 1947. For a list of the eight resolutions, see Bilinsky, *The Second Soviet Republic*, p. 395.
14. "Plenum TsK KP(b) Armenii," *Pravda*, September 26, 1947.

questions of annexation and Russian cultural influence on the annexed peoples. Iakovlev repeated the familiar charge that the historians had not examined "the concrete-historical conditions which led to the annexation of these peoples to Russia." Choosing as his example the touchy case of the Kazakhs, he noted that the new textbooks, while removing the old concept of conquest, had represented the annexation as an effort of Khan Abulkhair (1731) "to get Russian help against the Kalmyks." Thus annexation of the Kazakhs was represented as a kind of diplomatic deal for the advantage of a reactionary ruler—a view that was completely unsatisfactory for Iakovlev. The authors surely knew that there were many enemies (Kalmyks, Dzhungarians, and Oirots) who "strived to bring about the physical extinction of the Kazakhs." Russian annexation was a question of life itself for the Kazakh people. In the period after annexation, the historians had failed to give a true picture of the

> . . . national liberation struggles of the peoples, the source of the brotherly union of the working masses of the peoples in their common struggle against tsarism and capitalism. Appearing at the end of the nineteenth century in the arena of political activity, the Russian proletariat carried on a merciless struggle against tsarism. The Bolshevik party led the struggle of the working class and all workers, under the slogan of the rights of nations for self-determination up to the point of secession. All this created the conditions for the mutual struggle of the Russian people and the other peoples against the common enemy, tsarism.

This passage is far more revealing for what it omits than what it says. Iakovlev apparently dated the friendship of peoples from the period immediately before the Revolution. He skirted completely the status of relations during the long period between annexation and 1900, and did not mention the Kenesary Kasymov revolt, about which a storm was brewing. He failed to say how tsarist colonial policy should be discussed. He noted that the textbooks also failed to show the influence of Russian culture on the non-Russians, but the question of the alliance of the Russian peasant settlers and the non-Russian masses was still in the future.[15]

Voprosy istorii reported the proceedings of two scholarly conferences held in 1947 in the non-Russian areas devoted to the

15. N. Iakovlev, "O prepodavanii otechestvennoi istorii," *Bol'shevik*, No. 22, 1947, pp. 26-37.

problems of writing new historical works that would take recent developments into account. The First Scholarly Session of the Institute of History, Archeology, and Ethnography of the Kazakh Academy of Sciences, held at Alma-Ata in May, 1947, was devoted to correcting the errors of the 1943 survey history and speeding the publication of a second edition.[16] It featured a report on "nationalist distortions" in Kazakh historical writing by Kh. G. Aidarova, a candidate of historical science, who made her debut here as the party spokesman on historical interpretation. She criticized the idealization of the Kazakh past, particularly in the use of folklore and chronicle sources. She noted that the historians of Kazakhstan had not written from strict class positions, and had even gone to the extreme of characterizing counter-revolutionary groups of the period of the Revolution as progressive forces. Other reports dealt with the periodization of Kazakh history, the interpretation of the 1916 revolt in Kazakhstan, the elaboration of the progressive consequences of annexation of the Kazakhs and the failure of historians to write on the Soviet period. In many respects the other reports indicated that Aidarova's criticism was to the point; however, there seems to have been no forced consensus or vituperation which would characterize later conferences of this kind.

At the end of the year a session on the history of the Buriat-Mongols was held in Ulan-Ude. In many respects it appears to have been a carbon copy of the Alma-Ata meeting. The numerous works on the Buriat-Mongols by Okladnikov, Kudriavtsev, and Khaptaev, which were published on the eve of the War, were now so many albatrosses about the neck of scholarship, and the authors acknowledged their mistakes, including errors in periodization, idealization of the past, and a lack of concern for the Soviet experience. V. I. Shunkov's report on this meeting dealt almost entirely with "bourgeois nationalist distortions" that denied the friendship of peoples. The historians had "placed the Buriat people in opposition to the Russian people, thereby attempting to undermine the strengthening between them of the friendship and mutual labor for the building of socialism." They had failed to separate the policies of tsarism and the aims of the Russian peasants (one author had detected "national antagonism" resulting from the

16. Proceedings reported in *Izvestiia Akademii Nauk kazakhskoi SSSR, seriia istoricheskaia*, No. 49, Part 4 (Alma-Ata, 1948); brief summary in *VI*, No. 12, 1947, pp. 142-44.

change to Russian strip-farming). "The authors," said Shunkov, "did not take into account the positive results of the peaceful colonization of the Baikal region by Russian peasants; they did not take into account the common interests of the enslaved Russian peasantry and the enslaved Buriat population." They had not emphasized the dangers the Buriats faced from their "aggressive neighbors to the south" and the protection that came with inclusion in the Russian state. "In this connection," Shunkov continued, "it is necessary to reject the emphasis in the work of P. T. Khaptaev on the common struggle of the Buriats and the Mongols against Russian Cossacks." Finally, the influence of Russian culture on the Buriat-Mongols had been almost completely neglected.[17]

Generally speaking, party instructions did not state explicitly that the historiography of the non-Russian peoples must start from the friendship of peoples concept. Instead, it was usually emphasized that a Marxist-Leninist analysis of the history of these peoples would affirm the cordiality of Russian–non-Russian relations. The friendship of peoples was represented as a product of historical analysis, not as a premise. But it must have occurred to Soviet historians at some point that this view was really the party's *sine qua non* for the new history. The pragmatic nature of the party's position was clarified in a notorious episode at the height of the *Zhdanovshchina*. Muradeli's opera, *The Great Friendship*, which dealt with the sensitive question of relations among the peoples of the North Caucasus during the Revolution and Civil War, was condemned in a Central Committee resolution of February 10, 1948. The composer was ridiculed for writing "formalistic" music and also for falsifying the history of the peoples in question: "From the opera the erroneous impression is created that such Caucasian peoples as the Georgians and Ossetians, were, at that time, hostile to the Russian people. This is historically false, since the Ingushi and Chechens were the peoples who were a hindrance to establishing the friendship of peoples in the North Caucasus in that period."[18] Zhdanov, in explaining the resolution to a conference of musicians, repeated the charge that the Chechen and Ingush peoples had been hostile to the Russians, while all other members of the future Soviet family had been friendly.[19] *Voprosy*

17. V. Shunkov, "O razrabotke istorii Buriat-Mongolii," *VI*, No. 5, 1949, pp. 87-89.

18. "Ob opere 'Velikaia Druzhba' V. Muradeli," *Bol'shevik*, No. 3, 1948, pp. 10-14.

19. Referred to in *Pravda*, November 12, 1949.

istorii returned to the theme in a self-indicting editorial, in which the editors apologized for not taking a stand against I. M. Razgon, a specialist on the history of the North Caucasus who had given a "completely untrue picture of relations between the Russian people and the peoples of the North Caucasus" in an article for the *Great Soviet Encyclopedia*.[20] A. Gazzaev, the Chairman of the Council of Ministers of the North Ossetian Autonomous Republic, joined the chorus of denunciation in an article in *Pravda*, which was more explicit in its explanation of the unfriendliness of the Chechens and Ingushi than the vague reference to the "hindrance" in the resolution. Gazzaev charged that "in spite of historical truth, Razgon elaborates on the 'revolutionary nature' of the Chechens and Ingushi, although it is known that in 1917 and the beginning of 1918 these peoples plundered many villages and slaughtered thousands of peaceful inhabitants on the instructions of German-Turkish emissaries."[21]

For the conscientious Soviet historian, this episode must have been the extreme example of the perfidy of the politician in control of history. After several years of preaching about the friendship of Soviet peoples as a universal principle, Zhdanov had decided to "expel" two members of the family—obviously a consequence of their deportation during the War. (Apparently nobody had got around to saying before this time that the Volga Germans, Crimean Tatars, Karachai, Kalmyks, or Balkars had been friendly, and thus no attention was given to them; there will be more on this subject later.)

THE HISTORIANS' RESPONSE:

1. A NEW LOOK AT THE RESISTANCE MOVEMENTS

The uncertainty of historians about what constituted "correct" interpretations in the history of non-Russians was evident as the editors of the new journal *Voprosy istorii* surveyed the wreckage of their past work and took their first uncertain steps under the new directives. In the leading editorial of the first issue, the editors discussed the primary tasks of their profession, one of which was the writing of an acceptable history of the individual Union

20. "O zadachakh sovetskikh istorikov v bor'be s proiavleniiami burzhuaznoi ideologii," *VI*, No. 2, 1949, pp. 3-13.
21. A. Gazzaev, "Gruboe izvrashchenie istoricheskikh faktov," *Pravda*, November 12, 1949.

Republics. The editors saw dangers from two extreme positions. They deplored "the anti-Marxist tendencies in a number of works on the history of the various peoples of the U.S.S.R. . . . manifested in the forms of petty-bourgeois nationalism . . . [and] in the belittling of the role of the Russian state and its leaders." In other works they saw signs of the opposing evil, which they called "imperialistic chauvinism," characterized by "a complete rehabilitation of the aggressive colonial policy of tsarism . . . the denial of the revolutionary significance of the peasant rebellions, and an idealization of the leaders of the autocracy. . . ."[22]

In the third number of the journal M. P. Viatkin, one of the authors of the condemned Kazakh history, attempted to clarify some issues about the numerous uprisings in Kazakhstan. Pointing out that the class structure and the nature of class antagonisms at a given time had to be studied carefully in order to judge a particular movement, Viatkin postulated two ideas that would become standard theses in the re-examination of dozens of revolts and resistance movements. He demonstrated that the class nature of the societies in Central Asia was extremely complex, and that the character of a movement might change in the course of its development. The true nature of the class struggle in Kazakh society, according to Viatkin, was frequently disguised under the patriarchal system, because ownership was not easily detected, and therefore the identification of the exploiters and exploited was obscured. Furthermore, Kazakh society at that time was in a transition between "patriarchal-tribal" and "patriarchal-feudal" stages of development. According to the view of "nomad feudalism," propounded by V. Vladimirtsev, the Soviet specialist on the Mongols, the class struggle was not at all sharply defined in the earlier of these stages. Historians had made errors because they had not looked beneath the façade of Kazakh society.

Viatkin chose as his example the rebellion of Batyr Srym (1783-1797), which was aimed against both the Russians and Kazakh feudal leaders. He believed that the movement was an anti-colonial, anti-feudal, national liberation struggle, which had the support of the Kazakh masses. However, Srym had sought the support of feudal leaders in the latter stages of the movement

22. "Zadachi zhurnala 'Voprosy istorii'," VI, No. 1, 1945, pp. 3-5. See also the postwar plan of Soviet historians: "O perspektivnoi plane v oblasti istoricheskoi nauki," IZ, No. 3, 1945, pp. 60-75; abridged translation in Marin Pundeff (ed.), History in the U.S.S.R.: Selected Readings (Stanford, Calif.: The Hoover Institution, 1967), pp. 151-62.

and thus no longer worked in the interests of the masses. Viatkin contended that the masses had supported the movement at all times, but its leadership had not been consistent. The class struggle had not been sharp, and the movement gradually died out because "the patriarchal-tribal survivals prevailed over both the will of the popular masses and the consciousness of the leader of the struggle, Batyr Srym."[23]

Viatkin raised more questions than he answered. Working under instructions to analyze movements on the basis of class, he could only admit that the class struggle was obscure, if it existed at all. At one point he stated that "it was characteristic of that period in the development of the movement that the popular masses appeared together with the tribal *bii* [beys] and under their leadership. The movement was aimed against the steppe aristocracy, the sultans." Thus he had the feudal bey and *batyr* (a warrior leader, of indefinite class origin) leading the masses against higher feudal rule. Such a view could not stand for long. Viatkin continued this interpretation in his *Batyr Srym* the following year,[24] but would have to admit later that he was in error in suggesting that class lines were not clearly drawn in Kazakh society.

The only other attempt to analyze a resistance movement in the two years following the Morozov pronouncement was *The Inner Horde and the Rebellion of Isatai Taimanov*, by the Kazakh historian, V. F. Shakhmatov.[25] Since his task was uncomplicated, Shakhmatov succeeded. The popular nature of the rebellion of Isatai in the 1830's had never been questioned in the earlier discussion. The leader was a village elder, who had the support of a popular poet, Makhambet Utemisov. What was more important—though it was not stated—his revolt was aimed entirely against Kazakh sultans, and not against Russians. Isatai was one of few rebel leaders whose historic reputation was unchanged in the subsequent discussions.

The main difficulty faced by historians in their analysis of these movements was the necessity to fit facts to preconceived schemes, which meant, in this case, finding a clear class struggle where none

23. M. Viatkin, "K voprosu o krest'ianskikh voinakh v Kazakhstane, *VI*, Nos. 3-4, 1945, pp. 72-85.

24. M. P. Viatkin, *Batyr Srym* (Moscow-Leningrad, 1947). See Viatkin's explanation of his error in *VI*, No. 2, 1952, pp. 157-59.

25. V. F. Shakhmatov, *Vnutrenniaia orda i vosstanie Isataia Taimanova* (Alma-Ata, 1946). Not available to me. Reviewed in *VI*, No. 8, 1948, pp. 120-22.

was apparent. The ulterior purpose may not have been clear at the time: the class struggle was to be used to eliminate violence and animosities between the non-Russian masses and the Russian masses, and thus to promote the friendship of peoples. In the first two attempts to analyze movements, one was acceptable, the other was not. When E. Bekmakhanov made the third attempt in 1947, he touched a sensitive nerve and set off a controversy that raged for years. That story will be related in the next chapter.

2. THE REALIGNMENT OF CULTURAL TIES

The scholars' response to the party's call was much more satisfactory on the question of cultural relations. Here the problem did not involve complicated formulations, as did the evaluation of revolts and their leaders, but a new emphasis on cultural ties between Russians and non-Russians before the Revolution. This new interpretation involved some changes of view, but they were not as difficult to make as in the other case. New research uncovered names of cultural figures, Russian and non-Russian, whose almost forgotten contacts were now considered important. Cultural relations with peoples outside the Soviet family were played down, as required by the xenophobia of the emerging *Zhdanovshchina*.

The early issues of *Voprosy istorii* carried articles on the history of the relations of Russians with Moldavians, Georgians, Kabardinians, and Buriat-Mongols, as well as a report on the first meeting of the Iakut Scientific Research Institute, which was heavily laden with the theme. The Iakut meeting featured two papers on a subject that would be much publicized in the future—the cultural influence of the Decembrists and other political exiles on the non-Russians.[26] The articles on Moldavia and Kabarda were largely on the theme of Russian political and military aid, but they discussed such unlikely developments as the progressive role of the Orthodox church in the North Caucasus[27] and recorded the fact that "Ivan IV built monasteries in Moldavia, sent master artists to decorate them, protected them, and gave rich contributions for their endowment. In these monasteries educated people were gathered; here the young men of the kingdom were educated." The fact that Moldavia was not a part of the Russian state at any time during

26. "Pervyi plenum iakutskogo nauchno-issledovatel'skogo instituta," *VI*, No. 1, 1946, pp. 153-55.
27. G. Kokiev, "Russko-kabardinskie otnosheniia v XVI-XVII vv.," *ibid.*, No. 10, 1946, pp. 44-60.

the period covered by the article did not appear to detract in any way from the argument. The Turks were regarded as the "foreign enemy," the Russians as unselfish friends. Finding information to support such a view was difficult, as the author, I. Cheban, admitted at the outset:

> Nearly all Rumanian and certain Russian pre-revolutionary scholars erroneously represented Moldavia as an integral part of Rumania. However, Soviet historical science can completely truthfully represent Moldavia as a country developing without dependence on Wallachia or Rumania.
>
> Our task, in the main, consists of showing, on the basis of various materials (scattered in the works of authors who worked on the history of Russia, Bessarabia, Moldavia and Rumania) and documents, the diplomatic and cultural ties between Moldavia and Moscow and their importance for the history of both countries.[28]

The article on Georgia also set a pattern soon to become familiar: it presented a long list of Russians who were interested in Georgia and of Georgians who had a special interest in Russian culture.[29] The article on the Buriat-Mongols, by Kudriavtsev, recounted their debt to the Russians in such areas as agricultural techniques, the construction of houses, and the beginning of schools. It was also interesting because of a quotation which would shortly become highly heretical. Quoting Aleksandrov, Kudriavtsev noted that the subject of cultural relations was little understood because "our historians not infrequently described only that which divided peoples. Of course the hostility between peoples, artificially cultivated by tsarism, played no small [*nemaliuiu*] role. But the history of the peoples of Russia is a history of the diminishing of this animosity and of a gradual solidarity around the Russian people."[30] Soon there would be no diminishing of animosity because no animosity was considered to have ever existed.

One of the most fulsome of these early accounts of relations between Russians and non-Russians was a pamphlet by an Azerbaidzhani philosophy professor, Geidar Guseinov, *On the Historic Cooperation of the Russian and Azerbaidzhani Peoples.* The

28. I. Cheban, "O vzaimootnosheniiakh Moldavii s moskovskim gosudarstvom v XV-XVIII vekakh," *ibid.*, Nos. 2-3, 1945, pp. 59-71.

29. G. Khachapuridze, "K voprosu o kul'turnykh sviaziakh Rossii i Gruzii v pervuiu polovinu XIX veka," *ibid.*, Nos. 5-6, 1946, pp. 76-89.

30. F. Kudriavtsev, "Rol' russkoi kul'tury v razvitii buriat-mongol'skogo naroda v XVIII-XX vekakh," *ibid.*, No. 10, 1946, pp. 85-94.

author traced such cooperation from the twelfth-century poet Nizami, who "knew more about Russia than the people of Western Europe did at that time." Guseinov described a procession of literary and political figures who continued the "historic traditions of friendship" from that time to World War II, when "the Russian people not only saved the Azerbaidzhani people from the Hitlerite beasts, but also helped it to organize and train its own military cadres." In still another timely passage the author contrasted the historic attitudes of peoples toward Azerbaidzhani culture. The Russians had always been appreciative and helpful, but "certain German 'scholars' viewed the culture of our people with great arrogance."[31]

One cannot survey the yellowing pages of this pamphlet today without a feeling of profound irony. The author succeeded in producing a work that was considered a distinct service to the Party— so much so that it was favorably discussed in a Bol'shevik review.[32] But four years later when he incorporated these ideas into a book, he would commit an almost incidental political error that would make him the whipping boy in the most celebrated case regarding the friendship of peoples. The irony is intensified by Guseinov's generous quotations from the works of Mir D. Bagirov, the Azerbaidzhani Party Secretary, who would be his executioner (chapter 7).

Articles and pamphlets could be tailored to the new party line on cultural history with comparative ease, but this was not the case with recently published books. A major offender was A. A. Semenov's Physical Monuments of Persian Culture in Central Asia, which had been published by the Tadzhik Academy of Sciences in 1945. The work was the object of a scathing review in Voprosy istorii.[33] The reviewer, L. Bretanitskii, conceded that the book, which had been published originally in 1925, reflected profound scholarship, but regretted that the new edition did not make use of "the accomplishments of twenty years of Soviet scholarship." What made the book utterly unacceptable under the new conditions was its central idea: that most of the works of art in Central Asia

31. Geidar Guseinov, Ob istoricheskom sodruzhestve russkogo i azerbaidz-hanskogo narodov (Baku, 1946). The work had also appeared in Trudy Akademii Nauk azerbaidzhanskoi SSR Instituta filosofii (1945), Vol. I.

32. Sh. Mamedov, "Iz istorii obshchestvennoi mysli v Azerbaidzhane," Bol'shevik, Nos. 11-12, 1946, pp. 83-88.

33. A. A. Semenov, Material'nye pamiatniki iranskoi kul'tury v Srednei Azii (Stalinabad, 1945); reviewed in VI, No. 7, 1947, pp. 128-31.

showed the influence of Persian, and to a lesser degree, of Turkish and Chinese art. "The harmfulness of such a position is evident," observed the reviewer. Semenov had been the lackey of "foreign Orientalists," who had belittled the cultural history of Central Asia. In his deference to Persian art, the author had "ignored the culture of the other peoples of Central Asia." Obviously, the work did not "satisfy the mature needs of Soviet readers."

The editors of the major history textbooks were especially criticized for their lag in updating passages on cultural history. They were understandably reluctant to go all the way over to the Zhdanov line, and in most cases they made brief and subtle changes, which were in turn rejected as inadequate. From dozens of examples which might be cited, the following on medieval Georgia is typical, from two editions of the Pankratova textbook. The 1940 version stated that

> Georgia was located at the intersection of busy trade routes between countries of the East and West. Here the cultural influence of Asia Minor, Persia and Byzantium came together. Young Georgian feudal lords went to Constantinople to study. Georgian architecture reflected the influence of Byzantium, Georgian literature the influence of Persia. From the Arabs knowledge of medicine and astronomy came to Georgia. Thus a native Georgian culture was created, which, in turn influenced neighboring countries—in particular, Russian culture.[34]

This original version appeared in the early postwar editions. When it was belatedly rewritten, references to specific cultural borrowings were eliminated, the role of Georgia was enhanced, and the implied inferiority of Russian culture was deleted:

> Georgia was located at the intersection of busy trade routes between countries of the East and West. Hence, close ties with the cultural centers of Asia Minor and Byzantium were established very early. Young Georgian feudal lords went to Constantinople to study. Knowledge of medicine, astronomy and other sciences was extended. Georgian culture, which was based on and developed from many of the cultures of neighboring countries, had in turn a great influence on them. Thus, Georgian culture was in constant interaction [*vzaimodeistvii*] with the cultures of neighboring countries.[35]

34. *Istoriia SSSR*, ed. A. M. Pankratova (Moscow, 1940), I, 70.
35. *Ibid.* (13th ed. Moscow, 1954), I, 74-75.

Undoubtedly the greatest single boon to the new party views on cultural history was the publication of S. P. Tolstov's *Ancient Khorezm* in 1948. Basing his work on an archeological expedition to Central Asia between 1937 and 1939, this respected scholar put forth views that were eagerly appropriated and exploited by party theoreticians. Tolstov's data pointed to the existence of three advanced states in Central Asia in the first millennium, B.C.: Khorezm, Bactria, and Sogdiana. Their zenith predated that of Persia or the Arabs, and obviously they did not receive cultural influences from them. Furthermore, Tolstov held that there was a common culture of Central Asia, which was indigenous, or at least very ancient, from which the modern Uzbek, Kazakh, Kirgiz, Tadzhik, and Turkmen cultures were derived. The Persian, Arab, and Turkish invasions had not brought cultural progress to the region; they had in fact disrupted an advanced culture.[36] Thus Tolstov's book, which won a Stalin prize, furthered the coordination of the Soviet history of Central Asia by establishing a common link in ancient times. The break-up of that advanced Central Asian culture was laid to foreign invaders—a close parallel to the Soviet explanation of the disintegration of the budding Russian state, consisting of the "three brotherly peoples," at the hand of the Tatars.[37]

By the time B. G. Gafurov published his *History of the Tadzhik People* in 1949, the cultural flow was going in the other direction. His reviewer quoted a Gafurov passage to this effect with approval: "It should be pointed out that the peoples of Central Asia exercised a great influence on the cultural development of the western Persians of the Sassanid state. Thus, for example, silk production came to Persia from Central Asia. The epics of various Persian peoples consciously absorbed the works of the peoples of Central

36. S. P. Tolstov, *Drevnii Khorezm* (Moscow, 1948), pp. 341-45.
37. In a later article, Tolstov commented on the role of the Tatars in changing the cultural picture of the medieval world. Writing on the twenty-fifth anniversary of the delimitation of the Central Asian republics, he noted the superiority of the culture of that area to that of Western Europe in the middle ages. "Prior to the Mongol invasion, Western Europe had been an extremely backward corner of the Eurasian continent." Why had Central Asian culture declined, while that of Western Europe made a comparative advance? His ready answer was by this time standard in Soviet historiography. The Central Asian peoples had borne the brunt of the invasion, which led to feudal disintegration, while Western Europe, "taking advantage of the favorable historical situation, avoided this catastrophe through the shield thrown up by the heroic Russian people." See S. P. Tolstov, "Velikaia pobeda leninsko-stalinskoi natsional'noi politiki (K dvadtsatipiatiletiiu natsional'nogo razmezhevaniia Srednei Azii)," *Sovetskaia etnografiia*, No. 1, 1950, pp. 3-23.

Asia, especially those of Khorezm and Sogdiana. The culture of the period of the Sassanids, as well as that of the Achaemenids, was thus indebted to the activities of the Central Asian peoples." But the appetite for national pride is hard to satisfy. The reviewer, A. Iakubovskii, while holding up this view for praise, regretted that Gafurov had not gone further: "Unfortunately, the author nowhere mentions Bactria . . . [which] played an enormous role in the cultural development of Sassanid Persia."[38]

3. RUSSIAN COLONIALISM

Russian colonialism was understandably the least-developed topic in the early post-war period. Although the new concept of the pre-revolutionary friendship of peoples stood in flat contradiction to the well-established interpretation of Russia as a colonial power, the party made no direct effort to force a new interpretation on historians, and none was attempted immediately. But in time the contradiction became all the more glaring, not only because of the friendship theme, but also because of the rehabilitation of tsarist foreign policy, the growing pride in Russian accomplishments and in the superiority of Russian culture, and the thesis that annexation to Russia was always a progressive phenomenon. For a time historians allowed the contradictory views to glare at each other across the pages of the same book: tsarist colonialism retained all its brutality, but annexation was somehow progressive in the long run. The history of the revision of this theme is one of the most complicated of all. Russian colonialism was softened if not completely whitewashed under heavy party pressure, until a formula was found permitting the historian to argue the progress theme without denying well-known facts on the seamy side of the question.

The case of O. V. Ionova's *From the History of the Iakut People* points up the uncertainty of the moment. The study was written in 1938 as a thesis, but was not published until the early part of 1945, by which time it was out of step. Ionova had recounted in detail the techniques by which Russians collected the tribute: bribery of local leaders, taking hostages, holding people in chains. The Cossack raids (she called them "pogroms") had evoked mass rebellions, in which natives of all classes fought off the Russians.[39]

38. *VI*, No. 7, 1950, pp. 159-64.
39. O. V. Ionova, *Iz istorii iakutskogo naroda* (*pervaia polovina XVII veka*) (Iakutsk, 1945), pp. 50-55.

In her preface the author expressed appreciation for the help of Bakhrushin and S. Tokarev, under whose direction the work had been written seven years earlier. Tokarev made a rebuttal soon after the book appeared, noting that Ionova

> was not able to resolve correctly the most important question of the history of Iakutia—the question of the annexation of the Iakuts to Russia. The author depicts the history of the joining of the Iakuts with the Russians and the penetration of the Russians to the Lena only as the history of the "conquest" of Iakutia.
>
> Such an evaluation of the annexation of Iakutia to Russia is one-sided and consequently incorrect. O. V. Ionova does not see the fundamental role of tsarism and its agents in Iakutia and the progressive influence on its [Iakutia's] development by the Russian people. The great Russian people brought to Iakutia higher forms of economic life and culture in comparison to the backward life of the Iakuts at that time. Russian culture had a good influence on the development of the culture of the Iakut people. . . . The great Russian people helped the Iakut people to free itself from the yoke of tsarism and to create its national culture and national system. Unfortunately, O. V. Ionova does not show this in the book.[40]

The only work on tsarist colonialism to appear in the U.S.S.R. in the first two post-war years was V. I. Shunkov's *Sketches on the History of the Colonization of Siberia*.[41] It was a work of solid scholarship, and its emphasis on themes that were growing in favor—the role of the Russian peasant and economic progress— more than offset scattered references to the oppression of Russian colonialism. A reviewer, writing in the middle of 1947 in *Voprosy istorii*, dwelt almost exclusively on these positive influences of the Russian people, setting a tone not found in the book.[42]

Other historians would not be so fortunate. S. M. Abramzon, whose *Outline of the Culture of the Kirgiz People* appeared in 1946, was accused of falsely representing the Kirgiz annexation to Russia as "conquest," of idealizing reactionary Kirgiz historical figures, and belittling Russian cultural influences.[43] A. N. Bernshtam's

40. S. Tokarev, "Novaia nauchnaia literatura o Iakutii," *Propagandist*, No. 13, 1945, pp. 57-62.

41. V. I. Shunkov, *Ocherki po istorii kolonizatsii Sibiri v XVII-nachale XVIII veka* (Moscow, 1946).

42. N. Ustiugov in *VI*, No. 6, 1947, pp. 131-35.

43. S. M. Abramzon, *Ocherk kul'tury kirgizskogo naroda* (Frunze, 1946).

Great Heritage of the Kirgiz People was criticized on much the same grounds.[44]

The collections of documents on the history of non-Russian peoples, which by the early 1950's had become a major vehicle for the friendship of peoples, were conspicuously absent in the early post-war years. Apparently the editors of documentary series decided to wait for more settled times. The sole exception, the publication of three volumes of documents on Russia in Turkmenia and the development of the revolutionary movement there, was an ill-fated project.[45] N. A. Khalfin's review of the first of these volumes dealt almost entirely with sins of omission. "The compilers ignored an important event in the life of the Turkmen people—the union of the Pendinsk peninsula to the Turkmen lands already conquered by Russia." That annexation saved the Turkmen population from British imperialism. The volume contained only six documents on Russian-Turkmen trade, and "not a word on the mission of the Turkmen delegation to Russia with a request for the Russians to receive the Turkmens under their rule." There was nothing on the activities of "British agents," and nothing on early Russian expeditions to Turkmenia for the purpose of establishing fortified points against the British. The volume had failed to "show the objectively positive significance of the annexation of Turkmenia to Russia."[46]

The reticence of Soviet historians to soften their views on tsarist conquests and colonialism was evident in the new editions of the

For criticism of this book, see especially the leading editorial in *VI*, No. 4, 1951.

44. A. N. Bernshtam, *Velikoe nasledie kirgizskogo naroda* (Frunze, 1945). Not available to me. It was prominent in a resolution of the Academy of Sciences of the U.S.S.R., February 22, 1952 (*VAN SSSR*, No. 3, 1952, pp. 81-82).

45. The volumes were *Rossiia i Turkmeniia v XIX veke. K vkhozhdeniiu Turkmenii v sostav Rossii* (Ashkhabad, 1946); *Nachalo revoliutsionnogo dvizheniia v Turkmenii v 1900-1905 gg.* (Ashkhabad-Moscow, 1946); *Revoliutsionnoe dvizhenie v Turkmenii* (*1908-1917*) (Ashkhabad-Moscow, 1946). All were edited by A. G. Solov'ev. Only the first volume was available to me. My view that historians were cautious about publishing anything on this subject is supported by the subject matter of *Istoricheskie zapiski* (*Historical Notes*) during this period. In the first two years after the war, eight volumes containing over seventy articles appeared (Vols. 15-23). There was no article directly relating to the timely subjects of cultural relations between Russians and non-Russians, the non-Russian revolts and resistance movements, or tsarist colonialism. One article on Russian economic policy in the Caucasus was only indirectly related to these issues (Vol. 18, pp. 169-205).

46. *VI*, No. 10, 1948, pp. 155-57.

major textbooks. Slightly revised editions of the second volume of
both the secondary school and university textbooks, which surveyed
the period in question, were published in 1949. They retained the
wording of the 1940 editions, with minor changes. The issue was
particularly glaring in the university textbook edited by Nechkina
since it was devoted entirely to the Russian Empire in the nineteenth century and consequently went into tsarist aggression, brutality, and colonial oppression in detail. The book was marked
for quick extinction, largely for its treatment of this theme.

The most substantial survey history to be written in this period
(as opposed to revisions of earlier editions) was the first volume
of the *History of the U.S.S.R.*, written by the well-known historians
M. N. Tikhomirov and S. S. Dmitriev for use in the pedagogical
institutions.[47] Appearing in 1948, it is interesting as a transition
piece. It reflected the old view by continuing to describe Russian
expansion as "conquests," beginning with Kazan, and including
Siberia, the Caucasus, and much of Central Asia.[48] Georgia was
merely a *place d'armes* for tsarist expansion in the Caucasus—a
Pokrovskiian view.[49] There was very little about voluntary annexations or the progressive consequences of them. The controversial
Kenesary was mentioned only in passing; there was no clear assessment of his role or of the nature of his movement.[50] The book's
worst sin, from the view of two years later, was a lengthy section
on the Shamil movement, which retained all the superlatives of the
pre-war accounts.[51] Glimpses of the new interpretation could be
seen in passages on Russian leadership and greatness, on Russian
help for the non-Russian peoples, and several passages on the
friendship of peoples, including an especially glowing conclusion
entitled "Cultural Cooperation of the Peoples of Russia."

The survey histories of the Union Republics were far behind
schedule and as unsatisfactory as the revised textbooks. In spite of
frequent party reminders about the urgency of producing these
works, only four volumes of survey history on the larger non-Russian peoples in the pre-revolutionary period appeared in Russian
from the end of the war to the beginning of 1950, and all of them

47. M. N. Tikhomirov and S. S. Dmitriev, *Istoriia SSSR* (Moscow, 1948),
Vol I.
48. *Ibid.*, pp. 122-25, 132-34, 370-76.
49. *Ibid.*, p. 370.
50. *Ibid.*, p. 376.
51. *Ibid.*, pp. 373-74.

were, to use the Soviet editor's euphemism, "unsuccessful."[52] New histories of the Uzbeks, Georgians, and Tadzhiks all failed to anticipate the status of interpretations by the time reviews would be written. The long-awaited revision of the Kazakh history—the Central Committee resolution had set 1947 as a deadline—eventually appeared in 1949, and was withdrawn almost immediately.

52. I am not counting short surveys, apparently for elementary schools, which were published on the Belorussians and Uzbeks.

CHAPTER **6.**

THE BEKMAKHANOV CASE

"Creating a scholarly history of the Kazakh people is by no means an easy task." M. P. Kim in Voprosy istorii, *No. 6, 1949, p. 131.*

"Among a certain group of Soviet historians, incorrect views have become prevalent which hold that the advancement of historical science consists exclusively of the accumulation of new factual material and that the object of historical works is the fullest exposition of the facts. This is a harmful trend, which hinders the creative application of Marxist-Leninist theory in historical research. . . . The striving for the collection of facts means slipping into bourgeois-objectivist positions and a refusal to recognize the objective conformity to the laws of the historical process." Leading editorial in Voprosy istorii, *No. 11, 1949, p. 5.*

In the tortured rewriting of the history of the non-Russian peoples, the case of Kazakhstan has no rival. The central figure in that long struggle was Ermukhan Bekmakhanovich Bekmakhanov (1915-1966), the foremost native Kazakh historian of the first half century of Soviet power. Bekmakhanov was the author of two major monographs, two textbooks on Kazakh history, and more than a hundred articles, and was co-author of several other survey histories. He was a professor at the Kazakh State University and a director of the Institute of History, Archeology, and Ethnology of the Kazakh branch of the Academy of Sciences. He was editor of the journal *Obshchestvennye nauki* (*Social Sciences*) and of the large bibliography of historical works on Kazakhstan.

A *Voprosy istorii* obituary after Bekmakhanov's death in 1966 recounts all these accomplishments, and more—the numerous services to the party performed by this "staunch and devoted Communist," including many lectures to party officials, propaganda work, and the training of dozens of young cadres in the teaching profession. According to the eulogy, "of especially great significance was E. B. Bekmakhanov's elaboration of questions relating to the friendship of the Kazakh and Russian peoples and their mutual struggle against a common enemy, tsarism."[1] But the obituary omits all reference to an important part of Bekmakhanov's career: his three-year battle with the party (1947-50) for the integrity of the scholar; his long six-year silence as a bourgeois nationalist; his clever and well-reasoned "apology" and self-rehabilitation in the period of the thaw.

Bekmakhanov's first important scholarly assignment was as a member of the collective that produced the 1943 history of Kazakhstan. Apparently he was never singled out for criticism in the later denunciations of the book, and he indicated five years later, after the work had been repeatedly denounced, that he still held it in high regard. On October 14, 1946, Bekmakhanov successfully defended his doctoral dissertation and soon entered the higher ranks of the profession as a member of the faculty of the Kazakh State University. His dissertation, entitled "Kazakhstan from the 1820's Through the 1840's," was written under the direction of Viatkin, who served as the "opponent" at the examination. The work was a detailed study of the Kenesary movement, which was becoming an increasingly sensitive question after Morozov's article in *Bol'shevik* the previous year condemning the 1943 history. That the examination was uneventful is not surprising; Bekmakhanov's evaluation of the movement was in line with every Soviet historian who had written on the subject. But the failure of anyone to challenge the old interpretation, now elaborated in more detailed research than ever before, indicates that the historians were either not taking party guidance on the national movements seriously, or that they were quietly challenging the party view. It was only the following year, when Bekmakhanov published his dissertation in a book of the same title, that the party stirred itself to action.

THE ISSUE JOINED

Bekmakhanov's *Kazakhstan from the 1820's Through the 1840's* is a good example of that peculiarly Soviet phenomenon, the

1. VI, No. 9, 1966, p. 220.

instant rare book.[2] Although ten-thousand copies were published
and the book was hailed as an important work and widely discussed
for a time, its subsequent condemnation apparently cut it off from
export abroad. It has become so completely an "unbook" that its
author, in editing the detailed bibliography of Kazakh historical
works, does not mention it. One can get the main lines of argument
from the dissertation abstract, however, and from lengthy quotations of "erroneous" passages which appeared in the subsequent
discussion.

The Kazakh historian's main thesis was that the entire Kenesary
movement was progressive. According to the abstract of the dissertation, Bekmakhanov defended Kenesary on two main counts:
he was trying to eliminate tribal disintegration and create a strong
unified government (surely a worthy goal according to the party's
emphasis of the time) and he was opposing elements even more
reactionary than the tsars—the "steppe aristocracy" (sultans) and
the Central Asian khanates. It was true that Kenesary represented
the forces of patriarchal-feudalism and was acting from selfish
motives, but patriarchal-feudalism was a higher stage of development than the old patriarchal-tribalism, whose survivals were re-
tarding Kazakh society. The Kazakhs were wedged between the
"double aggression" of the tsars and Central Asian khans, and Kenesary himself preferred "a Russian orientation." Russia, however,
was busily penetrating Central Asia, and, not desiring the development of a strong unified Kazakh state, refused to support him.
Kenesary was characterized as "a talented reformer" who made
progressive land, fiscal, and legal reforms. He was a popular and
physically attractive leader who enjoyed mass support in a movement that was anti-colonial and of a national liberation character.

At the same time Bekmakhanov was careful not to idealize
Kenesary. He pointed out that his reforms were for the purpose
of building a powerful Kazakh state to be ruled personally by Kenesary, who held the traditional view that he, as the Khan, owned all
the property of the state. Kenesary was frequently cruel; he destroyed many Kazakh villages when their inhabitants would not
support him. Toward the end of his rebellion he had attacked the
Kirgiz. Bekmakhanov saw this attack as basically a defensive move:

2. E. B. Bekmakhanov, *Kazakhstan v 20-40e gody XIX veka* (Alma-Ata,
1947). The abstract of the dissertation was published in *Izvestiia Akademii
Nauk SSSR. Seriia istorii i filosifii*, IV (1947), No. 1, pp. 94-96. For a short
discussion of the issue see A. Uluktuk, "Natsional'no-osvoboditel'nye dvizheniia
v Turkestane v novoi sovetskoi otsenke," *Turkeli*, No. 1, 1951, pp. 26-33.

it was provoked by the tsar, who was seeking support of Kirgiz feudal leaders against the Kazakh rebel. Kenesary did not kill "ordinary Kirgiz people." Although Kenesary's movement was progressive, the eventual annexation of the Kazakhs to Russia was also of great progressive significance, because of the influence of Russian culture and the development of higher forms of economy.

It is clear that Bekmakhanov was not defying recent party directives altogether, but was attempting to work out a formulation that would find acceptance without basically changing a long-standing interpretation. To what extent he was prompted by the scholar's respect for facts and to what extent by Kazakh national pride it is impossible to know, but undoubtedly both elements were present. On only one point did he clearly cross an explicitly stated party opinion. He continued to justify the Kirgiz campaign, which had been condemned in the Morozov article. He sought to comply with party demands by his emphasis on building a powerful centralized government, on the sanctity of the struggle for independence (both of which had been strongly emphasized during the war and had not been repudiated), by his implicit acceptance of the "lesser evil" concept, by avoiding the idealization of Kenesary and his feudal system, and above all by his emphasis on the progressive significance of annexation. As it turned out, only the last point survived. The importance of centralized government and struggles for independence was acceptable only in the Russian context, as the party soon made clear. As for the non-Russians, all talk of strong central government or independence, aside from the Russian association, became an ideologically dangerous theme in the postwar situation. It is possible that this was not at all clear to any scholar in the rapidly changing ideological climate; it is also possible that Bekmakhanov understood it quite clearly and was unwilling to comply with it.

By the fall of 1947, when his book appeared, Bekmakhanov was rising rapidly in the profession. He reported on the periodization of Kazakh history at the May meeting in Alma-Ata (summarized earlier) and was the co-author of the summary of the proceedings of the meeting, which appeared in the *Vestnik* (*Bulletin*) of the Kazakh Academy of Sciences.[3] The *Vestnik*, which devoted much space to historical matters at that time, featured frequent articles and

3. E. Bekmakhanov and V. Shakhmatov, "Pervaia nauchnaia sessiia instituta istorii, arkheologii i etnografii akademii nauk kazakhskoi SSSR," *VAN kazakhskoi SSR*, No. 5, 1947, pp. 10-16.

book reviews by Bekmakhanov. Some of his articles must have been quite pleasing to party theoreticians, as for example "The Historical Roots of Friendship of the Kazakh and Russian People," in which he referred vaguely to the importance of the Battle of Kulikovo (1380) for the Kazakhs, and stated that "the history of the friendship of the Kazakh people with the great Russian people is many centuries old."[4] But more frequently than not, Bekmakhanov was on dangerous ideological ground, as in "The Folklore Sources on the Rebellion of Kenesary Kasymov,"[5] published at a time when the national epics of the non-Russian peoples were coming under fire for their "idealization of the warlike feudal past."

Bekmakhanov's most heretical article during this period was undoubtedly the one entitled "On the Question of the Social Nature of the *Batyrs* of the Nineteenth Century," in which he put forth a view that would further complicate the party's attempt to draw clean and simple class lines in Kazakh society.[6] Since the question of the nature of the class struggle was of primary importance in determining the character of military movements, and since many of their leaders were *batyrs*, the class identification of these figures was pivotal. The *batyr* was a military hero and popular warrior, whose class had not been considered important until the dictates of Marxism-Leninism made it necessary to label him. At the time Bekmakhanov was writing, the question was not settled. The authoritative *Great Soviet Encyclopedia*, whose article on the *batyr* was published in 1950, equates the *batyr* with the Russian *bogatyr*, who is in turn defined as a military hero, a protector of the land. But the non-Russian *batyr* did not enjoy the privileges of the Russian *bogatyr*, any more than the non-Russian struggle for independence got equal treatment. The *Encyclopedia* goes on to say that about the beginning of the nineteenth century the *batyr* was becoming a part of the "patriarchal-feudal nobility."[7] What makes the question crucial is the restriction of the Marxist class framework: a feudal exploiter could not lead a popular mass movement, which in this setting was usually considered an anti-feudal, anti-

4. E. B. Bekmakhanov, "Istoricheskie korni druzhby kazakhskogo i russkogo naroda," *ibid.*, No. 11, 1947, pp. 52-61. Party approval of this article is indicated by its simultaneous appearance in *Bol'shevik Kazakhstana*, No. 11, 1947, pp. 46-56.

5. "Fol'klornye istochniki vosstanii Kenesary Kasymova," *VAN kazakhskoi SSR*, No. 9, 1947, pp. 49-56.

6. "K voprosu o sotsial'noi prirode batyrov XIX v.," *ibid.*, No. 8, 1947, pp. 62-63.

7. *BSE*, 2nd ed., IV, 315-16.

colonial, national liberation movement. The feudal leader would by nature be opposed to all of these. Thus, if Kenesary's movement and others like it were to be given their old interpretation, their leader must be of lower class origin. Bekmakhanov argued that the *batyr* rose from the people as their leader. At the same time he had to admit that he had many of the characteristics of the feudal leader, and he repeated the long-established view that class lines in patriarchal-tribal society were not clearly drawn—an interpretation already condemned in the critique of the 1943 Kazakh history. He marshaled a quotation from the impeccable Chokan Valikhanov, the nineteenth-century Russophile Kazakh poet, who expressed the view that *batyrs* were popular leaders. Bekmakhanov concluded that the *batyr* of the early nineteenth century "played a significant role in the social-economic life of Kazakh society, in various positions of the governing feudal elite."

Late in 1947, before his book had been reviewed, Bekmakhanov wrote two articles summing up the accomplishments of Kazakh historical scholarship and outlining the tasks ahead.[8] He revealed that very ambitious projects were under way. In addition to the second edition of a survey history of the Kazakhs, which was to be ready for the press shortly, collectives of historians were busy compiling a five-volume history of Kazakhstan (which never appeared) and a collection of *Materialy* on Kazakh history. He pointed out the complexity of Kazakh history, particularly its class structure in certain periods, but appeared confident that true Marxist-Leninist interpretations were being formulated. These articles contained the standard trappings of the time: condemnation of earlier tsarist and Soviet interpretations, praise for the *Short Course* as a model for all historical interpretation, and generous mention of Russian influences and the friendship of peoples. It is evident from these articles that Bekmakhanov was not only prominent among Kazakh historians, he was also their spokesman and apparent leader.

The first public notice that Bekmakhanov was in trouble came in a sharp reply to one of these articles by A. Likholat, whose short note titled "A Muddled Article on the Tasks of Historical Science in Kazakhstan," in *Kul'tura i zhizn'* had all the markings of the party lash.[9] Likholat charged that Bekmakhanov had tried "to

8. "Nekotorye itogi raboty i ocheredyne zadachi istorikov Kazakhstana," *VAN kazakhskoi SSR*, No. 10, 1947, pp. 61-65; "O sostoianii i zadachakh istoricheskoi nauki v Kazakhstane," *Bol'shevik Kazakhstana*, No. 9, 1947, pp. 60-71.

9. A Likholat, "Putanaia stat'ia o zadachakh istoricheskoi nauki v Kazakh-

hide from the reader the unsatisfactory work of the Kazakh Institute of History, Archeology, and Ethnology." He had ignored
the errors in Viatkin's works, and had not written a word of criticism about his own book. But Likholat was particularly disturbed
about Bekmakhanov's attitude toward the condemned 1943 history
of Kazakhstan. It was apparent that he had not heeded either
Morozov's review or the Kazakh Central Committee resolution,
since he had stated that the book "possesses great merit and to this
day it is of distinct scholarly interest." Although he mentioned the
Morozov review several times, Bekmakhanov had "softened" its
views, adapting them to his own purposes. Furthermore, he had
presented a "muddled" picture of the class structure of Kazakh
society, had concentrated on ancient and feudal history to the near
exclusion of the Soviet period, and had discussed pre-revolutionary
historians under the headings of "Russian" and "Kazakh," categories which were national rather than ideological. Likholat expressed concern that Bekmakhanov was one of the co-authors of
the forthcoming history of Kazakhstan, and concluded his critique
with an ominous question: "For the reader, how is it comprehen-
sible that such a muddled article as that of E. Bekmakhanov could
be published in the journal of the Central Committee of the Communist party of Kazakhstan?"

Likholat here pointed to what must have been the most disturbing factor in the growing controversy. From statements made later
in the press, it is apparent that Bekmakhanov not only had the wide
support of his fellow scholars, but significant backing in the Kazakh
party itself. *Voprosy istorii* charged three years later that I. Omarov, the Secretary of the Kazakh Central Committee, "rose to the
defense of Bekmakhanov's nationalist views, opposing publication
of an article" criticizing the book, and that "former Vice President
Kenespaev of the Kazakh Republic Academy of Sciences compelled
historians by Arakcheev-like methods to refrain from a critical examination of it." The Kazakh newspaper *Socialist Kazakhstan* had
published a laudatory review, "in spite of the protests of a majority

---

stane," *Kul'tura i zhizn'*, December 20, 1947; reprinted in *Bol'shevik Kazakh
stana*, No. 1, 1948, pp. 50-51. Likholat would come to notoriety later on as
the author of a study on the Ukraine, which carried the myth of Bolshevik
leadership so far that it was rejected by the party itself as a bad example of
the influence of the cult of personality in historical writing (A. V. Likholat,
Razgrom natsionalisticheskoi kontrrevoliutsii na Ukraine, 1917-1922 gg. [Mos-
cow, 1954]). See below, pp. 199, 225.

of the historians of Kazakhstan," according to *Voprosy istorii's* belated criticism.[10]

There were further indications of official support. Bekmakhanov's book was given an award by the Kazakh branch of the Academy, and a highly favorable review in its *Vestnik*. The reviewer was E. Dil'mukhamedov, a fellow Kazakh who had written a dissertation on Kenesary before the War. He called the book "a significant work in Kazakh historical science." He took issue with the question of the class struggle within the movement, which he said was not sufficiently elaborated, but supported the author on the touchy question of Kenesary's Kirgiz campaign. The two Kazakh scholars were in complete agreement that this campaign was provoked by tsarism and was a strategic move rather than typical feudal aggrandizement.[11]

On February 28, 1948, the Institute of History of the U.S.S.R. Academy of Sciences held a discussion on Bekmakhanov's book.[12] Under the chairmanship of Grekov, the discussion included several of the most distinguished Soviet historians. A harsh critique of the book was presented at the beginning of the conference by Aidarova, who had given the report on bourgeois nationalist distortions in Kazakh history at the Alma-Ata meeting the year before. She declared that the book was "scientifically untenable, apolitical, without ideological substance [*bezideinoi*], and therefore also harmful." Bekmakhanov had ignored all party guidance on ideological questions. The new editions of the works of Lenin and Stalin should have helped him, but he obviously did not seek their views. The specific charges were familiar: he had idealized Kenesary, misinterpreted the movement, and confused the lines of the class struggle. In this connection Aidarova made an interesting statement relating historical interpretation to current political considerations. The book, she said, "confuses people who are struggling for their political freedom by confusing the class struggle."

After Aidarova's attack, the remaining six speakers[13] presented

10. *VI*, No. 4, 1951, p. 64; Serge A. Zenkovsky, "Ideological Deviation in Soviet Central Asia," *Slavonic and East European Review*, XXXII (1953-54), 424-37.

11. *VAN kazakhskoi SSR*, No. 1, 1948, pp. 62-68.

12. "Obsuzhdenie monografii E. Bekmakhanova 'Kazakhstana v 20-40 e. gody XIX veka,' " *ibid.*, No. 3, 1948, pp. 35-58.

13. I am not counting the short noncommittal comment by S. V. Iushkov, the Russian director of the Institute of History of the Kazakh Academy of Sciences, who merely found the book "interesting." Iushkov had also been rather uncritical at the Alma-Ata meeting, and was later taken to task for this (*VI*, No. 3, 1949, pp. 126-27).

a solid defense of Bekmakhanov's work and even took Aidarova to task by countering her arguments one by one. Bakhrushin and M. K. Rozhkova, a specialist on the economic history of Central Asia, defended the solid scholarship of the book ("a very great step forward" in Kazakh historiography, according to the latter). Druzhinin sided with the majority, by supporting the view that the Kenesary movement was of a national liberation character. Viatkin and A. P. Kuchkin led the counterattack on Aidarova, denying her characterization of the movement and the nature of the class struggle. Kuchkin denied that Bekmakhanov had idealized Kenesary by citing passages from the book that showed him to be cruel and selfish. A. Iakunin, who at this meeting began a long and ambivalent set of hypotheses on the national movements, offered a compromise. In his external policy (the struggle against tsarist colonialism) Kenesary was progressive; in his internal policy, in which he behaved like a typical feudal lord, Kenesary was reactionary.

At the conclusion of the meeting Bekmakhanov made a statement defending his work. He said that on the basis of careful research he had concluded that Kazakh society early in the nineteenth century was in a state of change and that class contradictions were not clearly drawn. He upheld every major thesis of his book, vigorously refuting Aidarova's charge that the Kirgiz campaign was a "reactionary plundering raid": "Nowhere has a single document been found which indicates that Kenesary considered the Kirgiz people to be his enemy. I categorically object to the assertion that the whole Kirgiz people carried on a struggle against Kenesary. That is absolutely untrue."

Grekov concluded the meeting by observing that certain corrections (all minor) that had been noted at this conference might be profitable in the work on the forthcoming survey history of Kazakhstan. There had been mention of a second edition of Bekmakhanov's book early in the meeting, but in the view of the majority of the speakers, such revision was unnecessary. This was Bekmakhanov's round.

Another discussion on the Bekmakhanov book was held in Alma-Ata in July, 1948, under the auspices of the Kazakh Institute of History, Archeology, and Ethnography. No details of this meeting appeared in the Russian language press, but a brief mention of the meeting in *Voprosy istorii* indicated that it had gone entirely in the other direction: "The broad public of Alma-Ata was represented at the discussion. The majority of the participants among the historians condemned E. Bekmakhanov's book as nationalistic, idealizing the activities of the sultans and Khan Kenesary Kasymov and other representatives of Kazakh society. It was noted that the author of the book had departed from Marxism, from the position of the class struggle."[14]

The manner of reporting these two meetings on the book is striking, and seems to support the view that a real Kazakh-Russian rivalry was in progress. Since there is little tangible evidence on this subject elsewhere, this clue is worth examining. The most interesting aspect of the reporting on the two conferences is that the earlier one, which was held in Moscow by the central Institute of History and which went overwhelmingly in Bekmakhanov's favor, was reported at great length (twenty-three pages) in the Kazakh scholarly press and only there. The second meeting, which was held in Alma-Ata by the Kazakh Institute, and which went against Bekmakhanov, was apparently not reported at all in the Kazakh press and only in the barest outline in the central press.

The length of the two reports is also suggestive. As for the Alma-Ata meeting, the quotation given above constituted the entire report, and was included in a summary of the activities of the Kazakh Institute for 1948. The Moscow meeting, on the other hand, was reported in fine detail, down to some sharp exchanges from the floor between Aidarova and Kuchkin. The Kazakh editors appended a footnote to the report in which they stated their aim in publishing this material. The discussion, they said, contained views on several "poorly studied questions . . . [which would] give significant help in the creation of fundamental scholarly work on the history of the Kazakh S.S.R." This is innocent enough, but such a footnote, as we shall see later in this study, is a standard procedure for editors who are publishing ideologically dangerous materials.

If this explanation of the disparity of reporting the two conferences is correct, how does one explain the failure of the central press to return *quid pro quo* by publishing the details of Bekmakhanov's humiliation in Alma-Ata? There are several possible reasons. The party may have wished at this point to keep the matter quiet, in the hope that the scholars would arrive at acceptable interpretations. The Alma-Ata meeting may not have been decisive enough to be used to advantage. Its lack of resolution was indicated

14. V. Shakhmatov, "V institute istorii, arkheologii i etnografii akademii nauk kazakhskoi SSSR," *VI*, No. 6, 1949, pp. 142-43.

later by a Kazakh reviewer who observed that "at the time of the discussion in the Academy of Sciences of the Kazakh S.S.R., along with correct criticism of the book, the mass character of the movement of 1837-46 and its progressive significance were groundlessly denied by other participants."[15] What is more certain is that Bekmakhanov had solid support from the best-known historians, both Kazakh and Russian. The editorial board of *Voprosy istorii* at that time included Grekov and Druzhinin, who had spoken in his behalf. They undoubtedly exercised caution in the controversy.

OTHER WORKS ON KAZAKH HISTORY

The criticism of Bekmakhanov's interpretation unfolded in slow motion. It was nearly a year after the book was published before the Kazakh Institute held its discussion; nearly two years before it was reviewed in the central press; more than three years before the authoritative voice of *Pravda* was heard; a full decade before the author made his peace with the party by publishing another book accepting its viewpoint. Meanwhile, other historians were publishing works on Kazakh history that indicated the development of the new formulation through trial and error. Since some of these works had a direct bearing on the later stages of the Bekmakhanov case, they will be considered here.

The publication of the monographs on Isatai Taimanov by Shakhmatov and Batyr Srym by Viatkin, and particularly their reception by reviewers and by the party press, furnished some guidance for the historians of Kazakh military movements. Their acceptance, with limited objections, indicated the direction of the revision which would be considered "correct" by the ideologists of the party. The next attempt to evaluate a Kazakh national movement after Bekmakhanov's ill-starred study was T. Shoinbaev's *The Rebellion of the Syr-Daria Kazakhs Under the Leadership of Batyr Dzhankhozhi Nurmukhamedov*, which appeared early in 1949.[16] Dzhankhozhi's movement, which took place in the middle 1850's, was sometimes regarded as a continuation of the Kenesary movement. The study is interesting as a transitional interpretation. It indicates broader opinion than that of its author, since Druzhinin was the editor, and Bakhrushin and Pankratova were thanked in the preface for their guidance.

15. K. Sharipov in *VI*, No. 4, 1949, p. 114.
16. T. Zh. Shoinbaev, *Vosstanie syr-dar'inskikh kazakhov pod rukovodstvom batyra Dzhankhozhi Nurmukhamedova* (*1856-1857 gg.*) (Alma-Ata, 1949).

Shoinbaev regarded this movement as a peasant movement, like Taimanov's. He characterized it as anti-colonial (it was aimed against Russia) and of national liberation character. He distinguished between it and the earlier movement by declaring that Kenesary's movement was of a feudal character, though he paradoxically left it in the category of national liberation movements. He complied with the new line by emphasizing (very modestly) the significance of annexation and by showing how the Kazakhs in question were better off under Russian control than they would have been under the Khans of Khiva and Kokand, who were threatening them.

Opinion on Shoinbaev's book was mixed. A Kazakh reviewer condemned it, charging that Dzhankhozhi was a feudal leader like Kenesary and that to declare such a movement a liberation movement denied the progressive nature of Kazakh annexation to Russia. The Kazakh Academy of Sciences held a discussion of the book and upheld the author. So did Iakunin in his review in *Voprosy istorii:* "M. Akhinzhanov [the Kazakh reviewer] evidently does not understand that the historical progressiveness of the annexation of Kazakhstan to Russia does not rule out the progressiveness of the popular-liberation struggle of the Kazakh people against the colonizing policy of tsarism. M. Akhinzhanov does not understand the peculiarities of the movement of Dzhankhozhi, the internal contradictions of this movement, the struggle between the feudal and peasant elements within it."[17] In view of the fact that the three Kazakh movements (Taimanov, Kenesary, and Dzhankhozhi) had been regarded as closely related, this discussion pointed up the thin line that divided feudal and peasant movements. It also emphasized Bekmakhanov's weak points: his failure to analyze the internal class conflicts within a movement and his reluctance to draw class lines sharply.

Whatever apparent clarification Shoinbaev's work may have brought to the treatment of the national movements was quickly dispelled in the second edition of the *History of the Kazakh S.S.R.,* which appeared at about the same time.[18] The collective of historians, headed by Pankratova and Kazakh Party Secretary I. Omarov, repaired many of the "errors" of the 1943 edition. They reduced the emphasis on military traditions, sharpened the class

17. *VI*, No. 8, 1950, pp. 125-27.
18. *Istoriia kazakhskoi SSR. S drevneishikh vremen do nashikh dnei,* ed. A. M. Pankratova and I. O. Omarov (2nd ed., Alma-Ata, 1949), Vol. I. Not available to me.

struggle, emphasized Russian cultural influences and the progressive consequences of annexation, and straightened out the periodization (the first edition had been most uncomplimentary to the Russians, dividing pre-revolutionary Kazakh history into two periods, "independence," from the beginnings up to 1868, and "Kazakhstan—a colony," 1868-1917). But on the national movements, and Kenesary's in particular, they stood their ground. In this chapter Bekmakhanov (the apparent author) maintained the view that the movement was anti-colonial and of a national liberation character, but conceded that "Kenesary's march into the territory of the Kirgiz tribes had aggressive aims."[19] In support of the progressive character of Kenesary's leadership, Bekmakhanov took a new tack. He dropped the old emphasis on the Kazakhs' struggle against the Russians (obviously a point of irritation) and stressed instead Kenesary's goal of creating a strong centralized state, which, according to a recent statement of Stalin, was a prerequisite for economic progress.

The new history of Kazakhstan was reviewed in *Voprosy istorii* by M. P. Kim, a "Moscow" historian. For the most part Kim praised the book. The authors and editors, he declared, had "in significant measure succeeded in fulfilling the task" of revising the condemned history. He took exception to the interpretation of the Kenesary movement, but here too he was surprisingly lenient, perhaps reflecting an uncertainty in his own mind. He chided the authors for giving the movement twice as much space (twenty-six pages) as the February Revolution, reminding them that they were veering in the direction of idealizing military traditions. But he refrained from condemning Kenesary, resorting merely to pointing out several reservations and noting that the progressive role of the Kazakh leader had been "overstated."[20]

The 1949 history of the Kazakhs, like its predecessor of 1943, had the ill fortune to appear on the eve of a shift in the party line. In a few months it joined the growing number of "unbooks." So complete was its liquidation that, although 25,000 copies of it were published, not a single one appears to have reached a Western library.

Also at this time there appeared a monograph that became the prototype for a whole new series. It was N. G. Apollova's *The*

19. Quoted in M. P. Kim's review in *VI*, No. 6, 1949, pp. 130-34.
20. *Ibid.*

Annexation of Kazakhstan to Russia in the 1730's.[21] Concentrating on the advantages of economic growth, cultural development, and political stability afforded by annexation, with passing references to the burdens of tsarist colonialism, the author expounded on "the profoundly progressive significance" of annexation, which "opened up the possibility for broad penetration into Kazakhstan of more advanced economics and culture." Annexation to Russia was "objectively progressive . . . from the point of view of the historical perspectives of the development of the Kazakh people."[22] In many respects Apollova was writing a corrective for the 1943 history. Emphasizing the chaos and external dangers the Kazakhs faced on the eve of submission to the Russians, she denied the assertion of that history that annexation had been brought about by the "deception" of Sultan Abulkhair. The broad Kazakh masses were in favor of joining Russia; they had not fought against the Russians as a protest against the loss of their independence—such military episodes were really "feudal attacks."

A PROPOSED COMPROMISE

Bekmakhanov's book was not reviewed in the central press until the spring of 1949, when *Voprosy istorii* published a long review by Kasym Sharipov.[23] Both the contents of the review and the identity of the reviewer must have been something of a surprise to readers of the journal, in view of the intensity of the controversy by that time. Sharipov was a leading Kazakh journalist, the editor of *Socialist Kazakhstan*, which had already published a favorable review of the work. Although accusing Bekmakhanov repeatedly of "gross political errors," his fellow Kazakh did not disagree on fundamental questions. He was in complete accord with the author about the nature of the movement: "The entire course of events shows that the movement of 1837-1846 had an anti-colonial character, and was a national liberation struggle of Kazakhs against foreign attackers." He also agreed that Kenesary had had mass

21. N. G. Apollova, *Prisoedinenie Kazakhstana k Rossii v 30-kh godakh XVIII veka* (Alma-Ata, 1948). The foreword was written by Bekmakhanov, who praised the author for her analysis of the Kazakh class struggle, her recognition of the external threat from the Dzhungars, and her view that "the annexation of Kazakhstan to Russia in the 1730's was prepared by long enonomic and political ties, which had begun already at the end of the sixteenth century."
22. *Ibid.*, pp. 246, 254.
23. *VI*, No. 4, 1949, pp. 109-14.

support against tsarist aggression. In this connection Sharipov offered one of several deft revisions: Bekmakhanov was correct about tsarist attacks, but he had underestimated the danger from the Khans of Khiva and Kokand, and furthermore had not drawn "a clear line between tsarism and the Russian people." He had not explained "the deeply progressive role of the Russian people and its advanced culture on the historical fate of the Kazakh people." The Kazakh people had had the full support of the Russian "revolutionary democrats," as Sharipov demonstrated by a quotation from Herzen's *Kolokol*.[24]

Sharipov's major objection concerned Kenesary's attack on the Kirgiz. Here he suggested that Bekmakhanov had been wrong in including this campaign in the category of a progressive movement. Sharipov proposed to solve the dilemma by dissecting the movement in the manner Viatkin had suggested in 1946. At the Moscow discussion it had already been suggested that the movement could be divided according to internal and external features (Iakunin). Sharipov recommended more radical surgery: he not only wanted to divide the movement into distinct progressive and reactionary periods, but went on to separate the mass movement from its leader. He said very little about Kenesary's leadership and his alleged reforms, referring always to "the movement of 1837-46." After dwelling on the consistently progressive character of the people's movement, he noted that

> it does not follow that Kenesary was the leader of the Kazakh people. The big fundamental mistake of E. Bekmakhanov was that he did not reveal the internal class contradictions in the movement of 1837-46. . . . To the extent that Kenesary, struggling with tsarism and the Central Asian khanates, was at the head of the movement, his activity was progressive and he, supported by the people, had formidable power. On the other hand, when Kenesary, out of clearly class feudal-monarchal interests, tried to strengthen his khanate by the method of carrying out pogroms against various nomads, by the method of attacks on the territory of the Kirgiz, his activity was reactionary, and losing the support of the people, he was reduced to nothing and perished.

24. An interesting note: the "revolutionary democrats" would be quoted generously in the coming arguments, but always on the other side of the question.

Thus the main sacrifice Sharipov made through this remarkable piece of casuistry was the fundamental thesis of Bekmakhanov that the creation of a strong central government was a progressive goal in itself.

Bekmakhanov was given the unusual opportunity of publishing an extensive reply to this review (but only in the Kazakh press, it should be noted). In an article titled "Fair Criticism," he accepted Sharipov's critique in almost every particular, and offered better-reasoned arguments in support of his new views.[25] He began by outlining three methodological mistakes he had made. First, he had not made a Marxist analysis of the class struggle within the movement. Refuting his former view of the solid front against Russia, he now acknowledged that "the struggle against external aggression at times drew the working masses together with the leading groups of the higher ranks of Kazakh society, but this collaboration never eliminated the class contradictions between them." Secondly, he had not studied the national liberation movement "in close relationship to the history of Russia. . . . As is known, the historic roots of ties between the Kazakh and Russian peoples go far into the past. They were strengthened by the historic acts of Khans Abulkhair and Ablai in putting themselves under Russian rule. . . . The national liberation struggle of the Kazakh people was inseparably tied with the struggle of the Russian people against the landlord system." In discussing the third of his "errors," Bekmakhanov made his most sweeping concession by admitting that "our previous treatment of the raids of Kenesary on the Kirgiz was deeply erroneous." But this statement, which bowed completely to the views of Sharipov, and of Morozov before him, was followed directly by others that showed clearly that Bekmakhanov was changing his mind for purely political considerations. He observed that "this war [on the Kirgiz] did not serve the interests of either of the brotherly peoples." Furthermore, he indicated that he had specifically changed his view by analyzing the war on the basis of the current usages of Marxism-Leninism: "Lenin and Stalin teach us to respect the best, progressive features of each people. Forgetting these positions of Marxism-Leninism inevitably leads to gross errors in the analysis of the mutual relations of peoples, as happened with us in the evaluation of Kenesary Kasymov's clash with the Kirgiz people." How complete Bekmakhanov's retreat on this

25. E. Bekmakhanov, "Spravedlivaia kritika," *VAN kazakhskoi SSR*, No. 9, 1949, pp. 108-10.

question was can be indicated by recalling his blunt answer to
critics the previous year, when he had stated that "nowhere has a
single document been found" to prove the aggressive nature of
the Kirgiz campaign; "I categorically object. . . . That is absolutely
untrue."

On another of Sharipov's points, Bekmakhanov was less clear.
He did not discuss the question of whether Kenesary's effort to
form a strong central government was a progressive move, but he
did concede that his "reforms" (he now put them in quotation
marks) were not in the interests of the Kazakh people. He agreed
that the Kirgiz campaign should be treated separately as a reactionary development, but he did not go all the way over to Sharipov's
illogical conception of a progressive movement with a reactionary
leader.

Bekmakhanov concluded with a conciliatory note which also
recorded what had been salvaged from his original interpretation:

> We, the historians of Kazakhstan, must sharply raise
> and resolve the problems of the mutual relations of the
> Russian and Kazakh peoples, not confusing the interests
> of the working masses with the interests of the exploiters.
> However, at the time of the discussion in the Academy of
> Sciences of the Kazakh S.S.R. certain historians (Comrades
> Kh. Aidarova, S. Tolybekov, T. Shoinbaev, B. Suleimenov)
> denied the mass character and progressiveness of the rebel-
> lion of the Kazakhs of 1837-46. Such a treatment objective-
> ly leads to the justification of the reactionary colonizing
> policy of tsarism. Comrade Sharipov is correct when he
> shows the mistakes of our individual historians in his ar-
> ticle.

Thus, when all was said and done, Bekmakhanov still held the
movement to be of a national liberation character, an anti-colonial
movement with mass participation. The concession was more apparent than real.

Sharipov's review and Bekmakhanov's reply raise more questions
than they answer. In the first place, why did *Voprosy istorii* entrust
the review to a Kazakh journalist who had already favored Bekmakhanov? Throughout this controversy the journal seems to have
been tolerant of bourgeois nationalist views and would later be
severely criticized for it. The Sharipov review was not a typical
party rebuke, but it met Morozov's review to the letter by condemning the Kirgiz campaign. The tone of the review, and the

almost eager agreement of Bekmakhanov, with his emphasis on the reviewer's correctness in standing by the interpretation of the mass character and progressiveness of the movement, all suggest that Sharipov and Bekmakhanov may have struck an alliance to save part of the old interpretation. Of course, too much of the controversy is hidden to allow more than speculation on this point.[26]

In the apparent alignment of forces in the controversy, Bekmakhanov received overwhelming support. In the profession he was supported by the prominent specialists and was treated leniently by *Voprosy istorii* (which, curiously enough, published almost favorable reviews of his book and his work on the 1949 Kazakh history but never published a line from his pen). He evidently had the backing of the Kazakh Academy of Sciences, which continued to publish a number of his articles and reviews up to the spring of 1950 when the party crackdown on Shamil forced it to be cautious. According to later criticism, significant elements in the Kazakh party supported him, and he was "protected" by the rector of the Kazakh State University, where he worked (see below, pp. 152-53). His opponents seemed to consist of the ideologues of the party in Moscow (but not in Alma-Ata!) and a few compliant Kazakh historians. The historians named by Bekmakhanov as his chief opponents were mostly Kazakhs, none of whom had established reputations. Thus the controversy cannot be considered to be purely a Kazakh-Russian clash.

Among historians, Bekmakhanov was perhaps the most frequent contributor to the *Vestnik* of the Kazakh Academy of Sciences throughout 1949 and early 1950. In some of these articles he tried to support his new positions. In an article on the structure of Kazakh society in the last half of the nineteenth century he attempted to repair fences on the question of class structure by maintaining that the proposition that Kazakh society was "classless" or a "tribal democracy" was bourgeois nationalist. Such a view implied that the Kazakhs were not ready for the October Revolution—an insult to

26. Another curious piece in this puzzle is the fact that Sharipov's review was published under a different title in two Kazakh newspapers (*Kazakhstanskaia pravda* and the Kazakh language *Socialist Kazakhstan,* July 9, 1949) and in the *Vestnik* of the Kazakh Academy of Sciences ("Po-marksistski osveshchat' istoriiu Kazakhstana," *VAN kazakhskoi SSR,* No. 8, 1949, pp. 13-23). This might indicate that Kazakh authorities hoped to establish this interpretation by wide circulation; it might, on the other hand, merely mean that Sharipov, who was later named head of the Kazakh telegraph agency, already had substantial control over the local press, and wanted to publicize his views.

his people. The class contradictions were always there, he said, but they were obscured by the "survivals of the patriarchal-tribal system."[27] In his last article before he disappeared from print Bekmakhanov emphasized the cooperation of the Russian and Kazakh people in the period of the 1905 Revolution, paying tribute to the great influence of the Bolsheviks on Kazakh workers.[28] Further indication of Bekmakhanov's scholarly good health (in Kazakh eyes, at least) was the appearance, early in 1950, of his pamphlet *The Historic Roots of the Friendship of the Kazakh People with the Great Russian People,* fifteen thousand copies of which were published in Alma-Ata.[29]

But as far as the central press was concerned, Bekmakhanov was talking to himself. His article accepting the main views of Sharipov was ignored. M. P. Kim's review of the new Kazakh history, of which Bekmakhanov was co-author, discussed the incorrect interpretation of Kenesary without mentioning the name of the outstanding exponent of that view. The Kazakh controversy was simply shelved for nearly two years by Soviet scholars. Meanwhile, in May, 1950, the party cracked down viciously on a work in which Shamil was characterized as a leader of a national liberation movement. There were so many obvious parallels between the historic roles of Shamil and Kenesary that Bekmakhanov was now obviously in line for a harsh official rebuke. But for more than half a year nothing was said; the only immediate result was that Bekmakhanov's articles disappeared even in the Kazakh press. The overdue reprimand came in a *Pravda* article on the history of Central Asia at the end of 1950.[30] Many Soviet historians—indeed all who had written on Central Asia—had made grievous errors in the evaluation of national movements, but the sins of Bekmakhanov were held up as a particularly dangerous example of bourgeois nationalism. The most serious charge against him was that he had persisted in error and offered rebuttal after numerous party warnings. *Pravda* dismissed his painstaking efforts to analyze the class

27. E. B. Bekmakhanov, "K voprosu o sotsial'nom stroe kazakov vtoroi poloviny XIX v.," *VAN kazakhskoi SSR,* No. 2, 1950, pp. 89-104.

28. E. B. Bekmakhanov, "Natsional'no-osvoboditelnoe dvizhenie v Kazakhstane v period pervoi russkoi burzhuazno-demokraticheskoi revoliutsii," *ibid.,* No. 4, 1950, pp. 61-75.

29. E. B. Bekmakhanov, *Istoricheskie korni druzhba kazakhskogo naroda s velikim russkim narodom* (Alma-Ata, 1950), apparently an expanded version of his article of 1947 (see note 3 above). Not available to me.

30. Since this article also involves questions of later developments, it will be discussed more fully in Chapter 7. See pp. 149-51.

structure of Kazakh society, charging that he "obliterates class boundaries" in his works. The authors of the articles found his "rapturous descriptions of Kenesary" to be a serious offense to the friendship of peoples. Sharipov's view was also rejected: he had correctly condemned Kenesary, but had tried "to rehabilitate the reactionary movement headed by him."

Although *Pravda* did not explicitly relieve Bekmakhanov of his duties, it clearly called on more compliant Kazakh historians to replace his harmful views with others which it outlined. As a result of this official condemnation Bekmakhanov became a silent exile in his own university for six years. He was humiliated in public discussions (without the right to reply this time), relieved of his professorship, and stripped of his doctor's degree. The freer atmosphere of 1956 would afford him an opportunity to redeem himself. That story will be told in its chronological context.

CHAPTER 7.

THE SHAMIL CONTROVERSY

"Today, the Bolsheviks fear the dead Shamil more than the Vorontsovs and Bariatinskiis feared him as a live, but honorable enemy." Editorial in Svobodnyi Kavkaz [The Free Caucasus], *No. 4, 1952, p. 2.*

While party officials postponed a pronouncement on Kenesary's proper place in history, no doubt hoping that historians would arrive at an appropriate interpretation through their own self-criticism, they were obliged to drench the fires of nationalism in the Caucasus by cutting down the fabulous Shamil. The move was all the more spectacular because it involved the revocation of a Stalin Prize that had just been awarded, and the undoing of virtually everything that had been written about the hero in the Soviet period up to May, 1950.

Unlike Kenesary, who was hardly known outside of Central Asia, Shamil had an international reputation as a guerrilla warrior. In the course of his quarter-century stand against Russian forces vastly outnumbering his armies (1834-59), he had become a legend in his own day. His honorable retirement, granted by Alexander II after his capture, was an indication of the admiration his Russian adversaries held for him.

The Shamil legend had been actively promoted before World War II through popular biographies, children's books, textbooks, and more scholarly works. Every Soviet schoolboy who studied the early editions of the Shestakov and Pankratova textbooks knew Shamil from a portrait showing a turbaned and bearded leader, with blazing eyes and a determined countenance, wearing a military jacket with sewed-in cartridge pockets, and a rifle slung over his

130

shoulder. The following description of the hero from the Shestakov textbook is typical: "The mountain people were united by the talented and energetic leader, Shamil. He was born in Dagestan, and in his childhood he distinguished himself for courage and determination. Shamil was strong, bold and agile, an excellent rider and a fine marksman, a tireless swimmer and runner. Shamil was a brave and experienced individual who had a great influence on the mountain people. Shamil became an able ruler and a talented general."[1]

Shamil's reputation had not been damaged by the beginnings of the rehabilitation of tsarist generals on the eve of World War II, or by the fact that the discredited Pokrovskii had admired him greatly. Indeed, up to the end of 1941, when the attempted popularization of Shamil as a military hero was unceremoniously stopped, it looked as though the Shamil cult would reach new heights. In 1939 S. K. Bushuev, who would be a major figure in the denigration of Shamil in the 1950's, began a discussion of the hero with a quotation from one of his lieutenants, who had stated in his journal that "Shamil was a well educated individual, pious, shrewd, brave, strong, resolute, a good horseman, marksman, swimmer, fighter, runner—in a word, no one was able to compete with him."[2] In addition to his military prowess, he had earned a considerable reputation as an administrator and reformer. "Shamil's brilliant epoch," a term first used by Chernyshevskii to refer to the middle years of his rule, became the topic head for lengthy discussions of his democratic government, his judicial and tax reforms, the removal of ancient privileges of the feudal aristocracy, and partial emancipation of the slaves of the area.[3]

Even after the failure to reprint the pamphlets on Shamil in 1941, there were signs that the party hoped to use the Shamil military tradition to arouse his countrymen to resist the Germans. Dagestanis were reported to have contributed the impressive sum

1. *Kratkii kurs istorii SSSR*, ed. A. V. Shestakov (Moscow, 1937), p. 90. In addition to the Shamil portrait, this book contained a second illustration, whose caption was "Mountain People Going to War With Tsarist Troops," and accompanying text, appropriate for the time: "Shamil lured detachments of Russian soldiers far into the mountains. The mountain people blocked the line of retreat with rocks and fallen trees. From ambush the mountain people exterminated the Russian troops."

2. S. K. Bushuev, *Bor'ba gortsev za nezavisimost' pod rukovodstvom Shamilia* (Moscow, 1939), p. 82.

3. *Ibid.*, chap. iv; *Istoriia SSSR*, ed. M. V. Nechkina (Moscow, 1940), II, 279-84.

of 25,000,000 rubles to equip a tank column named "Shamil." There was talk of having the mullahs of the North Caucasus proclaim a "holy war" against the Germans, but this plan was apparently called off.[4] Publication of works on Shamil, however, came to a standstill between 1941 and 1949, although the revised textbooks continued to reproduce their adulatory passages without any change.[5]

It was inevitable that Shamil's role would be reconsidered after the controversy arose over Kenesary. The two leaders had much in common. Their movements against the Russians were the most determined that had been made, and they had been evaluated in the same way. Both were aristocrats and both had reputedly formed strong governments and had made many administrative reforms. Both had resorted to brutal tactics late in their careers, had killed their own countrymen and invaded the territories of other peoples of the future Soviet family. They were frequently compared; the last published instance appears to have been in a speech by S. V. Iushkov at the session of the Kazakh Institute of History in May, 1947. It is characteristic of the confusion of the times, however, that when the proceedings of that meeting were reviewed by Iakunin in *Voprosy istorii* two years later, a strong objection was lodged on this point. By 1949 Kenesary was fading fast, but Shamil (in Iakunin's mind, at any rate) retained his former reputation. It was unfair to compare Shamil and Kenesary, said Iakunin, because the former had destroyed the feudal aristocracy, abolished slavery, proclaimed equality under the law, created an original "theocratic government" and worked out a complex army organization. Kenesary had done none of these things, but instead had "destroyed poor Kazakh clans which did not want to submit to him."[6]

The most difficult thing in Shamil's career to reconcile with the role of national liberation leader was the fact that he had been the *imam* (spiritual and political leader) of Muridism, a fanatical Moslem sect which sometimes carried out a *gazavat* (holy war) against all infidels. In the late 1940's Islam was regarded as the most reactionary of "religious ideologies," and Muridism was one

4. E. Genkina, *Obrazovanie SSSR* (Moscow, 1943), p. 76, cited by Robert Conquest in *The Soviet Deportation of Nationalities* (London: The Macmillan Co., 1960), p. 74.

5. The only work on Shamil during these years listed in the *Knizhnaia letopis'* (No. 13330 for 1946) is an Arabic text of the Chronicle of Mukhammed Takhir al Karakhi, his follower.

6. *VI*, No. 3, 1949, p. 127.

of the most reactionary sects of Islam. But in this case Soviet scholars had demonstrated the flexibility of Marxism-Leninism by either ignoring the association or by rationalizing it. A respectable rationalization had been formulated on the basis of an observation by Lenin that "political protests in a religious cloak *[obolochka]* are common to all peoples at a certain stage in their development."[7] By resorting ritualistically to this quotation, Soviet historians could dismiss the obvious contradiction of a progressive movement with a reactionary cause; religious movements were sometimes the natural vehicles of political revolt. B. V. Skitskii, a specialist on the North Caucasus, had tried in 1930 to divide Muridism into two periods—"old Muridism" (reactionary) and "new revolutionary Muridism," which he called "the *avant garde* of the revolutionary petty bourgeoisie."[8] Even after World War II, Skitskii continued to see Islam as "a common platform, on which the various peoples and social groups could unite against the approach of tsarism." Islam was "the symbol in the struggle with tsarism."[9] Shestakov had argued that the *gazavat* was in essence "a revolutionary slogan"; it was the best instrument by which leaders could get Moslems to participate in national liberation struggles. In support of this argument he noted that the *gazavat* had been proclaimed in Central Asia only after the Russians came.[10]

THE FIRST ATTACK ON SHAMIL

The first serious attack on Shamil came at a curious meeting of the Institute of History of the U.S.S.R. Academy of Sciences in 1947, called to hear and discuss a paper by an Armenian member of the Union of Soviet Writers, Kh. G. Adzhemian, "On the Historical Essence of Caucasian Muridism."[11] A distinguished gather-

7. V. I. Lenin, *Polnoe sobranie sochinenii* (Moscow, 1958-65), IV, 228.
8. B. V. Skitskii, *Klassovye kharakter miuridizma v poru imamata Shamilia* (Vladikavkaz, 1930), pp. 113-15.
9. B. Skitskii, "Ocherki po istorii osetinskogo naroda s drevneishikh vremen do 1867 goda," *Izvestiia severo-osetinskogo nauchno-issledovatel'skogo instituta,* XI (1947), 159. It is interesting that Skitskii, even in 1947, considered Islam to be a comparatively progressive force (by virtue of the religious cloak) against the Russian Orthodox Church, whose reactionary doctrines tsarism sought to spread in the Caucasus. The same general idea was found in his *Khrestomatiia po istorii Osetii* (Dzaudzhikau, 1949), I, 212-16.
10. *Trudy pervoi vsesoiuznoi konferentsii istorikov-marksistov* (Moscow, 1930), p. 523.
11. "Diskussiia o dvizhenii Shamilia," *VI,* No. 11, 1947, pp. 134-40. On the Shamil controversy of 1947-56, see Paul B. Henze, "Unrewriting History— the Shamil Problem," *Caucasian Review,* No. 6 (1958), pp. 7-29; Lowell R.

ing heard the obscure speaker declare that their long-established interpretation was one-sided and completely erroneous. Adzhemian's argument showed that he was well aware of the issues in the Kenesary controversy (Bekmakhanov's book had just been published). He began by declaring that the society of the North Caucasus in Shamil's day was patriarchal-tribal, and not early feudal, as had been supposed. It followed that Shamil could not have led an anti-feudal movement. One of the characteristics of patriarchal-tribal society was constant petty warfare and plundering raids, and Shamil's military activity should not be dignified by any other label. He denied that Shamil had created a government, freed slaves, or made any real reforms. Only the support of Turkey, backed by Britain, had enabled him to hold out for so long against Russia. The Russian Empire, he asserted, had brought these peoples "the first gleam of civilization." Since Shamil opposed this progressive development, his role must be assessed as reactionary. In support of all this Adzhemian demonstrated that the game of *tsitatnichestvo* (citation dropping) could be played both ways. The quotation of alleged pro-Shamil statements of Marx, Engels, and the Russian "revolutionary democrats" had been a favorite technique for building the heroic image of Shamil (Nechkina, who was in the audience, had edited a textbook that waxed eloquent with the views of Chernyshevskii and Lermontov on the subject). Against this tide of opinion Adzhemian referred vaguely to an article with an "anti-Shamil orientation" published in *The Contemporary,* and deduced that the journal's most illustrious contributor, Chernyshevskii, must have recognized that the movement was reactionary. He noted that the Azerbaidzhani scholar, M. F. Akhundov, as a determined crusader against Islam, had been of the same opinion. As for Marx and Engels, Adzhemian dared to state that they had been deluded by the anti-Russian bias of the British press.

Ten speakers rose to rebuttal, taking Adzhemian's paper apart piece by piece. Adzhemian, who had no real support, won only one unimportant concession (an agreement by one participant that Shamil had sometimes been idealized). Much of the criticism was scornful, questioning his knowledge of basic facts and lack of

Tillett, "Shamil and Muridism in Recent Soviet Historiography," *American Slavic and East European Review,* XX (1961), 253-69; A. Bennigsen, "The Muslim Peoples of the Soviet Union and the Soviets," Part 4, *Islamic Review,* XLIII (1955), No. 7, 27-36.

acquaintance with sources. In his concluding remarks Adzhemian stuck by all his basic arguments and warned of "the political harmfulness of the interpretation of Shamil as the leader of a progressive-liberation movement." Druzhinin, who was chairman, concluded the session with the observation that "the viewpoint of Kh. G. Adzhemian did not win the support of the participants. . . . The speaker gave no criticism of the sources and showed no acquaintance with many factual materials."

The reason for calling this meeting is not clear. The only clue given in the meeting itself was the remark of the chairman that "recently certain historians" had questioned the old interpretation. The parallel between Aidarova and Adzhemian, the devil's advocates, is inescapable. Both of them anticipated by two years what the new party line would be; both of them presented their views at public meetings and stood their ground against almost unanimous opposition. There is no evidence that they were party spokesmen in any formal sense. It is possible that they were able to reach their interpretations by a careful synthesis of all that had been said in the party directives on ideological matters, against the background of the deepening *Zhdanovshchina*. Having arrived at such views, which were in line with the drift of party thinking, they could hardly be denied a hearing. It is interesting, however, that they were heard at public meetings, which were in all probability arranged behind the scenes with the aid of party pressures, and not in the scholarly press. The seasoned scholars who were the responsible editors gave them no quarter: *Voprosy istorii* never published an article by Aidarova or Adzhemian; no book appeared on this subject until the party broke the dam in 1950.

What did the diviners of the new party line have in common? Besides these two we have only the names of three Kazakhs, S. Tolybekov, T. Shoinbaev, and B. Suleimenov, who had led the argument against Bekmakhanov. All of them seem to have been younger scholars who had not published very much.[12] By contrast,

12. Adzhemian, who was apparently a specialist in literature, made no further attempts in the field of history. According to the Soviet bibliography of historical works (*Istoriia SSSR. Ukazatel' sovetskoi literatury, 1917-1952* [Moscow, 1956-58]), he had not published as much as a book review by 1952. Aidarova had published a study on Chokan Valikhanov in 1945 and had edited a volume of articles on him in 1947. Shoinbaev's first book, on the Dzhankozhi rebellion, was published in 1949. Suleimenov edited a volume of documents on the 1916 rebellion in Central Asia in 1947 and another on the Revolution of 1905 in Kazakhstan in 1949. Tolybekov had not published anything before 1950.

it is remarkable that not a single older, well-known historian accepted these views before 1950, when party opinion was made crystal clear. Even such historians as Pankratova and Nechkina and the politician-historian Gafurov, who could ordinarily be counted on to follow the party line, persisted in the old interpretations through 1949.

The common factors which suggest themselves in this case are compliance and ambition. The spokesmen for the new line apparently had no respect for established interpretations and were willing to take party thinking as a beginning and to arrange the facts to suit it. The extreme example is Tolybekov, who, as we shall see, wrote such fantasies on the friendship of peoples in the 1950's that he was criticized by his colleagues during the thaw. These spokesmen were rewarded for their efforts: Aidarova, Tolybekov, and Shoinbaev were entrusted with editing still another survey history of the Kazakhs (the third). But in their attempts to anticipate the party's views they had undertaken a difficult task, and the casualty list was high. The editors of the Kazakh history were discredited when their work was aborted at the prospectus stage in 1952. Suleimenov had already been condemned for his evaluation of certain Kazakh leaders in the 1905 Revolution. Shoinbaev, who soared highest as party spokesman in *Pravda* and at several historical conferences, also fell hardest. His fellow historians published charges of gross plagiarism against him in the early 1960's, and he was stripped of his posts and denounced for unethical conduct.[13]

The discussion of Adzhemian's paper had no immediate result; there was if anything a studied silence on Shamil during the next two years while historians were exchanging views on Kenesary. *Voprosy istorii* reported the meeting routinely in its back pages, but did not publish anything further on the question. The text-

13. In 1963 N. G. Apollova wrote to the editor of the journal *Istoriia SSSR*, charging that Shoinbaev had plagiarized an unpublished manuscript of hers in an article he had published in a Kazakh journal the previous year. Proving her case with a dozen passages from the two works, which the journal published in parallel columns (*Istoriia SSSR*, No. 5, 1963, pp. 231-37), she also revealed that Shoinbaev had been paraphrasing other works and publishing them under his name for several years. Druzhinin had written him a personal letter calling for an explanation in 1958. Shoinbaev's paraphrasing of Apollova's work represented "a new stage in his offensive activity." In 1964 the journal published a notice that Shoinbaev had been dismissed from the Learned Council of the Kazakh Institute of History, Archeology, and Ethnography (*ibid.*, No. 4, 1964, p. 246).

books that were published in 1948 and 1949 contained the old interpretation. Collectives of historians who were at work on survey histories of the individual Soviet republics of the Caucasus were so far behind schedule that they were not embarrassed by committing their views to print.

Meanwhile, the scholar's lot was becoming more difficult. The particular bane of the historian was "bourgeois objectivism," which in simplest terms meant too much reverence for facts. "The accumulation of facts," according to numerous party spokesmen, might interfere with the formulation of "creative Marxist-Leninist interpretations." A leading editorial in *Voprosy istorii* pointed out that "Stalin angrily ridiculed and mercilessly denounced people who were capable only of 'the accumulation of historical facts'" but were unable "to explain their origin in relation to place and time" (he called such scholars "archive rats"). The journal pointed out the urgent need for a more "creative" approach to the writing of the history of the non-Russian peoples.

> One of the most important problems on which the Soviet scholarly community must concentrate is the writing of valuable works of high theoretical quality on the history of the different peoples who comprise the brotherly family of the Soviet union. At one time, in the performance of this task, serious errors of principle, of a bourgeois nationalist character, were committed in the individual Union and Autonomous Republics, and were noted in the directives of the Central Committee of the Communist Party of the Soviet Union. Now, on the basis of the guiding instructions of the Party on ideological questions, works on the history of individual peoples are being thoroughly revised.[14]

The editorial was unduly optimistic in hinting that such mistakes were in the past. The stormiest battles with the bourgeois nationalists were yet to come.

THE PARTY SPEAKS OUT

The turning point in the interpretation of national heroes and resistance movements came in a pronouncement on Shamil published on May 14, 1950. *Pravda* and *Izvestiia* of that date carried a brief report concerning some second thoughts by the Committee on Stalin Prizes, which had recommended a prize for Geidar

14. "Osnovye zadachi v izuchenii istorii SSSR feodal'nogo perioda," *VI*, No. 11, 1949, pp. 3-12.

Guseinov's *On the History of Social and Philosophical Thought in Azerbaidzhan in the Nineteenth Century*.[15] According to the report, the committee had discussed the matter further, had "recognized as erroneous" its earlier decision to nominate the book, and had petitioned the Council of Ministers to withdraw the nomination.

The dispatch then went on to give the reasons for the change of views, all of which concerned Shamil and Muridism. Guseinov's quotations on Shamil and his movement, which he had taken from completely respected sources, were repeated and contradicted. Against Shamil's "patriotism" and "love of the people," the *imam* was quoted as saying that he ruled over "brigands"; against the view of Muridism as a cover for a liberation movement, it was declared to be "reactionary, nationalistic, and in the service of British capitalism and the Turkish Sultan." In conclusion there was a hint of the future technique of revision in the citing of several quotations that showed the reactionary nature of the movement (three were from Marx and Engels, allegedly showing Shamil's ties with Britain and Turkey). Guseinov's error had been the result of dependence on reactionary bourgeois historians.

Two days later the newspapers, in a one-sentence announcement, stated that the Council of Ministers had granted the request of the committee to withdraw the nomination.[16] The arguments used to condemn Guseinov's book were the same ones Adzhemian

15. Geidar Guseinov, *Iz istorii obshchestvennoi i filosofskoi mysli v Azerbaidzhane v XIX veka* (Baku, 1949). A second edition was published in Baku in 1958. The statement of the Committee on Stalin Prizes is translated in full in the *Current Digest of the Soviet Press* [hereafter cited as *CDSP*], II, No. 17, 6-7.

16. In these transactions there are good examples of the party's technique of blaming others for its own errors and shortsightedness. Responsibility was lodged squarely on the Committee on Stalin Prizes, which had merely nominated a book that had been hailed by reviewers as an outstanding contribution to Soviet scholarship. According to the first report, the Committee had reconsidered its views "in connection with proposals of public organizations in Azerbaidzhan," but it was quite clear in the subsequent discussion that the impetus came from the highest authorities in the party. In another respect the reports contained a misleading statement, recognizable to Soviet readers. All the references to the event mentioned nomination for the prize, and it was the nomination which was withdrawn. But in reality Guseinov had actually been awarded the prize two months earlier. *Pravda* of March 8, 1950, listed Guseinov's name and book on the front page, the prize having been awarded in the third degree in the field of literary criticism and art. Guseinov presumably received 25,000 rubles, and entered the charmed circle (if only momentarily) occupied by Shostakovich, Khachaturian, Gladkov, and Simonov, who were on the same list.

had expounded to his hostile audience of historians nearly three years earlier.

The party's crackdown on Shamil came under ironic circumstances. Prior to the May 14 announcement Guseinov's book had been very well received. The author's real endeavor was to support two propositions which were in the forefront of the ideological campaign of the time: (1) that the Soviet cultural past was fully as rich as that of Western Europe, and (2) that Russian influence was foremost in Azerbaidzhani cultural achievement. How well he succeeded in this primary task was attested not only by the Stalin Prize, but in a highly favorable review by a watchdog of ideology, L. Klimovich, who praised Guseinov for "the restoration of the true history of the Azerbaidzhani people's culture" by refuting the former claims of bourgeois scholars about Arab, Persian, and Turkic influences. "A particularly strong feature of the book," added Klimovich, "is that it describes the age-old friendship of the Azerbaidzhani and Russian peoples and illustrates graphically the process by which the rich and glorious traditions of Azerbaidzhani culture were created."[17]

What is even more ironic about the author's plight is that as far as Shamil and Muridism were concerned Guseinov was almost an innocent bystander. He had made a half dozen passing references to Shamil and as many to the movement. Most of them were old quotations, well known and honored by Soviet scholarship. His most damning statement, judging from later criticism, was the repetition of a famous expression of Mirza Kazem-Bek, an Azerbaidzhani pioneer in Oriental studies, who remarked that Shamil "was a hero and a maker of heroes."[18] Guseinov had even taken the precaution to pen a disclaimer, albeit brief and per-

17. L. Klimovich, review in *Literaturnaia gazeta*, March 22, 1950. Klimovich's only reservation was that Guseinov had not gone far enough in attributing the origins of Azerbaidzhani thought to Russia. In a typical bit of didactic reviewing, he noted that Guseinov had stated that "the works of Belinskii, Herzen, Chernyshevskii and Dobroliubov exerted tremendous influence on the formation of M. F. Akhundov's philosophical and social-political views" but had not developed the theme. "In reality," Klimovich rejoined, "this claim could have been substantiated in detail and supported by a concrete analysis of Akhundov's works."

18. Guseinov, *Iz istorii*, 2nd ed., p. 43. The second edition purports to be unchanged except for minor corrections and deletions. Unfortunately I have not been able to see the first edition. However, as far as our question is concerned, the editions would seem to be the same, since the most sensitive and controversial passages, which were quoted in the campaign against the book, appear in the second edition without change.

functory: "However, it is necessary to note that M. Kazem-Bek was not able to show the social class origins of Muridism. He idealized Shamil."[19]

It seems probable that success itself was the greatest factor in Guseinov's defeat. The party could not tolerate such views on Shamil in a book receiving the wide publicity and the implied approval involved in the award of a Stalin Prize. There is also evidence, as we shall see later, that Guseinov was the victim of a personal clash with the most powerful Azerbaidzhani of the time, M. D. Bagirov.

Bagirov, the First Secretary of the Central Committee of the Communist Party of Azerbaidzhan, took a personal interest in the Shamil question and became the party spokesman on the whole question of the relations of Soviet peoples in the past. At this point in his career, Bagirov had been a full member of the Central Committee for ten years, and was the highest ranking official of Moslem background in the U.S.S.R. An associate of Beriia, he was the author of *On the History of Bolshevik Organizations in Baku and Azerbaidzhan,*[20] which in title and tone was reminiscent of Beriia's work on the party origins in Transcaucasia. Like Beriia, too, he used strong-arm methods, and made himself one of the most hated men in Azerbaidzhan. He lived in great luxury, traveled under heavy bodyguard, and was known among some of his countrymen as "the Khan of Azerbaidzhan."[21]

In July *Bol'shevik* published a long article under Bagirov's name entitled "On the Question of the Character of Muridism and Shamil."[22] This article did not add much to the arguments that had been made already, but it did indicate the line of reasoning and the emphases the party would impose in the interpretation. As the central statement and the basis of the whole discussion of the next three years, it deserves examination at some length. The arguments can be summed up under three headings.

1. Muridism was in essence a reactionary religious movement, having nothing in common with national liberation. Furthermore,

19. *Ibid.,* p. 146.
20. M. D. Bagirov, *Iz istorii bol'shevistskoi organizatsii Baku i Azerbaidzhana* (Moscow, 1946).
21. V. Astemirov, "Spoilers of a Literary Heritage," *Caucasian Review,* No. 9 (1959), pp. 91-97.
22. M. D. Bagirov, "K voprosu o kharaktere dvizheniia miuridizma i Shamilia," *Bol'shevik,* No. 13, 1950, pp. 21-37; condensed translation in *CDSP,* II, No. 13, 13-17.

Islam, with its periodic holy wars, had been an instrument of Turkish expansion since the sixteenth century, and the British had shrewdly employed it in Shamil's lifetime. "Foreign conquerors, colonizers, and imperialists have organized and supported various movements, giving them a national or religious character, with the aim of usurping them in their struggle against their rivals." With this strong implication that the Turks and British not only supported Muridism, but even organized it, Bagirov turned Lenin's "religious cloak" inside out.

2. Like Adzhemian, Bagirov argued that Shamil was a reactionary leader who had no popular support. He had not been elected *imam* by the people, as was formerly held, but "by the reactionary Moslem leaders and the feudal tribal aristocracy." One of his most reprehensible crimes was the destruction of whole villages that would not join in his fight against the Russians. "For a loyalty to Russia, for the slightest suspicion of ties with the Russians, Shamil destroyed even those people of his own faith—Moslems." On the other hand, Shamil's support from the Turks and British resulted from the services he had rendered to them; the "British lords and capitalists" had no reason whatever to support a popular national liberation movement, but were interested in helping a rebel leader who "was trying to detach the Caucasus from Russia, cutting off a large number of Russian troops and by this means was helping Russia's enemies. . . ."

3. "Annexation to Russia was for the peoples of the Caucasus the only possible path for the development of their economy and culture." Bagirov pointed up the historic alternative these people faced at that time: to be "swallowed up and enslaved by backward, feudal Turkey and Persia" or to be "annexed" to Russia. "In spite of the arbitrary acts of cruelty of tsarist colonizers [Bagirov's only reference in 15,000 words to unpleasantries resulting from inclusion in the Russian Empire], annexation of the Caucasus to Russia played a positive and progressive role for the peoples of the Caucasus." Annexation gave them security, conditions for economic development, and above all, contacts with advanced Russian culture and revolutionary thought. The "advanced people" of the area actually worked for annexation.

These arguments of Bagirov would be hardened into precise formulas immediately, and would be rehearsed hundreds of times in the new histories. Much of this reasoning would remain intact a decade after the denunciation of its author.

Bagirov concluded his article by firing parting shots at numerous scholars and writers. In addition to Guseinov, he condemned his editor, A. O. Makovelskii, who "led our public into error"; several historians, including Druzhinin, Pankratova, and Nechkina; a number of Guseinov's reviewers in Azerbaidzhan; and the Union of Writers, which had recommended Guseinov's work for the Stalin Prize. He declared that these people had slipped into "bourgeois objectivism," and many of them were "tied to the apron strings of bourgeois scholars, especially the British. . . ." These Soviet scholars "quite often omit and ignore numerous priceless documents and materials in our state archives, which make it possible to give a correct assessment of the true nature of Caucasian Muridism and the Shamil movement."[23] Turning to these materials, he gave the full text of a letter Shamil had written to the tsar after his capture. His purpose was to show that the hero was really an unprincipled double-dealer, seeking his own comforts above all. Suggesting that many of the statements of Chernyshevskii about Shamil were "ironic," Bagirov cited a number of Shamil's contemporaries who, in his view, had recognized the reactionary nature of the movement.

In July, Bagirov carried his campaign for ideological purification to his homeland. In a long speech to a specially convened group of "Baku intelligentsia," he reviewed the errors and shortcomings in Azerbaidzhani literature, history, and linguistics (Stalin's denunciation of N. Ia. Marr had just appeared).[24] Not only were scholars of the Azerbaidzhani Academy of Sciences still enslaved to bourgeois scholarship, but another important cause of their failings was that their work had been "divorced from industrial enterprises, collective farms, Machine and Tractor Stations, and state farms." He repeated his arguments of the *Bol'shevik* article on Shamil, vituperatively attacking Guseinov, his editor, his reviewers, and well-wishers. Most of them (but not Guseinov) then rose to engage in self-criticism.[25]

23. These references to the failure to use archives are especially ironic in view of the later complaints of historians during the "thaw" that most of these collections were under lock and key.

24. "Ob ocherednykh zadachakh intelligentsii Azerbaidzhana," *Bakinskii rabochii* [*The Baku Worker*], July 18, 1950. The Bagirov speech and the subsequent discussion filled almost all of the first three pages of this Baku Russian-language paper of that date. Curiously enough, publication of the text of the speech was delayed four days (it was delivered July 14), and appeared concurrently with a brief summary in *Pravda*.

25. *Pravda's* summary contains an interesting judgment on the self-criticism,

Other meetings in the Caucasus were held on the same pattern as the Baku meeting. In Shamil's home territory, the party *aktiv* of Makhachkala (the main city in Dagestan) held a session to hear a report on Shamil and Muridism by the local Party Secretary, A. D. Daniialov, and to engage in "party-principled criticism."[26] At Nal'chik, the Party Secretary of the Kabarda branch of the party, A. Keshokov, addressed a meeting of scholars "On Some Questions of the History of the Kabardinian People."[27] After condemning Shamil, he nominated proper heroes: Stalin, Kirov, and Ordzhonikidze. Great concern was expressed about delays in publishing a history of Kabarda, which had been started in 1949 and discussed as a *maket* earlier in 1950. But the collective, headed by the Russian specialist on the Caucasus, N. A. Smirnov, was understandably deliberate about committing itself to print: the history appeared in 1957.[28]

A second meeting was held in Baku in November. It was convened by the Central Committee of the Azerbaidzhani Party and consisted of historians, teachers and party workers. The Secretary of the Central Committee of the Azerbaidzhani Party, G. Gasanov, repeated the criticism of "Guseinov's defective, vicious book" and continued the familiar procedure of calling upon a number of scholars to recant. He spent considerable time on the shortcomings of the Azerbaidzhani Institute of History, which had done little work in recent years, and that from the wrong point of view. Graduate work in history was in poor straits, especially because of the approval of dissertations of poor quality. In this connection Gasanov's comment on two recent dissertations is revealing. G. Mekhti-

which indicates that the whole proceeding had been gone over very carefully in Moscow. "In general," *Pravda* said, "the meeting was on a high ideological-political level and was characterized by keen and convincing criticism." However, "the participants in the meeting were not satisfied with the empty speech" by M. A. Dadash-zade (Director of the Institute of Literature of the Azerbaidzhani Academy of Sciences). Also the statement of M. Ibragimov (Chairman of the Azerbaidzhani Union of Soviet Writers) "did not sound convincing enough." See *Pravda*, July 18, 1950; summary translation in *CDSP*, II, No. 29, p. 41.

26. This meeting apparently was not reported in the central press. It is mentioned in a review of developments given in *Izvestiia Akademii Nauk SSSR. Otdelenie literaturi i iazyka*, No. 3 [published in December], 1950, pp. 245-46.

27. I. Barits, "Pokhod protiv 'burzhuaznogo natsionalizma' v SSSR. Stat'ia chetvertaia: Severnyi Kavkaz," *Svobodnyi Kavkaz*, No. 7 (1952), pp. 19-27.

28. *Istoriia Kabardy. S drevneishikh vremen do nashikh dnei* (Moscow, 1957).

ev, in his dissertation on "The Annexation of Azerbaidzhan to Russia," was accused of holding that "between the sixteenth and nineteenth centuries, a real threat of the capture of the Caucasus by Persia or Turkey did not exist." From this premise he had concluded that "there could be no question of the progressive character of the annexation of Azerbaidzhan and the whole Caucasus to Russia." The dissertation of Dzhanaev (no initials given) on "The Annexation of Ossetia to Russia" was "written from a harmful, bourgeois nationalist position. Dzhanaev idealized the struggle of the mountain feudal leaders [!] against Russia." Both these dissertations had been approved by Professor I. Guseinov (not to be confused with Geidar Guseinov) of the faculty of the Azerbaidzhani State University. Matters went from bad to worse when Mekhtiev rose to acknowledge his errors. Trying to absolve his adviser from responsibility, he remarked that professors had far too much work to do, and only had time to read abstracts [*spetskursy*] of the dissertations of their graduate students. When all is said and done, perhaps the most revealing thing about this meeting is the fact that it had to be called at all. The bitter rebuke of several scholars in November for the same errors they had been criticized for in July by Bagirov indicates that they were stubbornly refusing to meet party demands.[29]

The wheels of rectification were also turning in Moscow. Most central publications were spared the humiliation of apologizing for favorable reviews of the Guseinov book by the plodding pace of their editors and reviewers. *Literaturnaia gazeta* was the exception, and it now gave more than equal space to a condemnation of "Guseinov's vicious book," repeating Bagirov's arguments and further incriminating the writers' organizations which had recom-

29. The full report on this meeting is in *Bakinskii rabochii*, November 16, 1950. A shorter report was published in *Kul'tura i zhizn'*, November 21, 1950 (complete translation in *CDSP*, II, No. 45, 38-39). The latter report, which confines itself to generalities about shortcomings and errors, contains nothing about the heretical dissertations. Mekhtiev later got back in step by writing an article for *Voprosy istorii* on the historical significance of the annexation of Azerbaidzhan. The article conformed to the Bagirov line perfectly and made frequent references to him. See G. G. Mekhtiev, "Istoricheskoe znachenie prisoedineniia Azerbaidzhana k Rossii," *VI*, No. 3, 1952, pp. 83-98. Mekhtiev also wrote a fifty-page pamphlet in the Azerbaidzhani language, entitled *The Annexation of Azerbaidzhan to Russia and its Historical Significance* (Baku, 1952), 10,300 copies of which were published (*Knizhnaia letopis'*, 1953, No. 697).

mended the book.[30] On September 22, the Presidium of the U.S.S.R. Academy of Sciences passed a sweeping resolution broadening the number of the condemned to include all the recent textbook authors who had written on the middle of the nineteenth century, as well as Bushuev and Magomedov, whose works had appeared more than a decade earlier.[31] The Institute of History was charged with laxity, especially for failing to carry out a resolution of the previous February "to extend scholarly assistance" to the Dagestan branch of the Academy.[32] The decree ordered several remedial measures. Magomedov was relieved of his duties as Vice Chairman of the Dagestan branch of the Academy. The Institute of History of the U.S.S.R. Academy of Sciences was to include assistance to the Dagestan branch in its 1951 plan, especially in writing a history of Dagestan. A subsidy of 150,000 rubles was allocated for the production of the new history. Scholarly meetings were to be held both in the central institutes of the Academy of Sciences and its Dagestan branch, with the results to be published. *Voprosy istorii* was asked to publish a number of articles elaborating the new interpretation. Rigid time limits were set for the scholarly meetings and the publication of their proceedings.[33]

The brief published reports of five of these meetings show how thoroughly the party drove its message home.[34] The new line was discussed not only by historians, but ethnographers, linguists, economists, and lawyers. Many speakers tried to make Pokrovskii responsible for the erroneous interpretation—an absurd argument, since after the middle 1930's, Pokrovskii's advocacy of any idea had the effect of the kiss of death. Most of the historians, including Druzhinin, Nechkina, and Bushuev, apologized in these sessions. Soviet writers repudiated fictional works on Shamil, attempting to show that Chernyshevskii, Dobroliubov, Lermontov, and Tolstoi had recognized the reactionary nature of the Shamil movement.

30. *Literaturnaia gazeta*, July 27, 1950; condensed translation in *CDSP*, II, No. 31, 42-43.

31. *Izvestiia Akademii Nauk SSSR. Otdelenie literaturi i iazyka*, No. 3, 1950, pp. 245-46; complete text translated in *CDSP*, II, No. 48, 13-14.

32. The February resolution and a report of the meeting at which it was adopted were published in *VAN SSSR*, No. 4, 1950, pp. 94-95. Magomedov, as head of the Dagestan history institute, was reprimanded on several counts for slovenly work of low ideological level, but the question of Shamil did not come up. The history of Dagestan, which was supposed to appear in 1951, actually went to press in 1957.

33. In general the central institutes met their deadlines. I can find no evidence, however, that the Dagestan branch ever held a meeting.

34. *VAN SSSR*, No. 12, 1950, pp. 89-90; No. 1, 1951, pp. 110-17.

In its September issue, *Voprosy istorii* published as a leading
article a discussion of the Bagirov article by the Dagestani party
leader, A. D. Daniialov, thus achieving almost instant compliance
with the resolution of the Presidium of the Academy of Sciences.[35]
Most of the arguments were shopworn. Daniialov spoke of the
"sympathy of the Dagestani people for Russia" and contended that
by the 1820's the area was on its way to peaceful unification with
Russia, when interference by Turkey and Britain was intensified.
He found new passages in Marx, Engels, and the "revolutionary
democrats" to support his view. Perhaps the most interesting rev-
elation was contained in a quotation from Magomedov, intended
to condemn him, but actually having the effect of showing party
censorship of publications on Shamil as far back as the 1930's:

> In 1937 [Magomedov had written], upon finishing my grad-
> uate work in Moscow, and arriving in Dagestan, I became
> fully engaged in studying the struggle of the mountain
> people for independence under the leadership of Shamil.
> I was struck by the fact that during the years of Soviet
> rule in Dagestan, not a single book was published about
> Shamil, and in the newspapers and journals published in
> Dagestan, there were no materials whatsoever about this
> subject. . . . Enemies of the people, bourgeois nationalists,
> who made their way into leading Party and Soviet posts,
> took all measures to show Shamil as a reactionary, fighting
> only for religious goals, and concealed documents about the
> real character of the struggle. I took it as my goal to show
> Shamil and his movement as a progressive phenomenon, as
> a bright page in the history of the peoples of Dagestan.[36]

35. A. Daniialov, "Ob izvrashcheniiakh v osveshchenii miuridizma i dvizheniia Shamilia," *VI*, No. 9, 1950, pp. 3-18. Since this issue of *VI* went to
press four days after the resolution, its editors may or may not have published
the article as a direct result of the meeting. It would have been possible to do
so because the article had already appeared as a ten-thousand-edition pamphlet
in Dagestan (see A. D. Daniialov, *Ob izvrashcheniiakh v osveshchenii miuridizma i dvizheniia Shamilia* [Makhachkala, 1950]). This appears to have been
Daniialov's speech to the Makhachkala party meeting in July.

36. R. M. Magomedov, *O dvizhenii Shamilia*, pp. 24-26, as quoted in A.
Daniialov, "Ob izvrashcheniiakh," pp. 16-17. I am unable to find even a solid
Soviet bibliographical reference to the Magomedov work quoted here. The
Daniialov footnote would indicate that it was a book or pamphlet, but it does
not appear in any of the official bibliographies of books and journal and
newspaper articles, or in the detailed bibliographies of historical works. It is
possible that Daniialov was referring to an unpublished manuscript, or to a
contribution to a larger work. It is also possible that the title was deleted
from bibliographies because it was considered a harmful "bourgeois nationalist" work. Deletions from the bibliographies of historical works are fairly

This passage was reproduced by Daniialov to prove that Magomedov's heretical views had been held many years ago. He also employed it to charge that "he uses local historical sources of a nationalist character, idealizing Shamil. . . ." But in view of the fact that
Magomedov was merely trying to publicize views that could be
found in any Soviet textbook, the quotation's main evidence was
something quite different. It clearly showed the party's restraining
hand on the popularization of Shamil by scholars working in his
homeland from local sources. Daniialov also made a serious tactical
blunder by giving wide currency to a quotation which might otherwise have gone almost unnoticed.[37]

In all this early discussion on the Shamil question, the voice of
Guseinov had been conspicuously silent. If he made any reply to
the charges against him, the editors must have considered it too
dangerous to publish. For a long time his fate was unknown, at
least to the outside world. More than a decade later, when detailed
accounts of the excesses of the Stalin period were in order, Bagirov's
successor as leader of the Azerbaidzhani party revealed, in the
course of a speech, that "Geidar Guseinov was driven to suicide
by Bagirov's threats."[38] The reason that was given was puzzling:
Guseinov had refused to allow Bagirov's name to appear as the
author of his book. If this charge is true, it is evident that Bagirov
only ascertained the villainous role of Shamil after 1949. In
this instance the high party official was no more skilled than the
scholar in divining the next turn of the party line.

---

common, but I have not yet found a clear case of a title being deleted from
the serial bibliographies, which are compiled immediately after publication.

37. Daniialov was not the only politician-turned-historian who used documents clumsily. W. W. Kulski has pointed out a self-defeating document
quoted by Bagirov in his *Bol'shevik* article. Inside the text of a Shamil letter,
which Bagirov intended to be incriminating, there is incontrovertible evidence
about the true nature of the struggle and the feeling of the mountain people
toward Russia. After referring to "Russia, this enemy of our whole nation,"
the letter goes on to state that "the only aspiration of the Cherkessi at all
times (as the whole world knows) is freedom, to which we have a true and
indisputable right." See W. W. Kulski, *The Soviet Regime: Communism in
Practice* (Syracuse, N.Y.: Syracuse University Press, 1954), pp. 104-5.

38. *Bakinskii rabochii*, November 30, 1961.

CHAPTER **8.**

CONSOLIDATING THE BAGIROV LINE

"Guided by Comrade Stalin's statements on the role of the great Russian people in the fraternal family of Soviet peoples, we must tirelessly educate our people, our youth, in the spirit of respect and love for our elder brother, the great Russian people. The work of elucidation and education on this question ought not to be done in trite phrases, such as fill many articles in certain of our journals, but must be based on historical documents, on concrete facts and examples from the common life and struggle of the peoples of our country under the leadership of our elder brother."
M. D. Bagirov in Kommunist, No. 3, 1953, p. 66.

Once the party had made its position clear on Shamil and Muridism, and had put its machinery in motion to impose the new view, Soviet historians were faced with a great deal of repair work. Not only did the Shamil case have numerous applications in the history of the other non-Russian peoples, but many long-held views on tsarist colonialism, foreign policy, and cultural history now stood in such stark contradiction to the new central themes of the party arguments that they had to be painstakingly re-examined. The task was further complicated by the fact that the party line was changing—pushed to greater extremes by party spokesmen and the more compliant historians. The Soviet historian was trying to measure an object that was itself in rather erratic motion. Between the spring of 1950 and Stalin's death in March, 1953 (and more important to our study, the fall of Bagirov a month later), the main preoccupation of Soviet historians concerned with the history of the non-Russian peoples was the frustrating task of bringing some semblance of order to this confused picture.

FROM SHAMIL TO KENESARY

The Shamil pronouncements could obviously be applied to Kenesary, but for six months the Kazakh problem lay dormant while the other controversy ran its course. Bekmakhanov disappeared from print at about the time of the retraction of Guseinov's Stalin Prize. During 1950 *Voprosy istorii* published only one article on Central Asian history in the modern period, a study on the question of the annexation of Northern Kirgizia, in which the author took the view, in line with current developments, that annexation of that area had been "voluntary and did not involve any serious opposition from the masses."[1]

The long overdue statement on Kazakh history came at the end of the year in *Pravda's* article, "For a Marxist-Leninist Elucidation of the Problems of the History of Kazakhstan," by a trio of historians who had been active in the discussion: Shoinbaev, Aidarova, and Iakunin.[2] In some respects it was parallel to the Bagirov article on the Caucasus, but it showed more evidences of the work of professional historians. The authors did not seem to be striving as much for documentary proofs and were far less fulsome in their praise for the elder brother. They derived their conclusions from a fresh analysis of the class struggle among the Kazakhs. They rejected the national liberation character of the Kenesary movement, resorting to the dissection technique, but with a new tack. They contended that there had been a popular national liberation movement in Kazakhstan in the 1830's: the rebellion of Isatai Taimanov, which preceded the Kenesary movement by two years. Kenesary had usurped this mass movement in an effort to restore the feudal privileges that had been abrogated by the Russians in 1822. "The political demands of Kenesary amounted to the restoration of the medieval power of the khan and separation of Kazakhstan from Russia"—both of which were reactionary. Thus the movement was popular up to 1838, and feudal thereafter. Such a neat scheme left the authors with one awkward contradiction: how to explain the large following of Kenesary's feudal movement. Their reasoning involved an admission that the masses are not always politically astute—that indeed they had been momentarily misled. According

1. A. Khasanov, "O prisoedinenii severnykh Kirgizov k Rossii," *VI*, No. 7, 1950, pp. 126-31.
2. T. Shoinbaev, Kh. Aidarova, and A. Iakunin, "Za marksistsko-leninskoe osveshchenie voprosov istorii Kazakhstana," *Pravda*, December 26, 1950; translation in *CDSP*, II, No. 52, 14-16.

to this new view, the Kazakh people had participated in the Taimanov rebellion, and even in the early stages of the Kenesary movement, but they had deserted Kenesary when his reactionary goals
became apparent:

> Certain groups of the Kazakh workers, which joined
> Kenesary's movement at the beginning, became convinced
> that Sultan Kenesary would not only not give them relief,
> but, on the contrary, would make the feudal-patriarchal yoke
> more oppressive. . . . As a result, the groups of Kazakh
> workers, which at first joined the Kenesary movement, later
> left it. The feudal bands of Kenesary, his kinsmen and
> other feudal lords, constituted the main force of the move-
> ment. . . . Numerous documents [none were cited] show
> that the Kazakh working masses not only did not want to
> join Kenesary but also in a number of cases rose in arms
> against him.

Bekmakhanov was blamed for the prevalence of the erroneous
view. His mistakes had resulted from "ignoring the class structure
of Kazakh society." The authors of the article denied that Kenesary had made reforms or had intended to lead the Kazakhs to a
peaceful existence under a strong government. "Actually Kenesary
did not extinguish the inter-tribal struggle, but inflamed it." Bekmakhanov had been "silent on the main point—the special interest
of the Central Asian khanates in Kenesary's struggle against Russia"; in reality their attempts "to extend their influence over Kazakhstan by support of Kenesary reflected their desire to hinder the
annexation of Kazakhstan to Russia." Bekmakhanov not only had
underestimated the threat from the British, but had treated Russia
and the "khanates on the same level, by reference to their aggression against Kazakhstan."

The conclusion of the article was printed in bold-faced type:
"All historical data indicate that the Kenesary movement was
neither revolutionary nor progressive. It was a reactionary movement which dragged the Kazakh people back, toward the strengthening of patriarchal-feudal principles, toward a restoration of the
medieval khan regime and the separation of Kazakhstan from Russia and the great Russian people."

Among the trio of authors, Aidarova had been the most consistent, having advocated most of these ideas since the beginning of
the controversy. The other two had held different views until recently. Shoinbaev had still maintained in 1949 in his book on the

Dzhankozhi revolt that the Kenesary movement was of a national liberation character, and Iakunin did not contest the point in his review of Shoinbaev's book, though he did mention the "feudal" nature of the revolt in passing.[3] The specific formula for the interpretation of the revolt smacks of Iakunin, who had, at the Moscow discussion early in 1948, suggested that the revolt be divided on the basis of its domestic and foreign policy aims,[4] and in 1949 had anticipated the newest view by stating that Kenesary usurped an already existing movement.[5]

Once *Pravda* had spoken, the historians and party leaders of Kazakhstan had their work cut out for them. In February, 1951, the Learned Council of the Institute of History of the U.S.S.R. Academy of Sciences held a discussion on the article.[6] The cast of characters was similar to the Moscow meeting on Bekmakhanov's book early in 1948: Pankratova, Viatkin, and Druzhinin were principal speakers. But the tone was entirely different. Bekmakhanov had no defenders, and in the session of self-criticism most of the speakers added new arguments against him. In the general confession of error, nearly everyone was involved. Pankratova, who had been associated with Kazakh histories all the way back to 1943, made a revealing confession. She and her colleagues, she said, "considered the participation in a movement by the popular masses with a liberation slogan to be the determining factor in the character of the movement." Indeed, one would think that Marxists would weigh heavily the action of the masses, but a wiser Pankratova now acknowledged some new party thinking on the question. It was evident that the masses could be misled, that they sometimes deserted a movement in midstream, and what was more perplexing, it was possible that the masses had never supported a given movement in the first place (Shamil's "feudal" movement). In her view the inconsistencies had nothing to do with Marxist theory or the party, but with the failure of historians to see the light: the errors had resulted from "an unskillful correlation of concrete research with profound study of the classics of Marxism-Leninism." Authors and editors of other recent textbooks acknowledged error; the editors of *Voprosy istorii* were reprimanded for publishing Sharipov's confusing review of the Bekmakhanov book; the authors of

3. *VI*, No. 8, 1950, pp. 125-27.
4. See Chapter 6 above, p. 118.
5. *VI*, No. 3, 1949, p. 127.
6. "V otdelenii istorii i filosofii akademii nauk SSSR," *Izvestiia Akademii Nauk SSSR. Seriia filosofii*, VIII (1951), No. 2, 195-201.

articles in the *Great Soviet Encyclopedia* had made numerous errors; the survey histories of the Uzbeks, Kazakhs, and Tadzhiks, which had appeared between 1947 and 1950, would have to be revised immediately.

On April 10, 1951, the Bureau of the Kazakh party's Central Committee discussed the *Pravda* article and issued a resolution accepting its criticism as correct. In the resolution, Bekmakhanov was accused of "juggling quotations and facts" in order to reach his erroneous interpretation. The tone of the resolution revealed a special effort of the Kazakhs to placate the central party on the sensitive question of Russian-Kazakh relations. One of the worst features of Kenesary's policy was that he had tried "to tear Kazakhstan away from Russia and restore the power of his line of khans." Bekmakhanov had made no effort "to reveal the deeply progressive significance of the annexation of Kazakhstan to Russia." Kazakh historians were told that they must "combat all attempts to destroy the history of the Kazakh people and its continuous friendship with the great Russian people."[7]

In the same month the Learned Council of the Institute of History, Archeology, and Ethnography of the Kazakh Academy of Sciences held a meeting in Alma-Ata to hear and discuss a report by Shoinbaev. The report, which was largely a repetition of the *Pravda* article, was followed by further condemnations of Bekmakhanov, and the adoption of a resolution to fulfill the order of the Kazakh party's Central Committee. At the conclusion of the discussion the scholars of the Council addressed themselves to the final degradation of their hapless colleague. An appeal was sent to the Ministry of Higher Education of the U.S.S.R. requesting it to deprive Bekmakhanov of the title of professor and "the degrees of *Kandidat* and doctor of historical science, which were incorrectly conferred on him for harmful, bourgeois nationalist works." The following October Bekmakhanov's title and degrees were rescinded, as were those of another Kazakh historian, Dil'mukhamedov, who had written a dissertation on Kenesary in 1940 and had given Bekmakhanov's book a favorable review in a Kazakh journal.[8]

Very little was heard of the Kazakh historian between this humiliation and his reappearance in print in 1956, but apparently

7. "Za marksistsko-leninskoe osveshchenie voprosov istorii Kazakhstana," *Pravda*, April 25, 1951; complete translation in *CDSP*, III, No. 17, pp. 12, 18.

8. "V institute istorii, arkheologii i etnografii akademii nauk kazakhskoi SSR," *VI*, No. 2, 1952, pp. 146-51.

he still had his friends and supporters. One of the rare references to Bekmakhanov occurred in *Pravda* late in 1952, in the course of a critical article on the Kazakh State University. In enumerating the sins of the rector, who had aroused the anger of his students by tearing down their wall newspaper, *Pravda* mentioned that he was still protecting "such exposed nationalists as Bekmakhanov, Suleimenov, and others."[9]

During the spring and summer of 1951 work on the third attempt at a survey history of Kazakhstan proceeded with urgency. The work was being edited by critics of Bekmakhanov, including Aidarova, Shoinbaev, and Tolybekov. A "prospectus" of the book, consisting of a thousand copies each in Russian and Kazakh, was distributed for broad discussion. Progress reports indicated that the Kazakh Central Committee resolution was being complied with in the book:

> A central place in the new edition of the *History of the Kazakh S.S.R.* is occupied by the question of the annexation of Kazakhstan to Russia. The historians of Kazakhstan are taking up their tasks not only to show the progressive character of the annexation of Kazakhstan to Russia, but to demonstrate by concrete historical materials the great significance of this event for the historic destiny of the Kazakh people, to demonstrate the historic roots of friendship of the great Russian and Kazakh peoples, to show how the liberation struggle of the Kazakh workers was influenced in the common current of the liberation struggle in Russia, to show the striving of the Kazakh workers for voluntary submission to Russian rule.[10]

A report of one of the discussions listed some recommendations of the participants: more emphasis should be given to "the ties of Kazakhstan with Rus in ancient and medieval times" [!]; further elaboration of "the preconditions of the annexation of Kazakhstan to Russia, and especially those underlying the voluntary nature of this annexation"; and a deeper study of "the economic development of Kazakhstan after annexation." At the same time some questions were not fully resolved at these discussions. These included the old sticklers: periodization, "the character of certain national movements," and the nature of feudal relationships in Kazakhstan.[11]

9. E. Makarov, "V kazakhskom universitete zazhimaiut kritiku," *Pravda,* November 22, 1952.

10. *VI,* No. 2, 1952, p. 149.

11. B. Sandzhiev, "Rabota nad pervym tomom 'Istorii kazakhskoi SSR,'"

Late in 1951 the Kazakh party carried out a widespread purge of scholars and party officials in its belated campaign against bourgeois nationalism. Among those who lost their positions were Omarov, the party secretary who had been co-editor of the 1949 history, and Sharipov, who was held responsible for too tolerant an attitude toward Bekmakhanov, and for writing articles about his book that confused the issue. It was pointed out that one of Sharipov's articles commemorated the one-hundredth anniversary of Sultan Kenesary's death, a tactical error in itself. At a meeting of the Kazakh Central Committee in October, charges of laxity on matters of Kazakh nationalism reached even the First Secretary of the Kazakh party, Zh. Shaiakhmetov, but he managed to save his post by apologizing profusely for his own past errors (including the writing of an article in 1944 for a Kazakh newspaper in which he idealized Kenesary) and by leading the purge of other bourgeois nationalists.[12]

In his report to the Nineteenth Party Congress a year later, Shaiakhmetov reported that all bourgeois nationalists had been removed, and allowed himself a little recrimination against the leadership in Moscow. "The Institute of History of the Academy of Sciences of the U.S.S.R.," he observed, "was of no help in clarifying our errors, but only succeeded in complicating them by officially recognizing that the Kenesary movement was a national liberation movement, although it was reactionary from beginning to end."[13]

THE OTHER REPUBLICS

Developments in Kazakh history were soon reflected in the rest of Central Asia. In its April, 1951, issue, the editors of *Voprosy istorii*, who had been under attack for detachment and lack of leadership on these questions, showed a more militant attitude in a long leading editorial "On Certain Questions of the History of the Peoples of Central Asia."[14] It was a blunderbuss attack on

VAN SSSR, No. 12, 1951, pp. 86-88. See also V. F. Shakhmatov and G. F. Dakhshleiger, "K itogam obsuzhdeniia maketa 1-go toma 'Istorii kazakhskoi SSR,'" *VAN kazakhskoi SSR*, No. 7, 1953, pp. 9-20.

12. *Pravda*, September 29, 1951; October 20, 1951; December 14, 1951; Serge A. Zenkovsky, "Ideological Deviation in Soviet Central Asia," *Slavonic and East European Review*, XXXII (1953-54), 429-31.

13. *Pravda*, October 8, 1952; condensed translation in *CDSP*, IV, No. 46, 9-10.

14. "O nekotorykh voprosakh istorii narodov Srednei Azii," *VI*, No. 4, 1951, pp. 3-15.

dozens of historians, for works written as much as a decade earlier (*Voprosy istorii* had never taken a public stand on the 1943 Kazakh history, whose "especially grave errors" it now condemned). Taking the friendship of peoples and the progressiveness of annexation as the central themes, the editorial picked out and condemned numerous passages in recent works. The high-ranking B. G. Gafurov was rebuked for a statement in his *History of the Tadzhik People* (1949) that capitalism would have developed in Central Asia whether the Russians had come or not "and possibly at an even faster pace than under the colonial conditions."[15] S. M. Abramzon's *Sketches on the Culture of the Kirgiz People* (1946) had belittled the cultural role of the Russians by limiting discussion "merely to the fact that the Kirgiz learned to whitewash their walls, to use forks, beds, and samovars, and to hang curtains over their windows."[16] The histories of the Kazakhs had grossly underestimated the economic improvements of the colonial period.

The editors indicated that there must be a re-examination of the whole range of Central Asian history, from ancient times to the present. Historians had failed to show that even in ancient times the Central Asian peoples had struggled against their "natural enemies," the Arabs and Persians (this theme would support the solidarity of the future members of the Soviet family and show that there had never been a tendency toward alliance with "foreigners"). As for recent history, the article gave detailed attention to events between 1905 and the formation of the U.S.S.R., noting the mistakes of several historians on the evaluation of leaders and movements in Central Asia. Although these arguments were put in terms of nationalism and reactionary religious ideology, it was easy to see from the total discussion that henceforth any leader or movement that had advocated separatism, either by the method of forming independent states or allying with foreign powers, was to be regarded as reactionary.

Among the historians of the other Central Asian republics, the

15. B. G. Gafurov, *Istoriia tadzhikskogo naroda v kratkom izlozhenii* (Moscow, 1949), p. 410. Gafurov replied in a long article in *Kommunist Tadzhikistana* in which he pointed out his errors and explained their cause. He stated that a corrected edition, based on Stalin's works, was in progress. His article devoted much space to the "urgent tasks ahead" theme, indicating that he was still in command of the situation. See "Za marksistskoe osveshchenie istorii tadzhikskogo naroda i istorii ego kul'tury," *Kommunist Tadzhikistana*, July 25-26, 1951.

16. S. M. Abramzon, *Ocherk kul'tury kirgizskogo naroda* (Frunze, 1946), p. 75.

Kirgiz received the most attention. Already in 1950 the Kirgiz Institute of Language, Literature, and History had been instructed by the U.S.S.R. Academy of Sciences to make staff changes, to revise its syllabus, and to send ten advanced graduate students to Moscow for study.[17] B. Dzhamgerchinov, who would later come to prominence by writing three monographs on the progressive significance of the annexation of the Kirgiz, became director of the Institute. The reform was apparently not considered satisfactory, and the Institute was the object of another resolution of the U.S.S.R. Academy of Sciences in February, 1952.[18] This resolution censured old works of Abramzon and Bernshtam, who had been attacked earlier for their bourgeois nationalist interpretations. Apparently they had not recanted and their influence was widespread. Kirgiz historians were asked to engage in self-criticism and to organize conferences on critical questions. Shortly thereafter, M. P. Kim filled in the details in an article "On Errors in the Scholarly Works on the History of Kirgizia."[19] Both historians had completely missed the significance of the annexation of the Kirgiz, and had considered reactionary feudal movements to be progressive. Bernshtam was in particular error for idealizing the nineteenth-century Kirgiz leader Ormon Khan and his regime, comparing it "in miniature to the century of Ivan Groznyi in Russia."[20] Kirgiz historians had not given a correct evaluation of the coming of the Russians; Abramzon had represented it "as typical colonial conquest" and Bernshtam had compared it to the conquest of Kirgizia by the Manchus, and by the Kalmyk and Kokand khans.

The Central Committee of the Turkmen Communist party discussed and criticized several bourgeois nationalist works at its meeting in December, 1951. Turkmen historians were accused of idealizing epic heroes, as well as reactionary groups at the time of the Revolution.[21] As has been noted earlier, the Turkmen scholars had been scolded in 1948 for bourgeois nationalist distortions in a collection of documents on Russian-Turkmen relations. Incorrect elaboration of this subject was still evident at the end of

17. *VAN SSSR*, No. 12, 1950, pp. 77-79; Zenkovsky, "Ideological Deviation," pp. 426-27.
18. *VAN SSSR*, No. 3, 1952, pp. 81-82.
19. M. P. Kim, "Ob oshibkakh v nauchnykh rabotakh po istorii Kirgizii," *ibid.*, No. 5, 1952, pp. 43-51.
20. This view had been stated in 1945, when the cult of Ivan was growing, and there was a great emphasis on the virtues of a strong central government.
21. *Turkmenskaia iskra*, January 12, 1952.

1952, when the Turkmen party journal, *Kommunist Turkmenistana,* reviewed the problem editorially.[22] The historian A. Karryev was singled out for reprimand for his views as expressed in two recent articles. Having chosen to write about the question of Russians and the peoples of Central Asia, Karryev, according to the editorial, was obliged "to show how the mutual relations of the Russian and Turkmen peoples were historically formed, how ties between them were strengthened, and how, in spite of the colonial policy of tsarism, these strengthened ties prepared the ground for the unbreakable and brotherly friendship which arose between them. . . ." This was not the case, however. Judging from the editorial, Karryev had formulated some highly original views on Russian-Turkmen relations. In one article, he was accused of asserting that "the Turkmen tribes strived for closer relations with Russia, but Russia spurned this closer relationship in every way." In the second article he advanced the idea that "only the weak and backward Turkmen tribes" sought closer ties, and that stronger tribes opposed annexation to Russia. Not only this, but Karryev maintained that such a strong tribe as the Akhal-teke "would have been able to unite Turkmenistan under its own aegis and to create an independent state." Completely wrong, said the editors of the party journal. Opposition to annexation to Russia was expressed only by Kirgiz feudal lords, who were hoping to retain their old privileges, and in view of the foreign predators waiting to take over the Kirgiz tribes, the chances of forming a unified independent government were nil.

Historians of the other Central Asian republics came off somewhat better. The history of the Uzbeks had been written to a considerable extent by Russians. The second volume of the survey history, covering the sensitive period of the nineteenth century, had the misfortune to appear before the first volume (and before the switch in the party line). Bakhrushin, the principal editor, came under heavy criticism for its assessment of revolts and relations with the Russians.[23] Volume I, on the earlier period, appeared

22. Reprinted in the Moscow *Kommunist:* "Vospityvat' kadry v dukhe neprimirimosti k ideologicheskim izvrashcheniiam," *Kommunist,* No. 2, 1953, pp. 113-20.

23. *Istoriia narodov Uzbekistana,* ed. S. V. Bakhrushin, V. Ia. Nepomnin, and V. A. Shishkin (Tashkent, 1947), Vol. II. This volume was still under attack at the Uzbek Central Committee meeting of February, 1952. See *Pravda,* February 27, 1952.

in 1950 and was somewhat better received.[24] Historical writing
on the Tadzhiks seems to have been under the control of Gafurov,
who made as many grievous errors as the rest, but hurried to correct them. His *History of the Tadzhik People*, which appeared in
Russian in 1949 and was severely criticized, was revised in 1952
and 1955. Gufurov, the Tadzhik Party Secretary, was the only individual historian to write a survey history of a Union Republic
in this period; all the others were written by collectives.

Along with their other bourgeois nationalist ideas, the historians
of Central Asia were criticized for the idealization of their great
folk epics. This is a vast subject in itself, but since it involved
historians and their interpretation of heroes, some brief mention
of it should be made here. Up to the end of World War II these
epics, of which the most famous were "Manas" (Kirgiz), "Korkut
Ata" (Turkmen and Azeri) and "Alpamish" (Uzbek), were considered to be among the most honored works in the literary heritage
of these peoples. In a real sense these oral epics constituted their
past history. But their main subjects, the feats of heroes in battle,
came into conflict with the new views. The main figures were
feudal leaders, and continued respect for them was now considered
an idealization of a class enemy, a reactionary past, and of warlike
activity in general. The ideological authorities cracked down fiercely on the epics during the drive on bourgeois nationalism. "Alpamish," according to one spokesman, "is impregnated with a reactionary and feudal sentiment, exhales Muslim fanaticism and preaches
hatred of the foreigner and of the unbeliever."[25] These epics disappeared from libraries; exhibits on their heroes were removed from
museums, and such Soviet editions as did appear were expurgated.[26]
Beneath the talk of idealization of the feudal past, there were two
considerations, related to history and the nationalities problem, that

24. *Istoriia narodov Uzbekistana*, ed. S. P. Tolstov, B. Iu. Zakhidov, and
Ia. G. Guliamov (Tashkent, 1950), Vol. I.

25. Quoted from *Literaturnaia gazeta* by A. Bennigsen in "The Muslim
Peoples of the Soviet Union and the Soviets," Part 3, *Islamic Review*, XLIII
(1955), No. 6, p. 15. See also Z. W. Togan, "Soviet Cultural Policy in Central
Asia," *The USSR Today and Tomorrow. Proceedings of the Conference of the
Institute for the Study of the History and Culture of the USSR, Munich, April
15-17, 1953* (Munich, 1953), pp. 42-48; Olaf Caroe, *Soviet Empire: The
Turks of Central Asia and Stalinism* (London: The Macmillan Co., 1953), pp.
234-37.

26. The purge of museums took place between February and May, 1952.
Museum directors were charged with underestimating Russian influence on
the non-Russian peoples. See Bertram D. Wolfe, "Operation Rewrite: the
Agony of Soviet Historians," *Foreign Affairs*, XXXI (1952-53), 39-57.

undoubtedly loomed large in the minds of those who ordered the condemnation of the epics. Study of the epics furthered not only a love of warfare, but of warfare among the ancestors of the Soviet peoples. Furthermore, it is probable that the ideological authorities thought that the cultivation of any national hero, no matter how far removed in the past, was a dangerous phenomenon in the current cultural climate of the non-Russian regions.

Condemnation of the epics was only one means by which the party sought to bring literature into line with the friendship of peoples. The journal *Druzhba narodov* (*Friendship of Peoples*), an organ of the Union of Soviet Writers, was considered of vital importance in this period in educating the masses by introducing them to the contemporary literature of other Soviet peoples, in Russian translation. This journal, which had been published since 1939, was expanded from two to six numbers per year in 1947, and became a monthly in 1955. The editors were periodically taken to task for choosing selections that did nothing to promote friendship and sometimes hindered it. Their most usual errors consisted of publishing materials that were apolitical, that idealized the past, belittled the Soviet present, or smacked of "local nationalism," which was not compatible with Soviet patriotism. In one such attack on the journal, *Pravda* singled out for ridicule a poem called "Road of the Horseman," by a Kabardinian writer, Alim Keshokov.[27] In this fantasy, the poet yearned for a magic horse that would give the dreamer a chance to ride away as far as the Milky Way. Without acknowledging that the poet probably alluded to physical escape from the U.S.S.R., *Pravda* scored it as a "muddled" work that idealized the past and contained nothing relevant to present problems. The editors had chosen works "divorced from life." In the last year and a half *Druzhba narodov* had ignored the problems of the working class, "American imperialism," and other current questions that bound Soviet peoples together. It had concentrated heavily on rural scenes and the past. At about the same time *Pravda* attacked the popular poem, "Love the Ukraine," by V. Sosyura, which had been highly praised during the war.[28] The trouble was that the poet extolled the "wide open spaces of ancient Ukraine," and said

27. P. Brovka and P. Panchenko, "Al'manakh, otstaiushchii ot zhizhni," *Pravda*, August 8, 1951.
28. "Protiv ideologicheskikh izvrashchenii v literature," *Pravda*, July 2, 1951; see also Yaroslav Bilinsky, *The Second Soviet Republic: The Ukraine After World War II* (New Brunswick, N.J.: Rutgers University Press, 1964), pp. 15-16.

nothing about the new industrial Ukraine. What was less clear, but no doubt more important, was that love of country, according to the requirements of Soviet patriotism, must involve the Soviet motherland, and not just one non-Russian part of it. A. Korneichuk, the author of many successful political plays, was criticized for the libretto of the opera "Bogdan Khmel'nitskii," because the work did not depict the attitude of the Ukrainians as being sufficiently anti-Polish or pro-Russian.[29]

The ritual of compliance carried out in Central Asia had no counterpart in the North Caucasus. If the scholarly assistance proffered by the Academy of Sciences in Moscow in 1951 for the North Caucasus was actually received, it was not reflected in print; the works in progress on the history of the area appeared only in the late 1950's. The historians and linguists of Northern Ossetia were lectured for their errors by *Pravda* in 1951 and 1952.[30] Apparently the most serious situation existed in Dagestan, Shamil's homeland, where the local branch of the party itself was implicated in bourgeois nationalist views and practices. In October, 1951, a *Pravda* correspondent reported from Makhachkala that the Dagestan party had not learned any lessons from recent events; that it was failing miserably in ideological work; that it was in fact looking the other way and was not aware of what was going on in its area.[31] The local party, jolted into action by this criticism, acknowledged its errors and organized a seminar to run for four months. It was to feature lectures and discussions on four critical subjects, including "the reactionary essence of Muridism and the Shamil movement."[32] Also indicative of the recalcitrance of the North Caucasus was the fact that no local historians rushed in to join in the denunciation of Guseinov, as had been the case in the Bekmakhanov controversy. M. S. Totoev, who would later become the most prominent historian of the area, was himself criticized for bourgeois nationalist views in the early 1950's.

29. "Ob opere 'Bogdan Khmel'nitskii,' " *Pravda*, July 20, 1951.
30. I. Barits, "Pokhod protiv 'burzhuaznogo natsionalizma,' " Part 4, *Svobodnyi Kavkaz*, pp. 25-26.
31. A. Zenchenko, "Chto pokazali pervye dni ucheby," *Pravda*, October 15, 1951.
32. Barits, "Pokhod protiv 'burzhuaznogo nationalizma,' " Part 4, p. 24. *Pravda* continued to complain about the low caliber of ideological work in Dagestan in articles published on December 19, 1951, and May 18, 1952.

LIQUIDATING THE EVIL IN THE "LESSER EVIL" FORMULA

With the growing emphasis on the progressiveness of all Russian annexations and the benefits derived by the non-Russians, discussion of the evils of Russian colonialism all but disappeared. Thus the old "lesser evil" formula became—to use the Soviet expression—further out of step with reality, divorced from life. Elaboration of two themes, at the extreme ends of the subject, contributed to the obsolescence of the formula. On the one hand there was a decided intensification of the "foreign threats" to the freedom of the non-Russians, particularly the threat of "British imperialism" in the Caucasus and Central Asia. At the other end of the spectrum there was a new emphasis on the cultural and economic blessings the annexed peoples had received from their Russian "elder brother," a theme which did not reach its full flower until the eve of Stalin's death. Thus the theoretical greater evil (being "swallowed up" by imperialists or reactionary feudal regimes) was multiplied, and the lesser evil of annexation disappeared so completely that the use of the term became embarrassing.

The new emphasis on the "foreign threat" to non-Russians on the eve of their annexation can be traced in the articles *Voprosy istorii* published on Shamil, in compliance with the Academy of Sciences resolution of September 22, 1950. In the course of the next two years the journal published five articles on the subject. All of them dealt with the theme of British and Turkish support for the Shamil movement, and the latter four were almost entirely on this subject. A. D. Daniialov's article on the whole range of distortions on the question (discussed in the last chapter) was peppered with references to Shamil's foreign support. In the second article, the almost legendary Sheik Mansur, who had been regarded as the predecessor of Shamil, and leader of a national liberation movement of the 1780's, was pictured as the coordinator of Turkish plots against Russia. The inhabitants of the Caucasus, it was said, had sought Russian protection since the sixteenth century against the Turks and Persians. Since the eighteenth century Britain and France had been active in intrigues designed to gain control of the areas.[33] The third article was apparently aimed at giving Soviet researchers some leads for establishing the relationship of Shamil and "foreign agents" who worked together on plans "aimed at set-

---

33. N. Smirnov, "Sheikh Mansur i ego turetskie vdokhnoviteli," *VI*, No. 10, 1950, pp. 19-39.

ting the Caucasian mountaineers against Russia." The authors called
attention to Shamil's correspondence, Russian foreign office papers,
and the letters of British agents as sources of this information. They
gave samples of the incriminating evidence from fifteen letters and
documents.[34] The path suggested by this article was followed in
two later ones, which emphasized the defensive nature of Russian
policies, in contrast to the aggressive plans of the British and Turks,
and sought to show that Shamil had close ties with the Turkish
army (holding the rank of marshal) and that Muridism was a mere
tool of the foreign powers.[35]

It was obvious, in view of this line of thinking, that the "lesser
evil" formula, in its original application, was not adequate to the
new interpretation, and *Voprosy istorii* carried out a discussion of
the concept in 1951. The veteran M. V. Nechkina, who had been
seeking Marxist formulations to historical interpretations as early
as the Conference of Marxist Historians in the late 1920's, opened
the question with a letter to the editors of the journal.[36] She
approached the problem with great caution, taking care not to
place any blame for the inadequacies of the "lesser evil" formula
on its real author, the party, and not admitting that Marxist-Leninist formulations had changed since 1937. Instead, she characteristically blamed the members of her profession, who had applied
it incorrectly. She argued that the formula had been intended for
a very restricted application, that the "evil" was only political
(tsarist colonial oppression) and was only temporary. Under no
circumstances was the formula intended to cover cultural or economic questions. "It is quite clear," said Nechkina, "that the expression 'evil' refers to the absence of state independence and the
suppression of the people by tsarism; it refers to the heavy weight
of the colonial policy of Russian tsarism." As for "the absence of
state independence," Bagirov and others had already shown that
under the historical conditions that existed, real independence was
out of the question. What it boiled down to was that the formula

34. E. Adamov and L. Kutakov, "Iz istorii proiskov inostrannoi agentury vo
vremia kavkazskikh voin," *ibid.*, No. 11, 1950, pp. 101-5.
35. A. Fadeev, "Miuridizm kak orudie agressivnoi Turtsii i Anglii na severozapadnom kavkaze v XIX stoletii, *ibid.*, No. 9, 1951, pp. 76-97; E. E. Burch-
uladze, "Krushenie anglo-turechikh planov v Gruzie v 1855-6 godakh," *ibid.*,
No. 4, 1952, pp. 10-24.
36. M. Nechkina, "K voprosu o formule 'naimen'shee zlo,'" *ibid.*, No. 4,
1951, pp. 44-48. See Konstantin F. Shteppa's essay "The 'Lesser Evil' Formula" in C. E. Black (ed.), *Rewriting Russian History* (New York: Frederick
A. Praeger, 1956), pp. 107-20.

was to be applied only to tsarist colonial policies in the period between annexation and the Revolution. Thus, application of the formula would in no way deny the great cultural and economic benefits derived from annexation, or the long-range political blessings brought by the Revolution. Nechkina was recommending that the technique of dissection, which had been successfully applied to revolts, should be applied to the formula. It was apparent, however, that the word "evil" itself grated on her: "any lesser evil is an evil all the same, that is, a negative conception."

The last half of her letter showed how the Nechkina version of the "lesser evil" formula would work in practice. The concept that "tsarism[37] was the prison of peoples," she said, "was profoundly true. In this prison also suffered the elder brother of the peoples of our country, the great Russian people." In reality tsarist expansion had had a part in creating the community of peoples that eventually destroyed tsarism. This association was to have major emphasis: "Consequently, when evaluating the results of the incorporation of peoples into tsarist Russia, historians must pay particular attention to the community of peoples, to the new and positive contributions made by the great Russian people, in spite of tsarism, to the economic and cultural life of the peoples. The task of historians is to depict in historical perspective the unification and the struggle of the working people of the various peoples under the leadership of the elder brother, the great Russian people. . . ."

In later issues of that year *Voprosy istorii* published several letters from historians in the non-Russian areas in reply to the Nechkina letter. The common factor in all of them was a recitation of new evidences of the friendship of peoples—even before annexation—and of the blessings of inclusion in the Russian state. The reader of the journal acquired such new pieces of information as these: that Moslems living in the Caucasus flooded General Paskevich with requests to join his armies against their "age-old enemies," and that their performance was highly praised by the

37. Nechkina "forgot" the exact wording of another well-known formula: "tsarist *Russia* was the prison of peoples." By substituting "tsarism" she removed any taint from the Russian people and blamed the class enemy. Moreover, she referred elsewhere to "Russian tsarism" by employing the term *rossiiskii,* referring to the whole empire, rather than the more usual *russkii,* connoting the Great Russian people. A small essay could be written on Nechkina's careful use of words in this letter. For example, peoples were "swallowed up" by Persia or Turkey, but were either "incorporated" or "found themselves within the frontiers" of Russia.

General;[38] that Lenin had shown how Russian annexation "historically played an objectively progressive role" in the economic life of the non-Russian peoples;[39] that Russian annexation saved the Armenian people from physical extinction;[40] that in the siege of Kazan, Ivan the Terrible's forces had no quarrel with the local inhabitants.[41]

Iakunin entered the discussion at the end of the year. His comment on Nechkina's letter was the only one that appeared to be in substantial disagreement. He could not agree to Nechkina's limited application of the formula, insisting that it was applicable to every situation. He also objected to Nechkina's emphasis on evaluating the experience of each people from the point of view of results alone. "The historian's task is to explain the entire complex of internal and external political conditions under which a people was annexed to Russia. The 'lesser evil' formula is scientifically correct and merely requires skillful application." Thus Iakunin did not disagree with Nechkina on basic matters; he merely thought that the same conclusions could be reached without use of the scheme she had suggested.[42]

If Iakunin was writing as a party watchdog, as the tone of his letter suggests, his error was more serious than Nechkina's because the party soon showed its displeasure with the whole discussion. In July, 1952, in the course of a general critique of the shortcomings of *Voprosy istorii*, *Bol'shevik* pointed out that the journal had not dealt correctly with the whole question of the progressiveness of annexation. It had failed to elaborate the importance of economic forces and the formation of "bourgeois nations" among the non-Russian peoples as a result of their economic advancement after coming into the Russian state. Furthermore, *Voprosy istorii* editors "introduced confusion on questions which were by no means under discussion and had long been decided by Marxism-Leninism. Mistaken views on these questions were evident in the discussion which the journal organized on Prof. M. V. Nechkina's letter 'On the Question of the "Lesser Evil" Formula.' "[43]

38. Letter of M. Mustafaev, *VI*, No. 9, 1951, pp. 97-101.
39. *Ibid.*
40. Letter of N. Tavakalian, *ibid.*, No. 9, 1951, pp. 101-7.
41. Letter of K. Naiakshin, *ibid.*, No. 9, 1951, pp. 108-11.
42. A. Iakunin, "O primenenii poniatiia 'naimen'shee zlo' v otsenke prisoedineniia k Rossii nerusskikh narodnostei," *ibid.*, No. 11, 1951, pp. 83-86.
43. L. Maksimov, "O zhurnale 'Voprosy istorii,'" *Bol'shevik*, No. 13, 1952, pp. 60-70.

Shortly thereafter, in his speech to the Nineteenth Party Congress, Bagirov also reprimanded *Voprosy istorii* for having "concocted a pointless discussion" on the question: "It is not known what the journal's goal was in this discussion, but in any event it did not help our cadres in the national republics in their struggle against bourgeois nationalism in matters of history, not to mention the actual harm done. This is what took place instead of a presentation of the full progressive and fruitful nature of Russia's annexation of non-Russian peoples on the basis of numerous historical sources, archive materials and documents."

Thus Bagirov indicated clearly that party policy comes first in matters of historical interpretation. His further remarks showed the party man's puzzlement with scholars who are bothered about facts and logic when party goals are at stake. What he wanted was something like an "absolute good" formula, with passing mention of tsarist oppression in general terms:

> Without underestimating in any respect the reactionary character of tsarist colonial policy, one should not lose sight of the fact that for many peoples, in their concrete historical situations, when they were threatened by the danger of complete enslavement and extermination by backward Turkey and Persia, supported by the Anglo-French colonizers, their annexation was the only path for them and had a very favorable effect on their later fate.
>
> There is no indication that the journal *Voprosy istorii*, guided by the statements of Comrade Stalin on the role of the great Russian people in the fraternal family of Soviet peoples, has worked out or clarified the current question, which is of vital importance to us for the further strengthening of the friendship of peoples of our country—the question of the invaluable assistance which our elder brother, the Russian people, has given and is giving to all the peoples of our country! (Applause.)[44]

The editors of *Voprosy istorii* promptly apologized in a reply to the *Bol'shevik* article for their "gross error" in publishing Nechkina's letter, which "brought confusion on questions which were by no means open to discussion, having been long decided by Marxist-Leninist scholarship."[45] P. N. Tretiakov, the principal

44. *Pravda*, October 7, 1952; condensed translation in *CDSP*, IV, No. 44, 15-16.
45. "Ot redaktsionnoi kollegii zhurnala 'Voprosy istorii,'" *VI*, No. 8, 1952, pp. 3-6.

editor, replied to Bagirov's charge at a meeting of the Institute of History, acknowledging that publication of the letter had been "one of the main mistakes" committed recently by the journal. Nechkina made a statement on her letter at the same meeting, acknowledging that its publication (but not its contents) had been in error. Her apology—if that is what it was—was unacceptable. The authors of the report of the meeting noted that "this statement provides a basis for believing that Professor M. V. Nechkina does not understand her errors and does not accept the correct positions of the critics."[46]

Nowhere in all this talk of confusion and political mistakes was the party's real objection to the discussion stated. Perhaps the most concrete evidence is to be found in the course of another of *Voprosy istorii*'s confessions of the time, this one in reply to charges made at the party congress: "The very fact of the organization of a discussion on the formula of the 'lesser evil' could be regarded as evidence that the editorial board of *Voprosy istorii* was openly making a debatable question of the beneficial nature of the annexation of the Ukraine, Georgia, Azerbaidzhan, Armenia and Central Asia, and its positive influence on the existence and subsequent fate of the peoples of these states."[47]

The discussion had unquestionably shown the irreconcilability of the facts and the theory. And incidental to the discussion, details of tsarist brutality and the aggressive nature of tsarist colonialism had come out in print—in direct contradiction to the prevailing practice of dealing with such matters in generalities. What was probably the most caustic characterization of the tsarist colonial policy to be published since the 1950 pronouncements was contained in the middle of the comment on Nechkina's letter by an Armenian, N. Tavakalian. To make matters worse, the argument was nailed to Stalin by two of his old statements, no longer in good odor:

> Of course, "the tsarist-Russian russifiers . . . who were hardly second in brutality to the Turkish assimilators [Stalin]," in giving "help" to the Armenian people (as to the other brotherly peoples of the Transcaucasus—the Georgians and Azerbaidzhanis), acted not in the interests

46. "V institute istorii akademii nauk SSSR," *ibid.*, No. 11, 1952, pp. 149-56.

47. A. L. Sidorov, "Zadachi instituta istorii akademii nauk SSSR v svete genial'nogo truda I. V. Stalina 'Ekonomicheskie problemy sotsializma v SSSR' i reshenii XIX s"ezda KPSS," *ibid.*, No. 10, 1952, pp. 3-32. Quotation on p. 7.

of these peoples, but for their own goals. "Tsarist Russia was a prison of peoples" and the government of the "international gendarme," Nicholas the Ramrod, eagerly went to the aid of the Armenians in their liberation struggle, led exclusively, as I. V. Stalin points out, by the "necessities of the military-feudal-merchant hierarchy of Russia for outlets to the sea, for seaports, for expansion of foreign trade and the possession of strategic points."[48]

In accord with party wishes, the "lesser evil" disappeared from discussion and from print. In one of the rare mentions of the formula, occurring in the course of a Soviet review of *Rewriting Russian History*, edited by C. E. Black, which contained Shteppa's essay on the subject, the Soviet writer referred to the "notorious 'lesser evil' formula," which "met with disapproval of Soviet scholars and was not propagated in historical literature."[49] The statement contains a claim that is equally rare: that Soviet historians were responsible for an accomplishment that clearly belonged to the party.

BAGIROV'S LAST ADVISORY

We are permitted a glimpse of what might have been through two publications that appeared at the time of Stalin's death, a volume of documents on Shamil and Bagirov's article on the elder brother.

The emphases on the "foreign threats" to the non-Russian peoples and on Shamil's relationship with foreign powers and agents reached their extreme statement in a volume of documents titled *Shamil, Henchman of the Turkish Sultanate and the British Colonizers,* published in Tbilisi.[50] The choice of Georgian scholars to compile such a work was logical. One of the black marks against the *imam*—even in the old days—was his attack on Georgian territory late in his career, which left Georgian scholars less inclined to idealize him. Now that the reinterpretation was under way, this campaign became as important a proof of Shamil's reactionary nature as the Kirgiz campaign of Kenesary's. The Georgian editors were apparently encouraged to use local archives to uncover incriminating evidence; they also drew their materials from a dozen other tsarist archive collections.

48. *VI*, No. 9, 1951, p. 103.
49. *Istoriia SSSR*, No. 6, 1959, p. 193.
50. *Shamil'—stavlennik sultanskoi turtsii i angliiskikh kolonizatorov*, ed. Sh. V. Tsagareishvili (Tbilisi, 1953).

On first encounter with this volume, one is impressed with the physical evidences of scholarship. There are 401 documents in three languages, with several hundred explanatory notes. A look at the preface, however, shows that the editors have set out to prove a preconceived thesis. They declare that the collection will elaborate the following subjects: (1) the role of Britain and Turkey in organizing the Muridist movement and in promoting by this means a "holy war" against Russia; (2) "the aggressive and reactionary nature of Muridism"; (3) the part played by Shamil and his lieutenants as "out-and-out champions of the Sultan of Turkey and his grasping policies in the Caucasus"; (4) Shamil's brutality—"pogroms, destruction, ruin and slaughter involved in the captivity of the peace-loving people of Georgia"; and (5) "the struggle of the Georgian people against Muridism and Shamil."[51]

In February, 1953, Kommunist published Bagirov's article "The Elder Brother in the Family of Soviet Peoples."[52] His last statement on the subject was his most obsequious, and is possibly the most extreme pronouncement on the subject ever made. It was obviously researched by others, since it contained dozens of quotations from sources the party leader would hardly have been familiar with. But the Bagirov flair was there—in the piling on of superlatives, the overstatements, and the striving for dramatic emphasis. The printer's usual method of emphasis proved inadequate for Bagirov, who employed three separate methods in this article: the spreading of letters, the use of italics (unusual in Soviet printing), and, for very special emphasis, the use of letters that were not only bold faced but twice the size of the print used in the text.

After the customary bow to Stalin as the ultimate authority on this subject, Bagirov offered his apotheosis to the Russian people:

> The leading, uniting, cementing and guidance force in the family of peoples of our country is their elder brother, the great Russian people. This position and role of the Russian people in the family of peoples of the Soviet Union has deep historic roots. The great Russian people, by its merits, commands the trust, respect and love of all peoples. . . .
>
> The peoples of our country regard the great Russian people with an attitude of special respect and gratitude. The peoples of the Soviet Union cannot think of strength-

51. Ibid., p. viii.
52. M. D. Bagirov, "Starshii brat v sem'e sovetskikh narodov," Kommunist, No. 3, 1953, pp. 64-88; condensed translation in CDSP, V, No. 23, 8-9.

ening of the friendship of peoples without the development, without the guidance of all Soviet peoples by the love, deep respect, gratitude and unbounded devotion to the elder brother, the great Russian people, who have the primary and guiding role in the construction of Communism.

Bagirov covered the whole range of arguments and expanded them somewhat. He emphasized the threat from "foreign aggressors," claiming that some of the peoples of the Caucasus faced extermination if Russia had not taken them in. In his view the historic alternative was quite clear in the minds of the non-Russian peoples, and he showed several instances of their eagerness to come into the Russian state. Quoting old travel accounts, he declared that the people living on the Caspian shore "pray[ed] for nothing so much as the coming of the Muscovites as quickly as possible to free them from the yoke of the Persian monarchy." The arrival of Russian troops in Derbent in 1722 and in Baku the following year "was greeted with joy, and everywhere they were given a warm welcome by the local people." He pushed the friendly ties of Russians and non-Russians further back in history by stating that economic ties had developed "long before" annexation, by which he evidently meant the medieval period, in view of the next statement that such ties "were strengthened in the fifteenth and sixteenth centuries."

In one section he enumerated the blessings gained by the non-Russians by annexation. He recounted the immediate economic gains and alluded to the political revolution that awaited these people with the coming of the Bolsheviks. But his special emphasis was on the cultural interchange among peoples, which was represented almost entirely as a process of radiation from the Russian center to the less advanced peoples. There was a lengthy statement on the importance of the Russian language and literature. Giving short snippets of quotations full of his own emphases, he called attention to more than a dozen of the great pre-revolutionary intellectuals of the Caucasus who loved the Russian elder brother, and twice as many Russian writers, diplomats, and revolutionaries who were concerned about the fate of the non-Russians. The whole article was studded with quotations from Marx, Engels, Lenin, and Stalin, which showed by their obliqueness how little they had had to say about the friendship of peoples.

Bagirov rebuked Soviet historians for not going into detail in elaborating the friendship of peoples, and his article was full of such details. But when it came to tsarist colonial policy, he wrote very briefly and in studied generalities. In the whole article of twenty-four pages, there were two short paragraphs of one sentence each on the subject. By contrast, his main point was brought up in endless repetition in his references to the great Russian people: "their remarkable qualities," their role as "head of the family of peoples," as "an example of self-sacrifice, of unselfish constructive labor," and above all their "position as elder brother in the family of peoples."

Bagirov, like so many of his countrymen who commit their views to print, was a victim of bad timing. For him, it was too late, though he could not know it when this article went to press on February 11, 1953. His own "historic fate" was running against him; in a month Stalin would be dead; in two he would be arrested as an associate of Beriia, to be charged, among other things, with membership in a nationalist, counter-revolutionary organization, with mistreating numerous intellectuals, with falsifying some documents and stealing others. In April, 1956, Bagirov was the object of a sensational five-day trial in Baku. He was found guilty of an assortment of political crimes and was executed. The local press published a long list of his innocent victims, including several scholars.[53]

For the Soviet historians who were undoubtedly contemplating the Bagirov article and rehearsing their commentaries on it at the time of Stalin's death and his arrest, his fall must have been welcome. What is remarkable about it all is that in later years, when Bagirov was a perfect scapegoat, they repudiated so little of his handiwork.

53. *Bakinskii rabochii*, May 27, 1956. According to this report, the trial was held between April 12 and 16, and was thus reported only six weeks later.

CHAPTER **9.**

CLASSIFYING

THE CENTRAL ASIAN REVOLTS

"The question of the evaluation of the nature of the national movements is by no means a narrow academic or scientific question, of concern only to historian-specialists. This question is of great political importance, a question of principle, of ideology, closely tied to the question of Communist training of our cadres, of our Soviet people. . . . The correct Marxist-Leninist evaluation of the nature of the national movements, a correct understanding of what happened in the past (particularly, in the territories of Central Asia and Kazakhstan) can facilitate an even greater strengthening of the friendship among the peoples of the U.S.S.R.—one of the basic motive forces of the Soviet state, one of the most important sources of the might and invincibility of the U.S.S.R." A. V. Piaskovskii's concluding remarks to the Second Tashkent Conference of Historians (Materialy nauchnoi sessii, posviashchennoi istorii Srednei Azii i Kazakhstana v dooktiabr'skii period [Tashkent, 1955], p. 372).

Among the hundreds of historical events that had to be re-examined and reinterpreted as a result of the new line on the friendship of Soviet peoples, no single subject was so troublesome as the proper classification of dozens of resistance movements and revolts in Central Asia during the tsarist period. The Bolshevik view of history dictates that every event of the past must be categorized as either progressive or reactionary within the framework of the Marxist laws of historical development. Before 1940 the question of the revolts was simple: all revolts against Russian colonialism had been regarded as progressive. But by the early

1950's several criteria for evaluating revolts had been imposed on the historian, and all previous interpretations that ignored them were considered naïve, one-sided, and un-Marxist. The historian now had to examine the internal class struggle in the society, the nature of the leadership, the goals of the movement, the involvement of "foreign enemies." And there was the hidden factor, which was seldom explicitly discussed, but was all important: to what extent was the revolt aimed against Russians? The historian was also obliged to employ empirical evidence with selectivity. Movements involving large numbers of people were not necessarily a reflection of the wishes of the masses: the masses might be misled; leaders who had been regarded as democratic might be proved to be representatives of the feudal class; the character of a movement might change from one time to another or from one locale to another.

Pouring the Central Asian revolts into the new party-manufactured molds proved to be a very difficult task. Movements that had been simple became extremely complex; very few of them could be placed in the progressive or reactionary category without qualifications. The task was complicated further by the fact that party pronouncements were not specific and detailed enough to cover all situations. It was left to the historians to apply general guidelines to many specific events, each having a different combination of the determinants.

As of early 1951 the guidelines on the interpretation of revolts were still sketchy. *Pravda* had spoken authoritatively on only two of them, pronouncing Kenesary's movement reactionary and Isatai Taimanov's progressive. Two others (Batyr Srym and Dzhankhozhi) had been treated in monographs with less than complete clarity, but the reviews and subsequent discussion offered some direction.[1] Some conclusions could be drawn from the Shamil discussion.[2] But this information, taken together, could hardly provide all the answers, and the historians held four large conferences on the nature of the revolts between 1951-54, but did not

1. The publication of Viatkin's *Batyr Srym*, with only minor retractions by the author, in an edition of 15,000 in the Kazakh language in 1951 was an indication of its general acceptance.

2. It was apparently hoped that the Bagirov article on Shamil would be enlightening. Fifteen thousand copies were published in pamphlet form in Alma-Ata in 1951 in the Kazakh language. See *Knizhnaia letopis'*, No. 31327, 1951.

arrive at interpretations that could win general acceptance until the end of the decade.

One of the first attempts to apply the new views to other revolts was made by Iakunin, in the April, 1951, issue of *Voprosy istorii*.[3] Confining himself to Kazakh revolts, Iakunin analyzed them largely in relation to their leadership and goals. He classified eleven revolts, finding two to be national liberation movements and all the others reactionary, mostly feudal-monarchal. The two progressive movements were the same ones that had passed the test earlier—Srym and Isatai (he did not mention the Dzhankhozhi movement). But Iakunin did not provide clear answers that would facilitate the evaluation of other revolts.[4] Although he claimed to be basing his arguments primarily on the class background of the leaders and their goals, it must have been clear to those reading between the lines that the prime consideration was whether a given movement was separatist, and whether it was aimed against Russians. These views were put forth only in a roundabout way. Without exception Iakunin indicated that struggles against states other than Russia were progressive. To take one example, he noted that "the struggle of the Kazakh and Kirgiz peoples against the Dzhungar Kalmyks in the eighteenth century and against the aggression of feudal China and the Central Asian khanates in the nineteenth century was a progressive struggle for independence." He was careful to point out that the progressive revolts of Srym and Isatai were directed mainly against feudal khans and sultans, and only secondarily against "the colonial policy of Russian tsarism." On the other hand, resistance to the Russians was a singularly reactionary feature, as indicated by the verdict against a revolt of the 1880's: "It was carried out under the reactionary slogan of *gazavat* (a holy war against 'infidels,' that is Russians)."

THE FIRST TASHKENT CONFERENCE

In March, 1951, a large conference was held at the Central

3. A. Iakunin, "K voprosy ob otsenke kharaktera natsional'nykh dvizhenii 30-40kh godov XIX v. v Kazakhstane," *VI*, No. 4, 1951, pp. 55-64.

4. The careful reader of the journal had another reason to take Iakunin's word lightly, even though he had just spoken in *Pravda*. He was criticized in the leading editorial in the same issue of *Voprosy istorii* which published his article for regarding some Kazakh leaders of 1905 as revolutionary, when in reality they were "bourgeois nationalists, striving to separate Kazakhstan from Russia and make an alliance with Turkey and Iran . . ." (p. 10). Obviously, Iakunin was not always to be trusted in his evaluation of Kazakh leaders.

Asian State University on "the character of the national movements in Central Asia and Kazakhstan in the colonial period."[5] The meeting apparently was intended to give guidance to many historians who were engaged in rewriting the histories of individual republics. The main report was given by Professor I. K. Dodonov, who was a co-editor of the history of Kazakhstan then in progress. Dodonov discussed more revolts than Iakunin, and was in general agreement with him, with one exception, the revolt in the Andizhan Valley in 1898.[6] This revolt had always been regarded as progressive before publication of the *Pravda* article, but it was clear from Dodonov's cautious approach and carefully reasoned statements that it had slipped into the doubtful column. His discussion illustrated the complexities of the problem. In his view the revolt was unquestionably a popular movement, aimed against tsarist colonialism and local feudal leaders. At the same time, reactionary leaders and religious forces "had tried to use this movement in their own interests." The movement followed the *gazavat* slogan, but according to Dodonov, who carefully used Lenin's exact words, such a manifestation was really "the religious cloak of the revolt." Thus the revolt obviously possessed contradictory characteristics; the question was, Which theme should be considered dominant? Dodonov's view was that the popular nature of the revolt was the overriding consideration; since it had had mass support throughout, he pronounced it a national liberation movement.

Dodonov's interpretation was challenged in the discussion that followed. Later the departments sponsoring the conference passed a resolution emphasizing the progressive features of annexation and referring without further clarification to "the reactionary essence of the feudal-nationalist Andizhan revolt of 1898."[7] Dodonov had made the same error to which Pankratova and her colleagues had

5. A. Zevelev and Sh. Abdullaev, "Diskussiia o kharaktere natsional'nykh dvizhenii v Srednei Azii i Kazakhstane v kolonial'nyi period," *VI*, No. 9, 1951, pp. 173-78. Baymirza Hayit believes that this meeting was heavily packed with Russians. Among the 374 participants, he finds only forty-seven names that appear to be native to Central Asia. See Baymirza Hayit, "Turkestan as an Example of Soviet Colonialism," *Studies On the Soviet Union*, I (1961), No. 2, 78-95.

6. Although Iakunin's article appeared after this meeting, it had probably already been written, so the two historians were making their interpretations independently.

7. A. Zevelev and Sh. Abdullaev, "Diskussiia," p. 178. This direct refutation of Dodonov's evaluation of the 1898 revolt in the report of the meeting was an early indication that the new Kazakh history on which he was working was in trouble. It was abandoned at the "prospectus" stage the following year.

confessed earlier: the evaluation of a revolt as a national liberation movement because it had received mass support. At the same time he and his colleagues must have contemplated a fact that was never aired at the conference or in the resolution: it was well known that the revolt was aimed primarily against Russian rule.

Dodonov's error proved to be instructive for other historians, notably the resilient Gafurov, who, like everybody else, had pronounced the Andizhan revolt progressive in his history of the Tadzhiks. In the second edition of the work Gafurov dwelt at length on the reactionary religious goals of the leaders of the revolt, specifically noting that his eyes had been opened by the discussion on Shamil. Not only had the main leader of the revolt, Dukchi Ishan, wanted to found a regime based on reactionary Sufism, he had also been supported by "numerous agents of the Afghan Emir" and "British imperialism," and had waged a holy war directed "not only against tsarist officials, but against Russians in general."[8] Gafurov followed this confession of error with an article on the revolt in *Voprosy istorii*.[9] His "glaring political error," he said, had resulted from his failure to detect the antagonism between the masses and their reactionary leader. His new interpretation of events was a carbon copy of the *Pravda* pronouncement on the role of the masses in the Kenesary movement. The people had followed a reactionary leader momentarily, but had deserted him when they became aware of his aims. One of the most important reasons for their change of heart was the growing realization that the movement was aimed against the Russian people.

THE MOST TROUBLESOME REVOLT

Gafurov's article apparently tied the ribbons on the Andizhan revolt of 1898. But other revolts were far too complicated to be dispensed with so easily. This was conspicuously apparent in the case of the large revolt in Central Asia in 1916, on which *Voprosy istorii* launched a discussion early in 1953. This revolt, the largest and most widespread rebellion against the Russian Empire, had always been considered progressive. Indeed it was regarded as the most glorious of insurrections, a curtain raiser to the October Revolution in the colonies. But the new criteria for evaluation of

8. B. G. Gafurov, *Istoriia tadzhikskogo naroda v kratkom izlozhenii* (2nd ed., Moscow, 1952), pp. 421-25.

9. B. Gafurov, "Ob andizhanskom 'vosstanie' 1898 goda," *VI*, No. 2, 1953, pp. 50-61.

revolts made this one extremely controversial, and the debate about it dominated three subsequent conferences of historians.

Since a proper evaluation of the Revolt of 1916 became the *pièce de résistance* for Soviet historians, a brief sketch of their previous thinking about it is in order. There was general agreement at all times among them that the revolt had been a mass movement, and that the immediate cause of the revolt had been a tsarist mobilization order which brought a series of smoldering grievances to flame. Beyond these points, nearly every feature of the revolt was subjected to criticism at one point or another. There were several particularly sensitive points:

1. *Causes.* In the old view the excesses of tsarist colonialism were foremost, but by the early 1950's, such factors, though not denied, were subordinated to the activities of "foreign agents" and the ambitions of reactionary leaders.

2. *Leadership.* Many of the leaders were of feudal or clerical origin. In the earlier view, it was possible for a popular movement to have such leadership, but this was no longer compatible with the party line.

3. *Ideology.* There could be no doubt of the religious nature of the movement in many areas, including the reactionary *gazavat.* This was no problem for earlier Soviet writers, but was now a factor to be weighed heavily on the side of reaction.

4. *Goals.* There had been general agreement that the rebels wanted independence. Such an interpretation was now vulnerable on two points: it accented separatism from the incipient Soviet family, and it meant in practice that the Central Asian peoples would have to ally themselves with a foreign power to maintain their independence or be "swallowed up" by another colonial power. Such an interpretation now smacked of Pan-Islam, Pan-Turkism, Pan-Iranism, or even Pan-Afghanism.

5. *Relations of Rebels with Russian Settlers.* In the old view there was no problem involved in armed clashes between rebels and ordinary Russian people, and early accounts were plentiful, from eyewitnesses and documents. The concept of the friendship of peoples demanded that some explanation be given which would deny large-scale clashes between non-Russian and Russian workers.

As if this complex of problems were not complicated enough, there were two other subjects that were currently receiving close attention by Soviet historians and could not be ignored. With the deepening of the Cold War, Soviet scholars had been delving into the intrigues of the "British imperialists" in Central Asia. What was their role in the events of 1916? There was also a growing emphasis on Bolshevik leadership before the Revolution. Historians were obliged to look closely for Bolsheviks in the 1916 revolt and to establish a continuity between it and the Bolshevik triumph of the following year.

The earliest Soviet interpretation of these events, by a Bolshevik eyewitness, G. I. Broido, held that tsarist officials deliberately provoked the rebellion in order to have an excuse to exterminate the natives and seize their land. This view was generally upheld by T. Ryskulov, who, in an article published in 1924, added that the land thus seized would serve as a *place d'armes* for further Russian penetration into Persia, China, and Afghanistan. This provocation theory was denounced by A. V. Shestakov two years later. He pointed out that such a move by the tsarist government, at a time when Russia had her back to the wall in World War I, would have been absurd. But Shestakov did not destroy Broido's theory of provocation altogether. He charged that Broido had merely drawn too broad a generalization; he had witnessed tsarist forces goading the peaceful Kirgiz into revolt and had assumed that this occurred all over Turkestan.[10]

There was also considerable disagreement among early Soviet writers on the role of the native aristocracy (*manaps*) in the revolt. One complicating factor was the absence of centralized leadership; the revolt was led by a variety of local leaders, and in some cases seemed to be almost without leadership. Some historians, including Shestakov, concluded that the *manaps* led the rebels in many areas, while others held that the native upper classes supported the tsarist regime. A report on the revolt among the Kirgiz by a tsarist official had stated that "in almost every volost the leaders of the revolt were the volost *starshinas* [native elders]."[11] But this interpretation, which fouled the clean class lines demanded by the new directives, had to be re-examined.

The most delicate question of all was the relationship of the

10. These views are summarized by Edward D. Sokol in *The Revolt of 1916 in Russian Central Asia* (Baltimore: Johns Hopkins Press, 1954), pp. 167–72. Unfortunately this study was published on the eve of the most intensive Soviet reappraisal of the revolt, but the author was able to anticipate much of the new line from leading statements in earlier articles.

11. *Vosstanie 1916 g. v Kirgizstane. Dokumenty i materialy,* ed. T. Ryskulov (Moscow, 1937), p. 112. The editor of this volume challenged this statement as "a clear distortion of fact" but went on to say that the *starshinas* had led the revolt "only in certain cases."

natives with the Russian people living there and with the Bolsheviks in particular. Early Soviet writers found no evidence of cooperation between Russian workers and the natives, but tended to put the bulk of the Central Asians on one side and the Russians on the other. The last Governor General of Turkestan, General A. N. Kuropatkin, had stated in a report that "during the past thirty years, we have not drawn any closer to, but farther away from the native population. The result of this has been disturbances over the provision of labor, bloodshed, havoc, mutual hostility and mutual lack of confidence." He also complained about the appropriation of nearly two million dessiatins of pasture land by Russians in the three years preceding the revolt, which contributed to native grievances. This view was supported in a Soviet study of 1931 by A. Alkin, who concluded that Russian settlers were to a great extent responsible for the unrest leading to the rebellion.[12] Soviet works of the middle 1930's upheld the view that lines were clearly drawn on the basis of nationality, rather than class, with the exception that some of the native aristocracy had sided with Russia.[13] The idea of Bolshevik participation and leadership seems to have been entirely of later vintage, though one Soviet work suggested an interesting variation on the theme of the future: that one of the positive gains of the revolt was the contact of some of its native leaders with the Russian proletariat and the Bolsheviks as a result of their deportation to Russia.[14]

As late as the fall of 1951 Voprosy istorii published an article on the Turkmen phase of the revolt that reiterated many of these themes, clearly out of line with the Bagirov view, which had been stated more than a year earlier. Iu. Tarasov, of the Institute of History of the Turkmen Academy of Sciences, drew heavily on the documents on Russian-Turkmen relations, published in 1946, and already under fire. Quoting from one of these documents, Tarasov

12. "Central Asia and the Russian People" [unsigned], Central Asian Review [hereafter cited as CAR], I (1953), No. 3, 1-8.

13. This is especially strong in S. D. Asfendiarov's National'no-osvoboditel'-noe vosstanie 1916 goda v Kazakhstane (Alma-Ata, 1936), in which the Kazakhs are said to have been worse off with the coming of Russian capitalism, and the few natives who cooperated with the conquerors are characterized as collaborators trained by the Russians (pp. 15-19, 35-37). See also Z. D. Kastel'skaia, Vosstanie 1916 v Uzbekistane (Tashkent, 1937) and the preface of Vosstanie 1916 g. v Kirgizstane, ed. Ryskulov.

14. S. Brainin and S. Shafiro, Vosstanie kazakhov semirech'ia v 1916 godu (Alma-Ata–Moscow, 1936), pp. 90-104, as cited in Sokol, The Revolt of 1916, p. 170.

related the events of the night of October 6, 1916, when the rebels, "armed with rifles, revolvers, swords, axes, knives, sticks and stones, moved into the town of Tedzhen for the purpose of destroying not only all the officials of the Russian government, but the whole Russian population."[15] Not content to let this contemporary account speak for itself, Tarasov added insult to injury on the question of Russian-Turkmen relations: "All the hatred which the *daikhane* [native peasants] harbored against the colonial regime was directed, under the influence of reactionary leaders, against the Russians as a whole, not distinguishing between the tsarist administrators and the rest of the Russian population."

It was true that Tarasov offered an extenuating circumstance: the rebels were misled by reactionary leaders. But the hostility and violence were still there, and could hardly be laid to leaders alone. No less devastating for the new interpretation were Tarasov's views on related matters. He maintained that the rebels had no revolutionary aims and "no contact with the Bolsheviks." He even held that the movement in Turkmenia "prevented the establishment of a single front between the workers of Turkmenistan and the Russian working class; the movement was anti-Russian."

Tarasov's article must have given the supporters of the new line on the friendship of peoples considerable discomfort. The views could not be dismissed as those of one heretical writer, since Tarasov had meticulously drawn his information from authentic sources—tsarist archives and documentary collections published by the Bolsheviks themselves. This article, which was condemned later, probably would not have been published in the embattled journal except for the fact that it placed a major emphasis on some welcome themes—the role of "foreign agents" and the reactionary role of some of the revolt's leaders.[16] It was to correct such views as those presented by Tarasov on Russian-Turkmen relations that increased pressure was brought on historians to find a "scientific Marxist-Leninist" interpretation of the events of 1916 in Central Asia.

On the eve of the Frunze Conference (March, 1953), which

15. Iu. Tarasov, "O kharaktere dvizheniia 1916 v Turkmenii," *VI*, No. 9, 1951, pp. 111-17. The documents referred to here are in *Revoliutsionnoe dvizhenie v Turkmenii (1908-1917)* (Ashkhabad-Moscow, 1946).

16. At the beginning of Tarasov's article the editors of the journal attached one of their curious notes of disclaimer: "In placing the article of Iu. Tarasov under discussion, the editors consider that the questions contained in it need further examination."

was to take up the 1916 revolt, *Voprosy istorii* published another
article on the revolt, in which the whole question was viewed in
an entirely new light from that of previous Soviet historians, including Tarasov. The authors of this article, Iakunin and O. K.
Kuliev, a historian of the Turkmen Academy of Sciences, continued
to see discontent with tsarist colonial policies as a major cause of
the revolt, but offered a whole series of contributory causes which
had received little or no attention earlier.[17] They claimed that the
Bolsheviks had been at work in Central Asia since 1905 organizing
workers, calling strikes, and forging an alliance of working people
of different nationalities. They produced the names of two genuine
proletarian leaders in the Kazakh revolt: an unknown Bolshevik,
Alibii Dzhangildin, and a poor peasant and Bolshevik to be, Amangel'dy Imanov. Iakunin and Kuliev emphasized the common struggle
of the Russian and Central Asian workers, and denied any large-
scale fighting between these groups. Such violence was darkly
hinted at, but was attributed to outside agitators—German, Turkish, British, and even American agents, who were all eager to gain
a foothold in Central Asia at the expense of Russia. It seems not
to have been important to the authors that the British were allied
with Russia at the time.

THE FRUNZE CONFERENCE

The three-day Frunze Conference on "the character of the
national movements of Kirgizia" was attended by about 250 scholars.[18] The main report, given by A. V. Piaskovskii, of the Institute
of History in Moscow, set the general tone of the conference.
Piaskovskii emphasized the progressive significance of annexation,
noting that the struggle against tsarism in no way contradicted the
concept of the friendship of peoples, since this was a mutual struggle
of the popular masses against their common enemy. Failure to
appreciate this fact accounted for many past errors in the works
of the historians of Kirgizia, who were called on to re-evaluate the
revolts as a first important step to the writing of a new history of
Kirgizia (then in progress).

In the second paper K. Usenbaev, of the Kirgiz Institute of

17. A. F. Iakunin and O. K. Kuliev, "Vosstanie 1916 goda v Srednei Azii,"
VI, No. 3, 1953, pp. 33-49.
18. "Nauchnaia konferentsiia o kharaktere natsional'nykh dvizhenii v
Kirgizii vo vtoroi polovine XIX-nachale XX veke," *VI*, No. 7, 1953, pp.
172-74.

History, Language, and Literature, showed what a creative application of Marxist-Leninist principles could do for the evaluation of the Kirgiz revolts of 1873-74 and 1875-76. The first, according to the speaker, was totally progressive: it was spontaneous, with mass participation, and directed against the Khan of Kokand. The rebels looked to Russia for aid and welcomed Russian intervention. "Feudal elements tried to suppress the spontaneous mass people's movement, in order to strengthen their class position," but they were unsuccessful. But the rebellion of 1875-76 was something else again. "Reactionary, feudal-clerical elements played a leading role in the leadership of this rebellion." They were "dissatisfied with the growing influence of Russia," now in control of three-fourths of the territory of the former Kokand khanate. Russian influence was opposed by "the powerful Kirgiz, Uzbek and other feudal lords, by military and bureaucratic aristocracy of Kokand, by the Moslem priesthood." The movement was accompanied by "a *gazavat* against Russia and against Russians. . . . Anglo-Turkish agents took part in the organization of the rebellion." How reactionary can a revolt be?[19]

Unfortunately for the cause, not all revolts were so simple, as was evident when the Kirgiz phase of the 1916 revolt came up for discussion. A. G. Zimma, a professor at the Kirgiz State University, resorted to the technique of dissection. The revolt had started as a spontaneous uprising of Kirgiz workers against tsarist exploitation, but complications soon set in. "The spontaneous movement of the masses, lacking proletarian leadership, was usurped in some places by feudal-clerical elements." In some areas these reactionary leaders changed the direction of the revolt away from "a national liberational struggle, and directed it to the detriment of the revolutionary movement. . . . Representatives of the exploiting aristocracy set the more backward elements of the native population against the Russian people, striving to kindle hatred between peoples." In other places German-Turkish agents, as well as the *manaps*, tried to capture leadership of the revolt. None of this, however, diminished in any way the growing friendship of the Kirgiz and Russian

19. Judging from the brief abstract of Usenbaev's paper published in *Voprosy istorii*, it seems the author omitted elements in both revolts that might have complicated his all-or-nothing interpretation. He said nothing about leadership in the first revolt, and nothing about the attitude of the masses in the second. In effect the first was leaderless, while the second consisted exclusively of leaders.

peoples. Zimma declined to put a label on the 1916 revolt as a whole.

In his concluding remarks to the conference A. L. Sidorov reminded the participants of their unfinished business. He "emphasized the necessity of studying the history of the 1916 revolt in Central Asia in its inseparable relationships with the general economic, social and political situation in Russia in that period."[20]

THE ASHKHABAD CONFERENCE

Shortly after the Frunze Conference, a large meeting was called at Ashkhabad for the purpose of evaluating the 1916 revolt in Turkmenia, where fighting had been especially fierce and historians had been unusually stubborn in holding their old views that it was an uprising against Russians in general. The Ashkhabad Conference, which met under the shadow of another meeting of the Central Committee of the Turkmen party on May 29-30, 1953, was apparently not reported in the press. But some of the details can be pieced together from references to the session by Turkmen historians at a subsequent conference. It was a large meeting, called by the Learned Council of the Institute of History of the Turkmen Academy of Sciences jointly with the Turkmen branch of the Institute of Marx-Engels-Lenin. Representatives were present from the Academy of Sciences in Moscow and the other Central Asian republics. After vigorous debate, the conference agreed to a rather contrived interpretation of the revolt in four key areas. Part of the resolution of that meeting was read into the record of the later Tashkent Conference by a Turkmen historian. It stated that the revolt in Turkmenia had been overwhelmingly spontaneous, popular, and progressive, but with some exceptions: "In certain, predominantly backward areas of Turkmenistan, where patriarchal-feudal relations were firmly preserved, the feudal-clerical aristocracy, closely tied to agents of foreign intelligence, were able to organize reactionary uprisings, into which the backward

20. During the Ninth Plenum of the Union of Kirgiz Writers, which met a month later, a plea was made for a relaxation of the harsh criticism of Kirgiz writers for their idealization of the events of the Central Asian revolt. The report indicates that the Kirgiz writers had displayed real national pride in giving accounts of the period, including a novel full of "bourgeois nationalist, pan-Islamic and pan-Turkic" ideas, a heroic poem about a *manap*, and an idealization of the Basmachi counter-revolutionaries who fought off the Bolsheviks for years after the Revolution. See the summary in *CAR*, I (1953), No. 1, 43-45.

ranks of the peasantry were partially drawn. Such was the armed uprising at Giurgen and the attack on Tedzhen on the night of October 5-6, 1916. However, these provoked uprisings did not win the support of the working masses of these areas."

Turkmen historians did not swallow this flimsy bill of goods easily. This was made quite clear by the irascible Tarasov, who, in the course of a lively argument at the later conference, stated that Turkmen historians had held two previous discussions on the subject, in May, 1951, and April, 1952, and had agreed, with only two dissenting votes, that these same revolts were "progressive, national liberational, revolutionary."[21] It is clear that the new interpretation was wrested from the same historians at the Ashkhabad Conference with the help of the Marx-Engels-Lenin Institute, the visitors from Moscow, and possibly the knowledge that the Central Committee of the Turkmen Party was meeting in another part of the city.

The new nearness to and dependence on the Russian elder brother, authoritatively set down for the Caucasus by Bagirov in his last article, which appeared shortly before the Frunze Conference, was quickly applied to the Central Asian younger brothers. Its emphasis was laid on heavily at Frunze, particularly in the main address of Piaskovskii and in the concluding remarks. Two articles appearing in the central-party and historical journals that summer broadened the discussion and suggested new kinds of supporting evidence which would be prominent in the subsequent discussion.

A. Niiazov, the Secretary of the Central Committee of the Uzbek Communist party, was the author of an article titled "In the Fraternal Family of Peoples of the Soviet Union," which appeared in *Kommunist*.[22] As Bagirov's counterpart in Central Asia, Niiazov was apparently trying to emulate him in the pages of the same journal. He fell far short, however, producing a "me too" statement which lacked the Bagirov dramatic touch and merely extended the interpretation to the Central Asian peoples. He gave expansive thanks to the Russians for their economic and cultural influences, but fell short of the Bagirov line by dwelling almost entirely on the Soviet period—a theme that was hardly new. Like Bagirov, he condemned the "gross ideological distortions and nationalist errors" of local historians. The bill of particulars against

21. See below, Note 24.
22. A. Niiazov, "V bratskoi sem'e narodov Sovetskogo Soiuza," *Kommunist,* No. 8, 1953, pp. 25-39; condensed translation in *CDSP*, V, No. 25, 9-10.

them indicated the peculiarities of Central Asian history. In addition to factors common to the Caucasus (failure to study class contradictions within movements, and incorrect evaluations of them) Uzbek historians had idealized despots of the Middle Ages and customs of the feudal past. Unlike Bagirov, who blamed scholars exclusively for the state of affairs, Niiazov acknowledged that "nationalist distortions occurred primarily because the republic's leading Party organizations underestimated the importance of ideological work."

Voprosy istorii's contribution to this theme was a long article by a troika of authors titled "On the Question of the Significance of the Annexation of Central Asia to Russia."[23] This article, based on a rich array of sources, including tsarist historians, documentary collections, and little-known monographs, was undoubtedly intended to broaden the range of discussion of relationships between the peoples. Using V. V. Barthol'd as their authority, they claimed that Soviet historians had badly underestimated the depth of the historic ties. Trade between Rus and Central Asia existed "possibly even earlier" than trade on the Baltic-Black Sea routes. Normal development of this trade had been broken off by the Tatar invasions, but had been solidly re-established in the sixteenth century. During the century before Russian annexation, the peoples of Central Asia had suffered from feudal warfare and the threat of foreign domination, which were attended by economic and cultural decline. But the coming of the Russians had turned the tide, and as a result of stable government, security, the introduction of capitalism, and the intense interest of many Russian experts in the area, Central Asia had made remarkable gains during the tsarist period. Lenin and Stalin had recognized this phenomenon, and so had many Central Asian and Russian intellectuals, who were mentioned. Only Soviet historians, it appeared, had failed to give a correct appraisal of this historic event, and the article called on them to correct their past errors.

Though it espoused Russian's cultural mission as completely as Bagirov had, this article signaled a significant retreat from his extreme views on the nature of Russian acquisition of territory: "The annexation of the peoples of Central Asia to Russia was far from a singular process. In some cases it was accomplished by means of conquest, and in others it proceeded in a peaceful way

23. I. S. Braginskii, S. Radzhabov, and V. A. Romodin, "K voprosu o znachenii prisoedineniia Srednei Azii k Rossii," *VI*, No. 8, 1953, pp. 21-40.

(the annexation of the Kazakh hordes, Northern Kirgizia, the Turk-mens of the Caspian area and Murgrab, and part of the Karakalpak people, etc., was accomplished by peaceful means). Therefore to characterize annexation as conquest without grounds would be in-accurate."

Having put the term conquest (*zavoevanie*) back into play, the authors quickly softened its implications. In the Central Asian khanates, the only areas they indicated to have been annexed by conquest, they emphasized the internal chaos, economic stagnation, and the British threat, rapping hard the authors of the *History of the Peoples of Uzbekistan* (Vol. II, 1947) for idealizing the govern-ment leaders of the khanates and implying that those states had some future independent of Russian influence. In sum, they ad-mitted that the territories had been conquered by Russian arms, but they considered the conquest entirely justified.

THE SECOND TASHKENT CONFERENCE

The climax of the discussion was reached in the Joint Scien-tific Conference on the History of Central Asia and Kazakhstan in the Pre-October Period, which was held in Tashkent between Jan-uary 30 and February 6, 1954. It was a large conference, whose published proceedings (lacking several speeches) run to nearly six-hundred pages.[24] The conference was sponsored by the U.S.S.R. Academy of Sciences jointly with the Academies of Science of the Central Asian republics, and was attended by delegations of his-torians from Moscow, Leningrad, the Central Asian republics, Azer-baidzhan, and interestingly enough, two troublesome autonomous republics—the Tatar and Dagestan A.S.S.R.'s. There were also present a number of teachers in higher schools, party and Soviet officials, students, writers, and journalists. There were five major topics for discussion, all of which were important to the rewriting of the history of Central Asia to party standards. They were (1) the nature of patriarchal-feudal relations among the nomads of Central Asia, (2) "the reactionary nature and treacherous role of Pan-Islam-ism and Pan-Turkism," (3) the formation of bourgeois nations in Central Asia, (4) the character of the revolt of 1916, and (5) the problem of periodization of the history of Central Asia.

24. *Materialy nauchnoi sessii, posviashchennoi istorii Srednei Azii i Kazakh-stana v dooktiabr'skii period* (Tashkent, 1955). My discussion of the earlier Ashkahbad conference is pieced together from references in this volume, pp. 320, 402; the excerpt from the resolution is on page 328.

The extent to which this conference was cut and dried can be ascertained by a comparison of an article published in the Tashkent newspaper, *Pravda vostoka*, two weeks before the conference and the final resolution of the conference itself.[25] On point after point the party newspaper indicated the errors in the old interpretations and the general lines of the new interpretations the scholars would publish as their "conclusions" after a week of "debate." There was no denial—either in the article or in the conference—that the interpretations sought were to be helpful in the solution of current political problems, usually stated euphemistically as the "further strengthening of the friendship of peoples." *Pravda vostoka* pointed out that the first two volumes of the history of Uzbekistan (1947 and 1950) contained harmful views on these questions and that a proper evaluation of them would aid enormously in the writing of the new history of the republic, which was then in progress. But the fact that the Uzbek party organ published the general conclusions of the conference in advance does not mean that the proceedings were uninteresting or unimaginative. It was up to the scholars to verify in detail what had been suggested in broad outline, and in doing so there was some vociferous wrangling that was not registered in the final resolution.

By far the most interesting question on the agenda was the 1916 revolt. *Pravda vostoka* had stated that it was a complex movement, that it was overwhelmingly progressive, but had reactionary "feudal-clerical" leadership in some areas (five were specified). Historians were enjoined not to "embellish" these manifestations, but, in effect, to show that they were exceptions, and to elaborate on the work of feudal class interests, clerical elements, and "foreign intelligence agents." This is exactly what came out of the conference, but not before very vigorous and revealing debate. Kh. T. Tursunov, an Uzbek historian, read a long paper on the general character of the revolt, after which four other speakers called attention to local characteristics in different areas. In the subsequent discussion, two of the eleven speakers sharply disagreed with the prevailing view that the revolt was progressive with a few minor reactionary pockets. The first dissenter was T. N. Kolesnikova, identified only as a *kandidat* of historical science. She saw two kinds of movements in the local uprisings of 1916: the *vosstanie*, a rebellion with some degree of leadership and program, and the

25. *Pravda vostoka*, January 16, 1954; summarized in *CAR*, II (1954), No. 4, 308-11. The resolution is in *Materialy nauchnoi sessii*, pp. 581-86.

volnenie, a riot or disturbance without leadership or aims, and without organized military action. She maintained that the *voss-tanie* part of the 1916 revolt was reactionary; in a long recitation of events she found the leaders to be feudal, clerical, German or Turkish agents, Pan-Islamists, or Pan-Turkists, but nowhere was there a genuine proletarian leader working for the good of the masses. As for the *volnenie,* she claimed that by its very nature it was neither progressive nor revolutionary, but merely an agitation against constituted government—in this case the Russian government, which was the only hope in the long run for the Central Asian peoples. Thus, in either case, the uprisings must be considered reactionary: "In the speech [of Tursunov] the events of 1916 were considered revolutionary, a national liberation mass movement. The speaker idealized these events. It must be stated plainly that the *vosstaniia* were reactionary. The popular *volneniia,* in a strictly scientific sense, cannot be regarded as either revolutionary or of a national liberation character."

Kolesnikova coupled this appraisal of the uprisings with some simple logic. Accepting fully what had been said about the progressiveness of annexation and association with Russians, she reasoned that the 1916 revolt must also be considered reactionary because it had the effect of bringing an end to this happy state of affairs. "Progressiveness is to be found not in revolts, but in the annexation of Turkestan to Russia, in new economic relations, in the development of proletarian ideology, which smashed the hopes of the Pan-Islamists, Pan-Turkists and Pan-Iranians." The leaders of the revolt were consciously trying to weaken Russia, the source of progress, and to weaken or dissolve ties with the Russian people. In all cases the uprisings tended to disrupt orderly processes of growth, as well as the economic and cultural benefits transmitted by the Russians. "The revolt," Kolesnikova concluded, "brought great harm to the working masses."[26]

In essence the argument was whether the Turkmen uprisings tipped the scales on the reactionary or progressive side. The dom-

26. *Materialy nauchnoi sessii,* pp. 342-56. Kolesnikova's minority report was accompanied by a footnote in the published report stating that she was unable to stay to the end of the meeting, and that her observations were being published from her manuscript. One cannot help wondering whether she might have softened her remarks if she had been able to ascertain the drift of the meeting. It is evident, in any case, that she knew the contents of Tursunov's report, and that other participants had read her statement, since they answered it in later discussion.

inant forces at Tashkent held that the reactionary manifestations
in Turkmenia should be regarded as exceptions, thus aligning the
Turkmen phase of the 1916 revolt with the larger rebellion, which
had been declared progressive. Kolesnikova's view that the reactionary uprisings were more characteristic of the larger movement
was argued even more pointedly by Tarasov, who charged that
proponents of the new interpretation had resorted to falsification to
give their case some foundation. Tarasov recalled that the Ashkhabad Conference had agreed on the reactionary character of uprisings in four areas, "that is to say, in reality, all the uprisings
that took place on the territory of Turkmenia." He charged
that Piaskovskii and Kuliev, who had made reports on the Turkmen phase of the revolt, had seized upon other minor disturbances,
and had magnified their significance in order to make the events
in Turkmenia predominantly progressive. Piaskovskii and Kuliev
had admitted that most of the Turkmen uprisings were reactionary,
but had "added to their reports two falsified 'revolutionary' revolts
in Turkmenia, at Serakhs and Atrek, and, incorrectly evaluating
them, contrasted them to the revolts in the Khiva Khanate, Tedzhen
and Giurgen. On this basis the joint scholarly council [at Ashkha-
bad] reached a decision on the national liberation, progressive
character of all the revolts of 1916 in Turkmenia."

What about these two "revolutionary" revolts, as Tarasov called
them? His listeners must have noted that he drew his arguments
straight from tsarist archives, not bothering with tangential Lenin
and Stalin observations, with which the conference abounded. On
the Serakhs case Tarasov quoted three documents. The first two,
from tsarist officials, reported that bands of thieves were stealing
cattle and raiding caravans, taking advantage of the unsettled
situation. Reference was made to particularly heavy raids on the
nights of October 1 and 2, 1916 (precisely the dates of the organization of the Piaskovskii-Kuliev national liberation movement). The
third document was the most convincing. It was an excerpt from
an affadavit made by the leader, one Kurban Durdy Essenov, under
questioning by tsarist officials. On the night in question Kurban
reported that he and about a hundred others attacked the Russian
garrison at Serakhs, firing about fifty shots in the course of two
hours. After he had been caught he admitted that he had been
going on pilfering raids regularly for three months. Tarasov observed that "it is difficult to see, as leaders of a revolutionary movement, these ringleaders of bands of thieves, who acknowledged at

the time of their questioning their raids and violence, shamelessly carried out against their comrades." As to the Atrek revolt, Tarasov charged that Piaskovskii and Kuliev had lifted it out of its setting and changed its character. It was in reality a part of the general reactionary movement of the Krasnovodsk area, led by the *starshina* Mergen, who was admitted by all to be a reactionary. Here the thin line seems to have been between Tarasov's view that Mergen actually led the movement and the prevailing view that he "tried to use" the revolt for his own ends. The early *volneniia* in Turkmenia, according to Tarasov, were potentially progressive, but were soon captured and held by reactionary leadership. The Turkmen phase of the 1916 revolt, taken as a whole, could only be characterized as reactionary. "All the leaders of the armed uprisings in Turkmenia in 1916 were enemies not only of the Turkmen people, but of the Russian people as well."

The intensity of Tarasov's rebuttal is pointed up by his frequent use of terminology usually reserved for the denunciation of bourgeois historians. Referring to the "pseudo-scientific, unobjective conclusion on the evaluation of the revolts in Turkmenia," he declared that "it was devoid of logic and sound thinking." Three times he specifically charged his two colleagues with falsification, and indicated that all the others had followed them without question: "Piaskovskii and Kuliev, by the method of plain falsification, succeeded in persuading the members of the joint Learned Council of the existence in Turkmenia in 1916 of even more revolutionary revolts in contrast to their reactionary revolts in Tedzhen and Giurgen. . . . By using all means, including falsification, to prove their untrue views, they bring harm to historical science."[27]

The accused historians apparently made no detailed reply to Tarasov and Kolesnikova. Kuliev, who in an earlier speech, had referred to the Serakhs event as the work of "a hundred young Turkmens, members of a workers' circle," made no further statement for the record.[28] Piaskovskii dealt with his differences with the pair of critics at some length, but offered no new facts. Their error, he said, was that they "put everything together into one common heap and do not trouble themselves with a detailed examination of the course of the revolt in each separate area."[29] This was, of course, precisely the charge Tarasov had placed against

27. *Ibid.*, pp. 402-5.
28. *Ibid.*, p. 325.
29. *Ibid.*, p. 372.

him. The final resolution of the conference generalized on the whole movement, which it characterized as progressive, with local reactionary manifestations, noting in passing that some historians considered all the revolts as reactionary, while others regarded all as progressive without exception. "The conference considers both of these points of view to be erroneous," the resolution added.

The minority reports of Kolesnikova and Tarasov not only represented a stubborn adherence to facts, but in a real sense they were a boomerang response to the party's emphasis. Both speakers referred repeatedly to the progressive advantages the Central Asian peoples enjoyed after annexation and to the meddling of foreign agents. The revolts inevitably brought about an alienation from the Russian people and worked to the advantage of the imperialists. There was even a hint in Kolesnikova's statement that opposition to orderly, stable government, particularly in times of war, was a treasonable activity and *ipso facto* reactionary. In this sense the two were *plus royaliste que le roi*.[30]

No such fireworks were heard in the other sessions of the conference, but since all the meetings touched in some way on the new interpretation, a brief summary of them will be included here. One of the subjects, "The Reactionary Nature and Treacherous Role of Pan-Islamism and Pan-Turkism," was apparently thought to be beyond need of debate. The conference heard a long lecture on the subject by Gafurov, and let it go at that. In this speech Gafurov was wearing his other hat as Secretary of the Central

---

30. At the end of this session the main speaker, Tursunov, undertook to answer the questions of participants. The tone of the three questions that were asked suggests that some people were trying to trap the speaker: (1) What had Lenin and Stalin said about the revolt of 1916? Tursunov said that "specific statements of V. I. Lenin . . . are not known to us" and went on for four paragraphs to reveal that they had said nothing directly on the subject but had made other statements that were applicable. This may have been a slam at speakers who had drawn so heavily on Lenin and Stalin in recent articles and in speeches to the conference (in the key article of Iakunin and Kuliev in *Voprosy istorii*, twenty-eight of the fifty-four footnote references were to Lenin and Stalin). (2) What was the relationship of the Russian people to the revolt? Tursunov replied that this question had been "studied very poorly by our historians" but that some eye-witnesses who had reported to the Frunze meeting the previous year recalled that "the Russian people had regarded sympathetically the revolt of the Kirgiz people." The whole question needed deep study from the archives. (3) What was the character of the Karakalpak revolt in the Sarybiisk and Chimbae regions? Replying that "materials on this question have not as yet been studied from all sides," the speaker immediately turned to a general discussion of local revolts elsewhere. This was the last question he replied to.

Committee of the Tadzhik party, revealing clearly the political motivation behind the conference.[31] His frequent references to the dark schemes of the imperialists (including Americans) in Central Asia before the Revolution and his warnings about the current dangers lurking on the border were unmistakable evidences of the connections between historical interpretations and contemporary political problems. His audience received his evaluation of the problem against a background of Soviet headlines on an "aggressive bloc" being formed in the Middle East, Iraqi-Turkish talks, U.S. pressure on Jordon and Syria, a Turkish-Pakistani treaty, and Pakistani negotiations in Washington.

On the question of patriarchal-feudal relations in Central Asia, the conference issued several pronouncements apparently intended to facilitate its analysis within the framework of Marxism-Leninism. In the conference resolution it was declared that there were no special cases, as some historians had stated, but that these complex societies were fully explicable by the laws of historical development. Feudal relations were said to have been based on land (not cattle), and the contention of some Soviet historians that nomads could not rise above the primitive stage of development was rejected.

The questions of the formation of bourgeois nations and periodization afforded new opportunities for extending the progressiveness of annexation. It was the decision of the conference that in the short period between annexation and the Revolution, there was not sufficient time for bourgeois nations to be formed. This process was telescoped by the Revolution, which brought about the formation of socialist nations. In any event the introduction of "capitalist relations" into Central Asia represented an economic leap for the peoples. In the session on periodization the idea that Central Asia was historically more backward than the West and that it had been locked in a long period of "universal feudalism" was rejected. The periodization of Central Asian history according to dynasties (the error of Uzbek historians) was rejected; the group declared that Central Asia's periodization fell within the general scope of that of the other peoples of the U.S.S.R. This finding, according to the resolution of the conference, would facilitate the production of general histories of the republics from a Marxist viewpoint.

31. Gafurov's speech was not published in the proceedings of the conference. The *Central Asian Review* compiled a summary of it from the Central Asian press (*CAR*, II [1954], No. 4, 308-10).

A week after the conference *Pravda vostoka* published a long report on its proceedings. It glossed all differences of opinion and expressed satisfaction with the meeting, which had made a "considerable contribution to the study of the history of the peoples of Central Asia and Kazakhstan . . . [and] helped to strengthen creative cooperation between scholars of the brotherly republics of the Soviet Union. . . ."[32] In March the Presidium of the U.S.S.R. Academy of Sciences heard a report on the conference and passed a resolution calling for further strengthening of work on Central Asian history through the cooperation of numerous research institutes which were "to give systematic consultative help to the scholars of Central Asia." The institutes were to draw up detailed and coordinated plans of work, and were to speed up the publication of documentary collections. The resolution called for further research and elaboration of some questions, but did not include the 1916 revolt, which was not apparently considered to be correctly evaluated.[33]

The impact of the second Tashkent Conference can be seen in the new history of the Uzbeks, which began to appear the following year.[34] This is especially noticeable in the history of the modern period up to the Revolution, when contrasted with the 1947 account, which had been the object of so much criticism. The earlier collective, headed by Bakhrushin, had represented tsarist expansion into Central Asia as typical conquest for economic and military gains, and had not even given lip service to the progressive consequences of annexation. Economic and cultural advances, when acknowledged, were said to have been for the benefit of the Russians living there.[35] Nothing was said about a growing friendship of peoples; it was actually denied by references to separate settlements of Russians and Uzbeks in the cities.[36] All revolts were considered to be progressive and of the national liberation type, including the Andizhan Revolt of 1898. On the 1916 revolt this history quoted an official

32. *Pravda vostoka*, February 12, 1954; complete translation in *CDSP*, VI, No. 7, 7-8.

33. "Ob itogakh ob"edinennoi nauchnoi sessii, posviashchennoi istorii narodov Srednei Azii i Kazakhstana," *VAN SSSR*, No. 5, 1954, pp. 60-61; reported in *Pravda*, March 25, 1954.

34. *Istoriia uzbekskoi SSR*, ed. S. P. Tolstov, R. N. Nabiev, Ia. G. Guliamov, and V. A. Shishkin (Tashkent, 1955), Vol. I, Part 1; *ibid.*, ed. M. G. Vakhabov, V. Ia. Nepomnin, and T. N. Kary-Niiazov (Tashkent, 1956), Vol. I, Part 2.

35. *Istoriia narodov Uzbekistana*, ed. S. V. Bakhrushin, V. Ia. Nepomnin, and V. A. Shishkin (Tashkent, 1947), II, 352-56.

36. *Ibid.*, p. 350.

document stating that in the Dzhizak area the revolt was considered by "all honorable natives to be a holy war against the Russians."[37] There were no Bolshevik heroes, and no German, Turkish, or British villains. By contrast the post-Tashkent history of the Uzbeks contains long passages on the economic and cultural growth under the influence of the Russian people. The Andizhan Revolt, discussed in the 1947 edition to the length of eight pages, is reduced to five paragraphs, and is of "a deeply reactionary, anti-popular character," organized mainly by the "Kokand aristocracy and the clergy," with a program of "Pan-Islamic propaganda." One of the leaders is said to have received two letters from the Sultan, offering the movement his blessing and support.[38] The 1916 revolt is dissected a dozen ways, with the Dzhizak area receiving lengthy explanation as a popular *vosstanie* that fell under the leadership of "feudal-clerical elements" so darkly reactionary that the term *miatezh* (mutiny) is employed from this point on in the course of the uprising. When the revolt was in its early national liberation phase, the fighting was directed against the native aristocracy (a full-page illustration shows Uzbek workers of Margelan in the act of killing two officials in native garb); in its later phase, however, it became a "separatist national movement" directed against Russians.[39]

But the Dzhizak revolt was an exception. Most of the Uzbek uprisings were progressive, and were regarded as a prelude to the great October Revolution. In one revolt, three Uzbeks who would soon become Bolsheviks held positions of leadership, and their names were listed in the history.[40] This new history of the Uzbeks indicated that the interpretation of the Central Asian revolts had been squared with the concept of the friendship of peoples.

37. *Ibid.*, p. 433.
38. *Istoriia uzbekskoi SSR*, ed. Vakhabov, Nepomnin, and Kary-Niiazov (1956), I, Part 2, 99-100.
39. *Ibid.*, pp. 388-91.
40. *Ibid.*, p. 398.

CHAPTER 10

THE THAW: AN ATTEMPT
TO REHABILITATE SHAMIL

*"The assertion that the mountain peoples' movement for
independence led by Shamil was reactionary contradicts
the facts. . . . We must put an end to the falsification of
the history of the mountain peoples of the Caucasus."* A.
M. Pikman in Voprosy istorii, No. 3, 1956, p. 84.

*"The publication in the Discussion and Debate Section of
A. M. Pikman's article on the Shamil movement (No. 3,
1956) was totally unjustified. The underlying theme of this
article is a veiled denial of the progressive significance of
the annexation of the Caucasus to Russia."* From the apology of the new editors of Voprosy istorii, No. 3, 1957, p. 12.

After April, 1953, Bagirov was a public enemy, and his
political activities were denounced in some of the same mass
meetings that reduced Beriia to a bandit and imperialist spy. His
historical ideas were not subjected to criticism for some time, however, and then only in a minor way. His accent on the "progressive
consequences" of the annexation of non-Russian peoples, to the
near exclusion of tsarist oppression, continued to prevail in Soviet
historical works. Ironically, the period of the most consistent elaboration of his ideas was the three years he spent in prison awaiting
his fate. Because of the time lag in publishing, works that were
in progress in Bagirov's heyday appeared in print in 1954 and 1955.
They emphasized the foreign threats to the non-Russian peoples,
the benefits of annexation, and the growth of the friendship of

peoples, and either omitted all reference to Russian colonialism or made brief generalized statements about it.

At conferences of historians held in the Caucasus during the year after Bagirov's fall, it was made clear that very little had changed. A meeting on the history of Kabarda, held in Nal'chik in August, 1953, was intended to force the hand of the specialists on the area who were reluctant to commit themselves to print, and to give them ideological guidance. A collective, headed by N. A. Smirnov, which had been upbraided at a similar meeting three years earlier, was still hesitating to submit a manuscript. The participants discussed still another *maket* on the history of Kabarda, by Bushuev, and found it unacceptable in several respects. It was deficient in its elaboration of the internal class struggle (it was too much a history of feudal princes, with too little attention to the popular masses), and on the social structure in the mid-nineteenth century ("semi-feudal—semi-patriarchal," said one historian, while another preferred "feudal, with semi-feudal survivals"). Vagueness on these points impeded a correct elaboration of the growing friendship of peoples. The local party secretary made a Bagirov-style speech, expressing alarm at both the paucity of historical works and the ideas expressed in those that had appeared. In the absence of scholarly works on local history, he turned to historical accounts contained in popular books. One author had made the mistake of referring to "the political conquest" of the area and "the bitterness and hatred of the mountain people against all the Russian people"; another did not show "the role of the Russian people in the liberation struggle of Kabarda against the Turkish-Crimean plunderers" and did not "reveal the historic roots of friendship of the Russian and Kabardinian peoples."[1]

At a much larger conference of social scientists of the three Union Republics of the Transcaucasus, held in Baku at the end of March, 1954, Pankratova gave a "tasks ahead" speech, calling for the correction of offending passages concerning the friendship of peoples and for more coordinated work by scholars of the Caucasus on this subject. Three speeches were presented on the progressive consequences theme—one for each republic. Other speeches on the formation of socialist nations in the Caucasus provided another vehicle for emphasizing Russian influence. There were three reports on "the influence of leading ideas of Russia" on the devel-

1. "Nauchnaia sessiia po voprosam istorii kabardinskogo naroda," *VI*, No. 10, 1953, pp. 150-53.

opment of philosophy, and two on "the ideas of friendship and brotherhood of peoples" as developed in literary ties. Although this conference was purportedly convened to facilitate the coordination of the work of the Union Republic Academies of Science in the social sciences, it was in reality devoted almost entirely to propagandizing the elder brother concept.[2] It is interesting, however, that although the elder brother permeated this meeting, the term itself, which was so closely associated with Bagirov, appears to have been tainted by his fall. Soviet scholars, who had never favored the term, avoided it at this meeting, and it has been used mainly in popular works since 1953.

There were small signs by 1954 that historians were ready to retreat from some of the extreme positions they had been obliged to take. One of the first retrograde motions can be detected in connection with the whitewashing of tsarist colonialism, which had been achieved mainly by silence on the matter in historical accounts. This reached its extreme, as far as the textbooks were concerned, in the 1954 revision of the Nechkina textbook on Russia in the nineteenth century, which ignored the whole matter so completely that a Soviet historian, five years later, when the climate had moderated considerably, charged that in the book "not a word is said about the aggressiveness of tsarist autocracy in Central Asia, and furthermore, the expansionist character of the tsarist offensive in that area is even denied."[3] In her speech to the Baku Conference, Pankratova cautiously asked for a more realistic view on this question. Sandwiched between her exhortations for more attention to progressive Russian influences was this comment:

> The history of the struggle of the non-Russian peoples for their social and national liberation must be presented truthfully, neither blackened nor embellished. One must not hush up or idealize the colonizing policies of peoples. In historical works it is necessary to demonstrate what divided peoples, as well as what united them. Therefore it follows that great emphasis should be given to the question of the historical roots of the friendship of peoples, of their growing closer together, of their common struggle against tsarism and capitalism. Historians face the task of studying the question of how, by the laws of historical de-

2. *Trudy ob"edinennoi nauchnoi sessii Akademii Nauk SSSR i Akademii Nauk zakavkazskikh respublik po obshchestvennym naukam (29 marta-2 aprela, 1954 g.)* (Baku, 1957).

3. Piaskovskii in *VI*, No. 8, 1959, p. 21.

velopment, the fighting union of the exploited peoples with the Russian people was strengthened, in opposition to the union of the feudal aristocracy and the Russian landlords.

Pankratova charged that Bagirov's emphasis had actually had an opposite effect from what he intended:

> In this connection it is important to note that Bagirov did not have this aim in his articles devoted to the unmasking of Shamil. For him it was not so much a question of showing the nature of the nationalistic ideology of Shamil as of emphasizing that he was a Turkish spy, which served mainly to irritate the Dagestani people and drive a wedge between the friendship of peoples.
>
> Such methods and aims have nothing in common with our struggle for the triumph of the ideology of the friendship of peoples.[4]

Pankratova's rejection of the characterization of Shamil as a spy received support from A. V. Fadeev, who added that the *imam's* followers were not acting primarily for any foreign power. One of the most absurd propositions used to denigrate the Shamil movement was the idea that it was a feudal movement without popular support and without roots in the Caucasus. In an article "On the Domestic Social Base of the Muridist Movement in the Caucasus in the Nineteenth Century," Fadeev showed evidences of some cautious re-thinking.[5] The burden of his argument was that although Muridism was "brought into the Caucasus from outside, and received the active support of the Turks, and subsequently from British emissaries," the larger resistance movement had an internal basis and support. He denied that Shamil was the leader of "a band of Murids," like foreign invaders, as recent works had stated. He specifically denounced the Tbilisi documents and several articles in which this view was stated (but did not include his own article on "Muridism as a Weapon of Aggressive Turkey and Britain," an important early contribution).[6] He also backed away slightly from the position that Muridism had no popular support by stating that "in the ranks of participants in the Muridist movement there were not a few workers of the mountain people, who saw it as a weapon in their anti-feudal and anti-colonial aims."

4. *Trudy ob"edinennoi nauchnoi sessii,* pp. 55-56.
5. A. V. Fadeev, "O vnutrennoi sotsial'noi baze miuridistskogo dvizheniia na Kavkaze v XIX veke," *VI,* No. 6, 1955, pp. 67-77.
6. See Chapter 8 above, p. 162, n. 35.

Fadeev's whole tone was one of moderation: for the first time in
five years an article involving Shamil did not contain the ritualistic
attack on him. The retreat from the Bagirov view represented by
these comments of Pankratova and Fadeev was not universal, however. Two other Soviet historians, Smirnov and Bushuev, who
would be on the side of caution throughout the coming discussion,
continued the unreconstructed Bagirov view in works they published during this period.[7]

The first substantial reappraisal of the question occurred in
the now-famous readers conference of *Voprosy istorii*, late in
January, 1956, two weeks before the opening of the Twentieth
Party Congress. In the discussion of a wide range of subjects, the
participants at this meeting showed that they had had advance
notice of many of the themes that would figure prominently in the
Congress. The conference lasted three days and was attended by
about six hundred people. E. N. Burdzhalov, the deputy editor,
introduced his campaign to clean the Augean stables at this meeting.[8] Referring pointedly to questions of distortion and even falsification by Soviet historians, Burdzhalov mentioned Shamil as a
case in point. He revealed that the editors had been under pressure
to re-examine the question, but their hands had been tied because of
the Bagirov articles (an argument that hardly held water, since
Bagirov had been in disgrace for nearly three years). Burdzhalov
stated that "we must return to this question and give a truthful,
correct appraisal of this movement." But he set the limits and the
direction of the reappraisal by stating carefully that the progressiveness of annexation of the Caucasus was not in question, and by
directing his remarks primarily against those who had covered up
the evils of tsarist colonialism.

The most thoroughgoing criticism on the question came from a
Moscow middle-school teacher, A. M. Pikman, who charged that

7. N. A. Smirnov, *Ocherki istorii izucheniia islama v SSSR* (Moscow, 1954);
S. K. Bushuev, *Iz istorii vneshnepoliticheskikh otnoshenii v period prisoedineniia Kavkaza k Rossii* (Moscow, 1955), pp. 38-63. Very little was published
on Shamil between 1952 and 1955. *Voprosy istorii* published only one
article, in which Shamil's operations during the time of the Crimean war were
pictured as being coordinated with Turkish military plans. See I. V. Bestuzhev,
"Oborona Zakavkaz'ia v krymskoi voine, 1853-56 godov," *VI*, No. 12, 1954,
pp. 53-66.
8. "Konferentsiia chiatelei zhurnala 'Voprosy istorii,'" *VI*, No. 2, 1956, pp.
199-213. Burdzhalov had lectured on the Shamil movement in 1940 to students
at the Higher Party School (see E. Skazin, *Dagestan v sovetskoi istoricheskoi
literature* [Makhachkala, 1963], p. 87).

there had been "gross falsification" in the matter, and that the views of Marx, Engels, and Dobroliubov had been distorted so as to give an opposite meaning from the original intent. He condemned Smirnov, Fadeev, and Daniialov by name, and charged that those who held opposing views had been denied space in journals since 1950. The sole criterion on which the Muridist movement should be judged, according to Pikman, was whether it contributed to the general movement of European workers for freedom from oppression. Concluding that it did, he implied that it was therefore progressive.

Several other speakers commented on the question. Some deplored the uncritical use of sources in past attempts to show Shamil's foreign connections, and the idealization of tsarist colonial policies. Three speakers, including Pankratova, disagreed with Pikman, persisting in their view that the movement was reactionary. The most revealing comment was made by B. D. Datsiuk of the Higher Party School, who noted candidly that Moscow historians had "corrected Kazakh histories, and proved the progressive and liberal character of the 1916 revolt." Implying that their evaluation of questions in the Caucasus might have been less accurate, he declared, "However, it would be incorrect to eulogize Shamil. This will not contribute to strengthening of the friendship of peoples —especially the recollection of the slaughter which Shamil carried out against other peoples."

The Twentieth Party Congress gave more attention to the problem of historical writing than any party congress before or since. Khrushchev, Mikoyan, Shepilov, and Suslov all discussed the matter, and Pankratova, who, as chief editor of *Voprosy istorii* and a member of the Central Committee, was probably the highest ranking historian, was given the floor to engage in a long exercise in self-criticism. "Scholarly work in the history of our Party and of Soviet society," remarked Mikoyan, "is perhaps the most backward sector of our ideological work."

Mikoyan's criticism of historians was the most detailed and biting. He covered a wide range of shortcomings: closed archives, hackwork, falsification, and the interference of Moscow historians in the work in the Union Republics (he drew laughter with a remark that Ukrainian historians, if given the chance, might produce a better history of the Ukraine than Moscow historians "who undertook the job, but perhaps would have been better advised not to do it"). His examples of falsification were the works on the party history of the Transcaucasus (Beriia) and Baku (Bagirov). Without mentioning the authors by name, he stated that their books "stretched the facts, arbitrarily exalted some people and failed even to mention others." His most caustic remarks were about the failure of Soviet historians to produce an acceptable history of the Revolution after forty years. He stated bluntly that one of the main drawbacks to their success had been the blind following of the *Short Course*.[9]

Khrushchev limited his remarks on history to a call for a new party history, but in the section of his report on nationality policy he made a remark that Soviet historians must have read with puzzled curiosity. He began by quoting Lenin to the effect that "only a great attentiveness to the interests of various nations removes the grounds for conflicts, removes mutual distrust." Using the same terms, he then stated that "our Party has succeeded in removing the mutual distrust which existed among the people of tsarist Russia, in uniting all the peoples of the Soviet Union by bonds of fraternal friendship. . . ."[10] This reference to mutual distrust before the Revolution was a denial of the whole legend of the solidarity of the Russian and non-Russian peoples that had been built up in the last decade. It seemed to put the emphasis back where it was before the War: that it was the Bolshevik nationality policy that had created a friendship of peoples in the period of Soviet power.

What did Khrushchev's two references to mutual distrust signify? Viewed in retrospect, it appears to have been a typical Khrushchevian off-the-cuff remark, but it may well have caused historians to ponder whether a change of interpretation was being called for. The remark occurred in a formal speech, which had presumably been given considerable thought and review. It came in the midst of criticism of the legacy of Stalin, of which this view was an indisputable part. It is entirely possible that Burdzhalov and others who were launching a campaign for the reform of historical writing were misled by this statement, and others like it,

9. *Pravda*, February 18, 1956; complete translation in *CDSP*, VIII, No. 8, 3-11.

10. *Pravda*, February 15, 1956; complete translation in *CDSP*, VIII, No. 5, 3-15. The Lenin quotation, in the first place, was completely out of context. Lenin had been answering a question about Soviet policy on the Straits. His reference to nations (*natsii*) clearly referred to the Great Powers. However, he did refer to "mutual distrust" of the peoples within the Russian Empire on other occasions.

which seemed to indicate that the Twentieth Party Congress was opening the way to a thoroughgoing change. The would-be reformers had to find out by trial and error that what the leaders wanted was a careful and selective review which would leave untouched some myths of political utility.

How attentive the profession was to Khrushchev's remark is revealed in the speech Pankratova made to the Party Congress a few days later.[11] She not only parroted his terms precisely, but also repeated his apparent turn of interpretation: "It is our duty to elucidate with concrete historical materials the question of how the Communist Party overcame the mutual distrust which used to exist among the peoples of tsarist Russia and united them in bonds of friendship, to show the past and present concern of the Party for the interests, the national distinctions and hopes of the peoples, large and small. . . ." She also indicated that a revision of the interpretation of tsarist colonialism was in order: "Our textbooks and works on the history of individual peoples give too little attention to exposing the national-colonial oppression of tsarist autocracy. A number of authors, while rightly emphasizing the progressive significance of the incorporation of these peoples into Russia, devote too little attention to the other side of the question. Tsarism brought to the peoples cruel oppression and held back their political, economic and cultural development." She characteristically blamed the historians themselves for the serious shortcomings, but added other culprits—the cult of the individual, and the cautious bureaucrats of the Academy of Sciences: "We have many resolutions, many meetings, but little research or creative discussion. . . . Scholarly problems cannot be solved by orders or by voting."

In its March issue, *Voprosy istorii* opened its columns to its critic, Pikman. His short article, "On the Struggle of the Caucasian Mountain People with Tsarist Colonizers," elaborated on his remarks at the readers conference.[12] A large part of the article was devoted to quotations from Marx, Engels, and Dobroliubov, in an attempt to restore what Pikman thought were their original views. His over-all appraisal of the leader and movement was reminiscent of the 1930's. Shamil was essentially democratic; his dictatorial

11. *Pravda*, February 22, 1956; complete translation in *CDSP*, VIII, No. 12, 9-11.
12. A. M. Pikman, "O bor'be kavkazskikh gortsev s tsarskimi kolonizatorami," *VI*, No. 3, 1956, pp. 75-84.

tendencies in the later years were to be attributed to his desperate circumstances. The movement was a popular one, and anyone who thought otherwise must account for the number of tsarist troops used against it for twenty-five years. Even the tsar's generals themselves had recognized the mass character of the movement, as Pikman tried to show by entering excerpts from their reports in evidence. As for support from Turkey and Britain, Pikman did not deny it, but pointed out that Shamil's primary goal was not to accomplish their goals, but to win independence for his people. When one's back is to the wall, one takes military aid from any quarter without question. Kossuth, Mazzini, Garibaldi, and the Polish rebels of 1863 had taken foreign assistance, and that did not prevent Soviet historians from declaring that their work was progressive. Pikman thought Shamil's case was comparable. By weakening tsarism, Shamil had assisted the general revolutionary movement in Europe, especially the revolutions of 1848. Shamil's shortcomings must not be overlooked, but neither should the fact that the movement was of a national liberation character with mass support.

Although Pikman's article was, for the most part, straightforward and well reasoned, there were omissions and passages of studied vagueness that indicated that the whole friendship of peoples idea was under re-examination—at least in the mind of this writer. He backed away slightly from his statement at the readers conference about the progressiveness of the Shamil movement, only inferring it in the article. He did not write a ritualistic passage about the unshakable friendship of the Russians and the mountain peoples, but merely stated that they had a common enemy, tsarism. He conformed to the new demands in terminology in a transparent way: in two instances when his quotations referred to fighting between the mountain people and "the Russians," he inserted a clarification in parenthesis—"that is, tsarist forces"; "that is, tsarism." He omitted any reference whatever to the progressive consequences of annexation. The editors tried to remedy this by adding a note at the end of the article stating that "the progressive consequences of the annexation of the peoples of the Caucasus to Russia are obvious," but that since questions had arisen about the character of the movement, the editors were publishing the Pikman article and calling for "a concrete historical elaboration of the mountain peoples' movement."

The unsettled state of Soviet historiography was further revealed in a conference of the history faculty of Moscow University on April 14, 1956, on "The Twentieth Party Congress and the Tasks of Soviet Historical Science."[13] The discussion showed how unaccustomed Soviet historians were to a degree of freedom that had not existed in twenty years. The directives of the Party Congress were entirely too generalized: the dogmatism and fabrication of the Stalin era were to be eliminated in favor of a return to positions of Marxism-Leninism. But what did that mean in concrete interpretations? How far were historians to go in reinterpreting sensitive questions the party had promoted? A wide range of subjects was discussed, including the Shamil question. Two well-known historians showed their displeasure with the way old interpretations were being unceremoniously discarded. A. M. Sakharov "spoke against the general denial of everything that has been done by historians in the last few years, against the dogmatic and flippant revision of several controversial questions, as for example, such a revision as that made by A. M. Pikman." Bushuev sounded the same note of caution about the question of tsarist colonialism. Acknowledging that the old imposed view had been one-sided, he declared that some historians were going to the other extreme. There had even been a suggestion that the work of Ivan IV in creating a strong centralized Russian state and expanding it had not been a progressive phenomenon. Such questions should not be revised without more investigation and discussion. But these views were challenged by several participants who had not figured in the controversy up to this time. One critic said that this was not simply a matter of interpretation, but of clearing up "distortions and plain fabrications." Another pointed out the inconsistency between the recent Soviet idealization of tsarist colonial policy and Soviet views on colonialism in the rest of the world. "A scientific, Leninist appraisal of tsarist colonial policy," he declared, would strike a blow at the contemporary colonial rulers of developing countries.

In the July issue, *Voprosy istorii* published a second article on Shamil, revising the old interpretation still further.[14] The author was G. D. Daniialov, a Dagestani *kandidat* of historical science (not to be confused with the Party Secretary, A. D. Daniialov),

13. M. I. Kheifets, "XX s"ezd KPSS i zadachi sovetskoi istoricheskoi nauki," *Vestnik moskovskogo universiteta. Seriia obshchestvennykh nauk,* No. 4, 1956, pp. 147-54.

14. G. D. Daniialov, "O dvizhenii gortsev pod rukovodstvom Shamilia," *VI,* No. 7, 1956, pp. 67-72; condensed translation in *CDSP,* VIII, No. 40, 3-5.

who would figure prominently in the coming controversy. For the first time since 1950 Shamil's movement was termed progressive without qualification. Daniialov rejected the view that the movement was supported mainly by feudal elements; they had in fact opposed Shamil. The movement was anti-feudal, with mass support, and was *ipso facto* progressive. In support of this view, he resurrected the positive accomplishments of the leader: setting up an orderly government, and organizing an army; establishing law and order, a state treasury, and an official language (Arabic). On the question of Shamil's foreign support, Daniialov went further than Pikman, declaring that "no documents have been found which would prove that Shamil received direct assistance from Turkey in the form of arms, soldiers or money." He admitted that Shamil had used repression and terror and that Muridism contained "much which was negative and reactionary," but that at the same time it "played a unifying role among the mountain peoples in their struggle against tsarism." Here he referred to Lenin's well-known dictum about political protests under a religious cloak. Like Pikman, Daniialov maintained complete silence on the related question of the progressive nature of the annexation of Dagestan.

CONFUSION IN THE CLASSROOM

Since 1950 Soviet teachers had faced a difficult problem in attempting to orient their students to changing views on heroes, national movements, and Russian colonialism. It will be recalled that Pikman, the first person to speak out on Shamil, was a middle-school teacher. In his remarks he referred to the difficulties in the classroom. Several speakers at the April conference at Moscow University also alluded to the problem. The editors and authors of textbooks were notoriously slow about incorporating revisions into their books, and in both 1950 and 1956 the party views had been expressed too late in the year to permit revision for the fall term, no matter how diligent the authors might have been. In both instances the educators had to resort to stop-gap methods, consisting of the publication of instructional articles in teachers' journals, pamphlets, and manuals.

The difficulties involved in teaching about Shamil in the fall of 1950 are described incidentally in the course of two articles intended to give the frustrated teacher some guidance. Writing in *Uchitel'skaia gazeta* (*The Teacher's Newspaper*) in September,

P. Leibengrub, a teacher in the Moscow public schools, warned his colleagues about conflicting viewpoints in the textbooks, suggesting that popular stories on Shamil and Sheik Mansur would have a harmful effect on students if they continued to read them.[15] The textbook situation, as Leibengrub described it, was bewildering. The Pankratova edition of 1949 was, of course, completely in error about Shamil and Muridism. A new edition was rushed to press in the summer of 1950, with this section rewritten to party requirements. But some schools had not received the new editions, and Soviet educators had issued a new manual with a revised section on "The Conquest of the Caucasus." Teachers were advised to lean heavily on this manual and the recent Bagirov article. The same topic was taught at the primary level from the Shestakov textbook, which had appeared in a new edition on the eve of the change of interpretation. No effort had been made to repair this textbook, and the teacher had to resort to his own devices. Thus a family that happened to include a fourth-grader and a ninth-grader might have some interesting discussions concerning homework, which had to be prepared from textbooks having diametrically opposed interpretations on a subject deemed politically vital. A later article, "On Teaching the Theme of 'The Conquest of the Caucasus by Russia' in the Ninth-Grade of Secondary School," went into far greater detail in its advice to teachers.[16] They were told to "ask students . . . not to use the old editions when studying this theme," but to make an outline in their notebooks based on materials the teacher would provide. The map in the old edition was also to be avoided, since it captioned Shamil's movement incorrectly. Sample questions were furnished, and the teacher was asked to "generalize and supplement" the answers given by pupils. A recommended generalization was also given, emphasizing the advantages enjoyed by the non-Russians as a result of annexation to Russia. At the conclusion of the lesson the teacher would refer to the current scene by calling attention to the fact that Muridism was the basis for the reactionary ideology of Pan-Islamism and Pan-Turkism, whose center "is mainly in Turkey, but also in the U. S. and British governments, which, not sparing any means, continue to use Islam, just as they use Christianity, for their own re-

15. *Uchitel'skaia gazeta*, September 26, 1950, as quoted in *CDSP*, II, No. 39, 10.
16. F. P. Korovin, "O prepodavanii temy 'Zavoevanie Kavkaze Rossiei' v IX klasse srednei shkoly," *Prepodavanie istorii v shkole*, No. 6, 1950, pp. 31-38; condensed translation in *CDSP*, II, No. 50, 6-7.

actionary aims." For the next day's assignment, it was suggested that the pupil be asked to prepare, "from the material studied earlier, examples showing the reactionary nature of Islam, and the bloody crimes inspired and supported by Islam."

Other less gentle methods were used to impose the new line. The Komsomol Congress which met in Alma-Ata in July, 1951, heard a report on the *Pravda* article on Kenesary, and the student members were asked to keep a vigil on the work in their schools in order to promote Soviet patriotism and "the Stalinist friendship of peoples."[17] The following year students in the history department at the Kazakh State University drew up a list of grievances against their professors in a student newspaper article entitled "On the Grave Deficiencies in Our Department," and succeeded in inspiring one of *Pravda's* periodic exposés of bourgeois nationalism.[18] The case of Bekmakhanov's revoked degree was by no means unprecedented: *Voprosy istorii* mentioned the revocation of twenty degrees in 1951; the leading institution, with four offenses, was Herzen Pedagogical Institute in Leningrad.[19]

In the fall of 1956 Soviet schools were once again opening with obsolete textbooks. Two veteran textbook authors, Pankratova and L. P. Bushchik, prepared a pamphlet on *Questions of Teaching the History of the U.S.S.R. in the Light of the Twentieth Party Congress*.[20] The views of this pamphlet are important, since they were written in the late summer of 1956, when the interpretation was unsettled, and undoubtedly were subjected to careful discussion and review, as they were intended for millions of Soviet school children. In the absence of anything more concrete we can consider this pamphlet the best reflection of party thinking on the question immediately after the Pikman-Daniialov critique.

Among the six topics Pankratova and Bushchik discussed, the greatest amount of space was given to the Shamil movement. The authors suggested that teachers drop some of the extreme positions of the Bagirov era, but they were by no means willing to go as far

17. *Kazakhstanskaia pravda*, July 8 and 12, 1951.

18. E. Makarov, "V kazakhskom universitete zazhimaiut kritiku," *Pravda*, November 22, 1952.

19. "Tvorcheskaia kritika i samokritika—moguchee oruzhie nauchnogo progressa," *VI*, No. 11, 1951, pp. 19-27.

20. The quotations given here are from an abridged version of the pamphlet that was published in the *Teacher's Newspaper* ("Nekotorye voprosy prepodavaniia istorii SSSR v shkole," *Uchitel'skaia gazeta*, September 22, 1956, complete translation in *CDSP*, VIII, No. 38, 3-5). The pamphlet was compiled from lectures given by the authors at a pedagogical institute.

as Pikman and Daniialov in the complete rehabilitation of the hero. Though they stressed all the eventual benefits gained by the mountain peoples by annexation, they pointed out that tsarist colonial policies "evoked a just protest and national liberation movement of the oppressed peoples." Teachers were to emphasize that the just war waged by the mountain people represented a brief interruption in an already developed friendship: "The colonizing policy of tsarism struck a heavy blow at the friendship of many centuries of the peoples of the Caucasus and the Russian people. Defending their lives, property and land, the small mountain peoples had to carry on a heroic struggle against the huge tsarist empire."

Pankratova and Bushchik made a concession to Pikman by agreeing that the Shamil movement, coming "at a time when tsarism was the all-powerful gendarme of Europe and the bulwark of European reaction . . . helped the liberation struggle of the Poles, Hungarians and other European peoples" by weakening the tsar. On the relationship of the movement to Muridism and foreign powers, however, they went only part of the way to the position of the revisionists:

> They [Shamil and his lieutenants] zealously propagated Muridism, one of the most reactionary Moslem teachings, throughout the Caucasus.
> Foreign powers, especially Turkey and Britain, *tried to use* this reactionary ideology, as well as the whole movement of the mountain peoples, against Russia. However, the opinion that the struggle of many years of the mountain people against tsarist troops was caused by Muridism, *a view spread in the Caucasus by Turkish and British agents,* is erroneous. Sources support the view that the mountain peoples' struggle against the tsarist conquerors was a fight for freedom and the independence of their country, which was being taken away *by tsarist generals and officials.*[21]

On the leader himself, the pamphlet was somewhat equivocal, conceding his talents, but guarding against making him a hero again. Shamil was mentioned only briefly in two short passages that were somewhat different in tone: "The talented ruler, warrior and mili-

21. This passage contains several interesting implications, noted by my emphasis. The authors do not retreat completely from Bagirov's views on Britain and Turkey, but only say that they tried to use the movement to their advantage. Their agents are now charged with the falsification about Muridism as the motive force of the Shamil movement. The mountain peoples were resisting tsarist generals and officials, not the Russian people.

tary leader, Shamil, a member of the mountain feudal hierarchy, led this struggle for a quarter of a century (1834-1859). . . . But Shamil and the mountain aristocracy around him were not consistent fighters against tsarism. Shamil and his associates exploited the mountain peoples' strong unrest with tsarist colonial policy in order to promote religious fanaticism and hatred of the 'infidels,' that is, of all Russians without distinction, among the masses."

The Pankratova-Bushchik interpretation of Shamil and Muridism was itself extremely ephemeral. Before the school year was out, Soviet teachers must have been surprised to read in their professional journal, *The Teaching of History in the School*, that this pamphlet designed to correct textbook errors was itself full of errors.[22] It seems that the authors were writing under the harmful influence of *Voprosy istorii*, during its heretical fling of 1956. Three of the pamphlet's propositions were emphatically rejected: the comparison of the Muridist movement with the European revolutionary movement, the equivocal elaboration of the social basis of the movement, and the "grave mistake" of denying the reactionary influence of Muridism on the whole anti-colonial movement. But this was the spring of 1957, and we are ahead of our story. We must first recount the reasons for the article that was designed to correct the corrective.

TWO CONFERENCES ON THE SHAMIL MOVEMENT

In the fall of 1956 two large conferences were held to discuss the Shamil problem. The first met in Makhachkala in October, the other in Moscow the following month. Both conferences are remarkable for the wide range of their interpretations, and for the intensity of the charges and counter-charges, which show through even in the formal reports of the meetings. It is also unusual that two conferences would have been held on the same subject within six weeks (some papers given at the first conference were repeated at the second), and that they should produce conclusions that were not in agreement in several respects. Evidence gleaned from these two meetings indicates strongly that the Dagestani historians, working from their base in Makhachkala, were making a strong and determined effort for a complete rehabilitation of Shamil and

22. P. P. Epifanov and M. E. Naidenov, "O broshiure 'Voprosy prepodavaniia istorii SSSR v svete reshenii XX s"ezda KPSS,' " *Prepodavanie istorii v shkole*, No. 5, 1957, pp. 113-17.

his movement, and that the Moscow authorities convened the second conference as a corrective to the first.

The Makhachkala Conference was attended by six hundred participants, almost entirely from the North Caucasus.[23] All the papers were given by historians from the area, and the U.S.S.R. Academy of Sciences was represented by only two delegates, whose contribution consisted of brief felicitous remarks. In the formal reports, the wide-ranging discussion from the floor, and the final resolution of the conference, the new Dagestani interpretation of the Shamil movement emerged. It was formulated concurrently with the dismantling of the Bagirov viewpoint, which the participants attacked with obvious relish.

The highlight of the work of demolition was a report on tsarist colonial policy in Dagestan by Kh. Ramazanov, a Dagestani historian, which had the devastating quality of Pokrovskii's essays on the subject. Ramazanov charged that the tsar preserved the worst features of the earlier feudal regime, that Ermolov's policies were harmful, that 200,000 dessiatins of Dagestani lands were usurped, that the tsarist land policy boiled down to cutting off the pastures, which led to the starvation of the mountain people.[24] Other speakers denounced the Tbilisi documents, maintaining that the whole idea of aid from Britain and Turkey was a pure myth. They rejected the idea that Shamil's support came primarily from feudal or clerical elements. In the discussion of these questions the evidences of local nationalism were unmistakable: the Dagestani speakers were particularly offended that the Georgian editors of the Tbilisi documents had considered Shamil a mere bandit; they resented references to the cultural backwardness of his followers. They were even sensitive about having Muridism pronounced reactionary. One speaker declared that Muridism was historically necessary: it was the only unifying force capable of welding the people together in their struggle for independence.

In their construction of a new interpretation, which was in reality a modification of the pre-1950 view, the historians of the Caucasus demonstrated that the game of far-fetched rationalization

23. An extensive (but incomplete) transcript of the proceedings was published in *O dvizhenii gortsev pod rukovodstvom Shamilia. Materialy sessii dagestanskogo filiala Akademii Nauk SSSR, 4-7 oktiabr, 1956 goda* (Makhachkala, 1957); a short summary was published in *Voprosy istorii*: "Obsuzhdenie voprosa o kharaktere dvizhenii gorskikh narodov severnogo Kavkaza v 20-50kh godakh XIX veka," VI, No. 12, 1956, pp. 188-98.

24. *O dvizhenii gortsev*, pp. 137-44.

could be played on both sides. Their task of producing an interpretation that would rehabilitate the Shamil movement, while at the
same time preserving an acceptable Marxist framework and protecting the party's two sacred cows—the friendship of peoples and
the progressiveness of annexation—involved some fancy footwork.
The central theme of the new interpretation was a separation of
the larger Shamil movement (progressive) from the clerical taint
of Muridism (reactionary). To accomplish this, various applications of the favorite technique of dissection were presented. One
speaker offered a three-part chronological division; another suggested four distinct periods, of which the last was reactionary. Still
another sought to divide the movement geographically, finding
Muridism to be more dominant in some areas than in others. It
was also suggested that historians should study the structure of
society in greater detail in order to detect the lines of division on
a class basis—a typical application of the Soviet technique of taking
an interpretation and going in search of a set of facts. There was
even a hint that dissecting the movement was perhaps unnecessary:
the participation of clerical and feudal elements in the movement
was further evidence that it was a broad, general movement involving all levels of society.

In the final resolution of the session, the conference participants
did not adopt any of these specific schemes; instead they strongly
asserted that narrow Muridism was not to be confused with the
broad Shamil movement: "The movement of the mountain people
under the leadership of Shamil, which has been represented as
Muridist, was in reality popular. It was aimed against the colonial
policies of tsarism. The movement of the mountain peoples was a
struggle of the broad working masses of the Northeast Caucasus for
their independence. The participation in this movement of the
clergy, as well as certain feudal elements, does not, in any sense,
make the movement feudal, or its leader, Shamil, a spokesman for
the interests of the feudal hierarchy."[25]

In the end, the historians at the Makhachkala Conference were
unable to remove some obvious contradictions in their interpretation. Their hair-splitting reasoning only served to put them in the
spotlight. The Muridist movement was Janus-like, good or bad,
depending on the angle of observation. Shamil's work was progressive, but so was his defeat, which consummated the annexation to

25. *Ibid.*, p. 249.

Russia. Tsarist colonialism was reactionary, but its results were objectively progressive. The most delicate point of all—so obviously contradictory that it was avoided or referred to only vaguely—was the remarkable view imposed on the conference that the friendship of the Russian and Caucasian peoples somehow existed and even grew while they were killing each other.

The Makhachkala Conference is also remarkable for the lack of the usual restraints imposed by the central Academy of Sciences in Moscow and by the party. These forces were present, but they were ineffectual. Only Fadeev and L. M. Ivanov attended from Moscow, and they had little to say. Fadeev's comments were those of a guest and peacemaker. Opening his remarks with his favorable impressions of the Caucasian scenery and climate, he went on to acknowledge that the views of 1950-52 were seriously in error. He agreed that the movement was popular, and was not generated from "external forces." But he did not go all the way with the consensus of the conference. He still hinted darkly that "foreign powers were interested in damaging Russia in the Caucasus," and continued in his view that clerical and feudal elements were prominent in the movement.

The only determined effort to hold the line was made by B. O. Khashaev, identified only as a representative of the Dagestan branch of the Institute of Marx and Engels. Khashaev charged that the discussion had neglected to elaborate several questions: (1) the social structure of Dagestan, (2) the reactionary nature of Muridism, (3) the aggressive policies of Britain and Turkey, and (4) the progressive significance of annexation. He accompanied this with a strange bit of involuted reasoning, by expressing doubts about the proposition that the movement had been provoked by tsarist colonial policy. Explaining that most of the tsarist troops were stationed in the lowlands, he stated that the mountain peoples had made few attacks on them in those locations.

These points Khashaev raised were precisely the ones that would be emphasized in the counter-attack on the Dagestani position a short time later. But they appear to have been ignored in the final resolution of the Makhachkala Conference, and when the proceedings were published by the Dagestan branch of the Academy of Sciences, Khashaev's report was deleted. The editor, G. D. Daniialov, a leader of the pro-Shamil forces, explained in the preface that he had not received a "revised manuscript" of Khashaev's report (see below, p. 216).[26]

The Moscow Conference, held under the auspices of the Institute of History, was attended by about five hundred participants, including most of the prominent specialists on the Caucasus.[27] Discussion at this meeting was no less frank than at the previous one, and there was a better balance of viewpoints, with a preponderance on the cautious side. At this conference the spokesmen for the extreme viewpoints—Pikman and Adzhemian—faced each other, and neither of them yielded an inch. There were six formal papers; three repeated from the Makhachkala Conference and three additional ones. The subjects of the new papers and their viewpoint strongly suggest that the Moscow Conference was deliberately planned as a corrective for the earlier discussion. They consisted of an analysis of the social structure of one section of the North Caucasus during the period (by M. V. Pokrovskii), a paper on the reactionary nature of Muridism (by Smirnov) and another on the Caucasus in international relations, in which Fadeev kept referring to British and Turkish plans and attempts to use Muridism, without giving concrete examples. Thus, three of the points the party spokesman, Khashaev, had raised at Makhachkala were dealt with prominently in Moscow. His remaining point, the progressiveness of annexation, received much emphasis throughout the meeting.

In the discussion Pikman took the floor first. The main thrust of his remarks was toward a further dissociation of Shamil and Muridism. The ties had been greatly overemphasized. He denied that there had ever been a distinctive Muridist ideology. Although Shamil was its titular head, he exercised no special religious authority and did not propound any religious teaching. Pikman was supported by V. G. Gadzhiev, a Dagestani historian, who stated that Fadeev, Bushuev, and Smirnov should have been correcting their own errors, instead of attacking Pikman. Another participant, with the suggestive name of Aliev, noted that Smirnov, the Russian authority on Islam, did not know much about Sufism. Burdzhalov, who was apparently the only Russian besides Pikman to support the pro-Shamil view, renewed the attack on tsarist colonialism. He maintained that one did not have to whitewash colonial policies

26. Apparently the only published statement on the Khashaev critique is the one-paragraph summary that appeared in the *Voprosy istorii* report.

27. *VI*, No. 12, 1956, pp. 188-98. The Makhachkala and Moscow Conferences are discussed in Paul B. Henze, "Unrewriting History—the Shamil Problem," *Caucasian Review*, No. 6 (1958), pp. 7-29.

in order to show the progressive consequences of annexation. The Russian acquisition of the Caucasus was plain conquest, and should be so labeled.

The emerging compromise was supported during the discussion by two delegates from the Institutes of Marxism-Leninism. B. O. Khashaev, who had single-handedly held the line at Makhachkala, restated the case: "We must show the popular-liberation character of the struggle of the mountain peoples and at the same time reveal the reactionary features of Muridism. The movement of the mountain peoples grew out of internal social forces, and was not inspired from outside. However, it is incorrect to consider the whole movement to be of an anti-feudal and anti-colonial character." Khashaev warned that *Voprosy istorii* had taken a one-sided position by publishing articles concealing the reactionary nature of Muridism. E. Iu. Bogush, of the Institute of Marxism-Leninism in Moscow, while tacitly admitting that the comments of Marx and Engels on Shamil had been grossly distorted in the early 1950's, showed his impatience with the current viewpoints of Bushuev and Adzhemian, who in his view simply proposed to forget that Marx and Engels had ever spoken on the subject. What was needed, he said, was a more profound analysis of their statements: "Marx and Engels came out in support of the liberation struggle of the mountain peoples of the Caucasus, as well as of other national liberation movements of the time."

The Moscow Conference is interesting for still another alignment of forces. The only participants from the Caucasus who stood against the pro-Shamil forces were one Armenian and two Georgians. Aside from the unreconstructed views of Adzhemian, who boasted that he had been the first to expose Shamil as a reactionary (in 1944), one Georgian tried to defend the Tbilisi documents, which had been severely attacked by participants from the North Caucasus, and another attacked Pikman, maintaining that the Shamil movement had strong Muridist motivation and Turkish ties and reminding the audience that Shamil had attacked the peoples of Georgia. There is a strong suggestion here that the old fires of enmity between Christian and Moslem in the Caucasus had not been put out.[28]

28. In an editorial review on Soviet policy on Islam, the *Central Asian Review* concluded in 1958 that "the latest attempt to rehabilitate Shamil . . . was probably abandoned because of the traditional anti-Muslim sentiment of the Georgians and Armenians." See *CAR*, VI (1958), No. 3, 242.

L. M. Ivanov, a "Moscow" historian, made the final remarks of the conference, summarizing the findings of the meeting. His report was hardly the statement of consensus it purported to be. The pro-Shamil forces must have listened with satisfaction to his remark that "the overwhelming majority of participants in the discussion recognized that the anti-colonial movement . . . was provoked by the aggressive and colonial policy of tsarism," and his call for a realistic appraisal of tsarist colonial oppression. But they could hardly agree with his repeated reference to the "intensification of the class struggle within the mountain society" as a cause of the movement, or his remarks about the importance of Muridism and the "striving of the ruling circles of Britain, Turkey and other powers to use the movement of the Caucasus mountain peoples in their own interests."

THE RESPONSE IN MOSCOW AND MAKHACHKALA

The strongest evidence of a scholarly tug of war between Dagestan and Moscow is to be found in the events immediately following these conferences. A group of Dagestani historians, with the active help of their local party organization and their branch of the Academy of Sciences, undertook to push the rehabilitation of Shamil as far as possible. In Moscow, however, a running attack on *Voprosy istorii* had already begun, obliging the editorial board to publish articles from a neo-Bagirov viewpoint. The central Academy of Sciences seemed eager to forget the matter.

The revisionists from Dagestan received the encouragement of no less an authoritative source than their local party organization. Shortly after the Moscow Conference, the Bureau of the Dagestan Regional Party Committee discussed the question and passed a sweeping resolution whose primary purpose was to revoke the group's 1950 decree on the Shamil movement and to facilitate a rapid rehabilitation of the local hero.[29] The new directive of the local party presented a statement of findings from the two conferences that had more of the ring of Makhachkala than of Moscow. It noted that "broad discussion established that the social-political basis of the movement was an anti-colonial and justifiable struggle

29. "K diskussii o kharaktere dvizheniia gortsev Dagestana pod rukovodstvom Shamilia," *VI*, No. 1, 1957, pp. 195-96; complete translation in *CDSP*, IX, No. 16, 33-34. Henze has pointed out that this is the only account of the resolution in the Soviet press ("Unrewriting History," p. 23). This is only a summary of the resolution, which was apparently never published.

against tsarist colonizers" and referred frequently to Shamil and to the "mountain peoples' struggle for independence and freedom." On the other hand, it specifically repudiated any connection between the movement and foreign powers, and said nothing at all about Muridism.

The Dagestan party resolution suggested a variety of remedial measures. It called for "comprehensive research" in several areas of local history, including a reappraisal of the revolt of 1877 and the works of condemned Dagestani writers—subjects that had not been raised in the previous discussion. In calling for further research on the Shamil movement, the resolution suggested a context that would appease central party ideologists: detailed research on "the struggle of these peoples for freedom and independence against foreign conquerors and national-colonial oppression" was to be accompanied by further elaboration of Russian-Dagestani relations, "the objectively progressive significance of Dagestan's entry into the Russian state, and the beneficial influence of Russian material and spiritual culture on Dagestan's cultural development." The proper study of the history of Dagestan, according to the resolution, would promote "Soviet patriotism, proletarian internationalism, and national pride" (which were apparently not considered to be contradictory). Finally, the resolution revealed—between the lines—how sweeping the restrictions had been since 1950: the Ministry of Culture was ordered to restore exhibits in the local museum and the Department of Agitation and Propaganda was to submit a plan for placing literature on the Shamil movement in the public libraries.

A group of Dagestani historians lost no time in complying with the resolution. At the turn of the new year, at a time when the Shamil discussion had been slowed to a halt in Moscow by increasing party criticism of *Voprosy istorii*, the scholars in Makhachkala seemed to be in a hurry to get their case into print. This is indicated by the sharp contrast in the published material on the two conferences on the Shamil movement. The Makhachkala Conference, with its strong pro-Shamil views, was given the widest coverage by local scholars. They ignored the Moscow Conference, which was much less to their liking. The central scholarly press, on the other hand, published very little about either conference.

On November 5, 1956, one month after the Makhachkala Conference, the Dagestan branch of the U.S.S.R. Academy of Sciences sent to press an incomplete transcript of the conference, containing the three main reports and the final resolution.[30] In May, 1957, a second version, twice as long, but still incomplete, was sent to press by Dagestani scholars. The editors noted that "unfortunately, the speeches of the remaining participants of the session (B. O. Khashaev, A. Kh. Agaev, and B. L. Itsikson) could not be published, because the editorial board, in spite of repeated requests, did not receive revised manuscripts from them."[31] Since Khashaev is known to have opposed the majority pro-Shamil view, this note raises some interesting questions about the editorial maneuvering involved in the publication of this volume. Unfortunately, there are few clues that provide answers: the only published report on the Khashaev speech appears to be the one paragraph in the *Voprosy istorii* summary of the proceedings, and there is no account at all of the other two speeches. It seems likely that the editors asked for the kind of revisions the anti-Shamil speakers were unwilling to make. It is also possible that some speakers made statements in October that they did not care to see in print the following May.

There are several unusual features about this first volume which suggest that the editors were rushing to publish their views. Why publish half the proceedings of a conference, and that only thirty days after it had met? At the head of each speech there is a note stating that the manuscript was being published without revision. Several printing errors suggest that the editors did not do an adequate job of proof-reading. (The later published proceedings have considerable routine revisions of those speeches which appear in both editions.) There is no table of contents, no preface or any other editorial comment. The page on which the editors, compilers, and others responsible for publication are usually listed in Soviet books is there, but it is completely blank. The volume is as anonymous as a Soviet book can be: the reader can only discern that it was published by the Dagestani branch of the Academy of Sciences.

Meanwhile the trio of Dagestani historians who read the main reports at the Makhachkala Conference (G. D. Daniialov, V. G. Gadzhiev, and Kh. Kh. Ramazanov) published a short collection of documents highly favorable to Shamil in the journal of the Dagestani Institute of History, Language, and Literature.[32] G. D. Dani-

30. *Dvizhenie kavkazskikh gortsev pod rukovodstvom Shamilia. Doklady i reshenie nauchnoi sessii dagestanskogo filiala Akademii Nauk SSSR v Makhachkale, 4-7 oktiabria, 1956 g.* (Makhachkala, 1956).
31. *O dvizhenii gortsev,* p. 3.
32. "Dokumenty o dvizhenii gortsev severo-vostochnogo Kavkaza 20-50 gg.

ialov's strongly pro-Shamil report to the Makhachkala Conference "On the Question of the Social Base and Character of the Movement of the Mountain Peoples Under the Leadership of Shamil," was published no less than four times, including publication in the Makhachkala newspaper, *Dagestanskaia pravda.*[33]

By contrast, the Moscow press reported these conferences only in short summaries in scholarly journals. The only account of the earlier conference was published in a four-page summary in *Voprosy istorii,* and the longer of two accounts of the Moscow Conference appeared in seven pages in the same journal.[34] In view of the closing statements at the Moscow Conference calling for extensive publication on the question (including collections of documents and an annual volume on new findings), one might expect an early edition of the conference's proceedings, but nothing ever appeared. By early 1957 the central party was making it clear that revision on the Shamil question had gone too far, and the authorities of the U.S.S.R. Academy of Sciences apparently decided on a policy of silence.

THE PARTY'S COUNTER-ATTACK

It had been apparent from the middle of 1956 that Burdzhalov had set *Voprosy istorii* on a dangerous course.[35] A running attack on revisionist historians who were using the journal as their mouthpiece was begun in July in party publications. E. Bugaev charged that in *Voprosy istorii* "very important problems in major articles are often treated and reviewed rashly, with unsubstantiated

XIX v. pod rukovodstvom Shamilia," *Uchenye zapiski dagestanskii filial Akademii Nauk SSSR, Institut istorii, iazyka i literatury,* II (1957), 262-87.

33. In addition to the two editions of the proceedings of the conference, it appeared in *Uchenye zapiski dagestanskii filial Akademii Nauk SSSR, Institute istorii, iazyka i literatury,* I (1956), 120-69, and *Dagestanskaia pravda,* December 14, 1956. Daniialov's paper had been the most unqualified statement of the progressive nature of the movement.

34. See notes 23 and 27, above. A second shorter summary of the Moscow Conference appeared routinely among accounts of scholarly sessions sponsored by the Academy of Sciences in its bulletin ("Dvizhenie kavkazskikh gortsev v pervoi polovine XIX v.," *VAN SSSR,* No. 2, 1957, pp. 121-23). According to a conference report made several years later, the proceedings of the Moscow Conference were set up in type, "but it was decided not to publish them" (*Vsesoiuznoe soveshchanie istorikov* [Moscow, 1964], p. 370).

35. Burdzhalov was only a deputy editor, but seems to have been in charge. Pankratova, the main editor, who was already suffering from a prolonged illness which resulted in her death the following year, was removed from the controversy in the summer of 1956.

and peremptory assertions."[36] *Kommunist* called attention to the journal's failings at least four times during the last half of 1956.[37] These attacks were directed mainly at attempts to revise party history. Burdzhalov himself had led this drive for reform with two articles on Bolshevik tactics in 1917, in which he tried to put the Mensheviks back in the historical picture, but also touched the most sensitive nerve of all—the question of the political infallibility of the Bolsheviks. The new interpretations on the national movements and tsarist colonial policy were secondary and were mentioned as supporting evidence of the journal's irresponsible course.

Burdzhalov's failure to heed party warnings is not easily explained. He was not a young idealistic crusader, but a veteran historian who had done his share of hackwork in behalf of the Stalin cult.[38] His editorial policy during the first half of 1956 is understandable, since the Twentieth Party Congress had explicitly called for revision. But his persistence in the last half of the year can only be explained by his hope of receiving support from some liberal elements in the party.[39] If such support was ever available, it faded quickly after October, when events in Hungary and Poland demonstrated the dangers of divided Communist parties and of the toleration of nationalist views.

In the late summer Burdzhalov's defiance of the authorities reached a point unprecedented in recent Soviet scholarship when he published two articles answering his critic, Bugaev.[40] Although he made it appear that this was a dialogue between historians (Bugaev was identified only as a *kandidat* of historical science), it could hardly be left at that, since Bugaev had spoken in the authoritative *Partiinaia zhizn'* (*Party Life*), an organ of the party's Central Committee, and was the deputy editor of that journal. Burdzhalov tried to put Bugaev on the defensive by accusing him of attempting

36. E. Bugaev, "Kogda utrachivaetsia nauchny podkhod," *Partiinaia zhizn'*, No. 14, 1956, pp. 62-72.

37. *Kommunist*, No. 10, 1956, pp. 14-26 (on party history); No. 15, pp. 44-58 (on the history of the Revolution); No. 16, pp. 122-28 (on socialist construction); No. 18, pp. 52-67 (on the periodization of party history).

38. See, for example, his article "Stalinskii 'Kratkii kurs istorii VKP(b)' i istoricheskaia nauka," *Bol'shevik*, No. 18, 1951, pp. 9-22, which held up the *Short Course* as a model for historians.

39. Merle Fainsod, "Soviet Russian Historians or: the Lesson of Burdzhalov," *Encounter*, XVIII (March, 1962), 82-89.

40. "O stat'e tov. E. Bugaeva," *VI*, No. 7, 1956, pp. 215-22. This article was unsigned, and although clearly an editorial, was placed at the back of the issue outside the usual categories of material. The other article was "Eshche o taktike bol'shevikov v marte-aprele 1917 goda," *VI*, No. 8, 1956, pp. 109-14.

to restore the Stalinist shackles on historical writing, of forgetting the directives of the Twentieth Party Congress. At about the same time Burdzhalov presided over another eventful conference of readers of *Voprosy istorii* in Leningrad, in which he carried his drive even further. Calling for a more objective look at party history in particular, he admitted that the older historians were too involved in the restrictions of the cult of personality to write truthfully. The hope of the future, he said, was in the recruitment of young cadres who are "freer from prejudices and the tendency to conform." The report of this meeting in the Leningrad press was thoroughly hostile, condemning not only Burdzhalov but a number of historians who agreed with him.[41]

In November *Pravda* joined the chorus against *Voprosy istorii* by publishing a letter to the editor from a Moscow professor, V. Smirnov, vigorously attacking an article on Lenin's early political views. Smirnov declared that the journal was undertaking "to revise . . . questions which have long been decided by the Party."[42] In December the annual report of the Chairman of the Academy of Sciences, A. N. Nesmeianov, noted the errors of the journal and hoped for early rectification.[43]

By the end of the year Burdzhalov was in retreat, although he did not apologize. In the December issue (not published until late January, 1957) there appeared an article "On Caucasian Muridism," by Bushuev, which reiterated the Stalinist position he had held throughout the controversy. The article was a specific rebuttal to Pikman's arguments. Bushuev scoffed at Pikman's comparison of the Shamil movement to the contemporary European revolutionary movements. Shamil's followers were mountain tribesmen "who never knew anything but war." And Shamil, far from being a democrat and reformer, was an unscrupulous warrior who did not hesitate to attack Georgia and to seek help from Britain. The British-Turkish tie was revived to the extent that they hoped for Shamil's victory and Russia's defeat. Throughout the article there were the old familiar emphases: the reactionary nature of Muridism and the progressive consequences of annexation.[44] This article happened to

41. *Leningradskaia pravda*, August 5, 1956; quoted in complete translation in *CDSP*, VIII, No. 39, 5-6. *Voprosy istorii* never reported the proceedings of this conference, although it had regularly reported the earlier ones.

42. V. Smirnov, "Nepravil'noe osveshchenie vazhnogo voprosa," *Pravda*, November 20, 1956.

43. *VAN SSSR*, No. 2, 1957, p. 36.

44. S. K. Bushuev, "O kavkazskom miuridizme," *VI*, No. 12, 1956, pp. 72-79.

appear in the same issue with the reports of the Makhachkala and
Moscow Conferences, which were full of pro-Pikman arguments,
giving the journal a blurred viewpoint unusual for a Soviet publication. Two months later *Voprosy istorii* continued its retreating
tactic by publishing the paper M. V. Pokrovskii had given at the
Moscow Conference "On the Character of the Movement of Mountain Peoples of the Western Caucasus from the 1840's to the 1860's."[45]
Though much more substantial and less polemical than Bushuev's
article, it upheld the same general views that Muridism was an
anti-popular movement, shunned by the masses; that there were
Turkish connections, particularly with the local aristocracy; that
annexation was a progressive event welcomed by the ordinary people
as an end of their tribulations. The fact that the editors of *Voprosy
istorii* chose this article for publication among all those given at
the conference was a further indication of their submission. As
events turned out, it was to be the last article the journal would
publish on the subject for several years.

In March *Voprosy istorii* suffered a double-barreled blow from
the Central Committee and *Kommunist*. A Central Committee
resolution of March 9 concerned itself primarily with errors in
party history. Burdzhalov was dismissed and Pankratova was let
off with a reprimand.[46] *Kommunist* went into chapter and verse.
Pikman's article was particularly offensive: "It is clamorous in tone,
weak in argumentation, and ignores the attained level of scientific
knowledge." Pikman was denounced for denying "the attempts by
Britain and Turkey to use the Shamil movement for their expansionist aims"; for viewing Shamil as a democrat; for not differentiating
the variations of the class struggle in different regions; and finally
for a sin of omission: for not mentioning the progressive nature of
annexation, a fact that "no serious Soviet scholar ever doubted."[47]
In the course of this critique, *Kommunist* revealed, more or less
between the lines, some points it considered well established and
not subject to revision. The most important of these were that (1)
annexation was progressive, (2) Muridism was linked to Britain

45. M. V. Pokrovskii, "O kharaktere dvizheniia gortsev zapadnogo Kavkaza
v 40-60kh godakh XIX veka," *ibid.*, No. 2, 1957, pp. 62-74.
46. "O zhurnale 'Voprosy istorii,'" *Spravochnik partiinogo rabotnika* (Moscow, 1957), pp. 381-82.
47. "Strogo sobliudat' leninskii printsip partiinosti v istoricheskoi nauke,"
Kommunist, No. 4, 1957, pp. 17-29. It is strange that G. D. Daniialov's article,
which went further than Pikman's on many of these points, was not mentioned.

and Turkey, though not inspired by them, and (3) Muridism became the ideology of "the warring feudal and clerical aristocracy."

The March issue of *Voprosy istorii*, which appeared two months late, carried a long leading editorial in which the new board of editors pointed out the errors of their predecessors.[48] They acknowledged that Pikman's article on Shamil should not have been published. The former editors had been "in a hurry to discuss the problem raised by the author without first studying the substance of the material." As for specific error, the editorial pointed only to a single sin of omission: Pikman had in effect denied that the annexation of the Caucasus was a progressive event.

If the old editors of the journal had been in a hurry to discuss the question, the new ones were singularly reticent. They published one article on Muridism the following year, but scarcely mentioned its leader. Six years later Shamil was discussed briefly in the course of a paradoxical essay on Guseinov's book—a review of sorts, affording the reader of the journal the editors' first critique of the work, fourteen years after its appearance and five years after the publication of the second edition.[49] The next full-scale article on Shamil did not appear until 1966.

48. "Za leninskuiu partiinost' v istoricheskoi nauke," *VI*, No. 3, 1957, pp. 3-19.

49. See Chapter 12 below, pp. 263-64.

CHAPTER **11.**

THE THAW ELSEWHERE

*"History must be dealt with as a science, not as an instru-
ment of daily propaganda." V. Miller, to a conference of
Estonian historians in December, 1956 (quoted in* Baltic
Review, *No. 14 [August, 1958], p. 53).*

The Shamil controversy was by far the most sensational
effort of Soviet historians to re-rewrite the history of the non-Russian nationalities during the brief period of comparative freedom
in 1956. The specialists on the other peoples undoubtedly followed
developments from the North Caucasus with great interest. In the
end, however, they made no attempt to rehabilitate Kenesary or any
other non-Russian military hero. But they lost no time trying to
tone down some of the extreme interpretations they had been obliged
to support in the early 1950's. Since the period of the thaw was
short, the new views can be found mostly in discussions, book reviews, and articles, rather than books. There were also a few cases
of survey histories that emerged from the press badly out of step
with the compromise interpretations of 1957.

In the comments and attempted revisions of the non-Russian
historians during this period, there are two fundamental themes
that must have been disquieting to the Moscow authorities who
continued to see history as the servant of nationality policy. The
greatest irritant for the non-Russian scholars was their recent obsequious dependence on the Russians. This is evident in their debunking remarks about the elder brother concept, and their efforts
to win some freedom from the slavish regimentation to current
directives from the center. Closely related to this is the unmistakable evidence of a still smoldering nationalism. The non-Russian

historians clearly preferred to recover their own distinctive histories; they wanted to do this at the expense of that contrived common heritage of Soviet peoples which the Party had been touting.

In the same issue of *Voprosy istorii* in which Pikman's article was published there appeared an article entitled "On Certain Questions of the History of Central Asia in the Eighteenth and Nineteenth Centuries," by O. D. Chekovich, identified only as being from Tashkent.[1] It was a refutation of the influential article published by Braginskii, Radzhabov, and Romodin in the journal in 1953. Chekovich declared that the earlier article's picture of Central Asia as a culturally and economically stagnant area on the eve of Russian annexation was badly distorted. He pointed out several examples of progress in the Central Asian khanates just before the Russians came: trade was increasing, cities were growing, and new irrigation canals were being constructed. The khanates were beginning to consolidate politically, and might have been unified in time. The gist of Chekovich's article was a denial of one of the favorite arguments in support of the progressiveness of annexation: that the peoples of Central Asia had no future except in the bosom of the Russian Empire.

Somewhat similar views were expressed at the First Congress of the Uzbek Intelligentsia, in October 1956, when the First Secretary of the Uzbek party, N. A. Mukhitdinov, demonstrated that expressions of national pride might come from a high party official as well as a scholar. Speaking to an overwhelmingly Uzbek audience, he praised at some length the greatness of Central Asian scholars and writers of the period before annexation, without the customary obeisances to the influences of Russian culture. He also indicated that the interpretation of some Central Asian revolts might be ready for reconsideration. Some of the historians of Central Asia had been "under the influence of the anti-scientific, anti-Marxist" statements of Bagirov, and had ignored Lenin's teaching about the "religious cloak" of certain movements.

> Those historians who attempt to deny the national-liberation character of the events of the second half of the nineteenth century and the beginning of the twentieth century, should not forget that the history of the peoples of

1. O. D. Chekovich, "O nekotorykh voprosakh istorii Srednei Azii XVIII-XIX vekov," *VI*, No. 3, 1956, pp. 84-95.

Central Asia is saturated with their struggles for freedom and independence. And it would be even more strange to assert, that in the period of the feudal and colonial yoke, in a situation in which a powerful revolutionary movement was developing in Russia, under the leadership of such allies and leaders as the Russian working class headed by the Communists, that the workers of Central Asia were somehow inactive.[2]

Although Mukhitdinov hinted that such movements as the Andizhan revolt of 1898 might be reassessed, he made no specific references to revolts other than that of 1916. It was clear from the latter part of this statement that the national pride of the Uzbek Communists themselves demanded that their revolts against the tsar, in alleged alliance with the Russian working class, not be considered reactionary.

But the most defiant challenge to the *status quo* came in a review of K. Beisembiev's book, *The World View of Abai Kunanbaev*, in which the great Kazakh intellectual's indebtedness to Russian thought was emphasized to the exclusion of all other influences.[3] The author's gesture to Moscow apparently nettled the reviewer, Kh. Suiunshaliev, a philologist. Reviewing the book in the authoritative *Kommunist Kazakhstana*, Suiunshaliev disagreed vigorously with Beisembiev's interpretation, charging that he had attributed Kunanbaev's views so completely to Russian influences that his subject seemed to be divorced from the life of his own country. It should be remembered that "the world view of the poet-thinker was formed first of all in the conditions of material life of the Kazakh people." He had also been well acquainted with Western thought, from Socrates to Byron. The reviewer's most devastating remark, however, was an aside: "Incidentally, it seems to us that the first chapter of this book on the historical significance of the annexation of Kazakhstan to Russia is superfluous [*izlishnei*]. This question is no longer new, is of doubtful importance [*spornykh momentov*], and not needed in a monograph on Abai, especially since the author keeps returning to the subject in all the following chapters."[4]

2. *I s"ezd intelligentsii Uzbekistana, 11-13 oktiabr 1956 goda. Stenograficheskii ocherk* (Tashkent, 1957), p. 27. See also Pavel Urban, "The New Soviet Drive Against Nationalism in Turkestan," *East Turkic Review*, No. 4 (1960), pp. 13-23. Urban points out that many scholars and academic officials who had been ousted in the early 1950's quietly returned to their posts during this period.

3. K. Beisembiev, *Mirovozzrenie Abaia Kunanbaeva* (Alma-Ata, 1956).

4. K. Suiunshaliev, "Kniga o mirovozzrenii Abaia," *Kommunist Kazakhstana,*

THE UKRAINE

The Ukrainians were quick to answer the challenges the Twentieth Party Congress seemed to pose. The next issue of *Voprosy istorii* to go to press after the meeting of the Congress carried a sharp review of A. V. Likholat's *Rout of the Nationalist Counterrevolution in the Ukraine* (1954), the book that had prompted Mikoyan's remark about the proper writing of Ukrainian history at the Congress. The work had already been favorably reviewed in the journal, but now it was re-reviewed by two Ukrainians identified as Old Bolsheviks with a firsthand knowledge of the events in question. Although they did not diminish the role of the Bolsheviks in the revolutionary period in the Ukraine, or the cooperation of the Russian and Ukrainian proletariat, they demanded that some of the Ukrainian leaders who had been condemned by Stalin (and of course by Likholat) as "left Communists" or "national Communists" be rehabilitated. They also brought up the dormant subject of Great Russian chauvinism, calling attention to Lenin's fears that "the slightest manifestation of Great Russian nationalism, which divides Russian and Ukrainian comrades, could do inestimable harm to the Revolution."[5] The revival of this subject would entail some reassessment of the idea of the friendship of peoples. The *Voprosy istorii* editors acknowledged in a footnote that their publication of the earlier review had been a mistake and called on "Old Bolsheviks, participants in the revolutionary events, scholars, and teachers, to help the journal study the historic-Party literature and place the study of the history of the CPSU and the revolutionary movement on a scientific, Marxist-Leninist basis."

Yaroslav Bilinsky has gleaned several cryptic remarks of Ukrainian scholars in 1956 indicating that they completely discounted recent Soviet historical writing on the Ukraine. The historian I. Boiko wrote that serious research work on the history of the period of the Ukraine's annexation to Russia did not exist, although there

No. 9, 1956, pp. 61-64. This was, however, a minority report. At about the same time Shoinbaev published a typical "historical significance" article in another Kazakh journal, rehearsing all the old arguments about Kazakh debts to Russian culture. See T. Shoinbaev, "Istoricheskoi znachenie prisoedineniia Kazakhstana k Rossii," *VAN kazakhskoi SSR*, No. 10, 1956, pp. 3-15.

5. E. S. Oslikovskaia and A. V. Snegov, "Za pravdivoe osveshchenie istorii proletarskoi revoliutsii," *VI*, No. 3, 1956, pp. 138-45. Still another reference to Great Russian chauvinism was made in the same issue of the journal by V. V. Pentkovskaia, who recalled Lenin's statement: "I declare a fight to the finish on Great Russian chauvinism" (*ibid.*, p. 21).

had been a flood of publications on these events at the time of the anniversary celebration two years earlier. Another Ukrainian scholar noted that the progressive significance of the annexation had perhaps been overstressed at the expense of "objective facts." Others complained that no one in recent years had written anything about Great Power Chauvinism in the Ukraine or had paid any attention to the accomplishments of bourgeois Ukrainian historians.[6]

In June Burdzhalov traveled to Kiev to preside over another Conference of Readers of *Voprosy istorii*.[7] This session, attended by about five hundred people, proved to be one of the most outspoken of the year, which was noted for free discussion. Many of the Ukrainian historians who spoke at the discussion showed that they were wholeheartedly in favor of the journal's new course (they congratulated Burdzhalov on his efforts to correct party history), but at the same time they subjected the editorial board to some sharp criticism. There was widespread complaint that *Voprosy istorii* had been slighting Ukrainian historians, and that what it had published recently on the Ukraine had been of little value or even harmful. Although the journal had published a leading editorial calling for "deep scientific study of the history of the Ukrainian people" (No. 7, 1955), it had proceeded to ignore much of the work Ukrainian historians were doing. Furthermore, A. D. Voina noted that "the journal has not liquidated harmful methods of criticism, growing out of cases in which certain people other than critics settle personal scores either by leading historians into error or by authoritative assertions. It is necessary to listen attentively

6. Yaroslav Bilinsky, *The Second Soviet Republic: The Ukraine after World War II* (New Brunswick, N. J.: Rutgers University Press, 1964), p. 207.

7. This meeting was not reported in the Soviet Ukrainian press, according to Bilinsky. The two published reports on it vary so widely that one might consider them to be accounts of different meetings. However, I am assuming that they are two partial, highly selective accounts of the same discussion. The earlier account is in *Voprosy istorii*: "Konferentsiia chitatelei zhurnala 'Voprosy istorii' v Kieve," No. 8, 1956, pp. 198-203. Another account appeared some months later in *Nashe slovo*, a periodical on cultural subjects published in Warsaw in Ukrainian for readers of Ukrainian origin living in Poland: "Ukrayns'ky istoriki v borot'b istorichnu pravdu," *Nashe slovo*, No. 16 (December 2), 1956. The latter report gives no date for the meeting, does not state explicitly that it was a conference of readers, and does not even mention the presence of Burdzhalov. It reports the remarks of only half as many speakers, and in a different order. However, the viewpoints of the speakers that appear in both accounts match, which leads me to believe that they refer to the same meeting. If this is true, we have here an interesting exercise in reporting to separate Russian and Ukrainian audiences. Some of the variations will be pointed out in the following notes.

to the voice of readers." The solution to these problems, said the Ukrainian historians, as in a chorus, was a separate journal on Ukrainian history. Their efforts were successful; the *Ukrayins'ky istorychny zhurnal* (*Ukrainian Historical Journal*) began to appear the following year.

The Ukrainian speakers noted in a variety of remarks the sad state of Soviet historiography in general and Ukrainian historiography in particular. E. F. Federenko complained about the low scholarly level of the *History of the Ukrainian S.S.R.*, published in 1953,[8] declaring that the "great deficiencies" of the book had resulted from "inadequate consideration of the opinions of specialist historians."[9] He went on to make it clear that not only had the history not been written by specialists, but that specialists had not even been consulted. Several of the speakers complained that they had been cut off in recent years from the best scholarly works of bourgeois historians—not only of Western Europe, but of pre-revolutionary Ukraine. Specific suggestions were made for deeper study of the works of Kostomarov and Dragamonov. In this connection, F. E. Los' asserted that the whole nationalist movement that had developed in the Ukraine in the nineteenth century contained progressive aspects worthy of study: "One must agree with the speaker,[10] that the history of national movements is not infrequently elaborated in an oversimplified manner in our literature; on these questions we sometimes slip into positions of nihilism. It is impossible, for example, not to see positive significance in the growth in the nineteenth-century Ukraine of a bourgeois national movement, which developed along with the national consciousness of

8. Federenko mentioned 1954 as the publication date, but he was evidently referring to the volume that appeared late in 1953. A second edition, with only minor changes, was published on the eve of the Twentieth Party Congress. See *Istoriia ukrainskoi SSR*, ed. A. K. Kasimenko, V. A. Diadichenko, F. E. Los', *et al.* (Kiev, 1953), Vol. I; *ibid.*, ed. V. A. Diadichenko, A. K. Kasimenko, F. E. Los', *et al.* (2nd ed., Kiev, 1956), Vol. I.

9. This remark is from the *Nashe slovo* account. The *Voprosy istorii* version is somewhat softer: "Comrade Federenko stated that although there were cadres of qualified historians in the Ukraine the first volume . . . did not satisfy the demands of readers; in this work it is impossible to find a full, truthful presentation of the history of the Ukrainian people. This results from the fact that scientific work is badly organized, that the opinions of specialists are inadequately listened to, and that certain comrades, who are inadequately prepared in scholarly matters, take part in the discussion of the work."

10. An earlier speaker had complained that "*Voprosy istorii* has not expressed a definite point of view on certain questions of history, for example, on the question of the movement of mountain peoples under the leadership of Shamil."

the Ukrainian people." At the same time two of the speakers derided
the recent idealization of tsarist colonial policies. K. G. Guslistyi
remarked that "Lenin branded tsarism as the cruel oppressor of the
Ukrainian people, but certain of our historians write about the
friendly attitude of tsarism toward the Ukrainian people."

The Ukrainian historians at this conference called for a new look
at several historical figures. Two speakers called for a more realistic
interpretation of the role of Bogdan Khmel'nitskii. Guslistyi remarked that "the report justly brings out the necessity of appraising
the role of Bogdan Khmel'nitskii more truthfully. In the last few
years many have become apologists for him. He was in reality an
important state leader, playing an important role in the history of
the Ukrainian people, but it is not necessary to transform him into
an icon." Other speakers called for a more realistic appraisal of
G. V. Plekhanov, N. A. Skrypnik, and K. G. Rakovskii.[11]

As has been noted, the sharpest criticism of the meeting came
from Guslistyi, identified in the reports as a member of the Institute
of Folklore, Ethnography, and Art Studies.[12] He concluded his
remarks with a general statement on historical science in the Ukraine
that seemed to sum up the general view of the participants.

> It must be clearly stated, that the question of criticism
> and self criticism among historians of the Ukraine is not
> satisfactory. Not infrequently friendly relationships inter-
> fere with decisions on serious scholarly problems. There
> are few fundamental principles [printsipal'nosti] in our
> scholarly work. It is necessary to create the conditions for
> healthy, business-like criticism—criticism which one can
> always distinguish from slander. It is necessary to train our
> historians in the spirit of high principles, to teach them to
> defend their point of view.

ESTONIA

The historians of Soviet Estonia also enjoyed—if only briefly
—the new scholarly climate of 1956. They met in two sessions (in

11. Interestingly enough, the Nashe slovo report makes no mention of
Khmel'nitskii, while the Voprosy istorii account does not mention Skrypnik or
Rakovskii. Thus the report for Ukrainian readers skips over remarks tending
to diminish the figure of Bogdan, and the rapporteur in Moscow is reluctant to
discuss the question of the reassessment of two of Stalin's victims.

12. In the Voprosy istorii account, Guslistyi's remarks appear to come at
the end of the meeting. The writer of the Nashe slovo account (who signed
himself M. Shch.) recognized that these comments would be most interesting
for Ukrainian readers and placed them at the beginning of his article.

October and December) to discuss a *maket* of a new history of Estonia. An unusually candid report on these conferences, written by the historian V. Miller, appeared in the monthly Estonian literary and political journal *Looming* (*Creativity*).[13] Many of the forty-five participants spoke with obvious cynicism about their working conditions and some of the interpretations they had been obliged to espouse during the period of the Stalin cult. Miller himself commented that the first edition of the *History of the Estonian S.S.R.* (1952) had been written at a time when the Stalin *Short Course* was regarded as "an irreproachable methodological example. Under these conditions history-writing had to follow ready-made schemes and conceptions. The task of the historian was only to select skillfully enough facts to prove them." The Estonian historians now hoped to remove such oversimplification and distortion, and subjected the new *maket* to "severe criticism." High on their agenda was what one participant cryptically referred to as "the unscientific treatment of the relations between the Estonian and Russian peoples." They had a variety of complaints on this subject: "Estonian territory has been recognized as an ancient Russian land"; Russification was regarded as "an objectively progressive event"; "losses are depicted as victories"; the periodization of Estonian history had been adjusted to that of Russia; the Socialist parties were not dealt with fairly ("it seems as though all the parties from their very inception were fascist"). Such distortions were to be expected during the period of the cult of personality, but when they were repeated in a manuscript of 1956, they seemed to be, in the words of one speaker, "an ugly prostration and singing of hallelujah to Great Russian chauvinism." The conclusion was that the new work "cannot be corrected by patching up; it must be written anew from its beginning."

When Miller's report on these meetings appeared in print in January, 1957, the tide was already beginning to recede. It created a furor in party circles, in the Estonian Academy of Sciences, and among the participants in the meetings, many of whom wrote letters to the editor dissociating themselves from Miller's account of the proceedings. The most important of these letters was one dated March 8, 1957, signed by both the director and the secretary of the

13. Apparently no account of these meetings appeared in the Russian language press. I am indebted for this account to Leonard Vahter, "History in the Clutches of Communism," *Baltic Review*, No. 14 (August, 1958), pp. 43-55.

Institute of History of the Estonian Academy of Sciences.[14] They charged that Miller had distorted the discussion by stating his own views; no one had presented such statements as he ascribed to them. This letter, too, indicated that Russian-Estonian relations was one of the most sensitive issues. Miller's version was "an insult to the Russian, as well as to Latvian, Lithuanian and to many Estonian comrades." The report gave "an impression that the author wishes to isolate the history of the Estonian people from that of the Russian people," which would be "a step back." Judging from the excerpts from this letter published by Leonard Vahter in the *Baltic Review*, its authors were sometimes self-defeating in their arguments. After denying that "unfriendly" statements about the friendship of peoples had been made at the meetings, they went on to charge that dangerous utterances had indeed been made in the speeches of three historians (including Miller), "who have to answer for their statements." They also took exception to the observation on Estonian subservience to the *Short Course*, but then admitted that such tendencies as did exist in this connection were not the fault of Estonian historians, but of Soviet historians in general. In conclusion, they complained that the editor of *Looming* had neglected his duties in publishing such an article. He was subjected to a campaign of criticism, and was shortly dismissed by the Presidium of the Communist Party of Estonia.[15]

When the new history of Estonia appeared in 1958, it was quite clear that it had not been rewritten but only patched up.

THE REAPPEARANCE OF BEKMAKHANOV

Bekmakhanov's appearance in print for the first time in over five years at the time of the thaw was not an occasion for the restatement of pre-1950 views but for a well-ordered retreat. Although his article, "The Feudal-Monarchal Movements in Kazakhstan," published in the scholarly journal of his university, revealed

14. It is surely no coincidence that the Director of the Institute, V. Maamiagi, was also a co-author of the history Miller had panned so severely.

15. A similar episode occurred at about the same time in Minsk, when a Belorussian writer challenged the importance of Russian cultural influences by publishing an article in which he argued that Belorussian culture was independent of and at certain points even superior to the Russian. In proving his point he noted that books had been published in Belorussia forty-seven years before those of the first Russian printer, Fedorov. The editor of the periodical that published this article was subjected to a campaign of criticism and dismissed in January, 1957. See St. Stankievic, "Recent Manifestation of National Opposition in the Belorussian SSR," *POP*, No. 2 (1959), pp. 35-40.

a complete surrender of his former views about the popular character of the Kenesary movement, it did not represent an apology.[16] Except for the first footnote, the article appeared to be a straightforward exposition of the reactionary nature of the Kenesary movement. Since it contained nothing that had not been said many times over since 1950, the only apparent reason for publishing it was to put the author on record as espousing the accepted view. In the footnote Bekmakhanov acknowledged that his earlier book on the subject had taken "an untrue, anti-Marxist position" on the movement, and stated that the *Pravda* article, "in which the movement of Kenesary Kasymov was evaluated as a feudal-monarchal, nationalistic movement, gave invaluable assistance to the author."

Bekmakhanov seemed to take care to reject in detail his former views and to accept explicitly those of the *Pravda* article. The *batyrs*, whom he had earlier defended as representatives of the people, he now lumped together with "representatives of the military-feudal aristocracy and their feudal cohorts." Kenesary's whole support had come from reactionary elements, once the masses deserted him early in the revolt. He rejected all of Kenesary's reforms and accepted the prevailing view on the aggressive character of the campaign against the Kirgiz. A close reading of this article, however, will show a clever technique of evasion, as subtle as any ever used by a nineteenth-century writer to get an idea past the tsar's censors. Bekmakhanov asserted repeatedly that Kenesary had stated aims he did not really intend to follow, that he had made promises he did not keep. Kenesary's policies were restated, anchored to the archival documents by footnote, and then rejected as bogus by Bekmakhanov. Could it be that Bekmakhanov's statement of Kenesary's policies was his primary goal, rather than his rejection of them? He recorded, for example, that Kenesary promised democratic reforms but did not carry them out. Also, "Kenesary fought against the annexation of Kazakhstan to Russia under the slogan of restoring the lands, belonging to 'kin of the Kasymovs,'"[17]

16. E. B. Bekmakhanov, "Feodal'no-monarkhicheskie dvizheniia v Kazakhstane," *Uchenye zapiski kazakhskii gosudarstvennoi universitet*, XX (1956), 66-85. Nothing was said about the restoration of his professorship or his degree. He was identified at the head of this article simply as a "senior teacher," whereas earlier articles identified him as a professor and doctor of historical science.

17. Bekmakhanov quotes these two words, *rodam kasymovykh*. He may have done so because of their double meaning. Soviet historians, including the chastened Bekmakhanov, contend that Kenesary appropriated all lands for himself and his family. The term is plural, however, and the word *rod* can

but he lost all support from the masses when they realized that he was appropriating all the land for his own family. The clearest example was the statement that "Kenesary promised 'to liberate the Kirgiz [i.e. Kazakh[18]] people from the yoke of the Russians, by the right of Khan Ablai, according to which all the Kirgiz belonged to him'" (this clause is quoted from an archive document of 1837). Bekmakhanov went on to say that what actually happened was that Kenesary "seized the best pasture lands for himself." Although the author's main emphasis was on the land seizure, his Kazakh readers might have been more interested in Kenesary's stated desire "to liberate the Kirgiz people from the yoke of the Russians," especially since the footnote indicated that the statement was authentic and showed where it could be found. Bekmakhanov even managed to reassert his old contention that Kenesary, early in his career, had tried to accept a Russian protectorate, but was denied it. This highly heretical item was sandwiched neatly between two propositions that would be welcomed by proponents of the new view:

> An analysis of the economic and political measures of Kenesary shows that his efforts to create his own khanate could only be regarded as an obstacle to the unification of the Kazakh people with the Russian people, since an autonomous khanate of Kenesary would mean nothing other than a stronger continuation of the struggle with Russia. Therefore, in spite of the fact that Kenesary begged for [*prosil*] a protectorate from Russia, he did not promote the solidarity of the Kazakh and Russian peoples by his long struggle, but on the contrary, strived to keep them apart.

Kenesary's proposed protectorate is not mentioned elsewhere, and it is difficult to see why Bekmakhanov interjected it here—where it weakened an already flimsy argument—unless he merely wanted to restate a fact.

This technique of statement and refutation served Bekmakhanov in another way. If the reader follows the line of argument, he must conclude that the Kazakh historian's earlier faulty interpretations had resulted from his taking Kenesary's statements of his aims and

mean, in addition to kin or family, a group of people with common ancestors, hence a tribe or clan. In this construction Kenesary's aim could have been to recover the lands Russia had taken and return them to the Kazakh people.

18. In pre-revolutionary usage, the term "Kirgiz" referred also to the Kazakhs, and since this statement is from the 1830's, several years before the Kirgiz campaign, it is clear that Kenesary meant the Kazakh people.

policies at their face value, as they were found in the archives. The party's interpretation rested on the proposition that such statements were hopelessly distorted, since they originated with class enemies (tsarist or Kazakh officials). In sum, Bekmakhanov admitted only to the error of believing that archive documents meant what they said.

Apparently Bekmakhanov's article did not arouse even a ripple of comment, and the following year he elaborated upon his arguments in *The Annexation of Kazakhstan to Russia,* which is easily the most ambitious and detailed of some twenty monographs to appear on the historical significance of the annexation of individual peoples to Russia.[19] The fourth chapter of the book is an enlarged version of the article, containing many of its passages verbatim. The article was, in all probability, a *ballon d'essai.*

In a long introduction, Bekmakhanov tells the reader something of the thought processes that were involved in his conversion. Stated euphemistically, it is simply that he came to see modern Kazakh history as a manifestation of the class struggle. But this is accomplished at the cost of jettisoning most of the sources he had formerly relied upon. From the viewpoint of the class struggle both archive documents and Kazakh folklore are suspect (the real history-makers, the Kazakh people, left few written records). Much of Kazakh folklore, according to Bekmakhanov's new view, originated from "feudal-bey" elements; most of the songs exude reactionary ideas. This is a major concession for Bekmakhanov, who had drawn so heavily from native folklore in arguing his earlier views. Reports from the tsars' *chinovniki* and the writings of tsarist historians suffer from a similar class bias (pp. 8-17). The archive materials must be sifted very carefully: "Most of the materials for the history of the revolutionary movement in Kazakhstan are scattered in various archives in Moscow. The facts of this movement, as a rule, are presented from the position of official circles, i.e. tendentiously. The history of social thought in Kazakhstan is reflected very weakly in the archives" (p. 17). The archives are not only very short on information about social thought in Kazakhstan, which in the new view was permeated with Russian cultural influences and a growing friendship of peoples. Bekmakhanov also admits that the archives shed little light on the leadership of the Bolsheviks, the political views of the ordinary people, the ideo-

19. E. B. Bekmakhanov, *Prisoedinenie Kazakhstana k Rossii* (Moscow, 1957).

logical struggle with "Pan-Islamism"—all major themes in the new "Marxist-Leninist" history of the period. In short, the new historian of the Kazakhs is liberated from objectionable sources; some of them are not used at all, and those that are may be regarded as tendentious.

As for what the historian relies upon instead of the old sources, Bekmakhanov makes that quite clear in frequent quotations from Lenin and Stalin (whose comments are usually tangential or very general) and in an introductory footnote acknowledging the helpfulness of the *Pravda* article on Kazakh history which led to his long intellectual exile. One wonders if Bekmakhanov might have written this introduction as a kind of covert disclaimer, knowing that his colleagues would understand its meaning. At any rate, he has maneuvered his source materials well enough to have accomplished the historian's goal as stated earlier by Pankratova: to achieve a correct "correlation of concrete research with profound study of the classics of Marxism-Leninism."

There are many passages in Bekmakhanov's book where glints of his former bourgeois nationalist views shine through. This is especially true in his frequent use of the device of statement and refutation, in which he seems intent to show that his old sources do not really mean what they seem to mean. As an example of reactionary folklore, he quotes this line about his erstwhile hero: "Kenesary was a sanctuary for the homeless, a refuge for the weak" (pp. 8-9). This does not mean that Kenesary was a champion of the Kazakh masses; it is merely the effort of a feudal poet to glorify his class leader. But the mere reappearance of this line in print would be welcome to Kazakh nationalists, who might prefer to put their own interpretation on it. Bekmakhanov states repeatedly that Kenesary's followers came only from his own class, but as one of his proofs he quotes from a contemporary document which begins "At the head of *all* the restless elements stood the Kasymov family ..." (p. 110, emphasis added). At another place, the author repeats the passage he had quoted in his article concerning Kenesary's promise to liberate his people from the Russian yoke. But this time there is a tantalizing one-word change: the phrase "from the yoke of the Russians" becomes "from the yoke of tsarism."[20] There

20. This purports to be a direct quotation, having a closing quotation mark and a footnote reference to the same source cited in the article. But unfortunately, one cannot tell where the quotation begins, since there is no opening quotation mark. It seems unlikely that a document of the 1830's would contain the term "tsarism." One might say that the omission of the

are enough such statements, whose authenticity is attested by citations to archive files, to permit another historian to write a thoroughgoing nationalist account of these events.

The last half of this book is a detailed, factual account of economic and cultural progress after the Kazakh annexation to Russia. This does not represent any change in view, since Bekmakhanov had emphasized this theme from the beginning. In the first five chapters, however, he emphasizes the disintegration of Kazakh society on the eve of the Russian annexation, the threat of the British, and the reactionary nature of the Kenesary movement—all revised interpretations which bring the author back to the party line. The book is also of interest for its long bibliographical essay, in which Bekmakhanov discusses the errors of the various Kazakh histories undertaken by Soviet scholars. He does not mention his own *Kazakhstan from the 1820's Through the 1840's*, either in the essay or in his bibliography. He discusses the errors on the Kenesary movement in the 1943 and 1949 histories, without mentioning the fact that he wrote these chapters.[21]

Bekmakhanov's *Annexation of Kazakhstan to Russia* was never reviewed by *Voprosy istorii*, or by the newly established journal, *Istoriia SSSR*, although at least three reviews appeared in Kazakh publications. In view of the fact that *Voprosy istorii* reviewed virtually all the other monographs on annexation—and this one is admittedly one of the most important of them—the failure to discuss this book is not easily explained.[22] Bekmakhanov's career prospered

---

quotation mark is a printing error, except that there are other errors of the same sort in vital places. The footnote reference to the *Pravda* article of December 26, 1950, which brought about Bekmakhanov's downfall, is misdated by nearly a year. Morozov's devastating *Bol'shevik* review of the 1943 Kazakh history, the beginning of the Kazakh historian's troubles, is given as 1943—two years off. These are the only references to these two articles in the book (Bekmakhanov does not mention them in his detailed bibliography); the reader who wishes to look them up would find a blind alley. Would a clumsy compositor just happen to foul up such vital dates? Would the author, in reading proof, overlook erroneous dates for the two most important events in his professional career?

21. The only mention of his earlier book is in a footnote, similar to that found in his article of the previous year, explaining his change of viewpoint. In this one he stated that the *Pravda* article "caused me to re-examine my views on this question. New factual material, which I discovered in the archives, made it possible for me to write the present chapter of the work from new positions" (p. 107).

22. The book is mentioned at least twice in survey articles on recent works on Central Asian history. In *Istoriia SSSR* it was praised for its appraisal of the national movements, but found deficient on the British threat (No. 2,

after 1957. He was a frequent reviewer of books in Kazakh journals, and was the main editor of the bibliography of historical works on Kazakhstan during the Soviet period. Beginning in 1959 he wrote a series of textbooks on the history of Kazakhstan for use in the Kazakh schools.[23]

In 1957 the long overdue new edition of the *History of the Kazakh S.S.R.* finally appeared.[24] It is impossible to determine whether it was a patched-up version of the *maket* that was written in the early 1950's and published in manuscript form for discussion on the eve of Stalin's death, or whether it was completely rewritten. Scanty available evidence suggests the latter. The editorial board of the 1957 history, nine strong, contains only one of the editors of the *maket*. One chapter of the history, "now in progress," had been published in a Kazakh journal in 1954. It was—significantly—the chapter on "The Voluntary Annexation of Kazakhstan to Russia," written by the authors of the 1957 chapter, N. Apollova and G. Dakhshleiger.[25] Although the two versions are in agreement on interpretation, they have little resemblance in actual wording. The finished product is longer, more detailed on the actual processes of annexation, and somewhat toned down.[26] There had been frequent mention of the forthcoming volume for several years, and periodic reminders about its failure to be sent to press, including a particularly sharp one in *Kommunist Kazakhstana* immediately after the Twentieth Party Congress.[27] The twenty-five editors and authors, who were understandably deliberate during the unsettled period of 1956, sent the work to press in February, 1957.

1959, p. 199); a Kazakh writer praised it without qualification as a significant new work, in *Voprosy istorii* (No. 11, 1961, pp. 164-65).

23. E. B. Bekmakhanov, *Istoriia kazakhskoi SSR. Uchebnoe posobie dlia 8-9-go klassov srednei shkoly Kazakhstana* (Alma-Ata, 1959). The following year he published a continuing volume for the tenth grade, which covers Kazakh history since 1905 (*Istoriia kazakhskoi SSR. Uchebnoe posobie dlia 10 klassa srednei shkoly Kazakhstana* [Alma-Ata, 1960]), and another survey history appeared in the year of his death (*Ocherki istorii Kazakhstana XIX v.* [Alma-Ata, 1966]).

24. *Istoriia kazakhskoi SSR*, ed. M. O. Auezov, S. B. Baishev, *et al.* (Alma-Ata, 1957), Vol. I.

25. G. Dakhshleiger and N. Apollova, "Dobrovol'noe prisoedinenie Kazakhstana k Rossii," *VAN kazakhskoi SSR*, No. 5, 1954, pp. 14-27.

26. For example, the topic on the "historical necessity for the annexation of Kazakhstan to Russia," which appears in the 1954 version, does not appear explicitly in the finished product, although the theme is implied in it.

27. P. Gavrilov, "O ser'eznykh nedostatkakh v razvitii obshchestvennykh nauk v Kazakhstane," *Kommunist Kazakhstana*, No. 3, 1956, pp. 18-26.

With this volume, the new Soviet historiography of the non-Russian peoples may be said to have come of age. The modern history of the Kazakhs is here thoroughly coordinated with the history of the Great Russians and subservient to it. The three long chapters on modern Kazakh cultural history might be more accurately titled "Russian Influences on Kazakh culture." The authors pay repeated tribute to the Russians for their economic development since the early eighteenth century, accepting many of the tsarist reforms almost at their face value. Though they point out that the reforms were primarily intended to strengthen the ruling classes, they conclude that these measures "objectively" were of great progressive significance for the Kazakh people. All the resistance movements of the first half of the nineteenth century are regarded as "feudal-monarchal" in character, with the exception of the Taimanov uprising. Kenesary's movement is reduced to two pages (from a long chapter in the 1943 history) and sketched in the darkest colors.

The first volume of the new history of the Kazakhs was a predictable success, as indicated by a long, favorable review in *Kommunist*.[28] To be sure, the trio of historians who wrote the review found shortcomings: there were not enough "references to sources," and there were oversimplifications on questions of class relationships and economic development during the tsarist period. But these objections were drowned in a chorus of hurrahs for the book's elaboration of Russia's good influences on Kazakh history. "Even from the first stages of its development," said the reviewers, "Kazakh culture felt the progressive influences of advanced Russian culture." Chapter XIX (dealing with the period when these influences reached their peak in the latter half of the nineteenth century) was called the "richest in the work." Thus, on the sixth attempt in a little over twenty years, Soviet historians had produced a history of the Kazakh Republic which the party found acceptable. But the acclaim of this work seems to have been restricted to the party and the Kazakh press. Although the publication of this long-awaited book—whether it was good or bad—could only be regarded as a major event in Soviet historical scholarship, the central historical journals never reviewed the book.

28. I. Braginskii, I. Zlatkin and N. Ustiugov, "Poleznaia kniga po istorii Kazakhstana," *Kommunist*, No. 16, 1957, pp. 86-95. It was reprinted in *VAN kazakhskoi SSR*, No. 1, 1958, pp. 103-9.

Because of the unsettled conditions of 1956, many historians held up works that were eventually published in 1957 or later, when the party's re-thinking could be taken into consideration. Their cautious attitude proved to be the better part of wisdom. Only three survey histories on the non-Russian peoples went to press during the twelve-month period beginning with the Twentieth Party Congress, and all were from the remoter parts of Central Asia and contained views that would be considered heretical by the time the ink was dry.

One of these was the two-volume *History of Kirgizia,* a first attempt at a Soviet survey history of that republic. The first volume of the work, covering Kirgiz history up to the Revolution, was produced by a stellar cast of editors and authors, including Abramzon, Bernshtam, Viatkin, Okladnikov, and the rising Kirgiz historians, B. D. Dzhamgerchinov and K. Usenbaev.[29] From the first sentence of the chapter on the annexation of the Kirgiz, the reader is aware that the process of demythologizing tsarist colonialism and the friendship of peoples is under way. The account begins with a deflating statement that Pokrovskii might have written: "The annexation of Kirgizia to Russia took place in the process of the conquest by tsarism of the Central Asian khanates." There is no description of the long preliminary historic process of growing "Russian orientation," of "striving" to collaborate with the Russian people, as usually given in the histories of Central Asian peoples written earlier and later. There are, to be sure, a number of statements on the progressive significance of annexation, and of the eventual benefits reaped by the Kirgiz. But these come later on, and do not soften the account of the brutal nature of tsarist colonialism, which is the dominant theme. The Russian interests in Central Asia were two: "as a source of state income and a new market for products for domestic production" and "as a new area for settlement of the surplus population from the central *gubernii.*" In their headlong rush for the new territories, the tsars "came into a collision with a no less forceful, aggressive attempt of capitalist Britain" (p. 255). May one infer from this statement that the British, were *no more* aggressive? The subsequent discussion would indicate as much; the Kirgiz are regarded as a pawn in the game of

29. *Istoriia Kirgizii,* ed. M. P. Viatkin, B. D. Dzhamgerchinov, A. P. Okladnikov, *et al.* (Frunze, 1956), Vol. I.

colonial rivalry. Such a view would be as emphatically rejected in the near future as it had been in the near past.

Much the same dark view of tsarist colonialism is continued in a lengthy discussion of colonial government in Kirgizia (p. 289 ff.). No immediate gains are reported for the Kirgiz; instead the class contradictions and problems of central Russia were transferred to the colony (p. 290). A realistic discussion of the settlement of Russian peasants on Kirgiz lands follows, without the customary sequel concerning the growing class alliance of the friendly peoples. Several Kirgiz uprisings are said to have been provoked late in the nineteenth century, and are not specifically condemned as reactionary. Regarding the 1916 revolt, the authors try to hold to the view that when clashes occurred between Kirgiz and Russians, the fault was that of the *manaps*, but the accounts are unconvincing, to say the least. In one area they note that the feudal leaders "directed the masses against all Russians"; in another they were able to stir up "national hatred," after which "the rebels burned the houses in Russian villages, not distinguishing between the rich and the poor" (pp. 399, 402). Evidences of friendship between the Kirgiz and Russian masses are there, but are stated so cautiously as to be a faint echo of the Bagirov view. The following statement will illustrate: "Both the *bey-manap* leadership of the uprising [1916] and the chauvinistic agitation of tsarist rule and the kulaks stirred up national dissensions, and interfered with manifestations of solidarity between the working masses of the Russians and Kirgiz. However, scattered glints [*otdel'nye probleski*] of such solidarity broke through along the way" (p. 403).

This history was the subject of a surprisingly gentle and uncritical review in *Voprosy istorii*, written by four obscure historians from Frunze.[30] The review was on the whole favorable, characterizing the appearance of the book as "a great event in the scholarly life of the country." The reviewers' minor objections were on old well-known bones of contention, such as periodization and the class structure in particular areas and periods. On the critical question of annexation, they confined themselves to restating a few platitudes about progressive consequences, which purported to summarize what the authors of the history had said. They skirted completely the obvious fact that the authors, in revising the pre-

30. *VI*, No. 8, 1957, pp. 201-8. The reviewers were I. Grishkov, A. Kats, Kh. Musin, and I. Skliar. None of them had published extensively, and none had figured in the discussion on the Central Asian revolts.

vailing view on tsarist colonialism, had produced an interpretation that was decidedly out of step by August, 1957, when the review was published.

We know that the 1956 *History of Kirgizia* was considered faulty, not from the reviews, but from the fact that a new collective soon went to work to produce another history of the Kirgiz. The old editorial board was considerably shaken up; it retained only Viatkin and Dzhamgerchinov and added a number of unknown authors. The successor volume, which was published in 1963, makes guarded references to the errors of the earlier one by stating that some materials were not used, which made it impossible to give a full account of the history of certain periods (fifteenth to the eighteenth centuries) and of the national movements.[31]

But the real faults of the 1956 history are to be discovered in the 1963 account. Kirgiz-Russian relations are restored to their former status; the aggressiveness of tsarist expansionist policies is not only toned down but converted into defensive moves against an aggressive Britain. All violence between Russian and Kirgiz is laid to the class enemy without any qualification. The "sympathy" of the Kirgiz people for their Russian brothers, their "striving for Russian citizenship," the pre-revolutionary alliance of workers, are all conspicuously there. Thus the "solidarity" of the Russian and Kirgiz peoples, which had been reduced to "scattered glints" by the 1956 authors, is once again in 1963 held to the radiant light of the morning sun.

Among the historians of the non-Russian republics, those of Turkmenia have been among the most deliberate and outspoken, and their works have frequently been out of step. One of the main reasons for this is undoubtedly the difficult task of reconciling the demands of the friendship of peoples with historical facts; it was the Turkmens who put up the most determined resistance to Russian expansion into Central Asia. In 1942 the Central Committee of the Turkmen party had discussed the need for a history of the Turkmen people and party organization. It had called for historical works dealing with the annexation of the area, the relations of the people with the Russians, and the development of the party. In 1944 the same body passed a resolution calling for the publication of documents on these subjects.[32] As has already been pointed out,

31. *Istoriia Kirgizii*, ed. M. P. Viatkin, M. P. Griaznov, *et al.* (Frunze, 1963), I, 9.
32. *Rossiia i Turkmeniia v XIX veke. K vkhozhdeniiu Turkmenii v sostav Rossii* (Ashkhabad, 1946), p. 4.

the first volumes of this collection, which appeared at the time of rapid change in Soviet historiography in 1946, were severely criticized. They not only contained materials on the armed clash of Turkmens and Russians but lacked the desired proofs of British interference and progress traceable to the Russians.[33] As fate would have it, these documents would become a mainstay of those historians who held out against the idealization of tsarist colonial policy. They were frequently quoted in articles and conferences on the Central Asian revolts. The historians of Turkmenia did not produce a survey history of their country for fifteen years after the first party requests. But they had evidently been holding their manuscripts for a favorable time, for they quickly surfaced in 1956.

Two small volumes on the history of the Turkmen Republic appeared that year. The authors, A. A. Rosliakov and A. Karryev, were already known as non-conformists who had never accepted the Bagirov view of tsarist colonialism and the voluntary nature of the annexation of their people to the Russian Empire. Rosliakov had stood with Tarasov at the Ashkhabad discussions on the 1916 revolt, refusing to accept the interpretation that the revolt had been largely progressive, with few instances of heavy fighting between natives and Russians. He was mentioned at the second Tashkent conference as the proponent of unscientific views. Karryev, it will be recalled, had been severely criticized for his articles refuting the friendly relations between Turkmens and Russians. Both of them demonstrated in 1956 that they had not changed their views, and—what is more surprising—they continued to state heretical propositions in the general history of the Turkmen S.S.R., which was published the following year.

The two books are complementary works with an identical title, *A Short Sketch of the History of Turkmenistan*, with subtitles dividing their accounts at the point of annexation to Russia.[34] Together with the second part of the *History of the Turkmen S.S.R.* (1957), they constitute the harshest critique of tsarist colonialism, particularly of the conquest of Central Asia, that has appeared since the late 1940's. The Turkmen annexation had always been one of the most difficult to put into the new framework, since it was well known that resistance had been long and determined. The

33. See Chapter 5 above, p. 107.
34. A. A. Rosliakov, *Kratkii ocherk istorii Turkmenistana* (*Do prisoedineniia k Rossii*) (Ashkhabad, 1956); A. Karryev and A. Rosliakov, *Kratkii ocherk istorii Turkmenistana* (*Ot prisoedineniia k Rossii do velikoi oktiabr'skoi sotsialisticheskoi revoliutsii, 1868-1917 gg.*) (Ashkhabad, 1956).

Turkmen phase of the revolt of 1916 had been the most explosive question at the second Tashkent conference, and although the final resolution of the meeting purported to state a consensus, the minority had never accepted it. Rosliakov and Karryev, who apparently regarded the Twentieth Party Congress statements on historiography to be a call for a more realistic interpretation of Russian-Turkmen relations, quickly responded with these little volumes, containing a short and popular account of the history of their republic, which would shortly be filled out in two stout volumes.[35]

Ninety-five per cent or more of the contents of these books would be considered "correct," either in 1955 or 1957. The most outstanding feature is perhaps the role of the British as the villain in Turkmenia in the nineteenth century. However, the small area of non-conformity, the 1956 ingredient, is the most sensitive one— the matter of Russian-Turkmen relations, especially from the time of annexation to the Revolution. The reader is first aware of a new climate in the use of the old terminology. Russian expansion is again referred to as "conquest."[36] The careful separation of "Russian" and "tsarist" is forgotten: one reads repeatedly of "Russian tsarist autocracy" and "Russian tsarism" in negative passages.[37] The studied vagueness on the actual clashes is gone; the authors speak of "fierce battles" between Russian and Turkmen forces, and of "the cruel military-colonial regime" that was established when the fighting was all over.[38]

Rosliakov, the sole author of the first volume, was less outspoken on the question of annexation. He stated that "a majority of the Turkmen tribes were annexed to Russia voluntarily, but in certain areas, the acts of violence of the tsarist troops, the requisitions and exactions, aroused the opposition of the people. In Akhal this

35. That Rosliakov and Karryev were in a hurry to get their account into print is suggested by the fact that two volumes of less than two hundred pages each appeared within five months, when they might have appeared in one volume of average size. In effect, Rosliakov admitted this. In a short note at the beginning of the first volume, he stated that the larger history was to appear soon, but that teachers, students, and scholars needed a short account "right now" (June, 1956). He asked for critical comments, which he said would be useful in preparing the other work. This suggests that these volumes may also have been offered as trial balloons.

36. Karryev and Rosliakov, *Kratkii ocherk*, p. 32.

37. *Ibid.*, pp. 5, 34; Rosliakov, *Kratkii ocherk*, p. 169.

38. Rosliakov, *Kratkii ocherk*, p. 169; Karryev and Rosliakov, *Kratkii ocherk*, p. 6. This terminology is also used in the *History of Kirgizia*, which appeared at the same time.

resulted in fierce battles in the area of the Geok-tepe fortress."[39] He followed this with a statement that did not conform to the accepted class lines, but suggested that the native upper class—momentarily, to be sure—had led the opposition to the Russians: "The Turkmen aristocracy put itself at the head of [*vozglavila*] the opposition of the tsarist forces, but soon made a deal with the autocracy."

In several other ways Rosliakov's account varied from the norm—sometimes by omission, implication, or shading of terminology. He made it quite clear, without saying so in as many words, that the annexation of Turkmenia was not the headlong rush of the people for protection against their enemies and for enjoyment of a better life which was described in other accounts. He devoted considerable space to the struggle among Turkmen feudal leaders who were oriented first toward Persia and then toward Khiva and Bukhara, noting that Russian annexation became a possibility only after tsarist armies had encroached on the borderlands. He also made it clear that independence was the first choice of the Turkmens and that annexation to Russia became interesting only when other possibilities failed: "Seeing the impossibility of liberating themselves from the feudal yoke by their own power, the Turkmens turned all the more to the Russian government with requests for help" (p. 160). He did not accept the concept of a united "Turkmen people" or the myth that future peoples of the Soviet family did not fight among themselves. He referred several times to divisions within the Turkmen family, and even to "the animosity between Turkmen tribes and the animosity toward neighboring peoples" (p. 167). He gave no lip service to an early friendship between the Russian and Turkmen peoples: such a development was linked with Lenin's nationality policy (p. 171). In contrast to developments elsewhere in Central Asia, trade between Russia and Turkmenia was said to have developed only slowly on the eve of annexation, and that event, albeit of great importance, was largely of potential significance for the Turkmens. "Russian tsarism" did all it could to preserve the worst features of the old feudal regime, and such benefits as the Turkmen people reaped before the Revolution were strictly the result of "objective economic laws" (pp. 169-70). At the end of a long list of reactionary measures of the Russian colonizers, Rosliakov found occasion for another jab at the idyll of Russian-Turkmen friendship: "All these brutal policies of tsarism

39. Rosliakov, *Kratkii ocherk*, p. 169.

provoked the hatred of the Turkmen people toward tsarist exploiter-officials, which was sometimes transferred to distrust of everything Russian [*nedoverie ko vsemu russkomu*]" (p. 170).

The second volume of *A Short Sketch of the History of Turkmenistan*, which was written jointly by Karryev and Rosliakov, and appeared in October, 1956, went even further in refuting the established views on tsarist colonial policies and the friendship of peoples. Very early in the account it is apparent that a view for which Karryev had been condemned four years earlier was being repeated: that the Russians had turned down repeated Turkmen requests for military aid. This was coupled with a statement on tsarist policies that hardly concealed the deep animosity between peoples:

> The Turkmen tribes needed the development of trade with Russia, from which they could and did receive food and handicraft products. At that time many Turkmens saw, in the presence of Russia, the power capable of cutting short the interminable wars, which tormented the Turkmen people, and of protecting the Turkmens from the raids of neighboring feudal lords. Therefore in the eighteenth and nineteenth centuries the requests of the Turkmen tribes, living near the Caspian, to take Russia citizenship, became more frequent and persistent.
>
> However, Russian - Turkmen collaboration was made more difficult by the reactionary policies of Russian tsarism and the determined circles of Turkmen feudal-clerical aristocracy.
>
> Russian tsarism, in carrying out its policies in Turkmenistan, was not guided, of course, by the common interests of the Russian and Turkmen peoples, but by its own plundering, colonizing efforts. The rude, violent activities of tsarist rule insulted and irritated the local population and frequently turned away from Russia even those, who earlier had been advocates of collaboration with her. . . . The dissatisfaction of the people, provoked by the plundering activities of tsarist forces, was utilized by the more reactionary part of the Turkmen feudal-clan leaders and Moslem clergy, in alliance with British agents, for their own aims. The aristocracy feared that the annexation to Russia would interfere with the raids by which they enriched themselves and would limit their power over the Turkmen workers. As a result tsarist troops, in certain

areas of Turkmenistan, especially in Akhal, met fierce opposition from the Turkmen tribes (pp. 5-6).

Thus armed resistance was real, but was attributed to the dissatisfaction of a misguided people—a proposition that would hardly be
accepted even by a naïve reader.

But that was not all. The historians went on to give more details in a later passage. They went to considerable length to describe how British agents and local reactionaries tried "to weaken
the position of the advocates of the annexation of Akhal to Russia,"
referring repeatedly to the "anti-Russian attitude" among the Turkmens. This attitude was engendered not solely by the local class
enemy and foreign agent, but by the "tsarist forces," and though
Russian generals and officials were held responsible for the excesses,
the role of the common Russian soldier was less than heroic:

> The arrival of tsarist forces, not without cause, was feared
> by a significant part of the working population of Akhal,
> who saw in them new conquerors. The haughty conduct
> of the tsarist generals and officials, the coarse treatment
> which the Turkmen representatives were subjected to in the
> Russian camp, as also the many kinds of requisitions and
> exactions practiced by the tsarist authorities, especially the
> mass requisition of camels, *kibitkas* [tents], and provisions
> for the troops, which sometimes degenerated into plain pil-
> laging [*grabezh*]—all this alienated from tsarist Russia even
> the former supporters among the natives . . . and strength-
> ened the position of the opponents of voluntary annexation
> to Russia (p. 43).

There is an account of the Turkmen defense of Geok-tepe against
the Russian siege from an unmistakably pro-Turkmen point of
view: "In spite of powerful artillery fire, the defenders of the fortress, with the arrival of aid from a contingent of the natives of
Merv, made a heroic defense. . . ." (p. 46). The 1916 revolt had
the same provocations and the same fierce fighting of Turkmens
against Russians, brought about by the ability of reactionary leaders to misguide the workers. The authors made it clear that these
deluded rebels were not highly selective in choosing their victims:
"The slogan of these uprisings was extermination of the *kapyr* ('the
infidel'), that is, the Russian, Armenian and non-Moslem population
in general, the plundering of cities, the destruction of Russian villages. For the most part the victims at the time of the uprisings

were not Russian capitalists and officials, but Russian settlers, rail-road workers, telegraph operators and working people" (p. 145).

Karryev and Rosliakov touched on other sensitive nerves. They referred to the migration of many Turkmen people from the Akhal oasis. Though they did not state explicitly that they were escaping the Russian invasion, their meaning was clear (p. 46). They re-jected the positive implications of the arrival of the Russian settler, the invaluable link in building the friendship of peoples. They reversed the proposition, giving it a Pokrovskian flavor: "In the country where a powerful peasant agrarian movement developed, tsarism tried to weaken it by the method of settling Russian peas-ants on part of the recently conquered lands" (p. 34). Along with their discussion of reactionary tsarist measures, they acknowledged considerable economic growth in pre-revolutionary Turkmenia, es-pecially the expansion of railroads, irrigation, and the textile indus-try. They saw these improvements coming in spite of tsarism, and made no further attempt to explain the progressive results of reac-tionary policies.

The History of the Turkmen S.S.R. (Volume I, Part 2), which appeared in 1957, contained no substantial revision of the interpre-tations of Rosliakov and Karryev the year before.[40] The chapter on the conquest, written by Karryev, contained a long verbatim passage from the second of the accounts of the previous year, with with its "anti-Russian" attitudes of the natives, their fear of Russia as "another conqueror," and the requisitions and pillaging (pp. 122-25). Since it was a much longer work, this history contained a much more detailed account, with many refinements and elabora-tions of ideas that were stated only briefly before. This discussion will be confined to some of these details. The villainous role of the British is one of the strongest features of the book. The destructive work of British agents is found everywhere; they are even said to have had a special interest in hindering good relations between Russians and Turkmens, and are thus useful in explaining why a friendship of peoples did not develop rapidly: "The anti-Russian attitude among the backward part of the Turkmens, and first of all among the natives of Akhal, was aggravated by British agents, who, taking advantage of the moment, began to organize anti-Russian provocations in different tribes. . . . The activity of the British agents, who were not sparing with their promises, played no small role in

40. *Istoriia turkmenskoi SSR,* ed. A. Karryev, O. K. Kuliev, M. E. Masson, *et al.* (Ashkhabad, 1957), Vol. I, Part 2.

weakening the position of the advocates among the natives of voluntary annexation to Russia" (p. 124). Even at the time of the 1916 revolt, when Britain was fighting for her life against the Central Powers, she was trying to weaken Russia in Central Asia: "Turkey and Germany, fighting against Russia, were especially active at this time in diversionist-intelligence work. But also the 'ally' [author's quotation marks] of Russia, Britain, and also the United States, did not hesitate to carry on underhanded work in Central Asia, trying to weaken Russia and prepare conditions for tearing her territories away from her" (p. 390).

The divisions among the Turkmen feudal leaders during the whole century before annexation are detailed and made more explicit: some are said to have preferred subservience to Persia rather than Russia, others sought aid from Britain and Afghanistan (p. 132). Armed clashes between the plain people of Turkmenistan and Russia are described without evasion, although qualifying clauses or extenuating circumstances are given:

> True, there took place in the Caspian area various armed clashes between Russian troops and Turkmens. . . . But on the whole, the basic mass of the Turkmen population along the Caspian shore and the Atrek valley happily greeted the Russian forces. . . .
>
> The Akhal-Tekinsk oasis was conquered by tsarist forces after fierce battles, as were other parts of Turkmenistan, for example, those described earlier, which were held by the anti-Russian "party" of the local feudal aristocracy (pp. 120; 137-38).

The pre-revolutionary alliance of the proletariat in Turkmenia was explicitly denied in the explanation of the failure of the 1916 revolt.

> The revolt in Turkmenistan was a constituent part of the revolt of 1916, taking place all over Turkestan. It was spontaneous, uncoordinated, not having centralized leadership and a clearly formulated program. The local national proletariat, because of its small numbers and its youth, was not yet able to be the leading force. The local Russian proletariat did not have as yet sufficiently firm ties with the native workers. Lacking proletarian leadership, the uprising of the national peasantry of Turkmenistan and the backward regions of Turkestan was doomed to defeat (p. 389).

The failure of the 1916 revolt because of the lack of strong, co-ordinated, proletarian leadership is a common Soviet view. But the specific statements about the failure of Russian and Turkmen workers to join forces, even on the eve of the Revolution, is a rare admission in recent Soviet historical writing of the emptiness of the high-sounding claims of proletarian solidarity.

Not one of these three volumes on the history of Turkmenia was reviewed in the central historical journals. Their failure to take notice of the two shorter books is not a conspicuous omission, al-though the journals frequently review works of a popular type, of less importance than these works. But passing over the survey history of Turkmenia, the product of several years work by a col-lective of historians, the first attempt at a survey history of the Turkmen people, is something else again.[41]

Anyone who examines the survey histories of the Kazakh and Turkmen republics, published within a few months of each other in 1957, cannot fail to notice a considerable variation in their treat-ment of the pre-revolutionary relations of their peoples with the Russians. The Kazakh history perhaps comes closest to the party ideal; the Turkmen history is clearly the most heretical of the recent histories of a Union Republic. The difference can hardly be ex-plained solely on historical facts themselves, even though it has always been admitted that Turkmen resistance to Russian expansion was the most determined among the non-Russian peoples. The peaceful coexistence of these two histories is indicative of a some-what freer scholarly atmosphere, a product of de-Stalinization. Al-though the Twentieth Party Congress' apparent mandate to his-torians to make thoroughgoing reforms proved to be illusory, the worst features of the Stalinist rigidity in historical writing were eliminated, permitting the Soviet historian a wider latitude of inter-pretation than would have been thinkable a few years earlier. The new climate and new party techniques will be discussed in the following chapter.

The circumstances under which the two histories were produced may help to explain their differences. The Kazakh historians had

41. In this connection, it should be pointed out that the history of Turk-menia is unusual for its scholarly apparatus. The narrative is closely tied by notes to the sources, which are impressive. There is an eighty-three page bibliography, including the bourgeois authors. Only the *History of the Uzbek S.S.R.* (1954-56), among the survey histories of the Union Republics, rivals it. Some of the histories, notably those of the Ukraine (1953 and 1956) and of the Kazakh Republic (1957) were criticized for shortcomings in this area.

been working under the searing spotlight of the party for over a decade. The collective that wrote the 1957 history had already drawn the main lines before the thaw; the Kazakhs had already capitulated and did not make a determined effort to rewrite their history along the lines suggested in 1956. The Turkmen historians, who had apparently been biding their time, published their survey immediately after the high tide of the reform movement. It should be pointed out that the Turkmen history conforms to the main lines of the friendship of peoples concept; it only questions the weakest propositions of the myth concerning the early development of friendly relations at the time of the Russian advance.

It has been noted that both party and history journals have taken a new tack since 1956. In most cases they have ignored the appearance of the new histories, and when they have reviewed them they have been surprisingly lenient with their faults. This is most remarkable in the failure of *Kommunist* or some other party organ to condemn the Turkmen history, and in the failure of the editors of the history journals either to praise their Kazakh colleagues, or to condemn the Turkmens. This seems to suggest a cautious "hands-off" policy for the historian as long as he meets the main lines of accepted interpretation. Actually the editorial boards of the history journals have neither approved nor disapproved of these histories; they have in effect said "no comment." The editors have always been reluctant disciplinarians, and, given the chance, they have shunned this duty.

CHAPTER **12.**

"THE FRIENDSHIP OF
PEOPLES" AFTER 1957

*"The utmost support should be given to the efforts of
the historians of the Soviet Republics who have strived to
reveal the objectively positive significance of the merging
[sblizhenie] of the history of their peoples with the Russians and of their annexation to Russia. The dialectic of
history is such that despite the reactionary goals and
methods of tsarism, the annexation of these peoples to
Russia and the combination of their forces with the forces
of the Russian people in the struggle against national and
social oppression prepared the way for the common front
of the empire-wide revolutionary movement, headed by the
proletariat and its Leninist Party, ultimately leading to the
liberation of all the peoples of the former tsarist empire
and to the establishment of a historically unprecedented
socialist community of dozens of nationalities populating
our country." Party spokesman B. N. Ponomarev to the All
Union Conference of Historians, December, 1962 (Voprosy
istorii, No. 1, 1963, p. 17).*

The direct interference of the party in the work of Soviet
historians has lessened considerably since early 1957, when the
campaign against the editors of *Voprosy istorii* resulted in the
silencing of those who wanted to make drastic reinterpretations.
The lesson of that crisis was that revision would have to be cautious
and selective, following party advice. This most stable decade in
Soviet historiography has resulted from work satisfactory to the
party. For more than twenty years earlier, the Soviet historian,
who had been in the toils of the party's directives on history, had

made frequent "errors," either by resisting the pressure to compromise his professional standards or by attempting to comply with party directives that were too general, vague, or contradictory, or were themselves changing because of new political considerations. But by the late 1950's historians had formulated interpretations that met with approval, and the editorial controls were perfected to the extent that a work as heretical as that of Bekmakhanov a decade earlier could never see the light of day. Thus, there are no more instant rare books in the Soviet Union (perhaps in literature, but not in history), and few completely unfavorable reviews. The survey histories will illustrate the point: since 1956 *all* the histories that have been published have been acceptable, receiving at worst minor criticism; before 1956 all except a few were rejected and are now considered obsolete.

If the stability of Soviet historiography is due in part to the fact that the historian has learned his lessons, it must also be said that the tactics of the party have also changed to the advantage of the scholars. This change is less substantial, but is nevertheless real. The watchdogs of ideology in the later period—men like L. F. Il'ichev and B. N. Ponomarev[1]—do not employ the sledgehammer tactics of Zhdanov or Bagirov. Their more moderate methods differ from those of their predecessors as much as those of Brezhnev differ from the methods of Stalin. Although the party's struggle against bourgeois nationalism continues, it is largely confined to the political arena. The historian has been able to do his work away from the constant supervision of the party.

The accommodation that has been reached between the party ideologist and the historian permits a range of interpretation considerably more flexible than that of Stalin's day, when a numbing uniformity was the rule. The limits of this tolerance have been demonstrated in our discussion of the survey histories of Kazakhstan and Turkmenistan, which are perhaps examples of the most orthodox and heretical extremes of the post-thaw interpretation of the friendship of peoples. Central Asia and the Caucasus remain the greatest problem areas in the historiography of the non-Russian peoples.

1. Il'ichev is Director of the Central Committee's Department of Propaganda and Agitation for the Union Republics; Ponomarev is Director of the Central Committee's International Department.

ANOTHER TASHKENT CONFERENCE ON CENTRAL ASIAN HISTORY

The views expressed in the histories coming out of Central Asia in 1956 and 1957 did not evoke an attack in the party press, as they surely would have a little earlier. But the general unhappiness with unresolved questions growing out of the abortive reexamination of historical questions following the Twentieth Party Congress can be detected in the repeated warnings about the vestiges of bourgeois nationalism and the positive role of the Soviet historian in the construction of a Communist society. The themes of the elder brother and the friendship of peoples were popularized in a growing number of publications on the cultural contacts of Russians and non-Russians, and of volumes commemorating various anniversaries of annexation (there will be more on this later). These themes were also given a prominent place in a number of scholarly conferences,[2] one of which was called in Tashkent specifically to deal with the question of the progressive significance of the annexation of Central Asia—a question that had presumably been settled by the conference that met in that city in 1954.

The Joint Scholarly Session on the Progressive Significance of the Annexation of Central Asia to Russia, which met in Tashkent at the end of May, 1959, was the largest conference called to discuss the question.[3] Seven hundred participants from all the Union

2. At a conference on the theoretical problems of the construction of communism in June, 1958, Gafurov lectured on bourgeois nationalism, warning particularly about "the idealization of the past, an uncritical attitude toward various movements" (*VI*, No. 9, 1958, pp. 183-84). A conference of Orientalists meeting in Tashkent in 1957 heard a paper on "The Role of the Great Russian People in the Historic Fate of the Peoples of Central Asia," beginning with the seventh century, A. D. (*Materialy pervoi vsesoiuznoi nauchnoi konferentsii vostokovedov v g. Tashkente, 4-11 iiunia, 1957 g.* [Tashkent, 1958], pp. 140-44). The themes of the proletarian alliance on the eve of the Revolution and of its Bolshevik leadership were prominent in conferences on Central Asian history in the Soviet period (Alma-Ata, 1957) and on the history of the October Revolution in the Transcaucasus (Baku, 1958). At the earlier conference O. K. Kuliev read a paper on "The Alliance of the Russian Working Class and the Turkmen Workers as a Decisive Condition for the Victory of the Great October Revolution in Turkmenistan." The history of Turkmenia, of which he was an editor, stated repeatedly that such an alliance did not exist one year earlier in many areas of Turkmenia (*Materialy ob"edinennoi nauchnoi sessii posviashchennoi istorii Srednei Azii i Kazakhstana (epokha sotsializma)* [Alma-Ata, 1958], pp. 114-23). At the Baku Conference, I. A. Guseinov, the Director of the Azerbaidzhan Institute of History, asserted that at the time of the Revolution "the proletariat of Azerbaidzhan had already been under the leadership of the Bolshevik Party for nearly fifteen years in the school of revolutionary struggle" (*VI*, No. 6, 1959, pp. 181-90).

3. "Ob"edinennaia nauchnaia sessiia, posviashchennaia progressivnomu

Republics attended. The meeting was well publicized in the Central Asian press, which revealed its cut and dried nature by discussing, as much as three months in advance, not only all the topics on the agenda, but the decisions of the conference as well. The *Central Asian Review*, in an analysis of the preliminary press notices, called attention to the main differences of opinion to be registered at the conference before it convened.[4]

This conference was characterized by the constant mixture of political considerations with scholarly questions. Not only in the opening and closing addresses, which are characteristically heavily political, but throughout most of the papers and discussion, the meeting concerned itself with the current plans of "the imperialists" in Central Asia, with bourgeois nationalist views of Central Asian scholars, and with the works of "bourgeois falsifiers." The participants showed a new sensitivity to Western studies questioning the merits of Soviet nationality policy and linking it to traditional imperialism. Soviet successes in nationality policy were held up as a guide for peoples still under the colonial yoke or just emerging from it. The threat of any kind of separatism within the Soviet family was uppermost in the minds of many: much was said on the old threadbare themes of Pan-Turkism, Pan-Islam, and Pan-Iranism, and the existence in early history of a Turkic language, common to peoples inside and just outside the Soviet Union, was denied. There were frequent references to the recent Twenty-First Party Congress' work, the new Seven-Year Plan, and the scholar's role in the construction of communism. The basic message was that further strengthening of "the unshakable friendship of peoples" was essential for the fulfillment of the party's long-range plans.

Most of the reports and discussion at the third Tashkent conference were hardly of concern to the serious scholar, but there was, at the same time, one attempt to reconcile some of the most obvious contradictions that had crept into the new Soviet interpretation of Russian expansion and its consequences. A new synthesis was offered in the report of A. V. Piaskovskii, who sought to analyze the two questions the *Central Asian Review* had predicted would constitute the bones of contention for the conference: the nature

---

znacheniiu prisoedineniia Srednei Azii k Rossii," *VI*, No. 8, 1959, pp. 173-83. There is a shorter report in *Istoriia SSSR*, No. 5, 1959, pp. 214-18.

4. "News Digest," *CAR*, VII (1959), No. 2, pp. 153-62, based on five articles in *Kommunist Tadzhikistana, Pravda vostoka*, and *Turkmenskaiia iskra* in February and March, 1959.

of Russian expansion, including the attitude of the Central Asian peoples toward it, and the extent of progress in the Russian colonies after annexation.

Piaskovskii was a well-known advocate of a new history of the last years of the Russian Empire. He had written a monograph on *Turkmenistan in the Period of the First Russian Revolution, 1905-1907* and was at this time working as editor on a large volume of documents on *The Rebellion of 1916 in Central Asia and Kazakhstan.*[5] In recent years he had expressed himself against some of the extreme interpretations he considered unwarranted. He acknowledged that the Social-Democratic organizations were very weak in Central Asia in 1905, and that they could hardly be credited with leading the native masses before the eve of the October Revolution.[6] At the Alma-Ata Conference on Central Asian history in the Soviet period he had made a conspicuous rebuttal to a paper attributing the successes of the Turkestan phases of the October Revolution to consistent and unerring Bolshevik leadership. Piaskovskii declared that he had been a participant in the events in Central Asia and could see little resemblance between the paper and reality. He called for an end of embellishment of the Bolshevik role and an acknowledgment that they had made mistakes.[7] On the other hand Piaskovskii had assigned a major role in revolutionary activities as far back as 1905 to such vague entities as "the Russian working classes" and the "working masses of the Central Asian peoples."[8] At the Tashkent conference of 1954 Tarasov had accused him of falsification by enlarging a small skirmish and characterizing it as a popular revolt.[9] Herein lay hints of the Piaskovskii thesis of 1959: historical interpretation was to turn largely on the actions, and even the opinions, of the working class, which Piaskovskii maintained were clearly discernible at any given stage of history. Since his paper to the conference appears to be the most serious attempt to offer a consistent interpretation of these troublesome historical events, it deserves summarizing here at some length.[10]

5. A. V. Piaskovskii, *Turkmenistan v period pervoi russkoi revoliutsii, 1905-1907 gg.* (Ashkhabad, 1955); *Vosstanie 1916 goda v Srednei Azii i Kazakhstane,* ed. A. V. Piaskovskii (Moscow, 1960).

6. Piaskovskii, *Turkmenistan v period pervoi russkoi revoliutsii,* p. 99.

7. *Materialy ob"edinennoi nauchnoi sessii* (Alma-Ata, 1958), pp. 160-64.

8. Piaskovskii, *Turkmenistan v period pervoi russkoi revoliutsii,* p. 99.

9. See Chapter 9 above, pp. 188-90.

10. The importance of Piaskovskii's views is also pointed up by the fact that *Voprosy istorii* singled out his paper for publication (A. V. Piaskovskii,

The Soviet view on the amount and nature of progress for the subject peoples between the time of their acquisition and the Revolution was extremely ambivalent. The early Soviet idea of the "double yoke" [*dvoinoi gnet*] imposed on these peoples by tsarism and native rulers was still current, and vague generalizations about tsarist oppression still abounded in historical accounts. On the other hand the friendship of peoples concept had been pushed to the extent that the immediate benefits of annexation were frequently recounted. This theme had been given a powerful impetus by Bagirov, who pictured the non-Russians as crying out for Russian aid and culture. This interpretation had not suffered at his downfall. As the latter view persisted, the concept of the "double yoke" ran into some of the same semantic difficulty that had plagued the "lesser evil." No amount of Marxist dialectical casuistry could get around simple arithmetic: two yokes must be somewhat worse than one. Early Soviet accounts had overwhelmingly followed this simple logic, but by the late 1950's Soviet histories, especially the popular ones, had painted progress in the tsarist colonies in such bright colors that not only had the "double yoke" become absurd, but in some cases progress marched so steadily under the tsars that the Revolution seemed almost superfluous.

The widely differing views offered at Tashkent on the question made Piaskovskii's views timely. A report by a group of Uzbek scholars emphasized that Central Asian production before the Revolution had been confined largely to agricultural products; the whole region had not produced more than 2 per cent of the Empire's output of manufactured and metallurgical goods. Lenin had called Central Asia "a colony of the purest type." Other speakers continued to refer to the benefits of transferring the economy to capitalism, the importance of the building of railroads and the textile industry, as well as the inclusion of Central Asia in the world market.

Piaskovskii tried to resolve the inconsistencies between tsarist oppression and economic progress by declaring that the two questions should be treated separately: "Here, without a doubt, two different questions are confused: the aggressive colonizing policy of the autocracy and the objective-progressive role which was played for the peoples of Central Asia by their annexation to Russia. In reality these questions have nothing in common. The progressive

"K voprosu o progressivnom znachenii prisoedineniia Srednei Azii k Rossii," VI, No. 8, 1959, pp. 21-46). The quotations that follow are from this version.

processes in the political life, economy and culture of the Central Asian peoples, which developed under the influence of Russia, occurred apart from tsarism and in spite of its national-colonial policies." Thus Piaskovskii pushed the doctrine of dual Russia to a new extreme. Having separated "official Russia" from "democratic Russia" in the colonies, he made the growing alliance of peoples the standard by which all progress could be explained. By placing the emphasis here, he could avoid the idealization of tsarist policies. Nor was it necessary to theorize that by some working of the laws of historic development, these oppressive policies had an objectively progressive result. Progress had come "apart from" and "in spite of" tsarism; the broad developments of peoples progressed by extra-governmental, extra-legal means. Inherent in this scheme is the doctrine of Great Russian leadership: progress flowed from the higher culture of the Russian people to their non-Russian friends.

Such a premise, according to its author, would clarify many questions that had confused Soviet historians. Some had reasoned that since annexation to Russia was progressive, revolts against the resulting *status quo* had to be reactionary. But such a view had resulted from relating elements that should be separated. The popular revolts "were not directed against Russia. The exploited peoples were struggling against autocracy. . . ." The sole determinant of the reactionary or progressive nature of a revolt was whether or not peoples (Russian and non-Russian, in this case) had fought together against autocracy.

Having made the friendship of peoples the nucleus of his interpretation, Piaskovskii was willing to toss overboard some of the propositions that had been offered in its behalf. He candidly admitted—in the face of many proud pronouncements at the conference about the achievements of Soviet historical science—that the whole question of the economic progress made in Central Asia on the eve of annexation and immediately thereafter had not been adequately studied. Instead of statistical studies the historians had produced empty arguments. He rejected the idea that the area had been economically stagnant, with no hope of progress except with Russian help. He also rejected the notion of an immediate blossoming of the economy after annexation. Simple facts about tsarist colonial policies would disprove it. Progress had come by a gradual process, in which the increased contacts of the peoples were the vital moving force. By 1905 there were 15,000 Russian workers and 100,000 Russian peasants in Central Asia. They engaged in a common revolutionary struggle with Central Asian peoples, and even in the defeat of 1905-7, they provided an important "school" for the successful Revolution later on. By 1917 there were 50,000 factory workers in Central Asia, of which 23 per cent were Russian. While emphasizing proletarian leadership, Piaskovskii continued to be cautious about giving credit to the Bolsheviks, who were still weak.

On the other main question—the nature of the Russian expansion and the attitude of the new subject peoples toward it—the Soviet interpretation had drifted to the absurd proposition that the Central Asian peoples welcomed the Russians, even when they were pushed off their hereditary lands. Only the Turkmen and Kirgiz historians maintained that there had been some armed resistance, but even here they claimed that it was confined to only a few places. At this conference the customary emphasis on the voluntary theme was made, notably by the Tadzhik historian, S. A. Radzhabov.

Piaskovskii's criticism of the voluntary nature of the annexations was perhaps the most important concession to reason in his report. Since the middle 1940's one people after another had been added to the list of those who were said to have joined the Empire voluntarily, and no attack on the proposition had been made up to now. Piaskovskii scored the "idealization of tsarist colonial policy," which had led to accounts that ignored altogether the violent, military nature of the tsarist conquests. "The desire of certain historians 'to prove' that the conquest of Central Asia by tsarism never happened, as though *all* its nationalities voluntarily came into Russia, is simply explained."[11] He laid it to an uncritical view of the progressiveness of annexation, i.e. a failure to see the role of the people, as against that of government.

> It is necessary to bring clarity to the thesis of so-called "voluntary"[12] annexation of Central Asia to Russia. Of course the peoples of certain areas of the countries (for example, Georgia, Ukraine, Kazakhstan, Northern Kirgizia), because of definite historical conditions, voluntarily joined with Russia, not wanting to be taken over by more backward eastern despots. But this does not mean that all peoples without exception (in particular the peoples of Central Asia) were annexed voluntarily to the Russian Empire. The historical fact is that a majority of the peoples of

11. Quotation marks and emphasis in the original (*ibid.*, p. 22).
12. Piaskovskii's quotation marks (*ibid.*).

Central Asia demonstrated a determined resistance to tsarist military forces.

Not only does this statement appear to limit severely the instances of voluntary annexation, but it circumscribes the others so much that they could hardly be offered as proofs of the friendship of peoples. But the statement is also tantalizing in its incompleteness. Who were the "majority" who resisted?

In sum, Piaskovskii seemed to be proposing a more modest friendship of peoples, which would emphasize the period between annexation and the Revolution. It would be a friendship based on proletarian solidarity, placing little or no emphasis on first encounters or "centuries-old" friendship (which he did not even mention). He reconciled some contradictions and took away the need for some extreme arguments. But he accomplished this by enlarging the scope of another part of the myth—the role of the alliance of peoples.

Subsequent Soviet historical writing has incorporated some of the main lines of Piaskovskii's argument, though it is impossible to know whether the new emphases are attributable directly to his report or to the general trend toward moderation. The emphasis on the alliance of peoples has been more marked than the negative aspects of tsarist conquest and colonialism. There seems to have been no significant retreat on the idea of a friendship of peoples before annexation, or on the voluntary nature of the annexations. Piaskovskii's report did not even change the drift of the Tashkent Conference. Other participants continued to speak of the significance of medieval contacts between Russians and the peoples of Central Asia. Some affirmed the voluntary annexation theme, and spoke of the sad state of affairs that prevailed before the Russians came. One speaker declared that "the annexation of Central Asia to Russia came when feudal exploitation had reached its apogee, therefore the broad popular masses in many regions did not oppose Russian forces." Another stated that "the opposition of local inhabitants of Central Asia to Russian forces was organized by agents of British imperialism."

The survey histories of Central Asian republics that appeared in the early 1960's gave increased attention to the growing alliance of peoples, especially on the eve of the Revolution.[13] This is also

13. *Istoriia Kirgizii*, ed. M. P. Viatkin, M. P. Griaznov, *et al.* (Frunze, 1963), Vol. I, chaps. xiii and xiv; *Istoriia tadzhikskogo naroda*, ed. B. I. Iskandarov and A. M. Mukhtarov (Moscow, 1964), II, Part 2, 158-70, 213-28.

a major theme of the studies on the Revolt of 1916.[14] At the same time the new works deal with the Russian conquest in far more realistic terms. This is particularly noticeable in the new *History of the Tadzhik People,* which goes into considerable detail on the many-sided struggle of the colonial powers for mastery of the area. Although Russian military actions are justified as essentially defensive, the violence is back in print. No particular claim is made about voluntary annexation of the Tadzhiks.[15] The evils of Russian conquest and colonialism have been discussed forthrightly, in a manner unthinkable in works published a decade earlier.[16]

Among the newer works, the histories of Kirgizia show the least change from the earlier views. Piaskovskii had implied that southern Kirgizia was not annexed voluntarily (by indicating that only northern Kirgizia was). But three studies on the annexation of the Kirgiz—all of which went to press later than Piaskovskii's report—firmly hold that all the Kirgiz were annexed voluntarily,[17] and the 1963 survey history of Kirgizia specifically states that the southern Kirgiz voluntarily chose to join the Russian state.[18] These works also continue the idealization of the Russian conquest and colonial administration.

UNSETTLED QUESTIONS FROM THE CAUCASUS

The party criticism that drove the editors of *Voprosy istorii* to rout in 1957 did not silence dissident voices from the North Caucasus. Dagestani historians have since that time been carrying on a curious tug of war with the "Moscow" historians, which has been characterized not by a direct disagreement on specific questions, but by the themes and emphases selected for detailed exposition from either quarter. The studies published in the central press have dealt with the social structure of the Caucasus in the nineteenth century, the reactionary essence of Muridism, and the blessings of annexation. Dagestani scholars have emphasized the

---

This is also prominent in E. B. Bekmakhanov's textbook, *Istoriia kazakhskoi SSR* (Alma-Ata, 1960), pp. 6-14.

14. Kh. Tursunov, *Vosstanie 1916 goda v Srednei Azii i Kazakhstane* (Tashkent, 1962). See also the preface of *Vosstanie 1916 goda* (1960), of which Piaskovskii was the chief editor.

15. *Istoriia tadzhikskogo naroda,* ed. Iskandarov and Mukhtarov, II, Part 2, 131-42.

16. See Chapter 15 below, p. 368.

17. See Chapter 13 below, p. 302.

18. *Istoriia Kirgizii,* ed. Viatkin, Griaznov, *et al.* (1963), I, 359-60.

national liberation character of the Shamil movement, almost to the exclusion of its Muridist "cloak," and although they have not been able to publish full-scale biographical works on Shamil, they have dealt with his heroic qualities at length in their works on the history of the area. Although they have given due regard to progressive consequences, the Dagestani historians have written considerably more than their Moscow colleagues about the oppression of Russian colonialism. In their struggle, the local historians have had the support of their branch of the Academy of Sciences, and to some extent the backing of the local party organization.

The Dagestani historians' winning first round—their hurried publication of two incomplete versions of the Makhachkala Conference, with its pro-Shamil views—has already been described. Shortly thereafter, in July, 1957, while the central press was already maintaining a prolonged silence on Shamil, the Dagestani Academy of Sciences published *A Survey of the History of Dagestan*, containing a long, well-argued and well-documented essay on Shamil.[19] Written by G. D. Daniialov, who was emerging as the main spokesman for the embattled hero, the essay reiterated the heroic qualities of the leader and extolled the national liberation quality of his struggle for independence. The maverick nature of the survey history of Dagestan can be detected if it is compared to two other histories of the region (Adygei and Kabarda) published in the same year. All three of these volumes were written by collectives, but whereas the Dagestan work was dominated by local historians, G. D. Daniialov and the rehabilitated R. M. Magomedov (both noted for pro-Shamil views), the others were directed by "Moscow" historians who had already expressed cautious views on the question. S. K. Bushuev was the most prominent editor of the history of Adygei; N. A. Smirnov was the main editor of the history of Kabarda.[20]

The most conspicuous difference in the histories is the treatment of Shamil. The history of Dagestan contained twenty-seven pages on his activities; the other two scarcely mentioned him. It is true that Dagestan was Shamil's homeland; but his movement was important to the whole area, and one gets the impression that Shamil was being suppressed in the other volumes. On the other hand, the

19. *Ocherki istorii Dagestana*, ed. M. O. Kosven, R. M. Magomedov, V. G. Gadzhiev, G. D. Daniialov, *et al.* (Makhachkala, 1957).

20. *Ocherki istorii Adygei*, ed. S. K. Bushuev, M. G. Autlev, and E. L. Kobzhesau (Maikop, 1957); *Istoriia Kabardy s drevneishkh vremen do nashikh dnei*, ed. N. A. Smirnov, Z. V. Angavadze, N. E. Gurevich, *et al.* (Moscow, 1957).

histories of Adygei and Kabarda emphasized at some length the progressive consequences of annexation, whereas the history of Dagestan devoted two paragraphs to it at the end of the Shamil epic—clearly a lip service. In his account of the Shamil movement in the history of Dagestan, Daniialov maintained the viewpoints of the Makhachkala Conference, with one slight nod to the neo-Stalinist line. Admitting that Muridism had gained control of the movement, if only at the last stages, he emphasized that the movement was originally indigenous, with popular following, aimed against the brutalities of tsarist forces, which had driven the inhabitants from their pastures, thereby threatening them with starvation. He defended Shamil's statesmanship and reforms. He also differed sharply with the other histories on foreign involvement. In the Adygei volume it was noted that Shamil wrote to the Sultan requesting help against the "infidels"; Daniialov quoted documents to show that the Turks themselves were reluctant to get involved in the Caucasian independence movement, and asserted that "Shamil not only was not a British-Turkish agent, but the existing documents show that he did not in the period of the Crimean war receive direct or indirect aid from British-Turkish forces" (p. 224).

S. K. Bushuev was the main spokesman for the Moscow line, which tolerated a limited rehabilitation of the Shamil movement without lionizing its hero. Bushuev, who had been publicly censured for pro-Shamil views in 1950, showed the resilience that is the secret of the successful Soviet historian by becoming the chief critic of the Dagestani historians and champion of a slightly moderated Bagirov line up to his death in 1958. In his study on foreign relations in the Caucasus, he devoted four chapters to the British-Turkish threat to the area, alleging Shamil's ties with these enemies of Russia.[21] This study went to the press in November, 1955, on the eve of the discussion in which many of Bushuev's colleagues renounced any ties between Shamil and British-Turkish agents. But Bushuev did not retreat an inch. The following year he published *From the History of Russian-Kabardinian Relations*, containing a chapter on "The Muridism of Shamil as a Weapon of Anglo-Turkish Aggression in the Caucasus."[22] Furthermore, he echoed the Bagirov view by maintaining that Russia's essential role in Kabarda

21. S. K. Bushuev, *Iz istorii vneshnepoliticheskikh otnoshenii v period prisoedineniia Kavkaza k Rossii* (Moscow, 1955), chaps. ii, iii, iv, and vi.
22. S. K. Bushuev, *Iz istorii russko-kabardinskikh otnoshenii* (Nal'chik, 1956), chap. ix.

had been as protector and civilizer. He had good words to say for
the Orthodox Church, the tsarist generals, and Russian colonial
reforms, which, although they had as their purpose "the strengthening of the Russian landlord, objectively had a progressive significance."[23] Early in 1958 Bushuev was the principal speaker at two
special meetings of the history faculty of Moscow University devoted
to the history of the Caucasus.[24] Although reported as a seminar,
these meetings consisted of polemical speeches by Bushuev, and
subsequent discussions that were so completely in support of his
views that they appear to have been staged. After a long condemnation of "bourgeois falsifiers" of the history of the area, Bushuev
turned to "the errors of a revisionist character" of his Soviet colleagues, which he regarded as no less dangerous. He mentioned
specifically three of the main speakers at the Makhachkala Conference—Gadzhiev, Ramazanov, and G. D. Daniialov—and Pikman,
who had raised the question at the readers' conference. In terms
echoing the party critic Bugaev, he noted that "the basis of the
revisionist errors of these historians is a loss of scientific approach
to historical reality, a running after cheap sensationalism, a tendency
to overlook questions of scholarship which are already decided and
uncontestable, the failure to bring essential arguments to substan-
tiate their point of view. In their works the accomplishments of
pre-revolutionary and Soviet historiography in the study of the
history of the peoples of the Caucasus are ignored." Repeating the
old arguments about the association of the Shamil movement with
reactionary Islam, Bushuev denounced the "revisionists" for using
such terms as "the people," "the nation," and "national liberation
movement" in referring to the struggle in the Caucasus. These historians had fallen into "the petit bourgeois illusion of 'the united
people'"; they were ignoring the internal class struggle.

The efforts of some conservative historians to clarify the resistance movements by analysis of the internal class struggle were
conspicuously less successful when applied to the Caucasus than
in the case of Central Asia. The disarming fact, for those who
would explain the Shamil movement in terms of the class struggle,
was that it had received support from all levels of society. This was
a strong point for the pro-Shamil forces, who maintained that this

23. *Ibid.*, pp. 38, 110-15, 162.
24. V. A. Fedorov, "Protiv fal'sifikatsii istorii narodov Kavkaza," *Vestnik
moskovskogo universiteta. Istoriko-filologicheskaia seriia*, No. 3, 1958, pp.
232-36.

fact proved the existence of a broad, popular basis for the movement. The impossibility of bringing order out of chaos was illustrated by Fadeev's article on the social structure of the North Caucasus of the nineteenth century, as treated in the three volumes of regional history published in 1957.[25] Fadeev found that these histories did not present a coordinated view of the stage of society at a given time and did not define the coherent groups that were allegedly involved in a class struggle. There were at least four stages of development and a half dozen classes, and all of them were changing rapidly. It all moved him to note in a gross understatement that the "question has not been fully clarified," and to give the customary call for further research and study.

The pro-Shamil forces received support from another quarter of the Caucasus in 1958 when a second edition of Guseinov's condemned book was published in Baku. The purpose of this project was not so much the rehabilitation of Shamil as of the book's author, editor, and the Azerbaidzhani Academy of Sciences, which had passed a special resolution calling for its publication. The book had the unusual feature of a full-page portrait of Guseinov as a frontispiece, though there was no mention of his death. The editor was the same A. O. Makovelskii who had been so badly badgered for sending the first edition to press. In the preface to this edition Makovelskii took exception to certain of the author's views, which, though they "were generally accepted in scholarship at that time," had since become "obsolete." Among such views he mentioned, inside a parenthesis, "the movement of Muridism and Shamil"—a subject he did not further clarify. According to the editor, the original version of the book was retained except for "corrections of a purely technical character" and what he called "useless ballast" (references to Stalin?).[26]

Fadeev eventually reviewed the second edition of the Guseinov book in *Voprosy istorii* in 1963.[27] In a detailed article, "On the Fate of One Book," Fadeev defended the book as a study "which has endured with honor the test of time." The author had been unfairly

25. A. V. Fadeev, "Vopros o sotsial'noi stroe kavkazskikh gortsev XVII-XIX vv. v novykh rabotakh sovetskikh istorikov," *VI*, No. 5, 1958, pp. 130-37; see also Kh. M. Khashaev, *Obshchestvennyi stroi Dagestana v XIX veke* (Moscow, 1961).

26. Geidar Guseinov, *Iz istorii obshchestvennoi i filosofskoi mysli v Azerbaidzhane XIX veka* (2nd. ed., Baku, 1958), p. 8. I have been unable to compare the two editions, having been unable to find the 1949 edition.

27. A. V. Fadeev, "O sud'be odnoi knigi," *VI*, No. 1, 1963, pp. 121-30.

attacked (Fadeev laid it all to Bagirov) and had "perished tragical-
ly in 1950 as a result of unfounded accusations." Guseinov had
made several errors, which Fadeev was generous enough to admit
were commonly held by Soviet scholars in 1949. Among these errors
was the idealization of Shamil. Fadeev avoided characterizing
Shamil, but dealt with the movement along the lines of the approved
view: it was originally a popular national liberation struggle, which
became reactionary under the influence of Muridism; the connections with Turkey were real; the progressive consequences of annexation were the overriding consideration.

A particularly strong move for the rehabilitation of Shamil was
made in 1959, when the Dagestan Branch of the Academy of Sciences published the volume of documents on the movement that
had been called for in the local party resolution three years earlier.[28]
The preface, written by G. D. Daniialov, as well as the selection of
documents, indicated that the local historians were still standing
by their views of 1956. Daniialov quoted passages from the 1956
conferences that were highly favorable to Shamil (interestingly
enough, an extensive passage from the Makhachkala Conference, a
short one from the Moscow Conference). He ignored differences
of opinion expressed at the conferences, and offered a rebuttal to
several points that had since been argued by the "Moscow" historians. He emphasized that the Shamil movement was an indigenous, popular movement for independence, whose sole cause was
the brutal colonial policy of tsarist colonialism. His most emphatic
point was that the movement had little connection with Muridism:

> Tsarist generals and officers subjected the mountain peoples
> to harsh repressions, destroyed their crops, laid waste their
> villages, confiscated their land and livestock, dooming the
> toiling masses of Dagestan and Chechnia to semi-starva-
> tion.
>
> The colonial yoke of the autocracy and the worsening
> yoke of the local feudal lords brought forth a profound
> protest from the popular masses. . . .
>
> Beyond a doubt, the movement of the mountain peoples
> of the Caucasus was not a movement inspired from the
> outside, even though powers hostile to Russia tried to make
> use of it in their aggressive purposes. All the factual ev-
> idence we have shows that it grew out of the social-economic
> soil of the north-eastern Caucasus. . . .

28. *Dvizhenie gortsev severo-vostochnogo kavkaza v 20-50 gg. veka. Sbornik
dokumentov,* ed. G. D. Daniialov (Makhachkala, 1959).

> Muridism became the religious cloak of the movement, but it must be emphasized, only the cloak, and not the motive force. There was no Muridist movement in the mountains of Dagestan and Chechnia, despite the assertions of individual researchers. . . .
>
> The struggle of the mountain peoples of Dagestan and Chechnia against tsarism went under the banner of Muridism, but they fought not so much for religion as for their freedom, for their native soil, for their homes, for the liquidation of every oppression. . . ."[29]

The disagreement over the historical assessment of Shamil and his movement continued in muffled tones into the 1960's. Characteristically, the Dagestani and "Moscow" historians did not argue with each other directly, but chose to emphasize different aspects of the same subject. The points of view are stated in two representative works by a leading protagonist of each view: N. A. Smirnov's *Muridism in the Caucasus* (1963)[30] and V. G. Gadzhiev's *The Role of Russia in the History of Dagestan* (1965).[31] Smirnov, it will be recalled, had been active in the Shamil controversy from the beginning, being influential as an editor of *Voprosy istorii* and author of many works on Islam and the Caucasus, especially tsarist foreign policy in that area. Gadzhiev, who participated in the 1956 conferences on the Shamil movement, was a compiler of the 1959 volume of documents and co-author of the Dagestan history. His book is under the general editorship of G. D. Daniialov, and although it was published in Moscow, it is a product of the Dagestan branch of the U.S.S.R. Academy of Sciences. Each book contains a chapter on the Shamil movement.

The general theme of the two works is indicative of the points of view. Smirnov's study is on Muridism, which in his view is at the base of the movement. It contains chapters on the reactionary role of the Moslem clergy and on "Muridist ideology," both of which the Dagestanis contend had little to do with the movement. Shamil, according to Smirnov, was largely the product of Muridism and was its cat's-paw. Gadzhiev, on the other hand, deals with "the mountain peoples' movement" and says little about Muridism. The subject of his book, as the title indicates, is the great influence of Russia on Dagestan from the early middle ages to the present. The themes

29. *Ibid.*, pp. 4, 7.
30. N. A. Smirnov, *Miuridizm na Kavkaz* (Moscow, 1963), pp. 104-35.
31. V. G. Gadzhiev, *Rol' Rossii v istorii Dagestana* (Moscow, 1965), pp. 211-47.

of Russian benefits, selfless service, and the progressive consequences of annexation recur throughout. It is evident that his long
essay on the Shamil movement, which comes in the middle of the
book, is a kind of counterpoint to the major theme so highly desirable to Moscow. The chapter on Shamil itself is sugar-coated: it
begins with a statement of praise about the inclusion of Dagestan
in the Russian Empire and ends with another on Dagestan's historic friendship with the Russian people. In the thirty-odd pages
between these passages, he reiterates and emphasizes most of the
arguments made in 1956.

If Smirnov's villain is "Muridist ideology," Gadzhiev's is the
Russian general and tsarist colonial policy. He begins by thoroughly
deflating Ermolov, who is still held in high regard by Smirnov as
an opponent of the *mullahs* (pp. 52-54). Ermolov's policy, according to Gadzhiev, was " 'to uproot all of the non-Russian nationality' on the border [by which] he created in the national regions, in particular, between Dagestan and Russia, a lack of faith
in everything Russian, called forth a profound protest, awakening
'the mountain people to new outbursts, new actions, new anger.' "[32]
As for the tsarist general, Pullo, he was "a cruel and unjust individual" (p. 219). The successes of the movement, writes Gadzhiev,
drawing on the incorruptible Dobroliubov, "can be explained by the
hostility of the mountain people for Russian rule" (p. 215).

Smirnov makes some small concessions on Shamil's domestic
policies. Some "elements of equality" appeared early in his rule,
"however they were not of a general character," and at any rate
such a concept under the Moslem customary law was inconceivable:
the only equality possible was "the equality of people before God,
in the next world, after 'judgment day' " (pp. 227-28). Shamil had
tried to limit the rights of the khans and beks, but they continued
to exploit the people. His law preserved medieval practices, and
did not in reality eliminate feudal practices (pp. 60-61). Gadzhiev,
as if in rebuttal, dwells at length on Shamil's reforms, by which he
characterizes the leader indirectly. These points, based on tsarist
archives and military reports, echo the old interpretations: Shamil
had created an administrative council and local officials; he had
taken all jurisdiction away from the beks and abolished the title

32. Gadzhiev, *Rol' Rossii*, p. 215. Here, as in much of his argument,
Gadzhiev relies on quotations from archives and trusted pre-revolutionary
sources. He does this so extensively as to suggest that he is protecting himself
by letting others speak for him.

itself; he had abolished feudal duties for the peasants; he had freed some of the slaves, and the owners of the others had been charged to "treat them humanely"; he had created courts and lightened penalties for crimes (pp. 221-23). But Gadzhiev does not insist that his hero was without fault. He admits that he had confiscated food and property, imposed heavy taxes, and had been unsuccessful in many well-intended reforms, and that these repressive measures had in fact caused some of the people to desert the movement. But Gadzhiev claims that these failures occurred late in the movement and were to be charged to the difficult situation of the last-ditch stand.

Gadzhiev is as eager to detach Shamil from Muridism and Turkish influence as Smirnov is to point up the connections. The movement, which was very complex, Gadzhiev says, contained many social streams. A majority of the fighters did not associate themselves with Muridism; they fought for freedom. The Moslem leaders had in fact attached themselves to the popular movement for their own ends, and the movement was hurt by the association. As for Shamil's involvement with Muridism, Gadzhiev tries to prove that it was merely a titular role by quoting General Romanovskii: "Muridism needed only a head, in order to bring it to a new strength. That head was Shamil, uniting in himself rare gifts as soldier and administrator" (pp. 215-17). As for the Turkish connection, the two authors are close to agreement on facts, but there is a different emphasis. Smirnov admits that there was no real Turkish aid, but dwells on the old themes of Turkish goals, intentions, and correspondence with Shamil. He points out frequently that Shamil and the Sultan were of the same faith and had the same immediate military goals. The only reason Shamil did not receive aid was that his ally was too weak and out of reach (pp. 67-73). Here Gadzhiev is less consistent, trying to balance the demands of Soviet patriotism and the reputation of his hero. He admits that Shamil had high hopes of receiving aid from those powers who opposed Russia, including Turkey, and that he was very disappointed in not receiving any. It is interesting, however, that this statement applies to the 1840's. As for the period of the Crimean War, when the Russian homeland was in danger, Gadzhiev approaches the subject from another angle. At this time the Sultan "was in the hands of Britain and France like a marionette," eager to cooperate in their underhanded plans for attacking the Caucasus. The Sultan sent emissaries to Shamil with promises of extensive aid, but Shamil had already become convinced of his perfidy. The important point Gadzhiev keeps returning to is that Shamil received no aid. At no time did the rebels actually receive arms or supplies, a fact proved by "numerous documents." The Sultan himself acknowledged that Shamil fought "without outside help, except from God." Furthermore, Gadzhiev tries to tear down the idea that Shamil and his followers were on good terms with the Turks. A workable alliance would not have been possible, he points out, quoting a contemporary Russian source on the "implacable hatred of the local population for the Turks." As for Shamil's attitude, he is quoted as saying "Oh, if they [the Turks] would but fall into my hands, I would cut them into twenty-four pieces, beginning with the Sultan" (pp. 227, 231).

A. D. Daniialov, First Secretary of the Dagestani party, who eagerly followed Bagirov in the early 1950's, appears to have been acting as a mediator in the Shamil controversy in recent years. In a 1959 pamphlet on the tasks of the local intelligentsia, he sought to make it clear that scholars, in carrying out the party resolution on the question, could restore the heroic qualities of the movement without idealizing its leader.[33] He specifically took the recent survey history of Dagestan to task for its claim that "in the activities of Shamil is found the idea of equality, the idea of the liberation of the majority from the yoke of the minority. . . ." He conceded that Shamil "was an individual of great organizational talent, brave and strong in war, an able commander, and we have no basis for considering him an agent of Turkey and Britain." But he warned historians against idealization of the leader, reminding them of his feudal background and his connections with Muridism. Nevertheless the progressive character of the movement itself was above question. In close proximity, Daniialov argued for "the progressive liberation struggle of the mountain peasantry against the colonial expansion of tsarism" and also for "the objectively progressive consequences" of annexation; he saw no contradiction in the two progressive historical developments. He continues the same line of argument in an article on the Shamil movement in *Voprosy istorii* late in 1966, the first article on Shamil to be published in that journal in a decade.[34] Here Daniialov is able to close the gap

33. A. D. Daniialov, *Semiletka Dagestana i zadachi intelligentsii* (Makhachkala, 1959), pp. 39-41.
34. A. D. Daniialov, "O dvizhenii gortsev Dagestana i Chechni pod rukovodstvom Shamilia," *VI*, No. 10, 1966, pp. 17-28.

between Smirnov and Gadzhiev somewhat, but does not improve the logic of his argument. Without regard for the official view that a friendship of peoples flourished in the North Caucasus before Shamil's time and was only interrupted by the movement, Daniialov returns to the idea of the "double yoke." The feudal lords of the area intensified their exploitation of the peasants upon the arrival of "tsarist forces" to the point that "the mountain people faced a dilemma: either physical extinction or the defense of their right to life with arms." Their movement, entirely justifiable in its early history, eventually came under the leadership of reactionary Muridism. Britain and Turkey tried to usurp the movement, but in the end gave only "moral support." The author praises Shamil as commander and administrator, but warns against making him a hero. He even acknowledges the validity of some of Shamil's reforms and thereby makes the dilemma concerning progress even more baffling. "The unification of the mountain peoples into a single government system, the *imamat,* was, in those historical conditions, without doubt a progressive step." But a far more progressive step, judging from Daniialov's emphasis, was the liquidation of that regime and the inclusion of its peoples in the Russian Empire. In the end, he tries to resolve the problem of logic by noting that "K. Marx, F. Engels and V. I. Lenin always drew a distinction between the progressive results of the annexation of the Caucasus to Russia and the means used by the tsarist government in the war with the mountain peoples." He offers half a dozen short quotations, none of which speak directly to the subject.

Thus, the basic argument of Daniialov and the "Moscow" historians is an application of the dissection technique used by the historians of Central Asia. A progressive, popular movement later came under reactionary leadership. The party's views on the role of the people and their national leaders are maintained without blemish, albeit at the expense of plain logic. The peoples act constructively and progressively in history. Their leaders play an equivocal role, perhaps as a hero in the early scenes, but as a villain in the last act.

THE PARTY'S NEW TACTICS

The fight against bourgeois nationalism continues on many fronts, but the historian is less in the forefront than he used to be.

The persistence of nationalist tendencies has been noticeable in many party undertakings—notably in the failure of Khrushchev's plan to decentralize economic planning and in educational reforms calling for more study of the Russian language by non-Russians. The party has wrestled with the continuing problem along two well-established lines: it has penalized the offenders and tried to sharpen its ideological weapons and make them more effective. In 1959 the party carried out a purge of considerable proportions in the Caucasus and Central Asia. The First Secretaries of the Communist parties of Azerbaidzhan, Turkmenistan, Kazakhstan, and Uzbekistan were removed, as well as many lesser officials. The charges made against them were largely concerned with their failings in administration, but they had the common factor of toleration of bourgeois nationalist ideology.[35] They were accused of failing to carry out the directives of the Twenty-First Party Congress on strengthening the friendship of peoples through a more intensive program of "international education."[36] There were specific charges of too much leniency with "bourgeois ideology," "nationalist prejudices," and "localism" (*mestnichestvo*). The failure of the party's never-ending drive for "strengthening the friendship of peoples" was admitted in charges common to all four republics. The carefully worded accusations barely concealed an admission that the non-Russian administrators still harbored animosity against Russians. *Kommunist Turkmenistana* charged that two ousted party secretaries had "distorted the sacred principle of internationalism in our party and treated the cadres of other nationalities with scorn . . ." and elsewhere it was noted that they selected people "according to criteria of local origin (*zemliachestvo*), personal devotion and servility." In Uzbekistan, the new First Secretary, Sh. R. Rashidov, indicated that his predecessor had tolerated serious breaches of discipline and emphasized the duty of party workers to "wage an implacable war against bourgeois ideology, revisionism, occurrences of nationalist rigidity, local patriotism and other survivals." In Azerbaidzhan, the ousted First Secretary, I. D. Mustafaev, had

35. The *Central Asian Review* compiled a set of the charges as published in the Central Asian press. See " 'Nationalism' in the Soviet Muslim Republics," *CAR*, VII (1959), No. 4, 341-43.

36. The term here is *internatsionalnyi*, which refers to relations among the peoples of the U.S.S.R., as contrasted with the term *mezhdunarodnyi*, the usual equivalent of the English "international." The term for education is *vospitanie*, which is not ideologically neutral, but has the flavor of "indoctrination."

failed to meet several specific demands of the Twenty-First Party Congress, among which was "educating the workers . . . in the spirit of the friendship of peoples and of socialist international-ism."[37] One of the most explicit statements on "localism" came in a speech by the First Secretary of the Tadzhik party, T. Uldshabaev:

> Some representatives of our intelligentsia are too willing, for any reason or for no reason at all, to emphasize that we Tadzhiks are an ancient people and have an ancient culture. Why these reminders now, one wonders? Yes, it is a fact that we are an ancient nation and have an ancient culture. But on the eve of the October Revolution our people, as is well known, were on the point of dying out, in fact the Tadzhik nation as such did not exist. . . .
> Whoever does not understand this, whoever tries to set the cadres of the local nationality against those of other nationalities, has no place in our Party, no place in our ranks.[38]

By such servility Uldshabaev saved himself; there was much criti-cism in the Tadzhik Republic in 1959, but no administrative changes.

In the Kazakh Republic, the First Secretary, N. I. Beliaev, and several officials just below the top level were removed late in 1959. In an article in *Kommunist* on "Certain Questions of International Education," N. Dzhandil'din revealed that the Kazakh difficulties were of a similar nature. Not only had local officials favored Kazakhs in their appointments, but Kazakh intellectuals, who had contended that knowledge of the Kazakh language should be a re-quirement for those in important positions, had started a modest campaign against "littering" the Kazakh language with Russian words, and had opposed the increased use of Russian. There was also the familiar charge that Kazakh historians, even after fifteen years of persistent party effort, continued "to idealize the patriarchal, feudal past."[39] There were also press campaigns in 1959 and 1960 against bourgeois nationalists in several other Union Republics, notably in the Ukraine, Kirgizia, Belorussia, and Moldavia.[40]

37. Quoted in "'Nationalism' in the Soviet Muslim Republics," *CAR*, VII (1959), No. 4, 341-43.

38. *Kommunist Turkmenistana*, July 17, 1959, as quoted in *ibid.*, p. 342.

39. N. Dzhandil'din, "Nekotorye voprosy internatsional'nogo vospitaniia," *Kommunist*, No. 13, 1959, pp. 30-43; excerpts translated in *CAR*, VII (1959), No. 4, pp. 335-40.

40. V. Borysenko, "The 1959 Purges in the Communist Parties of the Soviet National Republics," *POP*, No. 5 (1960), pp. 7-15; see also his "Ukrain-ian Opposition to the Soviet Regime, 1956-59," *ibid.*, No. 6 (1960), pp. 24-30.

Concurrently with these repressive measures, the party was intensifying its efforts on the constructive aspects of nationality policy. As a part of the general curriculum reform in 1959, plans were made to reintroduce history courses on individual non-Russian peoples at the republic level.[41] Thus a quarter-century after the Stalin decree that began the tight coordination of the histories of Soviet peoples, the authorities could allow the non-Russian pupils to study their own past without great fear of generating nationalistic views.

Strengthening the friendship of peoples, which is the positive way of approaching the elimination of nationalist survivals, was considered a prerequisite for the construction of a Communist society. The campaign reached a new pitch with the Twenty-Second Party Congress and the adoption of the new Party Program, which stated long-range objectives for nationality policy. Section four of the new program, "The Tasks of the Party in the Area of National Relations," begins with the dubious statement, "Under socialism the nations flourish and their sovereignty grows stronger."[42] But three sentences later the document notes that "the boundaries between the Union Republics of the U.S.S.R. are increasingly losing their former significance," and continues to explain that this is the result of social and economic equality achieved under socialism, the identification of all Soviet peoples with common goals, and the creation of a common Soviet culture. It is clear from the program that party leaders believe that they have reached the critical stage in the achievement of the merging of nations (*sblizhenie*), but also that it will be a long, drawn-out process:

> Full scale communist construction constitutes a new
> stage in the development of national relations in the
> U.S.S.R., in which the nations will draw still closer together
> until complete unity is achieved. The building of the
> material and technical basis of communism leads to still
> greater unity of the Soviet peoples. . . . Obliteration of dis-
> tinctions between classes and the development of com-

41. "O prepodavanii istorii v shkole," *Pravda*, September 16, 1959; text of the decree authorizing new textbooks on the history of the non-Russian republics is in *Uchitel'skaia gazeta*, November 3, 1959, trans. in Marin Pundeff, *History in the U.S.S.R.: Selected Readings* (Stanford, Calif.: The Hoover Institution, 1967), pp. 252-56.

42. *Programma kommunisticheskoi partii sovetskogo soiuza* (Moscow, 1961), pp. 112-16; English translation in Herbert Ritvo (ed.), *The New Society* (New York: The New Leader, 1962).

munist social relations make for a greater social homo-
geneity of nations and contribute to the development of
common communist traits in their culture, morals and way
of living, to a further strengthening of their mutual trust
and friendship.

With the victory of communism in the U.S.S.R., the nations will draw still closer together, their economic and
ideological unity will increase and the communist traits
common to their spiritual make-up will develop. However,
the obliteration of national distinctions, and especially of
language distinctions, is a considerably longer process than
the obliteration of class distinctions.

All of this was hardly new, but its restatement in the program
at great length, accompanied by many practical measures for bringing it about, brought a new emphasis and urgency to the question.
Even so, the program was quite vague about the actual nature of
the future polity and the date for its realization. During the discussion of the draft of the program, at least one Soviet commentator, the Armenian A. Egiazarian, asked that the final draft be
clarified with a statement specifying at what stage the "obliteration of national differences will occur."[43] This was not done, and
other Soviet writers have differed on whether nations will continue
to exist after the new stage of communism has been reached. We
need not concern ourselves here with the fine theoretical points
about the shape of the Communist future, which has received a
great deal of attention among both Soviet and Western scholars.
Our concern is the part to be played by the Soviet historian in
this achievement.

THE HISTORIAN'S ROLE

By the late 1950's Soviet historical science had arrived at
general interpretations that were acceptable to the party on the
sensitive questions of the history of the non-Russian peoples. Some
differences of opinion, encouraged by the freer discussions of 1956,
persisted, but the main lines were agreed upon. The task of the
historian in recent years has been to give further support to nationality policy, both through the popularization of views minimizing hostility among peoples and strengthening the friendship

43. Quoted by Aleksandr Yurchenko, "The New Party Programme and the
Nationality Question," *Studies on the Soviet Union*, New Series, II (1962-63),
No. 2, 14-24.

of peoples on the one hand, and to wage an ideological battle
against the "bourgeois falsifiers" on the other. His work has been
intensified and made more effective, from the standpoint of the
party, by an unprecedented degree of planning and coordination.

The further mobilization and regimentation of Soviet historians
can be traced to the *Voprosy istorii* episode of 1956, when a flirta-
tion with free expression proved to be embarrassing for the party.
One of the provisions of the Central Committee resolution on the
journal was to make its editorial board directly responsible to the
Academy of Sciences. The following year the work of coordination
was facilitated by the appointment of Nechkina as chairman of the
Learned Council of the Commission on the History of Historiography. While the primary task of the Commission was to prepare
the multi-volume *Survey of the History of Historiography in the
U.S.S.R.*, it has become, through its planning and discussions, a
kind of coordinating group for research and writing in history.[44]
Since 1958 it has held numerous conferences on periodization, the
re-evaluation of Pokrovskii, and the history of specific topics, including the history of the non-Russian nationalities. Beginning in
1957 the Academy of Sciences set up a list of priorities, consisting
of certain problems that were deemed most important for immediate
elaboration.[45] Scholarly councils were set up to coordinate and
direct research in these areas.[46] These working groups, which were
set up independently of existing research institutes, brought together the specialists on a particular question from all over the
U.S.S.R. Eight of them were eventually created in history, including one to work on the history of the U.S.S.R. in the eighteenth
and nineteenth centuries, with attention to the national liberation
movements and the progressive consequences of the annexation of
the non-Russian peoples. The extent of the coordination and planning is indicated by the fact that the table of contents for the eleven-
volume *History of the U.S.S.R.* planned for commemoration of the

44. Pavel Urban, "Discussions on Soviet Historiography," *Studies on the
Soviet Union*, New Series, II (1962-63), No. 4, 84-90.

45. "O nauchnoi deiatel'nosti i sostoianii kadrov instituta istorii," *VAN
SSSR*, No. 5, 1957, pp. 91-92; P. K. Urban, *Smena tendentsii v sovetskoi istoriografii* (Munich, 1959), pp. 35-37.

46. See the Central Committee resolution "O merakh po uluchsheniiu
koordinatsii nauchno-issledovatel'skikh rabot v strane i deiatel'nosti akademii
nauk SSSR," April 3, 1961, in *Spravochnik partiinogo rabotnika* (Moscow,
1963), pp. 397-403.

fiftieth anniversary of the Revolution could be published nearly seven years in advance, in early 1961.[47]

Still further coordination was effected in the early 1960's. L. F. Il'ichev called on social scientists to cooperate in the manner of the physical scientists in his speech to the Social Science Section of the Academy of Sciences in October, 1962.[48] Two months later B. N. Ponomarev put a major emphasis on the theme in his speeches at the All-Union Conference of historians.[49] Devoting a large section of his address to "the organization of scholarly research," Ponomarev noted that although Soviet historians had made great triumphs by coordinating their work, there were still serious short-comings. "Experience convincingly confirms the fruitfulness of *collective forms* of work. It is precisely such forms which are capable of assuring that we will overcome the predilection for petty themes, superficiality and empiricism *[empirizm]*. . . . The collective approach to a work assumes that scholars will be unified in studying the subject and in developing a common viewpoint."[50] Ponomarev made it clear that coordination of research had little in common with the large discussion sessions, such as those organized by the research institutes and journals. Such sessions had many drawbacks; speakers discussed petty themes or maintained dogmatic positions, and sometimes no positive answers were obtained. "Neither can we tolerate the use of a discussion to cast doubt on the actual triumphs of historical scholarship, or, even more, the basic propositions of Marxist-Leninist theory." The scholarly councils were to play the most important role. They were to "evaluate comprehensively the existing achievements, to chart the direction to further progress of a given trend in science, to analyze the existing shortcomings and to indicate measures to eliminate them." Ponomarev also advocated "a rational assignment of young scholars" to research projects, and the elimination of honorary editors, named on the basis of fame or prestige. He evidently intended the reorganization in favor of collectives to be sweeping, since he assured his audience at one point that the monograph by

47. *VI*, 2, 1961, pp. 43-53.
48. "Stroitel'stvo kommunizma i obshchestvennye nauki," *VI*, No. 11, 1962, pp. 3-8.
49. B. N. Ponomarev, "Zadachi istoricheskoi nauki i podgotovka nauchno-pedagogicheskikh kadrov v oblasti istorii," *VI*, No. 1, 1963, pp. 3-35; complete translation in *Soviet Studies in History*, II (1963), No. 1, 3-26.
50. *VI*, No. 1, 1963, p. 23. Emphasis in the original.

the individual was not completely obsolete and would continue to be valuable in some limited areas.

Evidently the scientific councils did not produce the desired results, since a further centralization of the whole Academy of Sciences structure took place in 1963. A resolution of the Central Committee "On Measures for Improving the Activities of the Academy of Sciences of the U.S.S.R. and the Academies of Sciences of the Union Republics" entrusted the supervision of all the Union Republic organs to the central Academy.[51] A new Social Sciences Section of the U.S.S.R. Academy of Sciences has general supervision over research and writing in the social sciences throughout the Soviet Union.[52] Although the result of this centralization is not readily apparent, it unquestionably limits even further the freedom of inquiry of historians studying the non-Russian peoples, whether they are attached to the institutes of the central Academy of Sciences or its branches in the Union Republics. With this degree of coordination of research and publication, and its attendant double and triple checking, it seems unlikely that the party will be embarrassed again by such publishing "errors" as occurred in several monographs of the late 1940's or the reform campaign of 1956.

As a result of the increasing pressures of coordination since 1957, the Soviet historian has been more effectively harnessed to current political goals than ever before. As far as the history of the non-Russian peoples is concerned, this has involved the affirmation of the friendship of peoples theme, with all its supporting arguments, and an intensification of the fight against bourgeois ideology, both the survivals at home and the "bourgeois falsifiers" abroad. Beginning with the Twenty-First Party Congress in 1959, the Soviet historian, like all other scholars, was called on increasingly to make practical, concrete contributions to the construction of communism. That the production of the historical guild in the Soviet Union has been made more topical is easily demonstrated by the steady growth of works on recent history, while the number of works relating to the period before 1850 has remained constant.[53]

51. "O merakh po uluchsheniiu deiatel'nosti akademii nauk SSSR i akademii nauk soiuznykh respublik," *VAN SSSR*, No. 6, 1963, pp. 3-22.
52. "O metodologicheskikh voprosakh istoricheskoi nauki," *VI*, No. 3, 1964, pp. 3-68. See especially pp. 66-68.
53. Pavel Urban, "Soviet Historical Science and the Position of Soviet Historians," *Bulletin of the Institute for the Study of the U.S.S.R.*, XI (1964), No. 9, 24-32. Urban calculates from a Soviet journal that in 1958 there were

An important step in implementing the construction of communism, as launched at the Twenty-First Party Congress, was the Central Committee resolution "On the Tasks of Party Propaganda in Present-Day Conditions," of January 9, 1960.[54] Recognizing that the chief shortcomings of propaganda were its "detachment from life" and the "narrowness of its sphere of influence," the Central Committee called on all ideological workers, including academicians, to perform a very difficult task: "to explain the ideas of Marxism-Leninism profoundly and comprehensively" and at the same time to make them intelligible and useful to the masses in the construction of communism. Coming to specific tasks for the social scientists, the resolution contained one of the most explicit and detailed statements on the complete identification of scholarly works with propaganda: "Party propaganda can be truly flexible and effective only when it is constantly enriched by keen, searching thought, when the best scientific forces take a direct and active part in it. In turn, social science can fulfill its functions only if it is organically linked with the practice of communist construction and ideological work, with the urgent requirements of Party propaganda. . . ." Historians, economists, and philosophers were called upon "to take a decisive part in the practice of oral and printed propaganda and to make a tangible contribution to the Communist education of the working people," to produce "popular mass publications on Marxism-Leninism, and to deliver lectures, reports and talks."

Several specific types of study were called for; most of them concerned current developments, but several touched on the correct elaboration of the history of the non-Russian peoples. Historians were asked repeatedly to explain the workings of the basic laws of historical development, to expose "bourgeois falsifiers," and to elaborate upon the "disintegration of the colonial system of imperialism and the development of the national liberation struggle of the peoples of Asia, Africa and Latin America," while at the same time contrasting the accomplishments of Soviet nationality policy.

The intensification of the effort to link the social scientists to present-day tasks is indicated by the great number of conferences,

---

34 research themes on the period before 1850 and 105 on the period since 1850. Five years later the figures were 36 and 131 respectively (p. 30).

54. "O zadachakh partiinoi propagandy v sovremennykh usloviiakh," *Pravda*, January 10, 1960; complete translation in *CDSP*, XII, No. 2, 17-23; see also Pavel Urban, "Propaganda as History," *POP*, No. 13 (1962), pp. 24-28.

speeches, and editorials which have been devoted to the subject since 1960. It was prominent at the Twenty-Second Party Congress and the new Party Program. In addition to the two general conferences of social scientists held in 1962 (discussed above) there was a conference of workers of the social science institutes in March, 1960, and M. A. Suslov spoke to an All-Union Conference of Social Science Workers in January, 1962.[55] The largest of the meetings was a "seminar-conference" devoted to "The Friendship of Peoples and Socialist Internationalism, a Great Force in the Struggle for the Building of Communism," which met for six days in April, 1961, in Tashkent.[56] Most of the sixteen speeches and the discussion dealt with post-revolutionary themes, but there were frequent references to the role of the Russian people, progressive consequences of annexation, and "bourgeois falsifiers." All these meetings betray a common theme: the attempts to coordinate scholarly work with ideological considerations is going badly and the party is trying to improve it. A further indication of dissatisfaction with current work was reflected in the Central Committee resolution of June 21, 1963, "On the Immediate Tasks of Ideological Work of the Party," which came in response to still another speech of Il'ichev.[57] The resolution called on ideological workers to "intensify work in rearing people in the spirit of socialist internationalism; to strengthen the fraternal friendship of peoples of the Soviet Union—the greatest achievement of socialism; to promote actively the mutual enrichment of the cultures of the peoples of the U.S.S.R." At the same time they were to busy themselves "with conducting an uncompromising struggle against the manifestations of nationalism: localism, the preaching of national exclusiveness and isolation, idealization of the past and the eulogising of reactionary traditions and customs." Nationalism, said the resolution, is by its very nature, "hostile to the Marxist-Leninist world view, to

55. "O zadachakh obshchestvennykh nauk v svete postanovleniia TsK KPSS ot 9 ianvaria 1960 g.," VI, No. 5, 1960, pp. 191-95; "XXII s"ezd KPSS i zadachi kafedr obshchestvennykh nauk," Pravda, February 4, 1962; L. Il'ichev, "Moshchnye faktor stroitel'stva kommunizma," Kommunist, No. 1, 1962, pp. 11-38; "Povysit' rol' istoricheskoi nauki v ideologicheskoi rabote," Istoriia SSSR, No. 4, 1963, pp. 3-9.

56. Druzhba narodov i sotsialisticheskii internatsionalizm—velikaia sila v bor'be za postroenie kommunizma. Materialy mezhrespublikanskogo seminara-soveshchaniia, sostoiavshegosia v Tashkente 10-15 aprelia 1961 g. (Tashkent, 1961).

57. "Ob ocherednykh zadachakh ideologicheskoi raboty partii," Pravda, June 22, 1963; complete translation in CDSP, XV, No. 25, 12-13.

the friendship of peoples, and runs counter to the objective process of the development and *sblizhenie* of socialist nations."

One tangible result of this campaign has been the appearance of a number of works on the "bourgeois falsifiers," and a growing sensitivity to Western writing on the U.S.S.R. Perhaps no area of Western historical writing has been more in the Soviet spotlight than the history of the non-Russian peoples, particularly the critique of the Soviet rationalization of tsarist colonial policy and Soviet nationality policy. Baymirza Hayit, the author of *Turkestan im XX. Jahrhundert* (1956), has noted that his book was reviewed in ninety Soviet publications.[58] Judging from the publications that have appeared on "bourgeois falsification," the recent history of Central Asia is the most sensitive point. Several works of a highly polemical nature have answered the "slanders and lies" of Western works on this subject.[59] Their solicitude for current political considerations is always evident. They try to draw a sharp contrast between the course of development in the Russian and British Empires, and rehearse the accomplishments of Soviet nationality policy. The reader of these works is always aware of the implications for Soviet policies toward the countries that are emerging from colonialism to independent status. It is interesting too that these works have come for the most part from little-known writers; the major historians have not dealt with the subject except for comparatively brief remarks in their books. The subject has been prominent in the speeches of the party secretaries of the Union Republics.

In addition to the continuing struggle with internal bourgeois nationalism and foreign "bourgeois falsification," the party has made a constant effort to popularize the friendship of Soviet peoples in the pre-revolutionary period. This was made clear in the authoritative speech of Ponomarev to the All-Union Conference of Historians. One of the major emphases of his report was that the

58. Baymirza Hayit, *Some Problems of Modern Turkistan History* (Düsseldorf, 1963), p. 7.

59. D. Kshibekov, *Klevetniki i fal'sifikatory istorii narodov sovetskogo Kazakhstana* (Alma-Ata, 1961); Kh. Sh. Inoiatov, *Otvet fal'sifikatoram istorii Srednei Azii i Kazakhstana* (Tashkent, 1962); D. A. Rzaev, *O fal'sifikatorakh istorii Srednei Azii* (Frunze, 1962); K. N. Novoselov, *Protiv burzhuaznykh fal'sifikatorov istorii Srednei Azii* (Ashkhabad, 1962); A. B. Tursunbaev, *Protiv burzhuaznykh fal'sifikatsii istorii Kazakhstana* (Alma-Ata, 1963); A. Nusupbekov and Kh. Bisenov, *Fal'sifikatsiia istorii i istoricheskaia pravda* (Alma-Ata, 1964); see also M. F. Puzrina, "Ubeditel'nyi otpor fal'sifikatoram istorii Srednei Azii i Kazakhstana," *Istoriia SSSR*, No. 5, 1964, pp. 166-70.

party would give "utmost support" to historians working on this theme. Ponomarev outlined once more the main tenets of approved interpretation: historians "must consider the long-term historical perspective" and show how the dialectic of history, in spite of the reactionary goals of tsarism, brought about "the common front of the empire-wide revolutionary movement, headed by the proletariat and its Leninist Party. . . . For certain peoples, annexation to Russia was at one time the sole means of salvation from outright physical extermination." In concluding his remarks on this subject, he emphasized the party's practical motive, the support of nationality policy: "In demonstrating the progressive significance of the annexation of peoples to Russia in the broad historical perspective, the historian promotes the strengthening of the friendship of peoples of our country and the further *sblizhenie* of the nations of the Soviet Union."[60]

60. B. N. Ponomarev, "Zadachi istoricheskoi nauki," p. 17.

Supporting Arguments for the Friendship of Peoples

Thus far, this study has been concerned with the background and development of the Soviet concept of the friendship of peoples, as applied to the past of the multi-national Soviet family. In order to prevent a chronological account of a complicated, many-sided subject from becoming too disjointed, discussion has been largely restricted to the main lines of development: the increasing party tutelage; the coordination of the histories of Soviet peoples; the growth of Soviet patriotism, Russian leadership, and respect for the centralized Russian state; the reassessment of historical figures; the re-examination of the non-Russian revolts and resistance movements.

These sweeping interpretations, which were imposed by the party, could not exist in compartments sealed off from the remainder of history. Each new view created contradictions in related areas, and the Soviet historian was obliged to reconcile a number of long-established interpretations with the concept of the friendship of peoples. In time the contradictory and ideologically harmful views of early Soviet historians on the military, cultural, and social history of the Russian Empire were transformed into supporting arguments for the new history. New evidences of historic ties between Russians and non-Russians were brought out. Newer writing on military history created a picture of all the Soviet peoples ranged on one side of a battle line against their common enemies. The processes of the expansion of the Russian state were reinterpreted in such a way as to blame "tsarism" for all excesses and give the Russian people a heroic role. New cultural contacts among Soviet peoples were emphasized.

The second part of this study will take up the most important of these recent arguments in support of the friendship of peoples.

CHAPTER **13.**

THE DEEPENING
OF HISTORICAL TIES

"*These backward, disintegrating, patriarchal-feudal Ossetian communities began to express their wishes to take Russian citizenship from the first days of the establishment of ties with Russia, that is, from the middle of the eighteenth century.*" M. S. Totoev, From The History of the Friendship of the Ossetian People with the Great Russian People (*1st ed., Ordzhonikidze, 1954), p. 7.*

"*From Russian chronicles, as well as from archeological information, it is well known that the Alan-Ossetians from the tenth to the twelfth centuries were engaged in lively economic, political and cultural relations with the Russian population of southern Rus'.*" Ibid. (*2nd "revised and enlarged edition," 1963), p. 7.*[1]

The emphasis on the long historic relations of friendship between the Russian and non-Russian peoples, which is universal in the newer Soviet history, seems not to have stemmed from any precise moment. One cannot find, among the instructions in a Stalin speech, a *Bol'shevik* article, or a party directive, a specific suggestion that historians look into the earliest ties between peoples as proof of the historic friendship. But once the view was established that such friendship had existed long before the Revolution, the question of the chronological length of all kinds of ties became an important supporting proposition. During World War II editorial writers and speakers frequently mentioned, in support of

1. M. S. Totoev, *Iz istorii druzhby osetinskogo narodov s velikim russkim naroda* (1st ed., Ordzhonikidze, 1954; 2nd ed., Ordzhonikidze, 1963).

their statements on the steadfastness of such friendship, that it was also strengthened by long historical experience. In the early post-war period articles touching on the friendship of peoples sometimes mentioned in general terms that these ties went far into the past. Among the non-Russian historians, Bekmakhanov perhaps had more to say on this subject than anyone else. In addition to many general references to the subject, he published the previously mentioned article on "The Historic Roots of Friendship of the Kazakh and Russian People," which referred vaguely to the fourteenth century as the time of the earliest contracts.[2] By late 1949 *Voprosy istorii* was calling on historians to study and elaborate on the subject more systematically. In stating the objectives for the projected eleven-volume history of the U.S.S.R., it was noted, among other things, that

> *the History of the U.S.S.R.* will reflect, together with the past of the Russian people, the past of the other peoples of our motherland. It will show their struggle of many centuries against national-colonial oppression by Russian tsarism, by the landlords and bourgeoisie, and against the social exploitation of their own ruling classes. The *History of the U.S.S.R.* must show the centuries-old friendship between the Russian people and the other peoples of our motherland and the progressive historical role of the Russian people as the "unifier of nationalities."[3]

Thus the adjective *nerushimyi* (unbreakable or unshakable), which had become the invariable modifier of the word "friendship," began to acquire a habitual companion, *vekovoi* (centuries-old).

Soviet historians went about their new task of grounding the friendship of peoples in history as methodically as stone masons constructing a new building. The building blocks in this case were hitherto little-known instances of contacts of any sort between peoples, which were magnified to new importance. Each of the new survey histories gives details of the very first known contacts between Russians and the people in question and elaborates on their historic significance. Earlier references to more recent first contacts are deleted. The search for early connections thus does not necessarily imply falsification; it is usually a question of changed emphases. However, the importance attached to a single account

2. See Chapter 6, above, p. 114, n. 4.
3. "Osnovnye zadachi v izuchenii istorii SSSR feodal'nogo perioda," *VI*, No. 11, 1949, pp. 3-12. Quotation on p. 6.

of early trade, a Russian military campaign, or the visit of a single diplomat is clearly overdone. The implication is frequently made that such tentative contacts served to "establish relations" between peoples, and that such relations were continuous from the first encounter.[4] In this chapter attention will be given to the beginnings of such relations and their significance; the much larger subject of subsequent relations will be discussed later.

EARLIEST CONTACTS

As proponents of Marxism, Soviet historians ascribe an all-important influence to economic developments. Thus the trade ties between future members of the Soviet family take on a significance other historians would not attach to them. In the Soviet view cultural relations grow with trade, and their nature is determined by that trade. And considering the Soviet elder brother concept of the historic role of the Russian people, friendship is so axiomatically a product of trade that its existence in the wake of trade is taken for granted. The idea of "unfriendly" Russian trade seems to be alien to current Soviet thinking. Soviet historians do not concern themselves with the possibility that some early traders might have driven such hard bargains that they created ill feeling, although one of the most active younger brothers—the Armenian—has sometimes been viewed as such a stereotype. Aside from their importance in establishing friendship, the early trade ties have a secondary significance: they support the Soviet contention that these peoples were in no sense backward or lagging behind the West.

The earliest of these trade contacts are necessarily rather nebulous. They predate the terms "Russian" and "Rus'," going back to the Eastern Slavs. Grekov claimed that trade existed between the Caucasus and the Dnieper area as early as the fifth and fourth centuries, B.C.[5] Trade between Central Asia and cities north of the Black Sea is said to have existed in the fourth century A.D.,

4. The act of "establishing relations" is construed very loosely in Soviet usage. In a recent campaign to popularize the trip of the first Russian to India (Afanasii Nikitin, in 1466) Soviet publications have repeatedly stated that relations between the two peoples were established by his visit, and they imply that relations were continuous thereafter, although there was a break of centuries. See my article, "Afanasy Nikitin as a Cultural Ambassador to India: A Bowdlerized Soviet Translation of his Journal," *Russian Review*, XXV (1966), No. 2, 160-69. When visiting Nikitin's statue in his home town, Kalinin, I heard an Intourist guide refer repeatedly to the fact that he had "established relations between the Russian and Indian peoples."

5. B. D. Grekov, *Kievskaia Rus'* (Moscow, 1953), p. 439.

and the point has been made by Central Asian historians that the Baltic-Caspian trade route is older than the Baltic-Black Sea route.[6] The Eastern Slavs began trading with the Kabarda area in the fifth century; and by the sixth century "close relations were established between the Adyzei and the Slavs."[7] In the seventh century trade is said to have existed between the Rus' and Armenians and the Uzbeks.[8] The Azerbaidzhanis follow in the ninth century and the Georgians in the eleventh.[9] The Baltic peoples are said to have had "lively trade" with Kiev Rus', which had a great influence on their political and cultural life. One of the histories of Latvia devotes three pages to the topic "Kiev Russia—a powerful factor in the progressive development of the peoples of the Eastern Baltic."[10]

Early Russian military campaigns into the homelands of the non-Russians are also important landmarks in establishing ties between peoples. A survey history of Armenia notes, in a statement that might be construed ironically, that "the Armenians, in coming into contact with the Russians, noted in the first instance their high military skill." The account goes on to quote an Armenian historian of the tenth century, who wrote that the Arabs were no match for the Russians, whose "might was insurmountable."[11] Fadeev has noted that although the chronicles are devoted largely to military events, it should not be forgotten that "the plain people" also had contacts in the Middle Ages that marked the beginnings of their long friendship.[12] In a later chapter attention will be given to the importance of Russian military aid to the friendship of peoples.

One cannot scan the successive editions of the survey histories without noting that Soviet historians are constantly improving on

6. Z. Radzhabov, *Iz istorii obshchestvenno-politicheskoi mysli tadzhikskogo naroda vo vtoroi polovine XIX i v nachale XX vv.* (Stalinabad, 1957), p. 31.

7. S. K. Bushuev, *Iz istorii russko-kabardinskikh otnoshenii* (Nal'chik, 1956), pp. 17-18; see also E. P. Alekseeva, I. Kh. Kalmykov, and V. P. Nevskaia, *Dobrovol'noe prisoedinenie Cherkesii k Rossii (k 400-letnemy iubileiu)* (Cherkessk, 1957), p. 4.

8. V. G. Gadzhiev, *Rol' Rossii v istorii Dagestana* (Moscow, 1965), p. 45; T. N. Kary-Niiazov, *Ocherki istorii kul'tury sovetskogo Uzbekistana* (Moscow, 1955), pp. 41-42.

9. *Istoriia Azerbaidzhana*, ed. I. A. Guseinov *et al.* (Baku, 1958), I, 130; *Istoriia Gruzii*, ed. N. Berdzenishvili and G. Khachapuridze (Tbilisi, 1962), I, 269.

10. *Istoriia latviiskoi SSR*, ed. K. Ia. Strazdin' *et al.* (Riga, 1952), I, 46-49.

11. *Istoriia armianskogo naroda*, ed. V. N. Arakelian and A. R. Ioannisian (Erevan, 1951), I, 163.

12. A. V. Fadeev, "Osnovnye etapy v razvitii russko-kavkazskikh sviazei," in *Uchenye zapiski kabardino-balkarskogo nauchno-issledovatel'skogo instituta. Seriia istoricheskaia*, XVII (1960), 39-60.

their earlier work on this subject—which is to say that the more recent works contain accounts of earlier contacts. Two examples will illustrate the point. In the preface to a volume of materials on Georgian-Russian relations, published in 1937, the statement was made that Ivan IV's embassy to a Georgian prince in 1547 was "the first known instance of relations between Georgia and Russia."[13] This statement may pertain strictly to diplomatic relations, but there are three other references to the beginnings of contacts in the sixteenth century, and none to earlier ties of any sort. The 1950 edition of the *History of Georgia* continued to refer to the sixteenth century as the time when the Russians became interested in the Caucasus, as their interests began to come into conflict with the Turks. Except for an unhappy episode involving the Russian bride-groom of a Georgian queen (see Chapter 14 below, pp. 327-29), in the thirteenth century, the Russians made no earlier debut in its pages.[14] The 1962 *History of Georgia*, on the other hand, reported that "Russian-Georgian relations have had a long history. Already in the eleventh and twelfth centuries Kiev Russia and Georgia knew each other well and had vital cooperation in economic, political and cultural areas. But in the 1230's the friendly countries were devastated, conquered and forced to pay tribute to the Tatar-Mongol Khans. After that Russian-Georgian relations were fully restored at the end of the fifteenth century."[15] *The History of the Armenian People*, published in 1944, displayed no interest in first contacts, merely mentioning the Russians in a list of peoples with whom Armenians were trading in the twelfth century. A survey history of 1951, which dealt vaguely with relations in the tenth century, quoted an Armenian historian's favorable reaction to the Russian performance in a battle of 943.[16] A volume of documents on Armenian-Russian relations of 1953 made no claims before the eleventh century, and as late as 1957 a popular volume of essays called *Friendship* continued to refer to the earliest date as "the middle of the eleventh century."[17] But the same year O. Kh. Khalpakhch'ian published a study on Armenian-Russian

13. *Materialy po istorii gruzino-russkikh vzaimootnoshenii, 1615-1640* (Tbilisi, 1937), p. xvi.

14. *Istoriia Gruzii*, ed. N. Berdzenishvili (Tbilisi, 1950), I, 343.

15. *Istoriia Gruzii*, ed. Berdzenishvili and Khachapuridze (1962), I, 269.

16. *Istoriia armianskogo naroda*, ed. K. G. Kafaderian and M. T. Nersisian (Erevan, 1944), p. 177; *ibid.* (Erevan, 1951), pp. 162-64.

17. *Armiano-russkie otnosheniia v XVII veka. Sbornik dokumentov* (Erevan, 1953), p. v; *Druzhba. Stat'i, ocherki, issledovaniia, vospominaniia, pis'ma ob armiano-russkikh kul'turnykh sviaziakh* (Moscow, 1957), p. 6.

cultural relations in which contacts dating to 913 were cited from Arabic sources.[18] A new edition of *Friendship*, appearing in 1960, contained an essay on "Russian-Armenian brotherhood," dating from the seventh century.[19]

Moldavian historians have done a most remarkable job of transforming their history. They have severed their cultural roots from "foreign aggressors" and found a very old tie with the Slavs. According to the *History of Moldavia* (1951) the Slavs came into Moldavia in the third century A.D., and they alone, of all the peoples who moved through that area in history, were never hostile or detrimental to the native population.[20] The Slavs helped the Moldavians in their battles against the Huns and Arabs, helped them resist Romanization, and "played a great role in the process of the formation of the Moldavian nationality (*narodnost'*)."[21] There must be few historical examples of one nation acting as midwife at the birth of another. At the same time Moldavian historians have betrayed their almost total lack of knowledge about these contacts by repeatedly pointing out that such an important subject has been written about very little, and usually from the wrong point of view. They have charged that bourgeois historians, chiefly the Rumanians, have falsified the early history of Moldavia by minimizing these ties with the East and linking Moldavian history excessively with the history of Rumania.[22]

Before leaving the subject of falsification, we might mention the special case of ancient ties with the Crimea. Here the argument is that the history of the Crimea has been inseparably linked with the Slavs since the third century A.D., and that bourgeois historians have falsified the history of the area by considering it a non-Russian area that was later annexed by the tsars. At a three-day conference on the history of the Crimea, held in Simferopol in 1952, Grekov charged that "the Crimea was the object of envy of many powers. The historians of these powers [unnamed] have falsified its history

18. O. Kh. Khalpakhch'ian, *Armiano-russkie kul'turnye otnosheniia i ikh otrazhenie v arkhitekture* (Erevan, 1957), p. 8.

19. *Druzhba. Stat'i, ocherki, issledovaniia, vospominaniia, pis'ma ob armiano-russkikh kul'turnykh sviaziakh* (Erevan, 1960), I, 13.

20. *Istoriia Moldavii*, ed. A. D. Udal'tsov and L. V. Cherepnin (Kishinev, 1951), I, 35-36, 55-58.

21. N. Mokhov, *Ocherki istorii moldavsko-russko-ukrainskikh sviazei* (Kishinev, 1961), pp. 11, 22.

22. *Istoriia Moldavii*, ed. Udal'tsov and Cherepnin, I, 36, 55; *Vekovaia druzhba. Materialy nauchnoi sessii instituti istorii moldavskogo filiala Akademii Nauk SSSR* (Kishinev, 1961), pp. 5, 7, 10, 12.

to suit their policies." According to another paper read at the meeting, the basic population of the Crimea was Slavic from the sixth century. Since the Crimea is considered to be an integral part of Slavdom which was severed from the trunk by the Tatar invasions, its later incorporation in the Russian state is referred to not as annexation (*prisoedinenie*) but as reunion or reunification (*vossoedinenie*).[23]

THREE BROTHERLY PEOPLES

One of the preoccupations of the party in Soviet historiography, as we have already noted, has been the coordination of the history of the Soviet peoples. Ukrainian historians have been particularly suspected of tending to create a separate history of their own. Warnings against this heresy are as old as the Conference of Marxist Historians in the late 1920's, and as new as the current Ukrainian press. In combating this tendency toward the "single stream," the Soviet view of the Old Russian State and its popular counterpart, the three brotherly peoples, has been an invaluable aid. The concept of the Old Russian State allows the historian to accent unity and to reject the idea of the separate historical development of Great Russians, Ukrainians, and Belorussians. It holds that these peoples, spread over a wide area, were of a common culture and were on their way to complete political unification when they were separated by the forces of feudal disintegration in the twelfth century. But even these divisive economic forces would have been overcome, a recent survey suggests, if the three brotherly peoples had been left alone. Prince Daniel of Galicia won impressive victories in the 1230's, victories which were progressive because they "objectively reflected the tendency to overcome feudal disunity." However, "this important historical process was interrupted by the Mongol-Tatar invasion."[24] Thus the failure to unite is laid to an insurmountable exterior force, which held the Great Russians, Ukrainians, and Belorussians in an artificial isolation for two centuries. It was during this period that most of the differences between these peoples developed—differences which are regarded as unimportant. The process by which the Moscow State put the

23. "Za glubokoe izuchenie istorii rodiny," *Pravda*, June 4, 1952; Edige Kirimal, "Soviet Historical Science in the Service of Russian Imperialism," *Caucasus*, No. 14 (1952), pp. 15-20.

24. *Kratkaia istoriia SSSR*, ed. I. I. Smirnov (Moscow-Leningrad, 1963), I, 61.

pieces back together is called reunification (*vossoedinenie*), as distinguished from simple unification or annexation.

The political utility of this theory has always been evident. It developed in the period of growing Soviet patriotism from the late 1930's to the early post-war years. Originally the main political necessity was probably the refutation of the Normanist theory, which was held to be belittling and of German origin. It was a powerful propaganda support during the War, but in the long run it has probably served the party best as a theoretical support for nationality policy, as a historical proof of the friendship of peoples.[25]

The political priority of the theory of the Old Russian State is indicated by the fact that discussion of it reached a climax toward the end of the War, impelled by Grekov's article on "The Formation of the Russian State" in *Bol'shevik*,[26] by the semi-popular book of N. S. Derzhavin, *The Origin of the Russian People: Great Russian, Ukrainian, Belorussian* (forty thousand copies of which were published under wartime conditions)[27] and by V. V. Mavrodin's *Formation of the Old Russian State*.[28] These works emphasized the significance of the Moscow state in reunifying peoples and the common military defenses these peoples had made, and linked these themes with the powerful Pan-Slav movement of the time. The unity of the Slavs was later de-emphasized in Soviet historical writing—again probably for political reasons. In the post-war years the new situa-

25. An early, well developed statement of the complete dependence of the Belorussians on Russian leadership was presented in the popular pamphlet *The Heroic Past of the Belorussian People*, which was based on a lecture given at the end of the war by T. Gorbunov, the Secretary of the Central Committee of the Belorussian Communist party. The heroic past of the Belorussians, in this account, consists of their complete reliance historically on Great Russian leadership (T. Gorbunov, *Geroicheskoe proshloe belorusskogo naroda* [Minsk, 1945]).

26. B. D. Grekov, "Obrazovanie russkogo gosudarstva," *Bol'shevik*, Nos. 11-12, 1945, pp. 25-34.

27. N. S. Derzhavin, *Proiskhozhdenie russkogo naroda: velikorusskogo, ukrainskogo, belorusskogo* (Moscow, 1944). Ironically, Derzhavin drew heavily on the linguistic evidence of N. Ia. Marr, who was so forcefully denounced by Stalin in 1950. But the denunciation of Marr was as selective as that of Pokrovskii; this part of his work was not mentioned. His contributions were simply appropriated as part of the general accomplishment of Soviet historical science. The very detailed account of the subject in the *Survey of the History of the U.S.S.R.* (1953-58) makes only passing negative references to Marr, and does not list him in the extensive bibliography. See *Ocherki istorii SSSR* (Moscow, 1958), II, 733-878, 891-94.

28. V. V. Mavrodin, *Obrazovanie drevnerusskogo gosudarstva* (Leningrad, 1945).

tion made it unnecessary and even undesirable. With Czechs, Poles, Bulgarians and Serbs in the Soviet orbit, there was little political need for the emphasis. And too great an emphasis on the common historic development of Slavdom would tend to exclude the non-Slavs of the Soviet family from their theoretical position of equality. Too much attention to the three brotherly peoples would have the same effect, nevertheless one receives the impression that in the Soviet family, the Ukrainians and Belorussians occupy a favored place nearest to the elder brother.

The date of the founding of the Old Russian State has been established as the second half of the ninth century. The specialist M. N. Tikhomirov, in an article published in 1962, declared that the precise date was 860, which marked the beginning of the reign of Prince Michael.[29] Tikhomirov did not hesitate to declare that by establishing and celebrating that date, Soviet historians would be scoring a victory over the Normanists, whose date is thus upstaged by two years. Earlier evidences of cooperation among the three brotherly peoples are found in the new histories, however, which describe the long processes of feudal formation, dating back to the early centuries of our era. The authors of the 1954 history of Belorussia declare that the "Old Russian nationality" was already in the process of formation at the beginning of the fifth century.[30]

It should be said, in behalf of the Soviet historian, that he does not care for the term "three brotherly peoples" any more than "elder brother." In scholarly works the term is seldom found; however, as in the case of the latter term, the concept is employed without the use of the popular terminology. In the survey histories of the Ukraine and Belorussia, for example, there are detailed accounts of the cooperation of the three peoples, as in the struggle against Poland in the middle of the seventeenth century, but the term "three brotherly peoples" is not used. One finds the three brotherly peoples mentioned most frequently in speeches, editorials, and popular works on Soviet patriotism and the successes of the Leninist nationality policy.

29. M. N. Tikhomirov, "Nachalo russkoi zemli," *VI*, No. 9, 1962, pp. 40-41.

30. *Istoriia belorusskoi SSR*, ed. V. N. Pertsev, K. I. Shabunia, and L. S. Abetsedarskii (Minsk, 1954), I, 23; *Istoriia ukrainskoi SSR*, ed. V. A. Diadichenko, A. K. Kasimenko, F. E. Los', *et al.* (Kiev, 1956), I, 28-35; *Istoriia belorusskoi SSR*, ed. L. S. Abetsedarskii, V. N. Pertsev, and K. I. Shabunia (Minsk, 1961), I, 28-29.

THE SIGNIFICANCE OF THE RUSSIAN CENTRALIZED GOVERNMENT

The new respectability of the Muscovite princes, the creators of the progressive Russian state, has already been noted as an important ingredient in the development of Soviet patriotism since the 1930's. Emphasis on this theme might be expected from Russian historians returning to a patriotic outlook, but the ring of truth is lessened when it appears in the newer histories of the peoples of the Baltic republics and the Caucasus, who were not themselves incorporated into the Russian state until centuries after the events described. That these historians should pay tribute to fourteenth- and fifteenth-century Muscovy is one further indication of their subservience to party wishes.

The triumph of the princes of Moscow, it is argued, created a stable and progressive base upon which the future commonwealth could grow. A strong central government checked feudal disintegration, with its petty warfare and economic stagnation. It promoted trade and urbanization, which raised the standard of living, and, what is more important historically, brought about an intensified class struggle, leading to revolution. It enabled Russian rulers to protect their immediate neighbors from "foreign enemies." It facilitated the flow of advanced Russian culture to these neighbors. All this is true, contemporary Soviet histories declare, in spite of the autocratic nature of the Russian government or its class composition.

It is argued further that the development of the Russian state as a multi-national state almost from the beginning is historically significant, since it afforded protection and progress for less advanced peoples who had not developed into full-fledged nations. The *Great Soviet Encyclopedia* puts it this way: "The Russian centralized state was formed as a multi-national state, including a number of peoples who had not developed into separate nations [*natsii*] but were united by membership in a common state. The unification of the country into a single state had a great historical significance. It facilitated the development of the economy and culture, and offered defense against foreign invasion."[31]

This kindly view of the early Moscow state represents another sharp reversal from the early Soviet interpretation, for which Pokrovskii was the spokesman. He held that Moscow had triumphed over her rivals, not because of her princes, who "were in no way

31. From the historical sketch on the U.S.S.R. in *BSE*, 2nd ed., L, 138.

remarkable," but because of her favorable location, which made possible the command of trade routes. Pokrovskii thought that Novgorod was comparatively more stable than Moscow in the early stages of the rivalry and "was ahead of the rest of Russia in economic development," but lost out because her merchants and peasants were lukewarm in their support of the rulers. The Moscow-Novgorod clash was regarded as a typical rivalry for economic control of the area, and although Pokrovskii did not say so directly, his reader might conclude that a more civilized state would have developed around a commercial Novgorod, rather than the brute force of Moscow, which "was all the more menacing because it had at its disposal the cavalry of the Tatars."[32]

The textbooks that were brought out on the eve of World War II stressed the military events leading to the consolidation of the Moscow state, reversing the Pokrovskii view on their significance.[33] But they made no claims about their historic meaning for the surrounding non-Russian peoples. These ideas developed as a part of the friendship myth during the war and immediately afterwards.[34] A much-quoted statement of Stalin, on the eight-hundredth anniversary of Moscow, served to bolster the emphasis: "The merit of Moscow, was, first of all, that it was the base for unifying the various parts of Russia into one state and one government, under one leadership. If a country is not able to preserve its independence, its serious economic and cultural growth, then it cannot free itself from feudal disintegration and governmental confusion. Only that country which is united under one central government, is able to count on the probability of serious cultural-economic growth, on the possibility of keeping its independence."[35]

The amount of space given to the consolidation of the Russian state in the histories of the republics seems to be proportional to their distance from Moscow. The most extensive passages are in the histories of Belorussia and the Ukraine. The *History of the Ukrainian S.S.R.* (1956) contains a six-page section of "The Formation of the Russian Centralized State and its Significance in the

32. M. N. Pokrovskii, *Russkaia istoriia v samon szhatom ocherka* (Moscow, 1934), I, 33-37.

33. *Kratkii kurs istorii SSSR*, ed. A. V. Shestakov (Moscow, 1937), pp. 32-39; *Istoriia SSSR*, ed. A. M. Pankratova (Moscow, 1940), I, 113-34.

34. S. Bakhrushin, "Obrazovanie russkogo natsional'nogo gosudarstva," *Propagandist*, No. 5, 1945, pp. 22-28.

35. *Pravda*, September 7, 1947.

History of the Ukrainian People."[36] It emphasizes in particular the Russian military protection of Ukrainians against Tatars, Turks, Poles, and Swedes. The *History of the Belorussian S.S.R.* (1961) states the case in the most fulsome fashion:

> An enormous influence on the continuing fortunes of the Belorussian and Ukrainian peoples was the creation of a centralized Russian state. . . . Under Ivan III the Russian state occupied a prominent place in international life. All attempts of the Lithuanian and Polish feudal leaders to interfere with the political successes of Moscow ended in complete failure. By the end of the fifteenth century Moscow became the hoped-for support in the struggle of the Belorussian and Ukrainian peoples against Lithuanian and Polish feudal leaders. The reunion of the Belorussian and Ukrainian lands to the Russian state fulfilled the vital interests of broad circles of the population of these lands.[37]

The histories of the Baltic republics also contain extensive passages on the subject. In dealing with Ivan IV's Livonian War—a major event in the formation of the Russian state—the Baltic historians have concluded that the Russian cause was just. In these histories the Baltic peoples are said to have been rescued by the Russians from the clutches of the Lithuanian and Polish feudal lords, the German merchants, and the Catholic church—a rescue operation no less noble for having failed for the time being.[38]

Lithuania constitutes a rather special case, since the Grand Duchy of Lithuania not only fought against the Russians but also won and held some Russian lands for a long period. In the 1940 edition of the Pankratova textbook, a whole chapter was given to the rise of the Grand Duchy, which was put on an equal footing with Moscow. By 1959 the successor to this textbook had cut the subject to a couple of paragraphs, giving the Soviet pupil the impression that the Lithuanian people were in alliance with the Russians all along against "Swedish and German feudal lords." The

36. *Istoriia ukrainskoi SSR*, ed. Diadichenko, Kasimenko, Los', *et al.* (1956), I, 163-68.

37. *Istoriia belorusskoi SSR*, ed. Abetsedarskii, Pertsev, and Shabunia (1961), I, 73. The reviewer of this book in *Voprosy istorii* declared that the discussion of this theme constituted "the best pages of the book" (*VI*, No. 3, 1963, p. 121).

38. *Istoriia latviiskoi SSR*, ed. Strazdin' *et al.* (1952), I, 138-45, 157-67; *Istoriia estonskoi SSR*, ed. G. I. Naan (Tallin, 1958), pp. 100-18; *ibid.*, ed. A. Vassar and G. Naan (Tallin, 1961), I, 326-47; Iu. Iurginis, *Istoriia litovskoi SSR* (Kaunas, 1958), pp. 12-30.

1940 version states that Prince Mindovg (d. 1263) "seized several Russian frontier lands." The 1959 textbook mentions the Prince, but gives the impression that when he got on his horse, he invariably rode to the West.[39] The textbook on Lithuanian history for the middle schools, written in 1958, is slightly more realistic. The entire course of the warfare is presented as rivalry among feudal leaders: "Certain Russian feudal lords, in order to escape the Tatar yoke, went over to the Livonian princes." The results are remarkable: the Grand Duchy received special benefits from having Russian lands in its possession. Cultural ties were strengthened and the Russian language became the official government language. The Lithuanian princes also went to school to the Russians in political matters: "From the Russians, who had already created a government in the ninth century, the Lithuanians adopted several legal customs and governmental procedures."[40]

Other histories contain briefer passages on the significance of the Russian centralized state for their people. A Moldavian survey contrasts the feudal wars in Russia, which produced the strong government and attendant progress, with the unhappy state of affairs in Moldavia, where the boyars were not beaten in the feudal wars of the same period.[41] The histories of Central Asia call attention to the Russian state as a trading partner and potential military ally. The *History of Azerbaidzhan* (1958) contains the following laconic appraisal: "The formation of the Russian centralized state had enormous significance for the fate of the peoples of our motherland"—a statement that is unquestionably true, and also susceptible to two interpretations.[42] The leaders of remote Turkmen tribes are said to have been greatly impressed with the growth of Russia: "Viewing the strengthening of the Russian state, whose international authority was growing higher and higher, certain Turkmen groups, who were exhausted by the raids of the Khivans and Kalmyks, went over to Russian allegiance at the end of the seventeenth century and transferred their territories to the Russian state, in order to secure for themselves a peaceful life."[43] The new Soviet histories would have us believe that the Turkmen leaders had many counter-

39. *Istoriia SSSR*, ed. Pankratova (1940), pp. 86-91; L. P. Bushchik, *Istoriia SSSR* (Moscow, 1959), I, 80-82.
40. Iurginis, *Istoriia litovskoi SSR*, p. 21.
41. *Istoriia Moldavii*, ed. Udal'tsov and Cherepnin (1951), I, 130-31.
42. *Istoriia Azerbaidzhana*, ed. Guseinov et al. (1958), I, 206.
43. A. A. Rosliakov, *Kratkii ocherk istorii Turkmenistana (Do prisoedineniia k Rossii)* (Ashkhabad, 1956), p. 114.

parts. Only in Soviet history do weak people look on the growth
of a neighboring state with hope and approval rather than suspicion
and dread.

TYPES OF SOVIET PUBLICATIONS ON HISTORIC
TIES OF SOVIET PEOPLES

In the preceding narrative on the major developments in
the dialogue between the party and scholar on this question, it has
been impossible to keep track of all the arguments and methods by
which the new interpretation has been established and popularized.
In this section we will survey certain kinds of publications by which
the party has reinforced its views.

The most important of these are the publications commemorating anniversaries, particularly the anniversaries of the annexation of individual non-Russian peoples. The large-scale celebration
of such anniversaries began in 1954, with the gigantic commemoration of the three-hundredth anniversary of the "reunion" of the
Ukrainian and Russian peoples by the Treaty of Pereiaslav. In
addition to popular celebrations, which included rallies, speeches,
concerts, theater productions, sports events, art displays, and the
renaming and redecoration of a major Moscow subway station, the
anniversary was marked by a tremendous flood of published material. For sheer numbers of published items commemorating a
single anniversary at one time, it is likely that the history of publishing knows no equal to this event. There were more than sixty
different published titles, as well as hundreds of articles. The anniversary was marked not only by the publishing organizations of
Moscow and the Ukraine, but by the other Union Republics: the
Kazakh Academy of Sciences, for example, published nine articles
on the event.[44] The publications ranged from *The Reunion of the
Ukraine with Russia, Documents and Materials*,[45] a collection of
three stout volumes in a deluxe edition of 15,000 copies, to popular
pamphlets "for the aid of propagandists." They included scholarly
monographs on diplomatic relations, the Cossacks, the treaty, biographical works on Khmel'nitskii, collections of articles, and lectures. The emphasis on the depth of the historic ties of the peoples,
and the genuineness of their friendship and its significance is in-

44. A list is given in *Bibliografiia izdanii Akademii Nauk kazakhskoi SSR,
1932-1959* (Alma-Ata, 1960), p. 857.
45. *Vossoedineine Ukrainy s Rossiei. Dokumenty i materialy*, ed. A. K.
Kasimenko, A. L. Sidorov, L. V. Cherepnin, *et al.* (Moscow, 1954).

dicated by some of the titles of popular works that were issued in the hundreds of thousands: *The Struggle of the Ukrainian People for Annexation to Russia; The Historic Significance of the Centuries-Old Friendship of the Ukrainian and Russian Peoples; The Unshakable Friendship of the Ukrainian and Russian Peoples; The Great Friendship; Together Forever;* etc.[46]

The most important of this mass of publications was the *Theses on the Three-hundredth Anniversary of the Reunion of the Ukraine with Russia,* adopted by the Central Committee of the Communist party of the U.S.S.R. on the eve of the anniversary.[47] This set of twenty-one propositions was published in all the major languages of the Soviet Union and many foreign languages as well (twenty-two altogether). A single Russian printing ran to a million copies, and one of several Ukrainian printings was 700,000. The *Theses* were concerned to a large extent with historical interpretations. They did not lay down any completely new views, although they canonized the most exaggerated version of Ukrainian dependence on Russia that had been stated up to that time. Their main significance was that they represented the most detailed official views of the Central Committee on this critical historical subject. The frequent citations of the *Theses* by Soviet historians in later years reflected their impact and their continued authority. The views expressed here were sometimes cautiously re-examined in 1956, but in the long run they were left untouched.

From the first paragraph of the introduction, the *Theses* equated the "long struggle for liberation of the Ukrainian people" and "reunion with the Russian people in a united Russian state," as though there had never been any thought of a separate Ukrainian state. The whole document abounds in references to friendship, mutual struggle against common enemies, and identity of political goals. Except for a passing condemnation of Ukrainian nationalists, there is no hint of differences of viewpoint, and even in this case the differences were not those of the people, but only of a remnant of their class enemies. The *Theses* are heavily laden with a sense of destiny: the whole history of the Ukrainian people pointed toward the focal point of the treaty of Pereiaslav, and its subsequent history was built on that event, which was historically necessary: "The

46. A complete list of the literature of book and pamphlet length is found in *Ezhegodnik knigi*, I, 1954, Nos. 638-98.

47. *Tezisy o 300-letii vossoedineniia Ukrainy s Rossiei* (1654-1954 gg.) (Moscow, 1954).

historic service of Bogdan Khmel'nitskii was that he, representing the centuries-old striving and hope of the Ukrainian people for a close union with the Russian people, and guiding the process of consolidation of the Ukrainian state, correctly understood his tasks and prospects and saw the impossibility of saving the Ukrainian people without their union with the great Russian people. . . ." The *Theses* became the formula for subsequent histories of the Ukraine. The survey histories of 1953[48] and 1956 not only echoed them but slavishly used the same terminology. A popular *History of the Ukrainian S.S.R.* of 1965, by A. K. Kasimenko, the main editor of the two earlier surveys, continues the pattern of elaborating on the *Theses* point by point.[49]

The Ukrainian anniversary was evidently regarded as a great success. In the next few years a number of Union Republics and Autonomous Republics celebrated the anniversaries of their annexation. This movement reached its climax in the late 1950's, and the eagerness of local authorities to enter the lists is suggested by the fact that some celebrations commemorated not only the even centuries, but half centuries and quarter centuries. The most conspicuous of these celebrations have been the four-hundredth anniversary of Kabarda's annexation in 1957 and the three-hundredth anniversary of the annexation of the Buriat-Mongols in 1959. On both occasions the Central Committee has issued resolutions[50] similar to the theses on the Ukraine, which have been held up to historians as guidelines.[51] Other anniversaries have included the Altais in 1956 (two-hundredth), the Iakuts in 1957 (three-hundred-and-twenty-fifth), the Bashkirs in 1957 (four-hundredth), the Udmurts

48. This volume was issued as part of the anniversary celebration. Although it has a 1953 publication date, it was sent to the press late in December and was issued in January. Its slavish following of the *Theses* indicates that they were prepared well in advance. The 1956 *History of the Ukrainian S.S.R.*, from the same editors, actually went to press in December, 1955, and thus does not show any marks of the Twentieth Party Congress; there are no substantial changes from the earlier edition.

49. A. K. Kasimenko, *Istoriia ukrainskoi SSR. Populiarnyi ocherk* (Kiev, 1965).

50. For the text of the resolution on Kabarda, see "Verkhovnomu sovetu kabardino-balkarskoi ASSR, Sovetu ministrov kabardino-balkarskoi ASSR, kabardino-balkarskomu obkomu KPSS," *Pravda*, July 6, 1957; the text of the Buriat decree is in "Verkhovnomu sovetu buriatskoi ASSR, sovetu ministrov buriatskoi ASSR, buriatskomu obkomu KPSS," *Pravda*, July 4, 1959.

51. In a leading editorial on writing the history of Siberia, *Voprosy istorii* used the resolution on the Buriat-Mongols as a point of departure (V. I. Shunkov, "Osnovnye problemy izucheniia istorii Sibiri," *VI*, No. 9, 1960, pp. 3-17).

in 1958 (four-hundredth), the Kalmyks in 1959 (three-hundred-and-fiftieth), the Khakasii in 1959 (two-hundred-and-fiftieth). The speeches and collections of essays published by the local publishing houses show a preoccupation with the themes of friendship, "progressive consequences," and affirmations of the voluntary nature of the annexation in many cases.[52]

The proletarian alliance and Bolshevik leadership themes have been important ingredients in other anniversary studies—in the dozens of works on the fiftieth anniversary of the 1905 revolution in various areas of the U.S.S.R., in others on the fortieth and fiftieth anniversaries of the October Revolution, and still others on the establishing of Soviet power in different places. Because of the centralized planning of research and writing in the U.S.S.R., these studies appear with assembly-line precision; they also have the uniformity of the assembly-line product in their main interpretations.

Another, no less important, type of publication is the monograph on the annexation of particular territories. These studies, which have been published in a steady stream since 1948, now number more than twenty.[53] They range in importance from serious studies on the pre-revolutionary economic development of a region to popular political exhortations. In the former group are the original study on Kazakhstan by Apollova and its successor by Bekmakhanov (both of which have been discussed) and N. A. Khalfin's *Annexation of Central Asia to Russia* (1965).[54] The areas covered range from whole regions, such as the Transcaucasus or Central Asia, to small areas, such as Merv, with a preponderance of them concerning the area inhabited by one people. Some of these studies

52. The anniversary publications include *Velikaia druzhba. 200 let dobrovol'nogo vkhozhdeniia altaitsev v sostav Rossii* (Gorno-Altaisk, 1956); P. Kuzeev and B. Iuldashbaev, *400 let vmeste s russkim narodom. Prisoedinenie Bashkirii k russkomu gosudarstvu i ego istoricheskoe znachenie* (Ufa, 1957); *Materialy nauchnoi sessii posviashchennoi 400-letiiu prisoedineniia Bashkirii k russkomu gosudarstvu* (Ufa, 1957); V. Chemezov and D. Petrov, *325 letie vkhozhdeniia Iakuti v sostav rossiiskogo gosudarstva* (Iakutsk, 1957); *325 let vmeste s russkim narodom* (Iakutsk, 1957); *400 let vmeste s russkim narodom* [Urdmurts] (Izhevsk, 1958); B. O. Dzhimbinov, *350 let vmeste c Rossiei* [Kalmyks] (Moscow, 1959); *250 let vmeste c velikim russkim narodom* [Khakasii] (Abakan, 1959); *300 let nerushimoi druzhby. Sbornik statei* [Buriat-Mongols] (Ulan-Ude, 1959).

53. A list of the annexation studies of book length is included below. See Bibliography, Section 2, pp. 430-31.

54. N. A. Khalfin, *Prisoedinenie Srednei Azii k Rossii (60-90e gody XIX v.)* (Moscow, 1965).

written before 1950 have been revised, either by the same author
or by another, to overtake the progress of the myth.[55] The later
studies in general devote more space to the progressive consequences of annexation; a few are simple recitations of the blessings
that came with association with the Russians. In some cases more
than one book has been published on the annexation of a people.
There are four on the Kirgiz, three of them by B. Dzhamgerchinov,
whose repetition and piling on of platitudes could only be excused
on grounds that the theme is politically useful.[56] On the other
hand, some cases of annexation have not yet been examined in
such a study. Although several studies on annexation of the Autonomous Republics have been published, two of the ideological
trouble spots, the Dagestan and Tatar A.S.S.R.'s, are not represented.
The most conspicuous absentee among the Union Republics is
Turkmenia.

Still another type of literature on the friendship of peoples is
the collection of documents on relations between the Russians and
non-Russian peoples. These range from diplomatic documents and
other governmental papers to materials relating to trivial contacts
and everyday administration. A stout volume on *Russian-Belorus-
sian Relations* in the sixteenth and seventeenth centuries, for example, contains lists of items of local trade, routine housekeeping
records of local government, and sketches penned by Belorussian
handicraftsmen who traveled to Russian cities. Though these materials are doubtless of some value to the historian, it is difficult to
imagine that they would have been published except for the fact
that every evidence of contacts between peoples is deemed important, and no occasion for demonstrating them is to be lost. This is
borne out in the preface, with its recurring references to the "economic pre-conditions of the struggle of the Belorussian people for
reunion with Russia," "the military cooperation" of the two peoples,

55. One can trace the elaboration of this theme in the work of a single
historian by a comparison of A. N. Usmanov's *Prisoedinenie Bashkirii k moskovskomu gosudarstvu* (Ufa, 1949) with his revised version, *Prisoedinenie
Bashkirii k russkomu gosudarstvu* (Ufa, 1960). The latter volume is one-third
longer, and is more detailed in every respect. The greatest expansion comes
in the author's discussion of the progressive consequences accruing to the
Bashkirs soon after annexation. In the first edition he discusses it in matter-
of-fact fashion in four pages (pp. 124-27); in the latter version he devotes a
twenty-five page chapter (pp. 150-75) to improved government, agriculture,
manufacturing, trade, and cultural life.

56. B. Dzhamgerchinov, *Prisoedinenie Kirgizii k Rossii* (Moscow, 1959),
O progressivnom znachenii vkhozhdeniia Kirgizii v sostav Rossii (Frunze,
1963), and *Dobrovol'noe vkhozhdenie Kirgizii v sostav Rossii* (Frunze, 1963).

and the "beneficial influences of the culture of the great Russian people."[57] In general, the prefaces to these collections make it clear that the reinforcement of the friendship of peoples is a prime consideration in the selection and publication of these documents.[58]

In addition to the documentary collections there are the studies on the relations of Russians and non-Russians. These range in scope from serious monographs on economic, military, or political relations for a short period to hortatory histories of friendship, putting on record even the most trivial of contacts, which are regarded as important in themselves. One of the most important of the former kind is M. K. Rozhkova's *Economic Relations of Russia with Central Asia, 1840's to 1860's*, a solid study from archive sources, which is remarkable for the almost complete absence of the usual trappings of friendship and progressive consequences.[59] Examples of the latter type are far more numerous. Typically they seize upon snippets of evidence of the historical good neighborly relations with Russians. They quote passages from poems and "songs of friendship" from travelers. They seek out and emphasize early contacts and examples of military aid. One such book, *From the History of Russian-Georgian Mutual Relations from the Tenth to the Eighteenth Centuries*, points out, for example, that "the progressive part of the peoples of the Transcaucasus" united against the Turks in the middle ages and looked to the north for help. "The advanced circles in Russia," it continues, watched the course of events in Georgia with great interest: neither the difficult mountains between them nor the raids of the Polovtsians could interfere with the development or close political ties between Russians and Georgians.[60] These works on relations with the Russians, as well as the

57. *Russko-belorusskie sviazi. Sbornik dokumentov* (1570-1667 gg.), ed. L. S. Abetsedarskii and M. Ia. Volkov (Minsk, 1963).

58. *Kazakhsko-russkie otnosheniia v XVI-XVIII vekakh* (*Sbornik dokumentov i materialov*) (Alma-Ata, 1961); *Kazakhsko-russkie otnosheniia v XVIII-XIX vekakh* (*Sbornik dokumentov i materialov*) (Alma-Ata, 1964); *Armiano-russkie otnosheniia v XVII veke. Sbornik dokumentov* (Erevan, 1953); *Armiano-russkie otnosheniia v pervoi treti XVIII veka. Sbornik dokumentov* (Erevan, 1964), Vol. II, Part 1; *Kabardino-russkie otnosheniia v XVI-XVIII vv.* (Moscow, 1957); *Russko-turkmenskie otnosheniia v XVIII-XIX vv.* (*do prisoedineniia Turkmenii k Rossii*). *Sbornik arkhivnikh dokumentov* (Ashkhabad, 1963); *Russko-dagestanskie otnosheniia XVII-pervoi chetverti XVIII vv.* (Makhachkala, 1957); *Russko-adygeiskie torgovye sviazi, 1793-1860 gg. Sbornik dokumentov* (Maikop, 1957).

59. M. K. Rozhkova, *Ekonomicheskie sviazi Rossii so Srednei Aziei, 40-60e gody XIX veka* (Moscow, 1963).

60. Sh. A. Meskhia and Ia. Z. Tsinadze, *Iz istorii russko-gruzinskikh*

documentary collections on the subject, have been published mainly since 1953; they apparently had their origin in the outpouring of similar works on Russians and Ukrainians at the time of the three-hundredth anniversary.

For sheer striving, the "friendship albums" have no equal. These productions have more of the stamp of the party propagandist and local branch of the union of writers than of the historian, but because of their subject and their inclusion of historical materials, they should be mentioned here. These collections, which seem to have originated with the Armenians, have been confined so far to the area of the Caucasus. The cycle began in 1956 with the publication in Erevan of a volume titled *Friendship: Articles, Memoirs, Sketches on Armenian-Russian Cultural Relations.*[61] The book consisted of a long essay on Russian-Armenian cultural relations and a series of tributes by Armenian writers, actors, and musicians to their Russian counterparts. The volume was answered the following year in a publication of almost identical title from Moscow, much longer, more elegant, and profusely illustrated.[62] It also carried a long essay on the same subject, with tributes by Russian writers, musicians, and scholars, including short pieces by Tarle on the Armenian historian I. A. Orbeli and by Grekov on Ia. A. Manandian. Two more volumes appeared in Erevan in 1960, on the occasion of the fortieth anniversary of Soviet power in Armenia.[63] Their illustrations demonstrate what socialist realism can contribute to the friendship theme. There are paintings of Pushkin standing by an oxcart on an Armenian road and visiting in an Armenian home. Others show a determined Lenin holding a telegraph tape in his hand

vzaimootnoshenii X-XVIII vv. (Tbilisi, 1958), p. 15. See also *Iz istorii russko-kabardinskikh otnoshenii* (Nal'chik, 1955); V. I. Savchenko, *Istoricheskie sviazi latyshskogo i russkogo narodov* (Riga, 1959); N. G. Apollova, *Ekonomicheskie i politicheskie sviazi Kazakhstana s Rossiei v XVIII-nachale XIX v.* (Moscow, 1960); Mokhov, *Ocherki istorii moldavsko-russko-ukrainskikh sviazei; Iz istorii russko-armianskikh otnoshenie* (Erevan, 1956), Vol. I; *ibid.* (Erevan, 1961), Vol. II; G. G. Paichadze, *K istorii russko-gruzinkikh vzaimo-otnoshenii* (Tbilisi, 1960); A. Guseinov, *Azerbaidzhano-russkie otnoshenie XV-XVII vekov* (Baku, 1963); G. G. Paichadze, *Russko-gruzinskie otnosheniia v 1725-1735 godakh* (Tbilisi, 1965); M. V. Pokrovskii, *Russko-adygeiskie torgovye sviazi* (Maikop, 1957); M. T. Aitbaev, *Istoriko-kul'turnye sviazi kirgizskogo i russkogo narodov (po materialam issyk-kul'skoi oblasti kirgizskii SSR)* (Frunze, 1957).
61. *Druzhba. Stat'i, vospominaniia, ocherki ob armiano-russkikh kul'turnykh sviaziakh* (Erevan, 1956).
62. *Druzhba. Stat'i, ocherki, issledovanii, vospominaniia, pis'ma ob armiano-russkikh kul'turnykh sviaziakh* (Moscow, 1957).
63. *Ibid.* (Erevan, 1960).

(titled "Armenia liberated") and Red Army troops entering Armenia to cheering crowds. Similar productions have come out of Georgia (two volumes), Azerbaidzhan, and Dagestan, whose entry is modest in size (250 pp.) but shows the greatest flexibility and imagination of the lot. It is entitled *Dagestan—Russia Forever Together! Documents, Letters, Poems, Views, Tales, Sketches.*[64]

64. *Letopis' druzhby gruzinskogo i russkogo narodov s drevnikh vremen do nashikh dnei* (Tbilisi, 1961); *Velikaia druzhba aberbaidzhanskogo i russkogo narodov (s drevnykh vremen do nashikh dnei). Dokumenty, pis'ma, stat'i vospominaniia, khudozhestvennye proizvedeniia* (Baku, 1964); *Dagestan —Rossiia naveki vmeste! Dokumenty, pis'ma, stikhi, vyskazyvaniia, rasskazy, ocherki* (Makhachkala, 1960).

CHAPTER **14.**

RUSSIAN MILITARY AID

"In the long and burdensome struggle with German en-
slavers they [the Baltic peoples in the late Middle Ages]
always pinned their hopes on help from their great Eastern
neighbor. To the Russian people history has repeatedly
assigned the role of saving other peoples from extinction or
enslavement by foreign conquerors." V. I. Savchenko,
Istoricheskie sviazi latyshskogo i russkogo narodov [The
Historic Ties of the Latvian and Russian Peoples] (*Riga,*
1959), *pp. 15-16.*

The new histories of the non-Russian peoples present a
picture of the Russians as the most consistent good neighbors in
history. Not only did they never initiate aggressive wars, but they
heroically offered help to their weaker neighbors when they were
threatened by aggression. Russian military aid is one of the con-
stants in the history of the Soviet family and is an important source
of the friendship of peoples. Such aid is as old as the established
Russian state. The princes of Kiev, Novgorod, and Moscow, one
gathers from the recent histories, were as concerned for the safety
of their non-Russian neighbors against the threats of aggressors as
the Soviet leadership ever was in the depths of the Cold War. If
all the recorded instances in which these princes rode off in the
performance of selfless heroic rescue for their neighbors be toted
up, one might wonder how they found time to concern themselves
with the more immediate threats from the Bulgars, Pechenegs and
Tatars.

In order to sustain this version of history, the Soviet historian
has had to employ vague and ambivalent terminology and to create
a military history full of anachronism. The military phase of the

artificially coordinated history of the Soviet family in medieval times is one of the clearest examples of the reinterpretation of the past according to the exigencies of the present. To begin with, the Soviet historian has no difficulty whatever in determining who is attacking and who is being attacked. Russians never attack; they only come to the rescue. It is interesting that the non-Russian victims of aggression have never regarded the Russians as foreign or alien when they have been engaged in military activity on their soil. What was the nature of the bonds which held these alliances of peoples together against a variety of foreign aggressors? Since Russian aid was offered in the Middle Ages to peoples of the Caucasus, Moldavia, and the Baltic, it is obvious that the common bond was neither ethnographic, linguistic, nor religious. Soviet historians are vague on this point; the only answer the reader can construe from the context is that these future members of the Soviet family recognized that the Russians had no ulterior motives. They were not interested in aggrandizement, but in defense against outside threats. Thus an anachronistic community of common interests is created, heavily foreshadowed by the blissful situation that is alleged to exist during the Soviet period.

From the accounts presented in recent Soviet histories of the Union Republics and Autonomous Republics, one can construct a composite view of the Soviet military past. It is the picture of a gigantic defense perimeter, inside which the forbears of the present Soviet family of peoples lived. The remarkable thing about this defense line is that it conforms to present Soviet boundaries. Historically the Russians have always been ready to defend the peoples within the perimeter; there is, however, no case in which they have crossed this defense line except when in hot pursuit of an aggressor who has invaded the homeland. This theoretical line of defense was activated at the time when the Russians established contacts with the peoples, which in most cases was long before the areas were annexed to the Russian state. The first line of defense would appear to have been established early in the tenth century, when the princes of Kiev helped the peoples of the Caucasus and the Caspian area against Arabs and Khazars; it was extended to Moldavia and the Baltic area before the coming of the Tatars in the thirteenth century, although those areas were not annexed to Russia until several centuries later. It reached the Pacific in the seventeenth century, and was virtually complete by the middle of the nineteenth century, with the growth of Russian interests in Central

Asia. The completed defense perimeter ran in a giant arc from Karelia to Kamchatka.

In reading the recent local histories, one views military history from a fixed point along this defense perimeter. The people in question face an enemy or combination of enemies beyond the perimeter; but in the direction of the center they always find a dependable friend in the Great Russian people. The foreign enemies are numerous; they wax and wane from one historical epoch to another. In the northwest the future Soviet peoples have been threatened by Swedish, Polish, Lithuanian, and German feudal leaders and by "Catholic aggression." Farther south the primary threat has been from the Turk, and later from "British imperialism," which imperiled more than half the line, from the Balkans to Central Asia, and even the Chinese border. The Caucasus and Central Asia have been threatened not only by the Turk, but by the Arab, the Persian, and the Moslem faith. In the Far East the threat has come from the Chinese, the Japanese, and a variety of imperialists, among whom the United States has recently been accorded a prominent place. Even the most vigorous of the Russian conquests, involving large armies engaged in hard fighting for long periods of time, have been interpreted to some degree as defensive actions to aid local populations attacked by foreign enemies. The particular rationale of that argument will be discussed later; in this section the earlier examples of Russian military aid will be considered, with their old and new interpretations.

In many cases, what is now regarded as Russian military aid is what used to be plain Russian conquest. When Soviet historians got seriously to the business of incorporating the friendship of peoples into the history of the U.S.S.R. in the late 1940's, they were obliged to take the friction out of relations among the peoples of the future Soviet family. Russian expeditions into non-Russian territories came to be justified not only for the defense of the neighbors, but for the protection of trade routes and the stabilization of frontiers.

KIEV RUS' AND THE PEOPLES OF THE CAUCASUS

A good example of the *volte-face* on the interpretation of Russian military actions is one of the earliest cases, the expeditions of the Kievan princes into the Caucasus in 913, 943, and 965. Up to 1950 Soviet historians, like virtually all others, considered these expeditions to be raids for booty and tribute. What has happened to these military operations can be gauged from parallel accounts in the Soviet history textbook for the eighth grade, in the editions of 1940 and 1959. The contrast is all the more telling because the book was never rewritten during this period, but was changed merely by deleting and adding short passages. The 1940 version states that the Rus', beginning in 912, "carried out an attack on the coast of the Caspian Sea. . . . The Russians robbed the inhabitants of the coast of the Transcaucasus (now Azerbaidzhan), but on their return route by land they were attacked by Khazars and suffered heavy losses."[1] In the 1959 version a new account is substituted: "On the Azerbaidzhan coast, held at that time by the Arabs, the Russian *druzhniki* captured one of the islands in the vicinity of Baku. On their return route they were attacked by Khazars."[2]

The earlier version recounted the conquests of Prince Igor in traditional fashion. "Igor continued the conquests of Oleg. He brought under control the Slavs living on the Southern Bug and imposed a tribute on the *Drevliane* who revolted against the rule of Kiev."[3] The later version confines itself here to a vague statement about the "extention of the boundaries of the Old Russian State" and omits altogether another 1940 passage reflecting on the Kievan princes' appetite for tribute and booty. Of the second expedition into the Caucasus the older account says: "In 943 Rus' once more mounted a big raid [*nabeg*][4] on the coast of the Caspian Sea. Russian warriors sailed up the Kura river and captured the city of Berdaa. Having fortified themselves in Berdaa, the Rus' carried out attacks on neighboring lands." According to the later account,

1. *Istoriia SSSR,* ed. A. M. Pankratova (Moscow, 1940), I, 37-38. A slight softening can already be detected in two places in this passage in the 1945 edition. Instead of reporting that the Kiev warriors "robbed the inhabitants" (*razgrabili zhitelei*), it says that they "devastated the coast" (*razorili poberezh'e*); instead of suffering "heavy" losses, they had only "certain" losses (*ibid.,* 1945 ed., p. 37).

2. L. P. Bushchik, *Istoriia SSSR: Uchebnik dlia 8 klassa* (Moscow, 1959), I, 38. Two revisions in this account on the sensitive point of past Russian greatness are worth noting. Russian defeats are minimized or eliminated altogether. In one case, a disastrous Russian encounter with "Greek fire" in the first campaign is eliminated; in the second campaign there is no mention of the climatic conditions contributing to Russian withdrawal. The collective of historians who wrote this textbook was apparently mindful of Tarle's discussion of the winter of 1812-13 as a factor in Napoleon's defeat.

3. *Istoriia SSSR,* ed. Pankratova (1940), I, 39.

4. Already in the 1945 edition (p. 38) the raid had become an expedition (*pokhod*).

Igor "started a new expedition [*pokhod*] by the Rus' on the Caspian coast. The Russian warriors sailed up the Kura river to the strong Azerbaidzhan city of Berdaa and took possession of it [*obladeli im*], but could not hold it for long."[5]

The third of these campaigns was led by the greatest of the Kievan military leaders, Sviatoslav (957-972), who has been transformed in the course of Soviet historiography from "a chieftain of a roving *druzhina* constantly in quest of booty and glory" (Bakhrushin, 1938) into an internationally known, fair-minded (he never attacked without giving the enemy a warning!) protector of Slavic peoples against a variety of natural enemies on their borders (Grekov, 1953).[6] In the 1940 version "Sviatoslav directed his arms first against the Slavic tribes east of the Dnieper, conquered the Viatichi on the Oka, and then attacked the other peoples. In the 960's he defeated the Volga states of the Bulgars and the Khazars, then marched to the North Caucasus, where he defeated the Kasogi (Circassians) and the Iasi (Ossetians)."[7] By 1959 Sviatoslav is projected as a statesman concerned with the stabilization of boundaries and the liberation and protection of friendly peoples. His military movements are justified by his high motives, and the terminology is softened: he no longer "attacks" or "conquers" other peoples and territories, but "subdues" [*podchinit'*] them and "takes possession of" [*obladat'*] their cities:

> Sviatoslav (957-972) continued to broaden the boundaries of the old Russian state and to levy tribute on the subject peoples. . . . In order to strengthen and broaden the eastern boundaries of Rus', an expedition under Sviatoslav was sent to the Oka, where the Slav-Viatichi living there were liberated from the Khazars. In the lower Volga the armies of Sviatoslav destroyed the rule of the Khazars, which had threatened the Slavs for several centuries. In the North Caucasus Sviatoslav subdued the tribes of the Iasi (Ossetians) and Kasogi (Circassians).[8]

The recent survey histories of the republics of the Caucasus area give a more detailed account of these tenth-century military operations and spell out their wholesome effects at some length.

5. *Istoriia SSSR*, ed. Pankratova (1940), I, 38; Bushchik, *Istoriia SSSR*, I, 38.
6. B. D. Grekov, *Kievskaia Rus'* (Moscow, 1953), pp. 459-61. Grekov took his senior colleague to task for his mistaken view of Sviatoslav.
7. *Istoriia SSSR*, ed. Pankratova (1940), I, 39-40.
8. Bushchik, *Istoriia SSSR*, I, 39.

In its account of the campaign of 943 the *History of Dagestan* states that it "created conditions for closer economic and cultural ties with the Caucasus." In this version inhabitants of Dagestan joined the forces of Rus' as allies, and their participation in the campaign "demonstrated the political and economic ties of Old Russia and Dagestan" (the area was not formally annexed until six centuries later).[9] From Arab sources the Dagestani historian V. G. Gadzhiev has found evidence of Rus'-Dagestani cooperation at least a century before Sviatoslav's campaign. He amplifies the view, which had been expressed earlier by Soviet historians, that these expeditions were in the nature of a joint effort of Russians and peoples of the Caucasus against the Arabs and Khazars: "The sources show, that at the time of the campaigns to the Transcaucasus, the mountain people of Dagestan not only joined with the Rus', but took a prominent part in these campaigns." Arab chronicles, according to Gadzhiev, noted that when the peoples of the Caucasus mounted a joint campaign, they were "accompanied by warriors of Rus'. . . . The Rus' gave the mountain people of Dagestan help more than once." The mountain people were impressed by the bravery and fairmindedness of the Russians: "After taking Berdaa, as [Arab] sources make clear, the Rus' 'announced an amnesty and behaved well (toward the inhabitants).'" After a campaign in alliance with the mountain people, the warriors of Rus' "always divided equally with them, the good and the bad," according to another fragment from Arab sources.[10] The observation on the Russian people by the Arab chronicler Ibn Miskaveikh is now repeated in the local Soviet histories: "This great people, characterized by well-built bodies and great virility, do not know retreat, and no one of them will retreat, but will turn (toward the enemy) until they kill or are killed."[11]

The historians of Northern Ossetia, whose ancestors, the Iasi, were, according to the new interpretation, among those who benefited from the 965 campaign, are particularly fulsome in their thanks for Russian aid on that occasion. M. S. Totoev, the best-known historian of that area, has had no difficulty finding mani-

9. R. M. Magomedov, *Istoriia Dagestana. S drevneishikh vremen do nachala XIX veka* (Makhachkala, 1961), pp. 101-2.

10. V. G. Gadzhiev, *Rol' Rossii v istorii Dagestana* (Moscow, 1965), pp 53-56.

11. *Ibid.*, p. 55; *Istoriia Azerbaidzhana*, ed. I. A. Guseinov *et al.* (Baku, 1958), I, 131. See similar passage in *Istoriia armianskogo naroda*, ed. V. N. Arakelian and A. R. Ioannisian (Erevan, 1951), I, 163.

festations of the friendship of peoples in the tenth century. Having noted that "in the tenth and eleventh centuries the Alan-Iasi had neighborly relations with the Russian population in the south of Rus'," he goes on to state that "The struggle of the Russian people with the Khazar kingdom, which had hindered the establishment of ties between Rus' and the peoples of the North Caucasus, brought about the first direct contacts between the ancient Rus' and the Iasi, particularly in the campaign of Sviatoslav to Khazaria in 965. The destruction of Khazaria by Sviatoslav had an important significance for the peoples of the North Caucasus, among them the Iasi: they were liberated from long and burdensome rule by the Khazars."[12] The *History of Northern Ossetia* notes that "the war of the Russian people with the Khazars" had the positive effect of bringing the peoples of the North Caucasus into closer contact with the Russians. In the course of two paragraphs it refers three times to "the strengthening of relations," "the strengthening of Russian influence," "the strengthening of political and economic ties"[13]— and this in spite of the fact that North Ossetia was annexed to Russia several centuries later. But historians consider these early ties to be important seeds of later friendship, and the lack of continuous relations, as we shall see, is laid entirely to the Tatars, and is a temporary and unavoidable break in the alliance.

THE PROBLEM OF DISTINGUISHING BETWEEN FRIENDS AND ENEMIES

As these quotations have demonstrated, the main technique by which Soviet historians have removed friction between Russian and non-Russian peoples of the future U.S.S.R. has been simply to change the roles of the protagonists. The Rus', who formerly clashed with Slavic peoples and inhabitants of the Caucasus, are now said to have been fighting against Arabs and Khazars. The peoples of the Caucasus were allied to the Rus' in a long and historically justifiable struggle. They are no longer regarded as being among the victims of the Rus'; at worst they were caught up in the larger struggle and added to Kiev's rule, in which case they were delivered from their enemies and benefited from their new Russian contacts.

12. M. S. Totoev, *K istorii doreformennoi severnoi Osetii* (Ordzhonikidze, 1955), p. 6.
13. *Istoriia severo-osetinskoi ASSR*, ed. S. K. Bushuev, M. S. Totoev, A. V. Fadeev, *et al.* (Moscow, 1959), pp. 77-79.

It is worth noting that the wars against the Arabs and Khazars are characterized as "struggles of the Russian people," a sure sign that the Arabs and Khazars are among the enemies of the yet unformed Soviet family of peoples. The case of the Arab is obvious enough: as a foreign aggressor and advocate of a "reactionary religious ideology," the Arab can be regarded as an enemy of the future U.S.S.R. without great difficulty. The case of the Khazars, however, is more complicated, and has its own story in Soviet historiography. Until about 1950 the Khazars were regarded by Soviet historians as a highly advanced people, and were said by some to have had an important influence on Kiev Rus'. In December, 1951, an unknown writer, P. Ivanov, put the scholars to retreat on this question. In an article in *Pravda* he denounced the foremost Soviet scholar on the Khazars, the archeologist M. I. Artamonov, who, "paying no attention to the facts, again pictured the Khazars in the role of an advanced people who allegedly fell victim to the 'aggressive' aspirations of the Russians." The Khazars were actually the aggressors. The "primitive" and "wild hordes of Khazars . . . seized wide expanses which had been inhabited from ancient times by Eastern Slavs and other peoples." The Khazars "played no positive role whatever"; Kiev not only owed them nothing, but was superior in every respect.[14]

Thus the new role as internal aggressor and enemy was assigned to the Khazars. (The term "internal enemy," as used here, refers to the present perimeter of the Soviet *rodina,* in contrast to the boundaries that may have existed at the time of the aggression.) The primary political reason for Ivanov's interpretation was probably that in the long established view, the Khazars, as a people more advanced than Kiev Rus', in effect upstaged the Old Russian State, reducing its prestige in the medieval world. In the climate of the fierce Soviet patriotism that existed in 1951, such a view was clearly "inadmissible." But the new interpretation had a useful secondary purpose: the Khazars, when viewed as aggressors, provided a key to a new interpretation of the military history of Kiev Rus'. They were now a legitimate target for the common struggle of future Soviet peoples, and their defeat could be celebrated in the same spirit as the later defeats of Tatars, Germans, Poles, Swedes, and Turks—as a milestone along the road of the friendship of peoples.

14. P. Ivanov, "Ob odnoi oshibochnoi kontseptsii," *Pravda,* December 25, 1951.

Ivanov's view of the Khazars was incorporated into Soviet historiography in the 1950's, albeit without the active participation of Artamonov, the Khazar specialist. The latter's compromise, offered a decade later in his *History of the Khazars,* is a case of saving half a loaf. His earlier view, put forward in his *Studies in the Ancient History of the Khazars* (1937), presented the Khazars as one of the most important peoples of the medieval world, a model for a new type of state, and an important cultural influence on Kiev Rus'. In the new book he saved part of his thesis by dividing Khazar history into two sharply contrasting periods. In their early history he held that the Khazars performed a historically progressive task by holding the Arab at bay, by spreading Byzantine culture, and by establishing order and safety in the Caspian and Black Sea areas. Later, however, after their adoption of Judaism ("a fatal step"), the Khazars abandoned agriculture and cattlebreeding and became traders and parsites. Artamonov accepted the imposed view that the Russians owed nothing to the Khazars, and that their destruction was a historically progressive event.[15]

It is of fundamental importance that the Khazars have disappeared as an entity in the Soviet family. If there were a Khazar A.S.S.R. today, it seems highly unlikely that the view of the Khazars as internal enemies could be held, since it would violate the principle that Soviet peoples have never been enemies in the course of history. The great historic friendship apparently applies to peoples presently constituting the Soviet family and their immediate forbears. The other internal enemies have also been peoples who disappeared. Thus one can find references to the struggle of the Russian people against Volga Bulgars, Pechenegs, and Polovtsy, but such terminology is not used involving any present members of the U.S.S.R. The reason is not difficult to find: Soviet leaders have no Volga Bulgar minority problem, and there are no Volga Bulgar political figures on the Soviet scene trying to cement a friendship of peoples with the aid of historic tradition. In this connection the most difficult—but not insurmountable—problem has been the case of the Kazan Tatars, who at first glance would seem to be an internal aggressor, against whom the Russian people fought, and

15. M. I. Artamonov, *Istoriia Khazar* (Leningrad, 1962), pp. 37, 457-59. Artamanov recognized that the *Pravda* article "played a positive role" in doing away with the idealization of the Khazars, and marveled, no doubt satirically, that such a "smashing blow" could be dealt "in a little critical note, published in *Pravda* by the unknown P. Ivanov."

at the same time a "friendly" member of the current Soviet family of peoples. The apparent contradiction is avoided by drawing a sharp distinction between the Tatar-Mongol invaders and the Kazan Tatars, who are said to be another people who lived in the area before the invasion. It is interesting that no such distinction was made until a conference on the question of Tatar ethnogenesis was held in 1946. The final resolution of that conference emphasized that the so-called Kazan Tatars were actually descended from Turkic-speaking Bulgar peoples inhabiting the area from an earlier time. Not only were they not a part of the Tatar invasion; they were in the new view enslaved and exploited by the Golden Horde. Since 1946 they have been referred to increasingly as "Kazantsy," to distinguish them from the invaders. Whatever the scholarly value of the ethnographic evidence presented at this conference, its utility for Soviet historiography is self-evident. In the new view, the "Kazantsy" were an exploited people who were liberated by the Russian army of Ivan IV, while their rulers were external aggressors who did not survive as an ethnographic entity. Thus the apparent conflict is resolved.[16]

One other case of contradiction involving an internal enemy has been resolved recently in Soviet historiography. It will be recalled that Zhdanov had named the deported peoples of the North Caucasus, the Chechen, Ingushi, and Balkars as enemies of the Revolution, and had explicitly excluded them from the friendship of peoples. Up to 1956 Soviet historians simply omitted mentioning these peoples in their works. But since Khrushchev referred to their deportation as one of Stalin's darker crimes, an adjustment on this question was in order. A Central Committee resolution, passed after the decision to rehabilitate these peoples, pointed out that Zhdanov's condemnation had no basis in history, and laid the error to the cult of personality.[17] Thus the deported peoples of the North Caucasus were returned to the ranks of the friendly Soviet family.

The meager writings on the history of the rehabilitated peoples dwell on the usual friendship themes, treating the unhappy events

16. Proceedings of the conference in *Sovetskaia etnografii*, No. 3, 1946, pp. 37-92, and in *Proiskhozhdenie kazanskikh Tatar* (Kazan', 1948). See also the standardized generalization based on the decision in *Materialy po istorii Tatarii* (Kazan', 1948), I, 3-4.

17. "Ob ispravlenii oshibok v otsenke oper 'Velikaia druzhba,' 'Bogdan Khmel'nitskii,' i 'Ot vsego serdtsa,'" in *Spravochnik partiinogo rabotnika* (Moscow, 1959), p. 494.

of 1944-57 as a momentary deviation which in no way interfered with friendly relations at the level of the masses. The *Survey of the History of the Balkarian People* reports friendly relations with Russians from the sixteenth century, as well as cooperation between Balkars and other peoples of the Caucasus. Although this survey, according to its subtitle, covers only the period before the Revolution, the authors have added an eleven-page postscript dealing largely with the World War II period—as though they wanted to set the record straight. Having noted Balkar cooperation in collectivization and socialist construction, they dwell on the patriotism of the area during World War II, listing names of Balkar heroes and noting their participation in partisan movements and their heroic defense and suffering during the brief German occupation of the area. The reader might conclude from this account that the "thirty-five day occupation of Balkar villages by the Fascist attackers," in which 500 adults and 150 children were killed, was a much more serious violation of the rights of the Balkars than the following total deportation of these people by the Soviet Government. Putting their best foot forward, the authors credit the Twentieth Party Congress for opening the road to the re-establishment of the Balkars' national autonomy. They cite the great material help the Russians, Kazakhs, and Kirgiz gave them, even in the period of their exile, adding that "today the Balkars consider Kazakhstan and Kirgizia as their second homeland and are proud that the economic and cultural developments of these allied republics are in part their work." On the other hand, Stalin is not mentioned, and the deportation is given one sentence: "In violation of the most important principles of Leninist nationality policy, the Balkar people, as well as other peoples of the North Caucasus, were deported to Central Asia and Kazakhstan, where they remained for thirteen years."[18]

A popular account of the friendship of Chechen-Ingush peoples with the Russians, E. I. Lin's *In the Friendly Family of Peoples of the Soviet Union*, follows the same approach, but speaks more immediately to the point. Without referring directly to the recent tragedy of these people, Lin declares that "the Chechen-Ingush A.S.S.R. furnishes a clear example of the working out of the nationality question, the life-giving force of the brotherly cooperation,

18. *Ocherki istorii balkarskogo naroda* (*s drevneishikh vremen do 1917 goda*), ed. T. Kh. Kumykov, P. G. Akritas, Z. V. Anchabadze *et al.* (Nal'chik, 1961), pp. 198-201.

the mutual help and friendship of Soviet peoples."[19] Lin not only denies that the deportation obstructed the friendship of peoples in any way but also says that it was the friendship of peoples that sustained the deported peoples and helped to return them to their homelands. He quotes officials from both the Kazakh and Kirgiz Republics who appeared at a session of the Chechen-Ingush Supreme Soviet in 1960 to thank their brothers of the North Caucasus for the "beneficial work" they had performed "shoulder to shoulder with the workers of our Republics in factories and mines, in the high mountain pastures of the Tian-Shan and Isul-Pal, in the fields of the Chuiskoi valley, in the orchards of Kirgizia." Furthermore, we are assured that "in the period 1944-56, the *oblast* party organizations, led by Leninist principles on nationality policy, showed constant concern for the development of the economy and culture, for the strengthening of friendship among the multi-national population of the *oblast*."[20]

A DETAILED CASE OF MILITARY AID: ESTONIA

The instances of Russian military aid to non-Russian peoples, as recorded in the recent local histories, would run into the hundreds. To give an account of them, even in the case of one of the smaller peoples, would be tedious and repetitive. The tone of the new Soviet history can be illustrated more palatably by the discussion of one segment of the history of one people, along with the comments of Soviet historians on its significance. What follows is a sketch of Russian-Estonian military solidarity up to the com-

19. Edip I. Lin, *V druzhnoi sem'e narodov sovetskogo soiuza* (Groznyi, 1964), p. 4.

20. *Ibid.*, pp. 36-37. The Soviet Government later made a more limited rehabilitation of the Volga Germans (1964) and the Crimean Tatars (1967) in decrees which exonerated them of mass guilt but did not resettle them. Up to the time of the completion of my research, I have not been able to examine any post-rehabilitation historical writing on these peoples.

The Kalmyks, who were also deported in 1944, were resettled in 1957. A survey history of the Kalmyks was reported in 1968 by *Voprosy istorii* (No. 5, p. 184), but was not available for this research. Among the few works of the first decade since the restoration of the Kalmyk A.S.S.R., the theme of military cooperation with the Russians is prominent. T. I. Belikov's *Kalmyks in the Struggle for the Independence of Our Homeland* is largely a recitation of Kalmyk aid to the Russian military cause in a long series of wars (see T. I. Belikov, *Kalmyki v bor'be za nezavisimost' nashei rodiny [XVII-nachalo XIX vv.]* [Stavropol', 1965]). There is also a volume of documents on Kalmyk participation in World War II (see *Kalmykiia v velikoi otechestvennoi voine, 1941-45. Dokumenty i materialy* [Elista, 1966]).

pletion of the German conquest of Estonian territory in 1227, based on the first volume of the *History of the Estonian S.S.R.*, published in 1961.

The earliest instance of Estonian military cooperation with the Slavs is dated from around 860, when the "Novgorod Slovene and Krivichi united with the Chuds (Estonians) in an alliance" against the Varangians. This appears to have been more than a casual alliance, since the partners also "ruled among themselves and built cities."[21] Estonian warriors participated in Oleg's campaigns to the south in the 880's and against Constantinople in 907. In 980 Estonians helped Kiev Rus' in a campaign against Polotsk and in 991 they helped construct a fortified line on the southern border. The authors make it clear that they see in these cases evidence of complete confidence and mutual cooperation. After describing these events, they conclude: "Thus it can be seen from the chronicles that Estonians took an active part in the Russian army, in widening the boundaries of the Old Russian State, and also in the struggle against foreign enemies." Furthermore the reader is assured that "in the written records there is not the slightest reference to any misunderstandings or conflicts during those years between the Estonians and the Rus'" (p. 108). To be sure, the Kiev princes were interested in "enlarging their lands and putting the area under tribute, and also in strengthening the power of the feudal lords," but such acts, which might ordinarily be considered unfriendly, counted for little with the Estonian people, who fully appreciated their larger gains—protection against the West and the opportunity to strengthen ties with the Russian people.

At the beginning of the eleventh century the Western threat to the Baltic peoples increased. There were coastal raids by Swedes, Danes, and Norwegians, to which the Kiev princes responded with characteristic effectiveness. Iaroslav the Wise (1019-1054) carried out "a particularly active policy of defense and broadening the borders to the West." His campaign of the 1030's, in which he established the town of Tartu and put the whole area under his administrative control, is presented in very guarded terms. To the uninitiated reader, this campaign has all the earmarks of a feudal conquest, but in this history of Estonia there is no hint of popular opposition. Iaroslav's expansion into the Baltic, described in the

21. *Istoriia estonskoi SSR*, ed. A. Vassar and G. Naan (Tallin, 1961), I, 107.

context of counterattacks against foreign enemies, seems to be entirely justifiable and even progressive (p. 109).

Some unpleasant events of the following hundred years are handled deftly in this history. According to the chronicle of Pskov, the people of Tartu rebelled in 1061 against Iaroslav's son, Iziaslav, who had placed the area under oppressive tribute. They burned the town, killed many people, and drove others away, and were subdued only after the prince had dispatched a large military force against them. Here the Estonian historians abruptly change their step and present the revolt in strictly class terms so that there is nothing anti-Russian about it and no break in the solidarity of the popular masses. Indeed, "This is the first known information in history about an uprising of Estonian peasants against feudal lords. The uprising was clearly aimed against Russian feudal lords, as well as their allies, representatives of the Estonian feudal aristocracy." We are reminded repeatedly that the rebels were peasants and that their victims were of the feudal class. In two separate passages, the authors emphasize that the rebels burned only the houses of feudal lords, and that Russian and Estonian feudal elements suffered equally (pp. 109-11). In the 1130's Russian soldiers marched once again to quell a rebellion of Estonians, who were protesting a famine and heavy feudal duties. The responsibility for this rebellion, which is also considered a class phenomenon, is laid to the greed of the Estonian feudal lords and to the eagerness of the Prince of Novgorod to maintain class solidarity with his Estonian vassals.

In both these rebellions, the history notes that soldiers from Novgorod and Pskov marched in to restore the feudal *status quo*. Although it does not comment on the role of the Russian soldier, it is quite clear that it has been reversed in these instances. In the midst of a long recitation of the heroic actions of the Russian soldiers sent to protect Estonians against their foreign enemies are these two cases in which Russian soldiers fight Estonian peasants. In the former instance the Russian soldier is a representative of the Russian people; in the latter he is the mere instrument of the Russian feudal state and bears no responsibility for his acts. The soldier's performance of his duty in quelling these popular rebellions does not interfere with the continuous development of the friendship of peoples.

The Russians came to the aid of the Estonians again in their wars with the Germans just after 1200. The Estonians appealed to Prince Mstislav of Novgorod for help in 1212. His action was less than brilliant: he arrived after much delay, and although he took a heavy tribute in payment for his services, he never met the enemy in battle. Nevertheless the authors of this history consider his response to be important. They point out that mustering 15,000 men was a remarkable accomplishment "under the conditions of those times," and demonstrated that the Novgorodians "were prepared to put an end to the attacks on Estonian lands": "Although the Russians did not come into contact with the German soldiers, their campaign had a great significance. It emphasized once more the ties of the Estonians with Novgorod and demonstrated the readiness to defend these lands from the grasp of the German aggressors. In addition to that, the arrival of the Russian army bolstered the fighting spirit of the Estonians and caused a suspension of the attacks of the German aggressors" (p. 150).

In 1216 military forces from Polotsk united with Estonians to form an "anti-German front." Following a "Russian-Estonian military plan," they were able to defeat the Germans at Otepia, in the southern part of Estonia. The Russians soon withdrew, however, and the Germans returned to overrun the area (pp. 153-55). The following year troops from Novgorod helped the Estonians retake Otepia. In the summer of 1217 the Estonians, who were hard pressed again, appealed to Novgorod for help, but the prince was fighting in the South, and did not appear until the following year. The Germans knew of the exchange of messages and "wanted to fight a battle with the Estonians before they were united with Russian soldiers." In September they took advantage of Russian delay and defeated the Estonians at Viliandi: "Having defeated the Estonians before the arrival of the Russian armies, the Germans hoped that this would lead the Russians to refuse further aid to the Estonians and other Baltic peoples. However, their calculations were not substantiated" (p. 159). The Russians eventually arrived, more than a year after they were called, and helped the Estonians to lay siege to the castle of Tsesis. After two weeks, however, the Russians abandoned the siege, having been called away to fight "Livonian feudal lords." The operation failed, but the authors find other considerable consequences of this joint military venture: "The campaign of 1218 is another of the series of demonstrations of the strength of Russian warriors in Estonian-Russian cooperation. Although Tsesis castle was not taken by the Russians, in the battles on the open field they showed unquestionable military superiority, forcing the German knights to withdraw with heavy losses. This obliged the German aggressors to take Rus' into account even more" (p. 160).

When the next crisis came in 1222, the Russian princes were deeply involved with the Tatars. The history implies that the Estonians got a sympathetic hearing in Novgorod, Pskov, and Vladimir-Suzdal. Prince Iaroslav of Novgorod, who "truly recognized that the main enemy at that time was the German attacker," changed his military plans "in order to conclude the liberation of all Estonia." For four weeks the Russian-Estonian forces laid siege to Tallin, which had been captured by the Germans. Then "the Russian warriors had to discontinue the prolonged siege to allow time to return home before the autumn season of bad roads" (p. 169).

The final loss of the Baltic during the next few years is attributed to a considerable extent to the Tatar invasion, which made it impossible for the Russians to continue the defense of the Baltic. The most heroic chapter in medieval Russian-Estonian military cooperation is the defense of Tartu against the Germans and Danes in 1224. Coming on the heels of the first major Russian encounter with the Tatars (Kalka, 1223), the Russian princes were heavily committed in the South and East. However, Prince Viachko of Novgorod was dispatched to Tartu with a detachment of two hundred Russian soldiers, and took charge of the defense of the city. After a determined stand, in which Viachko himself was killed, the city fell to the German-Danish forces in August, 1224. The Russian prince's part in Estonian history is commemorated in a piece of recent sculpture in the Tallin State Art Museum. It shows two intent figures, the prince and an Estonian archer, engaged in the defense of the city. This sculpture, which is symbolic of Russian-Estonian friendship, is widely reproduced. It is used in the 1961 survey history of Estonia twice; it is embossed on the cover and used as an illustration for the account of the battle (p. 170).

Within a few years after the unsuccessful defense of Tartu, the German domination was complete and Russian-Estonian military relations were suspended for a long period. But Aleksandr Nevskii won a victory in a neighboring territory, and the following six pages of this account are devoted to the "Battle of the Ice" in 1242. In their conclusion of this section of Estonian history the authors make the following statement:

In the struggle against aggression the Estonians received great help from their Russian neighbors, thanks to
which they were able to withstand the pressure of the
enemy longer. Fighting shoulder to shoulder, Estonians
and Russians inflicted serious blows on the attackers. When
the aggressors, because of their superior power, established
themselves on the Estonian land, many Estonians escaped
to Rus'. The mutual struggle of the Russian and Estonian
indigenous populations of the Baltic against German, Dan-
ish, and Swedish feudal-Catholic aggression is one of the
most important stages in the consolidation of ties between
the Russian people and the peoples of the Baltic (p. 184).

It would be quite easy to render a different interpretation from
the hard facts of this account. The *History of the Estonian S.S.R.*
points out, in passing, many facts that are damning to the Russians.
They repeatedly arrived too late to help their allies, and they left
the scene of battle prematurely, sometimes for definitely unheroic
reasons. They sent inadequate forces: two hundred men, however
heroically they may have fought, were a paltry force to throw into
the defense of Tartu. There is even a hint of bad faith here and
there. In 1212 the Russians took a heavy tribute from Estonians
as the price of their military aid (the exact amount is given in this
account, and the way it was divided), but never met the enemy
in the field—a clear breach of contract. No matter how conflicts
are dressed up in class trappings, it is evident that on at least two
occasions Russian soldiers came to Estonia to fight Estonians. But
none of this is allowed to interfere with the concept of Russian-
Estonian solidarity and the friendship of peoples.

THE TATAR YOKE

Soviet historians regard the Tatar invasion as the great dis-
rupter of a growing alliance of peoples. The Tatars broke up the
Old Russian State and separated the three brotherly peoples for
a prolonged period of isolation. Although the Russian principalities
were in a state of feudal disintegration, it has been argued that the
reunification process had already started under the princes of Galicia, and might have been successful if the Tatars had not interrupted it.[22] The temporary setback is thus attributed to an un-

22. *Kratkaia istoriia SSSR*, ed. I. I. Smirnov (Moscow-Leningrad, 1963),
I, 61. On the eve of the Tatar invasion the princes of Galicia-Volynia were
as active in helping weak neighbors as the other princes. The Moldavians
remember the help rendered by Roman Mstislavich around 1200 against

avoidable external force. The artificial coordination of the histories of Soviet peoples in the general survey histories creates the impression that resistance to the Tatar invasion was another example of a joint effort of peoples against an external foe. The discussion of the period under such a heading as "The Heroic Struggle of the Peoples of Our Country with the Tatar-Mongol Invaders" produces such an illusion, though actually there are few cases of coordinated defense.[23]

The histories of the Soviet republics point out that the Great Russians bore the brunt of the attack, lightening the burden of their people or, in the case of those located in the West, saving them from the Tatar yoke completely. The Russians are credited with saving Western Europe, and Western civilization as well, from the scourge of the Tatars. The History of Moldavia states that "the Russian people in their heroic and selfless struggle for their defense blocked the Mongol-Tatar path to Europe and saved Western European civilization from inevitable destruction."[24] A historian of the North Caucasus elaborates on the theme and summarizes the effects of the Russian resistance as follows:

> The Russian people, as is known, bore the full weight of the fight against the Tatar-Mongols. The successes of the Moscow government in that fight, among other things, weakened the rule of the Khans of the Golden Horde over other conquered peoples, strengthened the hope for the quick riddance of the yoke, and also stimulated the growth of resistance among the peoples. Therefore the struggle of the Russian people for their liberation turned out to be in reality the struggle for liberation of all the peoples who were under the Tatar-Mongol yoke.[25]

That Russians are to be credited as defender of all Soviet peoples against the Tatars is further demonstrated by the fact that the battle of Kulikovo (1380), their first major defiance of the Tatar yoke, is an important topic in the new histories of peoples as far removed from the scene as the Kazakhs and Moldavians.[26]

Hungarian, Polish, and Lithuanian feudal leaders (*Istoriia Moldavii*, ed. A. D. Udal'tsov and L. V. Cherepnin [Kishinev, 1951], I, 69), and his successor, Vladimir Vseslavich, defended Belorussian lands against the Teutonic Order (*Istoriia belorusskoi SSR*, ed. L. S. Abetsedarskii, V. N. Pertsev, and K. I. Shabunia [Minsk, 1961], I, 62).

23. *Istoriia SSSR*, ed. M. V. Nechkina (Moscow, 1964), I, 161-68.
24. *Istoriia Moldavii*, ed. Udal'tsov and Cherepnin (1951), I, 72-78.
25. Gadzhiev, *Rol' Rossii*, p. 62.
26. A full-page color print of A. P. Bubnov's painting "Morning on Kuli-

Even in the period of the Tatar yoke, Russian armies aided the Baltic peoples. Prince Boris Konstantinovich protected Karelia from the Swedes in the fourteenth century.[27] Other princes of Novgorod and Pskov aided the Baltic and Belorussian peoples repeatedly during this period.[28] And three Russian detachments from Smolensk were in the victorious Slavic army at Grünwald (1410), at which the Teutonic Order was given its most signal defeat.

With the rise of Moscow, the question of Russian military aid to the non-Russians becomes closely related to the more intricate arguments given to justify the expansion of the Russian state. Some examples of continuing Russian military aid will be described in the following chapter on the processes of Russian expansion.

APOLOGIES FOR RUSSIAN POLICIES

It has been noted already in the case of Estonia that the historians of the non-Russian republics strive to put Russian military actions in the best possible light, even when they would seem to have little connection with the friendship of peoples. In many instances the historians have gone further: they feel obliged to explain why the Russians did not come to the aid of their neighbors in their hour of peril; they show how the friendship of peoples developed in spite of numerous obstacles; they give examples of the Russian government's concern for the members of the future Soviet family, both before and after they became Russian subjects.

The survey histories of Moldavia and Georgia offer several examples of apology for the absence of Russian military aid and rationalizations of Russian military campaigns that were heretofore said to have been damaging to the non-Russian neighbors. Moldavian historians have explained that in the first half of the sixteenth century, when their homeland was overrun by the Turks, the Russians were unable to help Moldavia because they were occupied with "regaining Russian lands—the Ukraine and Belorussia" and had to maintain peaceful relations with Turkey in order to avoid a war on two fronts. Nevertheless, during this trying period, "when

---

kovo Field" appears in *Istoriia kazakhskoi SSR*, ed. M. O. Auezov, S. B. Baishev, *et al.* (Alma-Ata, 1957), I, 120, and also in *Istoriia ukrainskoi SSR*, ed. A. K. Kasimenko, V. A. Diadichenko, F. E. Los', *et al.* (Kiev, 1963), I, 124.

27. *Ocherkii istorii Karelii*, ed. V. N. Bernadskii, I. I. Smirnov, and Ia. A. Balagurov (Petrozavodsk, 1957), I, 66-71.

28. *Istoriia estonskoi SSR*, ed. Vassar and Naan (1961), I, 221 ff.; *Istoriia latviiskoi SSR*, ed. K. Ia. Strazdin' *et al.* (Riga, 1952), pp. 133-38.

there could be no question of open military activities against the Porte, the Russian government showed a lively interest in Moldavia." As proof of this the *History of Moldavia* mentions details of the instructions of the Russian envoy to the Moldavian *gospodar* in 1567. The envoy was asked to find out about the Sultan's military plans and to advise the tsar on Moldavia's defense plans and "financial problems." Although such sleuthing might be regarded as the routine business of a diplomat, this history makes more of it, concluding that "even though it could not help Moldavia with armed force, the Russian government obligated itself in this period to offering diplomatic and economic help to the Moldavian government." Such Russian moral support is made more conspicuous by a following statement that Moldavia appealed to Western European countries for help with completely negative results.[29]

Peter the Great's disastrous Pruth campaign, which not only failed to deliver Moldavia from the Turk, but brought in its wake unspeakable Turkish retribution to the Moldavian population, is also handled with delicacy by the historians of Moldavia. The old explanation of Peter's failure (Platonov and Kliuchevskii) was that he marched into unknown territory with too few soldiers (one-fifth of the Turkish forces) and did not receive the proffered aid of his allies, the King of Poland and the Moldavian *gospodar*. But in the new version, the *gospodar*, Kantemir, was ever faithful to his Russian ally, but was betrayed by "some of the higher feudal lords" of Moldavia, who sided with the Turks to protect their privileges. Peter's inglorious withdrawal from Moldavia is entirely justified: "In concluding the Pruth treaty, Peter I freed himself from the threat of having to fight two wars at the same time" so that he could concentrate on "the main war" with Sweden. And there were far-reaching consequences for the friendship of peoples:

> The Pruth campaign of the Russian armies did not bring freedom to Moldavia. However, its significance for the Moldavian people was great. This was the first campaign in history in which the Russian army fought on the territory of Moldavia, opening a whole series of wars between Russia and Turkey. These wars weakened the Turkish Empire. They objectively facilitated the liberation not only of Moldavia, but also all of the Balkan countries from the yoke of feudal Turkey. These wars showed once again the

29. *Istoriia Moldavii,* ed. Udal'tsov and Cherepnin (1951), I, 163.

sympathy of the Moldavians for the Russians and their hatred of the Turkish plunderer.[30]

Shortly after 1600 the Georgian king appealed twice to Moscow for help against the Turks and Persians. The Russians failed to respond in either case. The most recent history of Georgia gives the following explanation: "In the first quarter of the seventeenth century, Russia, occupied with domestic and foreign affairs, could not actively come out in the Transcaucasus against Persia and Turkey. However, the measures taken by Russia at the Shah's court demonstrated Moscow's active interest in the fate of Georgia."[31]

A century later King Vakhtang VI of Georgia received from Peter I a promise of aid against Persia, and in 1722 marched his army to a designated meeting place. He waited three months, only to receive a messenger who notified him that Peter had postponed the campaign until the following summer. Meanwhile the Sultan attacked Georgia and took Vakhtang's capital. Peter then made a treaty with the Sultan, which allowed Eastern Georgia, already weakened by the removal of troops for Vakhtang's ill-fated campaign, to fall to the enemy. This was the ruin of Vakhtang, who is reported to have said, "While Peter plans to succor Paul, Paul is being skinned." He died in exile. The 1962 survey history of Georgia contains not a word of recrimination against Peter's policy, and only a general reference to what occurred. In effect, it changes the subject by pointing out an unexpected bonanza: many Georgian soldiers, thus shanghaied by Peter, emigrated to Moscow, where they became the core of the Georgian colony, strengthening relations between the peoples and transmitting Russian culture to Georgia.[32]

The history of the last few years of the Georgian monarchy, which contains a number of Russian military moves formerly regarded as perfidious, has been smoothed in the retelling. Catherine the Great made a treaty with Georgia in 1783, agreeing to protect Georgia from her enemies. But five years later she withdrew her troops for action in a Russo-Turkish war, thus leaving King Iraklii II defenseless against the Persians. Iraklii protested the withdrawal of Russian troops, petitioning Catherine for their return. But Russian troops did not return to Georgia until several years later, after a Persian force had engulfed the Georgian capital. The 1962 history, which makes no mention of Iraklii's futile protest, avoids specifically stating that Russia broke her treaty by noting cryptically that "the Russian government did not hasten to fulfill the obligations she had undertaken."[33] Indeed, this history records a positive result from the withdrawal of Russian troops: the neighboring Moslem leaders looked on it as a friendly act, and relations between Georgia and Turkey became "less hostile."[34] The passage describing the belated return of Russian troops to Tbilisi, which the Shah had left in ruins, has been rewritten. In the 1950 version, "the Russian government fully realized its mistake. In not giving Georgia aid in time, Russia had deprived herself of an ally, and what is more, a *place d'armes* which would have a real significance for her further operations in the Near East."[35] In the 1962 version that passage gave way to this: "The Russian government was anxious (*obespokoeno*) about the situation in the Transcaucasus. Aga Mohamed Khan had already abandoned Tiflis when General Gudovich received an order from St. Petersburg to give aid to King Iraklii."[36] Thus the impression is left that Russia's tardiness was due either to slow communications or bumbling in St. Petersburg. There follows an account of how the Russian general came to the aid of Georgia with two separate expeditions.

These survey histories of Georgia also delineate another reinterpretation dictated by the friendship of peoples: the rehabilitation of the only Russian to figure in medieval Georgian history. Iurii Bogoliubskii, the son of Prince Andrei of Suzdal, was chosen as the husband for Georgia's brilliant Queen Tamara in 1185. Known in his adopted country as George the Russian, the foreign prince suffered at the hands of bourgeois and Soviet historians alike until the early 1950's. According to the old view George was a black sheep who was already in dishonorable exile in the Caucasus when Tamara's noble counsellors chose him over her objections. After two years with this drunken troublemaker, the queen asked the Church for a divorce and exiled George to Constantinople. He returned twice in attempts to take her throne, leading a band of Turks on his second futile attempt. In 1950, the authors of a survey history of Georgia recorded—blandly, and without editorializing,

33. *Ibid.*, pp. 399-400.
34. *Ibid.*, p. 398.
35. *Ibid.*, ed. N. Berdzenishvili (Tbilisi, 1950), I, 443.
36. *Ibid.*, ed. Berdzenishvili and Khachapuridze (1962), I, 400.

to be sure—the simple facts about George. They reported that he was exiled to Constantinople because of "negative personal qualities," and that later "he organized two revolts against Tamara."[37] The 1962 successor to this volume removes George the Russian from the role of villain, making him an almost innocent bystander who made a positive contribution to Russian-Georgian relations. The passage about George is introduced with a statement that "at that time political ties were strengthened between Georgia and Russia, with which Georgia had already for a long time had active relations." George is the victim of infighting among Georgian noble factions: "George the Russian, arriving in Georgia, was from the very beginning in the center of a fight which had already flamed up in the queen's court. After only two years they forced George the Russian to separate from Tamara, to leave Georgia and go to Constantinople." There is not a word about "negative personal qualities," or divorce or exile. His attempted revolts are also explained as a part of a series of uprisings by recalcitrant nobles: "In 1191 George the Russian came from Constantinople to Arzrum in order to survey the political situation, and to return to Georgia if the conditions were favorable. A group of high-born nobles . . . assured George of their support. At their urging the latter came to Western Georgia and sat on the tsar's throne at Geguti."[38]

Thus the way was cleared for George the Russian to make his contribution to the friendship of peoples. He has received short and honorable notice in other surveys. The revised history of the U.S.S.R. for the eighth-grade student disposes of him in this way: "Political and cultural relations between Georgia and Russia were significantly broadened. The husband of Queen Tamara was the Russian prince George, the son of Andrei Bogoliubskii."[39] The *History of Armenia* also has a good, brief word to say for him: "The Rostov-Suzdal prince Iurii, the son of Andrei Bogoliubskii, was married to Queen Tamara. In 1185 a Georgian-Armenian force led by Iurii liberated Dvin from the Seljuks."[40]

Sensitivity in the interpretation of George the Russian has also

37. *Ibid.*, ed. Berdzenishvili (1950), I, 216. A Western specialist on Georgian history is more explicit about the nature of George's troubles, reporting that he was expelled "for sexual conduct of an unnatural kind." See David Marshall Lang, *The Georgians* (New York: Frederick A. Praeger, 1966), p. 114.
38. *Istoriia Gruzii,* ed. Berdzenishvili and Khachapuridze (1962), I, 201.
39. Bushchik, *Istoriia SSSR,* I, 71.
40. *Istoriia armianskogo naroda,* ed. Arakelian and Ioannisian (1951), I, 163.

been indicated by the fate of a historical novel about him, originally entitled *The Unfortunate Russian*. Under party pressure, the Georgian author, Shalva Dadiani, revised both the title and the plot to bring it into line with the friendship of peoples. But apparently the damage had already been done; when the Georgian newspaper *Kommunist* published an article about the novelist and his works at the time of his death in 1959, it made no mention of this book.[41]

The new history of the non-Russian peoples is full of assurances of Russian concern and explanations for the interruption of close relations among Soviet peoples in the past. In his book *The Role of Russia in the History of Dagestan*, V. G. Gadzhiev feels obliged to explain why trade between his people and the Russians, established in 643 A.D., was not continuous. "The Russian government was always concerned about the development of trade with the peoples of the Caucasus and the East. But this was hindered for a number of reasons, mainly because many feudal lords, fighting among themselves, would not always be responsible for the security of the trade routes. . . ."[42] Gadzhiev goes on to praise the Russian government for sponsoring a clause in the Treaty of Georgievsk providing for the protection of caravans, which "played an extremely important role in the development of trade and economic ties between Dagestan and Russia, promoting the growth of productive forces of the area and strengthening the orientation of the peoples of Dagestan toward Russia." Friendship between the Latvian and Russian peoples was not weakened substantially even during the period when the Baltic area fell under the control of the Poles and Swedes.[43] Armenian traders could not be deterred from their growing commercial relations with the Russians by Turkish-Persian wars, the Livonian war, Tatar raids, or the Polish-Swedish intervention during the Time of Troubles.[44] Neither the formidable mountains nor the hostile Polovtsii, who held territories lying between Georgians and Russians in medieval times, could prevent the development of closer ties between those peoples.[45] One of the specific charges leveled at those foreign enemies of history—the Teutonic

41. *POP*, No. 2 (1959), p. 63.

42. Gadzhiev, *Rol' Rossii*, p. 178.

43. V. I. Savchenko, *Istoricheskie sviazi latyshskogo i russkogo narodov* (Riga, 1959), p. 18.

44. *Istoriia armianskogo naroda*, ed. Arakelian and Ioannisian (1951), I, 239.

45. Sh. A. Meskhia and Ia. Z. Tsinadze, *Iz istorii russko-gruzinskikh vzaimo-otnoshenii X-XVIII vv* (Tbilisi, 1958), p. 15.

Knights, the Swedish feudal lords, the Polish Pans, the Catholic and Moslem clergy, the Sultan, the Shah, "the British imperialists"— is that they purposefully pursued a policy of interfering with the development of friendly relations among the peoples of the future Soviet family.

CHAPTER **15.**

THE PROCESSES
OF RUSSIAN EXPANSION

"*Moscow appeared as a magnetic center for all peoples who were suffering disaster, such as the Ukrainians, Belorussians, Georgians, Armenians, Cherkessi, Kabardinians, Chechens, Avars, and other peoples presently constituting the Soviet Union.*" V. L. Tatishvili, Gruziny v Moskve (istoricheskii ocherk, 1653-1722) [Georgians in Moscow: An Historical Sketch, 1653-1722] (*Tbilisi, 1959*), *p. 8.*

With the advent of Soviet patriotism, it became axiomatic that Russian acquisitions of land were, regardless of the circumstances, historically progressive acts. In time the manner of acquisition itself has been re-examined and reinterpreted. In a large number of cases territories are said to have been acquired voluntarily, through the wishes of their leaders, and even of their peoples. Even when the use of force is admitted, it has been softened by a great variety of euphemisms and justified by extenuating circumstances, involving the defense of the local people, the growth of the Russian state, and the economic and cultural betterment of the population.

Underlying all these arguments is a kind of Russian manifest destiny. The old concept of "the gathering of the Russian lands," which is held more eagerly by recent Soviet historians than by their tsarist predecessors, has been extended to include non-Russian territory. The case is stated in *The Peoples of Siberia* (1956), a major Soviet work on the history and ethnography of Siberia, as follows: "The Russian state, growing economically and strengthening itself politically, required the expansion and fortification of its frontiers. The incorporation of Siberia, discovered by Russians, was in complete accord with this aim. In Siberia, which was the natural continuation of the territory of the Russian state beyond the Urals, and which had great natural wealth and was so sparsely populated, the Moscow government saw a major source of territorial and economic development for Russia."[1]

VOLUNTARY ANNEXATIONS

The most common technique for justifying Russian expansion, and at the same time removing all friction between the Russian and non-Russian peoples, is to propound the view that no military action took place. Well over half of all the annexations are said to have been voluntary, and to have reflected wise statesmanship on the part of non-Russian leaders as well as the will of the people. In nearly all cases of voluntary annexation, the immediate cause of the historic act was the threat from a foreign invader, and the Russian state is supposed to have been regarded as a natural ally and protector. Non-Russian leaders faced an historic alternative: either to cast the fate of their people with the Great Russian people, or to be absorbed by an external aggressor. The possibility of a separate existence as independent states is ruled out for the outlying territories of the present U.S.S.R.

The use of both parts of the expression "voluntary annexation" is questionable. The term used for annexation (*prisoedinenie*) is devoid of any suggestion of dominant action by one of the parties, referring to union on terms of equality. Earlier Bolshevik writers objected to the use of the expression altogether, suggesting that it was a term used by Great Russian chauvinists in their apologies for the brutalities of Russian conquests.[2] The accounts of voluntary annexation are full of explanations that in fact limit the meaning of the term. Invariably the decision for "voluntary" annexation was made in the face of an emergency that made it the lesser of two evils. In some cases the threat from Russia itself is acknowledged, and it is apparent that the decision was made to prevent bloodshed. Even these cases of annexation under duress are said to have been voluntary. This term, which was also considered to be a part of the vocabulary of the apologist for the tsars, was rejected by the

1. *Narody Sibiri*, ed. M. G. Levin and L. P. Potapov (Moscow-Leningrad, 1956), p. 118.
2. In an early article written in 1904, Stalin showed his contempt for the term by enclosing it in quotation marks, along with "the liberation of Georgia" (I. V. Stalin, *Sochineniia* [Moscow, 1946–], I, 32).

Bolsheviks until the eve of World War II. The first edition of the *Great Soviet Encyclopedia*, in its discussion of the history of the Kazakhs, stated that "the legend, which is increasingly spread by the great power chauvinists and Kazakh bourgeois nationalists, concerning the 'voluntary submission' of the Kazakh people, is an obvious lie [*iavnaia lozh'*]."[3] The first survey history of the Kazakhs of the Soviet period stated that "in spite of the statement of the great power chauvinists about the almost bloodless conquest, about peace, good deeds and culture which the Russian conquest supposedly brought; in spite of the statements of nationalists about the 'voluntary submission' of the Kazakhs—the conquest of Kazakhstan by tsarism, like all of Central Asia, was carried out with force and brutality."[4]

Between 1937 and the early 1950's the cases of voluntary annexation were gradually brought to light. The first instance, that of Georgia, was specifically prescribed in the *dictum* on the "lesser evil." In the first edition of the Shestakov textbook, only Georgia was said to have joined Russia voluntarily; all other cases were by conquest.[5] During the war period the Ukrainians and Belorussians were added to the voluntary list, but other areas were still said to have been annexed by conquest. The Kirgiz, for example, had "offered prolonged resistance to the Russians," according to the *Great Soviet Encyclopedia's* account, published in 1936.[6] A decade later Abramzon continued to recall the long struggle of the Kirgiz people for independence, pointedly denying that the annexation was voluntary.[7] As late as 1949, the Nechkina textbook noted that "the peoples of Central Asia offered prolonged resistance, and subordination to Russian rule was nowhere voluntary."[8] The authors, however, were badly out of step, and were reprimanded for merely reprinting an old passage from the 1940 edition. Up to the middle of 1950, the interpretation was still somewhat flexible. A Soviet reviewer of a study on the Bashkirs, for example, cited six historians who thought the annexation was voluntary, and five who called it a conquest.[9]

3. *BSE*, 1st ed., XXX, column 590.
4. S. D. Asfendiarov, *Istoriia Kazakhstana* (*s drevneishikh vremen*) (Alma-Ata, 1935), I, 110.
5. *Istoriia SSSR*, ed. A. V. Shestakov (1st ed., Moscow, 1937), p. 79.
6. *BSE*, 1st. ed., XXXII, column 377.
7. S. M. Abramzon, *Ocherk kul'tury kirgizskogo naroda* (Frunze, 1946), pp. 22-23.
8. *Istoriia SSSR*, ed. M. V. Nechkina (Moscow, 1949), II, 590.
9. N. Ustiugov in *VI*, No. 6, 1949, pp. 128-30. In the book under review,

In those cases in which military resistance by non-Russians was well known, Soviet historians resorted to the techniques of emphasizing the complexity of the situation and insisting that in many instances a people had been annexed in several stages, with resistance being offered only in a few exceptional cases. Thus the technique of dissection, which had been used in the analysis of revolts, was used also for annexation. The case of the Kirgiz is once again instructive. At first all the Kirgiz were conquered; later northern Kirgizia was said to have been annexed voluntarily; and more recently only small pockets of resistance have been noted. The new attention to the complexity of the annexation process is illustrated by a Soviet historian, writing in 1950, listing the following factors in the annexation of the Kirgiz: "The reasons which prompted the Kirgiz tribes to consider a request that they be brought under Russian rule were the following: the feudal-tribal struggle among the separate Kirgiz tribes, the colonization of Kirgizia by the Kokand khanate, the struggle between the Kirgiz and Kazakh feudal lords, the efforts of Chinese feudal lords to subjugate Kirgiz tribes, and finally, the warlike performance of tsarist troops in Central Asia."[10]

In their efforts to affirm the voluntary nature of annexations, Soviet historians have engaged in studied vagueness and euphemisms, and have been highly selective in their use of facts, choosing to "forget" those that would be damaging to the interpretation. R. Trakho has demonstrated the fragility of one case—the voluntary annexation of Kabarda, whose four-hundredth anniversary was celebrated in 1957. He believes that the indications are quite clear that the Kabardinian princes who sought the aid of Ivan IV against Crimean Tatars regarded their act as a military alliance and not a permanent surrender of their people to the Russian state. Kabarda was mentioned as an independent state in the Treaty of Belgrade, 1739. Histories and encyclopedias do not mention the voluntary annexation until about 1950. Maps of the Russian Empire, published by tsars and Soviets alike, give a variety of much later dates for the annexation. Trakho found one map published in Moscow in 1950 which gave the date as 1825.[11] Occasionally a Soviet his-

---

A. N. Usmanov, *Prisoedinenie Bashkirii k moskovskomu gosudarstvu* (Ufa, 1949), the Bashkir annexation was considered voluntary, and the reviewer agreed.

10. A. Khasanov, "O prisoedinenie severnykh Kirgizov k Rossii," *VI*, No. 7, 1950, p. 126.

11. R. Trakho, *Cherkesy* (Munich, 1956), pp. 20-26.

torian will comment on the confusion. M. S. Totoev, writing in 1955 about the annexation of Northern Ossetia, noted the lack of agreement among Soviet historians on both the nature of the annexation and its date. He mentioned three dates (1774, 1830, 1859) and complained that Soviet historians had not understood that the military resistance against the Russians had been entirely the responsibility of a "separatist, feudal-nationalist movement of part of the Ossetian feudal lords," having nothing to do with the Ossetian people.[12]

The most incredible part of the theme of voluntary annexation is the contention that the non-Russian peoples themselves had a part in the process. In all cases annexation was in accord with their will; in some cases they initiated the undertaking and were instrumental in carrying it through; in a few instances the people even sought annexation against the will of their rulers. The picture presented by the new history is that these peoples—who were in many cases illiterate and were widely scattered—had a foreign policy. At least they were agreed on one vital principle: that Russians were friendly and the people living in the opposite direction from Russia were enemies. According to the Director of the Institute of History of the Kirgiz Academy of Sciences, "from the end of the eighteenth century and during the entire first half of the nineteenth century the external orientation [*vneshniaia orientatsiia*] of several of the Kirgiz tribes turned in the direction of *rapprochement* with Russia."[13] A later account characteristically detects this manifestation somewhat earlier and more widespread in the country: "Beginning at the end of the eighteenth century the foreign political orientation of the Kirgiz people was strongly directed toward *rapprochement* with Russia."[14] And from the beginning of the nineteenth century, "the Turkmens, seeing the impossibility of freeing themselves from the feudal yoke by their own power, more frequently turned to the Russian government with requests for help."[15] After describing the suffering of the Kazakhs under feudal leaders, Shoinbaev stated that "in these circumstances,

12. M. S. Totoev, *K istorii doreformennoi severnoi Osetii* (Ordzhonikidze, 1955), pp. 3-4.

13. B. Dzhamgerchinov, *Prisoedinenie Kirgizii k Rossii* (Moscow, 1959), p. 12.

14. K. Orozaliev, "Istoricheskoe znachenie dobrovol'nogo vkhozhdeniia Kirgizii v sostav Rossii," *Izvestiia Akademiia Nauk kirgizskoi SSR. Seriia obshchestvennykh nauk*, V, Part 3 (1963), 5-12.

15. A. A. Rosliakov, *Kratkii ocherk istorii Turkmenistana (Do prisoedineniia k Rossii)* (Ashkhabad, 1956), p. 160.

the striving of the broad masses of the Kazakh people for a union with Russia, which alone could assure them a peaceful life, grew all the more. The Kazakh people were sure that the strengthening of ties with Russia represented the only way in which they could be saved from a war with Dzhungaria."[16] In connection with the arrangement Khan Abulkhair made with the tsar in 1731, we are told that "the greater part of the [Kazakh] people regarded that act as a distinctive military union with Russia, which provided for their change from the old nomadic way to peaceful labor."[17]

But more frequently than not the beginnings of voluntary annexation are found in an instinctive groping for the better life and a working out of the will of the people. There are dozens of references in the new history to *stremlenie* (yearning or striving). Such striving is both old and persistent. The Pereiaslav Treaty fulfilled "the centuries-long striving and hopes" of the Ukrainian people for union with Russia. There are four references to "the striving of the Ukrainian people" for annexation in a two-page passage in the 1956 edition of the *History of the Ukrainian S.S.R.*[18] On the fifteenth anniversary of the formal annexation of Tuva (1944), *Pravda* acknowledged the "centuries-long striving of the Tuvinian people to live in one family with their great neighbor."[19] Other euphemisms are as vague as *stremlenie*. In their long association with the Russian people before annexation, the peoples of Tuva, Kirgizia, and Moldavia are said to have developed *simpatiia* (sympathy or liking) for the Russians,[20] and other accounts note the *nadezhdy* (hopes or aspirations) of Ukrainians and Buriats for closer ties with their elder brother.[21] An essay written for the anniversary of the annexa-

16. T. Zh. Shoinbaev, "K voprosu o prisoedinenii srednego zhuza k Rossii," in *Voprosy istorii Kazakhstana* (Alma-Ata, 1962), pp. 41-60.

17. *Kazakhsko-russkie otnosheniia v XVI-XVIII vekakh. Sbornik dokumentov i materialov* (Alma-Ata, 1961), p. viii.

18. *Istoriia ukrainskoi SSR*, ed. V. A. Diadichenko, A. K. Kasimenko, F. E. Los', *et al.* (Kiev, 1956), I, 282-83; see also *Istoriia Kirgizii*, ed. M. P. Viatkin, M. P. Griaznov, *et al.* (Frunze, 1963), I, 277, 332; *Istoriia Tuvy*, ed. L. P. Potapov (Moscow, 1964), I, 270.

19. S. Toka, "V sem'e narodov-brat'ev," *Pravda*, October 10, 1959.

20. *Istoriia Tuvy*, ed. Potapov, I, 275; *Istoriia Kirgizii*, ed. M. P. Viatkin, B. D. Dzamgerchinov, A. P. Okladnikov, *et al.* (Frunze, 1956), I, 280; *Istoriia Moldavii*, ed. A. D. Udal'stov and L. V. Cherepnin (Kishinev, 1951), I, 147.

21. V. A. Golobutskii, *Osvoboditel'naia voina ukrainskogo naroda pod rukovodstvom Khmel'nitskogo, 1648-1654 gg.* (Moscow, 1954), p. 135; *Trista let nerushimoi druzhby (sbornik statei)* (Ulan-Ude, 1959), p. 26; B. Tsibikov, *K voprosu o dobrovol'nam prisoedinenie Buriat-Mongolii k Rossii* (Ulan-Ude, 1950), p. 9.

tion of the Khakassian people (South Central Siberia) states that "historical sources reveal that during the whole of the seventeenth century the Khakassian working people struggled for annexation with the Russian state," though the nature of the struggle is not described.[22]

Arguments in favor of the striving of non-Russian peoples are not only vague, but sometimes quotations from tsarist archives are used in an uncritical manner when they seem to speak to the point. For example, a Kirgiz scholar quotes a statement by a delegation of Southern Kirgiz to the Russian Governor-General of Turkestan as a proof of the strong desire of the people to unite with Russia: "So many of our fellow tribesmen, they said, are subject to the white tsar in the Orenburg district, in Siberia and in Turkestan, and all of them give thanks to God. This we also hope for."[23] Such a statement, designed for the attention of the Russian official, appears to be typical Oriental flattery. But in this account it is accepted completely at face value.

When annexation climaxed such striving and struggling, and fulfilled the hopes of the non-Russian peoples, we are assured in the new histories that the will of the people had been realized and that they consciously approved of the actions of their leaders. Such statements of purported public opinion are universal in the accounts of annexation and are rather standardized: the reunification of Belorussian lands "answered the vital interests of broad circles of the population of these lands"; the Pereiaslav Treaty represented "the powerful will of the freedom-loving Ukrainian people"; "the historic act of incorporation into Russia accorded with the vital interests of the broad masses of the countries of the Transcaucasus."[24] In the extreme statement of the case, it would appear that the governments concerned took their historic steps in response to the peoples' wishes. In 1957 a Kazakh party journal stated that "the tsarist government, in the interests of strengthening the state, supported the will of the Kazakh people for union with Russia."[25]

22. *Dvestapiat'desiat' let vmeste s velikim russkim narodom* (Abakan, 1959), p. 5.
23. *Istoriia Kirgizii*, ed. Viatkin, Dzhamgerchinov, Okladnikov, *et al.* (1956), I, 280.
24. *Istoriia belorusskoi SSR*, ed. L. S. Abetsedarskii, V. N. Pertsev and K. I. Shabunia (Minsk, 1961), I, 73; *Istoriia ukrainskoi SSR*, ed. Diadichenko, Kasimenko, Los', *et al.* (1956), I, 282; M. Mustafaev, in *VI*, No. 9, 1951, p. 97.
25. N. N. Poppe, "Ideological Work in Central Asia since World War II," *East Turkic Review*, No. 2 (1959) pp. 3-27, quoting from *Kommunist Kazakhstana*. Poppe points out that such an assertion is "pure nonsense" from a

In connection with the wishes of the population of the Merv Oasis to join Russia, one account declares that "the striving to unite with Russia was so strong that under the pressure of the popular masses the influential feudal lords of Merv had to address the Russian command with a request that they come under Russian rule."[26]

But the masses were not the only ones who were interested in union with Russia. According to these accounts, certain leaders and "progressive people," who are never named or numbered, also worked for the goal. "The most far-sighted political leaders" of Tuva, who were referred to also as "the progressive people of the day in Tuva," appealed to the tsarist government in 1914 for annexation and were not disappointed.[27] "The advanced people of the Georgian, Armenian, Azerbaidzhani and Dagestani nationalities . . . always directed their gaze to Russia and sought help and support from her."[28] And "progressive representatives of the Uzbek, Tadzhik, Kirgiz, Turkmen and Karakalpak peoples understood the progressive significance of the annexation of Central Asia to Russia."[29]

Marxist historians are expected to write from positions of economic determinism and to find the logical working out of the laws of historical development. The new Soviet history, however, pushes the rationale of such propositions to extreme limits with numerous vague references to the common historical destiny of the peoples of the future U.S.S.R., as though some immutable historical law determined that Estonians and Kirgiz, Moldavians and Iakuts had been for many centuries on a common historic path to membership in the multi-national Soviet state. These references, which are seldom clarified, seem to have become an unquestioned stock-in-trade in the jargon of Soviet historiography. It is a curious kind of element to be found in a body of scholarship which calls itself "historical science."

One occasionally finds an opaque reference to a sort of predestination in Soviet history, more suggestive of Calvin than Marx.

Marxist viewpoint, since Russia was a bourgeois state whose goal was to oppress the masses, not to follow their will.

26. A. Karryev and A. Rosliakov, *Kratkii ocherk istorii Turkmenistana* (*Ot prisoedineniia k Rossii do velikoi oktiabr'skoi sotsialisticheskoi revoiutsii, 1868-1917 gg.*) (Ashkhabad, 1956), p. 47.

27. "Slavnyi iubilei sovetskoi Tuvy," *Pravda*, August 17, 1946; Toka, "V sem'e narodov-brat'ev."

28. M. Mustafaev "O formule 'naimen'shee zlo,'" *VI*, No. 9, 1951, pp. 97-101. Quotation on p. 97.

29. *VI*, No. 8, 1959, p. 174.

The historical sketch on the U.S.S.R. in the second edition of the *Great Bolshevik Encyclopedia,* for example, states the following: "Prepared [*podgotovlennoe*] by the whole course of social-economic development, the unification of Russia proceeded successfully in the period of Ivan III (1462-1505) and Vasilii III (1505-1533)."[30] The annexation of the Ukraine is also said to have been "prepared by the whole course of the historical life of both brotherly peoples." Some historical events are inevitable or historically necessary. A survey history of the Ukraine refers to the "historical inevitability of the liberation war," and a monograph on the annexation of Eastern Armenia calls the event "an historic necessity."[31] This theme can also be used as an apology for Russian expansion, as when T. Gorbunov, Secretary of the Central Committee of the Belorussian party explained that "all people in the U.S.S.R. possess equal rights and are free. At the same time, because of certain conditions in our country, the process of unifying all the peoples around the Great Russian people was historically necessary."[32]

Much mention is made in the survey histories of common destinies and common paths of Soviet peoples. The 1943 history of Kazakhstan, speaking of the period immediately after annexation, stated that "Russian tsarism was not able to block the progressive course of historical development which now linked the destinies of Russia with Kazakhstan."[33] The 1957 version speaks more broadly of "the development of friendly ties of the Kazakh people with the Russians and other brotherly peoples of our country, the community of their historical fate, the history of their mutual struggle against tsarism, against the social and national yoke."[34] The histories of Tadzhikistan report that the peoples of Central Asia, from the most remote times "all followed the same historic path" and refer to the "historic common fate of the peoples of Central Asia."[35] "The

30. *BSE,* 2nd. ed., L, 138.

31. *Istoriia ukrainskoi SSR,* ed. Diadichenko, Kasimenko, Los', *et al.* (1956), I, 283, 240; Z. T. Grigorian, *Prisoedinenie vostochnoi Armenii k Rossii v nachale XIX veka* (Moscow, 1959), p. 4.

32. Quoted by Pavel Urban, "Changing Trends in Soviet Historiography," *Caucasian Review,* No. 9 (1959), pp. 11-24.

33. *Istoriia kazakhskoi SSR, S drevneishikh vremen do nashikh dnei,* ed. M. Abdykalykov and A. Pankratova (Alma-Ata, 1943), p. 308.

34. *Istoriia kazakhskoi SSR,* ed. M. O. Auezov, S. B. Baishev, *et al.* (Alma-Ata, 1957), I, 5.

35. B. G. Gafurov, *Istoriia tadzhikskogo naroda v kratom izlozhenii* (2nd ed., Moscow, 1952), pp. 5-6; *Istoriia tadzhikskogo naroda,* ed. B. G. Gafurov and B. A. Litvinskii (Moscow, 1963) I, 3-4. In his review of Gafurov's first edition, A. Iakubovskii considered this theme one of the strong points

history of Karelia in the seventeenth century," according to an historical sketch on that republic, "records quite a number of remarkable facts reflecting the unity of the historic paths of the Russian and Karelian peoples."[36]

The new histories dramatize the historic turning point when the non-Russian peoples came into the Russian state. The historic alternatives faced by the peoples are described in black and white: to be engulfed by a foreign enemy or to unite with the Russian people. The decision, once made, is described as "the only right and historically progressive course of development," or "the only reasonable path—the path of drawing together with Russia."[37] The 1956 *History of the Ukrainian S.S.R.* contains one of the most dramatic instances of the historical alternative facing a people. In this account, Khmel'nitskii speaks before the Rada at the time of the Pereiaslav Treaty, recalling past suffering at the hand of foreign enemies, and outlining for the delegates the dire fate awaiting the Ukrainian people unless they decide to unite with Russia. The account gives the impression that the decision was made democratically and by the will of the Ukrainian people. It has the ring of a current newspaper account of proceedings of the Supreme Soviet or a party congress, even down to the conclusion: "the Rada approved with stormy applause. . . ."[38]

Finally in this connection, one sometimes encounters a word a serious historian should hesitate to use with reference to decisions or acts of mortal leaders—the word "forever." In the Ukrainian history, for example, the reader is told that "the Ukrainian people, by tying their fate forever to that of their blood brothers, the fraternal Russian people, in whom they always saw their hoped-for protector and ally, saved themselves as a nation."[39]

---

of the book: "In the short preface the author notes the close intertwining of the destinies of the Tadzhiks and other peoples of Central Asia—the Uzbeks, Turkmens, Kazakhs and Kirgiz: 'All these peoples united even in the distant past in the common struggle against domestic and foreign exploiters. They all followed the very same historical path: from feudalism, with the help of the victorious proletariat of Russia, directly to socialism, passing up the agonizing stage of capitalism.'" (*VI*, No. 7, 1950, p. 159).

36. *Karel'skaia ASSR*, ed. A. A. Grigor'ev and A. V. Ivanov (Moscow, 1956), p. 122.

37. *Vossoedinenie Ukrainy s Rossiei. Dokumenty i materialy*, ed. A. K. Kasimenko, A. L. Sidorov, L. V. Cherepnin, *et al.* (Moscow, 1954), I, xxi; *Istoriia Kirgizii*, ed. Viatkin, Griaznov, *et al.* (1963), I, 353.

38. *Istoriia ukrainskoi SSR*, ed. Diadichenko, Kasimenko, Los', *et al.* (1956), I, 281-82.

39. *Ibid.*, p. 282. This point is emphasized further with an accompanying

SECOND THOUGHTS ON TSARIST CONQUESTS—
THE CASE OF KAZAN, 1552

Ivan IV's conquest of the Kazan Tatars has generally been regarded as the beginning date of the Russian Empire, since it expanded Russia into clearly non-Russian lands. The early Soviet view of that campaign was that it was a particularly brutal example of a tsarist conquest. The reinterpretation of this event and its significance, made just after World War II, is typical of the patterns of rethinking that have been employed by Soviet historians in many other cases of Russian expansion.

An essential condition for the reinterpretation of the Kazan campaign was met by the new view on the ethnogenesis of the Kazan Tatars, made in 1946. It will be recalled (pp. 314-15) that the "people" living in Kazan had been completely separated from the Golden Horde, which had enslaved them. The way was thus cleared for Ivan's campaign to be relabeled a rescue operation for the purpose of liberating the inhabitants of Kazan. But such an interpretation was not made universal for several years in Soviet historical writing. Tatar historians, who had been in difficulty with Moscow since their ill-fated idealization of Idegei in 1943, did not publish a survey history of their A.S.S.R. until 1955. The question came into the spotlight after the 1950 edition of the Pankratova textbook appeared with the old version of the conquest reproduced intact from its 1940 edition. A letter to the editors of *Voprosy istorii* angrily condemned the book for its discussion of Ivan's motives for attacking Kazan: (1) to provide new lands for his nobles, (2) to stop raids by Kazan Tatars on Russian lands, and (3) to open trade routes to the Caspian and Urals. The correspondent, K. Naiakshin, charged that the Pankratova account had missed two essential points. The Sultan's Janissaries were on the move and their agents were already within Kazan's walls. Ivan's campaign was thus a just war against a foreign enemy, albeit a potential one. Furthermore, Naiakshin objected to the reference to prolonged resistance by the inhabitants of Kazan. Russian troops fought "not against the local population, but against the surviving remnants of the Kazan feudal

color reproduction of a painting by M. I. Khmel'ko titled "Forever with Moscow—Forever with the Russian People," which shows Khmel'nitskii and the Russian envoy meeting the crowd in the square at Pereiaslav at the time of the signing of the treaty. All classes of Ukrainians applaud and throw their hats into the air.

lords, members of the Golden Horde."[40] The revision of the textbook showed the result. The section was completely rewritten,
including the topic head, which was changed from "The Conquests
of Tsar Ivan IV" to "The Annexation of the Volga Khanates to
Russia." The Sultan was now the villain: he encouraged the Khans
of the Crimea and Kazan to raid Russian lands, and sent artillery
for the defense of Kazan. The position of the local inhabitants was
also made clear: "The native population of the Volga area was
subjected to plunder and violence from the Tatar feudal lords.
For the Volga peoples, among them the working Tatar masses, the
aggressive policy of the Crimean-Kazan feudal lords was deeply
foreign."[41] It is now possible for the later version to regard the
storming of Kazan as a great patriotic victory for the future Soviet
peoples. No doubt taking a cue from Naiakshin's assertion that the
"foreign engineers" in the earlier Pankratova version were in reality
Russians, the author of the newer account attributes the victory to
the superiority of Russian artillery over that supplied by the Turks,
pointing with patriotic pride to the "leadership of the talented Russian master of artillery, Ivan Vyrodkov."

The histories of the Volga peoples have fallen into line with
this view. Viatka is said to have sided with Moscow more than a
half century before the siege of Kazan, even though such a policy
put the city in danger of reprisal from the Khans of Kazan. After
Kazan fell, the Udmurts continued to be raided by the Khan's forces,
but in the summer of 1554 "the arrival of Russian troops saved the
Udmurts from reprisals" and they were voluntarily annexed to Russia.[42] The Chuvash people gave "significant support to the Russian
forces" in the battle for Kazan by building roads and bridges and
even by participating in storming the walls.[43] We are even assured
by Armenian historians that those Armenians living in the Middle
Volga area "went under Russian rule with gladness."[44] But the prize

40. K. Naiakshin, "K voprosu o prisoedinenii srednego povolzh'ia k Rossii,"
VI, No. 9, 1951, pp. 108-11.

41. L. P. Bushchik, Istoriia SSSR: Uchebnik dlia 8 klassa (Moscow, 1959),
I, 122-23. See also N. F. Kalinin, Kazan'. Istoricheskii ocherk (Kazan',
1952), p. 18; Istoriia tatarskoi ASSR, ed. N. I. Vorob'ev et al. (Kazan', 1955),
I, 133-38.

42. Ocherki istorii udmurtskoi ASSR, ed. I. P. Emel'ianov (Izhevsk, 1958),
I, 30-38.

43. V. D. Dimitriev, Istoriia Chuvashii XVIII veka (do krest'ianskoi voiny
1773-1775 godov) (Cheboksary, 1959), p. 30.

44. Istoriia armianskogo naroda, ed. V. N. Arakelian and A. R. Ioannisian
(Erevan, 1951), I, 239.

is taken by the *Survey of the History of the Mordvinian A.S.S.R.*, particularly if one recalls Pokrovskii's view that Mordvinia "was surrendered to Russian colonists as booty and plunder. . . . It was rape and oppression of a rather densely populated agricultural land." The new version says that the Mordvinian people were under the cultural influences of the Slavs well before the thirteenth century, when they were enslaved by the Golden Horde, and that they "have always seen and now see in the great Russian people their true friend and teacher." In the crisis of the 1550's "the Mordvinian people placed their hopes on help from the great Russian people, who led the struggle of the exploited peoples against the yoke of the Khans. In this struggle the Mordvinian people took an active part in the events which gradually led to liberation from the rule of the Golden Horde, and with the fall of the Kazan Khanate finally entered into the Russian state and came under the protection of the Russian people."[45]

SIBERIA: FROM "CONQUEST" TO "SETTLEMENT"

Russia's expansion across the vast reaches from the Urals to the Pacific constitutes a special case in the history of colonialism. The acquisition of Siberian lands obviously did not involve the same kind of pitched battles as in the case of parts of Central Asia and the Caucasus; at the same time it involved more violence than the annexations made primarily by diplomacy—Georgia and the Ukraine. Moreover, it is easier to make a case for the cultural advantages for the local population than in those areas where an advanced civilization existed before annexation. These factors have no doubt made the writing of the new history of the Siberian peoples somewhat easier for Soviet historians, but the transformation is nevertheless remarkable and has not been achieved easily.

One reason for the difficult transition was that several historical studies of the 1930's, as previously noted, had emphasized the brutality of the conquest of Siberia and of tsarist colonial policies there. These studies were occupied with the fierce and brutal nature of the Cossack attacks, the prolonged native resistance, and later revolts—all of which highlighted the class struggle in the colonization of Siberia. They spoke of the "terror of the *voevody*," of special punitive expeditions, of the starvation of the natives and attacks on their women, land seizure, and heavy tribute. The Orthodox mis-

45. *Ocherki istorii mordovskoi ASSR*, ed. V. N. Vochkarev (Saransk, 1955), I, iv, 61, 86 ff. Quotation on p. 62.

sionaries in Siberia were mere instruments of oppressive tsarist policies. The natives resisted heroically, at times killing all the Russians in the area. Sometimes in desperation they committed mass suicide or escaped into Mongolia. There is no hint in these accounts that annexation was progressive, or that it brought cultural advantages.[46]

Just after World War II, the Soviet interpretation of Russian expansion in Siberia began to change, in keeping with the newer views on the history of Soviet peoples. The transition was soon made from the emphasis on the sufferings of the Siberian peoples to the long-range progressive consequences of the coming of the Russians.[47] By the early 1950's the roles of the main characters in these events had shifted considerably. Ermak, the fierce Cossack leader, who had been pictured in the pre-war textbooks as the raider dispatched by a greedy tsar and the acquisitive Stroganovs, was now seen in a new light. His campaign became a noble one, and the erstwhile brigand, while no less fierce and courageous, was given the qualities of a heroic general leading a justifiable campaign. The revised Pankratova textbook reported that "Ermak himself was an individual with the strength of a *bogatyr*, bold, courageous, with a good knowledge of the military art."[48] His reputation is enhanced in part by finding a new villain for the piece: Khan Kuchum, the head of the Siberian Khanate, a remnant of the Golden Horde. The reader is told that Kuchum represented reaction—that he was a tyrant who constantly conducted punitive raids, pitted Siberian peoples against each other, and laid unbearable tribute on his victims. "The Siberian Khanate possessed neither strength nor stability," and furthermore the Siberian peoples "showed little desire to support Kuchum"; therefore his regime "collapsed at the very first clash with Ermak's forces, which freed the tribes of northwest Siberia from Kuchum's tyranny."[49] The role of

46. A. P. Okladnikov, *Ocherki iz istorii zapadnykh Buriat-Mongolov* (*XVII-XVIII v.*) (Leningrad, 1937), pp. 15, 385 ff. See also P. T. Khaptaev, *Kratkii ocherk istorii buriat-mongol'skogo naroda* (Ulan-Ude, 1936), pp. 28-33; V. G. Kartsov, *Ocherk istorii narodov severo-zapadnoi Sibiri* (Moscow, 1937), pp. 33-38; F. A. Kudriavtsev, *Istoriia buriat-mongol'skogo naroda* (Moscow-Leningrad, 1940), pp. 39-60; S. A. Tokarev, *Ocherki istorii iakutskogo naroda* (Moscow, 1940), pp. 39-64.

47. An important "programmatic" article calling for this change was published by Kudriavtsev late in 1946. See F. A. Kudriavtsev, "Rol' russkoi kul'tury v razvitii buriat-mongol'skogo naroda v XVIII-XX vekakh," *VI*, No. 10, 1946, pp. 85-94.

48. Bushchik, *Istoriia SSSR*, I, 124.

49. *Narody Sibiri*, ed. Levin and Potapov, p. 119.

the Stroganovs, formerly the robbers of Siberian peoples and the epitome of the evils of merchant capital, has been reduced to a minor and anomalous one. Their acts of exploitation are subordinated to the over-all progressive results of the growth of the Siberian trade and the development of Siberian resources.[50]

No better example of the reversal of interpretation on Russian expansion into Siberia can be cited than the views of the function of the *ostrog*, the wooden fortress built by the Russians at regular intervals on the Siberian frontier. Until 1950 the ostrogs were considered a symbol of tsarist colonialism. They were the fortified bastions which enabled the Russians to control a large, sparsely settled area. From the ostrogs, the Cossacks mounted raids (sometimes referred to as pogroms) far afield, bringing more natives under subjection and tribute. The native population was kept at a distance from the ostrog, lest they learn some of its military secrets or organize a plot against it; in some cases native labor was not employed in their construction for fear that they might acquire information that would enable them to destroy the forts later on. The early Soviet accounts were full of futile revolts by natives, who fought manfully with primitive weapons to capture ostrogs defended by Russian guns.[51] When Bakhrushin wrote an introductory essay for a Soviet edition of the tsarist historian G. F. Miller's [Müller] *History of Siberia* in 1937 he complained that Miller had been an apologist for tsarist colonialism by considering the ostrog to be a necessary evil in the Russian conquest of Siberia. He especially scorned Miller's references to the role of the ostrogs as "the protection" of the peoples of the area. In Bakhrushin's view the ostrogs were the instruments of an aggressive colonial policy.[52]

The progress of the ostrog in Russian colonial history can be seen in two works of the historian B. D. Tsibikov, a specialist on

50. It is interesting that Potapov, in his historical sketch on Siberia in *Narody Sibiri*, is so preoccupied with the settlement of Siberia as a peoples' movement that he does not discuss the Stroganovs at all. A picture of the Stroganov mansion in Siberia, published in the early Pankratova editions (1940, p. 141), apparently as an example of the fruits of exploitation, is omitted in later editions.

51. Tokarev, *Ocherki istorii iakutskogo naroda*, pp. 39-64; Khaptaev, *Kratkii ocherk istorii buriat-mongol'skogo naroda*, pp. 27-33; Kartsov, *Ocherk istorii narodov severo-zapadnoi Sibiri*, pp. 28-34; Kudriavtsev, *Istoriia buriat-mongol'skogo naroda*, pp. 42-45; Okladnikov, *Ocherki iz istorii zapadnykh buriat-mongolov*, pp. 385-90; George V. Lantzeff, *Siberia in the Seventeenth Century: A Study of the Colonial Administration* (Berkeley, Calif.: University of California Press, 1943), pp. 87-90.

52. G. F. Miller, *Istoriia Sibiri* (Moscow, 1937), I, 44-45.

the Buriat-Mongols. His book on the voluntary annexation of these people, published early in 1950 on the eve of the historiographical upheaval, was full of friendship and progress, but when it came to the ostrog, it was traditional. The purpose of the ostrog was "to conquer new territory and to hold the territory in between" existing ostrogs.[53] In a similar work of 1957, which appears to be an up-dating of the earlier book, Tsibikov has nothing to say about the conquering role of the ostrogs, but notes another use: "With the mass flight of the Buriats out of Mongolia the danger of attacks by the Mongol Khans on the Buriat nomads increased. Therefore the Buriats turned to the Russian ostrogs with a request that they pro-tect them from these possible attacks from the Mongol Khans; that they construct ostrogs along the paths of march of their detach-ments."[54]

The ostrogs are being viewed increasingly as having a complete-ly non-military role, and in some cases they are even seen as friendly meeting places and cultural centers. A volume on the annexation of the Khakassians, published to commemorate the two-hundred-and-fiftieth anniversary of that event, refers to the ostrog as "an administrative center," without any negative connotation what-ever. Elsewhere in the same volume, which is published by the local branch of the Academy of Sciences, one learns that "the Rus-sian ostrogs . . . [five are enumerated] became not only strong points for protection against raids from the Khans, but they were also the first source of Russian peasant culture among the local popu-lation."[55] A similar volume on the Buriat-Mongols notes also that "along with the agents of tsarism, the working population—peas-ants and handicraftsmen—came from Russia to the ostrogs," where they befriended the native people and helped them.[56]

Thus the once uninviting ostrog has taken its place as another focal point in the history of the friendship of peoples. The emer-ging picture seems to be that the native, in his frequent visits to the big wooden house, was not disturbed by the guns or ammunition kept there for his protection; he looked forward to resting in a warm

53. Tsibikov, *K voprosu o dobrovol'nam prisoedinenii Buriat-Mongolii*, p. 13.
54. B. D. Tsibikov, *Nerushimaia druzhba buriat-mongol'skogo i russkogo naroda* (Ulan-Ude, 1957), p. 8.
55. *250-let vmeste s velikim russkim narodom* [*Khakasii*] (Abakan, 1959), pp. 37, 39.
56. *300 let nerushimoi druzhba. Sbornik statei* [*Buriat-Mongols*] (Ulan-Ude, 1959), p. 27.

place, where the samovar was always lit and a friendly Russian peasant was usually on hand to teach him how to weave a better basket.

When Russian force and violence are discussed in these accounts, the gory details of the early Soviet accounts are conspicuously absent, having been replaced by euphemism, studied vagueness, and bland generality. Potapov's historical sketch in *The Peoples of Siberia* deals with this theme at some length, but never quite openly. Potapov broaches the subject by stating that "there are historical facts which show that in addition to the other methods there was enforced annexation of some nationalities and territories." He refers to "the subjugation and devastation of the local population" in one campaign, and to "extremely cruel methods" of another, but suggests that these methods were not entirely typical of the period of exploration. He acknowledges that the tsars "prescribed firm reprisals," which took the form of "punitive expeditions, accompanied by harsh treatment of an often innocent population." He notes that "historical documents give some vivid accounts of these 'pogrom' raids," but he does not choose to repeat any of them.[57] Rebellious populations, or those not yet under Russian control, are referred to as "unquiet territories." Potapov admits that hostages were taken by the Russians to ensure the payment of tribute, but their fate is less than clear: in case of continued refusal to pay, "the hostages were severely dealt with. . . ."[58] As for the tribute itself, there is every indication that it was entirely justified, particularly in view of the more stable conditions the Russians provided in exchange for it. It is noted that the tribute paid to the Russian masters was intentionally made light, and that the tsars repeatedly sent orders to keep it that way. Furthermore, there was a definite advantage to paying one regular tribute instead of many irregular ones to the old "nomadic aristocracy" (referred to in this case as "the extortion of tribute," as against its "collection" by Russians). Potapov explains it this way: "The incorporation into the Russian state improved the political situation, replaced the

57. *Narody Sibiri*, ed. Levin and Potapov, p. 126. The quotation marks around "pogrom" are Potapov's.

58. *Ibid.*, pp. 121, 126. Potapov indicates a trace of the old view in two telltale phrases which occur in this passage, and are not referred to further. The most severe reprisals, he indicates, were taken when "groups of the population . . . sometimes even attacked the tax collectors and other peaceful Russian or tributary inhabitants"; also in cases in which "the dissenting tribesmen had carried out armed attacks on the Russians or on peaceful tributary citizens."

system of numerous tributes by one *iasak* payable to the Russian tsar, and made for a more peaceful existence."[59] Thus the Siberian native appears to have been in a situation comparable to the harried taxpayer of today who is invited by the friendly banker to pool all his financial worries by taking out a consolidation loan. Potapov sums up with the choice euphemism of them all: "The considerate behavior of the local population towards the pioneers helped the Russians to advance speedily into Siberia and to reach the shores of the Pacific."[60]

One of the most transparent cases of updating a Soviet historian can be observed in the Soviet publication of the collected works of Bakhrushin, who wrote extensively on Siberian history before the historiographical revolution and staunchly defended his position in the face of the new pressures after World War II, making only a limited compromise with the new views before his death in the early 1950's. The editors have republished his works without changing the text, but have presented the new interpretation in accompanying essays, prefaces, and editorial footnotes. They contend that Bakhrushin himself became thoroughly convinced of the new positions, and regretted his earlier errors. At the beginning of the third volume, devoted to works on Siberia, V. I. Shunkov presents a bibliographical essay, the last half of which is devoted to Bakhrushin's late conversion. Shunkov leaves the impression that the old historian's change of views came entirely through more profound research and reflection—there is no hint of party pressure. When he wrote his works on Siberia, Bakhrushin was "under the influence of the traditional representatives of *dvorianstvo* and bourgeois historiography," which caused him to regard the tsarist expansion into Siberia as "military occupation" and to exaggerate greatly the themes of military conquest, cruelty, and exploitation. Later, however, "taking into account the extremely small numbers of the first Russian detachments, and the striving of various groups of the

59. *Ibid.*, pp. 110, 115. See also L. P. Potapov's *Ocherki po istorii Altaitsev* (Moscow, 1953), p. 171. On the subject of the Russian *iasak* it should be said that a detailed and unapologetic study, N. S. Romanov's *Iasak in Iakutia in the Eighteenth Century*, was published during the historiographical thaw in 1956. Although it was written before World War II, publication was obviously held up for nearly twenty years because its viewpoint was unacceptable. In the preface, the editor makes specific reference to Pankratova's speech to the Twentieth Party Congress, in which she called for a more realistic appraisal of tsarist colonial policy (N. S. Romanov, *Iasak v Iakutii v XVIII veke* [Iakutsk, 1956], p. 3).

60. *Narody Sibiri*, ed. Levin and Potapov, p. 120.

Siberian population for voluntary inclusion into the Russian state, Sergei Vladimirovich began to deny the theory of plain conquest and to emphasize a new position on the annexation of the peoples of Siberia to Russia."[61]

In another prefatory essay to the same volume the editors warn further that Bakhrushin "remained wholly in the position of bourgeois historiography" concerning Siberian history:

> In his *Essays [on the History of the Colonization of Siberia]*, the author is inclined to equate the Russian colonization of Siberia in the seventeenth century with colonial aggression of European states, not dealing with the basic differences between them. In this connection the author not infrequently gives a false evaluation of the relations between Russians and the local population. Only in his very last works did the author make an effort to re-examine his positions on these questions. Therefore a correct use of many of the materials of the author demands a critical approach to the text.[62]

Throughout the four volumes of the *Collected Works*, the editors "correct" Bakhrushin in their footnotes. To his comments on the resistance of the Buriats, the editors reply that he was generalizing on a few isolated reports (III, 151). When Bakhrushin explains that the vast reaches of Siberia could be held by "this unimportant little group of people" because they were heavily armed and got "continual reinforcements," the editors point out that he missed the most important reason for the ease with which Russia controlled the area: "This reason is the growing friendly ties of the Russian working population and the local inhabitants" (III, Part 2, 29). When Bakhrushin remarks on the wild, savage nature of the Evenks, who brought "terror" to the service gentry who conquered them, the editors remark that his views were "due to the Russians' lack of knowledge" of these people. His eye-witness sources were unreliable, and the chronicles were greatly exaggerated and "highly colored" (III, Part 2, 21). One reason why Bakhrushin greatly overemphasized the cruelty and military activity of the service gentry was that he was basing his accounts on their reports to Moscow, and since they were constantly trying to get greater "governmental favors" from the tsars, they exaggerated the dangers under which

61. S. V. Bakhrushin, *Nauchnye trudy*, eds. A. A. Zimin, N. V. Ustiugov, L. V. Cherepnin, and V. I. Shunkov (Moscow, 1952-59), III, 9.
62. *Ibid.*, pp. 15-16.

they worked (III, Part 2, 215). One case of Bakhrushin's uncritical use of sources, as corrected here, could hardly fail to produce amusement, even for the most unquestioning Soviet reader. Remarking that "the cultural level of the masses of the new [Russian] settlers was not high," Bakhrushin quoted a contemporary account of their "unbelievable drunkenness." The service gentry "spend their nights in the tavern [*kvasnaia isba*]" and the peasants drank up all their money and pawned their supplies. "Many people beat each other to death because of drunkenness, and others inform on them to the authorities, and many of them tell about robberies. . . ." The editors discount all this: Bakhrushin was "under the influence of *voevoda* notes, which were spicy, overly colored . . ." (IV, 95).

In another case, Soviet editors have been even more direct in updating Bakhrushin. When one of his old articles was reprinted in a volume entitled *The Leading Role of the Russian People in the Development of the Peoples of Iakutiia*, the following note was appended: "In publishing the article without change, the editors state that in their view, S. V. Bakhrushin used the term "colonization" in the sense of "settlement" and "assimilation."[63]

RUSSIAN ARMIES VS. FOREIGN ENEMIES

In the new Soviet view, the ends clearly justify the means concerning the Russian advance across Siberia. The progressive consequences for the native population far outweighed any difficulties that attended the annexation processes. Indeed, it could be said that the Russians saved the Siberian peoples from themselves, and from their old accustomed way of life. One of the strongest proofs of the progressive quality of these events is that it put a stop to the internecine fighting which prevented these peoples from having stable living conditions. A similar argument is given in the case of the more recent and forceful annexations in Central Asia and the Caucasus, the main difference being that in the latter instances there are always foreign enemies threatening them with all the evils of colonialism and imperialism. The enemies in these cases are far more palpable and formidable: whereas the Siberian peoples were saved from the ravages of their own internal feudal leaders for the most part, the peoples of Central Asia and the Caucasus were rescued from the clutches of the British, French, or American imperialists, or their Turkish or Persian henchmen.

63. *Vedushchaia rol' russkogo naroda v razvitii narodov Iakutii. Sbornik statei* (Iakutsk, 1955), p. 49.

Thus Russian expansion into these areas has a strong defensive quality. Russian armies moved to protect the Russian state and at the same time to save the local people from an incomparably worse threat from "outside." These operations are viewed as an extension of the selfless military aid offered by the Russians in medieval times, except that in these cases the reward for such aid was the incorporation of the territories located between the Russians and the foreign enemies into the Russian Empire.

"British imperialism" is the overwhelming villain in the history of modern Russian expansion. But the cast of supporting characters is large. The Germans have threatened the Baltic republics and Eastern Siberia. Poles, Hungarians, and Rumanians have threatened Moldavia. Turks and Persians, usually backed by the British, have sent peoples of the Caucasus and Central Asia to seek aid from Russia. The Khans of Khiva, Khorezm, and Bukhara, at the instigation of the British, threatened the peoples of Central Asia (who in many cases happened to be their subjects at the time), preventing them from gravitating toward Russia. "Feudal China" acted as a brake on the progress of the Kirgiz people.[64] The Japanese imperialists have threatened eastern Siberia and especially the Kurile Islands, which have had a predominantly Russian culture since 1632.[65] The United States is said to have had a supporting role behind the British threat to Central Asia as early as the 1850's,[66] and threatened Siberia more directly later in the century. According to the recent survey history of Tuva, that region in middle Asia was threatened by U.S. imperialism by 1900.[67] The historian V. Dulov described the threat in Eastern Siberia graphically:

> Foreign capitalists, taking advantage of the negligence and corruption of tsarist officials, plundered and robbed the wealth of Siberia. Their predatory intrigues in Chukotka, where, as a result of the criminal activity of foreign entrepreneurs and traders, the local indigenous nationalities died out, are well known. American business sent armed schooners to our Pacific coast for the contraband export of Siberian

64. Dzhamgerchinov, *Prisoedinenie Kirgizii*, p. 136.
65. L. N. Kudashev, "Iz istorii kuril'skikh ostrovov," *VI*, No. 8, 1963, pp. 42-58.
66. N. A. Khalfin, *Politika Rossii v Srednei Azii (1857-1868)* (Moscow, 1960), p. 54. Hubert Evans has done an abridged translation. See N. A. Khalfin, *Russia's Policy in Central Asia, 1857-1868* (London: Central Asian Research Centre, 1964).
67. *Istoriia Tuvy*, ed. Potapov, I, 275.

gold. The business activity of Morgan, Harriman, Guggenheim, Herbert Hoover and McCormick, who with such English capitalist ravagers as Leslie Urquhart, tried to suppress local industry, to seize the region's material resources and to make Siberia their colony, is well known.[68]

But among the foreign enemies, none come close to the British in their continuous provocations of the non-Russian peoples of the future Soviet family. In the current view they were constantly probing the perimeter of the Russian Empire, from the late eighteenth century to the present (they are charged with complicity in many anti-Soviet nationalist movements since World War II). Current accounts are full of British diplomatic intrigues, the activities of British agents, British military and economic aid for Russia's enemies, British backing of separatist movements, the attempts of British merchants to exploit the peoples of the border areas, and of course British intervention during the Civil War. The British have been charged with a great variety of black deeds, ranging from conspiring to have the Russian poet-diplomat Griboedov murdered in Persia in 1829 to a persistent effort to block the natural tendency of the non-Russian peoples to form friendlier ties with Russia.[69] "Hindering" the development of the friendship of peoples is a fairly common charge against the British.

Like the other parts of the friendship myth, the development of the British threat has had its own evolution, conforming closely to political needs and the status of British-Soviet relations at the time of writing. The development of this theme is a good example of how a question that has been either unknown or little discussed can suddenly blossom under party tutelage. In this case 1950 seems

68. *CDSP*, V, No. 14, pp. 8-9, translated from *Izvestiia*, April 9, 1953.

69. The Nechkina textbook stated that the Persian riot that resulted in the death of Griboedov broke out "with the active complicity of the British resident" (1954 ed., II, 160); in later editions, the Shah's forces are said to have organized the riot, "having found support from the British mission" (1965 ed., I, 708). Two recent Soviet studies on the diplomat are less direct, but still implicate the British (S. V. Shostakovich, *Diplomaticheskaia deiatel'nost A. S. Griboedova* [Moscow, 1960], pp. 235-36; O. I. Popova, *Griboedov-diplomat* [Moscow, 1964], pp. 185-87). Two western scholars who have studied the problem find no direct British complicity. David Lang believes that Griboedov's fatal error was his own lack of tact and "contemptuous disregard for the religious susceptibilities of a proud and independent nation" (D. M. Lang, "Griboedov's Last Years in Persia," *American Slavic and East European Review*, VII [1948], No. 4, 317-39). D. P. Costello concludes that the Persian government was solely responsible ("The Murder of Griboedov," *Oxford Slavonic Papers*, VIII [1958], 66-89).

to be the dividing line. N. A. Khalfin, the specialist on Central Asia who has probably written more on this question than any other scholar, demonstrates this in his impressive bibliographies. Almost every item is either from the pre-revolutionary period, or post-1950.[70]

It will be recalled that Pokrovskii and his "school" emphasized the Russian threat to the non-Russian peoples. These writers believed that the Russian armies followed the demands of expanding Russian capitalism in a typical search for new markets and raw materials, and that the British rivalry for the politically weak but economically rich borderlands was a logical counter-move. The critics of Pokrovskii considered this view erroneous, but still held that the Russian threat was real. In 1940 A. L. Popov charged that "Central Asia, as the object of an Anglo-Russian struggle, did not exist for Pokrovskii." Pokrovskii had been blind to the British threat in the Caucasus in the 1850's and in Central Asia in later decades. He had not noted the activities of British spies; he had overlooked British subsidies to the Shah; he had even suggested that British rule in India was superior to Russian rule in Central Asia.[71] This article was published during the period of the German-Soviet Non-Aggression Pact, when it was proper to condemn British imperialism; it probably could not have been published a year earlier or a year later, because of the rapid changes in Soviet-British relations at that time. But while condemning British imperialism, Popov held Russian imperialism equally culpable. He wrote two other articles on the conquest of Central Asia in the same year, in which he held that Central Asia was regarded by tsarist forces as a potential *place d'armes* for Russian thrusts into British-held territories. As far as the peoples of Central Asia were concerned, both Russia and Britain represented a threat to their freedom.[72]

Most of the authors and editors of the survey histories of the Union Republics published in the 1940's discussed the British threat, but continued to hold that there was a Russian threat as well. The 1943 history of the Kazakhs, which went to press at the apogee of

70. N. A. Khalfin, *Angliiskaia kolonial'naia politika na Srednem Vostoke* (Tashkent, 1957); *Politika Rossii* (cited above); and *Prisoedinenie Srednei Azii k Rossii (60-90e gody XIX v.)* (Moscow, 1965). Each volume has an extensive bibliography on the British threat.

71. A. L. Popov, "Vneshniaia politika samoderzhaviia v XIX veke v 'krivom zerkale' M. N. Pokrovskogo," in *Protiv antimarksistskoi kontseptsii M. N. Pokrovskogo. Sbornik statei* (Moscow, 1940), pp. 306-11.

72. A. L. Popov, "Bor'ba za sredneaziatskii platsdarm," *Istoricheskie zapiski,* VII (1940), 182-235; "Iz istorii zavoevaniia Srednei Azii," *ibid.,* IX (1940), 198-242.

Soviet-British cooperation, said nothing at all about the British threat to the Kazakhs in the nineteenth century, although it was as harsh as ever toward tsarist designs in the area. Gafurov was still within the tolerable limits of the party line in 1949 when he wrote in his *History of the Tadzhik People* that "the leading role of Britain in organizing the defeat of tsarism in the Crimean campaign forced tsarism to seek out new territory, from which it was possible to threaten the power of Britain in India. Such was the territory of Central Asia, which provided the possibility for the creation of a *place d'armes* for further expansion into India."[73] But the party line switched on this question early in 1950, most conspicuously in the pronouncements on the role of Shamil, which linked British designs in the Caucasus with the resistance movement there. Gafurov was specifically taken to task for this passage in the *Voprosy istorii* review of his book: "First of all, Britain attacked not tsarism, but Russia, although the Crimean defeat was not a defeat of Russia but of tsarism. The main thing is that Russian tsarism did not take as its special task the threatening of Britain in India. It wanted to capture Central Asia in order to get its cotton. By such means it tried to widen its markets, which were required especially by the rapid development after the 1861 reform of the Russian bourgeoisie."[74] In this case, Gafurov was not the only victim of bad timing. His reviewer, A. Iakubovskii, argued against him by presenting evidence which would become "inadmissible" by the time it got to print. Since early 1950, no Soviet historian would have the Russians moving into Central Asia for so base a motive as the seizure of its cotton.

One of the arguments that has been stressed in Soviet writing on this subject since 1950 is that the Russian threat to India ("the Russian Bogey") was imaginary.[75] Help has come from India, where K. S. Menon, in his book, *The Russian Bogey and British Aggression in India and Beyond,* has tried to prove that from the beginning the speculation of British officials about the Russian threat to India was motivated by a hope of getting larger funds from London.[76] Soviet striving on this question is unnecessary,

73. Gafurov, *Istoriia tadzhikskogo naroda* (1949), p. 400.

74. VI, No. 7, 1950, p. 164.

75. E. L. Shteinberg, "Angliiskaia versiia a 'russkoi ugroze' Indii v XIX-XX v.," *Istoricheskie zapiski*, XXXIII (1950), 47-66. See also Khalfin, *Politika Rossii*, pp. 13-18.

76. K. S. Menon, *The Russian Bogey and British Aggression in India and Beyond* (Calcutta: Eastern Trading Company, 1957), chap. ii.

since British scholars for the most part agree on this point. The Soviet purpose is to show that Russia was on the defensive in Central Asia. In the opinion of Geoffrey Wheeler, Soviet historians go too far, however, in assuming that all the British in India knew at the time that there was no Russian threat, that it was a mere pretext for a British military build-up. By asserting that the British were aggressive and the Russians were peace-loving, Soviet scholars have substituted an "English bogey" for the "Russian bogey."[77]

British threats and Russian counter-moves have become a standard feature of post-1950 historical writing on Central Asia in particular. The survey histories of the area, which barely mentioned it earlier, now devote considerable space to it.[78] Several special studies have been written on British "aggression," British "expansion," and British "colonial policy" in Central Asia.[79] The studies on the annexation of these areas contain chapters or substantial sections on the British threat.[80]

The resulting interpretation of the essentially defensive nature of Russian expansion into Central Asia has brought tsarist foreign policy back to a position of reasonableness. Prince Aleksandr Gorchakov, the Russian Foreign Minister during much of this period, has been largely rehabilitated: his stated views are remarkably in line with current interpretations. This "statesman of marked talent . . . one of the most important diplomats of the nineteenth century," has recently been the subject of two popular biographies.[81]

77. Geoffrey Wheeler, in a review of Khalfin's *Politika Rossii* in *Royal Central Asian Society Journal*, XLIX, Part 1 (January, 1962), p. 61.

78. *Istoriia tadzhikskogo naroda,* ed. Gafurov and Litvinskii, II, Part 2, 77-79; *Istoriia uzbekskoi SSR,* ed. M. G. Vakhabov, V. Ia. Nepomnin, and T. N. Kary-Niiazov (Tashkent, 1956), I, Part 2, 55-59; Karryev and Rosliakov, *Kratkii ocherk,* pp. 35-38; *Istoriia turkmenskoi SSR,* ed. A. Karryev, O. K. Kuliev, M. E. Masson, *et al.* (Ashkhabad, 1957), I, Part I, 123-27; *Istoriia kazakhskoi SSR,* ed. Auezov, Baishev, *et al.* I (1957), 352-55; *Istoriia Kirgizii,* ed. Viatkin, Griaznov, *et al.* I (1963), 329-31.

79. In addition to Khalfin's *Angliiskaia kolonial'naia politika,* these studies include his *Proval britanskoi agressii v Afganistane (XIX v.-nachalo XX v.)* (Moscow, 1959); F. Iuldashbaeva, *Iz istorii angliiskoi kolonial'noi politiki v Afganistane i Srednei Azii (70-80 gody XIX v.)* (Tashkent, 1963); A. Kh. Babakhodzhaev, *Proval angliiskoi politiki v Srednei Azii i na srednem vostoke (1918-1924)* (Moscow, 1962). There are numerous articles, listed in the Khalfin bibliographies.

80. E. B. Bekmakhanov, *Prisoedinenie Kazakhstana k Rossii* (Moscow, 1957), chap. iii; Dzhamgerchinov, *Prisoedinenie Kirgizii, passim.,* in chaps. iii and iv; M. N. Tikhomirov, *Prisoedinenie Merva* (Moscow, 1960), pp. 100-23.

81. Khalfin, *Politika Rossii,* p. 76; S. K. Bushuev, *A. M. Gorchakov* (Moscow, 1961); S. Semanov, *A. M. Gorchakov, russkii diplomat* (Moscow, 1962).

It is surely one of the crowning ironies of Soviet historiography that Gorchakov's famous circular of November, 1864, in which the diplomat sought to justify Russian expansion in Central Asia on the grounds that it created stable political conditions and was a civilizing mission—a statement that was once regarded as the epitome of hypocrisy—is now taken at face value. Gorchakov's references to Russia's desire "to put a stop to this state of permanent disorder" in Central Asia, and "to prepare a future of stability and prosperity for the occupied country, by gaining over the neighboring populations to civilized life," are perfectly acceptable to the Soviet historian. So is his observation that "very frequently of late years the civilization of these countries, which are her neighbors on the continent of Asia, has been assigned to Russia as her special mission." There is even a reference in the circular to the obvious differences between Russia's basically defensive colonization and "the undefined path of conquest and annexation which has given to England the empire of India. . . ." Only one element in the circular prevents its complete rehabilitation: Prince Gorchakov obviously knew nothing of the friendship of peoples. He spoke condescendingly of these "half-savage, nomad populations, possessing no fixed social organization . . . [whose] turbulent and unsettled character make most undesirable neighbors. . . . It is a peculiarity of Asiatics to respect nothing but visible and palpable force; the moral force of reason and the interests of civilization have as yet no hold upon them."[82] But the rationale of the friendship of peoples provides a ready answer to this anomaly. The Prince was obviously blinded by his own class outlook, and would not be able to observe accurately the relations between natives and Russians at the popular level.

Much of Soviet writing on Russian expansion into Central Asia is highly colored with emotional accounts of the aggression of the British. But even the more scholarly accounts, like those of Khalfin, based heavily on tsarist archives, fail to consider the question objectively. Khalfin's terminology will illustrate. Central Asia seems to have been full of British "agents" and "spies" engaging in "intrigue" and "espionage." The British are said to have sent in swarms of merchant-spies trained at a "special spy school" in India.[83] It is freely admitted that the Russians were unofficially penetrating

82. The text of the Gorchakov circular is in "An Indian Officer," *Russia's March Toward India* (London: Sampson Low, 1894), II, 302-8.

83. Khalfin, *Politika Rossii*, p. 54. The other expressions mentioned here occur in Khalfin's long discussion of the British threat, *ibid.*, chaps. i and ii.

the area to gain all the information possible, but there are no Russian agents or spies. Khalfin refers to "a political officer," "an Orenburg merchant," and groups of exploring scientists as those who provided valuable information. British diplomacy is full of "duplicity," "blackmail," and "intimidation." The Russian government was a model of restraint. By about 1860, however, "the methods of diplomacy proved incapable of improving Russia's position," and a decision was made "to push her frontiers into Central Asia as far as Tashkent." Thus, in answer to the British, who "unscrupulously waged colonial wars in the East" and "interfered in the affairs of the borderlands," the "tsar's troops began their advance over a wide front deep into Central Asia." Scrupulously avoiding all suggestions of blood and gunpowder, Khalfin fills out his narrative by noting that "the forward movement into Central Asia progressed" and that "preparations for the advance into Turkestan were completed in 1864."

CHAPTER **16.**

THE PROGRESSIVE
CONSEQUENCES OF ANNEXATION

"The annexation of Kabarda to the Russian state was of decisive significance in the historic destiny of the Kabardinian, Balkarian and other peoples. It provided these peoples with the possibility of further national development, saved them from enslavement and destruction by foreign attackers, and created favorable conditions for economic and cultural contacts with the Russians and other peoples of our country." From the Central Committee resolution on the four-hundredth anniversary of the annexation of Kabarda (Pravda, July 6, 1957).

"The voluntary entry of the Buriats into the Russian state under historically complex conditions was the only correct path. Forever tying their fate with Russia, the Buriat people established close ties with the great Russian people, acquiring from them their high material and spiritual culture, and a mutual struggle of the Russians and Buriats against their common enemy—tsarist autocracy, which led to establishing between them relations of fraternal friendship." From the Central Committee resolution on the three-hundredth anniversary of the annexation of the Buriats (Pravda, July 4, 1959).

The historian S. S. Dmitriev, writing in the 1940 edition of the standard college textbook on the history of the U.S.S.R., concluded his account of the Russian conquest of Central Asia with a flair: "The conquest of Central Asia was finished. Central Asia became a colony of the Russian Empire. The peoples of Central Asia came under the rule of tsarist Russia—the prison of peoples." That

358

was the end of the story. Soviet historians, from the viewpoint of 1940, regarded the colonial period as one of darkness and oppression for the Central Asian peoples. There would be several heroic attempts to regain freedom, but they would be brutally put down. Dawn would come with the Russian Revolution. When the same historian rewrote this section for the 1954 edition, this point in the history of Central Asia became a beginning. Not only was this gloomy passage eliminated but the wording of the chapter title was changed from "conquest" to "annexation" and a section on "the progressive consequences of the annexation of Central Asia to Russia" was added.[1]

The reader will have gathered from the earlier account of the growth of the friendship myth that much emphasis has been given to the progressive consequences of annexation. In this chapter an attempt will be made to outline the arguments given in support of the proposition and to examine a much-quoted Engels statement on the matter, as well as to give an account of an earlier Soviet debate on the question.

The progressiveness of all acquisitions of territory by the Russian Empire, and more recently by the U.S.S.R., became axiomatic in Soviet historical writing by about 1945. The Soviet historian who fails to give this proposition adequate affirmation in his writing will be taken to task by his reviewers. The survey histories, which seldom mentioned the subject before World War II, have more recently given lengthy and detailed treatment to the progressive consequences of annexation, in contrast to their shortened and generalized accounts of the methods of acquisition. In some of the monographs on the annexation of particular territories, more than half the space is devoted to progressive consequences. One of the ritualistic elements of public speeches by non-Russian leaders is a passage in which thanks is extended to the Russian elder brother for helpfulness given before the Revolution.

THE DEBATE ON PROGRESS IN THE
RUSSIAN COLONIES (1929-1934)

In earlier Soviet historical writing, before scholarship was so firmly harnessed to ideology, the progressiveness of the tsars'

1. *Istoriia SSSR*, ed. M. V. Nechkina (Moscow, 1940), II, 554; *ibid.*, 1954, pp. 548-60. For a survey of recent Soviet writing on this subject, see D. I. Gusev, "Literatura poslednikh let po istorii druzhby i bratskogo sotrudnichestva narodov SSSR," *VI*, No. 10, 1963, pp. 126-30.

annexations was an open question, with the great majority of historians taking the negative view. Pokrovskii scoffed at the idea, regarding anyone who saw progressive results of tsarist conquests as a Great Russian chauvinist. Most other historians either ignored the question or implied a negative answer by dwelling on the evils of tsarist colonialism. In 1929, the historian V. Karpych disagreed with the prevailing view that tsarist colonialism in Central Asia had been an unrelieved tragedy. He attacked this proposition (and specifically its presentation by Galuzo in *Turkestan, a Colony*) in an article titled "On the History of the Conquest of Turkestan by Russian Capitalism."[2] Karpych contended that the Russian role in breaking up the old stagnant feudal order and in stimulating trade in Central Asia had been progressive in the long run. He also disagreed with other historians who claimed that Russian "merchant capital" had not made any significant changes in the feudal structure before the Revolution. In his view the Russians had definitely put Central Asia on the path of capitalist development, and regardless of the hardships attending the process, it had to be regarded as progressive. He cited Marx's observation that the British had played a progressive role in India by breaking up the patriarchal order and isolation of the area. He hinted that Marx, who had made this evaluation on the British in India in 1853, might have reached the same conclusion about Russia in Central Asia if he had lived to see the rapid economic growth that came in the late 1880's and thereafter. He also quoted Lenin's view that colonial wars sometimes had the progressive effect of sharpening the class conflict and bringing the revolutionary pot to a boil more quickly. These Karpych arguments were very modest harbingers of later Soviet contentions.

Karpych's views were sharply challenged. The most thoroughgoing critique was given by E. Shteinberg, in his history of Turkmenia.[3] In view of the later Soviet interpretation, these arguments *against* the progressiveness of annexations, published in 1934, deserve detailed attention. Shteinberg's reply to Karpych was that he

2. V. Karpych, "K istorii zavoevaniia Turkestana rossisskim kapitalizmom," *Turkmenovedenie*, Nos. 10-11, 1929, pp. 43-52. Karpych was not the first to argue for a modest progressive result from annexation. He cited an article by L. Reztsov, in *Kommunisticheskaia mysl'*, No. 6, 1927 (not available to me). In a later discussion of the question, in G. Togzhanov, *Kazakskii kolonial'nyi aul* (Moscow, 1934), I, 60-62, the author also held that Russian annexation was progressive, but only in a limited economic sense.

3. E. Shteinberg, *Ocherki istorii Turkmenii* (Moscow-Leningrad, 1934), pp. 47-59.

had taken both Marx and Lenin out of context. Although Marx had noted that this one feature of British policy in India was progressive, he had disclosed at much greater length the reactionary nature of British colonialism in India as a whole. Moreover, the two cases were not comparable, because the colonial rulers were so different: "Marx, as well as Engels, always underlines the characteristics of Russian colonial expansion as a movement which was reactionary, Asiatic, and semi-medieval. . . . Therefore one cannot equate British policy in India, a policy which was carried out by a young capitalistic, manufacturing state, and Russian aggression in Central Asia, coming from a barbaric, half-Asiatic, feudal, gendarme empire."[4] In answer to Karpych's contention that Lenin had recognized a possible progressive effect of Russian expansion in Central Asia, Shteinberg presented other Lenin quotations that in his view proved that Russian colonialism was peculiarly oppressive, so much so that the colonial peoples were held at too low a level to mount a revolutionary movement. In *Socialism and War* Lenin had remarked that for Russia "the possibility of oppressing and exploiting other nations perpetuates economic stagnation, because the source of income is frequently not the development of productive forces, but the semi-feudal exploitation of non-Russians." Russian colonialism had even had the effect of stagnating the revolutionary movement in Russia itself. Lenin had argued that the expansion of Russian capitalism "in breadth" (into new territories) had helped to perpetuate the old semi-feudal institutions precisely because it "temporarily postponed" the solution of the contradictions in the system at home.[5]

For good measure, Shteinberg added some points of his own against the progress view: (1) the Russians did not solve Central Asia's primary problem, irrigation; (2) Russia did not take local customs into account, and actually suppressed local education; (3) Russian land policies benefited Russian settlers and the native aristocracy exclusively; and (4) the economic gains went to Russian and Armenian capitalists, who controlled the means of production. "In the light of Lenin's position," Shteinberg concluded, "the absurdity of declaring the progressiveness of Russia's conquest of Central Asia is clear." Only after the October Revolution did the transformation of Central Asia begin.[6]

4. *Ibid.*, pp. 47-48.
5. *Ibid.*, pp. 48-51.
6. *Ibid.*, pp. 52-59.

Shteinberg's view that the economic activity in the Russian colonies helped only the capitalists and Russian settlers was widely held at the time. Although Soviet historians generally acknowledged that great economic strides had been made in the Russian colonies, they contended that none of the fruits went to the native population. Indeed, many held that the native population was worse off on the eve of the Revolution than when the Russians came.[7] Another proposition that would be sharply reversed later was the question of Russia's civilizing role. No one who called himself a Bolshevik would have suggested such a thing before the middle 1930's. G. Togzhanov, who went along with the view that there had been modest economic progress in Central Asia before the Revolution, reserved his special scorn for this proposition: "Apologists for Russian imperialism, beginning with the Black Hundred monarchist generals and ending with Cadet-liberals, in their evaluation of the role of the imperialist policies of the Russian autocracy, always sought to emphasize the special 'civilizing role' of the latter in the Kazakh steppes."[8] As for his contemporaries, Togzhanov called the proponents of such a view "social-Fascists," and associated them with "Trotsky, Roy, and Company—the contemporary leaders of world counter-revolution." Apparently neither Karpych, nor any other historian who saw evidences of gains as a result of Russian expansion, claimed to have detected any growing alliance between the Russian settlers and the population of the colonies.

THE TRANSITION TO "PROGRESSIVE CONSEQUENCES"

The party's decrees and observations on historical writing of the middle 1930's did not bring forth any immediate recognition by Soviet historians of the progressive aspects of Russian expansion. Up to World War II the emphasis continued to rest on the brutal nature of tsarist conquests and Russian colonialism, and there seems to have been no attempt at that time to reconcile this theme with subsequent progress, though in the post-war years historians would find a formula for resolving this apparent contradiction. In an article on the Kirgiz (published in 1936) the *Great Soviet Encyclopedia* declared that "the colonizing policies of tsarist Russia led to the

7. S. D. Asfendiarov, *Istoriia Kazakhstana* (*s drevneishikh vremen*) (Alma-Ata, 1935), I, chaps. viii-x; N. Samurskii, *Dagestan* (Moscow, 1925), pp. 50-51; G. Safarov, *Kolonial'naia revoliutsiia: Opyt Turkestana* (Moscow, 1921), pp. 42-44.
8. Togzhanov, *Kazakhskii kolonial'nyi aul*, p. 62.

impoverishment and extinction of the Kirgiz population, whose number decreased by 7 to 10 percent in the decade from 1903-1913. The Kirgiz were driven into the valleys and mountains; in only five years (1902-1907) the number of cattle herded by the Kirgiz decreased by 27 percent."[9]

The "lesser evil" formula was originally applied in a very narrow sense to indicate that the lot of non-Russian peoples might have been even worse had they not been annexed. There was no mention of marked economic progress in the colonies in the textbook surveys appearing just before the War, and the thought of cultural or political progress under the tsars was still the exclusive property of bourgeois apologists for the tsars. The historical studies on the non-Russian peoples published in this period also continued in the view that tsarist colonial policy was so oppressive as to preclude the idea of concurrent progress.[10] Okladnikov's study on the Buriat-Mongols noted the beginnings of a common struggle among Russian settlers and the natives, but did not find any cultural progress deriving from it; indeed Okladnikov repeated the old view that the standard of living of the local population had suffered under the Russians.[11]

The idea of progress in the colonies seems to have emerged gradually in the latter part of World War II, when the new concept of the friendship of peoples was eclipsing the uglier aspects of tsarist ,conquest and colonialism. But its acceptance was by no means consistent. Abramzon denied that the Kirgiz had made progress under the tsars in his study of 1946, and even as late as 1949 and 1950 the Pankratova and Nechkina textbooks were criticized for repeating their old views on this question. The 1943 history of Kazakhstan had denied the existence of progress in the Kazakh colony, and one of the main purposes of Apollova's study on the

9. *BSE*, 1st ed., XXXII, col. 377.

10. V. G. Kartsov, *Ocherk istorii narodov severo-zapadnoi Sibiri* (Moscow, 1937), pp. 33-37; S. A. Tokarev, *Ocherki istorii iakutskogo naroda* (Moscow, 1940), pp. 51-64; F. A. Kudriavtsev, *Istoriia buriat-mongol'skogo naroda* (Moscow-Leningrad, 1940), pp. 53-60.

11. A. P. Okladnikov, *Ocherki iz istorii zapadnykh Buriat-Mongolov (XVII-XVIII v.)* (Leningrad, 1937), p. 387. Okladnikov continued in this negative view in his 1943 study on the Iakuts. He noted the development of a friendship of Russian and Iakut workers, but looked at the consequences of annexation almost entirely as exploitation by the "Russian landlords, merchants and capitalists." See his *Istoricheskii put' narodov Iakutii* (Iakutsk, 1943), pp. 80-82.

annexation of the Kazakhs (1948) was to give a corrective on this subject.[12]

The post-war transition to a new emphasis on progressive consequences of annexation was accomplished by fits and starts, with frequent resort to the party lash. Ironically, it was Bekmakhanov and Guseinov, the chief victims of the party's over-all program, who wrote earliest and in the most detail about progressive consequences, while many of their colleagues, who were successful in the long run, stumbled badly. Bekmakhanov had written a number of articles between 1946 and 1950 emphasizing the benefits enjoyed by the Kazakhs after annexation, and it was a major emphasis in his condemned book. It will be recalled that Guseinov had written his pamphlet on "Historic Cooperation" in 1946, which extolled Russia's help for the Azerbaidzhanis, and that emphasis on Russian cultural influences was the main factor in winning his short-lived Stalin Prize in 1950. On the other hand, such successful historians as Gafurov and Tolstov learned their lesson late. Gafurov's failure to note the progressive consequences of the annexation of the Tadzhiks, in his survey history of 1949, was severely criticized, and this section was thoroughly rewritten for the 1952 edition.[13] Tolstov, a principal editor of the history of the Uzbeks, incriminated himself early in 1950 by stating that though the annexation of Central Asia "had an objectively progressive role" for its peoples, "tsarist autocracy and Russian capitalism had no part [in it]. . . . On the contrary, they did everything in their power to minimize this role." Tolstov then quoted a Stalin passage that had gone out of style:

> Tsarism deliberately cultivated patriarchal feudal oppression on the frontiers, so as to keep the masses in slavery and ignorance. Tsarism deliberately settled the best localities on the frontiers with colonizing elements, in order to crowd the national masses into inferior places and to aggravate national discord. Tsarism curbed and sometimes suppressed the local school, theater and educational institutions to keep the masses in ignorance. Tsarism suppressed every sign of initiative among the best people of the local

12. N. G. Apollova, *Prisoedinenie Kazakhstana k Rossii v 30-kh godakh XVIII veka* (Alma-Ata, 1948), chaps. ii and iv. This theme was emphasized as a strong point of the study in Ustiugov's review in *VI*, No. 4, 1949, pp. 117-21.

13. "O nekotorykh voprosakh istorii narodov Srednei Azii," *VI*, No. 4, 1951, pp. 7-8.

population. Finally, tsarism stamped out all activity among the masses of the people on the frontiers.[14]

If it was easy to find quotations from the Marxist oracles to disprove the new contention that Russian influences had had a great immediate impact on the subject peoples, it was difficult to find usable quotations that would verify the point. This was a heavy handicap, in view of the Soviet penchant for grounding all arguments with citations from recognized authorities. Lacking this essential tool, the Soviet historian has resorted to using a few quotations out of context. By far the most familiar one is a carefully excised passage from a letter Engels wrote to Marx in 1851. Its utility lies in the obvious fact that Engels uses the magic terms "progressive" and "civilizing role" in characterizing Russian colonialism. But in order to use the quotation, the historian must substitute an ellipsis for a distinctly derogatory phrase that falls between these terms, and must badly distort the whole meaning of Engels' letter. The emasculated Engels quotation is employed typically in such a passage as this:

> The founders of scientific Communism already in the 1850's stressed the progressive significance of annexation to Russia. In a letter to Marx in 1851 Engels wrote of Russia as a country which was playing a progressive role in the East: "Russia, by comparison, really plays a progressive role in relation to the East. . . . Russian rule plays a civilizing role on the Black and Caspian Seas and Central Asia, for Bashkir and Tatar. . . ."[15]

In reality, Engels' letter was a polemic against Poland, in which he tried to persuade Marx of the utter worthlessness of the Poles in history. Compared to the Poles, he said, even the Russians were progressive. A longer excerpt of the letter will show its misuse in Soviet hands:

> The Poles have never done anything in history except to play at brave, rowdy stupidity. One cannot point to a single moment when Poland represented progress, even in relation to Russia, or did anything at all of historical importance. Russia, by comparison, really plays a progressive

14. S. P. Tolstov, "Velikaia pobeda leninsko-stalinskoi natsional'noi politiki (k dvadtsatipiatiletiiu natsional'nogo razmezhevaniia Srednei Azii)," *Sovetskaia etnografia*, No. 1, 1950, pp. 21-22.

15. B. Dzhamgerchinov, *Prisoedinenie Kirgizii k Rossii* (Moscow, 1959), p. 345.

role in relation to the East. For all its baseness and Slavic filthiness [*mit all ihrer Gemeinheit, all ihrem slawischen Schmutz*], Russian rule plays a progressive role on the Black and Caspian Seas, Central Asia, for Bashkir and Tatar, and Russia has absorbed far more civilizing and especially industrial elements than the Poles, whose whole nature is that of the idle cavalier.[16]

Soviet historians have also employed quotations from tsarist historians, taken out of context, to verify current interpretations on the friendship of peoples. For example, Tsibikov, in a work on the Buriat-Mongols, edited a passage out of the works of A. P. Shchapov, the eminent tsarist historian of Siberia, in such a way as to badly distort its original meaning. Tsibikov quoted Shchapov as saying that "Almost every Buriat came to have in the nearby villages and countryside a comrade or opposite number, and the Russians did exactly the same thing on their side, securing comrades or partners in the *ulus*. This cooperative practice has continued to the present."[17] According to Tsibikov, "Such was the picture of the relations of Russian workers and the Buriats, as given by A. Shchapov, who knew well the life of Eastern Siberia." Shchapov's passage immediately preceding this one presents a different picture:

> At first the Buriats were afraid of the Russians, especially the Cossacks, and looked on them as some sort of terrible monster. "Mangud irebe—the terrible monster has come." Thus they cried with horror as they saw the Russians for the first time. But after a few decades, the Buriats, because of more and more frequent clashes with the Russians, gradually began to look on the Russians as people like themselves, and began little by little to associate with them, and finally, even to establish a mutual friendship. Almost every Buriat . . . [etc.].[18]

In recounting the progress brought by the Russians to the colonies, Soviet scholars sometimes stretch their data to the breaking point. They can take some of the same figures that were used earlier to show the lack of progress, and use them to support the opposite viewpoint. The most recent history of Kirgizia devotes seven pages (and an illustration) to the Russian-native schools.

16. Karl Marx and Friedrich Engels, *Werke* (Berlin, 1963), XXVII, 267.
17. B. Tsibikov, *K voprosy o dobrovol'nam prisoedinenii Buriat-Mongolii k Rossii* (Ulan-Ude, 1950), p. 53.
18. A. P. Shchapov, *Sobranie sochinenii. Dopolnitel'nyi tom k izdaniiu 1905-1908 gg.* (Irkutsk, 1937), pp. 254-55.

In spite of their scarcity (there were sixteen in 1917), in spite of the fact that they were attended almost entirely by Russian children, and were tools for Russification, their existence is termed "a great progressive step in the cultural life of the Kirgiz people."[19] The history of the Kazakhs attributes a cultural revival in the area to a small number of Russian schools, and the efforts of a handful of Russian scholars; it credits the direction of the nascent Kazakh proletariat to a few Russian revolutionists. Dzhamgerchinov names over the pitifully small number of medical stations in colonial Kirgizia. There were three each in two of the *uezdy,* which were larger than Belgium. The author states that the number of doctors was inadequate, but that they were effective in preventing the spread of epidemics.[20] Elsewhere, Dzhamgerchinov discusses the great significance of the building of railroads in Central Asia, and then states that there were no railroads in Kirgizia, the subject of his study. Presumably the Kirgiz benefited from being nearer to the railroads than they had formerly been. Dzhamgerchinov says that at the beginning of the twentieth century the major cities—he names four—had telegraphic connections, and that "there was already some electrification" in one oblast.[21]

By no means all of the recent Soviet works go to such lengths to affirm the progress theme, and some make very modest claims. The question of how much progress came to the tsars' colonial subjects is one of the main unsettled issues in this area of Soviet historiography. It will be recalled that there was a difference of opinion in the papers read at the Tashkent conferences of 1954 and 1959, and the Piaskovskii interpretation sought to separate tsarist colonialism and progress, which was attributed to the Russian people. Some recent historical works have returned to detailed accounts of tsarist oppression. They do not reject progress, however; instead, they indicate that it came through the influence of the Russian people in spite of tsarist policies. Such arguments inevitably begin with the term *nesmotria* (in spite of), which has been reduced to a formula no less set than the extinct "lesser evil" formula. Some works contain dozens of "in spite ofs," coming after accounts of tsarist policies and before contrasting accomplishments through the influence of the Russian people. Among the longer surveys,

19. *Istoriia Kirgizii,* ed. M. P. Viatkin, M. P. Griaznov, *et al.* (Frunze, 1963), I, 492-98.
20. Dzhamgerchinov, *Prisoedinenie Kirgizii,* p. 374.
21. *Ibid.,* pp. 369-70.

368   THE GREAT FRIENDSHIP

the second volume of the history of Iakutia is perhaps the most
cautious on the progress theme and is one of the most explicit on
tsarist colonial policies. The authors frequently remind their readers that progress was modest, and that it was accomplished against
the tsarist brake. In some cases, their statements recall the earlier
version, when all progress came in the Soviet period: "Only the October Revolution in fact put science at the service of the national
economy and the culture of the country."[22] A particularly strong
indictment of tsarist colonialism appeared in a popular book on the
peoples of the Soviet North, written by an Evenk, V. Uvachan.
His bill of particulars against tsarist colonialism is reminiscent of
the "Pokrovskii school." In his view, the tribute was definitely
exorbitant, and was collected by village elders who took hostages to
force its payment. After greedy traders brought about "the rap-
acious extermination of all fur-bearing animals . . . the economic
situation of the native inhabitants grew rapidly worse, due to
uniform trade practices that could be better described as outright
robbery." Evenks were swindled by traders, who sold them liquor
on credit. The Orthodox faith was forced on the Northern peoples.
There was only one hospital in the region, and there were frequent
epidemics of smallpox, tuberculosis, and measles. There was not
a single native language school before the Revolution, and as late
as 1926 the literacy rate was 2 per cent.[23] Nevertheless, Uvachan
manages to view all these evils as class oppression, and considers the
annexation of the area progressive because of the resulting alliance
with the ordinary Russian people who came to the area.

PEOPLE TO PEOPLE

The special vehicle of progress in the Russian colonies was
the people, "the makers of history." In propounding this view, the
Soviet historian draws on the old concept of "dual Russia," which
he views through the prism of the Marxist class struggle. He sees
a cultural flow from the center to the colonies, transmitted by the
popular masses, as well as certain designated groups whom he re-
gards as the vanguards of the Russian people. If progress comes
from the people, it is also true that reaction and oppression come
from the people's class enemy, the tsars, his *chinovniki*, local feudal
lords, and foreign enemies. The formula is made highly flexible by

22. *Istoriia iakutskoi ASSR*, ed. S. A. Tokarev, Z. V. Gogolev, and I. S.
Gurvich (Moscow, 1957), II, 364.
23. V. Uvachan, *Peoples of the Soviet North* (Moscow, 1960), pp. 21-32.

studied vagueness: an aristocrat can be regarded as a representative of the people if his actions are considered progressive. In some cases tsarist generals and Orthodox priests are ambassadors of the Russian people. At the same time, reactionary roles are kept indistinct by the use of such terms as "tsarist colonizers," "the ruling circles," and "imperialists." In many cases when the Russian government, the army, or the aristocracy were involved in progressive acts, the accomplishment is nevertheless attributed to the people. "It was not the tsarist government, but the Russian people . . . who brought progress and civilization. . . ." Having so stated, a Kirgiz scholar goes on to mention the building of railroads and schools, without mentioning the government, and the elimination of internecine fighting without crediting the army.[24] Another account notes that in Central Asia "Russian scholars organized for the people libraries, museums, scientific societies, schools, hospitals and polyclinics, and popularized the achievements of Russian science and culture."[25] If the reader is to know that the government had a hand in any of these activities, he might deduce it from Soviet practice; he will not find it in this account. After enumerating a number of scientific expeditions and describing their progressive results for his country, an Uzbek scholar feels obliged to state that "their expeditions were mostly subsidized not by the tsarist government, but by the Geographical Society, the Society of Friends of Natural Science, Anthropology and Ethnology, and other scientific societies."[26] He also notes that "the progressive Russians of the time" tried to form a university in Turkestan after 1905. The Tashkent Duma was compelled by "progressive public opinion" to recommend the founding of a university, but the tsarist authorities said that it would be "untimely." So the university was established only under Soviet rule.[27]

In order to make this view of progress credible, the historian must scrupulously protect the proposition that a class alliance of the masses, Russian and non-Russian, was formed upon first contacts and that it was frictionless. Whereas the early Soviet history viewed clashes in the colonies along nationality lines, the new his-

24. B. D. Dzhamgerchinov, *Vazhnoi etap iz istorii kirgizskogo naroda* (*k stoletiiu prisoedineniia Kirgizii k Rossii*) (Frunze, 1957), pp. 79-92.

25. Sh. Rashidov, "Naveki vmeste s russkim narodom," *Kommunist*, No. 10, 1959, pp. 39-52. Quotation on page 41.

26. T. N. Kary-Niiazov, *Socialist Culture of the Uzbek People* (Moscow, 1958), p. 5.

27. *Ibid.*, pp. 7-8.

tory sees it exclusively on class lines. This has involved a great deal of reinterpretation and "forgetting" of facts that were recorded earlier. The revolts in which the natives killed all the Russians in sight, regardless of their class, are now eliminated except in a few cases in which there was reactionary leadership. Observations about the low cultural level and boisterous behavior of Russians living in the colonies have been repudiated or forgotten.

It has also been necessary to ignore a number of common-sense considerations posing barriers to the budding friendship of peoples in the colonies. The new history assumes that Russians and non-Russians had no language barriers, religious prejudices, or the usual suspicion of foreigners. It was well known, as late as the 1947 survey history of the Uzbeks, that Central Asian cities were divided into "Russian" and "Asiatic" sections, and that there was little communication between them. Russian culture and science developed in Central Asia, but for the benefit of the Russian population.[28] A "wall of demarcation," which a Turkmen historian wrote about in 1946, was repudiated by *Voprosy istorii* in 1951.[29]

Aside from the usual barriers, one might ask how much of the Russian cultural heritage could be conveyed by those who went to the colonies, since a great majority of them were illiterate. Nevertheless, the people are credited with botanical and zoological studies, mining and metallurgical techniques, and geographical discoveries.[30] Obviously such technical advances could not be credited to ordinary people, but they are usually not specifically credited to the upper classes or intelligentsia either.

Of all the special groups within the charmed circle labeled "the Russian people," none has been more publicized or idealized than the peasant settler. To some extent his heroism is to be explained by the peculiar features of the Russian Empire. Larger numbers of Russians emigrated to the colonies than in other empires, and they were from the lower classes. Soviet historians have frequently contrasted this feature of Russian colonization with the British situation, in which a handful of civil servants and military personnel regarded themselves superior to the natives. It is also true that the Russian settlers carried with them agricultural and

28. *Istoriia narodov Uzbekistana*, ed. S. V. Bakrushin, V. Ia. Nepomnin, and V. A. Shishkin (Tashkent, 1947), II, 12-13.
29. *VI*, No. 4, 1951, p. 10.
30. *Narody Sibiri*, ed. M. G. Levin and L. P. Potapov (Moscow-Leningrad, 1956), pp. 129-34.

handicraft skills which were usually higher than those of the indigenous population, and that the concept of racial superiority was largely absent. Then, too, both Russian settlers and natives were subjected to grinding exploitation, which might be expected to engender some cooperation.

But none of these factors enabled the early Soviet historian to detect the friendship of peoples. He saw the role of the Russian settler to be largely passive. Only in the period after World War II did the call go out for more research on the role of the settler. It has been answered in a number of studies, which cast the lowly Russian peasant in the colony as hero and teacher.[31]

Another line of cultural transmission was through the foreign colonies of peoples of the future Soviet family in major Russian cities. These people assimilated Russian culture and facilitated its transmission by their contacts with their homeland. It is emphasized that people from the areas that would later become part of the Russian state emigrated to Russia for protection and opportunity.[32]

The Decembrists have always been popular with Soviet scholars. Since World War II, however, there has been a virtual explosion of writing about them. Their role in putting together a revolutionary alliance of Russian and non-Russian peoples is undoubtedly one of the factors involved in their new prominence. The newer works emphasize not only their political views, but give an important place to a theme almost forgotten in earlier work: their role as teachers, writers, and engineers among the non-Russian peoples. Popular biographies of even the most obscure Decembrists have

31. These include the two works of V. I. Shunkov, *Ocherki po istorii kolonizatsii Sibiri v XVII-nachale XVIII veka* (Moscow, 1946), and *Ocherki po istorii zemledeliia Sibiri XVII vek* (Moscow, 1956); V. N. Sherstoboev, *Ilimskaia pashnia* (Irkutsk, 1949) Vol. I; two works of F. G. Safronov, *Krest'ianskaia kolonizatsiia basseinov Leny i Ilima v XVII veke* (Iakutsk, 1956) and *Russkie krest'iane v Iakutii (XVII-nachale XX v.)* (Iakutsk, 1961); V. N. Skalon, *Russkie zemleprokhodtsy XVII veka v Sibiri* (Moscow, 1951); M. S. Alferov, *Kres'tianstvo Sibiri v 1917 godu* (Novosibirsk, 1958); E. P. Busygin and N. V. Zorin, *Russkie naselenie chuvashskoi ASSR. Material'naia kul'tura* (Cheboksary, 1960); A. N. Kopylov, *Russkie na Enisee v XVII v. Zemledelie, promyshlennost' i torgovye sviazi eniseiskogo uezda* (Novosibirsk, 1965).

32. L. S. Abetsedarskii, *Belorusy v Moskve XVII v.* (Minsk, 1957); V. L. Tatishvili, *Gruziny v Moskve (istoricheskii ocherk, 1653-1722)* (Tbilisi, 1959); P. T. Arutiunian, *Osvoboditel'noe dvizhenie armianskogo naroda v pervoi chetverti XVIII veka* (Moscow, 1954), pp. 185-87. About one-third of the volume of documents, *Russko-Belorusskie sviazi*, ed. L. S. Abetsedarskii and M. Ia. Volkov (Minsk, 1963), deals with activities of Belorussians who fled to Russia.

appeared; papers about their activities are read at regional history meetings; volumes of their papers have been published. They are accorded considerable space in the histories of the Union and Autonomous Republics, in the areas of the Caucasus and Siberia where they were scattered in exile. A *History of Moldavia* devotes five pages of discussion to the Decembrists in a section entitled "Russian progressive social thought and its significance for the development of the culture of Moldavia."[33] Their main influence on Moldavia appears to be that some of them were stationed there before the revolt. Greater significance is claimed for those areas where the Decembrists were in exile. They are said to have had a great influence on the literary life of Georgia and Armenia,[34] for example, and the fourteen who were sent to Iakutia helped to develop and popularize that almost unknown region.[35]

Russian political exiles, who in general are held in high esteem in the new Soviet history, constitute an important link between the Russian center and the more distant colonies. The political exile has a certain inherent heroism in the Soviet view, since he has found himself among the non-Russian peoples because of political ideas that are considered advanced and progressive. He is therefore an ideal vanguard of "democratic Russia." Even the religious exiles are said to have had a progressive influence on the non-Russian peoples, although their ideas are regarded as reactionary. Putting aside their religious ideas, current writers point out that the exiled religious sects "objectively played a progressive role" in the development of agriculture.[36]

It goes without saying that the Bolshevik exiles play the leading role in transmitting progressive Russian culture to the colonies on the eve of the Revolution. The local histories feature their portraits and give details of their political and cultural activities among non-Russian peoples at great length. One gets the impression that during World War I Emel'ian Iaroslavskii and Sergo Ordzhonikidze were more important to the life of the Iakuts than any officials or

33. *Istoriia Moldavii*, ed. A. D. Udal'tsov and L. V. Cherepnin (Kishinev, 1951), I, 420-25.

34. G. V. Khachapuridze, *K istorii Gruzii pervoi poloviny XIX veka* (Tbilisi, 1950), pp. 240-52. A. A. Olonetskii, *Iz istorii velikoi druzhby (Ocherki iz istorii gruzino-russkikh vzaimootnoshenii v pervoi polovine XIX stoletiia)* (Tbilisi, 1954), pp. 5-58; *Iz istorii russko-armianskikh otnoshenii*, ed. M. Nersisian (Erevan, 1956), I, 179-220, and (Erevan, 1961), II, 39-332.

35. *Istoriia iakutskoi ASSR*, ed. Tokarev, Gogolev, and Gurvich, II, 231-34.

36. *Vedushchaia rol' russkogo narod v razvitii narodov Iakutii. Sbornik statei* (Iakutsk, 1955), p. 72.

cultural figures, Russian or native.[37] The myth of Bolshevik leadership has been established in disregard for earlier well-known facts about their scarcity in the colonies, the weakness of their movement, and their political mistakes. Georgii Safarov, a Bolshevik leader sent to Central Asia, wrote that "before the revolution of 1917 there was no revolutionary ideology tied with conditions in Turkestan, not even any ties linking to the weak ranks of the revolutionary movement in the Russian population; there was no revolutionary organization of the masses, no revolutionary tradition—nothing. Between the heavily oppressed nation and the alien Russian population there was an impenetrable wall of mutual misunderstanding because of national inequality."[38] The February Revolution, remarked Safarov, "arrived by telegraph." Stalin's speeches while he was Commissar for Nationalities contain many references to the acute shortage of Bolshevik leadership in the colonies, the errors of tactics, and the distrust of the non-Russian inhabitants.[39] Nevertheless, the recent local histories paint a glowing picture of a solid alliance between the Russian proletariat in the colonies and the growing native working class, under the leadership of the Bolsheviks. The Russian Revolution has become the heritage of the whole Soviet family. It is considered a widespread multi-national class revolt, but with its Russian leadership carefully preserved.

One indication of the weakness of the Soviet historian's case for the solid revolutionary front of the Russian and non-Russian proletariat is the shortage of non-Russian Bolshevik leaders. To date only one pre-1917 Central Asian native has reached the first rank in Soviet historiography. He is Amangel'dy Imanov, a Kazakh leader of the 1916 revolt in Central Asia. Although Amangel'dy did not join the party until after the Revolution, he has, for all purposes, been admitted to the pantheon of Bolshevik heroes. His spectacular rise from near oblivion to a position resembling the father of his country is a by-product of the friendship of peoples. There was no entry for his name in the first edition of the *Great Soviet En-*

37. *Istoriia iakutskoi ASSR*, ed. Tokarev, Gogolev, and Gurvich, II, 398-416.
38. Safarov, *Kolonial'naia revoliutsiia*, p. 54.
39. I. V. Stalin, *Sochineniia* (Moscow, 1946-), IV, 280, 360; V, 333. The paucity of Bolshevik leadership in pre-revolutionary Kazakhstan is revealed between the lines in a recent study by a Kazakh historian, who bases his case largely on the journal *Aikap*, whose editor was not Bolshevik, but was influenced by Bolsheviks. See K. Beisembiev, *Progressivno-demokraticheskaia i marksistskaia mysl' v Kazakhstane nachala XX veka* (Alma-Ata, 1965), p. 11.

cyclopedia, and he was not mentioned in Asfendiarov's history of the Kazakhs. But he was discovered as a Kazakh military hero during World War II and his work was praised in the 1943 history (for six pages, as against twenty-four for Kenesary). In the 1957 history his role as the main Kazakh leader of the revolutionary period is established; his activities during the whole period are described, and his place in Kazakh history is punctuated by a full-page color portrait.[40] His imposing monument, rivaling that of Lenin, stands in a main square of Alma-Ata. Amangel'dy is apparently the Bolshevik antidote for Kenesary.

PROGRESSIVE CONSEQUENCES: POLITICAL

The arguments that have been given in support of the progressive nature of all Russian annexations of territory are so numerous that they defy brief description. At a minimum, the recent histories of each non-Russian people mention benefits for the tsar's subjects in their political, economic, and cultural life. Attention will be given here to the most frequently stated reasons in the political and economic areas; the cultural arguments are so numerous and complex as to require a separate chapter.

Perhaps the most basic political benefit said to have been bestowed by the Russians was the right to continue living as a united people. Many of the non-Russian peoples were, according to these accounts, marked for physical extinction had they not been annexed to Russia. The Khakassian and Altai peoples of Siberia are in this category,[41] as are several peoples of the Caucasus. It has even been argued that a people as numerous as the Armenians might have been exterminated by the Turks. In other cases the Russians provided conditions under which a nomadic people could settle in one place (some tribes of the Kazakhs, Kirgiz, Karakalpaks, and Turkmens).[42] Many of the peoples of the Caucasus, Central Asia, and Siberia were saved from their own internecine fighting; in the preferred terminology of the class struggle, the common people were

40. *Istoriia kazakhskoi SSR,* ed. M. Abdykalykov and A. Pankratova (Alma-Ata, 1943), pp. 384-90; *ibid.,* ed. M. O. Auezov, S. B. Baishev, *et al.* (1957), I, 584-95. There is a popular biography of Amangel'dy: A. Nurkanov, *Amangel'dy Imanov* (Alma-Ata, 1959).

41. *Dvestipiat'desiat let vmeste s velikim russkim narodom* (Abakan, 1959), p. 37; L. P. Potapov, *Ocherki po istorii Altaitsev* (Moscow, 1953), p. 373.

42. *Istoriia kazakhskoi SSR,* ed. Auezov, Baishev, *et al.* (1957), I, 244-45; *Istoriia Kirgizii,* ed. Viatkin, Griaznov, *et al.* (1963), I, 333.

rescued from the exploitation of their feudal lords. Still others were relieved from an enervating anarchy. The notable case is Georgia, where internal political chaos at the end of the eighteenth century invited Turkish and Persian attacks.[43] In all cases, Russian annexation provided more stable political conditions that were basic to a better life.

Once they were brought into the Russian Empire, the non-Russian peoples enjoyed continued military assistance against their internal and external enemies: "The inclusion of the Altais in the Russian state not only saved them from extinction in the period of the heart-breaking internecine attacks from Dzhungaria, but provided a decided influence on their whole future destiny. Under the protection of the Russian state the Altais in the course of their history were defended against various eastern aggressors and lived under peaceful conditions."[44] Such examples are legion. The Russian construction of fortresses in the Caucasus after the annexation of the area is now regarded exclusively as evidence of a long-range commitment to protect these peoples from the Turk and Persian.[45] It has already been noted that the Siberian ostrog has become, in the new view, a place of refuge for the inhabitants of the area when they were threatened. The Kazakh historian, S. E. Tolybekov, has stated that the Russian construction of fortified lines on the Kazakh borders had a protective and stabilizing effect. Arguing against Viatkin's old view of 1941 that the purpose of this long process was the systematic conquest of the Kazakh lands, Tolybekov contended that the fortified lines brought better conditions and were welcomed by the Kazakh people themselves:

> The ravaged and starving Kazakhs constantly approached the Russian fortified lines, seeking to subject themselves to Russia. This gave the Kazakhs the possibility of engaging in fishing and agriculture. . . .
> The construction in the eighteenth and nineteenth centuries of military outposts on the borders of, and further, into the depths of the Kazakh steppes, was a completely reasonable and progressive measure of the Russian government by which the military-semi-feudal and tribal-nomadic life of the Kazakh people was gradually put on the

43. Khachapuridze, *K istorii Gruzii,* pp. 49-55.
44. Potapov, *Ocherki po istorii Altaitsev,* p. 372.
45. S. K. Bushuev, *Iz istorii russko-kabardinskikh otnoshenii* (Nal'chik, 1956), pp. 112-14.

path to agriculture and the introduction of the Russian system of government.[46]

The role of the Russian generals who became administrators in the colonies has been softened, and there have been scattered attempts to rehabilitate some of them. The general histories of the U.S.S.R. have, in successive editions, turned their emphasis from their brutalities to their constructive work in pacification and defense. One of the most determined efforts in behalf of the tsarist generals was made by Bushuev. In his study on Russian-Kabardinian relations, he credited General Ermolov with the defense of the area, especially the strengthening of fortifications, and indicated that he received considerable support from the inhabitants, who "took a more and more active part in the struggle with Turkish agents, who had penetrated into their lands." Bushuev considered Ermolov's proclamation of 1822 on civil courts to be a significant development (one indication of its progressiveness is the fact that it was strongly opposed by the local Muslim leadership). He also discussed the nine points of General Paskevich's governmental reform as a progressive step.[47] In another surprising case, General Cherniaev, the tsar's sensational commander in Central Asia, has found a friend in Dzhamgerchinov, who gives a glowing account of the general as defender of the Kirgiz against the Kokand khanate in the middle 1860's. Dzhamgerchinov quotes the general's patriotic order of the day at the beginning of the campaign, and indicates that he had popular support. By contrast, the latest survey history of Kirgizia barely mentions Cherniaev, and Khalfin pictures him as a brash officer who made many errors of judgment.[48] All in all, the rehabilitation of the generals has been modest.

In the stable conditions resulting from annexation, many of the non-Russian peoples are said to have formed into modern nations. The early Soviet view emphasized that tsarist policy was aimed at dispersing nationalities to break up national unity; the new view not only holds that tsarist colonial government nurtured national unity by creating stable conditions, but in some cases it is said to have fostered unity in drawing administrative boundaries.

46. S. E. Tolybekov, "O reaktsionnoi bor'be kazakhskikh sultanov i batyrov mladshego zhuza protiv dobrovol'nogo prisoedineniia k Rossii," *VAN kazakhskoi SSR*, No. 6, 1955, pp. 43-59.

47. Bushuev, *Iz istorii russko-kabardinskikh otnoshenii*, pp. 112-17.

48. Dzhamgerchinov, *Prisoedinenie Kirgizii*, pp. 277-312; *Istoriia Kirgizii*, ed. Viatkin, Griaznov, *et al.* (1963), I, 348; N. A. Khalfin, *Politika Rossii v Srednei Azii (1857-1868)* (Moscow, 1960), pp. 197-217.

As late as the beginning of 1950, Tolstov stated that "the administrative organization of the Russian possessions in Central Asia was not in the least set up to contribute to national consolidation. On the contrary the dispersion and demarcation of the different nationalities became even more pronounced." Tolstov illustrated his point with concrete examples of the scattering of segments of the Uzbeks, Tadzhiks, Turkmens, Kirgiz, and Karakalpaks among other peoples.[49] But the newer survey histories of the Central Asian republics see it differently. In the history of the Uzbeks the tsars' administrators delimit boundaries according to good Soviet practice: "The oblasts were drawn in such a way that one nationality or another had a collective predominance, giving the oblast a definite national character."[50] Whereas the 1943 version of Kazakh history stated that "all the Kazakh lands were intentionally divided between various administrative divisions for the purpose of breaking up the unity of the Kazakh people, in order to subdue them more easily," the 1957 version views the divisions as a design to reduce the power of the reactionary Kazakh feudal leaders.[51]

The tsars' administrative, legal, court, and land reforms are discussed in detail and in many cases accepted at near face value. There is a standard formula by which the historians explain how the administration performed progressive acts in spite of itself. It points out that the primary aim was to strengthen tsarist colonialism, but that "objectively" it proved to be a progressive event for the inhabitants by improving their lives in a variety of ways.[52] In the early Soviet view, tsarist colonial policies were formulated in complete disregard for the local culture, but the new history of Kirgizia declares that "in order to create a new system of administration, the tsarist government thoroughly studied the customs, traditions, economy and current system of administration of the Kazakhs and Kirgiz."[53] Some Russian reforms are accepted as entirely progressive and a part of Russia's civilizing mission. These include the elimination of the slave trade in some areas and the prohibition of local

49. Tolstov, "Velikaia pobeda," pp. 20-21.

50. *Istoriia uzbekskoi SSR*, ed. M. G. Vakhabov, V. Ia. Nepomnin, and T. N. Kary-Niiazov (Tashkent, 1956), I, Part 2, 101.

51. *Istoriia kazakhskoi SSR*, ed. Abdykalykov and Pankratova (1943), p. 269; *ibid.*, ed. Auezov, Baishev, *et al.*, I (1957), 387.

52. *Ibid.* (1957), I; chap. xvii; *Istoriia Kirgizii*, ed. Viatkin, Griaznov, *et al.* (1963), I, 404-26; T. Kh. Kumykov, *Prisoedinenie Kabardy k Rossii i ego progressivnye posledstviia* (Nal'chik, 1957), pp. 84-88.

53. *Istoriia Kirgizii*, ed. Viatkin, Griaznov, *et al.* (1963), I, 404.

customs on feuding, the seclusion of women, and the bride price.[54] There can be no argument that such moves were progressive; what is unusual is that the recent studies should give credit to those who had recently been denounced as "tsarist colonizers" in earlier Soviet histories. Even in those cases when tsarist reforms are considered to be completely reactionary or a hoax, as in the Stolypin period (1906-11), they are not without progressive results, since they tended to drive the oppressed inhabitants and the Russian people living in the colony into a closer alliance, which sharpened the class struggle and hurried revolutionary activity.[55]

The most nebulous of the political benefits for the non-Russian peoples was a matter of political destiny, over which their colonial masters had no control. The new histories universally note that through annexation these peoples were put on the road to the Revolution and the socialist state. Since membership in the Soviet family is considered the best of all possible political situations, this is the crowning event in the long list of progressive consequences.

PROGRESSIVE CONSEQUENCES: ECONOMIC

Many of the newer works on the history of the non-Russian peoples in the tsarist period are as replete with graphs and charts on economic growth as are those volumes dealing with the Soviet period. While it is recognized that much of the profits from such economic growth were never enjoyed by the people of the tsarist colony, the long-range economic benefits for the people are recounted at length. In the earlier Bolshevik view, the expeditions of Russian scientists and engineers who went to the colonies to survey and develop their natural resources were instruments of tsarist exploitation; in the new view the same expeditions are hailed as pioneer efforts to unlock the riches of the area and improve the standard of living for all.[56]

54. *Istoriia kazakhskoi SSR,* ed. Auezov, Baishev, *et al.* (1957), I, 244; Dzhamgerchinov, *Prisoedinenie Kirgizii,* p. 351; N. A. Khalfin, *Prisoedinenie Srednei Azii k Rossii* (Moscow, 1965), p. 427; Potapov, *Ocherki po istorii Altaitsev,* p. 373.

55. Ts. P. Agaian, *Krest'ianskaia reforma v Azerbaidzhana v 1870 gody* (Baku, 1956), pp. 359-68; *Istoriia kazakhskoi SSR,* ed. Auezov, Baishev, *et al.* (1957), I, 516-24; *Istoriia Kirgizii,* ed. Viatkin, Griaznov, *et al.* (1963), I, 447-57.

56. N. A. Gvozdetskii, V. N. Fedchina, A. A. Azam'ian, and Z. N. Dontsova, *Russkie geograficheskie issledovaniia Kavkaza i Srednei Azii v XIX-nachale XX v.* (Moscow, 1964). This book contains information on more than a hundred Russian geographers, explorers, and engineers, and their work in the

The progressive economic consequences for the non-Russian peoples are different for those who were in various stages of development, but they are universal. In the case of the more primitive peoples, the Russians are credited with removing them from complete economic isolation and stagnation, and with promoting simple trade. The Russian settlers brought new ideas about handicrafts, and in some cases introduced agriculture and a settled life for the first time.[57] The coming of the Russians brought an economic leap for many peoples of Siberia, who skipped the feudal stage, experienced an abbreviated capitalist stage, and emerged to socialism thanks to the October Revolution. Thus many members of the Soviet family are said to have escaped the full weight of capitalist exploitation. The specific advantages brought by the Russians are many, and need only be summarized here. The Russian settler brought farming implements, cultivated crops hitherto unknown, and introduced better agricultural methods. He introduced fishing and the breeding of domestic animals, and taught handicrafts. He opened up simple trade, and was influential in eliminating stifling tribal or feudal dues. He taught the native how to build Russian-style houses and how to wear Russian-style clothes.

The most bothersome problem about this interpretation is the basic question of land possession. There is general agreement among Soviet historians, early and recent, that there was widespread land seizure, but there is a great difference of opinion concerning responsibility for it and its results. Early Soviet historians drew no fine distinctions between "tsarist colonizers" and plain Russian settlers, and in many cases they assigned to the ordinary Russians a large role in driving the natives off their lands and exploiting them thereafter. The Russian peasants "quickly changed from the exploited to exploiters," according to the Bolshevik observer Safarov.[58] Another Soviet account of the middle 1920's stated that the Kirgiz were driven from their lands, not by the tsarist forces alone, but by the "Russian population": "Not satisfied with seizure of land, the Russian population, holding the Kirgiz in contempt as an inferior nation, exploited them in every possible way, cheating

Caucasus and Central Asia. See also S. S. Daniiarov, *O progressivnom znachenii russkoi kul'tury v razvitii kul'tury kirgizskogo naroda v kontse XIX i nachale XX vekov* (Frunze, 1961), pp. 9-16.

57. *Istoriia buriat-mongol'skoi ASSR*, ed. A. P. Okladnikov (Ulan-Ude, 1951), I, 138-39; *Istoriia iakutskoi ASSR*, ed. Tokarev, Gogolev, and Gurvich (1957), II, chap. iii.

58. Safarov, *Kolonial'naia revoliutsiia*, p. 42.

them at every turn, preventing them from cultivating their lands."[59]
The 1943 history of the Kazakhs still discussed the "mass seizure"
of Kazakh lands, quoting Lenin's condemnation of the tsar's "re-
settlement fund," which reserved vast areas for Russian use. In
some parts of Kazakhstan, according to this history, the Russian
population, constituting 10 per cent of the whole, held all the
arable land, and the Kazakhs, who were driven to poor lands, suffered mass impoverishment.[60] In most recent accounts such events
are forgotten or glossed over; in a few cases the argument has been
put forward that among the settlers there were *kulak* elements who
exploited the lower peasants, or that the upper ranks of the Cossacks were exploiters.[61] But usually when injustices about land use
are admitted, they are charged vaguely to "tsarist policies." Tolybekov has rehabilitated colonial policy to the extent of claiming that
in some areas the amount of land available to the Kazakhs was
"significantly increased" by the coming of the Russians, because
they stabilized the area.[62]

In the areas where the Russians found a more advanced economy, they are credited with removing the economic stagnation of
peoples who had found themselves in the backwaters of the world
economy, and with putting them in touch with world markets for
the first time. They introduced a single monetary system, banking,
and eliminated customs barriers. They built roads and canals, and
introduced a regular postal system. The survey histories give details
about the construction of railroads, the development of the oil
industry in the Caucasus, and of mining and the textile industries
in Central Asia.[63]

Thus, while it is possible to argue that skipping the capitalist
stage was a progressive move for some non-Russian peoples, intensive capitalist investment and industrialization were progressive

59. A. Briskin, *V strane semi rek. Ocherki sovremennogo semirech'ia*
(Moscow, 1926), pp. 34-35.
60. *Istoriia kazakhskoi SSR*, ed. Abdykalykov and Pankratova (1943),
pp. 289-93.
61. *Narody Sibiri*, ed. Levin and Potapov, pp. 146-47; *Istoriia kazakhskoi
SSR*, ed. Auezov, Baishev, *et al.* (1957), I, 403.
62. Tolybekov, "O reaktsionnoi bor'be," p. 45.
63. See especially two volumes of essays on Azerbaidzhan: *Prisoedinenie
Azerbaidzhana k Rossii i ego progressivnye posledstviia v oblasti ekonomiki
i kul'tury*, ed. A. N. Guliev and V. D. Mochalov (Baku, 1955), pp. 21-30;
*Prisoedinenie Azerbaidzhana k Rossii i ego progressivno-ekonomicheskie re-
zul'taty*, ed. E. S. Sumbatzade and M. E. Ismailov (Baku, 1957); A. V.
Fadeev, "Ekonomicheskie sviazi severnogo Kavkaza s Rossiei v doreformennyi
period," *Istoriia SSSR*, No. 1, 1957, pp. 135-60.

for others. But the flexibility of the historian's arguments does not stop here. He can argue for the progressiveness of Russian capital investment either when it benefited the non-Russian worker or oppressed him. The historian sometimes acknowledges that the advanced economic system brought by the Russians increased the general standard of living, but even when he emphasizes the exploitation of the system he can argue for the progressive consequences, by pointing out that it brought about a native proletariat and a revolutionary movement. Thus one can find a statement that "the working masses of Azerbaidzhan suffered from domestic and foreign capital" in the midst of a glowing account of the progressive development of the area at the end of the nineteenth century.[64] One Soviet historian, N. P. Egunov, has tried to solve this apparent contradiction by stating that "the *process* of economic and cultural merging . . . had a deeply progressive significance, while the *forms* of that merger were extremely reactionary. . . ."[65] But the most commonly used argument for explaining the economic progress of the colonial peoples while under tsarist exploitation stems from Piaskovskii's emphasis on the growing alliance of peoples against their common oppressor. The idea is well stated in P. G. Galuzo's recent work on Kazakh agriculture. Galuzo strongly rejects the Stalinist thesis of a "politics of reaction, economics of progress" in the colonies; he sees progress coming out of a mutual "struggle for the development of a democratic path of capitalism" among the Russian and non-Russian peoples.[66]

64. Adil' Nadzhafov, *Formirovanie i razvitie azerbaidzhanskoi sotsialisticheskoi natsii* (Baku, 1955), pp. 30-31.
65. N. P. Egunov, *Kolonial'naia politika tsarizma i pervyi etap natsional'nogo dvizheniia v Buriatii v epokhu imperializma* (Ulan-Ude, 1963), p. 301. Emphasis added.
66. P. G. Galuzo, *Agrarnye otnosheniia na iuge Kazakhstana v 1867-1914 gg.* (Alma-Ata, 1965), pp. 25-32.

CHAPTER **17.**

THE CULTURAL SCENE

"Learn from the Russians—that is the key to life." Abai
Kunanbaev, nineteenth-century Kazakh poet, quoted in E. B.
Bekmakhanov, Prisoedinenie Kazakhstan k Rossii (*Moscow,*
1957), p. 239.

The Soviet historians of the non-Russian peoples are in
their most obsequious position when discussing cultural history.
Some of the more extreme claims for Great Russian cultural leadership of the Zhdanov period may have been quietly abandoned, but
the basic argument is unchanged. The new histories proclaim the
superiority of Russian culture in every field and every age; they
contend that it had considerable influence on the non-Russian peoples even before annexation, and that after annexation the non-
Russian cultural leaders owed everything to their elder brother.
The frequency and subservience of the references to Russian cultural influences are stultifying. In the cultural sections of the
survey histories, references to Russian culture and its influence on
the people in question occur at a rate approaching one per paragraph. It is customary to introduce each cultural subject—literature,
art, the theater, music—with a statement on Russian accomplishments and influences in the period under discussion, and their
relationship to the local culture. There is no pretense of equality
in cultural relations; the non-Russians make new accomplishments
"under the influence of the culture of the great Russian people," as
the stock phrase emphasizes.

Early Soviet historians drew perhaps too harsh a picture of
Russian cultural influences on the colonies because they could see
only cultural oppression and Russification. They dismissed Russia's

paltry efforts at building schools as a part of Russification policy, and regarded the Orthodox church's cultural activity as black reaction. They contended that the non-Russians appropriated little of the alien culture of the conqueror, and in most cases were worse off because their own culture was suppressed.[1] Pokrovskii was well known for his view that Russian culture was inferior to that of most of the conquered peoples. In some cases it was said that the ignorant Russian settler learned from the natives.[2] Even after World War II, when Russian culture was being extolled, Abramzon limited the benefits gained by the Kirgiz to simple material things —learning to use forks, to whitewash walls, to sleep on beds, and to hang curtains on windows.[3] For this he was severely rebuked in *Voprosy istorii* for belittling "the influence of progressive Russian culture on the Kirgiz people."[4]

Although mention is frequently made of the mutual cultural relations of Russians and non-Russians, the cultural flow seems to have gone almost entirely from the superior Russian culture to the non-Russians. Examples of the Russians learning from the other members of the future Soviet family are comparatively rare. Progressive Russian culture was a treasury of the people, and was transmitted by the people. However, the concept of "dual Russia" is applied very flexibly here, and nobles and churchmen can be the ambassadors of this culture. A particularly productive transmission line was established between a number of the nineteenth-century Russian intelligentsia and their counterparts in the colonies—aristocrats almost to a man. Only one element of old Russia did not transmit progressive cultural ideas—the vague and ambiguous ruling force, "tsarism." When the Russian government sent Griboedov to the Caucasus on diplomatic missions, we might expect that he had some connection with "tsarism," that he perhaps carried out "tsarist" policies, but the reputation of the great Russian poet and revolutionary is absolutely untainted by the experience. As for the cultural outlook of "tsarism," a history of the Ukraine put it this way:

1. S. D. Asfendiarov, *Natsional'no-osvoboditel'noe vosstanie 1916 goda v Kazakhstane* (Alma-Ata, 1936), p. 35; G. Togzhanov, *Kazakskii kolonial'nyi aul* (Moscow, 1934), pp. 60-62; S. V. Bakhrushin, *Istoricheskie sud'by Iakutii* (Leningrad, 1927), pp. 26-31.

2. E. Shteinberg, *Ocherki istorii Turkmenii* (Moscow-Leningrad, 1934), p. 58.

3. S. M. Abramzon, *Ocherk kul'tury kirgizskogo naroda* (Frunze, 1946), p. 75.

4. "O nekotorykh voprosakh istorii narodov Srednei Azii," *VI*, No. 4, 1951, pp. 3-15.

"Tsarism prostrated itself before Western European reactionary culture, asserting it in Russia by every means, and disclaimed the world significance of Russian progressive culture, which in the second half of the nineteenth century had taken a leading place in a number of branches of science, in literature and art. In the Ukraine the ideology of tsarism supported the Ukrainian landlords and bourgeoisie."[5]

RUSSIFICATION: THE ROLE OF SCHOOL AND CHURCH

In viewing the cultural scene from the new vantage point of Great Russian leadership and Soviet patriotism, the historian has projected the issues and processes of the current ideological struggle into the past. He sees an ideological battle in the colonies between Russian culture and other cultures, and for him the comparative values of each are as clear as those of communism and its rivals in today's world. His values are thus reversed from those of the early Soviet historian: Russian culture, even when it is promulgated by the Orthodox faith or by a policy of Russification, is all-important for the non-Russian peoples. This puts current Soviet writing on the Orthodox church in an anomalous position, and Russification into a state of limbo. The reader is assured that the Ukrainian and Belorussian peoples were not ideologically neutral in the seventeenth and eighteenth centuries; they hated the Polish government and the Catholic church and its schools as much as they liked the Russian counterparts. The authors of a survey history of the Ukraine state that

> The Polish government, trying to Polonize the Ukrainian population, supported in every way possible the Jesuit colleges . . . and also the Uniat schools, whose curriculum had a clearly expressed Polish-Catholic character. In their opposition to this policy the Ukrainian population supported the schools of the Orthodox brotherhoods, where, besides the humanities, mathematics, astronomy and music were taught. The activities of these schools were carried on under conditions of constant restriction and persecution by the Polish government.[6]

The Soviet historians of Belorussia describe "a fierce national religious oppression" in which the Polish Pans and the Catholic

5. *Istoriia ukrainskoi SSR*, ed. A. K. Kasimenko, V. A. Diadichenko, F. E. Los', *et al.* (Kiev, 1953), I, 574.
6. *Ibid.*, p. 398.

church worked together for centuries not only to Polonize the Belorussians, but failing that, to interfere in every way with the growing friendship and "sympathy" of the people with the Russians.[7]

It is ironic that the theme of Russification has dropped out of the new histories most completely in those areas where it was carried out most intensely—the Ukraine and Belorussia. Indeed, Russification has become almost heroic: the peoples yearn for Russification, although the term is not used. If the non-Russian peoples actively turned to the Russians, with a desire to acquire their superior culture, as the current view has it, then the whole question of forceful measures for Russification becomes absurd. In most cases historians dodge the contradiction by omitting any mention of it, or by making oblique references to it. Sometimes the non-Russian historians are taken to task for failing to touch on such delicate questions. A lengthy review of the *History of the B.S.S.R.* criticized the authors for leaving out completely "the resistance of the best sons of Belorussia to the Russification policy of the autocracy."[8] In this rare instance Moscow was telling Minsk that it was not necessary to bow so low. The histories of the Ukraine, for all their discussion of Polonization, say very little about Russification. In one section of eleven pages on cultural history, in which there are twenty-four explicit references to positive Russian influences, the authors come no closer than this to the troublesome question of Russification: "The development of culture and education in the Ukraine was affected negatively by the Polish-*szlachta* and Austro-Hungarian rule, and also by the influence of the colonial policies carried out by the tsarist government. In the eighteenth century tsarism carried out various restrictions on publishing and instruction in the Ukrainian language, etc. However, all of this could not destroy the cultural ties of the fraternal Russian and Ukrainian peoples."[9]

When Russification is discussed at all in the newer histories, it is put in class terms and thus separated completely from the Russian people. It is usually confined to generalities, and is found only in those areas, like Siberia, where there was no strong ideological struggle with other religions or political systems.

7. *Istoriia belorusskoi SSR*, ed. L. S. Abetsedarskii, V. N. Pertsev, and K. I. Shabunia (Minsk, 1961), I, 113-18; 128-32.

8. *VI*, No. 3, 1963, pp. 120-25.

9. *Istoriia ukrainskoi SSR*, ed. Kasimenko, Diadichenko, Los', *et al.* (1953), I, 397-408.

Russian educational activity in the colonies is said to have preceded the construction of schools. The Orthodox missionaries carried on some educational work, which is sometimes approved in the local histories, and sometimes condemned because of its religious nature. The literate Russian settlers are praised as pioneer teachers. The history of the Udmurt A.S.S.R. describes the work of one Anfim Bushmakin, a Russian peasant teacher. It also reports that "Some of the Udmurts, who lived in the neighborhood of the Russians, gave their children to the literate Russian peasants for instruction. This was one of the factors in the cultural influence of the Russian people on the spiritual development of the Udmurts. For the plain Russian people, the first teachers of the Udmurts, the repressions and harsh measures used by the missionaries and other servants of tsarism, were alien."[10] Many families of North Ossetia are also said to have sent their children into the Russian settlements in order to learn the Russian language.[11] Some of the histories point out that Russian specialists first reduced their spoken language to writing, and compiled the first grammars and dictionaries.[12]

Soviet opinion on the role of the Russian schools in the colonies is ambivalent. In the great majority of cases the schools win qualified praise: they "objectively" played a progressive role, in spite of their purpose of promulgating reactionary political views and the Orthodox faith. In the recent histories of the Kazakhs and Kirgiz the Russian schools are declared to have been a vast improvement over the Moslem *mekteb* and a progressive force in the struggle against the reactionary Moslem faith—their association with the Orthodox church is largely forgotten.[13] In many cases the connection between the schools and Russification is either overlooked or its implications reversed: study of the Russian language and culture is in itself progressive. One writer has unwittingly pointed

10. *Ocherki istorii udmurtskoi ASSR*, ed. I. P. Emel'ianov (Izhevsk, 1958), I, 105.

11. *Istoriia severo-osetinskoi ASSR*, ed. S. K. Bushuev, M. S. Totoev, A. V. Fadeev, et al. (Moscow, 1959), p. 219.

12. *Ocherki po istorii Komi ASSR*, ed. K. V. Sivkov et al. (Syktyvkar, 1955), I, 72-75; *Istoriia iakutskoi ASSR*, ed. S. A. Tokarev, Z. V. Gogolev, and I. S. Gurvich (Moscow, 1957), II, 261-62; V. G. Gadzhiev, *Rol' Rossii v istorii Dagestana* (Moscow, 1965), pp. 315-16.

13. *Istoriia kazakhskoi SSR*, ed. M. O. Auezov, S. B. Baishev, et al. (Alma-Ata, 1957), I, 365-67; *Istoriia Kirgizii*, ed. M. P. Viatkin, M. P. Griaznov, et al. (Frunze, 1963), I, 489-503; T. T. Tazhibaev, "Shkoly vnutrennei (bukeevskoi) ordy vo vtoroi polovine XIX veka," *Voprosy istorii Kazakhstana XIX-nachala XX veka* (Alma-Ata, 1961), pp. 126-153.

up this anomaly in an article quoting General Kaufmann's statement that Russian schools were for "Russian interests,"—to make the population fit for Russian life—and then proceeding to argue that these schools brought about the *sblizhenie* of Kazakh and Russian peoples, contacts with the best Russian thinkers, and the new intelligentsia of the Central Asian peoples.[14]

Other historical accounts still recall the pitifully small numbers of schools built in the Russian colonies and their reactionary outlook. In the history of the Udmurts, written during the brief cultural thaw, it is stated that the "policy of tsarism, the landlords and bourgeoisie was to cripple the culture of these peoples, to stifle their language, to keep them in ignorance, to Russify them." It notes that there was one school in the region during the reign of Peter the Great. After training a total of thirty-two children, it closed its doors in 1709. A later church school, which is heavily condemned for its reactionary ideology, lasted only twenty-five years.[15] The sad state of education in the colonies is frequently recounted as a foil for the recitation of Soviet accomplishments in education.[16]

ENLIGHTENERS AND REVOLUTIONARY DEMOCRATS

The most publicized channel of cultural relations between Russians and non-Russians before the Revolution is the dialogue between intellectuals in the nineteenth century—specifically between the Russian "revolutionary democrats," a group of writers and critics, whose most famous members were Pushkin, Lermontov, Chernyshevskii, and Griboedov, and their non-Russian counterparts, frequently referred to as "the enlighteners." The latter are said to have approved of the annexation of their homelands, and to have appreciated the superiority of Russian culture. They voluntarily became cultural ambassadors for Russia and interpreters of Russian culture for their countrymen. The term *prosvetitel'* (enlightener) originally referred to proponents of the eighteenth-century Enlightenment, and has sometimes been employed to refer to "progressive" Russian thinkers of the nineteenth century. But since

14. N. Sabitov, "Russko-kirgizskie shkoly," *VAN kazakhskoi SSR*, No. 7, 1949, pp. 74-79.

15. *Ocherki istorii udmurtskoi ASSR*, ed. Emeli'anov, I, 104.

16. See, for example, the damning statistical survey of education among the Buriats in A. A. Durinov, "Narodnoe obrazovanie v buriatskoi ASSR," *Issledovaniia i Materialy po istorii Buriatii* (Ulan-Ude, 1963), pp. 42-53.

World War II the term has come into much wider use to designate a remarkable band of non-Russian writers, teachers, and civil servants.[17] The number of enlighteners referred to in all the histories of the Union Republics, Autonomous Republics, and local areas would probably exceed a hundred. A great majority of them were completely obscure outside their own areas until the last twenty years. But recent Soviet scholarship has catapulted them to fame: their works have been published widely,[18] they have been publicized in biographies, special studies, and historical novels,[19] and their careers are discussed at length in the newer histories.

It must seem strange to the Soviet reader that these obscure men, most of whom were not even mentioned in the first edition of the *Great Soviet Encyclopedia,* now light the cultural sky like super-novae. The official explanation is that tsarist historians, blinded by their own class interests, were not concerned with these "progressive" figures, and that the first generation of Soviet historians did not write from a Marxist-Leninist position. But another explanation suggests itself: the enlightener is extremely useful in affirming the concept of the friendship of peoples in its pre-revolutionary setting. He is the vital link between the Russian intelligentsia and the non-Russian people, the assimilator, translator, and transmitter of Russian culture, the catalyst in an historical process.

The enlighteners are too highly individualistic to permit discussion of a typical representative of the group, but the recent Soviet treatment of the careers of a trio of Kazakh enlighteners will illustrate some characteristics of Soviet writing about them. They are Chokan Valikhanov (1835-1865), poet, scientist, linguist, and army officer; Abai Kunanbaev (1845-1904), patriarch of Kazakh

17. The term is not applied uniformly to all non-Russian nationalities. It is most frequently used with reference to the non-Western peoples of Central Asia and the Caucasus, and to peoples who were less advanced than the Russians. Thus the term is not applied to the Georgian, Ukrainian, or Belorussian intellectuals, although they are also regarded as cultural ambassadors in exactly the same way as the others. However, a number of figures in the Baltic area who were from a Western and advanced culture are referred to as enlighteners.

18. The works of only one enlightener (Valikhanov) were published before the Revolution. Three others had appeared by 1940 (Bakikhanov, Akhundov, and Khetagurov). Since World War II there have been editions of selected works, the complete works, and the correspondence of Valikhanov, and editions of either selected or complete works of a dozen others.

19. Among the most popular of these works have been the historical novels of M. Auezov, *Abai* and *Put' Abaia,* which won a Stalin Prize in 1948 and a Lenin Prize in 1959.

literature; and Ibrai Altynsarin (1841-1889), a foremost educator.

The recent Soviet attention given to these men represents a sharp reversal of attitude from the first generation of Soviet scholars. Only one of them, Altynsarin, was given a biographical sketch (one paragraph) in the first edition of the *Great Soviet Encyclopedia*. Their work was appreciated by some tsarist scholars, but they were never popularized. Early Soviet scholars paid almost no attention to them: they were class enemies, being men of aristocratic birth (Valikhanov was the grandson of the last khan of the Middle Horde), and the fact that they had been in the tsar's service was damaging to their reputation.

It is apparent from current Soviet writing about these men that their most highly regarded trait (and one which seems to be the *sine qua non* for designation as an enlightener) was their attitude toward Russia. All of them, in the current Soviet interpretation, approved of the Russian annexation of their country. They eagerly learned from the Russians and sought to reform their educational system along Russian lines. Each of these enlighteners was thoroughly Westernized, having attended Russian schools and mastered the Russian language. Their high regard for Russian culture is emphasized by frequent repetition of some of their testimonials. Valikhanov is quoted as saying that "we Kazakhs would be lost without Russia. Without Russians we would be unenlightened, in despotism and in darkness. Without Russia we are only Asia and can be nothing without her."[20]

A point of special emphasis is the contact these men had with the leading Russian "revolutionary democrats" of their day, who are said to have greatly influenced their views, and in some cases to have had a formative influence on their *Weltanschauung*. The list of Russian mentors is frequently formidable. In the case of Abai Kunanbaev, a minimum list would include Pushkin, Tolstoi, Lermontov, Belinskii, Saltykov-Shchedrin, Chernyshevskii, Pisarev, Nekrasov, Turgenev, and Dobroliubov. Valikhanov's list would include many of the same figures, as well as the Orientalists N. P. Grigoriev and G. N. Potanin, and geographer P. P. Semenov (Tian-Shanskii). Valikhanov was particularly influenced by Dostoevskii, with whom he had a long correspondence. Altynsarin's special mentor was the educator N. I. Ilminskii.[21]

20. Quoted by Serge A. Zenkovsky, in *Pan-Turkism and Islam in Russia* (Cambridge, Mass.: Harvard University Press, 1960), p. 62.

21. *Ibid.*, p. 64.

Their association with the Russian intelligentsia, Russian schools, and the tsar's civil service was so extensive that it raises a question about them as spokesmen for their own people. Although the current Soviet view is that they were the vanguard of their people, and representatives of the most advanced Kazakh thought, it seems likely that they were regarded as turncoats by their contemporaries. They were removed from the daily life of the people and were seeking to bring in a foreign culture. As late as the middle 1930's the Kazakh historian Asfendiarov referred to Valikhanov as a representative of the noble-landlord class (*dvoriansko-pomeshchich'ego klassa*) and an advocate of the missionary-colonizing (*missionersko-kolonizatorskoi*) policy of tsarism.[22]

Ranking slightly below this trio of Kazakhs in current fame are a number of other enlighteners from Central Asia. The most cursory list would have to include the Tadzhik philosopher and poet, Akhmad Donish (1827-1897); the Uzbek poets Furkat (1858-1909) and Mukimi (1851-1903); and the Kirgiz folk-poets and singers (*akyny*), Togolok Moldo (1860-1942) and Toktogul Satylganov (1864-1933). These men have much in common with the Kazakh enlighteners: all sought to introduce Russian culture and education in their countries, and all were influenced by Russian intellectuals. Along with the Kazakhs, they are said to have recognized the reactionary essence of the traditional religion of their region and to have opposed it actively.

Next to Central Asia, the Caucasus is the most conspicuous habitat of the enlightener. Two literary men from this area rival the Kazakh trio for fame. They are Mirza Fatali Akhundov (1812-1878), the Azerbaidzhani philosopher, linguist, and dramatist ("the Mussulman Molière"), and Khachatur Abovian (1805-1848), the Armenian novelist, educator, and ethnographer. In popular Soviet accounts each of these men is considered to be the first important modern figure in the literature of his country. Both were Russian-educated in part, and both were in the Russian service, Akhundov as an associate of the diplomat, Baron Rosen, and Abovian as an inspector of schools. Recent Soviet writing on them emphasizes three common struggles of their careers: (1) their efforts to reform their native schools and literary language, (2) their opposition to the religious practices of their day, and (3) their allegiance to

22. S. D. Asfendiarov, *Istoriia Kazakhstana* (*s drevneishikh vremen*) (Alma-Ata, 1935), I, 203; *Natsional'no-osvoboditel'noe vosstanie*, p. 37.

Russia as the savior of their countries against Turkish and Persian threats.

The list of secondary enlighteners from the Caucasus would run into the dozens. Among the best known are the Azerbaidzhanis Abbas Kuli Aga Bakikhanov (1794-1847), a historian and philosopher; Kasumbek Zakir (1784-1857), poet and satirist; Mirza Kazem-Bek (1802-1870), linguist and Orientalist; and Gasan Bek Zardabi (1837-1907), educator and reformer. The Armenian philosopher and literary critic Mikael Lazarevich Nalbandian (1829-1866) is remembered as a precursor of the Bolsheviks. In the North Caucasus the most famous enlighteners are Shora Nogmov (1801-1844), linguist and historian, from Kabarda, and the Ossetian poet, Kosta Khetagurov (1859-1906).

Another cluster of enlighteners can be found in the Baltic area. The best known are three Estonian writers, Christian Peterson (1801-1822), Frederick Felman (1798-1850), and Frederick Kreitswald (1803-1882).

In the encyclopedia articles on the enlighteners and accounts of their activities in local histories fully half of the space is devoted to establishing their ties with Russian cultural leaders and affirming their pro-Russian views. The recitation of this information is so standardized as to be almost ritualistic. Following the usual biographical information about the enlightener, his contacts with "progressive" Russians will be related according to their extent and closeness. In some cases there were long friendships and correspondence: Valikhanov with Dostoevskii, Semenov, and S. F. Durov of the Petrashevskii Circle; Altynsarin with Ilminskii; Bakikhanov with Griboedov and the Decembrist A. A. Bestuzhev-Marlinskii; Zardabi with A. N. Pleshchev, the Petrashevist, etc. Occasional meetings with the Russians are considered worthy of emphasis. Thus it is reported that Nalbandian met Herzen and Ogarev while on a trip abroad, and that Bakikhanov met Pushkin twice. Even an uncertain encounter is noteworthy: "It is possible," the encyclopedia reports, "that Akhundov met Lermontov."

Indirect contacts are also considered significant. Abai Kunanbaev, who had few direct connections with the better-known Russian intellectuals, is linked with them through two of the followers of Chernyshevskii. This is how the encyclopedia article on Abai establishes the tie:

> Representatives of the Russian democratic intelligentsia—
> Chernyshevskii's pupil Mikaelis, N. I. Dolgopolov and

others, who were exiles in Semipalatinsk, were the friends
and teachers of Abai. They played a decisive role in the
intellectual development of Abai, helping him to study the
works of the great Russian writers and thinkers Pushkin,
Lermontov, Nekrasov, Pisarev, Saltykov-Shchedrin, Tolstoi,
Turgenev, Chernyshevskii, and Dobroliubov, which contributed to the formation of the views of the poet-en-
lightener.[23]

In demonstrating these contacts the travels of the enlighteners
and their Russian mentors take on great significance. Many of the
enlighteners lived for a time in Russian cultural centers. Nogmov,
Khetagurov and Nalbandian attended school in St. Petersburg, and
Valikhanov spent two years there. Zardabi attended Moscow University, and Abovian studied at Tartu University. Akhmad Donish
was stationed in St. Petersburg in the diplomatic service of the
Emir of Bokhara. The Russians also traveled widely, facilitating
contacts with the enlighteners. Pushkin, Lermontov, Griboedov,
Tolstoi, and the young Gorkii all traveled or worked in the Caucasus.
The Russian scientists Semenov, N. A. Severtsov, and P. K. Kozlov
did much work in Central Asia and are said to have had a great effect on the local intelligentsia.[24] The newer histories contain long
lists of Russians whose work in some part of the Empire made a
contribution to the friendship of peoples. A history of the Uzbek
Republic discusses the work of thirty-one Russian intellectuals, and
a study on the Tadzhiks piles up a list of fifty-two Russian literary
and scientific benefactors.[25]

Russian influence in the arts is not left out. Vereshchagin's trip
to Central Asia is celebrated, as is Ippolitov-Ivanov's work in the
Caucasus.[26] The Kazakhs are said to have learned Tatiana's aria

23. *BSE*, 2nd ed., I, 6. See also A. M. Zhirenchin, "O sviazi Abai s
russkimi revoliutsionerami-demokratami," *VAN kazakhskoi SSR*, No. 1, 1948,
pp. 49-54.
24. P. K. Kozlov, *Russkii puteshestvennik v tsentral'noi Azii. Izbrannye
trudy k stoletiiu so dnia rozhdeniia* (Moscow, 1963); *Istoriia tadzhikskogo
naroda*, ed. B. I. Iskandarov and A. M. Mukhtarov (Moscow, 1964), II,
Part 2, 154-58; T. N. Kary-Niiazov, *Ocherki istorii kul'tury sovetskogo Uzbekistana* (Moscow, 1955), pp. 50-55.
25. *Istoriia uzbekskoi SSR*, ed. M. G. Vakhabov, V. Ia. Nepomnin, and
T. N. Kary-Niiazov (Tashkent, 1956), I, Part 2, 180-83; Z. Radzhabov, *Iz
istorii obshchestvenno-politicheskoi mysli tadzhikskogo naroda vo vtoroi polovine
XIX i v nachale XX vv.* (Stalinabad, 1957), pp. 54-57.
26. *Obzor russkikh puteshestvii i ekspeditsii v Sredniuiu Aziiu*, (Tashkent,
1956), Vol. II, contains accounts of Vereshchagin and seventeen other Russian
cultural figures. See also *Istoriia kazakhskoi SSR*, ed. Auezov, Baishev, *et al.*

from *Eugene Onegin* and to have sung it as a popular song. Russian influence in architecture and the theater is also emphasized.[27]

Another indispensible part of the current format of Soviet writing on the enlighteners is an explicit statement about the subject's attitude toward Russia and the friendship of peoples. Here are some samples from the biographical articles in the *Great Soviet Encyclopedia:*

> Abovian saw in Russia the salvation of the Armenian people and became an ardent spokesman for Armenian-Russian friendship. This affirmation of friendship with the Russian people fills Abovian's works.
>
> . . . .
>
> [Akundov:] He passionately loved his people and in his works called for their progress and freedom, which he could not conceive of without the friendship and help of the Russian people.
>
> . . . .
>
> Altynsarin was a persuasive advocate of the cooperation of the Russian and Kazakh peoples, and of the appropriation by the Kazakhs of the culture of Pushkin, Krylov, Belinskii and Chernyshevskii.
>
> . . . .
>
> [Donish:] Recognizing the positive aspects of the annexation of Central Asia to Russia, he sought to broaden economic and cultural ties with Russia. He was a fervent advocate for the study of the Russian language and Russian culture by the peoples of Central Asia.

The enlighteners' admiration for Russia and their views on the friendship of peoples are illustrated by direct quotations from their works, which punctuate current writing on them. In the history of the Kirgiz S.S.R., Toktogul Satylganov is cited in lines indicating the common bond between Russian and native on the eve of the Revolution:

(1957), I, 477-78; Iu. Aksenov and G. Il'in, "Vliianie russkoi kul'tury na razvitie kul'tury Ukrainy, Belorussii i Zakavkaz'ia v XIX v.," *Prepodavanie istorii v shkole,* No. 2, 1956, pp. 24-36; L. A. Perepelitsyna, *Rol' russkoi kul'tury v razvitii kul'tur narodov Srednei Azii* (Moscow, 1966).

27. B. Erzakov, "Istoricheskie sviazi russkoi i kazakhskoi muzyky v dooktiabr'skii period," *VAN kazakhskoi SSR,* No. 10, 1953, pp. 48-53; *Istoriia kazakhskoi SSR,* ed. Auezov, Baishev, *et al.* (1957), I, 475-78; Aksenov and Il'in, "Vliianie russkoi kul'tury," pp. 33-35; V. Shleev, "O sviaziakh russkogo i ukrainskogo iskusstva vtoroi poloviny XIX veka," *Iskusstvo,* No. 2, 1954, pp. 43-49.

> I see, side by side, Kazakh
> Russian, Kirgiz, Uzbek.
> I see them: they stand about
> Unhappy, just as I am.
> Each is to me a brother and friend,
> A prisoner, as I too am.[28]

Furkat is remembered for writing:

> There is no limit to the inventions of science.
> Great Russia has brought them to us. . . .
> Learned minds produced the telegraph,
> And I praise it, having chosen the role
> Of the singer.
> O youth! The priceless light of Russian wisdom
> Has overshadowed the traditions of past years.[29]

The role of the Russians as the savior of peoples against the attacks of greedy neighbors is much emphasized. Of the Azerbaidzhani people, Akhundov says: "Thanks to the protection of the Russian government we have escaped from our former condition of endless inroads and raids of aggressive hordes and have turned finally, to rest."[30] One can even find in these quotations statements of praise for the tsar's armies. Reflecting on the policy of Britain, France and Turkey in the Crimean War, Kasumbek Zakir wrote that

> A prudent man never exposes himself to a storm.
> Really, they are all three imbeciles—imbeciles.
> To take a stand against the Russian army
> One needs an iron head and a steel body.

Remarking that the poet thus "glorifies the strength and power of the Russian army," the Soviet commentator goes on to write about the enthusiasm of the Azerbaidzhani people for the Crimean War and their heroism in its battles.[31]

The enlighteners are fighting the current ideological battles of the Soviet Union, even at the cost of anachronistic terminology. Thus Nalbandian is said to have been "a resolute opponent of bourgeois nationalism," as was Valikhanov, who also fought against

28. *Istoriia Kirgizii*, ed. Viatkin, Griaznov, *et al.* (1963), I, 476.

29. *Istorii uzbekskoi SSR*, ed. Vakhabov, Nepomnin, and Kary-Niiazov (1956), I, Part 2, 174.

30. Aksenov and Il'in, "Vliianie russkoi kul'tury," p. 26.

31. *Prisoedinenie Azerbaidzhana k Rossii i ego progressivnye posledstviia v oblasti ekonomiki i kul'tury*, ed. A. N. Guliev and V. D. Mochalov (Baku, 1955), p. 262.

Pan-Islamism and Pan-Turkism. Both Bakikhanov and Khetagurov are praised for having advocated the *sblizhenie* of their people with the Russians. "In all his creative work Abovian was dedicated to the interests of the working people." Donish fought for "education of the masses and propagandized secular learning." Soviet readers, who are constantly warned about hostile and predatory enemies just beyond their borders, learn in these accounts that Abovian and Akhundov were active in the struggle against Turkish and Persian aggressors, that Kreitswald opposed German incursions into the Baltic, and that Nalbandian "unmasked the aggressive policies of Britain in India and China." As for the war on "reactionary religious ideology," it is said that most of the enlighteners of Central Asia and the Caucasus fought against the backward influences of the Moslem religious leaders, and the Baltic enlighteners carried the battle against the Catholic church. It is greatly to the credit of Akhundov that he was an atheist and materialist.[32]

The enlighteners are also active in the Soviet linguistic campaign of the 1960's—the effort to increase the study of Russian and make it the "second mother tongue" of all non-Russian Soviet citizens. Without exception the enlighteners are reported to have loved the Russian language, and a few of them wrote some of their works in Russian. Abai, Altynsarin, and Akhundov favored reform of their traditional alphabets; the latter saw the Arabic alphabet as "one of the obstacles in the way of Azerbaidzhani national education." Abovian is remembered for writing that "the Russian language is one of the most widespread and important languages of the world. . . . The Russian language helps us to enrich our thought and feeling. The works of Russian literature help us to catch the spirit of that people, bringing us closer to their culture and uniting us with the great Russian people, whose name inspires in every foreigner love and self sacrifice."[33] Akhundov's estimate of the Russian language is useful in the present effort: "I know the Russian language well. In the present century the Russian language . . . is developing in the scientific field and in other areas as an excellent language for the expression of the most subtle thoughts."[34] And Abai's advice to his countrymen is added: "Remember above all, that one must study Russian science. . . . In order to overcome

32. All the quotations in this paragraph are from the biographical articles in the second edition of the *BSE*.
33. Aksenov and Il'in, "Vliianie russkoi kul'tury," p. 34.
34. *Prisoedinenie Azerbaidzhana*, ed. Guliev and Mochalov (1955), p. 263.

our ills and do good, it is necessary to know the Russian language
and Russian culture. The Russians view the world. If you know
their language, then you can open your eyes to the world."[35]

One of the pitfalls the scholar encounters when using such
quotations to further current Soviet policies is that his selections
are likely to become obsolete or even ideologically incorrect. The
following stanza from Furkat, published in 1956 (and not likely
to appear in the next edition), will illustrate:

> Great Russia and China—collaborators and friends
> Their lands since olden times have been linked together.
> Their union brings peace,
> Beauty for the grandeur of the world.[36]

Although Soviet writing on the enlighteners is almost entirely
laudatory, these men are not immune from criticism. One sometimes
finds their shortcomings enumerated, particularly concerning their
religious or class views. Some Soviet scholars have been charged
with idealizing the enlighteners and crediting them with advanced
thinking which would have been impossible in their day. Bakikhanov, we are reminded, always remained feudal in his thinking.
He erroneously regarded the history of his people as a series of
military events and could not see the "objective historical consequences of national mass movements."[37] Nogmov also "followed a
tendency to see questions of the history of the Kabardinian people
from a nobleman's point of view."[38] In the *History of the Uzbek
S.S.R.* it is stated that "Akhmad Donish, Furkat, and Mukimi, in
spite of their progressive actions and views, were all children of
their age. They were not free of religious views and positions.
This is evident in their ideological and political limitations."[39]

The enlightener is permitted to express his views only through
the prism of Soviet interpretation. His anti-tsarist views can sometimes be aired and even praised, since they show him to be sympathetic with the coming revolutionary movement. But he can never

35. A. Tursunbaev, *Nerushimaia druzhba russkogo i kazakhskogo narodov*
(Alma-Ata, 1955), p. 19.
36. *Istoriia uzbekskoi SSR,* ed. Vakhabov, Nepomnin, and Kary-Niiazov
(1956), I, Part 2, 175.
37. *VI*, No. 1, 1963, p. 124; *Prisoedinenie Azerbaidzhana,* ed. Guliev and
Mochalov (1955), pp. 269-70.
38. *Istoriia Kabardy,* ed. N. A. Smirnov, Z. V. Angavadze, N. E. Gurevich,
et al. (Moscow, 1957), p. 114.
39. *Istoriia uzbekskoi SSR,* ed. Vakhabov, Nepomnin, and Kary-Niiazov
(1956), I, Part 2, 179.

be anti-Russian. Any of the enlightener's acts or writings that can be construed as anti-Russian are either omitted or passed over in silence by Soviet scholars. It is known, for example, that Valikhanov was sickened by the Russian atrocities he witnessed, and that he withdrew from "civilized" (i.e. Russian) society for a time in protest. This episode was described in the 1943 history of Kazakhstan, but has been omitted in subsequent histories.[40] Abai's criticism of the narrowness of Russian education for the Kazakhs is generally passed over in favor of other passages emphasizing his high regard for Russian culture.[41] Many of Khetagurov's verses reflect the typical desperation of a people under colonial rule:

> With fetters of iron our bodies entrammelled
> The dead in their graves are bereft of repose
> Our country is slandered, our mountains sequestered.
> We are covered with shame and beset with the lash,
> Deprived of our homeland and scattered asunder
> Like cattle are driven by some maddened beast.
> Where art thou our leader? O draw us together,
> Command us to seek now a happier life.[42]

Is this not a call for a national leader to come forward to liberate a people? But these verses, as published under Soviet auspices, can be interpreted to mean that Khetagurov was condemning the common oppression of all future Soviet peoples and was looking toward the October Revolution.

The most difficult instance of coordinating an enlightener's views has been what has been referred to as "the struggle for Shevchenko."[43] The official Bolshevik views on the greatest Ukrainian poet have vacillated sharply, reflecting Russian-Ukrainian relations during the fifty years of Soviet rule. The first Bolshevik soldiers who entered the Ukraine in 1918 are reported to have torn down

40. Richard A. Pierce, *Russian Central Asia, 1867-1917: A Study in Colonial Rule* (Berkeley, Calif.: University of California Press, 1960), p. 330, note 1.

41. Thomas G. Winner, *The Oral Art and Literature of the Kazakhs of Russian Central Asia* (Durham, N.C.: Duke University Press, 1958), pp. 115-17.

42. Quoted by R. Takoev, "Kosta L. Khetagurov: On the Occasion of the Centenary of his Birth (1859-1959)," *Caucasian Review*, No. 9 (1959), pp. 123-27.

43. This expression was first used in 1925 in a series of newspaper articles by V. Koriak. It is also the title of a more recent article: P. Odarchenko, "The Struggle for Shevchenko," *The Annals of the Ukrainian Academy of Arts and Sciences in the U.S.*, III (1954), No. 3, 824-37.

his portraits and trampled them. Soon thereafter, the ideological authorities, recognizing the unbounding respect of the Ukrainians for their national poet, tried to interpret him as a people's poet and prophet of the Revolution. At the time of the purge of the Ukrainian nationalists in the early 1930's the party reversed itself again and published theses on Shevchenko declaring him to be a "bourgeois democrat," expressing the ideology of petit-bourgeois peasantry, with its reactionary nationalist and religious views. By the eve of World War II Shevchenko was represented as a spokesman for Soviet patriotism. From this time on his connections with Russian writers and his alleged love of the Russian people have grown rapidly. His poems containing anti-Russian themes are omitted from editions purporting to be unexpurgated, and in other cases slanted annotations are employed to tailor his views. It is stated, for example, that Shevchenko's caustic remarks about the plunderers of the Ukraine were aimed exclusively against the Poles. His many statements looking toward Ukrainian freedom and independence are viewed as the poet's anticipation of Soviet society.

The extent to which Shevchenko has been fitted into the current Soviet view can be illustrated by a sampling of the themes of *The Historical Views of T. G. Shevchenko*, by Iu. D. Margolis, one of the most recent works in an enormous Soviet literature on the poet.[44] Margolis contends that Shevchenko regarded the Treaty of Pereiaslav as a progressive event, a turning point in the life of the Ukrainian people ("The Muscovites grabbed whatever they saw," had been the poet's now-forgotten comment). Shevchenko is said to have struggled for freedom, not for the Ukrainians alone, but for all the oppressed peoples, and for the destruction of the tsarist "prison of peoples." He recognized that "the overthrow of the autocratic-landlord power could only be accomplished by the united force of all the exploited peoples of tsarist Russia." He is thus the champion of the future multi-national Revolution, for he saw that the great source of the future freedom was the Russian people: "The unbounded respect and tremendous faith of Shevchenko in the growing power of the Russian people was the vital source of his revolutionary democracy. In friendship with the Russian people Shevchenko saw a guarantee of future freedom for the Ukraine. Shevchenko implored the Ukrainian people to master the great democratic culture of the Russian people, and he himself

44. Iu. D. Margolis, *Istoricheskie vzgliady T. G. Shevchenka* (Leningrad, 1964).

was a remarkable example of his advice."[45] In the old view, Shevchenko was the archetype of the Ukrainian patriot and nationalist, but Margolis declares that "in all his works, Shevchenko opposed the ideology of nationalist limitations and narrow-mindedness." Indeed, the poet was aware of the class struggle and, one gathers, was almost a Marxist:

> Of great significance in the historical views of Shevchenko was his conception of the antagonistic divisions of society, and of the role of the struggle of hostile social groups on historical development. Shevchenko observed antagonistic divisions of society even in the ancient past. . . . Shevchenko clearly understood that the schism of society into hostile groups of people resulted from opposing material interests. The poet skillfully applied his views on the class divisions of society both in the history of society and to his own times.[46]

And he clearly envisioned the Soviet future: "Shevchenko deeply believed that as a result of popular revolutions there would be established an epoch of the triumph of social justice, an epoch of 'great,' 'voluntary,' 'new' union of free peoples."[47] Oddly enough, the Margolis work was written as a corrective to certain "vulgarized" works on the poet written during the personality cult. Margolis points out that Shevchenko had certain limitations of his age; he idealized some historical figures and events, and he did not clearly see the role of the proletariat.

Much the same editorial treatment has been given to two Belorussian poets, Ianka Kupala (1882-1942) and Iakub Kolas (1882-1956). Their early opposition to the Soviet regime has been forgotten, and their so-called collected works do not contain some works inimical to the friendship of peoples. On the other hand they have been made consistent champions of the class struggle and of the Soviet society by editorial annotations and the work of Soviet literary critics.[48]

Another obvious control the Soviet scholar has over cultural history is the privilege of choosing his spokesmen, and of cutting off others completely. The enlighteners constitute only a fraction of the

45. *Ibid.*, pp. 283-84.
46. *Ibid.*, p. 289.
47. *Ibid.*, p. 292.
48. S. Stankievic, "Kupala in Fact and Fiction," *Belorussian Review*, No. 3 (1956), pp. 31-55; *Istoriia belorusskoi SSR*, ed. Abetsedarskii, Pertsev, and Shabunia (1961), I, 591-605.

outstanding intellectuals among the non-Russians of the empire. The case of Ismail Bey Gasprinskii, the eminent educator of Crimean Tatar origin, suggests itself. Gasprinskii had much in common with the enlighteners. He was a better-known educator in his day than Altynsarin; he was influenced by Chernyshevskii, Belinskii, Herzen, and Pisarev; he worked for educational reform and a better life for his people. But Gasprinskii lacks the main ideological qualification for inclusion among the enlighteners, since he was pro-Turkish and favored a reformed Moslem society, rather than a closer tie with Russian culture. He is therefore almost an unperson for the Soviet reader, unworthy of mention in the cultural history of his time.

Although the usual Soviet practice is to omit all mention of a rejected figure, there are cases in which an active campaign is launched against a would-be enlightener, and sometimes a figure is admitted to the ranks only after considerable deliberation. The authors of the most recent history of Kirgizia resort to the unusual procedure of pointing out why Moldo Kylych (1866-1917), a popular philosopher-poet, should not be considered an enlightener. He is accused of idealizing the feudal way of life, of advocating Pan-Turkism and Moslem theology. And significantly, he is charged with anti-Russian views and a failure to grasp the significance of the annexation of Kirgizia to Russia.[49] In the case of Khetagurov, it has been reported that Soviet cultural authorities postponed a decision about him for years. Only after long urging by intellectuals of the North Caucasus did the government decide to erect a monument to him in Ordzhonikidze in 1955. Soviet anthologies of Khetagurov's poems have omitted his works on religious themes.[50]

Sometimes the line between the "progressives" and "reactionaries" can be very difficult to draw. A good recent example is the tortured analysis of Jadidism which has been offered by M. G. Vakhabov. As a reform movement within Moslem thought, Jadidism has long been condemned as a bourgeois nationalist movement. But many impeccable enlighteners were associated with Jadidism. Vakhabov's solution is to divide the movement into two parts, and to assert that the term was used very loosely. Some of those who called themselves Jadids were not really Jadids at all. He thus

49. *Istoriia Kirgizii,* ed. Viatkin, Griaznov, *et al.* (1963), I, 472-73.
50. Takoev, "Kosta L. Khetagurov," p. 127; V. Astemirov, "Spoilers of a Literary Heritage," *Caucasian Review,* No. 9 (1959), pp. 91-97.

removes the taint of Jadidism from the enlighteners without altering the long-standing interpretation of the movement.[51]

There was much concern in the early 1950's about the uncritical idealization of intellectuals in Iakutia just before the Revolution. In 1951 *Pravda* dealt a heavy blow to two works that had gone too far in attempting to promote the friendship of the Iakut and Russian peoples.[52] In his book, *Three Iakut Realist Enlighteners* (1944), G. Basharin had failed "to separate the positive in their heritage from the erroneous and negative." The author had resorted to "idealizing literally everything they wrote," although it was well known that their works contained bourgeois nationalist ideas, which sometimes used "vile and deeply insulting slander against the Russian people." One of the enlighteners, A. Kulakovskii, had even joined the White Guards. To make matters worse, this idealization of literary figures had been continued in a symposium, *The Progressive Influence of the Great Russian People on the Development of the Iakut People,* which had just received a completely favorable review in *Voprosy istorii.*[53] *Pravda* called on scholars to separate the early reactionary ideas of these men from their later progressive ones, and thereby to give a true picture of their progress under the influence of the Russian people. The article evoked a resolution from the Iakut branch of the party.[54] The later *History of Iakutia* (1957) shows the result: it reduces the three to minor roles (far below Ordzhonikidze and Iaroslavskii, who were in Iakutia at the time) and divides their works precisely along the lines laid down by *Pravda.*[55]

The popularization of the enlighteners serves Soviet cultural policy well, but it has an inherent danger. The more heroic the role of the enlightener, the greater the possibility that he will become a symbolic figure for nationalist feelings in the non-Russian

51. M. G. Vakhabov, "O sotsial'noi prirode sredneaziatskogo dzhadidizma i ego evoliutsii v period velikoi oktiabr'skoi revoliutsii," *Istoriia SSSR,* No. 2, 1963, pp. 35-56, and his *Formirovanie uzbekskoi sotsialisticheskoi natsii* (Tashkent, 1961), pp. 234-36.

52. "Za pravil'noe osveshchenie istorii iakutskoi istorii," *Pravda,* December 10, 1951.

53. *Progressivnoe vliianie velikoi russkoi natsii na razvitie iakutskogo naroda. Sbornik* (Iakutsk, 1950), I, reviewed in *VI,* No. 1, 1951, pp. 140-44.

54. *VI,* No. 9, 1954, p. 122.

55. *Istoriia iakutskoi ASSR,* ed. Tokarev, Gogolev, and Gurvich, II, 351-55. Basharin apologized for his "political error," explaining that when he wrote in the early 1940's he knew nothing about archival materials on the "anti-Soviet activities" of the trio. He also revealed that he had rewritten his doctoral dissertation to meet party requirements (*VI,* No. 9, 1954, pp. 122-23).

republics. Questions about the attitudes and views of the enlighten-ers are not left to the scholars, but are discussed in the highest echelons of the party. The case of Moldo Kylych, for example, reached the agenda of the Central Committee of the Kirgiz party and a party conference in Frunze.[56] This fear of the centrifugal forces of nationalism undoubtedly explains why Soviet scholars take such pains to make the enlighteners not only pro-Russian, but to reduce their role as nationalists.

56. *POP*, No. 5 (1960), p. 14; No. 6 (1960), p. 56.

CHAPTER 18.

FRIENDSHIP AMONG
THE NON-RUSSIAN NATIONALITIES

"The brotherly peoples of the Caucasus were prepared to stand shoulder to shoulder with the Georgians against their common enemy. The expulsion of the Seljuk Turks was necessarily tied to the political unification of the peoples of the Transcaucasus. Georgia took the role of the unifier."
Istoriia Gruzii (*Tbilisi, 1962*), *I, 163.*

As a logical extension of the friendship of peoples concept, the newer Soviet histories proclaim the existence of historic friendship, not only bilaterally between individual non-Russian peoples and Russians but also among the non-Russian peoples themselves. Readers of the new history discover a unique phenomenon: dozens of peoples of different religions, languages, and historical backgrounds, living together for centuries in harmony and in close alliance against their enemies. To be sure, the rulers of these peoples sometimes went to war, grasping merchants exploited neighboring peoples, and reactionary religious leaders held peoples in darkness. But as far as the peoples themselves were concerned, there was only mutual respect and helpfulness.

In the old view, the peoples of the future Soviet family had more than their share of strife. They clashed not only with the Russians, but fought among themselves. Internecine warfare was endemic to parts of the Caucasus, Central Asia and Siberia. Medieval Georgia and Lithuania conquered and annexed neighboring peoples—Armenians, Azerbaidzhanis, Belorussians, and even some Russians. Christian-Moslem tensions led to some particularly bloody riots in the Caucasus, even as late as the eve of the Revolution. These events have not been forgotten, but they have been sub- ordinated to evidences of cooperation, and have been reinterpreted in the context of the class struggle, which attributes warfare to the exploiting classes, leaving the peoples with clean hands.

One of the standard ingredients of the new survey histories is a general statement affirming friendly relations among peoples. From the early Middle Ages, according to the history of Azerbaid- zhan, "close cultural ties existed among the peoples of Azerbaid- zhan, Armenia, Georgia, Iran, and other countries of the East."[1] According to the recent history of the Kirgiz, "the nearness and friendship between the Uzbek and Kirgiz popular masses was not restricted to the common struggle against the feudal-khan yoke. These peoples had much in common in economics, culture, and also in their way of life, manners and customs; thus, finding them- selves close neighbors, they had a common influence one on the other."[2] And in the North Caucasus, formerly regarded as a seedbed of petty warfare and religious intolerance, peoples lived together for centuries as good neighbors: "The Balkarian people, dwelling from time immemorial in the almost inaccessible high mountain regions of the Caucasus, lived for many centuries side by side with the Kabardinians, Ossetians, Georgians and other peoples of the Caucasus, and established many kinds of ties with their neighbors. These ties were of an economic, as well as cultural and political character. Among these neighboring peoples, the Balkars had especially close ties with the brotherly Kabardinian people."[3]

The friendship of the non-Russian peoples is always subordi- nated to the role of the Russian people, who are given the greatest credit for developing and maintaining good relations among neigh- boring peoples. A Moldavian historian has stated the proposition this way:

> The friendship of the exploited peoples of our country
> in their struggle against exploiters grew and was strength-
> ened during the period of capitalism. The main force and
> leadership in this struggle of the peoples of tsarist Russia
> against the yoke of Russian, Ukrainian, Moldavian, Tatar,
> and other landlords and capitalists was from the Russian

1. *Istoriia Azerbaidzhana*, ed. I. A. Guseinov, *et al.* (Baku, 1958), I, 103.
2. *Istoriia Kirgizii*, ed. M. P. Viatkin, M. P. Griaznov, *et al.* (Frunze, 1963), I, 296.
3. *Ocherkii istorii balkarskogo naroda*, ed. T. Kh. Kumykov, P. G. Akritas, Z. V. Anchabadze, *et al.* (Nal'chik, 1961), p. 38.

working class. In the class struggle, there grew a class solidarity and faith of the other peoples of our motherland in the Russian people, as the main leading force, uniting the multi-national family. For each of the Soviet peoples, there was in its past its own path, by which it came into the brotherly multi-national family, the U.S.S.R.[4]

THE TECHNIQUES OF REINTERPRETATION: COORDINATION AND THE CLASS STRUGGLE

Cooperation among the non-Russian peoples is impressed on the reader by the extreme coordination of historical development in the survey histories. In their efforts to discuss the great majority of Soviet peoples in a severely restricted space, the authors treat events and developments on a regional basis, emphasizing the common factors and minimizing the differences. It is now fashionable to discuss the history of a particular period for "the peoples of Central Asia," or of the Caucasus, the Baltic, or Siberia. In the most recent edition of the college-level survey history of the U.S.S.R., for example, one can find dozens of topic headings such as "The Struggle of the Peoples of the Transcaucasus against the Arab Yoke," "The Culture of the Peoples of Central Asia," "The Position of the Baltic Peoples in their Liberation Struggle." The impression is given that the peoples of a whole area cooperated in their political life and military activity, and that their cultural life was very close. The great cultural figures are pictured as representative of the area, not just their own people. One gathers that all the peoples of an area cooperated in defense against their common enemies. But the cooperation of peoples, as discussed in these topics, is more apparent than real. The reader will find few concrete cases of cooperation, and a great many broad statements of studied vagueness: "The working population actively continued to fight against the invaders" or "The foreign yoke in the Baltic called forth a popular mass movement."[5]

Another sort of coordination is accomplished by the radical rewriting of a topic with a changed emphasis. A good example is the survey treatment of the history of the Grand Duchy of Lithuania, as previously noted in connection with the rise of the centralized Russian state. The old discussion of Lithuania's conquest

4. N. Mokhov, *Ocherki istorii moldavsko-russko-ukrainskikh sviazei* (Kishinev, 1961), p. 4.
5. *Istoriia SSSR*, ed. M. V. Nechkina (Moscow, 1964), I, 132, 198.

of Belorussian, Russian, and Ukrainian lands, to the length of a whole chapter in both the elementary and college-level textbooks, could have only a negative effect on the historic friendship of peoples. Beginning in editions of the middle 1950's, the discussion of the Grand Duchy is reduced to a few paragraphs, and the emphasis is placed on the mutual struggle of the peoples of the area against foreign invaders and "the aggression of Polish-Lithuanian feudal lords," who "prevented a union with Moscow."[6] According to the college textbook, "In the struggle with the Teutonic Order, the whole Lithuanian people took part, supported by the population of the Russian, Ukrainian, and Belorussian lands. Lithuanian military forces, together with Russian cavalry, struck the Teutonic Order on the borders of the Grand Duchy of Lithuania. Thus, in 1370, a stubborn battle took place between Russian-Lithuanian military forces and the German knights not far from Koenigsberg."[7] The greatest battle of all was at Grünwald (1410), which has blossomed from a mere mention in the early editions of the textbooks to one of the decisive battles of world history. This battle fits the new line of interpretation perfectly, since it involved a joint force of Polish, Lithuanian, Russian, Ukrainian, Belorussian, and Czech forces in a great Slavic victory over the Germans.[8] Thus the old aggression of the Lithuanian state is engulfed in a military struggle of a completely different nature.

The concepts of the class alliances and the class struggle are applied to this theme with considerable flexibility. In the new history there are two kinds of warfare, the progressive mass movements, and the reactionary wars of the ruling classes. Frequently a single event is dissected into separate military aspects. The Lithuanian case in the fourteenth and fifteenth centuries is once again instructive. There was a popular movement of all the peoples for their defense and union with the Russians, and a concurrent series of aggressive actions by the Lithuanian and Polish feudal lords. Indeed, the feudal leaders did all they could to impede the progress of the other military movements: "The local landlords were hostile

6. L. P. Bushchik, *Istoriia SSSR* (Moscow, 1959), I, 99.

7. *Istoriia SSSR*, ed. Nechkina (1956), I, 215-16.

8. Khrushchev gave considerable attention to the battle of Grünwald in a speech in Stettin in 1959: "Why are we concerned today with this old page from history?" he asked. "Grünwald stands forever as a monument of the people, as an example not only of the brave opposition to foreign attackers, but also to the road to victory against attackers—through the unity of peoples who are threatened." *Istoriia SSSR. Uchebnoe posobie*, ed. B. D. Datsiuk (Moscow, 1960), p. 52.

to the mass movements of the people against the power of the
Grand Duchy of Lithuania, protecting the class interests not only
of the Lithuanian and Polish, but also the Russian, Ukrainian and
Belorussian feudal lords."[9] The people possessed political wisdom,
but their leaders were selfishly short-sighted: "After the battle of
Kulikovo [1380] the population of the Ukraine and Belorussia
gravitated even more toward the Moscow principality. At the same
time the dangers for the Duchy of Lithuania from the Teutonic
Order increased. Under these conditions the vital political interests
of the Lithuanian people called for the conclusion of a union with
Russia, for which they struggled in Moscow. But the ruling section
of the Lithuanian feudal lords prevented a union with Moscow."[10]
But where are the same feudal lords in the great progressive victory
of Grünwald? Obviously, they were there in positions of command,
but the authors of the new history see the battle as a peoples' victory,
ignoring the presence of the nobles. Another indication of the great
flexibility on this subject is the representation of Ivan IV's Livonian
War in the following century as a just war of liberation. The
Lithuanian people are said to have been on Ivan's side; this was
a war to liberate the Baltic peoples from "the yoke of the Livonian
Order," and Ivan's failure resulted not from lack of popular support,
but from the designs of Swedes, Germans, and Polish feudal lords.[11]

The precepts of Marxism-Leninism dictate that the popular
masses do not engage in aggressive warfare. The goal of Soviet
historians is to reinterpret the many wars in the past of Soviet
peoples to bring them into line with this view. In most cases aggressive wars are charged to the reactionary ruling classes, the
enemies of the people. In still other cases, groups of warriors are
re-labeled as brigands or raiders, and are thus divorced from the
popular masses. This probably explains what has happened to the
Lezgins in Georgian history. The 1950 edition of the history of
Georgia contained three passages on the depredations of these
fierce Dagestani tribesmen, who came out of the mountains to pillage
and rob Kakhetia, to kill its inhabitants or sell them into slavery.
Their raids lasted two centuries and sometimes decimated whole
towns. Although the history stated that they were urged on by
reactionary Moslem leaders, there could be no doubt that this

9. *Istoriia SSSR*, ed. Nechkina (1956), I, 185.
10. *Ibid.*, p. 183.
11. *Ibid.*, pp. 252-57.

aggression involved large numbers of "the people."[12] In the 1962 edition of this history, the Lezgins as such are hardly mentioned. In their place we find several instances of "bands of brigands from Dagestan, led by feudal lords," of raids by "Dagestani bands," which are linked with Turkish intrigues.[13] It is emphasized that their numbers were not large, and that they consisted of brigands, whose leaders were either class enemies or foreigners.

Raids and incursions of nomads are also substituted for older, more specific references to warfare between peoples. Petty warfare is considered by Marxism to be a characteristic of nomadic societies, and apparently scattered groups of nomads are not considered to be in the sacrosanct classification of the masses. Sizeable wars are sometimes attributed to "nomadic incursions." The history of Georgia furnishes an example of a reinterpretation along these lines. The 1950 edition includes a discussion of a war between the Georgian army and a Turkmen tribe called "the Black Sheep." The war lasted several years and in one battle in 1407 King George VII and "the greater part of his army" were killed. Several references indicate that this was a sizeable war between Georgians and Turkmens.[14] The 1962 edition covered all the military events of the war years with this passage: "With the death of Timur [1405] the incursions of nomadic tribes into Georgia did not cease. Only in 1416 was the country restored to peace and tranquility. Such were the circumstances when the Georgian King Alexander I came to the throne in 1412. He regained control of all of Georgia, whose territory had up to that time been severely restricted."[15]

THE MILITARY ALLIANCES OF THE NON-RUSSIAN PEOPLES

Although some attention is given to the economic and cultural ties that bound the non-Russian nationalities together historically, the overwhelming cooperation was military. The concept of the historic defense perimeter, discussed earlier in connection with Russian military aid, is very much in evidence here, even in ancient times. Assignment of the role of invader and defender is as easy for the Soviet historian in earlier epochs as in the Soviet period. The newest history of the Tadzhiks devotes a whole chapter to "The Struggle of the Peoples of Central Asia against Greco-Mace-

12. *Istoriia Gruzii*, ed. N. Berdzenishvili (Tbilisi, 1950), I, 393, 401, 405.
13. *Ibid.* (1962), I, 342-44, 358.
14. *Ibid.* (1950), I, 300-1.
15. *Ibid.* (1962), I, 259-60.

donian Attackers"—the invasion of Alexander the Great. The reader is told that in the uprising of 329 B.C., "under the leadership of Spitamen, settled people and nomads fought shoulder to shoulder. Particularly in that period the courage and heroism of the nationalities and tribes of Central Asia were displayed with exceptional clarity."[16] A Georgian scholar has found evidence of military cooperation of the peoples of the Caucasus against Roman incursions in the first century, A.D., as well as an alliance against Persian and Arab threats in the fifth and sixth centuries.[17] The Moldavians received the aid of the neighboring Slavs against Romanization from about the sixth century.[18]

In the Middle Ages the regional alliances of the peoples of Central Asia, the Caucasus, and the Baltic against foreign aggressors became established on a more permanent basis. In the new history, cases of warfare that were formerly seen as pitting the non-Russian nationalities against each other are reinterpreted as mutual defense efforts against foreigners, in much the same way as was noted in connection with Russian military aid. An outstanding example is the case of Georgia. The histories written in the 1940's still bristled with warfare in the Caucasus involving the future Soviet family. In the early editions of the Pankratova textbook King David the Builder (1089-1125), after recovering his capital from the Seljuks, "conquered Azerbaidzhan, and sent an expedition into Armenia. . . ." His successors "extended their rule in Armenia to Erzerum."[19] The college textbook reported also that King David took the northern part of Azerbaidzhan and "a significant part of the territory of Armenia."[20] Although it was stated that the Armenians welcomed the Georgian king as their liberator from the Seljuks, his campaigns were nevertheless presented as conquests, with the conquered areas becoming vassal states. In the later editions of the survey histories these campaigns are changed to heroic mutual defense; all hint of conquest is gone. The peoples of the Caucasus looked to Georgia as a strong centralized state capable of leading their liberation, in exactly the same way as the Baltic

16. *Istoriia tadzhikskogo naroda*, ed. B. G. Gafurov and B. A. Litvinskii (Moscow, 1963), I, chap. v and p. 274.

17. A. I. Shavkhelishvili, *Iz istorii vzaimootnoshenii mezhdu gruzinskim i checheno-ingushskim narodami* (Groznyi, 1963), pp. 46-47.

18. Mokhov, *Ocherki istorii moldavsko-russko-ukrainskikh sviazei*, p. 5; *Istoriia Moldavii*, ed. A. D. Udal'tsov and L. V. Cherepnin (Kishinev, 1951), I, 35-36.

19. *Istoriia SSSR*, ed. A. M. Pankratova (Moscow, 1940), I, 69.

20. *Istoriia SSSR*, ed. B. D. Grekov (1947), I, 136.

peoples, the Belorussians, and Ukrainians looked to Moscow. King
David the Builder has taken on the role of the Ivans for his own
area. The 1959 edition of the Pankratova textbook, in the course of
singing the praises of King David for subjugating his own feudal
lords, driving out the Seljuks, and establishing a strong monarchy,
makes the following observation:

> The successes in uniting the country permitted the
> Georgian people, with the support of the Armenian and
> Azerbaidzhani peoples, to mount a struggle against the Sel-
> juk-Turks, who had dominated the Transcaucasus since the
> middle of the eleventh century. In 1122, after a long strug-
> gle with the Turks, Tbilisi, the capital, was liberated. The
> expulsion of the Seljuks from the country increased the
> political significance of Georgia in the eyes of all the peo-
> ples of the Transcaucasus. By the end of the twelfth cen-
> tury and the beginning of the thirteenth century, a united
> Georgian-Armenian force liberated all of Armenia from
> Turkish power.[21]

As a result of this common struggle, "the economic, political and
cultural ties, which had existed among the peoples of the Transcaucasus from the remote past, were now strengthened even more."[22]
Later editions of the college textbook follow the same pattern.
Territories of the Transcaucasus were "conquered" by the Seljuks
and "liberated" by the common efforts of the local population. "Outstanding heroism in this liberation struggle was displayed by the
Georgian working masses, supported by the Armenian and Azerbaidzhani peoples."[23] The *History of the Armenian People* reports,
in an echo of the purported thoughts of Moscow's neighbors, that
"the strengthening of the Georgian state aroused considerable hopes
in the Armenian population, which was under Seljuk rule."[24]

Although the early Soviet histories seldom noted alliances between the non-Russian peoples, they did occasionally mention joint
military efforts of these peoples *against the Russians.* Such alliances
were noted between Buriats and Kazakhs, Kirgiz and Kalmyks,
Bashkirs and Kazakhs, and Bashkirs and Karakalpaks at one time

21. Bushchik, *Istoriia SSSR*, I, 70. See also *Istoriia Gruzii*, ed. Berdzenishvili
(1950), I, 195-98; *ibid.*, ed. N. Berdzenishvili and G. Khachapuridze (Tbilisi,
1962), I, 160-64.
22. Bushchik, *Istoriia SSSR*, I, 70-71.
23. *Istoriia SSSR*, ed. Nechkina (1956), I, 96-97.
24. *Istoriia armianskogo naroda,* ed. V. N. Arakelian and A. R. Ioannisian
(Erevan, 1951), I, 161.

or another, as they faced Russian encroachments.[25] These alliances have disappeared in the new history, and instead the reader finds much evidence of non-Russian peoples working together in their struggle for closer ties with the Russian people. This is a logical theme, since further *sblizhenie* with the Russians is said to have been historically tied up with disengagement from "foreigners," whose purpose was not only to exploit the non-Russian peoples, but to prevent closer relations with the Russians or with the other non-Russian nationalities.[26] Georgians and Ukrainians are said to have assisted each other in their struggle against Turkish oppression in the sixteenth century, and the Zaporozhian Cossacks are credited with helping the people of Wallachia and Moldavia in their revolts against the Turks between 1594 and 1601.[27] In their struggle to unite with the Russian people, the Ukrainians received the support of Moldavians and Belorussians. Pointing with pride to an alliance between a Moldavian *gospodar* and Khmel'nitskii, a Ukrainian scholar has declared that "one of the brightest pages in the history of the fraternal relations of the two peoples is found in the relations of the Ukraine and Moldavia at the time of the liberation wars of the Ukrainian people."[28] At a critical moment in the Ukrainian-Polish struggle in the middle of the seventeenth century, it is claimed that the Belorussians revolted, at Khmel'nitskii's request, against their Polish masters, thus increasing the military pressure on the Poles and enabling the Ukrainians to accomplish their aim: "The revolt of the national masses of Belorussia had a great significance for the liberation struggle of the brotherly Ukrainian people. The Polish Pans lost a chance to group their military forces in

25. P. T. Khaptaev, *Kratkii ocherk istorii buriat-mongol'skogo naroda* (Ulan-Ude, 1936), pp. 27; A. P. Chuloshnikov, *Vosstanie 1755 g. v Bashkirii* (Moscow, 1940), pp. 108-9; S. M. Abramzon, *Ocherk kul'tury kirgizskogo naroda* (Frunze, 1946), pp. 19-20; *Materialy po istorii Karakalpakov. Sbornik* (Moscow-Leningrad, 1935), p. 63.

26. A Georgian scholar contends that one of the Arab objectives in the Caucasus, even in the early Middle Ages, was "to break up the ties between the peoples of the North Caucasus and Georgia" (Shavkhelishvili, *Iz istorii vzaimootnoshenii*, p. 68).

27. Sh. A. Meskhia and Ia. Z. Tsinadze, *Iz istorii russko-gruzinskikh vzaimootnoshenii, X-XVIII vv.* (Tbilisi, 1958), p. 58; Mokhov, *Ocherki istorii moldavsko-russko-ukrainskikh sviazei*, p. 69; *Istoriia Moldavii*, ed. Udal'tsov and Cherepnin (1951), I, 210.

28. A. F. Ermolenko, "Ukrainsko-moldavskie otnosheniia v gody osvoboditel'-noi voiny ukrainskogo naroda," in *Vossoedinenie Ukrainy s Rossiei, 1648-1654. Sbornik statei* (Moscow, 1954), pp. 223-41.

Belorussia and Lithuania for intervention in the Ukraine."[29] Furthermore, "in the course of that struggle, the unshakable friendship of brotherly peoples was strengthened and tempered."[30]

And military aid also went in the other direction. Khmel'nitskii is said to have given military assistance to Moldavia, and in the winter of 1649, when Belorussian-Polish talks were in progress, he strengthened the hand of his Belorussian brothers by sending an army of ten thousand into their territory.[31] It is emphasized repeatedly in the histories of Belorussia and the Ukraine that their struggle against the Poles and for union with Russia was a joint campaign, in which each gave the other vital aid at critical times.[32]

In more recent times, the instances of military cooperation among the non-Russian nationalities multiply and become more diverse. There are the more recent liberation struggles. In the eighteenth century "one of the main sources of the power and scope of the liberation movement of the Armenian people was their friendship and alliance with the Georgian and Azerbaidzhani peoples."[33] It is emphasized that in the rebellions of Bolotnikov, Razin, and Pugachev many of the non-Russian nationalities participated. The Pugachev revolt, for example, is presented as a multi-national class revolt involving Ukrainians, Kazakhs, Bashkirs, Kalmyks, and Tatars. The participation of the Kazakhs in the Pugachev revolt has become a bright page in the Kazakh class struggle, although earlier historians thought their role to be minor. "In the course of the struggle against tsarist power," according to the recent Kazakh history's discussion of the revolt, "the *sblizhenie* of the workers of various nationalities proceeded further."[34] The survey histories of individual peoples make a point of their participation in the Russian wars from the time of Peter the Great to the Revolution. The Baltic,

29. *Istoriia belorusskoi SSR*, ed. L. S. Abetsedarskii, V. N. Pertsev, and K. I. Shabunia (Minsk, 1961), I, 167.

30. L. S. Abetsedarskii, "Bor'ba belorusskogo naroda za vossoedinenie Belorussii s Rossiei v seredine XVII veka," in *Vossoedinenie Ukrainy. Sbornik*, pp. 178-222. Quotation on p. 222.

31. *Istoriia Moldavii*, ed. Udal'tsov and Cherepnin (1951), I, 222-23; *Istoriia belorusskoi SSR*, ed. Abetsedarskii, Pertsev, and Shabunia (1961), I, 174.

32. *Ibid.*, I, 122, 158, 165-67, 174 ff.; *Istoriia ukrainskoi SSR*, ed. A. K. Kasimenko, V. A. Diadichenko, F. E. Los', *et al.* (Kiev, 1953), I, 226-27, 248, 250-52.

33. P. T. Arutiunian, *Osvobitel'noe dvizhenie armianskogo naroda v pervoi chetverti XVIII veka* (Moscow, 1954), pp. 182, 282.

34. *Istoriia kazakhskoi SSR*, ed. M. O. Auezov, S. B. Baishev, *et al.* (Alma-Ata, 1957), I, 269-80. Quotation on p. 275.

Belorussian, and Ukrainian peoples are said to have contributed to Peter the Great's victory over the Swedes and to the defeat of Napoleon; the peoples of the Caucasus have volunteered repeatedly for service in the Russo-Turkish Wars.[35] The Armenian and Georgian colonies in Ukrainian and Belorussian cities have fought shoulder to shoulder with the local people in their struggle with the Poles.[36] Scholarly sessions were held to commemorate the one-hundredth anniversary of the 1863 revolts in Poland, Belorussia, Lithuania, and the Western Ukraine, in which discussion of the military cooperation of these peoples played a prominent role.[37] Taken together, these histories give the impression that the Soviet family fought together in as solid a front in the past as it was purported to have fought in the Revolution or World War II.

THE FRIENDSHIP CONFERENCES

The most conspicuous development on the question of the friendship of the non-Russian nationalities has been the convening of several scholarly conferences on the subject in recent years. Such conferences have been held on Moldavian-Ukrainian-Russian friendship and Armenian-Ukrainian friendship, and plans for further meetings have been announced. An impetus for such conferences has come from the new Party Program, with its many exhortations to all Communist workers for "a further *sblizhenie* of peoples and the attainment of their complete unity," for "the even greater union of Soviet peoples," for "the intensive interchange of the material and spiritual riches among peoples, growing out of the contribution of each republic in the mutual pursuit of communist construction." According to the editors of the published proceedings of one recent conference, "research on the historic ties and fraternal friendship of Soviet peoples has become the center of attention for historians, economists, literary writers, and many other scholars."[38]

While the political motivation for these conferences has been

35. See especially V. E. Shutoi, *Bor'ba narodnykh mass protiv nashestviia armii Karla XII, 1700-1709* (Moscow, 1958).

36. V. A. Parsamian, *Uchastie pol'skikh armian v vosstanii David-Beka. Novye materialy ob armianskom osvoboditel'nom dvizhenii XVIII veka* (Erevan, 1962), p. 41.

37. *VI*, No. 4, 1963, pp. 157-58, 194.

38. *Istoricheskie sviazi i druzhba ukrainskogo i armianskogo narodov. Sbornik materialov vtoroi ukrainsko-armianskoi nauchnoi sessii* (Kiev, 1965), p. 5.

apparent, especially in the opening remarks made at each meeting by the officials of the Academies of Science, and in the prefaces to the published proceedings, it is also true that most of the papers that have been presented are of high caliber, reflecting intensive research into previously neglected archives, and a new emphasis on this aspect of local and regional history. Historians in the Union Republics have been seriously at work uncovering the data necessary to verify the generalizations that have been made about the historic friendship of the non-Russian nationalities. In connection with these conferences the various Academies of Science have announced plans for elaborate publication of archive materials, statistics, and bibliography.[39]

In November, 1958, the Institute of History of the Moldavian Academy of Sciences sponsored a conference in Kishinev on "the history of Russian-Moldavian-Ukrainian relations." A preliminary meeting on Russian-Rumanian relations had been held in Bucharest a few months earlier, and some Rumanian historians attended the Kishinev conference, at which they presented four papers in line with the others on the close historic ties of Moldavians with the Russians and Ukrainians. Apparently, one purpose of the conference was to orient Moldavian history more toward Russia and the Ukraine, and to do so with the active participation of Rumanian historians, who helped to correct the alleged errors of their bourgeois predecessors who tied Moldavia historically to the West. The tendentious nature of the scholarly quest was suggested in several passing statements made at the conference. It was admitted repeatedly that the facts about the historic relations of the Moldavian peoples with Ukrainians and Russians were little known; they had not received any serious scholarly attention until after World War II. The "mistaken views" on Moldavian history had been the work of the bourgeois historians, who concentrated on the relations of states, which were sometimes in conflict with each other. On the other hand, "Relations among the popular masses have invariably been friendly. Unfortunately, these latter relations have been studied least of all, even though they represent the greatest interest, since the creators of history are first of all the popular masses." It was also admitted that the old mistaken views were still found "in the works of certain Soviet and Rumanian historians"; the meet-

39. *Istoricheskie sviazi i druzhba ukrainskogo i armianskogo narodov. Sbornik materialov nauchnoi sessii* (Erevan, 1961), pp. 36-37.

ing was thus convened to deal with problems of the present as well as those of the past.[40]

N. A. Mokhov, the historian who has written more on Moldavian-Russian relations than anyone else, read the leading paper "On the Forms and Stages of Moldavian-Russian-Ukrainian Relations from the Fourteenth to the Eighteenth Centuries." He claimed that Moldavia had established firm trading relations with the Ukraine, and especially with the city of Lvov, from the beginning of the fifteenth century. He admitted that there was no significant trade between Moldavians and Russians in this period, but there was a reason: "Direct trade between Moldavia and Moscow was insignificant, because its development was impeded by the Polish Pans. They deliberately hindered the development of friendly Moldavian-Russian relations."[41]

One of the main points of Mokhov's paper was the emphasis on a "common uprising" of Ukrainian and Moldavian peasants between 1490 and 1492. Here again there was a question of obscurity and an erroneous interpretation by earlier historians. Bourgeois historical literature had largely ignored the uprising, and some historians had named the *gospodar*, Stephen III, as its leader. But the movement was a genuine peasant revolt, led by one Mukhi, according to Mokhov's research. It was entered in the record here as evidence of the common class interests and cooperation of the Ukrainian and Moldavian masses at that early date. Moldavians had also assisted the Ukrainians in later military operations against the Turks.[42]

In other sessions of this conference papers were read on the evidences of the friendship of peoples in Ukrainian chronicles, on the history of social thought in Russia and Moldavia in early modern times, the Russian-Moldavian alliance of 1711 against the Turks, the mission of a Moldavian diplomat to St. Petersburg in the 1730's, and the Moldavian role in the Russo-Turkish War of 1768-1774. The emphasis on Moldavian-Ukrainian friendship was thus secondary to Moldavian-Russian relations.

Two conferences have been held on "the historic ties and friendship of the Ukrainian and Armenian peoples," the first in Erevan in October, 1959, and the second in Kiev and Lvov in November, 1962.

40. *Vekovaia druzhba. Materialy nauchnoi sessii instituta istorii moldav-skogo filiala A. N. SSSR* (Kishinev, 1961), pp. 5, 10, 20.

41. *Ibid.*, p. 12.

42. *Ibid.*, pp. 20-23; see also *Istoriia Moldavii*, ed. Udal'tsov and Cherepnin (1951), I, 109.

These meetings were attended not only by the historians of the two republics, but also by archivists and museum personnel. Some fifty papers were presented at these sessions, ranging chronologically from Armenian ties with Kiev Rus' to "the participation of the sons of the Armenian people in the struggle for the Ukraine, 1941-1944." Aside from the opening speech by A. B. Arutiunian, Director of the Armenian Institute of History, on "The Leninist Friendship of Peoples of the U.S.S.R.," the Erevan conference was remarkable for its high level of scholarship and comparative freedom from propaganda.[43] The papers showed the evidence of extensive research by Lvov historians on the Armenian colony living in that city, as well as work from Armenian archives on the history of the Ukraine. The propaganda content of the Kiev-Lvov conference was somewhat greater, but there were also scholarly papers on Armenian trade, population figures, and the Armenian colonies in Ukrainian towns. One of the most interesting scholarly exercises in behalf of the friendship of peoples was the paper of F. N. Shevchenko on "Armenians in the Cossack Forces in the Seventeenth and Eighteenth Centuries."[44] Admitting at the outset that he was skating on very thin ice, Shevchenko tried to prove that Khmel'nitskii's war of liberation in the Ukraine was a multi-national movement, involving the Armenians prominently. From his study of names on the Cossack rosters, he concluded that twenty-one nationalities fought with Khmel'nitskii's Cossacks. Remaining true to his class outlook, Shevchenko made the flat statement that the "prosperous Armenians were in agreement with the Polish ruling classes and came out against the liberation struggle of the Ukrainian people. But as for the Armenian workers, they, on the other hand, regarded the mighty popular movement with great sympathy." On the basis of a few Armenian names on the military rosters (no numbers were given), Shevchenko stated that the Armenian workers, who had made the Ukraine "their second home," made a great contribution to the Ukrainian struggle for union with Russia.

It seems likely that such conferences on the friendship of peoples will become a part of the pattern of coordinating research in the U.S.S.R. Past conferences have been praised in other meetings, and the planners have stated their intentions to convene new ones. Speaking to the All-Union Conference of Historians in December, 1962, the Ukrainian historian, A. K. Kasimenko, pointed to the

43. *Istoricheskie sviazi i druzhba* (1961), pp. 9-34.
44. *Istoricheskie sviazi i druzhba* (1965), pp. 93-100.

Ukrainian-Armenian conferences as examples of "positive experience in the joint scholarly treatment of the historic ties between peoples," and called for setting up research and writing teams "to prepare works which comprehensively treat the fraternal mutual aid and friendship among peoples."[45]

45. Quoted in *Soviet Studies in History*, II (1963), No. 1, p. 40.

CHAPTER **19.**

CONCLUSION

" 'You see this text? It is good for this year only' ... [snickers
from the audience]." A Moscow history teacher, complain-
ing to his school administrator, in the recent Soviet film
Let's See What Monday Will Bring, *as quoted in the* New
York Times, *December 26, 1968.*

The universal affirmation in Soviet historical works of the
concept of historic friendship among the peoples of the U.S.S.R.
has become one of the distinctive accomplishments of Soviet historical science. Soviet historians have made their contribution to
"Communist construction" by their elaborations upon the sketchy
blueprints of the party, verifying the claims of Soviet nationality
policy and giving them an historical dimension. The role of the
Russian people as cultural leader, military defender, and political
genius has become an axiom of Soviet historiography, as has the
perennial good relations among Soviet peoples in all historic epochs.

The new interpretations have in the course of time been refined
and put into the acceptable framework of Marxism-Leninism. However, they have been formulated at great cost. Almost every Soviet
historian who had written anything about the non-Russian peoples
before 1950 has been obliged to repudiate his work, and some have
become complete professional casualties. The new history is replete
with studied vagueness, awkward arguments, and far-fetched generalizations. On the advice of the party, the historian has placed
severe restrictions on empirical evidence, and has come to cite
Central Committee resolutions as prime historical sources. He has
detected and analyzed the class struggle in many obscure eras and
places, and has given great weight to such faceless historical forces

418

as "tsarism" and "the people." He has contrived his interpretations by artificially dividing historical events into progressive and reactionary components, sometimes dividing a single event on the basis of time, geography, or a shift in the class struggle. Not even "the people"—the sacrosanct makers of history—have escaped the ambiguities of these politically inspired interpretations: "the people" have at times been misled, or have failed to discern their class interests.

The historical works on the non-Russian nationalities that were appearing a decade after the party's crackdown on *Voprosy istorii* indicate that the ideological battles with the bourgeois nationalists are over, and that the party has won its predictable victory. The new interpretations have been standardized, and are put forward in a matter-of-fact way with a new sophistication. It is no longer necessary for the historian who is affirming the party interpretation to argue his points effusively, or to take a defensive stance. This new uniformity and stability can be attributed largely to recent successes in coordination and collective scholarly work.

This is the tone characterizing the new histories of Moldavia, Kazakhstan, and Turkmenia,[1] and the first parts of the long awaited eleven-volume *History of the U.S.S.R.*, which began to appear on the eve of the fiftieth anniversary of the October Revolution.[2] The main lines of the recently established interpretations concerning Russian colonial history and the friendship of peoples are presented routinely in these works, as a generally accepted accomplishment of Soviet historical science. These themes are given somewhat less proportionate space than in Soviet works of a few years ago, and the rough edges of the Stalinist arguments have been honed off. Footnotes and the bibliographies lead the reader to numerous Soviet monographs of the last fifteen years and to a few carefully selected older works. Soviet historical works that were the center of controversy a few years ago have vanished like the melted snow. In general, these histories also pass over the contentions of the "bourgeois falsifiers," so that the reader might conclude that these are solid interpretations, which have not been challenged either at

1. *Istoriia moldavskoi SSR*, ed. L. V. Cherepnin *et al.* (Kishinev, 1965), Vol. I; E. B. Bekmakhanov, *Ochecki istorii Kazakhstana XIX v*, (Alma-Ata, 1966); *Istoriia Turkmenistana* (*Uchebnoe posobie dlia vuzov*), ed. A. Karryev *et al.* (Ashkhabad, 1966).

2. *Istoriia SSSR. S drevneishikh vremen do nashikh dnei. V dvukh seriiakh v dvenadtsati tomakh*, gen. ed., B. N. Ponomarev (Moscow, 1966-). The first three volumes, on the history of the U.S.S.R. from ancient times to the seventeenth century, had appeared by early 1967.

home or abroad. One gathers that there are few unsettled questions in this area. These new histories also present a more orderly synthesis of the history of Soviet peoples, and a somewhat more modest account of the historical relations of the Russian and non-Russian peoples—a visible sign of more efficient coordination of historical writing through large collectives of editors and authors, and of a *modus vivendi* among Soviet historians.[3]

The new multi-volume *History of the U.S.S.R.* marks a new refinement in scholarly coordination and collective work. The general editor of this series is B. N. Ponomarev, the party theoretician who has been the strong advocate of collective scholarly work. It is doubtful that so many Soviet historians have cooperated before on a work of this size. There are three levels of editorial boards. The Main Editorial Council has thirty-two members; the Editorial Commission of the First Series (Volumes I-VI) consists of twenty; there are two to five editors for each of the first three volumes to appear. The authors of the individual volumes number between twenty and thirty. Not counting duplications, it seems likely that some two hundred editors and authors will have worked on this series by the time it is completed. There is a good representation of non-Russian historians in these collectives, but the names of the controversial scholars—the Bekmakhanovs, Magomedovs, Karryevs, and Gadzhievs—are not listed.

Another significant indication of the end of ideological battle and a new stability in Soviet historical scholarship is the appearance of the *Selected Works* of Pokrovskii, who has resumed his place as the pioneer Bolshevik historian.[4] This most outspoken critic of Russian colonialism has been corrected by editorial footnotes, as was the case with Bakhrushin. But the corrections are less conspicuous and are not argued: Pokrovskii's editors point out that he had not entirely freed himself of bourgeois concepts, and of course he could not benefit from the researches of later Soviet historians. Their corrections of his views are unaccompanied by any of the angry attacks of the Stalin era. Thus Pokrovskii could hardly be expected to perceive the nature of the "Old Russian State," or see the significance of the centralized Moscow state, since the true "Marxist-Leninist" interpretation of these subjects was de-

3. These conclusions are based on an examination of the pertinent sections of these works. All of the books cited in this chapter came into my hands too late to permit a detailed incorporation of their views into this study.

4. M. N. Pokrovskii, *Izbrannye proizvedeniia*, ed. M. N. Tikhomirov *et al.* (Moscow, 1965-67).

termined later by Soviet historians. He misunderstood the historical role of the expansion of the Russian state among the non-Russian nationalities, and failed to detect the development of a class alliance among the downtrodden, multi-national mass in the Russian colonies.[5] The editors quietly correct Pokrovskii, apparently ignoring evidence of his that is detrimental to current interpretations. But Pokrovskii's successors have not been entirely equal to their task. They have avoided doing battle with his two most acrimonious condemnations of Russian colonialism; neither his *Diplomacy and War in Tsarist Russia* nor *Historical Science and the Class Struggle* was included in the *Selected Works*. Correcting those works by editorial footnotes would be a formidable task indeed.

Pokrovskii's editors take in stride even the most sensitive themes. It is necessary for them to turn his version of the Ukrainian annexation upside down, and they do so with maximum economy of words by trumping their predecessor with the citation of a more recent and authoritative source, the Central Committee's *Theses* of 1953.[6] Thus the old Bolshevik's well-known dictum that history is "politics retrojected into the past" is given a practical application at his own expense.

Although the ideological fires seem to have been put out, there is still a small cloud of smoke hanging over the North Caucasus, sufficient to obscure the scene in the late 1960's. Scanty evidence from Shamil's homeland suggests that the historians of Dagestan have not only been subjected to unusual coordination measures, but have perhaps been restricted in their publications, as they were before 1956. Since 1965 very few historical works have been published by these scholars, and they have been published in Moscow, and not in Makhachkala, the center of earlier dissension. It was noted previously that Gadzhiev's *The Role of Russia in the History of Dagestan* (1965), although published under the auspices of the Dagestan branch of the Academy of Sciences, appeared from the press in Moscow. This seems to be the emerging pattern. In 1965 only five historical works were published in Makhachkala—a decline from earlier years. During the following three years, not a single book on history was reported out of the Dagestan capital. The multi-volume *History of Dagestan,* probably the most ambitious undertaking of Dagestan historians, also began to appear from Mos-

5. *Ibid.,* I, 180-82; 208 ff., 495-99; III, 24-34.
6. *Ibid.,* III, 82.

cow. It is worth noting that the volumes have appeared out of order. The first volume, dealing with Dagestan's history up to 1800,
was published in 1967; the third volume, covering the period since
the Revolution, appeared early in 1968; but the second volume
on the sensitive nineteenth century had not appeared almost
a year later, suggesting that the authors and editors may continue
to have difficulty producing an acceptable version.[7]

It is too early to determine whether the new Soviet history, with
its strong emphasis on the friendship of Soviet peoples in the past,
will make the desired contribution to the reduction of nationalist
tensions among the peoples of the Soviet family. But there are
indications in recent party propaganda work that efforts are being
redoubled to indoctrinate the Soviet citizen to the concept that
he belongs to a commonwealth of peoples with a long record of
good relations.

The party appears to be well pleased with this accomplishment
of Soviet historians, as is indicated by the recent cordial relations
between party and scholarly forces, and the lack of controversy.
The emphasis now is on elaboration and popularization of the new
interpretations. In view of the party's new controls and coordination of scholarship in recent years, there is little likelihood that
these welcome interpretations will be seriously re-examined in the
near future. But the resistance of some Soviet historians in the late
1940's and their quick rebuttal in 1956 made it quite clear that if
they were given the choice they would base their interpretations on
more solid stuff than the generalizations of party theoreticians,
offered under the pressures of political developments.

7. *Istoriia Dagestana,* ed. G. D. Daniialov, G. A. Alikberov, V. G. Gadzhiev, *et al.* (Moscow, 1967–). My observations on these publications are
based on an examination of the monthly list of new books in *Voprosy istorii,*
which presumably includes all works on history published in the U.S.S.R.

GLOSSARY

batyr—a Kazakh popular hero, a military leader. Formerly considered equal to the Russian *bogatyr*, but more recently regarded as a reactionary feudal or tribal leader.

bogatyr—Russian folk hero, usually a military hero.

chinovnik—tsarist official, a bureaucrat.

dvorianstvo—the Russian service gentry.

gazavat—a Moslem holy war.

gospodar—the ruling prince of Moldavia.

iasak—tribute paid by the Siberian peoples.

imam—the spiritual, military, and governmental leader of the Murids, a fanatical Moslem sect in the North Caucasus.

kandidat—a post-graduate degree, lower than the doctorate; the standard degree of Soviet academicians.

maket—a model or dummy. A preliminary version of a book circulated for discussion and revision.

manap—a member of the Kirgiz feudal aristocracy.

miatezh—a mutiny. In the Soviet categories of just and unjust wars, the *miatezh* is usually reactionary, having none of the progressive qualities of other terms for revolts.

muridism—the fanatical sect of Moslems of the North Caucasus.

oblast—a Russian province. In this case, a frontier area ruled by a military governor.

ostrog—a wooden fortress constructed along the line of Russian advance in Siberia.

prisoedinenie—annexation; joining together. In current Soviet usage, the term refers to a joining of two territories, without reference to their size or importance.

prosvetitel'—literally, enlightener. Refers to a group of literary and cultural leaders in the Russian colonies.

rodina—the land of one's birth; used in a patriotic sense, as the equivalent of motherland.

sblizhenie—merging; coming together. Used in the sense of *rapprochement*, but also to refer to the eventual Soviet goal of complete disappearance of all national differences among Soviet peoples.

starshina—a Cossack military leader; in Central Asia a native elder.

starshii brat—elder brother, referring to the position of the Russian people in relation to the non-Russian peoples. The term does not refer to chronological seniority, but to the sense of importance and cultural advancement.

strel'tsy—the standing infantry of the Russian state between the fifteenth and seventeenth centuries.

stremlenie—striving, yearning. Used here to describe the alleged orientation of non-Russian peoples for annexation to the Russian state.

szlachta—the Polish gentry.

uezd—a lesser Russian governmental unit, a subdivision of an *oblast* or *guberniia.*

voevoda—a Russian military governor.

volnenie—literally, agitation. Used here to refer to an uprising without definite leadership or political goals.

vossoedinenie—reunion or reunification.

vosstanie—uprising. In contrast to the *volnenie*, the *vosstanie* has a definite leadership and political goals.

zhdanovshchina—the period of Zhdanov, referring to the cultural regimentation of the years immediately after World War II.

BIBLIOGRAPHY

In a few cases books that have been mentioned in this study were not available to me. In most cases these are works that have been condemned and withdrawn from circulation in the U.S.S.R. They are listed in this bibliography in brackets.

This bibliography does not include works published after the middle of 1967.

Abbreviations of works frequently cited are as follows:

BSE	Bol'shaia sovetskaia entsiklopediia
CAR	Central Asian Review
CDSP	Current Digest of the Soviet Press
IM	Istorik-Marksist
IZ	Istoricheskii zhurnal
POP	Problems of the Peoples of the USSR
VAN	Vestnik Akademii Nauk. . .
VI	Voprosy Istorii

1. COLLECTIONS OF DOCUMENTS; PROCEEDINGS AND REPORTS OF CONFERENCES; RESOLUTIONS AND DIRECTIVES OF THE PARTY, GOVERNMENT, AND ACADEMY OF SCIENCES

Armiano-russkie otnosheniia v XVII veka. Sbornik dokumentov. Erevan, 1953.

Armiano-russkie otnosheniia v pervoi treti XVIII veka. Sbornik dokumentov. Vol. II, Part 1. Erevan, 1964.

Bekmakhanov, E., and V. Shakhmatov. "Pervaia nauchnaia sessiia instituta istorii, arkheologii i etnografii akademii nauk kazakhskoi SSSR," *VAN kazakhskoi SSR,* No. 5, 1947, pp. 10-16.

Direktivy VKP (b) i postanovleniia sovetskogo pravitel'stva o narodnom obrazovanii. Sbornik dokumentov za 1919-1947 gg. Moscow-Leningrad, 1947.

"Diskussiia o dvizhenii Shamilia," *VI,* No. 11, 1947, pp. 134-40.

"Dokumenty o dvizhenii gortsev severo-vostochnogo Kavkaza 20-50 gg. XIX v. pod rukovodstvom Shamilia," *Uchenye zapiski dagestanskii fiilial akademii nauk SSSR. Institut istorii, iazyka i literatury,* I (1956), 120-69.

Dokumenty po istorii Balkarii (konets XIX-nachalo XX v.). Nal'chik, 1962.

Druzhba narodov i sotsialisticheskii internatsionalizm—velikaia sila

v bor'be za postroenie kommunizma. Materialy mezhrespubli-
kanskogo seminara-soveshchaniia, sostoiavshegosia v Tashkente
10-15 aprelia 1961 g. Tashkent, 1961.
Druzhba narodov RSFSR (materialy v pomoshch' propagandistu i
agitatoru). Leningrad, 1938.
Dvizhenie gortsev severo-vostochnogo kavkaza v 20-50 gg. XIX veka.
Sbornik dokumentov. Ed. G. D. Daniialov. Makhachkala, 1959.
Dvizhenie kavkazskikh gortsev pod rukovodstvom Shamilia. Doklady
i reshenie nauchnoi sessii dagestanskogo filiala akademii nauk
SSSR v Makhachkale, 4-7 oktiabria, 1956 g. Makhachkala, 1956.
"Dvizhenie kavkazskikh gortsev v pervoi polovine XIX v.," *VAN*
SSSR, No. 2, 1957, pp. 121-23.
Istoricheskie sviazi i druzhba ukrainskogo i armianskogo narodov.
Sbornik materialov nauchnoi sessii. Erevan, 1961.
Istoricheskie sviazi i druzhba ukrainskogo i armianskogo narodov.
Sbornik materialov vtoroi ukrainsko-armianskoi nauchnoi sessii.
Kiev, 1965.
"Itogi obsuzhdeniia uchebnikov institute istorii A N," *IM*, No. 9,
1940, pp. 144-48.
"K diskussii o kharaktere dvizheniia gortsev Dagestana pod rukov-
odstvom Shamilia," *VI*, No. 1, 1957, pp. 195-96.
KPSS v rezoliutsiiakh i resheniiakh s"ezdov, konferentsii i plenumov
Ts. K. 7th ed. Moscow, 1953.
Kabardino-russkie otnosheniia v XVI-XVIII vv. 2 vols. Moscow,
1957.
Kazakhsko-russkie otnosheniia v XVI-XVIII vekakh (sbornik doku-
mentov i materialov). Alma-Ata, 1961.
Kazakhsko-russkie otnosheniia v XVIII-XIX vekakh (sbornik doku-
mentov i materialov). Alma-Ata, 1964.
Kolonial'naia politika rossisskogo tsarizma v Azerbaidzhane v 20-60
gg. XIX v. Moscow, 1936.
Kolonial'naia politika tsarizma na Kamchatke i Chukomke v XVIII
veke. Sbornik arkhivnykh materialov. Leningrad, 1935.
Kolonial'naia politiki moskovskogo gosudarstva v Iakutii v XVII v.
Sbornik dokumentov. Leningrad, 1936.
"Konferentsiia chitatelei zhurnala 'Voprosy istorii,'" *VI*, No. 2, 1956,
pp. 199-213.
"Konferentsiia chitatelei zhurnala 'Voprosy istorii' v Kieve," *VI*, No.
8, 1956, pp. 198-203.
Materialy nauchnoi sessii, posviashchennoi 400-letiiu prisoedineniia
Bashkirii k russkomu gosudarstvu. Ufa, 1957.
Materialy nauchnoi sessii, posviashchennoi istorii Srednei Azii i
Kazakhstana v dooktiabr'skii period. Tashkent, 1955.

Materialy ob"edinennoi nauchnoi sessii posviashchennoi istorii Sred-nei Azii i Kazakhstana (epokha sotsializma). Alma-Ata, 1958.
Materialy pervoi vsesoiuznoi nauchnoi konferentsii vostokovedov v g. Tashkente, 4-11 iiunia, 1957 g. Tashkent, 1958.
Materialy po istorii bashkirskoi ASSR. 5 vols. Moscow-Leningrad, 1936-60.
Materialy po istorii gruzino-russkikh vzaimootnoshenii, 1615-1640. Tbilisi, 1937.
Materialy po istorii Karakalpakov. Sbornik trudy instituta vostok-ovedeniia. Vol. VII. Moscow, 1935.
Materialy po istorii Tatarii. Vol. I. Kazan', 1948.
Nachalo revoliutsionnogo dvizheniia v Turkmenii v 1900-1905 gg. Ashkhabad-Moscow, 1946.
"Nauchnaia konferentsiia o kharaktere natsional'nykh dvizhenii v Kirgizii vo vtoroi polovine XIX-nachale XX veke," *VI*, No. 7, 1953, pp. 172-74.
"Nauchnaia sessiia po voprosam istorii kabardinskogo naroda," *VI*, No. 10, 1953, pp. 150-53.
O dvizhenii gortsev pod rukovodstvom Shamilia. Materialy sessii dagestanskogo filiala akademii nauk SSSR, 4-7 oktiabr, 1956 goda. Makhachkala, 1957.
"O merakh po uluchsheniiu deiatel'nosti akademii nauk SSSR i akademii nauk soiuznykh respublik," *VAN SSSR*, No. 6, 1963, pp. 3-22.
"O merakh po uluchsheniiu koordinatsii nauchno-issledovatel'skikh rabot v strane i deiatel'nosti akademii nauk SSSR," *Spravochnik partiinogo rabotnika.* Moscow, 1963. Pp. 397-403.
"O perspektivnoi plane v oblasti istoricheskoi nauki," *IZ*, No. 3, 1945, pp. 60-75.
"O podgotovke 2-go izdaniia 'Istorii kazakhskoi SSR,' " *Bol'shevik Kazakhstana*, No. 6, 1945, pp. 49-51.
"O sostoianii i merakh uluchsheniia agitatsionno-propagandiskoi raboty v bashkirskoi partiinoi organizatsii," *Propagandist*, Nos. 3-4, 1945, pp. 16-18.
"O sostoianii i merakh uluchsheniia massovo-politicheskoi i ideo-logicheskoi raboty v tatarskoi partiinoi organizatsii," *Propagandist*, Nos. 15-16, 1944, pp. 19-22.
"O zadachakh partiinoi propagandy v sovremennykh usloviiakh," *Pravda*, January 10, 1960.
"O zhurnale 'Voprosy istorii,' " *Spravochnik partiinogo rabotnika.* Moscow, 1957. Pp. 381-82.
"Ob itogakh ob"edinennoi nauchnoi sessii, posviashchennoi istorii narodov Srednei Azii i Kazakhstana," *VAN SSSR*, No. 5, 1954, pp. 60-61.

"Ob obsuzhdenii I toma uchebnika dlia vuzov po istorii SSSR," *IM*, Nos. 4-5, 1940, pp. 107-13.

"Ob ocherednykh zadachakh ideologicheskoi raboty partii," *Pravda*, June 22, 1963.

"Ob opere 'Velikaia druzhba' V. Muradeli," *Bol'shevik*, No. 3, 1948, pp. 10-14.

"Ob"edinennia nauchnaia sessiia, posviashchennaia progressivnomu znacheniiu prisoedineniia Srednei Azii k Rossii," *VI*, No. 8, 1959, pp. 173-83.

"Obsuzhdenie monografii E. Bekmakhanova 'Kazakhstana v 20-40 e. gody XIX veka,'" *VAN kazakhskoi SSR*, No. 3, 1948, pp. 35-58.

"Obsuzhdenie v redaktsii 'Istoricheskogo zhurnal' knigi 'Istoriia kazakhskoi SSR,'" *IZ*, Nos. 11-12, 1943, pp. 85-90.

"Obsuzhdenie voprosa o kharaktere dvizhenii gorskikh narodov severnogo Kavkaza v 20-50kh godakh XIX veka," *VI*, No. 12, 1956, pp. 188-98.

"Pervyi plenum iakutskogo nauchno-issledovatel'skogo instituta," *VI*, No. 1, 1946, pp. 153-55.

[Pervyi] *I s''ezd intelligentsii Uzbekistana, 11-13 oktiabr 1956 goda. Stenograficheskii ocherk*. Tashkent, 1957.

"Plenum TsK KP(b) Armenii," *Pravda*, September 26, 1947.

Prisoedinenie Turkmenii k Rossii (sbornik arkhivnykh dokumentov). Ashkhabad, 1960.

Programma kommunisticheskoi partii sovetskogo soiuza. Moscow, 1961.

Proniknovenie revoliutsionnykh idei i razvitie revoliutsionnogo dvizheniia v Turkmenistane v 1881-1907 gody (dokumenty i materialy). Ashkhabad, 1962.

Revoliutsionnoe dvizhenie v Turkmenii (1908-1917). Ashkhabad-Moscow, 1946.

Rossiia i Turkmeniia v XIX veke. K vkhozhdeniiu Turkmenii v sostav Rossii. Ashkhabad, 1946.

Russko-adygeiskie torgovye sviazi, 1793-1860 gg. Sbornik dokumentov. Maikop, 1957.

Russko-belorusskie sviazi. Sbornik dokumentov (1570-1667 gg.) Minsk, 1963.

Russko-dagestanskie otnosheniia XVII-pervoi chetverti XVIII vv. Makhachkala, 1957.

Russko-turkmenskie otnosheniia v XVIII-XIX vv. (do prisoedineniia Turkmenii k Rossii) Sbornik arkhivnikh dokumentov. Ashkhabad, 1963.

Sbornik rukovodiashchikh materialov o shkole. Moscow, 1952.

Shakhmatov, V. F., and G. F. Dakhshleiger. "K itogam obsuzhdeniia maketa 1-go toma 'Istorii kazakhskoi SSR,'" *VAN kazakhskoi SSR*, No. 7, 1953, pp. 9-20.

Shamil'—stavlennik sultanskoi turtsii i angliiskikh kolonizatorov. Ed. Sh. V. Tsagareishvili. Tbilisi, 1953.

Tezisy o 300-letii vossoedineniia Ukrainy s Rossiei (1654-1954 gg.). Moscow, 1954.

Trudy ob"edinennoi nauchnoi sessii akademii nauk SSSR i akademii nauk zakavkazskikh respublik po obshchestvennym naukam (29 marta-2 aprela, 1954 g.). Baku, 1957.

Trudy pervoi vsesoiuznoi konferentsii istorikov-marksistov. Vol. I. Moscow, 1930.

"Ukrayns'ky istoriki v borot'b istorichnu pravdu," *Nashe slovo*, No. 16 (December 2), 1956.

"V institute istorii, arkheologii i etnografii akademii nauk kazakhskoi SSR," *VI*, No. 2, 1952, pp. 146-51.

"V otdelenii istorii i filosofii akademii nauk SSSR," *Izvestiia akademii nauk SSSR. Seriia istorii i filosofii*, VIII (1951), No. 2, 195-201.

Vekovaia druzhba. Materialy nauchnoi sessii instituti istorii moldavskogo filiala akademii nauk SSSR. Kishinev, 1961.

"Verkhovnomu sovetu buriatskoi ASSR, Sovetu ministrov buriatskoi ASSR, buriatskomu obkomu KPSS," *Pravda*, July 4, 1959.

"Verkhovnomu sovetu kabardino-balkarskoi ASSR, sovetu ministrov kabardino-balkarskoi ASSR, kabardino-balkarskomu obkomu KPSS," *Pravda*, July 6, 1957.

Vossoedinenie Ukrainy s Rossiei. Dokumenty i materialy. Ed. A. K. Kasimenko, A. L. Sidorov, L. V. Cherepnin, *et al.* 3 vols. Moscow, 1954.

Vosstanie 1916 goda v Srednei Azii i Kazakhstane. Ed. A. V. Piaskovskii. Moscow, 1960.

Vosstanie 1916 g. v Kirgizstane. Dokumenty i materialy. Moscow, 1937.

Vsesoiuznoe soveshchanie o merakh uluchsheniia podgotovki nauchno-pedagogicheskikh kadrov po istoricheskim naukam, 18-21 dekabr, 1962 Moscow, 1964.

Zevelev, A., and Sh. Abdullaev. "Diskussiia o kharaktere natsional'nykh dvizhenii v Srednei Azii i Kazakhstane v kolonial'nyi period," *VI*, No. 9, 1951, pp. 173-78.

2. SOVIET STUDIES ON THE ANNEXATION OF
THE NON-RUSSIAN NATIONALITIES

Alekseeva, E. P., I. Kh. Kalmykov, and V. P. Nevskaia. *Dobrovol'noe prisoedinenie Cherkesii k Rossii (k 400-letnemy iubileiu).* Cherkessk, 1957.

Aminov, A. M., and A. Kh. Babakhodzhaev. *Ekonomicheskie i politicheskie posledstviia prisoedineniia Srednei Azii k Rossii.* Tashkent, 1966.

Apollova, N. G. *Prisoedinenie Kazakhstana k Rossii v 30-kh godakh XVIII veka.* Alma-Ata, 1948.

Bekmakhanov, E. B. *Prisoedinenie Kazakhstana k Rossii.* Moscow, 1957.

Bliev, M. M. *Prisoedinenie severnoi Osetii k Rossii.* Ordzhonikidze, 1959.

Dzhamgerchinov, B. *Dobrovol'noe vkhozhdenie Kirgizii v sostav Rossii.* Frunze, 1963.

———. *O progressivnom znachenii vkhozhdeniia Kirgizii v sostav Rossii.* Frunze, 1963.

———. *Prisoedinenie Kirgizii k Rossii.* Moscow, 1959.

Dzidzariia, G. A. *Prisoedinenie Abkhazii k Rossii i ego istoricheskoe znachenie.* Sukhumi, 1960.

Grigorian, Z. T. *Prisoedinenie vostochnoi Armenii k Rossii.* Moscow, 1959.

Ioannisian, A. R. *Prisoedinenie Zakavkaz'ia k Rossii i mezhdunarodnye otnosheniia v nachale XIX stoletiia.* Erevan, 1958.

Iskandarov, B. I. *Vostochnaia Bukhara i Pamir v period prisoedineniia Srednei Azii k Rossii.* Stalinabad, 1960.

Khalfin, N. A. *Prisoedinenie Srednei Azii k Rossii (60-90e gody XIX v.).* Moscow, 1965.

Kumykov, T. Kh. *Prisoedinenie Kabardy k Rossii i ego progressivnye posledstviia.* Nal'chik, 1957.

Mirzoev, V. G. *Prisoedinenie i osvoenie Sibiri v istoricheskoi literature XVII veka.* Moscow, 1960.

Prisoedinenie Azerbaidzhana k Rossii i ego progressivno-ekonomicheskie rezul'taty. Ed. E. S. Sumbadze and M. E. Ismailov. Baku, 1957.

Prisoedinenie Azerbaidzhana k Rossii i ego progressivnye posledstviia v oblasti ekonomiki i kul'tury. Ed. A. N. Guliev and V. D. Mochalov. Baku, 1955.

Tikhomirov, M. N. *Prisoedinenie Merva.* Moscow, 1960.

Tsibikov, B. *K voprosu o dobrovol'nam prisoedinenie Buriat-Mongolii k Rossii.* Ulan-Ude, 1950.

Usenbaev, K. *Prisoedinenie iuzhnoi Kirgizii k Rossii.* Frunze, 1960.

Usmanov, A. N. *Prisoedinenie Bashkirii k moskovskomu gosudarstvu.* Ufa, 1949.
——. *Prisoedinenie Bashkirii k russkomu gosudarstvu.* Ufa, 1960.
Verein, L. E. *Prisoedinenie nizhnego povolsh'ia k russkomu gosudarstvu. Nachalo stroitel'stva russkoi Astrakhani; k 400-letiiu Astrakhani.* Astrakhan', 1958.
Zalkind, E. M. *Prisoedinenie Buriatii k Rossii.* Ulan-Ude, 1958.

3. SOVIET SURVEY HISTORIES AND TEXTBOOKS

Since this study is primarily concerned with the period of the Russian Empire, the volumes listed here deal mainly with that period. Survey histories of earlier or later periods have not been listed except when they have been referred to in the text.

Asfendiarov, S. D. *Istoriia Kazakhstana (s drevneishikh vremen).* Vol. I. Alma-Ata, 1935.
Bekmakhanov, E. B. *Istoriia kazakhskoi SSR. Uchebnoe posobie dlia 8-9-go klassov srednei shkoly Kazakhstana.* Alma-Ata, 1959.
——. *Istoriia kazakhskoi SSR. Uchebnoe posobie dlia 10 klassa srednei shkoly Kazakhstana.* Alma-Ata, 1960.
——. *Ocherki istorii Kazakhstana XIX v.* Alma-Ata, 1966.
Bushchik, L. P. *Istoriia SSSR.* Vol. I. Moscow, 1959.
Dimitriev, V. D. *Istoriia Chuvashii XVIII veka (do krest'ianskoi voiny 1773-1775 godov).* Cheboksary, 1959.
Gafurov, B. G. *Istoriia tadzhikskogo naroda v kratkom izlozhenii.* Moscow, 1949.
——. 2nd ed. Moscow, 1952.
——. 3rd ed. Moscow, 1955.
Gafurov, B., and N. Prokhorov. *Tadzhikskii narod v bor'be za svobody i nezavisimost' svoei rodiny. Ocherki iz istorii tadzhikov i Tadzhikistana.* Stalinabad, 1944.
Iavorskii, M. *Istoriia Ukrainy v styslomu narysi.* Kharkov, 1928.
——. *Korotka istoriia Ukrainy.* Kharkov, 1923.
——. *Kratkaia istoriia Ukrainy.* Kharkov, 1925.
——. *Narys istorii Ukrainy.* Kharkov, 1922.
Istoriia armianskogo naroda. Vol. I. (*S drevneishikh vremen do kontsa XVIII veka*). Ed. K. G. Kafadarian and M. T. Nersisian. Erevan, 1944.
Istoriia armianskogo naroda. Vol. I. Ed. V. N. Arakelian and A. R. Ioannisian. Erevan, 1951.
Istoriia Azerbaidzhana. Vol. I. Ed. I. A. Guseinov *et al.* Baku, 1958.

Istoriia belorusskoi SSR. Vol. I. Ed. V. N. Pertsev, K. I. Shabunia, and L. S. Abetsedarskii. Minsk, 1954.

Istoriia belorusskoi SSR. Vol. I. Ed. L. S. Abetsedarskii, V. N. Pertsev, and K. I. Shabunia. Minsk, 1961.

Istoriia buriat-mongol'skoi ASSR. Vol. I. Ed. A. P. Okladnikov. Ulan-Ude, 1951.

Istoriia buriat-mongol'skoi ASSR. Vol. I. Ed. P. T. Khaptaev *et al.* Ulan-Ude, 1964.

Istoriia chuvashskoi ASSR. Vol. I. Ed. I. D. Kuznetsov *et al.* Chekobary, 1966.

Istoriia estonskoi SSR. Ed. G. I. Naan. Tallin, 1958.

Istoriia estonskoi SSR. Vol. I: *S drevneishikh vremen do serediny XIX veka.* Ed. A. Vassar and G. Naan. Tallin, 1961.

Istoriia estonskoi SSR. Vol. II: *S 50kh godov XIX veka po mart 1917 goda.* Ed. I. Saam, A. Vassar, *et al.* Tallin, 1966.

Istoriia Gruzii. Vol. I: *S drevneishikh vremen do nachala XIX veka.* Ed. N. Berdzenishvili. Tbilisi, 1950.

Istoriia Gruzii. Vol. I: *S drevneishikh vremen do 6okh godov XIX veka.* Ed. N. Berdzenishvili and G. Khachapuridze. Tbilisi, 1962.

Istoriia iakutskoi ASSR. Vol. II: *Iakutiia ot 1630kh godov do 1917 g.* Ed. S. A. Tokarev, Z. V. Gogolev, and I. S. Gurvich. Moscow, 1957.

Istoriia Kabardy. S drevneishikh vremen do nashikh dnei. Ed. N. A. Smirnov, Z. V. Angavadze, N. E. Gurevich, *et al.* Moscow, 1957.

Istoriia kazakhskoi SSR. Vol. I. Ed. M. O. Auezov, S. B. Baishev, *et al.* Alma-Ata, 1957.

Istoriia kazakhskoi SSR. S drevneishikh vremen do nashikh dnei. Ed. M. Abdykalykov and A. Pankratova. Alma-Ata, 1943.

[*Istoriia kazakhskoi SSR.* 2nd ed. Ed. A. M. Pankratova and I. O. Omarov. Alma-Ata, 1949.]

Istoriia Kirgizii. Vol. I. Ed. M. P. Viatkin, B. D. Dzhamgerchinov, A. P. Okladnikov, *et al.* Frunze, 1956.

Istoriia Kirgizii. Vol. I. Ed. M. P. Viatkin, M. P. Griaznov, *et al.* Frunze, 1963.

Istoriia latviiskoi SSR. Vol. I. Ed. K. Ia. Strazdin' *et al.* Riga, 1952.

Istoriia latviiskoi SSR (S drevneishikh vremen do 1953 g.). Ed. K. Ia. Strazdin'. Riga, 1955.

Istoriia Moldavii. Vol. I. Ed. A. D. Udal'tsov and L. V. Chrerepnin. Kishinev, 1951.

Istoriia moldavskoi SSR. Vol. I: *S drevneishikh vremen do velikoi oktiabr'skoi sotsialisticheskoi revoliutsii.* Ed. L. V. Cherepnin *et al.* Kishinev, 1965.

Istoriia narodov Uzbekistana. Vol. I. Ed. S. P. Tolstov, B. Iu. Zakhidov, and Ia. G. Guliamov. Tashkent, 1950.

Istoriia narodov Uzbekistana. Vol. II. Ed. S. V. Bakhrushin, V. Ia. Nepomnin, and V. A. Shishkin. Tashkent, 1947.

Istoriia severo-osetinskoi ASSR. Ed. S. K. Bushuev, M. S. Totoev, A. V. Fadeev, *et al.* Moscow, 1959.

Istoriia SSSR. Ed. A. M. Pankratova. Vol. I [to 1700], Moscow, 1940; Vol. II [1700-1900], Moscow, 1940; Vol. III [1900 to present], Moscow, 1941. [There are more than twenty subsequent editions; beginning in 1959 L. P. Bushchik has been listed as author. Translation of first edition, with a few changes, in A. M. Pankratova, *A History of the USSR,* Parts 1-3. Moscow, 1947-48.]

Istoriia SSSR. Vol. I: *S drevneishikh vremen do kontsa XVIII v.* Ed. V. I. Lebedev, B. D. Grekov, and S. V. Bakhrushin. Moscow, 1939. Vol. II: *Rossiia v XIX veke.* Ed. M. V. Nechkina. Moscow, 1940. [Editors and subtitles change in subsequent editions. Abridged translation of the first part of second volume in M. V. Nechkina, *Russia in the Nineteenth Century, Volume II of the History of Russia.* Ann Arbor, Mich.: J. W. Edwards, 1953.]

Istoriia SSSR. S drevneishikh vremen do nashikh dnei. V dvukh seriiakh v dvenadtsati tomakh. Ed. B. N. Ponomarev *et al.* 12 vols. Moscow, 1966–.

Istoriia SSSR. Uchebnoe posobie. Ed. B. D. Datsiuk *et al.* Moscow, 1960.

Istoriia tadzhikskogo naroda. Vol. I, ed. B. G. Gafurov and B. A. Litvinskii. Moscow, 1963. Vol. II, ed. B. I. Iskandarov and A. M. Mukhtarov. Moscow, 1964.

Istoriia tatarskoi ASSR. Vol. I: *S drevneishikh vremen do velikoi revoliutsii.* Ed. N. I. Vorob'ev *et al.* Kazan', 1955.

Istoriia Turkmenistana (Uchebnoe posobie dlia vuzov). Ed. A. Karryev *et al.* Ashkhabad, 1966.

Istoriia turkmenskoi SSR. Vol. I, Part 1: *S drevneishikh vremen do kontsa XVIII veka.* Vol. I, Part 2: *S nachala XIX veka do velikoi oktiabr'skoi sotsialisticheskoi revoliutsii.* Ed. A. Karryev, O. K. Kuliev, M. E. Masson, *et al.* Ashkhabad, 1957.

Istoriia Tuvy. Vol. I. Ed. L. P. Potapov. Moscow, 1964.

Istoriia ukrainskoi SSR. Vol. I. Ed. A. K. Kasimenko, V. A. Diadichenko, F. E. Los', *et al.* Kiev, 1953.

Istoriia ukrainskoi SSR. Vol. I. Ed. V. A. Diadichenko, A. K. Kasimenko, F. E. Los', *et al.* Kiev, 1956.

Istoriia Ukrainy. Korotkyi kurs. Kiev, 1940.

Istoriia Urala. Ed. F. S. Gorovoi. Perm', 1963.

Istoriia uzbekskoi SSR. Vol. I, Part 1, ed. S. P. Tolstov, R. N. Nabiev, Ia. G. Guliamov, and V. A. Shishkin. Tashkent, 1955. Vol. I, Part 2, ed. M. G. Vakhabov, V. Ia. Nepomnin, and T. N. Kary-Niiazov. Tashkent, 1956.

Iurginis, Iu. *Istoriia litovskoi SSR.* Kaunas, 1958.

Ivanov, P. P. *Ocherki po istorii Srednei Azii.* Moscow, 1958.

Kalinin, N. F. *Kazan'. Istoricheskii ocherk.* Kazan', 1952.

Karryev, A., and A. Rosliakov. *Kratkii ocherk istorii Turkmenistana (Ot prisoedineniia k Rossii do velikoi oktiabr'skoi sotsialisticheskoi revoliutsii, 1868-1917 gg.).* Ashkhabad, 1956.

Kartsov, V. G. *Ocherk istorii narodov severo-zapadnoi Sibiri.* Moscow, 1937.

Kasimenko, A. K. *Istoriia ukrainskoi SSR. Populiarnyi ocherk.* Kiev, 1965.

Khaptaev, P. T. *Kratkii ocherk istorii buriat-mongol'skogo naroda.* Ulan-Ude, 1936.

Kratkaia Istoriia SSSR. Vol. I. Ed. I. I. Smirnov. Moscow-Leningrad, 1963.

Kratkii kurs istorii SSSR. Ed. A. V. Shestakov. Moscow, 1937.

Kudriavtsev, F. A. *Istoriia buriat-mongol'skogo naroda.* Moscow-Leningrad, 1940.

Magomedov, R. M. *Istoriia Dagestana. S drevneishikh vremen do nachala XIX veka.* Makhachkala, 1961.

Ocherk istorii abkhazskoi ASSR. Vol. I. Ed. G. A. Dzidzariia, I. G. Antelava, A. V. Fadeev, *et al.* Sukhumi, 1960.

Ocherki istorii Adygei. Ed. S. K. Bushuev, M. G. Autlev, and E. L. Kobzhesau. Maikop, 1957.

Ocherki istorii balkarskogo naroda. S drevneishikh vremen do 1917 goda. Ed. T. Kh. Kumykov, P. G. Akritas, Z. V. Anchabadze, *et al.* Nal'chik, 1961.

Ocherki istorii Dagestana. Ed. M. O. Kosven, R. M. Magomedov, *et al.* Makhachkala, 1957.

Ocherki istorii karakalpakskoi ASSR. Vol. I. Ed. S. P. Tolstov. Tashkent, 1964.

Ocherki istorii Karelii. Vol. I. Ed. V. N. Bernadski, I. I. Smirnov, and Ia. A. Balagurov. Petrozavodsk, 1957.

Ocherki istorii mordovskoi ASSR. Vol. I. Ed. V. N. Vochkarev. Saransk, 1955.

Ocherki istorii SSSR. Ed. B. D. Grekov *et al.* 9 vols. Moscow, 1953-58.

Ocherki istorii udmurtskoi ASSR. Vol. I. Ed. I. P. Emel'ianov. Izhevsk, 1958.

Ocherki po istorii bashkirskoi ASSR. Vol. I. Ed. S. M. Vasil'ev. Ufa, 1956.

Ocherki po istorii Komi ASSR. Ed. K. V. Sivkov, A. A. Zimin, and L. N. Surno. Syktykar, 1955.

Ogorodnikov, V. I. *Ocherk istorii Sibiri do nachala XIX stol.* Vol. I: *Vvedenie istoriia do russkogo Sibiri.* Irkutsk, 1920. Vol. II: *Zavoevanie russkimi Sibiri.* Vladivostok, 1924.

Okladnikov, A. P. *Ocherki iz istorii zapadnykh Buriat-Mongolov, XVII-XVIII v.* Leningrad, 1937.

Okun', S. B. *Ocherki istorii SSSR. Konets XVIII-pervaia chetvert' XIX veka.* Leningrad, 1956.

——. *Ocherki istorii SSSR. Vtoraia chetvert' XIX veka.* Leningrad, 1957.

Pokrovskii, M. N. *Russkaia istoriia s drevneishikh vremen.* Vol. I. Moscow, 1933.

——. *Russkaia istoriia v samon szhatom ocherke.* Vol. III. Moscow, 1934.

Potapov, L. P. *Ocherki po istorii Altaitsev.* Moscow, 1953.

Rosliakov, A. A. *Kratkii ocherk istorii Turkmenistana (Do prisoedineniia k Rossii).* Ashkhabad, 1956.

Senchenko, I. A. *Ocherki istorii Sakhalina (Vtoraia polovina XIX v. nachalo XX v.).* Iuzhno-Sakhalinsk, 1957.

Shteinberg, E. *Ocherki istorii turkmenii.* Moscow-Leningrad, 1934.

Tikhomirov, M. N., and S. S. Dmitriev. *Istoriia SSSR.* Vol. I. *S drevneishikh vremen do 1861 goda.* Moscow, 1948.

Tokarev, S. A. *Ocherki istorii iakutskogo naroda.* Moscow, 1940.

Viatkin, M. *Ocherki po istorii kazakhskoi SSR.* Vol. I: *S drevneishikh vremen po 1870 g.* Moscow, 1941.

4. OTHER WORKS

Abetsedarskii, L. S. *Belorusy v Moskve XVII v.* Minsk, 1957.

——. "Bor'ba belorusskogo naroda za vossoedinenie Belorussii s Rossiei v seredine XVII veka," *Vossoedinenie Ukrainy s Rossii. Sbornik statei.* Moscow, 1954. Pp. 178-222.

Abramzon, S. M. *Ocherk kul'tury kirgizskogo naroda.* Frunze, 1946.

Adamov, E., and L. Kutakov. "Iz istorii proiskov inostrannoi agentury vo vremia kavkazskikh voin," *VI*, No. 11, 1950, pp. 101-5.

Agaian, Ts. P. *Krest'ianskaia reforma v Azerbaidzhana v 1870 gody.* Baku, 1956.

Aitbaev, M. T. *Istoriko-kul'turnye sviazi kirgizskogo i russkogo narodov (po materialam issyk-kul'skoi oblasti kirgizskoi SSR).* Frunze, 1957.

Aksenov, Iu., and G. Il'in. "Vliianie russkoi kul'tury na razvitie kul'tury Ukrainy, Belorussii i Zakavkaz'ia v XIX v.," *Prepodavanie istorii v shkole*, No. 2, 1956, pp. 24-36.

Alferov, M. S. *Krestianstvo Sibiri v 1917 godu.* Novosibirsk, 1958.

Aleksandrov, G. "O nekotorykh zadachakh obshchestvennykh nauk v sovremennykh usloviiakh," *Bol'shevik*, No. 14, 1945, pp. 12-29.

———. "O reshaiushikh usloviiakh pobedy nad vragom," *Pravda*, July 13, 1942.

———. "Otechestvennaia voina sovetskogo naroda i zadachi obshchestvennykh nauk," *Bol'shevik*, No. 9, 1942, pp. 35-47.

"An Indian Officer," in *Russia's March Toward India*, Vol. II. London: Sampson Low, 1894.

Anan'ev, N. "Velikaia sila nerushimoi druzhba narodov SSSR," *Propagandist*, Nos. 11-12, 1942, pp. 16-21.

Apollova, N. G. *Ekonomicheskie i politicheskie sviazi Kazakhstana s Rossiei v XVIII-nachale XIX v.* Moscow, 1960.

Armstrong, Terence. *Russian Settlement in the North.* New York: Cambridge University Press, 1965.

Artamonov, M. I. *Istoriia Khazar.* Leningrad, 1962.

Arutiunian, P. T. *Osvoboditel'noe dvizhenie armianskogo naroda v pervoi chetverti XVIII veka.* Moscow, 1954.

Asfendiarov, S. D. *Natsional'no-osvoboditel'noe vosstanie 1916 goda v Kazakhstane.* Alma-Ata, 1936.

Astemirov, V. "Spoilers of a Literary Heritage," *Caucasian Review*, No. 9 (1959), pp. 91-97.

Auezova, L. M. "K voprosu o pereselenii krest'ian i ikh roli v razvitii zemledeliia v Kazakhstane v 70-90kh godakh XIX veka," *Izvestiia akademii nauk Kazakhskoi SSR. Seriia istorii, arkheologii i etnografii*, No. 1, 1958, pp. 28-41.

Azizian, A. "Narody kavkaza nikogda ne budut rabami," *Bol'shevik*, No. 15, 1942, pp. 28-37.

Babakhodzhaev, A. Kh. *Proval angliiskoi politiki v Srednei Azii i na srednem vostoke (1918-1924).* Moscow, 1962.

Backus, Oswald P. "The History of Belorussia in Recent Soviet Historiography," *Jahrbücher für Geschichte Osteuropas*, XI (1963), 79-96.

Bacon, Elizabeth E. *Central Asians under Russian Rule: A Study in Cultural Change.* Ithaca, N.Y.: Cornell University Press, 1966.

Bagirov, M. D. *Iz istorii bol'shevistskoi organizatsii Baku i Azerbaidzhana.* Moscow, 1946.

——. "K voprosu o kharaktere dvizheniia miuridizma i Shamilia," *Bol'shevik,* No. 13, 1950, pp. 21-37.

——. "Starshii brat v sem'e sovetskikh narodov," *Kommunist,* No. 3, 1953, pp. 64-88.

Bakhrushin, S. V. *Istoricheskie sud'by Iakutii.* Leningrad, 1937.

——. *Nauchnye trudy,* ed. A. A. Zimin, N. V. Ustiugov, L. V. Cherepnin, and V. I. Shunkov. 4 vols. Moscow, 1952-59.

——. "Obrazovanie russkogo natsional'nogo gosudarstva," *Propagandist,* No. 5, 1945, pp. 22-28.

——. *Ocherki po istorii kolonizatsii Sibiri v XVI i XVII vv.* Moscow, 1927.

Barghoorn, Frederick C. "Nationality Doctrine in Soviet Political Strategy," *Review of Politics,* XVI (1954), No. 3, 283-304.

——. "Stalinism and the Russian Cultural Heritage," *Review of Politics,* XIV (1952), No. 2, 178-203.

Barits, I. "Pokhod protiv 'burzhuaznogo natsionalizma' v SSSR," in nine parts in *Svobodnyi Kavkaz,* No. 4, 1952–No. 4, 1953.

Basharin, G. P. *Istoriia agrarnykh otnoshenii v Iakutii (60-e gody XVIII-seredina XIX v.).* Moscow, 1956.

Beisembiev, K. *Iz istorii obshchestvennoi mysli Kazakhstana vtoroi poloviny XIX veka.* Alma-Ata, 1957.

——. *Mirovozzrenie Abaia Kunanbaeva.* Alma-Ata, 1956.

——. *Progressivno-demokraticheskaia i marksistskaia mysl' v Kazakhstane nachala XX veka.* Alma-Ata, 1965.

Bekmakhanov, E. B. "Feodal'no-monarkhicheskie dvizheniia v Kazakhstane," *Uchenye zapiski kazakhskii gosudarstvennoi universitet,* XX (1956), 66-85.

——. "Fol'klornye istochniki o vosstanii Kenesary Kasymova," *VAN kazakhskoi SSR,* No. 9, 1947, pp. 49-56.

——. "Istoricheskie korni druzhby kazakhskogo i russkogo naroda," *VAN kazakhskoi SSR,* No. 11, 1947, pp. 52-61.

[——. *Istoricheskie korni druzhba kazakhskogo naroda s velikim russkim narodom.* Alma-Ata, 1950.]

——. "K voprosu o sotsial'noi prirode batyrov XIX v.," *VAN kazakhskoi SSR,* No. 8, 1947, pp. 49-56.

——. "K voprosu o sotsial'nom stroe kazakov vtoroi poloviny XIX v.," *VAN kazakhskoi SSR,* No. 2, 1950, pp. 89-104.

[——. *Kazakhstan v 20-40e gody XIX veka.* Alma-Ata, 1947.]

——. "Natsional'no osvoboditelnoe dvizhenie v Kazakhstane v

period pervoi russkoi burzhuazno-demokraticheskoi revoliutsii,"
VAN kazakhskoi SSR, No. 4, 1950, pp. 61-75.
——. "Nekotorye itogi raboty ocherednye zadachi istorikov Kaz-
akhstana," *VAN kazakhskoi SSR,* No. 10, 1947, pp. 61-65.
——. "O sostoianii i zadachakh istoricheskoi nauki v Kazakhstane,"
Bol'shevik Kazakhstana, No. 9, 1947, pp. 60-71.
——. "Spravedlivaia kritika," *VAN kazakhskoi SSR,* No. 9, 1949,
pp. 108-10.
Belikov, T. I. *Kalmyki v bor'be za nezavisimost' nashei rodiny
(XVII-nachalo XIX vv.).* Elista, 1965.
Bennigsen, A. "Les limites de la déstalinisation dans l'Islam soviét-
ique," *L'Afrique et l'Asie,* No. 39, 1957, pp. 31-40.
——. "The Muslim Peoples of the Soviet Union and the Soviets,"
Parts 3 and 4, *Islamic Review,* XLIII (1955), No. 6, 13-18; No.
7, 27-36.
Bernshtam, A. N. *Velikoe nasledie kirgizskogo naroda.* Frunze,
1945.
Bestuzhev, I. V. "Oborona Zakavkaz'ia v krymskoi voine, 1853-56
godov," *VI,* No. 12, 1954, pp. 53-66.
Bilas, Lev. "How History is Written in the Soviet Ukraine," *The
Ukrainian Review* (London), V (1958), No. 4, 39-47.
Bilinsky, Yaroslav. *The Second Soviet Republic: The Ukraine after
World War II.* New Brunswick, N.J.: Rutgers University Press,
1964.
Black, Cyril E. (ed.). *Rewriting Russian History.* New York:
Frederick A. Praeger, 1956.
——. (ed.). *The Transformation of Russian Society.* Cambridge,
Mass.: Harvard University Press, 1960.
Bliev, M. M. *Osetiia v pervoi treti XIX veka.* Ordzhonikidze, 1964.
[Borodin, S. *Dmitrii Donskoi.* Moscow, 1942.]
[——. *Mikhail Kutuzov.* Moscow, 1942.]
Borysenko, V. "The 1959 Purges in the Communist Parties of the
Soviet National Republics," *POP,* No. 5 (1960), pp. 7-15.
——. "Ukrainian Opposition to the Soviet Regime, 1956-59," *POP,*
No. 6 (1960), pp. 24-30.
Braginskii, I. S., S. Radzhabov, and V. A. Romodin. "K voprosu o
znachenii prisoedineniia Srednei Azii k Rossii," *VI,* No. 8,
1953, pp. 21-40.
Braginskii, I., I. Zlatkin, and N. Ustiugov. "Poleznaia kniga po
istorii Kazakhstana," *Kommunist,* No. 16, 1957, pp. 86-95.
Brainin, S., and S. Shafiro. *Vosstanie kazakhov semirech'ia v 1916
godu.* Alma-Ata-Moscow, 1936.
Briskin, A. *V strane semi rek. Ocherki sovremmenogo semirecha'ia.*
Moscow, 1926.

Brovka, P., and P. Panchenko. "Al'manakh, otstaiushchii ot zhizhni," *Pravda*, August 8, 1951.

Bugaev, E. "Kogda utrachivaetsia nauchny podkhod," *Partiinaia zhizn'*, No. 14, 1956, pp. 62-72.

Burdzhalov, E. N. "Eshche o taktike bol'shevikov v marte-aprele 1917 goda," *VI*, No. 8, 1956, pp. 109-14.

———. "O stat'e tov. E. Bugaeva," *VI*, No. 7, 1956, pp. 215-22.

———. "Stalinskii 'Kratkii kurs istorii VKP (b)' i istoricheskaia nauka," *Bol'shevik*, No. 18, 1951, pp. 9-22.

Bushuev, S. K. *A. M. Gorchakov*. Moscow, 1961.

———. "Aleksandr Nevskii," *Propagandist*, No. 1, 1942, pp. 42-44.

———. *Bor'ba gortsev za nezavisimost' pod rukovodstvom Shamilia*. Moscow, 1939.

———. *Iz istorii russko-kabardinskikh otnoshenii*. Nal'chik, 1956.

———. *Iz istorii vneshnepoliticheskikh otnoshenii v period prisoedineniia Kavkaza k Rossii*. Moscow, 1955.

———. "Muzhestvennye obrazy nashikh velikikh predkov," *Bol'shevik*, No. 8, 1942, pp. 57-64.

———. "O kavkazskom miuridizme," *VI*, No. 12, 1956, pp. 72-79.

Busygin, E. P., and N. V. Zorin. *Russkie naselenie chuvashskoi ASSR. Material'naia kul'tura*. Cheboksary, 1960.

Caroe, Olaf. *Soviet Empire: The Turks of Central Asia and Stalinism*. London: Macmillan, 1953.

Carrère d'Encausse, H. "La 'Déstalinisation' dans l'Islam soviétique," *L'Afrique et l'Asie*, No. 37, 1957, pp. 30-42.

———. "La politique culturelle du pouvior tsariste au Turkestan (1867-1917)," *Cahiers du Monde Russe et Soviétique*, III (1962), No. 3, 374-407.

———. "Tsarist Educational Policy in Turkestan, 1867-1917," *CAR*, XI (1963), No. 4, 374-94. [Abridged translation of "La Politique culturelle."]

Cassirer, Ernst. *The Myth of the State*. New Haven, Conn.: Yale University Press, 1946.

"Central Asia and the Russian People," *CAR*, I (1953), No. 3, 1-8.

Cheban, I. "O vzaimootnosheniiakh Moldavii s moskovskim gosudarstvom v XV-XVIII vekakh," *VI*, Nos. 2-3, 1945, pp. 59-71.

Chekovich, O. D. "O nekotorykh voprosakh istorii Srednei Azii, XVIII-XIX vekov," *VI*, No. 3, 1956, pp. 84-95.

Chemezov, V., and D. Petrov. *325 letie vkhozhdeniia Iakutii v sostav rossiiskogo gosudarstva*. Iakutsk, 1957.

[Chetyresta] *400 let vmeste s russkim narodom*. Izhevsk, 1957.

Chuloshnikov, A. P. *Vosstanie 1755 g. v Bashkirii*. Moscow, 1940.

Conquest, Robert. *The Soviet Deportation of Nationalities*. London: Macmillan, 1960.

Costello, D. P. "The Murder of Griboedov," Oxford Slavonic Papers, VIII (1958), 66-89.
Curzon, Lord George. Russia in Central Asia in 1889; and the Anglo-Russian Question. London: Longmans, 1889.
Dagestan-Rossiia naveki vmeste! Dokumenty, pis'ma, stikhi, vyskazyvaniia, rasskazy, ocherki. Makhachkala, 1960.
Dakhshleiger, G., and N. Apollova. "Dobrovol'noe prisoedinenie Kazakhstana k Rossii," VAN kazakhskoi SSR, No. 5, 1954, pp. 14-27.
Daniialov, A. "Ob izvrashcheniiakh v osveshchenii miuridizma i dvizheniia Shamilia," VI, No. 9, 1950, pp. 3-18.
———. "O dvizhenii gortsev Dagestana i Chechni pod rukovodstvom Shamilia," VI, No. 10, 1966, pp. 17-28.
———. Semiletka Dagestana i zadachi intelligentsii. Makhachkala, 1959.
Daniialov, G. D. "O dvizhenii gortsev pod rukovodstvom Shamilia," VI, No. 7, 1956, pp. 67-72.
Daniiarov, S. S. O progressivnom znachenii russkoi kul'tury v razvitii kul'tury kirgizskogo naroda v kontse XIX i nachale XX vekov. Frunze, 1961.
Danilevskii, V. Aleksandr Nevskii. Moscow, 1942.
———. Dmitrii Donskoi. Moscow, 1942.
[———. Dmitrii Pozharskii. Moscow, 1942.]
Davletov, D. "Ukreplenie pozitsii tsarisma na vostochnom beregu kaspiiskogo moria i prisoedinenie zapadnogo Turkmenistana k Rossii," Izvestiia akademii nauk turkmenskoi SSR. Seriia obshchestvennykh nauk, No. 4, 1962, pp. 3-12.
Davletshin, Tamurbek. "The Party Congresses of the Turkestani Republics," Studies on the Soviet Union, II (1962), No. 3, 18-32.
Derzhavin, N. S. Proiskhozhdenie russkogo naroda: velikorusskogo, ukrainskogo, belorusskogo. Moscow, 1944.
Diadichenko, V., and E. Stetsiuk. Bor'ba ukrainskogo naroda za vossoedinenie Ukrainy s Rossiei. Kiev, 1954.
Druzhba. Stat'i, ocherki, issledovaniia, vospominaniia, pis'ma ob armiano-russkikh kul'turnykh sviaziakh. Moscow, 1957.
———. 2 vols. Erevan, 1960.
Druzhba. Stat'i, vospominaniia, ocherki ob armiano-russkikh kul'turnykh sviaziakh. Erevan, 1956.
Dubrovskyi, V. "The Current Soviet Approach to Ukrainian History," Ukrainian Review (Munich), No. 3 (1956), pp. 122-45.
Duishemaliev, T. "Iz istorii druzhby kirgizskogo i kazakhskogo narodov," Trudy instituta istorii akademii nauk kirgizskoi SSR, V (1959), 113-18.
Durinov, A. A. "Narodnoe obrazovanie v buriatskoi ASSR," in Issle-

dovaniia i materialy po istorii Buriatii. Ulan-Ude, 1963. Pp. 42-53.

[Dvestapiat'desiat'] *250 let vmeste s velikim russkim narodom.* Abakan, 1959.

Dzhamgerchinov, B. D. "Iz istorii prisoedineniia severnoi Kirgizii k Rossii," *Trudy instituta istorii akademii nauk kirgizskoi SSR,* IV (1958), 3-18.

———. "Nachalo utverzhdeniia vliianiia Rossii v severnoi Kirgizii," *Trudy instituta istorii akademii nauk kirgizskoi SSR,* V (1959), 3-38.

———. *Vazhnoi etap iz istorii kirgizskogo naroda (k stoletiiu prisoedineniia Kirgizii k Rossii).* Frunze, 1957.

Dzhandil'din, N. "Nekotorye voprosy internatsional'nogo vospitaniia," *Kommunist,* No. 13, 1959, pp. 30-43.

Dzhimbinov, B. O. *350 let vmeste s Rossiei.* Moscow, 1959.

Egunov, N. P. *Kolonial'naia politika tsarizma i pervyi etap natsional'nogo dvizheniia v Buriatii v epokhu imperializma.* Ulan-Ude, 1963.

Epifanov, P. P., and M. E. Naidenov. "O broshiure 'Voprosy prepodavaniia istorii SSSR v svete reshenii VV s''ezda KPSS,'" *Prepodavanie istorii v shkole,* No. 5, 1957, pp. 113-17.

Ermolenko, A. F. "Ukrainsko-moldavskie otnosheniia v gody osvoboditel'noi voiny ukrainskogo naroda," *Vossoedinenie Ukrainy. Sbornik statei.* Moscow, 1954. Pp. 223-41.

Erzakov, B. "Istoricheskie sviazi russkoi i kazakhskoi muzyky v dooktiabr'skii period," *VAN kazakhskoi SSR,* No. 10, 1953, pp. 48-53.

Fadeev, A. V. "Antikolonial'nye dvizheniia narodov severnogo Kavkaza v 20-60kh godakh XIX v.," *Prepodavanie istorii v shkole,* No. 6, 1957, pp. 34-45.

———. "Ekonomicheskie sviazi severnogo Kavkaza s Rossiei v doreformennyi period," *Istoriia SSSR,* No. 1, 1957, pp. 135-60.

———. "Miuridizm kak orudie agressivnoi Turtsii i Anglii na severozapadnom Kavkaze v XIX stoletii," *VI,* No. 9, 1951, pp. 76-97.

———. "O sud'be odnoi knigi," *VI,* No. 1, 1963, pp. 121-30.

———. "O vnutrennei sotsial'noi baze miuridistskogo dvizheniia na Kavkaze v XIX veke," *VI,* No. 6, 1955, pp. 67-77.

———. "Osnovnye etapy v razvitii russko-kavkazskikh sviazei," in *Uchenye zapiski kabardino-balkarskogo nauchno-issledovatel' skogo instituta. Seriia istoricheskaia.* XVII. Nal'chik, 1960. 39-60.

———. "Vopros o sotsial'noi stroe kavkazskikh gortsev XVII-XIX vv. v novykh rabotakh sovetskikh istorikov," *VI,* No. 5, 1958, pp. 130-37.

Fainsod, Merle. "Soviet Russian Historians or: the Lesson of Burdzhalov," *Encounter*, XVIII, March, 1962, pp. 82-89.

Faseev, K. F. *Iz istorii tatarskoi peredovoi obshchestvennoi mysli (vtoraia polovina XIX-nachalo XX veka)*. Kazan', 1955.

Fateev, P. "Knigi dlia naroda," *Bol'shevik*, No. 6, 1942, pp. 59-64.

Fedenko, Panas. "Hetman Ivan Mazepa in Soviet Historiography," *Ukrainian Review* (Munich), No. 9 (1960), pp. 6-18.

Fedorov, V. A. "Protiv fal'sifikatsii istorii narodov Kavkaza," *Vestnik moskovskogo universiteta. Istoriko-filologicheskaia seriia*, No. 3, 1958, pp. 232-36.

Fridman, Ts. L. *Inostrannyi kapital v dorevoliutsionnom Kazakhstane*. Alma-Ata, 1960.

Gadzhiev, A. S. *Rol' russkogo naroda v istoricheskikh sud'bakh narodov Dagestana*. Makhachkala, 1964.

Gadzhiev, V. G. *Rol' Rossii v istorii Dagestana*. Moscow, 1965.

Gafurov, B. G. "Ob andizhanskom 'vosstanie' 1898 goda," *VI*, No. 2, 1953, pp. 50-61.

———. "Za marksistskoe osveshchenie istorii tadzhikskogo naroda i istorii ego kul'tury," *Kommunist Tadzhikistana*, July 25-26, 1951.

Galuzo, P. G. *Agrarnye otnosheniia na iuge Kazakhstana v 1867-1914 gg.* Alma-Ata, 1965.

———. "Pereselencheskaia politika tsarskogo pravitel'stva v Srednei Azii," *Kommunisticheskaia mysl'*, No. 2, 1927, pp. 22-47; No. 3, 1927, pp. 9-78; No. 4, 1927, pp. 25-49.

———. *Turkestan—koloniia (ocherk istorii Turkestana ot zavoevaniia russkimi do revoliutsii 1917 goda)*. Moscow, 1929.

Gavrilov, P. "O ser'eznykh nedostatkakh v razvitii obshchestvennykh nauk v Kazakhstane," *Kommunist Kazakhstana*, No. 3, 1956, pp. 18-26.

Gazzaev, A. "Gruboe izvrashchenie istoricheskikh faktov," *Pravda*, November 12, 1949.

Genkina, E. *Obrazovanie SSSR*. Moscow, 1943.

Golobutskii, V. A. *Chernomorskoe Kazachestvo*. Kiev, 1956.

———. *Osvoboditel'naia voina ukrainskogo naroda pod rukovodstvom Khmel'nitskogo, 1648-1654 gg.* Moscow, 1954.

Gorbunov, T. *Geroicheskoe proshloe belorusskogo naroda*. Minsk, 1945.

———. *Vossoedinenie belorusskogo naroda v edinom sovetskom sotsialisticheskom gosudarstva*. Moscow, 1948.

Gorkin, A. "Osnova prochnosti i istochniki sily sovetskogo stroia," *Bol'shevik*, No. 16, 1942, pp. 11-25.

Grekov, B. D. *Kievskaia Rus'*. Moscow, 1953.

———. "Obrazovanie russkogo gosudarstva," *Bol'shevik*, Nos. 11-12, 1945, pp. 25-34.

Grosul, Ia. S. "Istoricheskoe znachenie prisoedineniia Bessarabii k Rossii dlia sudev moldovskogo naroda," *VI*, No. 7, 1962, pp. 48-68.

——. *Reformy v dunaiskikh kniazhstvakh i Rossiia* (*20-30 gody XIX veka*). Moscow, 1966.

Guseinov, Akhmed. *Azerbaidzhano-russkie otnoshenie XV-XVII vekov.* Baku, 1963.

[Guseinov, Geidar. *Iz istorii obshchestvennoi i filosofskoi mysli v Azerbaidzhane v XIX veka.* Baku, 1949.]

——. 2nd ed. Baku, 1958.

——. *Ob istoricheskom sodruzhestve russkogo i azerbaidzhanskogo narodov.* Baku, 1946.

Gvozdetskii, N. A., V. N. Fedchina, A. A. Azam'ian, and Z. N. Dontsova. *Russkie geograficheskie issledovaniia Kavkaza i Srednei Azii v XIX-nachale XX v.* Moscow, 1964.

Hayit, Baymirza. *Some Problems of Modern Turkistan History.* Düsseldorf, 1963.

——. *Sowjetrussische Orientpolitik am Beispiel Turkestans.* Köln, 1962.

——. "Turkestan as an Example of Soviet Colonialism," *Studies on the Soviet Union,* I (1961), No. 2, 78-95.

——. *Turkestan im XX. Jahrhundert.* Darmstadt, 1956.

Henze, Paul B. "Unrewriting History—the Shamil Problem," *Caucasian Review,* No. 6 (1958), pp. 7-29.

History of the Communist Party of the Soviet Union (Bolsheviks): Short Course. New York: International Publishers, 1939.

Hostler, Charles W. *Turkism and the Soviets.* New York: Frederick A. Praeger, 1957.

Iakovlev, N. "O prepodavanii otechestvennoi istorii," *Bol'shevik,* No. 22, 1947, pp. 26-37.

——. "O shkol'nykh uchebnikakh po istorii," *Kul'tura i zhizn',* November 30, 1946.

Iakunin, A. "K voprosu ob otsenke kharaktera natsional'nykh dvizhenii 30-40kh godov XIX v. v Kazakhstane," *VI*, No. 4, 1951, pp. 55-64.

——. "O primenenii poniatiia 'naimen'shee zlo' v otsenke prisoedineniia k Rossii nerusskikh narodnostei," *VI*, No. 11, 1951, pp. 83-86.

Iakunin, A. F., and O. K. Kuliev. "Vosstanie 1916 goda v Srednei Azii," *VI*, No. 3, 1953, pp. 33-49.

Iaroslavskii, E. "Bol'sheviki—prodolzhateli luchshikh patrioticheskikh traditsii russkogo naroda," *Pravda,* December 27, 1941.

——. "O blizhaishikh zadachakh istoricheskoi nauki v SSSR," *IZ,* No. 6, 1942, pp. 17-24.

——. "Za boevuiu, dokhodchivuiu, pravdivuiu agitatsiiu," *Pravda*, July 10, 1942.

Il'ichev, L. "Moshchnye faktor stroitel'stva kommunizma," *Kommunist*, No. 1, 1962, pp. 11-38.

Inoiatov, Kh. Sh. *Otvet fal'sifikatoram istorii Srednei Azii i Kazakhstana*. Tashkent, 1962.

Ionova, O. V. *Iz istorii iakutskogo naroda (pervaia polovina XVII veka)*. Iakutsk, 1945.

Istoriia kommunisticheskoi partii sovetskogo soiuza. Ed. B. N. Ponomarev. Moscow, 1959.

Istoriia vsesoiuznoi kommunisticheskoi partii (Bol'shevikov). Kratkii kurs. Moscow, 1938.

Iuldashbaeva, F. *Iz istorii angliiskoi kolonial'noi politiki v Afganistane i Srednei Azii (70-80 gody XIX v.)*. Tashkent, 1963.

Ivanov, P. "Ob odnoi oshibochnoi kontseptsii," *Pravda*, December 25, 1951.

Iz istorii russko-armianskikh otnoshenii. Ed. M. Nersisian. Vol. I, Erevan, 1956. Vol. II, Erevan, 1961.

Iz istorii russko-kabardinskikh otnoshenii. Nal'chik, 1955.

Kadyrov, Sh. *Zapiski i otchety russkikh puteshestvennikov kak istochnik po istorii kirgizii vtoroi poloviny XIX veka*. Frunze, 1961.

Kalnberzin, Ia. "Latyshskii narod v bor'be s nemetskimi zakhvatchikami," *Bol'shevik*, No. 14, 1942, pp. 27-34.

Karel'skaia ASSR. Ed. A. A. Grigor'ev and A. V. Ivanov. Moscow, 1956.

Karpych, V. "K istorii zavoevaniia Turkestana rossisskim kapitalizmom," *Turkmenovedenie*, Nos. 10-11, 1929, pp. 43-52.

Kary-Niiazov, T. N. *Ocherki istorii kul'tury sovetskogo Uzbekistana*. Moscow, 1955.

——. *Socialist Culture of the Uzbek People*. Moscow, 1958.

Kastel'skaia, Z. D. *Vosstanie 1916 v Uzbekistane*. Tashkent, 1937.

Kasumov, M. M. *Ocherki po istorii peredovoi filosofskoi i obshchestvenno-politicheskoi mysli azerbaidzhanskogo naroda v XIX veke*. Baku, 1959.

Kazemzadeh, Firuz. *The Struggle for Transcaucasia, 1917-1921*. New York: The Philosophical Library, 1951.

Keep, John (ed.). *Contemporary History in the Soviet Mirror*. New York: Frederick A. Praeger, 1964.

Kenesbaev, S. K. "K voprosu o vliianii russkogo iazyka na kazakhskii," *VAN kazakhskoi SSR*, No. 6, 1953, pp. 11-19.

Khachapuridze, G. V. *K istorii Gruzii pervoi poloviny XIX veka*. Tbilisi, 1950.

————. "K voprosu o kul'turnykh sviaziakh Rossii i Gruzii v pervuiu polovinu XIX veka," *VI*, Nos. 5-6, 1946, pp. 76-89.

Khalfin, N. A. *Angliiskaia kolonial'naia politika na Srednem Vostoke.* Tashkent, 1957.

————. *Politika Rossii v Srednei Azii (1857-1868).* Moscow, 1960.

————. "Prisoedinenie Srednei Azii k Rossii i ego progressivnye posledstviia," *Istoriia SSSR*, No. 2, 1959, pp. 196-99.

————. *Proval britanskoi agressii v Afganistane (XIX v.-nachalo XX v.).* Moscow, 1959.

————. *Russia's Policy in Central Asia (1857-1868).* London: The Central Asian Research Centre, 1964. [An abridged translation of *Politika Rossii* by Hubert Evans.]

Khalpakch'ian, O. Kh. *Armiano-russkie kul'turnye otnosheniia i ikh otrazhenie v arkhitekture.* Erevan, 1957.

Khanazarov, K. Kh. *Sblizhenie natsii i natsional'nye iazyki v SSSR.* Tashkent, 1963.

Khasanov, A. "O prisoedinenii severnykh Kirgizov k Rossii," *VI*, No. 7, 1950, pp. 126-31.

————. *Vzaimootnosheniia Kirgizov s kokandskim khanstvom i Rossiei v 50-70 gg. XIX veka.* Frunze, 1961.

Khashaev, Kh. M. *Obshchestvennyi stroi Dagestana v XIX veke.* Moscow, 1961.

Kheifets, M. I. "XX s"ezd KPSS i zadachi sovetskoi istoricheskoi nauki," *Vestnik moskovskogo universiteta. Seriia obshchestvennykh nauk*, No. 4, 1956, pp. 147-54.

Khrushchev, N. "Stalinskaia druzhba narodov—zalog nepobedimost nashei rodiny," *Bol'shevik*, No. 24, 1949, pp. 80-85.

Kim, M. P. "O zadachakh izucheniia istoricheskogo opyta sotsialisticheskogo stroitel'stva v SSSR v svete reshenii XXII s"ezda KPSS," *VI*, No. 2, 1962, pp. 3-19.

————. "Ob oshibkakh v nauchnykh rabotakh po istorii Kirgizii," *VAN SSSR*, No. 5, 1952, pp. 43-51.

Kirimal, Edige. "Soviet Historical Science in the Service of Russian Imperialism," *Caucasus*, No. 14 (1952), pp. 15-20.

Kokiev, G. "Russko-kabardinskie otnosheniia v XVI-XVIIvv.," *VI*, No. 10, 1946, pp. 44-60.

Kolarz, Walter. *Communism and Colonialism: Essays.* New York: St. Martin's Press, 1964.

Kopylov, A. N. *Russkie na Enisee v XVII v. Zemledelie, promyshlennost' i torgovye sviazi eniseiskogo uezda.* Novosibirsk, 1965.

Korneev, M. *Druzhba narodov SSSR—zalog nashei pobedy.* Kuibyshev, 1942.

Korovin, F. P. "O prepodavanii temy 'Zavoevanie Kavkaze Rossiei' v IX klasse srednei shkoly," *Prepodavanie istorii v shkole*, No. 6, 1950, pp. 31-38.

Kostiuk, Hryhory. *Stalinist Rule in the Ukraine: A Study of the Decade of Mass Terror* (*1929-1939*). Munich, 1960.

Kozachenko, A. I. *Bor'ba ukrainskogo naroda protiv inozemnykh porabotitelei za vossoedinenie s Rossiei.* Moscow, 1954.

———. *Vossoedinenie Ukrainy s Rossiei. K 300 letiiu pereiaslavskoi rady.* Moscow, 1954.

Kozlov, P. K. *Russkii puteshestvennik v tsentral'noi Azii. Izbrannye trudy k stoletiiu so dnia rozhdeniia.* Moscow, 1963.

Krikunov, V. P. *Sovmestnaia bor'ba russkikh i kabardinskikh krest'ian protiv feodal'nogo gneta v 60kh godakh XIX veka.* Nal'chik, 1956.

[Kroviakov, N. *Shamil'. Ocherk iz istorii bor'by narodov kavkaza za nezavisimost'.* Groznyi, 1941.]

Krupnycky, B. "Bohdan Khmelnitsky and Soviet Historiography," *Ukrainian Review* (Munich), No. 1 (1955), pp. 65-76.

Kruzhkov, V. "Velikaia sila leninsko-stalinskoi druzhby narodov," *Pravda,* February 21, 1942.

Kshibekov, D. *Klevetniki i fal'sifikatory istorii narodov sovetskogo Kazakhstana.* Alma-Ata, 1961.

Kudashev, L. N. "Iz istorii kuril'skikh ostrovov," *VI,* No. 8, 1963, pp. 42-58.

Kudriavtsev, F. "Rol' russkoi kul'tury v razvitii buriat-mongol'skogo naroda v XVIII-XX vekakh," *VI,* No. 10, 1946, pp. 85-94.

Kulski, W. W. *The Soviet Regime: Communism in Practice.* Syracuse, N.Y.: Syracuse University Press, 1954.

Kuzeev, P., and B. Iuldashbaev. *400 let vmeste s russkim narodom. Prisoedinenie Bashkiri k russkomu gosudarstvu i ego istoricheskoe znachenie.* Ufa, 1957.

Lambton, Ann K. S. *Islam and Russia.* London: Central Asian Research Centre, 1956.

Lang, David Marshall. *The Georgians.* New York: Frederick A. Praeger, 1966.

———. "Griboedov's Last Years in Persia," *American Slavic and East European Review,* VII (1948), No. 4, 317-19.

Lantzeff, George V. *Siberia in the Seventeenth Century: A Study of the Colonial Administration.* Berkeley, Calif.: University of California Press, 1943.

Lashauri, Mindiia. *Istoriia Gruzii XIX-XX vekov v sovremennoi sovetskoi interpretatsii.* "Issledovaniia i materialy," Second Series, No. 44. Munich: Institute for the Study of the USSR, 1956.

———. "The State of Historical Science in the Georgian SSR," *Caucasian Review,* I (1955), 93-99.

Lebedev, V. "Iz istorii zavoevaniia Kazakhstana tsarskoi Rossiei (1730-1732 goda)," *Bor'ba klassov,* No. 10, 1936, pp. 60-65.

Lenin, V. I. *Polnoe sobranie sochinenii.* 55 vols. Moscow, 1958-65.

Leonidov, N. "Patrioticheskaia ideia v istorii nashei rodiny," *Bol'-shevik*, No. 10, 1942, pp. 27-45.

Leonov, M. "Boevye traditsii bol'shevizma vdokhnovliaiut krasnuiu armiiu v bor'be s vragom," *Bol'shevik*, No. 14, 1942, pp. 8-17.

Letopis' druzhby gruzinskogo i russkogo narodov s drevnikh vremen do nashikh dnei. 2 vols. Tbilisi, 1961.

Likholat, A. V. "Putanaia stat'ia o zadachakh istoricheskoi nauki v Kazakhstane," *Kul'tura i zhizn'*, December 20, 1947.

——. *Razgrom burzhuazno-natsionalisticheskoi direktorii na Ukraine.* Moscow, 1949.

——. *Razgrom natsionalisticheskoi kontrrevoliutsii na Ukraine, 1917-1922 gg.* Moscow, 1954.

Lin, Edip I. *V druzhnoi sem'e narodov sovetskogo soiuza.* Groznyi, 1964.

Litvin, K. "Ob istorii ukrainskogo naroda," *Bol'shevik*, No. 7, 1947, pp. 41-56.

Low, Alfred D. "Patriotism, 'Bourgeois nationalism,' and the Nationality Policy of the USSR after Stalin," *The Annals of the Ukrainian Academy in the U. S.*, IX (1961), 126-46.

[Magomedov, R. M. *Imam Shamil'.* Makhachkala, 1941.]

[——. *Iunost' Shamil'.* Makhachkala, 1941.]

[——. *Shamil'.* Makhachkala, 1941.]

——. *Vosstanie gortsev Dagestana v 1877 g.* Makhachkala, 1940.

Makarov, E. "V kazakhskom universitete zazhimaiut kritiku," *Pravda*, November 22, 1952.

Maksimov, L. "O zhurnal 'Voprosy istorii,'" *Bol'shevik*, No. 13, 1952, pp. 60-70.

Mamedov, Sh. "Iz istorii obshchestvennoi mysli v Azerbaidzhane," *Bol'shevik*, Nos. 11-12, 1946, pp. 83-88.

Manning, Clarence A. "The Soviets and Khmelnitsky," *The Ukrainian Quarterly*, III (1946-47), No. 1, 10-15.

Margolis, Iu. D. *Istoricheskie vzgliady T. G. Shevchenka.* Leningrad, 1964.

Markosian, S. "Kolonial'naia politika tsarizma i Armiane v XVIII veke," *Bor'ba klassov*, No. 11, 1936, pp. 92-98.

Matiushkin, N. V. I. *Lenin o druzhbe narodov.* Moscow, 1954.

Matossian, Mary. *The Impact of Soviet Policies in Armenia.* Leiden: E. J. Brill, 1962.

Mavrodin, V. V. *Obrazovanie drevnerusskogo gosudarstva.* Leningrad, 1945.

Mazour, Anatole G. *Modern Russian Historiography.* 2nd ed. Princeton, N. J.: Van Nostrand, 1958.

Megrelidze, Sh. V. *Gruziia v russko-turetskom voine, 1877-1878 gg.* Batumi, 1955.

Mekhtiev, G. G. "Istoricheskoe znachenie prisoedineniia Azerbaid-zhana k Rossii," *VI*, No. 3, 1952, pp. 83-98.
Menon, K. S. *The Russian Bogey and British Aggression in India and Beyond.* Calcutta: Eastern Trading Company, 1957.
Meskhia, Sh. A., and Ia. Z. Tsinadze. *Iz istorii russko-gruzinskikh vzaimootnoshenii X-XVIII vv.* Tbilisi, 1958.
Mikhailov, N. N., *et al. Nasha velikaia rodina.* Moscow, 1953. [Many subsequent editions.]
Mikirtitchian, L. "Soviet Historiography of the Armenian Nation," *Caucasian Review*, No. 9 (1959), 98-122.
Miller, F. G. *Istoriia Sibiri.* Vol. I. Moscow, 1937.
Mirchuk, I. "The Brotherhood of the Slavic Peoples and Bolshevik Reality," *Ukrainian Review* (Munich), No. 1 (1955), 104-10.
Mokhov, N. *Ocherki istorii moldavsko-russko-ukrainskikh sviazei.* Kishinev, 1961.
Mokhov, N. A., and K. V. Stratievskii. *Rol' russkogo i ukrainskogo narodov v istoricheskikh sud'bakh Moldavii.* Kishinev, 1963.
Morozov, M. "Ob 'Istorii kazakhskoi SSR,'" *Bol'shevik*, No. 6, 1945, pp. 74-80.
——, and V. Slutskaia. "Broshiury mestnykh izdatel'stv o geroi-cheskom proshlom nashego naroda i o geroiakh velikoi otechest-vennoi voiny," *Propagandist*, No. 17, 1942, pp. 46-48.
Musabai, V. "Russification of the Tatars," *POP*, No. 5 (1959), 31-38.
Mustafaev, M. "O formule 'naimen'shee zlo,'" *VI*, No. 9, 1951, pp. 97-101.
Nadzhafov, Adil'. *Formirovanie i razvitie azerbaidzhanskoi sotsial-isticheskoi natsii.* Baku, 1955.
Naiakshin, K. "K voprosu o prisoedinenii srednego povolzh'ia k Rossii," *VI*, No. 9, 1951, pp. 108-11.
Narody Sibiri. Ed. M. G. Levin and L. P. Potapov. Moscow-Lenin-grad, 1956.
" 'Nationalism' in the Soviet Muslim Republics," *CAR*, VII (1959), No. 4, 341-43.
Nechkina, M. V. "K itogam diskussii o periodizatsii istorii sovetskoi istoricheskoi nauki," *Istoriia SSSR*, No. 1962, pp. 57-68.
——. "K voprosu o formule 'naimen'shee zlo,'" *VI*, No. 4, 1951, pp. 44-88.
"Nekotorye itogi raboty i ocherednye zadachi istorikov Kazakh-stana," *VAN kazakhskoi SSR*, No. 10, 1947, pp. 61-65.
"Nekotorye voprosy prepodavaniia istorii SSSR v shkole," *Uchitel'-skaia gazeta*, September 22, 1956.
Nepesov, G. "Vozniknovenie i razvitie turkmenskoi sovetskoi sot-sialisticheskoi respubliki," *VI*, No. 2, 1950, pp. 3-24.

Nersisian, M. G. *Otechestvennaia voina 1812 goda i narody Kavkaza.* Erevan, 1965.

Niiazov, A. "V bratskoi sem'e narodov Sovetskogo Soiuza," *Kommunist,* No. 8, 1953, pp. 25-39.

Novikov, A. "Aleksandr Nevskii," *Pravda,* December 24, 1941.

Novonashennaia, K. "Istoriia narodov Srednei Azii v kurse istorii SSSR," *IZ,* No. 10, 1940, pp. 108-14.

Novoselov, K. N. *Protiv burzhuaznykh fal'sifikatorov istorii Srednei Azii.* Ashkhabad, 1962.

Nurkanov, A. *Amangel'dy Imanov.* Alma-Ata, 1959.

Nusupbekov, A., and Kh. Bisenov. *Fal'sifikatsiia istorii i istoricheskaia pravda.* Alma-Ata, 1964.

"O metodologicheskikh voprosakh istoricheskoi nauki," *VI,* No. 3, 1964, pp. 3-68.

"O nauchnoi deiatel'nosti i sostoianii kadrov instituta istorii," *VAN SSSR,* No. 5, 1957, pp. 91-92.

"O nekotorykh voprosakh istorii narodov Srednei Azii," *VI,* No. 4, 1951, pp. 3-15.

"O prepodavanii istorii v shkole," *Pravda,* September 16, 1959.

"O zadachakh obshchestvennykh nauk v svete postanovleniia TsK KPSS ot 9 ianvaria 1960 g.," *VI,* No. 5, 1960, pp. 190-95.

"O zadachakh sovetskikh istorikov v bor'be s proiavleniiami burzhuaznoi ideologii," *VI,* No. 2, 1949, pp. 3-13.

"Ob ispravlenii oshibok v otsenke oper 'Velikaia druzhba,' 'Bogdan Khmel'nitskii,' i 'Ot vsego serdtsa,'" *Spravochnik partiinogo rabotnika.* Moscow, 1959. p. 494.

"Ob ocherednykh zadachakh intelligentsii Azerbaidzhana," *Bakinskii rabochii,* July 18, 1950.

Obzor russkikh puteshestvii i ekspeditsii v Sredniuiu Aziiu. Vol. II. Tashkent, 1956.

Ocherki istorii istoricheskoi nauki v SSSR. Ed. M. V. Nechkina *et al.* 3 vols. Moscow, 1955-63.

Odarchenko, P. "The Struggle for Shevchenko," *The Annals of the Ukrainian Academy of Arts and Sciences in the U. S.,* III (1954), No. 3, 824-37.

Ohloblyn, Olexander, "Ukrainian Historiography, 1917-1956," *The Annals of the Ukrainian Academy of Arts and Sciences in the U. S.,* V-VI (1957), 360-63.

Okladnikov, A. P. *Istoricheskii put' narodov Iakutii.* Iakutsk, 1943.

Olonetskii, A. A. *Iz istorii velikoi druzhby (ocherki iz istorii gruzino-russkikh vzaimootnoshenii v pervoi polovine XIX stoletiia).* Tbilisi, 1954.

Orozaliev, K. "Istoricheskoe znachenie dobrovol'nogo vkhozhdeniia

Kirgizii v sostav Rossii," *Izvestiia Akademiia Nauk kirgizskoi SSR. Seriia obshchestvennykh nauk*, V, Part 3 (1963), 5-12.

Osipov, K. *Bogdan Khmel'nitskii*. Moscow, 1939.

Oslikovskaia, E. S., and A. V. Snegov. "Za pravdivoe osveschenie istorii proletarskoi revoliutsii," *VI*, No. 3, 1956, pp. 138-45.

"Osnovye zadachi v izuchenii istorii SSSR feodal'nogo perioda," *VI*, No. 11, 1949, pp. 3-12.

"Ot redaktsionnoi kollegii zhurnala 'Voprosy istorii,'" *VI*, No. 8, 1952, pp. 3-6.

Paichadze, G. G. *K istorii russko-gruzinskikh vzaimootnoshenii*. Tbilisi, 1960.

——. *Russko-gruzinskie otnosheniia v 1725-1735 godakh*. Tbilisi, 1965.

Pankratova, A. M. *Druzhba narodov SSSR—osnova osnov mnogonatsional'nogo sotsialisticheskogo gosudarstva*. Moscow, 1953.

——. " 'Kratkii kurs istorii VKP(b)' i zadachi sovetskoi istoricheskoi nauki," *VAN SSSR*, No. 10, 1948, pp. 17-30.

——. "Nasushchnye voprosy sovetskoi istoricheskoi nauki," *Kommunist*, No. 6, 1953, pp. 55-67.

——. "Velikii russkii narod i ego rol' v istorii," *Prepodavanie istorii v shkole*, No. 5, 1946, pp. 18-31.

Parsamian, V. A. *Uchastie pol'skikh armian v vosstanii David-Beka. Novye materialy ob armianskom osvoboditel'nom dvizhenii XVIII veka*. Erevan, 1962.

Perepechenova, P. "Kreshchenie buriat," *Bor'ba klassov*, No. 8, 1936, pp. 110-14.

Perepelitsyna, L. A. *Rol' russkoi kul'tury v razvitii kul'tur narodov Srednei Azii*. Moscow, 1966.

Petrov, P. U. *Iz istorii revoliutsionnoi deiatel'nosti ssyl'nykh bol'shevikov v Iakutii*. Iakutsk, 1952.

Petrovskii, N. "Prisoedinenie Ukrainy k Rossii v 1654 godu," *IZ*, No. 1, 1944, pp. 47-54.

——. "Vossoedinenie ukrainskogo naroda v edinom ukrainskom sovetskom gosudarstve," *Bol'shevik*, No. 2, 1944, pp. 42-45.

——. *Vossoedinenie ukrainskogo naroda v edinom ukrainskom sovetskom gosudarstve*. Moscow, 1944.

Piaskovskii, A. V. "K voprosu o progressivnom znachenii prisoedineniia Srednei Azii k Rossii," *VI*, No. 8, 1959, pp. 21-46.

——. *Turkmenistan v period pervoi russkoi revoliutsii, 1905-1907 gg*. Ashkhabad, 1955.

Pierce, Richard A. *Russian Central Asia, 1867-1917: A Study in Colonial Rule*. Berkeley, Calif.: University of California Press, 1960.

Pikman, A. M. "O bor'be kavkazskikh gortsev s tsarskimi koloni-zatorami," *VI*, No. 3, 1956, pp. 75-84.

Pokrovskii, M. N. *Diplomatiia i voiny tsarskoi Rossii v XIX stoletii.* Moscow, 1923.

——. *Istoricheskaia nauka i bor'ba klassov.* Vol. I. Moscow, 1933.

——. *Izbrannye proizvedeniia,* ed. M. N. Tikhomirov *et al.* 4 vols. Moscow, 1965-67.

——. "Vozniknovenie moskovskogo gosudarstva i 'velikorusskaia narodnost,'" *IM*, Nos. 18-19, 1930, pp. 14-28.

Pokrovskii, M. V. "O kharaktere dvizheniia gortsev zapadnogo Kavkaza v 40-6okh godakh XIX veka," *VI*, No. 2, 1957, pp. 62-74.

——. *Russko-adigeiskie torgovye sviazi.* Maikop, 1957.

Ponomarev, B. N. "Zadachi istoricheskoi nauki i podgotovka nauchno-pedagogicheskikh kadrov v oblasti istorii," *VI*, No. 1, 1963, pp. 3-35.

Popov, A. L. "Bor'ba za sredneaziatskii platsdarm," *Istoricheskie zapiski,* VII (1940), 182-235.

——. "Iz istorii zavoevaniia Srednei Azii," *Istoricheskie zapiski,* IX (1940), 198-242.

——. "Vneshniaia politika samoderzhaviia v XIX veke v 'krivom zerkale' M. N. Pokrovskogo," in *Protiv antimarksistskoi kontseptsii M. N. Pokrovskogo. Sbornik statei.* Vol. II. Moscow, 1940. Pp. 210-390.

Popova, O. I. *Griboedov—diplomat.* Moscow, 1964.

Poppe, N. N. "Ideological Work in Central Asia since World War II," *East Turkic Review,* No. 2 (1959), pp. 3-27.

"Povysit' rol' istoricheskoi nauki v ideologicheskoi rabote," *Istoriia SSSR,* No. 4, 1963, pp. 3-9.

Progressivnoe vliianie velikoi russkoi natsii na razvitie iakutskogo naroda. Sbornik. Vol. I. Iakutsk, 1950.

Proiskhozhdenie kazanskikh tatar. Kazan', 1948.

Prokop, Myroslav. "Current Trends in Moscow's Nationality Policy," *Ukrainian Quarterly,* XIV (1959), 13-28.

Protiv antimarksistskoi kontseptsii M. N. Pokrovskogo. Sbornik statei. Vol. II. Ed. A. Sidorov, B. D. Grekov, E. Iaroslavskii, *et al.* Moscow, 1940.

Protiv istoricheskoi kontseptsii M. N. Pokrovskogo. Sbornik statei. Vol. I. Ed. A. Sidorov, B. D. Grekov, E. Iaroslavskii, *et al.* Moscow, 1939.

Pundeff, Marin (ed.). *History in the USSR. Selected Readings.* Stanford, Calif.: The Hoover Institution, 1967.

Puzrina, M. F. "Ubeditel'nye otpor fal'sifikatoram istorii Srednei Azii i Kazakhstana," *Istoriia SSSR*, No. 5, 1964, pp. 166-70.

Rabinovich, I. "Zavoevanie Turkmenii tsarskimi voiskami (1883-1885 gg.)," *Bor'ba klassov*, No. 8, 1936, pp. 1-11.

Radiuk, D. *Torzhestvo leninskikh idei druzhby narodov.* Minsk, 1957.

Radzhabov, S. *Rol' velikogo russkogo naroda v istoricheskikh sud'bakh narodov Srednei Azii.* Tashkent, 1955.

Radzhabov, Z. *Iz istorii obshchestvenno-politicheskoi mysli tadzhikskogo naroda vo vtoroi polovine XIX i v nachale XX vv.* Stalinabad, 1957.

Ramzin, K. *Revoliutsiia v Srednei Azii v obrazakh i kartinakh.* Moscow, 1928.

Rashidov, Sh. "Naveki vmeste s russkim narodom," *Kommunist*, No. 10, 1959, pp. 39-52.

Rauch, Georg von. "Grundlinien der sowjetischen Geschichtsforschung im Zeichen des Stalinismus," *Europa Archiv*, V (1950), 3383-88, 3423-32, 3489-94.

Romanov, N. S. *Iasak v Iakutii v XVIII veke.* Iakutsk, 1956.

Rozhkova, M. K. *Ekonomicheskaia politika tsarskogo pravitel'stvo na srednei vostoke vo vtoroi chetverti XIX veka i russkaia burzhuaziia.* Moscow-Leningrad, 1949.

———. *Ekonomicheskie sviazi Rossii so Srednei Aziei 40-60e gody XIX veka.* Moscow, 1963.

Rybakov, B. *Early Centuries of Russian History.* Moscow, 1965.

Ryskulov, T. "Protiv izvrashcheniia istorii kazakhskogo naroda i kharaktera oktiabria v Kazakhstane," *Revoliutsiia i natsional'-nosti*, No. 6, 1936, pp. 62-67.

Rywkin, Michael. *Russia in Central Asia.* New York: Collier Books, 1963.

Rzaev, D. A. *O fal'sifikatorakh istorii Srednei Azii.* Frunze, 1962.

Sabitov, N. "Russko-kirgizskie shkoly," *VAN kazakhskoi SSR*, No. 7, 1949, pp. 74-79.

Safarov, G. *Kolonial'naia revoliutsiia. Opyt Turkestana.* Moscow, 1921.

Safronov, F. G. *Krest'ianskaia kolonizatsiia basseinov Leny i Ilima v XVII veke.* Iakutsk, 1956.

———. *Russkie krest'iane v Iakutii (XVII-nachale XX v.).* Iakutsk, 1961.

Sairanov, Kh. S. *Druzhba rozhdalas' v bor'be.* Moscow, 1959.

Samurskii, N. *Dagestan.* Moscow, 1925.

Sandzhiev, B. "Rabota nad pervym tomom 'Istorii kazakhskoi SSR,'" *VAN SSSR*, No. 12, 1951, pp. 86-88.

Savchenko, V. I. *Istoricheskie sviazi latyshskogo i russkogo narodov.* Riga, 1959.

Schlesinger, Rudolf. "Recent Soviet Historiography," *Soviet Studies,* I (1950), No. 4, 293-312; II (1951), No. 1, 3-21.

Schuyler, Eugene. *Turkistan: Notes of a Journey in Russian Turkistan, Khokand, Bukhara and Kuldja.* 2 vols. New York: Scribner, Armstrong, 1877.

Semanov, S. *A. M. Gorchakov, russkii diplomat.* Moscow, 1962.

Semenov, A. A. *Material'nye pamiatniki iranskoi kul'tury v Srednei Azii.* Stalinabad, 1945.

Semichaevskii, M. A. "Knigi o velikom bratstve narodov," *Istoriia SSSR,* No. 1, 1964, pp. 167-69.

[Shakhmatov, V. F. *Vnutrenniaia orda i vosstanie Isataia Taimanova.* Alma-Ata, 1946.]

Sharipov, K. "Po-marksistski osveshchat' istoriiu Kazakhstana," *VAN kazakhskoi SSR,* No. 8, 1949, pp. 13-23.

Shaskol'skii, I. P. *Normanskaia teoriia v sovremennoi burzhuaznoi nauke.* Moscow-Leningrad, 1965.

Shavkhelishvili, A. I. *Iz istorii vzaimootnoshenii mezhdu gruzinskim i checheno-ingushskim narodami.* Groznyi, 1963.

Shchapov, A. P. *Sobranie sochinenii. Dopolnitel'nyi tom k izdaniiu 1905-1908 gg.* Irkutsk, 1937.

Sherstoboev, V. N. *Ilimskaia pashnia.* Vol. I. Irkutsk, 1949.

Shevchenko, F. *Istoricheskoe znachenie vekovechnoi druzhby ukrainskogo i russkogo narodov.* Kiev, 1954.

Shleev, V. "O sviaziakh russkogo i ukrainskogo iskusstva vtoroi poloviny XIX veka," *Iskusstvo,* No. 2, 1954, pp. 43-49.

Shoinbaev, T. "Istoricheskoe znachenie prisoedineniia kazakhstana k Rossii," *VAN kazakhskoi SSR,* No. 10, 1956, pp. 3-15.

———. "K voprosu o prisoedinenii srednego zhuza k Rossii," in *Voprosy istorii Kazakhstana.* Alma-Ata, 1962. Pp. 41-60.

———. *Vosstanie syr-dar'inskikh kazakhov pod rukovodstvom batyra Dzhankhozhi Nurmukhamedova (1856-1857 gg.).* Alma-Ata, 1949.

———, Kh. Aidarova, and A. Iakunin. "Za marksistsko-leninskoe osveshchenie voprosov istorii Kazakhstana," *Pravda,* December 26, 1950.

Shostakovich, S. V. *Diplomaticheskaia deiatel'nost' A. S. Griboedova.* Moscow, 1960.

Shteinberg, E. L. "Angliiskaia versiia o 'russkoi ugroze' Indii v XIX-XX v.," *Istoricheskie zapiski,* XXXIII (1950), 47-66.

Shteppa, Konstantin F. *Russian Historians and the Soviet State.*
    New Brunswick, N. J.: Rutgers University Press, 1962.
Shunkov, V. I. "O razrabotke istorii Buriat-Mongolii," *VI,* No. 5,
    1949, pp. 87-89.
————. *Ocherki po istorii kolonizatsii Sibiri v XVII-nachale XVIII
    veka.* Moscow, 1946.
————. *Ocherki po istorii zemledeliia Sibiri XVII vek.* Moscow,
    1956.
————. "Osnovnye problemy izucheniia istorii Sibiri," *VI,* No. 9,
    1960, pp. 3-17.
Shutoi, V. E. *Bor'ba narodnykh mass protiv nashestviia armii
    Karla XII, 1700-1709.* Moscow, 1958.
————. "Izmena Mezepy," *Istoricheskie zapiski,* XXXI (1950), 154-
    90.
Sidorov, A. L. "Zadachi instituta istorii akademii nauk SSSR v
    svete genial'nogo truda I. V. Stalina 'Ekonomicheskie problemy
    sotsializma v SSSR' i reshenii XIX s"ezda KPSS," *VI,* No. 10,
    1952, pp. 3-32.
Sivkov, K. "Epizody iz istorii kolonial'nogo ogrableniia Kavkaza
    (XIX vek)," *Bor'ba klassov,* No. 8, 1936, pp. 24-35.
Skalon, V. N. *Russkie zemleprokhodtsy XVII veka v Sibiri.* Mos-
    cow, 1951.
Skazin, E. *Dagestan v sovetskoi istoricheskoi literature.* Makhach-
    kala, 1963.
Skitskii, B. V. *Khrestomatiia po istorii Osetii.* Vol. I. Dzaudzhikau,
    1949.
————. *Klassovye kharakter miuridizma v poru imamata Shamilia.*
    Vladikavkaz, 1930.
————. "Ocherki po istorii osetinskogo naroda s drevneishikh vremen
    do 1867 goda," *Izvestiia severo-osetinskogo nauchno-issledovatel'-
    skogo instituta,* XI (1947), 3-197.
"Slavnyi iubilei sovetskoi Tuvy," *Pravda,* August 17, 1946.
Smal-Stocki, Roman. *The Nationality Problem of the Soviet Union
    and the Russian Communist Imperialism.* Milwaukee: Bruce
    Publishing Co., 1952.
Smirnov, N. A. *Miuridizm na Kavkaz.* Moscow, 1963.
————. *Politika Rossii na Kavkaze v XVI-XIX vekakh.* Moscow,
    1958.
————. *Ocherki istorii izucheniia islama v SSSR.* Moscow, 1954.
————. "Sheikh Mansur i ego turetskie vdokhnoviteli," *VI,* No. 10,
    1950, pp. 19-39.
Smirnov, V. "Nepravil'noe osveshchenie vazhnogo voprosa," *Pravda,*
    November 20, 1956.

Sokol, Edward D. *The Revolt of 1916 in Russian Central Asia.* Baltimore: Johns Hopkins University Press, 1954.

Solovey, D. "Fresh light on the Nationality Policy of the Communist Party and the Soviet Government," *Ukrainian Review* (Munich), No. 4 (1957), pp. 67-122.

Stackelberg, G. "Otrazhenie politiki SSSR v smene sovetskikh istoricheskikh kontseptsii," *Vestnik instituta po izucheniiu istorii i kul'tury SSSR,* No. 2, 1952, pp. 34-53.

———. "The Tashkent Conference on the History of the Peoples of Central Asia and Kazakhstan, 1954," *Bulletin of the Institute for the Study of the USSR,* I (1954), No. 2, 8-13.

———. "The Twentieth Party Congress and the Soviet Evaluation of Historical Figures," *Bulletin of the Institute for the Study of the USSR,* IV (1957), No. 6, 30-39.

Stalin, I. V. *Sochineniia.* 13 vols. (incomplete). Moscow, 1946- .

Stankievic, Jan. "The Soviet Falsification of Belorussian History," *Belorussian Review,* No. 4 (1957), pp. 56-82.

Stankievic, S. "Kupala in Fact and Fiction," *Belorussian Review,* No. 3 (1956), pp. 31-55.

———. "Recent Manifestation of National Opposition in the Belorussian SSR," *POP,* No. 2 (1959), pp. 35-40.

"Strogo sobliudat' leninskii printsip partiinosti v istoricheskoi nauke," *Kommunist,* No. 4, 1957, pp. 17-29.

"Stroitel'stvo kommunizma i obshchestvennye nauki," *VI,* No. 11, 1962, pp. 3-8.

Suiunshaliev, K. "Kniga o mirovozzrenii Abaia," *Kommunist Kazakhstana,* No. 9, 1956, pp. 61-64.

Sullivant, Robert S. *Soviet Politics and the Ukraine, 1917-1957.* New York: Columbia University Press, 1962.

Sumbatzade, A. S. "Progressivnye ekonomicheskie posledstviia prisoedineniia Azerbaidzhana k Rossii v XIX v.," *Trudy instituta istorii i filosofii akademii nauk azerbaidzhanskoi SSR,* V (1954), 194-96.

Svetlov, V. "O prepodavanii obshchestvennykh nauk v vysshei shkol," *Pravda,* March 10, 1947.

Takoev, R. "Kosta L. Khetagurov: On the Occasion of the Centenary of his Birth, (1859-1959)," *Caucasian Review,* No. 9 (1959), pp. 123-27.

Tarasov, Iu. "O kharaktere dvizheniia 1916 v Turkmenii," *VI,* No. 9, 1951, pp. 111-17.

Tarle, E. V. *Pavel Stepanovich Nakhimov.* Moscow, 1942.

Tatishvili, V. L. *Gruziny v Moskve (istoricheskii ocherk, 1653-1722).* Tbilisi, 1959.

Tazhibaev, T. T. "Shkoly vnutrennei (bukeevskoi) ordy vo vtoroi

456 BIBLIOGRAPHY

polovine XIX veka," *Voprosy istorii Kazakhstana XIX-nachala XX veka.* Alma-Ata, 1961. Pp. 126-53.

Tikhomirov, M. N. "Nachalo russkoi zemli," *VI*, No. 9, 1962, pp. 40-41.

Tillett, Lowell R. "Afanasy Nikitin as a Cultural Ambassador to India: A Bowdlerized Soviet Translation of His Journal," *Russian Review*, XXV (1966), 160-69.

———. "Nationalism and History," *Problems of Communism*, XVI, No. 5 (September-October, 1967), 36-45.

———. "Shamil and Muridism in Recent Soviet Historiography," *American Slavic and East European Review*, XX (1961), 253-69.

———. "Soviet Second Thoughts on Tsarist Colonialism," *Foreign Affairs*, XLII (1963-64), 309-19.

Togan, Z. W. "Soviet Cultural Policy in Central Asia," *The USSR Today and Tomorrow. Proceedings of the Conference of the Institute for the Study of the History and Culture of the USSR.* Munich, 1953. Pp. 42-48.

Togzhanov, G. *Kazakskii kolonial'nyi aul.* Vol. I. Moscow, 1934.

Toka, S. "V sem'e narodov-brat'ev," *Pravda*, October 10, 1959.

Tokarev, S. "Novaia nauchnaia literatura o Iakutii," *Propagandist*, No. 13, 1945, pp. 57-62.

Tolstov, S. P. *Drevnii Khorezm.* Moscow, 1948.

———. "Velikaia pobeda leninsko-stalinskoi natsional'noi politiki (k dvadtsatipiatiletiiu natsional'nogo razmezhevaniia Srednei Azii)," *Sovetskaia etnografiia*, No. 1, 1950, pp. 3-23.

Tolybekov, S. E. "O reaktsionnoi bor'be kazakhskikh sultanov i batyrov mladshego zhuza protiv dobrol'nogo prisoedineniia k Rossii," *VAN kazakhskoi SSR*, No. 6, 1955, pp. 43-59.

———. *Obshchestvenno-ekonomicheskii stroi kazakov v XVII-XIX vekakh.* Alma-Ata, 1959.

Totoev, M. S. *Iz istorii druzhby osetinskogo naroda s velikim russkim naroda.* Ordzhonikidze, 1954.

———. 2nd ed. Ordzhonikidze, 1963.

———. *K istorii doreformennoi severnoi Osetii.* Ordzhonikidze, 1955.

Trakho, R. *Cherkesy.* Munich, 1956.

[Trista] *300 let nerushimoi druzhby. Sbornik statei.* Ulan-Ude, 1959.

[Tristadvadtsat'piat] *325 let vmeste s russkim narodom.* Iakutsk, 1957.

[Tristapiat'desiat] *350 let vmeste s Rossiei.* Moscow, 1959.

Tsamerian, I. *Sovetskoe mnogonatsional'noe gosudarstvo, ego osobennosti i puti razvitiia.* Moscow, 1958.

Tsamerian, I. P., Ronin, S. L. *Equality of Rights Between Races and Nationalities in the USSR.* Paris: UNESCO, 1962.

Tsibikov, B. D. *Nerushimaia druzhba buriat-mongol'skogo i russkogo naroda.* Ulan-Ude, 1957.

Tursunbaev, A. *Nerushimaia druzhba russkogo i kazakhskogo narodov.* Alma-Ata, 1955.

——. *Protiv burzhuaznykh fal'sifikatsii istorii Kazakhstana.* Alma-Ata, 1963.

"Tvorcheskaia kritika i samokritika—moguchee oruzhie nauchnogo progressa," *VI,* No. 11, 1951, pp. 19-27.

Uluktuk, A. "Natsional'no-osvoboditel'nye dvizheniia v Turkestane v novoi sovetskoi otsenke," *Turkeli,* No. 1, 1951, pp. 26-33.

Urban, Pavel. "Changing Trends in Soviet Historiography," *Caucasian Review,* No. 9 (1959), pp. 11-24.

——. "Discussions on Soviet Historiography," *Studies on the Soviet Union,* New Series, II (1962-63), No. 4, 84-90.

——. "The New Soviet Drive Against Nationalism in Turkestan," *East Turkic Review,* No. 4 (1960), pp. 13-23.

——. "The Policy of the CPSU Towards the Nations of Central Asia," *Studies on the Soviet Union,* [Old Series] No. 4, 1960, pp. 64-82.

——. "Propaganda as History," *POP,* No. 13 (1962), pp. 24-28.

——. *Smena tendentsii v sovetskoi istoriografii.* Munich, 1959.

——. "Soviet Historical Science and the Position of Soviet Historians," *Bulletin of the Institute for the Study of the USSR,* XI (1964), No. 9, 24-32.

——. "The Twentieth Party Congress and the National Question," *Belorussian Review,* No. 4 (1957), pp. 83-95.

Ustiugov, N. V. *Bashkirskoe vosstanie 1737-1739 gg.* Moscow-Leningrad, 1950.

Uvachan, V. *Peoples of the Soviet North.* Moscow, 1960.

Vahter, Leonard. "History in the Clutches of Communism," *Baltic Review,* No. 14 (1958), pp. 43-55.

Vakhabov, M. G. *Formirovanie uzbekskoi sotsialisticheskoi natsii.* Tashkent, 1961.

——. "O sotsial'noi prirode sredneaziatskogo dzhadidizma i ego evoliutsii v period velikoi oktiabr'skoi revoliutsii," *Istoriia SSSR,* No. 2, 1963, pp. 35-56.

Vambery, Arminius. *Western Culture in Eastern Lands: A Comparison of the Methods Adopted by England and Russia in the Middle East.* London: John Murray, 1906.

Varonic, A. "The History of Belorussia in the Works of Soviet Historiography," *Belorussian Review,* No. 2 (1956), pp. 73-97.

Vedushchaia rol' russkogo naroda v razvitii narodov Iakutii. Sbornik statei. Iakutsk, 1955.

Velikaia druzhba azerbaidzhanskogo i russkogo narodov (s drev-

nykh vremen do nashikh dnei). *Dokumenty, pis'ma, stat'i, vos-pominaniia, khudozhestvennye proizvedeniia.* 2 vols. Baku, 1964.

Velikaia druzhba. 200 let dobrovol'nogo vkhozhdeniia altaitsev v sostav Rossii. Gorno-Altaisk, 1956.

"Velikaia druzhba narodov SSSR," *Pravda*, July 29, 1941.

Viatkin, M. P. *Batyr Srym.* Moscow-Leningrad, 1947.

———. "K voprosu o krest'ianskikh voinakh v Kazakhstane," *VI*, Nos. 3-4, 1945, pp. 72-85.

———. "Pis'mo v redaktsiiu," *VI*, No. 2, 1952, pp. 157-59.

"Vospityvat' kadry v dukhe neprimirimosti k ideologicheskim izvrashcheniiam," *Kommunist*, No. 2, 1953, pp. 113-20.

Vzaimootnosheniia narodov Srednei Azii i sopredel'nykh stran vostoka v XVIII-nachale XXv. Ed. M. A. Babakhodzhaev. Tashkent, 1963.

Werth, Alexander. *Russia at War: 1941-1945.* London: Barrie and Rockliff, 1964.

Wheeler, Geoffrey. *The Modern History of Soviet Central Asia.* London: Weidenfeld and Nicolson, 1964.

Winner, Thomas G. *The Oral Art and Literature of the Kazakhs of Russian Central Asia.* Durham, N.C.: Duke University Press, 1958.

Wolfe, Bertram D. "Operation Rewrite: The Agony of Soviet Historians," *Foreign Affairs*, XXXI (1952-53), 39-57.

Wurm, Stefan. *Turkic Peoples of the USSR: Their Historical Background, Their Languages and the Development of Soviet Linguistic Policy.* London: Central Asian Research Centre, 1954.

Yakobsen, Sergius. "Postwar Historical Research in the Soviet Union," *Annals of the American Academy of Political and Social Science*, CCLXIII (1949), pp. 123-33.

———. "The Rise of Russian Nationalism," *Nationalism: A Report by a Study Group of the Royal Institute of International Affairs.* London, 1939.

Yakovliv, Andriy. "The Reunion of the Ukraine with Russia," *The Annals of the Ukrainian Academy of Arts and Sciences in the U. S.*, IV (1955), No. 3, 1002-34.

Yurchenko, Aleksandr. "The New Party Programme and the Nationality Question," *Studies on the Soviet Union*, New Series, II (1962-63), No. 2, 14-24.

"Za glubokoe izuchenie istorii rodiny," *Pravda*, June 4, 1952.

"Za leninskuiu partiinost' v istoricheskoi nauke," *VI*, No. 3, 1957, pp. 3-19.

"Za marksistsko-leninskoe osveshchenie voprosov istorii Kazakhstana," *Pravda*, April 25, 1951.

"Za pravil'noe osveshchenie istorii iakutskoi istorii," *Pravda*, December 10, 1951.

"Zadachi sovetskikh istorikov v oblasti novoi i noveishei istorii," *VI*, No. 3, 1949, pp. 3-13.

"Zadachi zhurnala 'Voprosy Istorii,'" *VI*, No. 1, 1945, pp. 3-5.

Zenchenko, A. "Chto pokazali pervye dni ucheby," *Pravda*, October 15, 1951.

Zenkovsky, Serge. "Ideological Deviation in Soviet Central Asia," *Slavonic and East European Review*, XXXII (1953-54), 424-37.

———. "Kulturkampf in Pre-Revolutionary Central Asia," *American Slavic and East European Review*, XIV (1955), No. 1, 15-41.

———. *Pan-Turkism and Islam in Russia*. Cambridge, Mass.: Harvard University Press, 1960.

Zhirenchin, A. M. "O sviazi Abai s russkimi revoliutsionerami-demokratami," *VAN kazakhskoi SSR*, No. 1, 1948, pp. 49-54.

Zhiugshda, R., and A. Smirnov. *Litovskaia SSR (kratkii istoriko-ekonomicheskii ocherk)*. Moscow, 1957.

Zimanov, S. Z. *Politicheskii stroi kazakhstana kontsa XVIII i pervoi poloviny XIX vekov*. Alma-Ata, 1960.

Zinoviev, M. A. *Soviet Methods of Teaching History*. Ann Arbor, Mich.: Edwards Brothers, 1952.

INDEX